Jeff's Book

A chronology of Jeff Beck's career, 1965–1980

From the Yardbirds to jazz-rock

Christopher Hjort and Doug Hinman

Dear John!
Thanks for your help –
Christopher

(((Rock 'n' Roll Research Press)))
P. O. Box 4759, Rumford, Rhode Island 02916-0759 USA

2000

Copyright © 2000 by Rock 'n' Roll Research Press

All rights reserved

No part of this data may be reproduced, stored in a retrieval system, or transmitted in any form or by any means, electronic, mechanical, photocopying, recording, or otherwise, without written permission of the copyright proprietor thereof.

Cover photo: Electric Theatre, Toronto, Canada, March 9, 1969. Photo by John Pinto.
Inner cover (front): Detroit Lakes, Minnesota, August 8, 1966. Poster courtesy of the Greg Paul Collection.
Inner cover (back): Arnolds Park, Iowa, August 9, 1966. Poster courtesy of the Tom W. Tourville Collection.

Editing, design and layout: Christopher Hjort

Published by Rock 'n' Roll Research Press, PO Box 4759, Rumford, RI 02916-0759 USA.
Europe: Rock 'n' Roll Research Press, c/o Hjort, Hjørungveien 5, 0375 Oslo, Norway
Visit our website at: **http://www.rocknrollresearchpress.com**

    Jeff's book : a chronology of Jeff Beck's career, 1965–1980 : from
the Yardbirds to jazz-rock / Christopher Hjort and Doug Hinman.
240 p., 16 p. of plates : ports. ; 30 cm.
Rumford, R.I. : Rock 'n' Roll Research Press, 2000

    Includes bibliographic and discographic references and indeces.

    1. Beck, Jeff, 1944- - -History- -Chronology. 2. Guitarists- -
Great Britain- -History- -Chronology. 3. Yardbirds (Musical group)- -
History- -Chronology. I. Hinman, Doug, 1953- II. Title.

ML419 .B393 H677 2000   787.87092 B393h–dc21
ISBN 0-9641005-3-3 (pbk.) $29.95
Library of Congress Card Number: 00-104571

First edition – June 2000.

Printed and bound in Oslo, Norway.
Text is set in Stone Serif 8,5/11 pt, headers are set in News Gothic and Serpentine.
The book is printed on G-Print 100g/G-Print gloss 130g/cover G-Print 240g acid-free paper.

"Jeff was the guy for developing sounds. He used to get into motorbike sounds on a guitar and detuning, playing with the strings over the top of the nut, and detuning the thing while he was playing. He used to go out on stage without tuning up. He hardly ever tuned up properly. He'd get a semblance of tuning up and then he'd go on stage and just play – he'd bend to the notes. He never really played chords or anything. If the thing was out of tune he'd just bend to it. You could never get him to tune up. He'd go out on stage with the guitar totally out of tune – but whatever he'd play would be in tune."
Keith Relf on Jeff Beck in the Yardbirds (1965–66), interview with William Stout and Baby Ray for 'More Golden Eggs' bootleg, 1974

"He's probably the most wonderful intuitive guitar player and so much fun to play with. He's a genuine rock star of the 60s. I think a guy who has really been touched by God. He doesn't know what he's doing but his fingers are just unlike anyone else's. He gets a sound and a feel that are incredible and his rhythmic feel is great ... He's really on top of it. He'll play one note on the guitar and play a melody with the whammy bar and it sounds like it's quantized, like it goes to the right pitch and stops. He's adapt as a musical saw player or something."
Terry Bozzio, MUSIC NEWS NETWORK #54, October 1997

Acknowledgements

In 1991 – inspired by David Terralavoro's first of four editions of the JEFF BECK FANZINE (1991–93) – I decided to try to put together a chronology of Jeff Beck's career, along the same lines of similar-styled books that have been published on other rock artists. I found the Jeff Beck project to satisfy my love for rock 'n' roll history and research neatly combined with my professional occupation as a typesetter and my linguistic interests. By December 1995 I had completed "Jeff Beck – A Chronology 1965–1970", a 48-page xerox-copied publication. As time passed my ambitions grew from that first simple attempt to produce a definite chronology on Jeff Beck, which should also embrace my own personal essays on Beck's career.

It was Doug Hinman who proved crucial in making this book a reality, and he quickly moved from being a contributor to being a collaborator since we first got in touch in February 1997 via the magic of the Internet. His unselfishness has known no boundaries and combined with his deep understanding of rock 'n' roll research, his keen eye for details and his access to literally hundreds of sources beyond my own reach, we have managed to put the book together by painstaking e-mail correspondence. To say this book would have been lesser without Doug's involvement is a gross understatement. More than for anyone else, this book is for him.

I am indebted to the following for their encouragement and contributions: Felix Aeppli, Eric Anderson, Tony Bacon, Roy Bernhus, Bob Brennan, Joan Bryant, Warren Cherry, Alan Clayson, Fred Dellar, Bob Elliot, Nigel Flannigan, John Forrest, Danilo Galluzzi, Caesar Glebbeck, John Gourley, John Gray, Chris Groom, Volker Grupe, Johan Heidenbauer, Claude Hubain, Peter Jacob, Rolf Jarn, Robert Knight, Dave Lewis, Jeff Little, Bruce McNally, Pete Moody, Andy Neill, Benoit Pascal, Justin Purington, Rosko Melo-Lizana, Greg Russo, Marc Roberty, Peter Robinson, Thomas Schmid, Roland Schmitt, Børge Skilbrigt, Jan Inge Sommerseth, David Terralavoro, Jean-William Thoury, Bill Tikellis, Edgar Türk, Uli Twelker, Ben Valkoff, and Willy B.

Toshiaki Igarashi and Annette Carson have proved helpful way beyond the call of duty and deserve my special thanks.

I also extend my sincere thanks to Paul Wilson, who has supplied the book with hithertho unresearched areas regarding Jeff Beck's countless visits to the BBC.

I furthermore want to thank the musicians who have worked with Jeff who have contributed to this project; Jim McCarty, Alan Hope (aka Kerry Rapid), Chris Dreja, Tony Newman, Noel Redding, Pete Brown, Kim Gardner and Mo Foster.

For contributing photographs I want to thank John Abrams, Bill Armstrong, R.E. Barnes, Jon Berle, Gerry Clarke, Chris Dixon, Bob Elliot, Marti Herring, Cheryl 'Pinkie' Jennings, Bob Lampard, Jeff Little, Pete Moody, Mike Peters, John Pinto, Norwood Price, Rancurel Photothèque and Ben Valkoff.

Every effort has been made to acknowledge correctly and contact the copyright holder of illustrations and pictures, but I apologize for any unintentional errors or omissions, which will be corrected in future editions of this book.

A special mention goes to Dick Wyzanski and Bill Armstrong for keeping the Jeff Beck fans updated with their web-page.

Christopher Hjort
Oslo, Norway
June 2000

Through a bit of a roundabout way, I came in on this project early in 1997 initially strictly as a researcher but ultimately as a partner. The three years I worked on this have proven to be intense ones but where I once again realise and would like to acknowledge that no such project happens without an almost unspeakable amount of help from many other people and institutions. Many new acquaintances have been made in the process and to each and every one who helped with even the smallest tidbit you are my friend for doing so. Thank you all!

Special thanks to my research partner and archiving buddy, noted Who-ologist Joe McMichael, for the countless favours and hundreds of hours on the phone sharing leads, theories, tips and assorted information from the Miscellaneous Tour File, and for being there throughout this project. (Look for our joint project covering more of the Yardbirds career in the future). Also to some of my other concert-history researcher pals Andy Neill, Greg E. Shaw and Stuart Rosenberg; and Jason Brabazon for decades of sharing his expertise of rock 'n' roll history.

Also, in absolutely no particular order, everyone who helped from a single piece of information to mountains of it: Julian Bailey, Peter Robinson, Rick Clark, Andrew Sandoval, Greg Paul, George Paul, Dave Hoffman, Giorgio Gomelsky, Jim McCarty; Chris Dreja; Tony Newman; Greg Russo, Gerry Clarke, Jack Hill, Ian McLeod, Mike Ober, Sam Rapallo, Eddy Smit, Garrett Hashimoto; Kathryn Fitchett Schumann, Janet Englebrecht, Kevin Walsh, Miriam Moore, Fred Case. Steve Kent, Tom W. Tourville, Ray Rivers, Ed Mertz, Gary Dottowick, Jim Guentner, Blake English, Barry Tucker (The Old Hippie), Billy Blackmon, Gert Eggens, Peter Seeger (GOOD TIMES magazine), Bill Small, Larry Marion, Bruce Kawakami, Jon Paris, Erik Lindgren, Steve Ingless, Keith Badman, Thomas Sielck, Neil Skok, Greg Shaw (California), Doug Calgaro, Richard Groothuizen, Johnny Rogan, Pete Long, Jim Oldsberg, Helge Buttkereit, Art Sides, Paul S. Williams, Alec Palao, Liz Crawford, Bill Finneran, Ed Dougherty, Dave Cutter, Jim McVeety, Mark Green, Doug Schenker, Jim Fetsch, Chris Klein, Ronnie Warner, Kenny Collins, Bob Watkins, Tommy Tripplehorn, Marti Herring, Gene Triplett, Eric Shoaf, Bobby Poe; Ed Halbrook, Bobby Velline, John Platt, Dick Stewart, Mark Snyder, Joey Dryfka, Mike Mitchell, Linda Arnold Dodson, Steve Brown (Iowa Rock 'n' Roll Hall of Fame), Gary Peterson, Bill Inglot, Phil Cohen, Craig Moore, Cliff McLenehan, Francesco Lucarelli, Peter Stupar, Elliot Sears, Susan Milbrath, Marianne Spellman, Joy Travisano, Urs Steiger, Russell M. Smith, Dave Emlen, Chris & Virginia Locke, Christophe Le Public, Dewey Martin, Juliann France, Paul Surratt, Duke Robillard, Jimmy Karstein, John Beecham, John Platt, Steve Kolanjian, Jerry Miller, Norm Meder, Doug Hanners, Carl Becker, Chris Gerniottis and the late Alan Betrock.

Anyone else I inadvertantly omitted, you know who you are and please know I appreciate your help!

And a special thanks of course to Chris for starting, and later including me in, this great project; for being on the same musical wavelength as I; for being a part of the culture of "detail and accuracy"; and for the fun, satisfaction and the thrill of the hunt which has driven this project all along. I hope we will eventually speak or even meet in-person some day!

And finally, love and thanks as always to Nancy, Ned and Amie who bear with me through "my projects" and always make it worthwile.

Doug Hinman
Rumford, Rhode Island
June 2000

Acknowledgements

Public Libraries: **United States:** Little Rock, Magnolia, AR; Phoenix, Tucson, AZ; Yuba County (Marysville), Chico, Monterey, Santa Barbara, San Luis Obispo, Hayward, Oakland, CA; Colorado Springs, Denver; Pueblo, CO; Jacksonville, FL; Columbus, Macon, Albany, GA; Honolulu, HI; Angola, Fort Wayne, IN, Arnolds Park, Cedar Rapids, Clear Lake, Davenport, Storm Lake, IA; Rockford, IL; Wichita, Topeka, Salina, Emporia, Chanute, KS; Boston, Seekonk, Worcester, MA; Jackson, Houghton Lake, Flint, Detroit, Saginaw, MI; Crookston, Detroit Lakes, MN; Kansas City, MO; Great Falls, MT; Albuquerque, Santa Fe, NM; New York City (main library and the Rodgers & Hammerstein Archives of Recorded Sound at Lincoln Center), Buffalo, Newburgh, NY; Grand Forks, Fargo, ND; Oklahoma City, Tulsa, OK; Salem, OR; Philadelphia, Pittsburgh PA; Providence, RI; Memphis, TN; Amarillo, Austin, Harlingen, San Antonio, Beaumont, Corpus Christi, Lubbock, Houston, Harlingen, San Angelo, Fort Worth, Dallas, TX; Providence, RI; Olympia, Tacoma, WA; District of Columbia, Washington D. C. **United Kingdom:** Buxton, Chelmsford, Aylesbury, Ashton, Dundee, Dumfries & Galloway, Dunfermline, High Wycombe, Montrose, Farnborough, Perth, Bury, Tunbridge Wells, Salisbury, Stirling, Wick, Burnley, Nelson, Swansea, Ipswich, Portsmouth, Glasgow, Wolverhampton, Kirkcaldy, Edinburgh, King's Lynn, Matlock, Surrey County **France:** Lyon, Marseilles, Nice, **Italy:** Milan, **Denmark:** Roskilde, **Switzerland:** Luzern, St. Gallen, Chur, **Sweden:** Trelleborg, Gothenburg, Uddevalla, Jönköping, Kristinehamn **Belgium:** Antwerp, Koninklijke Bibliotheek Albert I, Brussels **Canada:** Winnipeg, Calgary **Germany:** Munich, Nurenberg, Frankfurt

State Libraries: Arkansas; Texas; California; Kentucky; Connecticut; Stockholm, Sweden; Royal Library, Copenhagen, Denmark; Bibliothèque Royale de Belgique, Belgium; Mediatheque national, Brussels, Belgium; Bibliothèque national de France, Paris, France

University Libraries: **United States:** Lamont Library-Harvard University, Rockefeller Library-Brown University; University of California-Los Angeles Library; University of Kansas-Lawrence; University of Massachusetts-Lowell; Temple University; Angelo State University; University of California-Santa Barbara; Southern Methodist University, Alma College, Yale University, University of Connecticut (Storrs); University of Florida (Gainesville); University of New Orleans, Tulane University; University of Alabama (Tuscaloosa); U.S. Naval Academy (Annapolis, MD); **United Kingdom:** Universities of Birmingham, Reading, Leeds, Nottingham, University of Essex, Colchester; University of Manchester; University of Brighton, University of Durham, University of Bristol; **Germany:** Frankfurt; **France:** Ecole Polytechnique, Palaiseau

Historical Societies: Becker County (Detroit Lakes, MI); Iowa, Illinois, Indiana

Private: Philadelphia Convention & Visitors Bureau; the Astrodome; Dick Clark Productions; National Museum of Roller Skating, North of Scotland Newspapers (Wick)

Literally thousands of sources have been sifted through in the the research process. Musical periodicals include AMUSEMENT BUSINESS, BEAT INSTRUMENTAL, BEST, BILLBOARD, CASHBOX, CIRCUS, CRAWDADDY, CREEM, DISC AND MUSIC ECHO, DISC WEEKLY, DOWNBEAT, EXTRA, EYE, FUSION, GO!, GOLDMINE, GUITAR PLAYER, GUITAR WORLD, GUITARIST, HIT PARADER, INTERNATIONAL RECORDING AND MUSIC WORLD, KRLA BEAT, MAXIPOP, MELODY MAKER, MOJO, MUZIEKKRANT OOR, NATIONAL BLAST WEEKLY, NEW ENGLAND SCENE, NEW MUSICAL EXPRESS, POPULAR 1, Q, RAVE, RECORD BEAT, RECORD COLLECTOR, RECORD MIRROR, RECORD WORLD, ROCK & FOLK, ROLLING STONE, SOUND, SOUNDS, TEEN SET, VIBRACIONES, VIBRATIONS, VOX.

The backbone of this book is a chronological presentation and documentation of Jeff Beck's live peformances in the years 1965–1980, but also other events and activities related to his musical career.

- Tour dates and concert information are presented as regular bold; first name of venue, then name of city or locale, e.g. **The Marquee Club, London.** All live performances take place in England unless noted under specific "tour" headings, i.e. "First North American Tour" – where the following dates will all be in the United States. In the United States, the name of cities are always presented in conjunction with the name of the state; e.g. **Shrine Exposition Hall, Los Angeles, California.**
- Magazines, newspapers and other literary references are presented in regular small capitals, e.g. NEW MUSICAL EXPRESS
- Television and radio programmes are shown in quotation marks, e.g. "Discs A Go Go"
- Song titles and thus also singles and album titles are presented in italics, e.g. *Heart Full of Soul, Blow By Blow.*
- Chart positions in the separate "discography boxes" are restricted to American and British charts only, and the sources are what are termed "official", i.e. in the case of the United States the source is the BILLBOARD charts, while in Great Britain the source is the RECORD RETAILER charts.
  For further discographical detail consult: *Yardbirds – The Ultimate Rave-Up* by Greg Russo (Crossfire Publications, P. O. Box 20406, Floral Park, New York 11002-0406)
- The separate set lists are not definitive in the sense that Jeff's repertoire at any specific time may naturally have strayed from a basic set list.

⊡ Denotes a live tape review. It should made be clear that whereas the running text is sprinkled with excerpts from actual concert and record reviews and press announcements, these tape reviews – like the separate essays throughout the book – are purely the author's personal opinions.

✸ An asterisk indicates an estimated date and/or venues not confirmed. An asterisk can also denote a best guess, e.g. in the Radio and TV appearance index, where an asterisk signals the likely song(s) performed.

The authors welcome correspondence in conjunction with a revised (and expanded) edition, which will also cover 1981–2000, and is planned for publication in the future. Besides first hand accounts, anecdotes, corrections, additions, reviews and advertisements, we are in particular looking for unpublished photographs.

Please write:

Christopher Hjort
Hjørungveien 5
0375 Oslo
Norway
e-mail: hjort@gazette.no

or

Rock 'n' Roll Research Press
PO Box 4759
Rumford,
RI 02916-0759
USA
e-mail: info@rocknrollresearchpress.com

Introduction

A word about the research in this book....

One of the main goals of this book was to remove the shroud of mystery which surrounds Jeff Beck's performing and recording activities in the '60s. Very little reliable research had previously been done into this crucial era. While a fair amount of British concert dates – fairly easily available from the British weekly music papers – have long been in circulation, such dates are not always very reliable and really require cross-checking in local newspapers to verify. We have painstakingly done this whenever possibe, resulting in far more accurate information than existed before. For the US tours, little such concert coverage was widely published at the time and combined with the sheer enormity of the country, tracking concert information from this era is another matter entirely. And as Jeff's career, both with the Yardbirds and his subsequent bands, quickly shifted to the US, there has never been much complete information available on this aspect of his career at all.

Unlike researching other high-profile bands of that era like the Beatles or the Rolling Stones, both in fact being well-run businesses backed by well-fueled publicity machines, Jeff Beck is a mercurial character who seems to respond best to spontaneity and whim and has always been somewhat in conflict with his own career. In the early days he was equally likely to book or cancel dates – or an entire tour – on a moment's notice. Such tendencies make unraveling his activities all these years later somewhat of a nightmare.

Often, rock 'n' roll events were not promoted through printed advertisements or even acknowledged in listings of upcoming events in the local established press such that, in some cases, no print evidence may survive which might properly date or confirm a concert ever occured. With the '60s especially, unless there is a clear paper trail, reconstructing events based on recollections alone can prove disastrous. While such research becomes an easier task as rock music became much more mainstream, even some of Beck's activities in the 70s have proved elusive as well.

Reliable recording information on Jeff too has, so far, been sketchy at best and we feel we have made great strides here too. It is with great pride that through dilligent reconstruction of the Yardbirds' US tours that we have been able to unravel details of their important recording activities in US studios. Furthermore, full details of the abundant and important recording activity at the BBC can now finally be revealed here in detail straight from the BBC's files.

Many of the dates and information included here for the first time represent untold hours of effort and frustration. In some cases, it has taken years trying to confirm just a single fact. A few we just couldn't get. While the advent of the internet has certainly speeded up aspects of this kind of research, it still often gets down to convincing a stranger to plough through reels of microfilm for the briefest piece of evidence of a concert or spending weeks waiting for borrowed microfilm to arrive, only to find nothing of use within it and being forced to start the process all over again with another potential source. Sadly, the instant information age applies mainly to events of the last decade where one can now search hundreds of on-line newspapers for the smallest mention of someone with the push of a few buttons, rendering almost complete media coverage of a worldwide tour in a matter of minutes. By contrast tracking a rock 'n' roller's activities around the globe 25–35 years ago takes almost as long to document as it did for the artist to accomplish the activity himself in the first place. But such is the challenge and where the puzzle-solving skills come in handy.

So, that we have been able in the end to present hundreds upon hundreds of exact and confirmed dates and new pieces of information, in fact, a very high percentage of all his performances, we think is a very significant accomplishment. We are proud of the research which has been assembled within this book. While it is not yet definitive, or the last word, it is extremely comprehensive and we hope the reader will agree, is light-years ahead of the collective knowledge which had existed about Mr. Beck before. But beyond the pure thrill of the hunt, we tried not to ever lose sight of the fact that the point of it all is to not only properly document but celebrate the career of a true original, Jeff Beck. We both salute your talent and thank you for all the great music.

Contents

1944–1964: The First Twenty Years	9
1965	14
Five Live Yardbirds	15
A Map of Early Influences	17
A Yardstick To The Future	25
Trailblazing Experiences	29
1966	41
Zeppelin Unledded	49
This Band Ain't Big Enough	59
Turmoil In Texas	63
1967	67
The Most of Beck	71
The Singing Beck	77
1968	82
Truth And Consequences	89
The Chicken and The Egg	93
1969	96
Beeb Pop A Beck	105
1970	106
Panic in Detroit	107
1971	110
The Importance of Being Ernest	111
1972	115
Rough, Ready, Go!	121
Picture Section: "Blowup"	
1973	132
Strange Interlude	133
The Electric Larynx	137
1974	148
Unfinished Business	149
1975	155
Slide Projector	159
Show By Show	163
1976	167
Guitar As Voice	171
Wang Bar Doodles	179
1977	181
1978	185
1979	188
The Beck–Clarke Expedtion	189
1980	191
Here And Gone	193
Fast Forward: 1981–2000	198
Appendix 1: "Quote Rightly So" – Other guitarists on Jeff Beck	199
Appendix 2: "The Nuts 'n' Bolts of Jeff Beck" – Equipment file	202
Appendix 3: Live performances	207
Appendix 4: Radio- and TV-appearances	220
Appendix 5: Recording sessions	228
Appendix 6: Bibilography and sources	231
Appendix 7: Index	236

Preface

◀◀ Rewind

Freeze-frame # 1 [Date: March 8, 1965. Location: Marquee Club, London, England] It is a cold Monday night, and house regulars the Yardbirds are about to step on stage at the Marquee in the middle of Soho. The group has played here innumerable times already, but tonight the group's popular lead guitarist is missing as he has just left the band a few days earlier. Eric Clapton, who has played lead with the Yardbirds up till now, has built a fervent fan following – his own crowd who stand in front of stage left and cheer him on. In fact, many of his fans are not even aware that he has left the band, while those who have heard the news are here just to heckle the newcomer. The new boy cuts a pale, thin figure who takes up Clapton's regular position on stage left. "Where's Eric?" and "We want Slowhand!" voices in the crowd call out as the unknown guitarist nervously plugs in his white Telecaster. The Yardbirds kick in their opening number. Above the din of the massive rhythm, Keith Relf's voice can barely be heard. Suddenly, the lead guitar cuts through the music – a vibrant and stinging sound, unpolished and raw. Then the guitarist motions towards his Vox amplifier which is perched on a small chair, moving closer and closer until the unmistakable earsplitting sound of a pickup feeding back rings out. But wait! As if by magic, while the one note sustains, the guitarist is able to tame the feedback into a long snake-like melody. From his horn of plenty he then pulls sounds never before heard from a guitar; one moment a steam train coming down the tracks, the next moment a coop full of squawking chickens. At the end of the night he lifts the guitar above his head in an act of triumph as he acknowledges the standing ovation from the audience.

Freeze-frame # 2 [Date: June 29, 1968. Location: Boston Tea Party, Boston, Massachusetts, USA] A new English group has played here in Boston for four days running. Although the first night was slow, word of mouth has spread rapidly and tonight the club is packed wall to wall with people. The group is named after its guitar player and although he had toured the US earlier with the Yardbirds, that was almost two years ago and even then he never appeared in Boston. In the meantime, not much has been heard of him but Jimi Hendrix has talked generously of his talent and his influence is still felt through his contribution to classic Yardbirds hit singles. To underline both the hot atmosphere in the club and his cool image, he plays bare chested. Rod Stewart, the rusty voiced singer, stands to his left in a frilly shirt, while the bassist and the drummer line up the rear. A sweet scent fills the air. One! Two! Three! Bang – the group jumps headlong into a tough Earl Hooker song, before a gear shift to a comfortable Buddy Guy-borrowed boogie. The centre of attention is the empathy between the guitar and the vocal, closely coordinated and carefully worked out yet clearly intuitive and musical. The formula is as genial as it is simple, but ultimately it will be up to someone else to convert the concept into really big cash.

Freeze-frame # 3 [Date: September 23, 1972. Location: Grangemouth, Falkirk, Scotland] It is a dismal September night way up in Scotland and the "Great Caledonian Express" festival is about to grind to a halt. It has not been a great success. A pair of the announced attractions have cancelled at the very last moment, and the crowd – which at one point counted 12,000 spectators – is down to a mere 2,000 souls as a brand new English–American power trio takes the stage for a ferocious set. Warmed by the sounds from the stage, the cold crowd demands an encore, and the three ramble back on with knowing smiles on their faces. The guitarist looks at the bassist and drummer and rips off the opening to the boogie bearing his name. With startlingly unpredictability he moves from lo-fi to sci-fi; from an old blues riff to a banjo hoedown in the blink of an eye. Alternately he runs riot across the fretboard or coaches phrases of pure beauty from the strings – in the process perhaps surprising himself just as much as the listener. The gasps of astonishment from the stagehands, musicians and journalists standing in the wings are clearly audible as the encore reaches its rattling conclusion and the trio leaves the stage.

Freeze-frame # 4 [Date: July 10, 1976. Location: Comiskey Park, Chicago, Illinois, USA] The United States is in the middle of its Bicentennial celebration, and a series of huge open air concerts are staged around the country this long hot summer. Today at Chicago's huge Comiskey Park – usually reserved for White Sox baseball games – "The World Series of Rock Games #1" is about to kick off. A big, rowdy audience with more than 60,000 people has filled the park. In the middle of the day, a group performing primarily instrumental music in the already dubious 'fusion' category walks on stage. An inter-continental, inter-racial five-man group featuring a Czech-born jazz pianist and a black rhythm section, their secret weapon is the English guitarist whose professional career stretches back more than ten years to the time when he replaced Eric Clapton in the Yardbirds. The music they perform today injects the 'jazz-rock' label with a new meaning. The guitarist moves around the stage with all the flamboyancy befitting a true rock star. He looks uncannily like he did ten years ago; same black, ruffled hair style, wearing street clothes of the jeans variety. Actually, he even *sounds* like he did ten years ago, although his technique is of course refined and his ability to improvise is improved. Although once prone to smash his equipment in a rage when it malfunctioned, now he is comfortable with the instrument and amplifier as they are well behaved and co-operate his slightest whims. The guitar sings wild and free as the music moves from spine tingling ballads to funky instrumentals. At his best it sounds like the guitarist's fingers are bypassing his brain and are wired straight to his soul.

The First 20 Years

Geoffrey Arnold Beck was born June 24 1944, in Wallington, Surrey, England, the only son of Ethel Florence Dixie and Arnold Herbert Beck. The couple already had a daughter, Annetta, born four years previously. Beck senior worked as a departmental manager at a bottle manufacturer. Nestling just south of London and a little west of Croydon, Wallington was one of the many suburban towns that later were incorporated into Greater London. The family home was at 206 Demesne Road, where baby Beck was brought up in normal British post-war surroundings with food rationing and shortages, but also a great deal of optimism for the future.

Jeff has always described his childhood as happy, with parents who took a keen interest in their two kids. After passing the 'Eleven Plus' examination, Jeff was sent to Sutton East Secondary School on Greyhound Road in nearby Sutton, presumably beginning here in September 1955. In November the same year, Jeff was involved in a serious accident: "I was on a red bicycle, pedalling up this narrow street. I tried to pass a car ahead but it swerved unexpectedly, smashing me up against the wall of a building on the right-hand side. Several stitches had to be taken in the back of my head ... I was covered with blood by the time I got to the nearby hospital", was how Jeff graphically described the accident to an American teen magazine ten years later.

In the mid-fifties, the sounds of modern jazz and early rock and roll came to Britain from America. Jeff's interest in music and arts developed at this time, and it was the sounds from the radio that first pricked his ears. He would turn the dial on the radio and find Radio Luxemburg late at night: "[It] was one of these stations you could just tune into, as if it was coming from the far flung regions of Africa or something." He has vivid memories of hearing Les Paul and Mary Ford singing and playing one of their many adaptations of popular jazz standards. Les Paul, the 'Wizard of Waukesha', developed overdub methods and trick recordings making his guitar sound like an orchestra. Always interested in sketching and drawing, at Sutton East Jeff was allowed to take part in a special two-year junior art class. Like kids do, Jeff tried to assemble a guitar consisting of some cigar boxes for the body, an unsanded fence moulding for the neck, strings of aircraft control wire and painted-on frets.

Sensing the young boy's love of music, already as a ten-year old Jeff was urged by his mother to sing in the local church choir. At the same time he took piano lessons for about two years. Jeff also dabbled on other instruments in his pre-teens; an uncle who was greatly interested in classical music, tried to teach him to play the cello. Jeff did not come to terms with the bow, although he also attempted the double bass for a short time.

The watershed moment came when Jeff's sister Annetta brought home records by Elvis Presley. *Hound Dog* was the landmark, a brilliant little record propelled by DJ Fontana's shoot out on drums and Scotty Moore's remarkable guitar. Coming to grips with this new sensation, Jeff first acquired a snare drum and tried to play along to the records. But like hearing Les Paul earlier, it was the sound of the guitar that again struck the impressionable boy. He duly borrowed an acoustic guitar from a friend and taught himself the intro to the Buddy Holly classic *That'll Be The Day*. Another record Annetta brought home was the LP *Gene Vincent & The Blue Caps*. With an image even rowdier than Elvis, Vincent also sported a fearsome backing group with a 30-year old Virginia guitarist called Cliff Gallup, who had the rare ability of playing solos set in stone; perfectly hummable mini-compositions, naturally mixing swinging jazz into a bluesy rockabilly stew.

Around 1957, Jeff was inspired by a poster for the movie "The Girl Can't Help It" (which starred Jayne Mansfield and featured Gene Vincent and Eddie Cochran) to try to build himself an electric guitar: "I'd sussed out in my mind how to make it without any plans, and I went to buy some wood, which was about half-an-inch thick plywood, so the front and the belly and the back were all half-inch ply, making a total weight equivalent to about six electric guitars", Jeff Beck later recalled to John Tobler in a BBC interview: "I just did it from a scaled up picture in my mind of how it should look, so it was about fourteen feet long and ridiculously out of proportion ... It was a good thing to get hold of, and wield about, and that's where it all started, with that one guitar – I used to prop it up in an armchair, and just look at it more than play it, because I loved the way guitars looked." Reportedly Jeff had another pass at building his own guitar, this one sprayed yellow, and although the result wasn't any more playable, it again looked good; Jeff used to bike around with the guitar strapped to his back.

In March 1958, seminal American rocker Buddy Holly with his Crickets (just Joe B. Mauldin on bass and Jerry Allison on drums), began a UK tour in London. Jeff, not yet fourteen, caught Holly's concert at Croydon's stately Davis Theatre on Wednesday March 12, and was shellshocked: "It was so great. Coming out of that theatre, I just couldn't see anything, I'd walk under buses and not care," Jeff recalled to the BBC. (Holly, just twenty-two, tragically died within a year in an airplane crash in Iowa.)

Beck's first stage appearance apparently took place circa spring 1958 or '59, when he backed up a singer – "who sang *Be-Bop-A-Lula* or something" – on a May Day parade at Carshalton Park on Ruskin Road, halfway between Sutton and Wallington. The ensemble was completed by a 'double bassist' who toted a cello! The rather impromptu performance generated enough excitement locally to give Jeff a reputation.

Beck never took formal lessons, instead he practised and perfected his guitar technique like countless other would-be guitarists across Britain; perched in front of the gramophone, slowing down the speed to 16 rpm, carefully lifting the needle back again and again to try to learn exactly what was being played. Jeff's early favourites were all Americans and thus the genuine article: Buddy Holly, Scotty Moore, Eddie Cochran, Cliff Gallup, Chuck Berry and Ricky Nelson (with the string bending phenomenon James Burton). Jeff taught himself Cochran's *Twenty Flight Rock,* and as his technique quickly improved he learned James Burton solos parrot-fashion from Ricky Nelson's *It's Late* and *My Babe*. Briefly commissioned to write a column in BEAT INSTRUMENTAL in the mid-sixties, Jeff Beck recounted: "I went through several phases. First I decided that I was going to be a folk guitarist. I bought a pile of thumb and finger picks, stuck 'em all over my right hand and thought I was great. I learned the usual folksy numbers. After a while I decided I'd move on and launched into a sort of jazz-education kick. I bought a book of dance-band chords and ploughed through it finding different chords to use. In the end I taught myself to play about two bars of a couple of jazz standards." The 'folksy' period included a fascination of US country guitarists Chet Atkins and Merle Travis, and Jeff religiously taught himself to play Atkins' *Trambone* finger picking style.

In the late 1950's Annetta Beck introduced Jeff to another guitarist through her friend Barry Matthews: "You gotta see this weird thin guy playing a weird shaped guitar like yours." This was Jimmy Page, six months Beck's senior, who lived on Miles Road in nearby Epsom (about six miles west of Wallington). The two boys hit it off right away and became close friends, spending their time listening to records and forever playing guitars at Jimmy's house.

Another neighbourhood acquaintance was Roger Mayer from Sutton. Page and sometimes Beck would go to Mayer's house for informal strumming sessions. The electronically-inclined Mayer later made fuzz devices for both Page and Beck.

Also sharing Beck's great interest in guitars was his best friend John Owen. Either with John or alone, Jeff would travel to London by train, looking at the unobtainable American Fender guitars displayed in the music shops: "I found my way to Charing Cross Road, looked at this guitar, and dreams floated off in the distance. I actually saw it, touched it, and that was enough. I had a catalogue way before then, which I used to look at, an American one from Fender in Fullerton. I always remember it was on ritzy looking paper, and I always thought these guitars have got to be about a thousand quid ...", Beck later recalled to the UK magazine GUITAR.

By now, Jeff had acquired his first electric guitar, a Japanese Guyatone: "I'll always remember that Guyatone because it had a big toggle switch, and that was the business. It looked like it'd be more at home at a railway station. I made a case for the guitar, but I didn't allow for the switch. It was about 1/8 of an inch out. I put the guitar in the case, slammed the lid down, and pressed the switch right through the plastic. So I stuck it back together and went off to a gig. Stood at the bus stop and the guitar case fell over and did it again! Did the gig and it was all right, went home, plugged in and it just buzzed. So I stuck it back together again, painted it black ... [and] got a Burns", Jeff explained to NEW MUSICAL EXPRESS in 1974. So Jeff now had a Burns, presumably a Vibra Artiste, which featured three single coil pickups, an array of switches and a tremolo arm – a guitar as close to a Fender Stratocaster as the British could make.

Beck also built himself a homemade amplifier at school: "[to] be honest, I never bothered to pick it up from the woodwork room because of its size. There was a straightforward 30-watt unit, but the speaker cabinet was about 15 ft. x 1 ft. and it was packed with different speakers."

Jeff himself succinctly summed up the years until 1960 to Mike Ledgerwood of DISC AND MUSIC ECHO: "I've been interested in the guitar since I was 11. My mind was a bit of a blank between then and 16 when I left school."

1960

It was probably during Gene Vincent's first UK tour in January/February 1960 that Jeff got to see his idol. Sadly, the great Cliff Gallup had long since left the Blue Caps; he had lasted barely seven months and a handful of recordings with Gene before he returned to peaceful Virginia, leaving behind him a lasting legacy and a fervent fan following. Vincent came back to Great Britain for a second time in March 1960, and subsequently survived the same car crash that killed Eddie Cochran on April 17.

As for his academic aspirations, Beck enrolled at Wimbledon School of Art on September 19, on a two-year Fine Art course. By doing this he did what many of his British rock-contemporaries all did – e.g. John Lennon, Keith Richards, Ray Davies, Ron Wood, and two other Surrey boys, Jimmy Page and Eric Clapton. They all found that the art school's bohemian attraction went hand in glove with their own love of rock 'n' roll and rhythm and blues.

In 1960, armed with his Burns guitar, Jeff Beck joined what is believed to be his first proper group, **the Deltones** from Croydon. The opportunity arose because their lead guitarist Ian Duncan had decided to leave to go play with one of the Sarstedt brothers. The group's ex-bass player and then manager, Roger Jarvie, recalls in his memoir in 'Rockin' And Around Croydon': "... a young art student about sixteen years old, asked for an audition as lead guitarist. My first reaction was 'no way', he was far too young to play with us 'established veterans', but as we had no other offers, we agreed to give him an audition. He came along to one of our rehearsals, in Bowaters canteen on Purley Way [Croydon] one Thursday night, carrying a long cardboard box under his arm. I thought 'Christ he hasn't even got a guitar case, what kind of old junk has he got in that box.' Then he opened it and took out a guitar that made all the rest of our equipment ready for the scrapyard. The most beautiful red and gold Burns London guitar, and when he started playing we all froze in disbelief – he was magic". Apparently Beck made enough of an impression to also squeeze in his friend John Owen on rhythm guitar! The rest of the band was Derek "Del" Burchell on vocals, drummer Mick Godfrey and an unknown bass player. The group played regularly around Croydon (at the Park Lane Ballroom), Wimbledon (the Palais), Hammersmith (another Palais), Tonbridge (Dowgate Hall) and likely the Public Hall on Stafford Road, Wallington. The group also used to rehearse at the Prince of Wales, a pub in Thornton Heath. They played a wealth of Shadows material, and accordingly Jeff was required to recreate Hank Marvin's crystalline guitar instrumentals. Local Croydon guitarist John Edmed was impressed when he heard Beck: "I was absolutely mesmerised by this guitarist who sounded just like Hank Marvin, same guitar, same sound, in fact the whole bloody band was a rip-off of the Shadows! Even then Beck was special, completely special you know? He always had the knack of getting sounds out of the guitar that nobody else could do, he was a very good technician."

Peter Sarstedt also insists that his older brother Rick used to sing with the Deltones at the point when Beck was with them; Rick Sarstedt was better known under his adopted guise Eden Kane, who had a sizeable British hit in June 1961 with *Well I Ask You*.

The First Twenty Years

1961

Jeff spent around a year with the Deltones, performing regularly with them until the latter part of 1961. The constant playing also had some financial rewards for Jeff, who decided to upgrade his equipment and went and bought the ultimate; a sunburst Fender Stratocaster, while his friend John Owen bought the simpler sibling, the Telecaster. Roger Jarvie personally had to assure Ethel Beck that the group would be able to honour the down payments on the new guitars. To recreate the Shadows' sound, Jeff also got a German echo unit called a Klempt. A picture of the Deltones is reproduced in the *Beckology* CD-set, with a high-quiffed Jeff proudly displaying his Stratocaster.

After completing only the first year of a two year course, on May 22 Jeff left Wimbledon School of Art. Soon 17 years old, this was to be Jeff's first and last brush with academia.

Around this time Jeff also met Patricia Rose Brown, who became his girlfriend. Martin Nighy, a local Croydon boy who sat in with the Deltones when Derek Burchell could not make it, recalls a funny story: "I remember a gig that I was due to do with the Deltones, Jeff was very late in turning up and when he did arrive he had no guitar or amp with him. When the band asked him about it, he admitted that he had sold them to buy an engagement ring – and needless to say the gig didn't go ahead!"

It was likely after his time with the Deltones, in the autumn of 1961, that Jeff adopted the short-lived alias 'Jeff Mason', and landed the job as guitarist for a local Gene Vincent lookalike called **Cal Danger**, being allowed to impersonate Cliff Gallup as much as he fancied. Danger worked for Bob Potter's Entertainment Agency, playing ballrooms around South London. On the tour bus one day Jeff met **Kerry Rapid**, a singer fronting a band called the **Bandits.** Rapid, or rather Alan Hope as he was christened, managed to talk Jeff into joining his band. Hope takes up the story: "I first met Jeff Beck in the back of a tour bus ... he was a spotty faced youngster, who looked much like Alfred E. Neuman (!) The one problem with Cal was that he only knew the popular Vincent songs. The reason Jeff and I hit it off was that I knew a lot of Vincent's rarer material ... [Beck] played a Fender Stratocaster ... I don't recall him being around for long, but he certainly played the Aldershot Palais and the Agincourt Ballroom in Camberley. The one gig he definitely won't forget is the Newark Corn Exchange in Nottinghamshire [and] the whole evening ended in one massive fight."

The Stratocaster had gone through some changes by then: "I ruined that by trying to re-wire it. Trouble was that I'd seen a Gene Vincent LP cover with white Fender Strats ... I thought that I'd try and get their sound out of mine, so for a start I painted it white, and then set to work on the electrics. That was a big mistake! I just couldn't get the right sound no matter what I did, so I threw it off the end of my bed one night in a rage. It cracked, of course, just down the back where the neck meets the body. I decided to sell it and jack the whole thing in", Jeff wrote in his BEAT INSTRUMENTAL column. The guitar was put back together, the crack was covered with nail varnish, and it was sold for a fair price at a West End music shop, and the money was promptly plowed into his first car – and probably a fraction into the aforementioned engagement ring! The episode is Jeff Beck in a nutshell; although dedicated to music it was not going to stand in the way of his other devotion – cars – and despite his reverence for the exotic and very expensive Stratocaster, he was not afraid to take it apart in search of a new sound or to repaint it for a cooler look.

The column continued: "For a time I was happy to drive around but, after a while, I felt like playing again ... I didn't have a guitar of my own so another of the blokes let me use his Fender Telecaster." This was John Owen's guitar, which Jeff actually kept for several years before – as the story goes – it finally ended up in the hands of Jimmy Page, ostensibly the instrument used on the solo on Led Zeppelin's *Stairway To Heaven*.

1962/1963

Upon leaving art college, Jeff took on several odd jobs, briefly driving a tractor on a golf-course, doing carpentry and – closer to his heart – working as a panel beater and a car painter at South Croydon Motors. On his lunch break he would pop into Ted Potter's Music Shop in High Street, in oil stained overalls. The shop served as the place where musicians would meet.

After the Deltones, Jeff Beck was unable to find a comfortable setting to suit him, so he drifted from group

The Tridents 1964 diary:

▶ **APRIL**
Sunday ?
Eel Pie Island, Twickenham

Tuesday 14th
100 Club, Oxford Street, London
The Tridents and Mark Leeman Five supported the Pretty Things.

▶ **MAY**
Wednesday 6th
Ealing Club, Ealing

Wednesday 20th
Ealing Club, Ealing

Wednesday 27th
The Cellar Club, High Street, Kingston-upon-Thames, London
A club also frequented by the Yardbirds.

Friday 29th
Ealing Club, Ealing

▶ **JUNE**
Wednesday 3rd
Ealing Club, Ealing

Wednesday 17th
Ealing Club, Ealing

Wednesday 24th
Ealing Club, Ealing

▶ **JULY**
Wednesday 1st
Ealing Club, Ealing

Thursday 2nd
100 Club, Oxford Street, London

Monday 13th
The Attic, Hounslow

Wednesday 15th
Ealing Club, Ealing

Thursday 16th
100 Club, London

Friday 17th
Ealing Club, Ealing

Thursday 23rd
100 Club, London

Tuesday 28th
100 Club, London

to group, freelancing with whomever cared to ask him or whomever he cared to join. Consequently, the chronology of groups and events post-Deltones is chaotic at best.

Seemingly, he first went with **the Crescents**, with whom Jeff made his debut in Tunbridge Wells, Kent. Another Shadows-type group, they again included Derek Burchell on vocals, and performed around West London at venues like the Boathouse at Kew Bridge on the Thames.

Rob Stearns, a musician on the South London scene, remembers Jeff ("a dynamite guitar player") playing with a group called **Brian Howard & the Silhouettes** with drummer Barry Gilford, who played locally at a club called the Rock n' Twist in Wimbledon.

Jeff is also believed to have played with **Johnny Howard**, which does seem a bit unlikely. From the Croydon area, Howard ran a big dance orchestra which regularly played the Orchid Ballroom in Purley.

Asked by singer Phil Somerville to deputise for some gigs, Jeff played about eight or nine times with '**Im And the Uvvers**, including a performance at the Foresters Hall in Epsom.

Then there was a brief tenure with **Rodney Walsh & the HotRods**, who held down a regular residence at Addington Community Centre.

Some flings were even *more* short-lived; for a single night Jeff freelanced with bass player **Brian Gregg** (who had served time with Johnny Kidd & the Pirates) – who met Jeff after answering an advertisement Gregg had placed in MELODY MAKER.

On the recommendation of Jimmy Page, Jeff auditioned for **Neil Christian's Crusaders**, but was turned down. Christian had a succession of famous guitarists in his band, including Page, Ritchie Blackmore, and Albert Lee. "The only mistake I ever made", Christian said years later.

Jeff also failed an audition for Croydon group the **Alphabeats**, who were looking for a replacement for Steve Carroll, who had just died in a road accident. (The Alphabeats over time evolved into the Herd.)

Jimmy Page, whose frail physique forced him to quit live playing temporarily, began working as a studio musician in early 1963. Sometimes, Page would arrange for Beck to do some session work as well. Much speculation concerns the many sessions Beck allegedly played on during the early Sixties. Beck himself has never discussed these in detail – nor denied them for that matter – but highly likely his contributions were scarce and limited to a few selected appearances. Unlike Jimmy Page who worked full weeks as session guitarist, Jeff was never in such a position, but he has mentioned in passing that he did sessions for Pye Records. Another guitarist Beck bumped into when doing sessions was Ritchie Blackmore, who had created some noise on his own as a member of the Savages, a group that backed the eccentric Dave 'Screaming Lord' Sutch.

Ex-Deltones manager Roger Jarvie is sure that Beck's studio debut was on an unreleased version of Eddie Fisher's sugary *Wedding Bells*.

1963

According to his own recollections, Jeff was vaguely offered two positions around 1963 which he turned down. One offer was to join the **Roosters**, a group put together by two wayward blues enthusiasts from Oxford, Tom McGuinness and Ben Palmer. The twosome had moved to Kingston-upon-Thames, but in the end, it was Eric Clapton who got his start with this amateur group. The other position was to play with **John Mayall**. Mancunian Mayall came to London to assemble his first Bluesbreakers in the summer of 1963, and Jeff was urged by a guitar salesman in Charing Cross Road to check him out: "He's the guv'nor, you'd better see him!"

Sometime in 1963 Jeff met Ian Stewart, who would instill in Beck a love for the blues: "It was old Stew, the Rolling Stones' road manager who really started things off for me. As you probably know, he is a fair blues pianist ... he was the one who introduced me to people like Buddy Guy, Otis Rush, B. B. King and the guitarists who used bottleneck." One record in particular impressed Beck: an EP by Muddy Waters and Earl Hooker featuring the vibrant *You Shook Me* (UK Pye, September 1963). In fact, Jeff was present at Croydon's Fairfield Halls when the American Folk & Blues Festival came through town for two appearances this year, on October 18 and 20, starring Muddy Waters, Willie Dixon, Matt "Guitar" Murphy and many others.

With his new-found love for the blues, Jeff rounded up drummer Dave Elvidge, singer Brian Wiles and a forgotten bassist to complete the **Nightshift**. The group played around locally at venues like the Palais in Wimbledon, the Tolworth Co-Op, and Eel Pie Island in Twickenham, Middlesex.

The Tridents 1964 diary:

▶ **AUGUST**

Monday 3rd
100 Club, London

Monday 10th
100 Club, London

Wednesday 12th
Ealing Club, Ealing

Thursday 13th
Studio 51, London

Friday 14th
Allnighter Club, Windsor

Saturday 15th
Allnighter Club, Windsor

Monday 17th
100 Club, Oxford Street, London
The Tridents played support to the Birds tonight, featuring Ron Wood on guitar.

Wednesday 19th
Ealing Club, Ealing

Thursday 20th
Studio 51, London

Saturday 22nd
Studio 51, London

Sunday 23rd
• Flamingo Club, London
• Studio 51, London
The Tridents supported Georgie Fame & The Blue Flames before they headed off to an "all-nighter" at Studio 51.

Monday 24th
100 Club, Oxford Street, London
The Tridents opened while the Birds headlined.

Thursday 27th
Studio 51, London

Monday 31st
100 Club, Oxford Street, London

▶ **SEPTEMBER**
Thursday 3rd
Studio 51, London

Thursday 10th
Studio 51, London

The First Twenty Years

That was an old Victorian hotel in the middle of the River Thames, and its only access was by a footbridge. Although some sources insist Beck's talents grace the Nightshift single *That's My Story/Stormy Monday* (Piccadilly Records), this is unlikely as this was released in the autumn of 1965.

Meanwhile, on July 13, Jeff Beck married Patricia Rose Brown at the Parish Church of St. Mary in Southgate, Sussex. The couple had moved in at 5 Dickens Road, Tilgate, Crawley, some miles straight south from Wallington. (It was not a long lasting marriage; on November 15, 1967 Patricia successfully sued for divorce.)

By 1963, London was teeming with rhythm and blues groups that popped up in the wake of the Rolling Stones, who had released their debut single *Come On* in June. One such band was the **Tridents**, lining up John Lucas on guitar, Paul Lucas on bass/vocals, Ray Cook on drums and Mike Jopp on lead guitar, who had decided to leave when the others wanted to go professional. Performing one evening with the Nightshift – presumably late 1963 – Jeff was spotted by the brothers Lucas, and they had found their man. Outfitted with John Owen's trusted Fender Telecaster, a Binson Echorec and John Lucas' Vox AC30 amplifier, Jeff finally found a musical home. The revamped Tridents made a recording this year Regent Sound; *Keep Your Hands Off My Baby* (presumably the Little Eva US #12 hit from 1962) and the blues standard *Trouble In Mind*. Reportedly, a few acetate copies were made to promote club dates. *Trouble In Mind* resurfaced almost thirty years later on the *Beckology* box in 1991.

1964

The Tridents jumped up a league when they became represented by the Rik Gunnel Agency from February 1964 onwards, and the group quickly gathered a fan following in the Richmond area, particularly due to their regular Sunday residence at Eel Pie Island, where they could pack in 800–1,000 people. But the Tridents played all over London, including the cradle of British blues, the Ealing Club; Studio 51 on Newport Street (Ken Colyer's Jazz Club, which was 'Studio 51' on its blues nights); the Flamingo in Wardour Street and of course the 100 Club on Oxford Street. Out of town bookings included the Memorial Hall in Holsworthy, Devon.

In 1964, the group again intended to make a single, this time at the small Oriole Studio, preserving on tape the group compositions *That Noise* and *Wandering Man Blues*. Again the recordings were at best manufactured in a limited amount with no commercial release, but *Wandering Man Blues* was also dusted off and included on the *Beckology* box.

On March 9, the group sent an application to the BBC, requesting an audition. Oddly enough, the form was signed by a lead guitarist calling himself Leslie Jones; perhaps a temporary stand-in or another of Beck's aliases? All the same, the request was politely rejected by the BBC Audition Panel due to the group's lack of professional experience. BBC documents show no further Tridents applications or session details.

In April, the group taped a storming live version of Bo Diddley's *Nursery Rhyme* during an engagement at Eel Pie Island, which was also issued on the 3 CD-set *Beckology* in 1991.

Jeff Beck's reputation as a guitarist was rapidly spreading, as shown by an entry in Bill Wyman's diary for May 6; Jeff, Bill, Jimmy Page, Ian Stewart, drummer Wint, and harp-player Knocker all indulged in a late-night jam at Eel Pie Island.

By July, the Tridents seemed to have secured a regular residence at the 100 Club, allowing at least one weekly appearance at the club.

Strangely enough, Jeff rejoined the Nightshift for their support slot at the 4th National Jazz & Blues Festival in Richmond, Surrey on August 7, 1964, when they played on a bill topped by the Rolling Stones. Indeed, the Nightshift did a stretch of dates at London's Marquee Club between August and November 1964 – including supporting the Yardbirds on October 30! – but is has been impossible to determine if Beck played with the group on these occasions.

In the second half of 1964, Jeff did a pair of guest appearances, first when he turned up for Screaming Lord Sutch's *Come Back Baby*, which was the B-side of Sutch's single *Dracula's Daughter* (released October 23 on Oriole Records). Next he appeared on *I'm Not Running Away*, a straight pop number by the totally obscure Fitz 'n' Startz (released December 11 on Parlophone).

In late 1964, despite their local success, the Tridents had neither a proper management nor a record deal, and it was only a question of time before Jeff would move on. ■

The Tridents 1964 diary:

Thursday 17th
- 100 Club, Oxford Street, London
- Studio 51, London

Thursday 24th
Studio 51, London

Saturday 26th
'Cavern' Olympia, Reading

Tuesday 29th
100 Club, Oxford Street, London
With Brian Knight's Blues By Six.

▶ **OCTOBER**
Thursday 15th
100 Club, Oxford Street, London
Supported by the Epitaphs.

Thursday 29th
100 Club, Oxford Street, London
Supported by the Blues By Night.

▶ **NOVEMBER**
Tuesday 10th
100 Club, Oxford Street, London
With Brian Knight's Blues By Six.

Tuesday 17th
100 Club, Oxford Street, London

Tuesday 24th
100 Club, Oxford Street, London

▶ **DECEMBER**
Friday 4th
Town Hall, East Ham
Also with the Herd.

Tuesday 8th
100 Club, Oxford Street, London
Supported by The Long And The Short And The Tall.

Tuesday 15th
100 Club, Oxford Street, London
With King B Four.

Saturday 19th
Mitcham R&B Club, Romany Dance Hall, Mitcham

(This is by no means a complete list of the Tridents' exhaustive schedules. Although Eel Pie Island was a Tridents' stronghold and they played here innumerable times during 1964, it has been impossible to confirm exactly when they performed here as the venue did not advertise in the regular music press.)

1965

JANUARY

Presumably the Tridents keep up the pattern of regular club dates set throughout 1964; for some reason, however, there are no high-profile appearances on the London club circuit this month.

> RHYTHM 'N' BLUES
> **TRIDENTS**
> BAND & GENERAL AGENCY
> 8 Great Chapel Street, W.1
> GER 0337

THU 28TH
T-Bone Walker plays the Marquee, leaving a lasting impression on Beck: "He used to finish off his act by playing with one hand while carrying his amp off with the other. I thought that was the coolest thing in the entire universe when I saw that."

SAT 30TH
Playhouse, Walton-on-Thames
The Tridents play a small town in Surrey along the Thames.

FEBRUARY

TUE 9TH
100 Club, London
The Tridents resume their 100 Club residence after not having played here all of January.

SAT 13TH
Waterfront Club, Southampton
A Tridents date down in Hampshire.

MID–LATE
Faced with the need for a replacement for the dissatisfied Eric Clapton, Yardbirds' manager Giorgio Gomelsky phones another South London guitarist and friend of the band Jimmy Page, who everyone agrees is a perfect choice.

Page in fact had been asked once before by Gomelsky to replace Clapton during Clapton's Christmas 1963 holiday furlough from the band, but had turned them down out of loyalty to his friend Eric in not wanting to appear to move in on his territory. Faced with the proposition again, Page, now comfortably employed as a guitarist in the prosperous London recording scene, does not want to leave his secure session life, and suggests his long-time friend Jeff Beck instead.

MON 15TH
100 Club, London
As best as can be determined, this is the night when Giorgio Gomelsky and Hamish Grimes personally approach Jeff Beck, who's playing with the Tridents at the 100 Club on Oxford Street. They invite him to audition for the Yardbirds, who incidentally play just a few blocks away tonight at the Marquee Club on Wardour Street.

TUE 16TH/WED 17TH✱
The day or so following Gomelsky's invitation, Jeff gets to audition for the Yardbirds at the Marquee, where the band regularly rehearses. Anecdotally Beck is offered the vacant spot after impressing Relf with his knowledge of bluesman Matt 'Guitar' Murphy. (This scenario could possibly also take place on February 24–25, refer to the Tridents' 100 Club appearance on the 23rd.)

Although reluctant to leave the Tridents, Beck accepts the position because the Yardbirds "appeared to have good management, and seemed to be going places", as he would later put it. Though it would have been difficult to predict the runaway success *For Your Love*, having a very commercial record poised for release by one of Britain's major record labels could easily be considered an opportunity too good to pass by.

TUE 23RD
100 Club, London
Jeff Beck and the Tridents pick up their 100 Club residency.

> **100 CLUB**
> 100 OXFORD ST., W.1
> 7.30 to 11 p.m.
> (Sat. 7.30 to 11.30 p.m.)
>
> Thursday, February 11th
> **GRAHAM BOND**
> THE BLUES BY KNIGHT
> Friday, February 12th
> Final appearance of
> **WILD BILL DAVISON**
> with
> **FREDDIE RANDALL**
> and His Band
> Members 5/-, Guests 7/6
> Saturday, February 13th
> **ALAN ELSDON**
> MICK EMERY'S FOLK GROUP
> THE EVERGLADES
> Sunday, February 14th
> **Mr. ACKER BILK**
> and the PARAMOUNT JAZZ BAND
> THE FREEWHEELERS
> Monday, February 15th
> **TRIDENTS**
> Tuesday, February 16th
> Return visit of the
> Great American Blues Singer
> **MAE MERCER**
> with
> **THE ART WOODS**
> Members 5/-, Guests 6/-
> Wednesday, February 17th
> **BACK O'TOWN**
> Thursday, February 18th
> **GRAHAM BOND**
> THE LOOSE ENDS
> Full details of the Club from the secretary,
> 100 Club, 8 Great Chapel St., W.1 (GER 0337)

THU 25TH
Jeff Beck witnesses Chicago bluesman Buddy Guy's searing performance at the Marquee. Guy is backed by Rod Stewart & the Soul Agents, who include drummer Mickey Waller. Also in the audience is Eric Clapton.

MARCH

MON 1ST✱
Eel Pie Island Hotel, Twickenham
American folk singer Jesse Fuller arrived in Britain on February 19 ahead of a UK tour to commence today. Reportedly, the Tridents back Fuller on a booking at Eel Pie Island, attracting a record audience of 1,500.

TUE 2ND
According to Paul Lucas's diary, Jeff leaves the Tridents today.

WED 3RD
Eric Clapton makes his last appearance as a Yardbird at the Bristol Corn Exchange. According to a vivid account of the evening provided by fan Julian Bailey, the band turns in a breathtaking performance despite Clapton's imminent departure. The memorable impressions are of Clapton playing a red Fender Telecaster, nonchalantly leaning against the venue's mock Greek columns and slowly sliding down as his solos became more frantic – and that they definitely did play the contentious new single *For Your Love*, a fact corroborated by another fan sighting around this time.

Prior to his stage debut with the Yardbirds, Jeff's appearance undergoes a quick "Yardbirdization". His hair – which has been down below the collar – is trimmed à la Mick Jagger (a resemblance which will not go unnoticed by the music press). As it turns out, Beck is the same size as Clapton, so he merely inherits Eric's stage suit. Some rehearsals to learn the existing stage show are also squeezed in, but Beck is a quick study, and the material he needs to learn is not dissimilar to what he has already been playing with the Tridents.

•

Upon his formal departure, Clapton

Newsflash March 1965: Jeff Beck debuts with the Yardbirds in Croydon ...

initially considers joining Mick O'Neil and the Soultones, but after a brief hiatus accepts an offer to join John Mayall's Bluesbreakers in mid-April. After little more than a year with Mayall, Eric Clapton embarks upon a well documented career whose route takes a number of twists before achieving superstar status as a solo performer. His path will cross Jeff's many times in the ensuing years.

FRI 5TH
"Sounds of '65"
Fairfield Hall, Croydon

Tonight Jeff Beck makes his live debut with the Yardbirds at a benefit concert for the pirate station Radio Caroline. The other acts on the bill are the Moody Blues, the Mark Leeman Five, Ronnie Jones & the Nightimers, Barry St. John, and Jimmy James & the Vagabonds – all compèred by deejay Simon Dee. As is common at the time, there are two shows (6.45 and 9 pm) and, typical of such package shows, the Yardbirds' set would only consist of about four songs – taking some of the initial pressure off Jeff to know more than a handful of their numbers. The CROYDON ADVERTISER gives Beck what is perhaps his first ever review: "The lead guitarist of the Yardbirds, a five man solid rhythm and blues group, demonstrated his versatility in *For Your Love*, their latest record." In summing up, the reviewer does not find all to his taste: "The Yardbirds in particular, must learn to choose suitable numbers to play to a sitting audience, rather than keep pounding away at something that would make excellent dance music, but is a little boring to listen to."

A press release claims that after the concert, the Yardbirds host a farewell party in honour of Clapton. Considering the acrimony of his departure, this is likely a publicity ploy.

This same day, the Yardbirds' third single, *For Your Love* coupled with the instrumental *Got To Hurry* (credited to O. Rasputin, technically Oscar Rasputin – an appropriate Russian-sounding alias for Giorgio Gomelsky), is released in Great Britain on Columbia Records, a subsidiary of the behemoth EMI Ltd. Jeff Beck is not heard on the disc, as both sides feature Clapton on guitar. Faith in the song's potential will be proved justified when the single makes #1 in the UK on the NEW MUSICAL EXPRESS chart (in the 'official' British chart it peaks at #2) during the second week of April, sandwiched between chart-toppers by the Rolling Stones (*The Last Time* on April 3) and

HERE 'TIS

Five Live Yardbirds

The Yardbirds, a rhythm and blues group from the Richmond and Surbiton areas in the southern reaches of Greater London were formed in the spring of 1963 through the combining of members of two school-based bands the Metropolitan Blues Quartet (vocalist/harmonica player Keith Relf and bassist Paul Samwell-Smith) and the Country Gentlemen (drummer Jim McCarty, guitarists Chris Dreja and Tony 'Top' Topham). The band quickly established itself by inheriting the Sunday residency at the Crawdaddy Club in Richmond, taking over from the Rolling Stones whose last performance there was September 22, 1963. The Yardbirds forged their own distinct R&B style based on improvisation and spontaneity and developed their 'rave-up' style through extended jams and employing simple effects of dynamics overlooked by many of the purist acts of the day.

A conflict with school duties and a desire by the band to turn pro necessitated the departure of Topham and ex-Rooster member Eric Clapton came in as new lead guitarist in October of that year. Concurrently, the Crawdaddy Club's mentor Giorgio Gomelsky became the Yardbirds' manager. (Gomelsky had been the Rolling Stones' manager before they were whisked away by the young entrepreneur Andrew Loog Oldham). On December 8, 1963, a live show at the Crawdaddy was captured on tape as the Yardbirds backed up American blues legend Sonny Boy Williamson. Days later the band made its first studio demos at the tiny R.G. Jones Studios in Morden, Surrey. The group was signed to a master lease deal with EMI's Columbia subsidiary in March 1964. Their debut single, recorded independently at Olympic Studios in London, *I Wish You Would/A Certain Girl*, was issued on May 1st. Despite a strong recording and a solid push by both Columbia and the band, the record faltered in the lower reaches of the charts. Probably in early April, the band also independently recorded an energetic live performance at London's famed Marquee Club where they held a prestigious Friday residency. Although not issued until December that year, it was a coup for the band in both capturing the excitement of their live sound and for having a major label issue such an LP with no chart success to back it up.

Recording for a second single in August was halted by the nearly fatal collapse and hospitalisation of Keith Relf who suffered from acute asthma. Following his recuperation the band resumed its efforts at commercial R&B success completing their second single *Good Morning Little Schoolgirl/I Ain't Got You*, issued on October 30, 1964. Despite promotional efforts and the band's high-level visibility the single died a death. Determined to create a commercially viable interpretation of their R&B style, the boys set their sights on finding the perfect vehicle for the all-important make-or-break third single. In November and December they made two separate failed efforts in the studio, first with a cover of Major Lance's *Sweet Music* recorded under the direction of Manfred Mann, and then with the Shirelles' *Putty (In Your Hands)*, neither of which made the cut for single release. During the band's participation in the Beatles Christmas show (at the Astoria Theatre, Finsbury Park, December 24, 1964–January 16, 1965), budding young songwriter Graham Gouldman of the Mockingbirds from Manchester wrote a song with their sound in mind.

The song was warmly received and Gomelsky and Samwell-Smith both heard unusual arrangement possibilities for it, including use of a harpsichord as the predominant instrument and a sparse non-traditional accompaniment of upright bass and bongos in the main section, only breaking into a boogie in the middle. For Clapton, however, the ideas were totally at odds with his own desire to play pure blues. In his 16 month tenure with the Yardbirds, Clapton developed in great strides and also had a strong fan base of his own, who gave him the nickname "Slowhand".

Likely in the early days of February, the band committed *For Your Love* to tape at IBC Studios, with Eric Clapton's only grudging cooperation. So thrilled was everyone else involved with the results that a second alternate choice for consideration, the Otis Redding song *Your One And Only Love* favoured by Clapton was not even recorded.

Once its chart potential was agreed upon, *For Your Love* was quickly slated for release on March 5. The first known mention of the bands' recording was included in publisher B. Feldman's advertisement placed in the February 12 edition of NEW MUSICAL EXPRESS, where interestingly the Yardbirds were also listed as recorders of Snooky Pryor's 1956 recording *Someone To Love Me*. It was likely shortly after this time that Clapton's departure was formally stated and a search began immediately for a suitable replacement. ■

March 1965: Jeff Beck plays the Marquee with the Yardbirds ...

the Beatles *(Ticket To Ride* on April 17). In the US the song hits #6 (although not until June), becoming the Yardbirds' biggest single ever there.

Today's RECORD MIRROR is the first to report on Clapton's departure, and also the first national music press reporting of his replacement Jeff Beck.

SAT 6TH
University of Manchester, Manchester
An announced appearance by the Yardbirds on BBC's Light Programme "Easy Beat" for broadcast March 7, with a scheduled taping at Playhouse Theatre today, is evidently cancelled in deference to the induction of the new guitarist.

While a contract exists for this booking at the University of Manchester, it has not been possible to confirm if it was carried out.

MON 8TH
Marquee Club, London
The Yardbirds play one of their favourite London clubs, where they have an irregular monthly residency. Unlike the Croydon debut a few nights earlier, the pressure is from two fronts tonight: The new guitarist has to be familiar with at least a full-length show's worth of material, and – most importantly – he must face the throngs of Clapton loyalists. After an opening set by Mark Leeman Five, Beck's moment of truth is witnessed by a packed crowd. Over 30 years later, the evening is still vivid in Jeff's mind, as he recounts in GUITAR WORLD (October 1999): "... the next thing you know I'm in the bloody Yardbirds, facing Eric's audience at the Marquee. I was a little nervous, but I also knew that it was the best break I was ever going to get. So I just went for it. And luckily I had a great night. I pulled out every trick I knew and got a standing ovation." Yardbirds fan Peter Robinson remembers a very pale, thin and nervous Jeff.

The band's repertoire is basically built around their one album and three singles, with a slew of other Jimmy Reed, Chuck Berry and Bo Diddley songs thrown in for ballast. One number Jeff reportedly introduces into the group's act right away is his own extension of Chuck Berry's *Guitar Boogie*. Beck is also given his own vocal showcase (probably an Elmore James number like *The Sun Is Shining*), and he also features slide guitar extensively from the outset.

Stuck for a guitar for a few shows, Jeff briefly borrows the striking red Fender Telecaster that belongs to the management – a guitar both Clapton and Dreja had used on occasion.

Earlier today, the Yardbirds also presumably tape their guest spot on Radio Luxembourg's "The Friday Spectacular" in front of a live audience at EMI's headquarters at 20 Manchester Square, London, to be broadcast on March 12. This marks Jeff's radio debut with his new band.

TUE 9TH
Grosvenor Ballroom/Borough Assembly Hall, Aylesbury

WED 10TH
Wolsey Hall, Cheshunt

THU 11TH
Thorngate Ballroom, Gosport
The Yardbirds appear with the Roadrunners, who subsequently will become Simon Dupree & the Big Sound.

The headline for MELODY MAKER (dated March 13) on sale today reads "Clapton Quits Yardbirds – Too Commercial", where Keith Relf says: "He has been replaced by Jeff Beck, who is very good, and was recommended to us by session man Jimmy Page." From semi-obscurity and only local notoriety, Jeff Beck becomes a national pop music celebrity overnight when he joins the Yardbirds. He is duly introduced to the music press by way of promotional pictures supplied by Hamish Grimes. Well-known photographer Dezo Hoffman takes the first colour picture of the group at this time, published in the March 20 edition of RECORD MIRROR. And on this date the Yardbirds begin their trip up the charts, entering at #30.

FRI 12TH
Hillside Ballroom, Hereford
The Yardbirds play a dance from 8 pm to 12.30 am supported by the Soulents, who years later would evolve into Mott The Hoople. Also, the Yardbirds are heard tonight on EMI-sponsored "The Friday Spectacular" between 10.00–11.00 pm (► March 8).

SAT 13TH
• **Loughborough College, Loughborough**
• **Twisted Wheel, Manchester**
A double booking finds the Yardbirds first at a Leicestershire college, then at a popular Manchester nightspot.

SUN 14TH✴
Crawdaddy Club, Richmond Athletic Association Club House, Richmond
The new-look Yardbirds possibly make their Crawdaddy Club debut this night; the club, where the nascent Yardbirds got their first big break back at the end of September 1963. Once again Jeff has to prove himself to the hardened Clapton loyalists who have assembled en masse to pass judgement on the new recruit. Again as Jeff would recall years later (GUITAR WORLD, October 1999) following his frightening debut at the Marquee: "After that, the big test was to play this club in Richmond because that's where all the real blues fanatics went. It was kind of an athletic, smelly kind of place to play, and the audience would actually stand on each other's shoulders. It was the first time I really felt like I was going to be slaughtered. But I was cocky. It was like 'All right you bastards, get a load of this!'"

This date is likely but not documented (the first documented Crawdaddy date with Jeff in the band is March 28). Advance advertisements show the T-Bones as slotted for this night but secondary evidence immediately after the fact points to the Yardbirds being there instead.

A contract for a booking tonight at Agincourt Ballroom, Camberley also exists, but seemingly this was replaced by a booking in nearby Farnborough just days later on March 20.

MON 15TH✴
This is almost certainly the day of the Yardbirds' first recording session with Jeff Beck, which had been booked to produce sides for an EP release planned to be issued in May according to a press release in NEW MUSICAL EXPRESS, March 12, 1965. While definitive documentation for this and all the early sessions seem lost to time, both Jeff and Giorgio vividly recall that *Steeled Blues*, considered only a studio warm up number, was the first performance captured on tape by the Beck line-up of the Yardbirds. Gomelsky further elaborates that recordings for this EP were Jeff's baptism by fire in the studio. Sonic evidence at least links the track *I Ain't Done Wrong* as being from the same session as *Steeled Blues* in the form of a badly over-recorded bass guitar distorting the snare drum beats. *Steeled Blues* is a straight-ahead blues instrumental featuring Jeff on slide while the Keith Relf composition *I Ain't Done Wrong* is actually a thinly disguised take on Elmore James' *Done Somebody Wrong* also highlighted by

March 1965: Radio- and TV promotion for the new single "For Your Love"...

slide guitar. While *Steeled Blues* will be used instead as a B-side to the as-yet-unrecorded *Heart Full Of Soul*, it seems if any other tracks recorded for the intended EP, that they were not used or were re-recorded at another documented session next month (▶ April 13). The distortion on these two tracks may be partly attributable to the equipment at Advision not being able to handle capturing a loud rock band on tape at the time. Indeed the studio's equipment was evidently upgraded shortly after this session. (Advision is at the time staffed by head engineer Roger Cameron and assistant Eddie Offord.)

The likelihood of this date being Jeff's debut is further strengthened in that it is conclusively documented that the band records the following day for their first BBC session with Jeff and by then his studio abilities would have been proven.

Originally announced for today but cancelled is a show in Woking, likely at the Atlanta Ballroom.

TUE 16TH

Now with a certifiable hit record on their hands the Yardbirds begin the customary rounds of the media where they suddenly are in great demand. The band make radio and TV appearances this week to promote *For Your Love*, and today Jeff Beck makes his BBC recording debut with the Yardbirds. The state-owned BBC is the crucial promotional outlet for every sixties group, and the Yardbirds with Clapton did their trial broadcast on October 29, 1964, and received an unanimous pass from the Talent Section Group, who concluded "a driving commercial British R & B sound". (The test cuts in question were broadcast on November 21, 1964 on the BBC World Service series "Rhythm & Blues".)

Today, at BBC's Playhouse Theatre studio on Northumberland Avenue in London, the Yardbirds pre-record the newly introduced Mose Allison-cover *I'm Not Talking* (a song that Giorgio has suggested), *Guitar Boogie*, the Vibrations' *My Girl Sloopy*, *For Your Love* (with Jeff playing a 12-string guitar to re-create the harpsichord on the original record), and Howlin' Wolf's *Just Like I Treat You*, all broadcast on BBC Light Programme's key show "Saturday Club" on March 20. The group receives the standard BBC fee of around £36.

WED 17TH

A tentatively scheduled date in Oxford is uncertain if done.

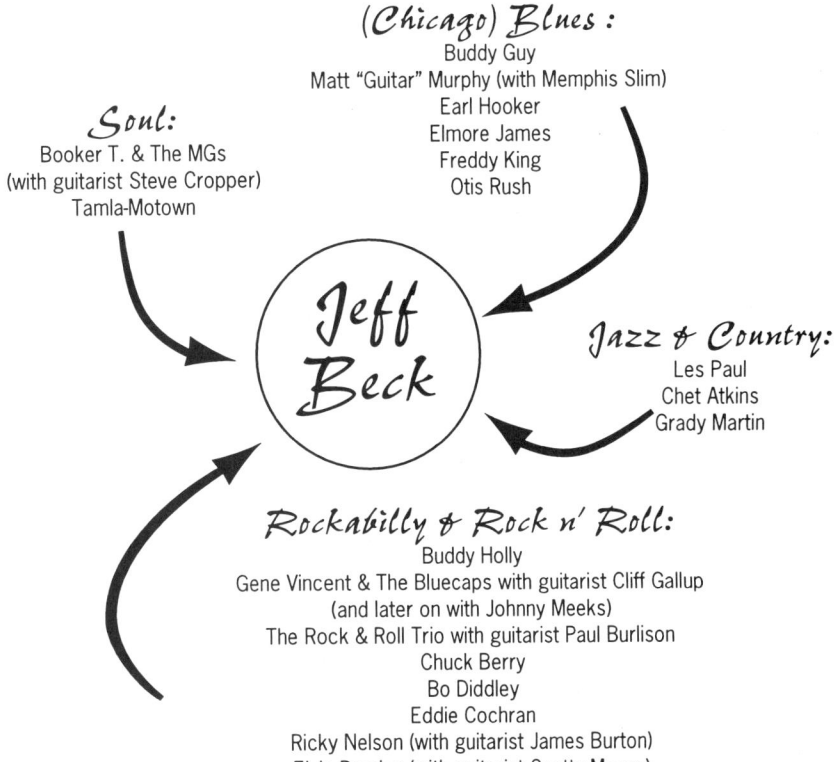

OVER UNDER SIDEWAYS DOWN

A Map Of Early Influences

(Chicago) Blues:
Buddy Guy
Matt "Guitar" Murphy (with Memphis Slim)
Earl Hooker
Elmore James
Freddy King
Otis Rush

Soul:
Booker T. & The MGs
(with guitarist Steve Cropper)
Tamla-Motown

→ **Jeff Beck** ←

Jazz & Country:
Les Paul
Chet Atkins
Grady Martin

Rockabilly & Rock n' Roll:
Buddy Holly
Gene Vincent & The Bluecaps with guitarist Cliff Gallup
(and later on with Johnny Meeks)
The Rock & Roll Trio with guitarist Paul Burlison
Chuck Berry
Bo Diddley
Eddie Cochran
Ricky Nelson (with guitarist James Burton)
Elvis Presley (with guitarist Scotty Moore)

THU 18TH

The band evidently makes two television appearances today marking Jeff's debut in this medium. They presumably tape a segment on "Scene At 6.30" for the independent company Granada at their Television Centre on Quay Street in Manchester, miming to *For Your Love* (for the first of many times!) and aired later in the day (6.30 pm). The band also appears on BBC Television's weekly chart-show "Top Of The Pops" (BBC 1 every Thursday at 7.30–8.00 pm), importantly transmitted on the national network as opposed to local, independent TV stations which often only air in their limited areas. "Top Of The Pops" is as a rule at this time produced at BBC's Dickenson Road Studios, Rusholme, Manchester. The show was inaugurated in January 1964, and is along with "Ready, Steady, Go!" a vital piece of mid-sixties pop promotion. The BBC uses various hosts on this programme, usually their most popular disc-jockeys like Alan Freeman, David Jacobs, Pete Murray and Jimmy Savile.

FRI 19TH

Wimbledon Palais, Wimbledon, London
Back in London, fueled by the sudden popularity of *For Your Love*, the Yardbirds are also a late addition to this week's line-up for Rediffusion's "Ready, Steady, Go!". Tonight's show, hosted by Keith Fordyce, also includes the Dave Clark Five, the Marvellettes, Martha & the Vandellas, Them, Bobby Vee, Dave Berry and one Judi Johnson. This is the first of many appearances by the Yardbirds on this popular music programme where the group is often allowed to stretch out from strictly performing its latest hit à la the BBC "Top Of The Pops". This week's program is transmitted from Television House, Kingsway, London.

SAT 20TH

Assembly Hall, Farnborough Technical College, Farnborough
In the morning the Yardbirds are heard on the airwaves on BBC Light Programme's "Saturday Club" (▶ March 16), broadcast between 10 am and noon, and hosted by Brian Matthew. Other guests are Alex Harvey & His Soul Band and Terry Lightfoot & His Jazzmen.

This evening they play a dance in Farnborough, Hampshire for the student union of the local college supported by the Tom Cats in a show running 8 pm to midnight.

◉ March 20, 1965: Opening night of the Tamla-Motown Revue's tour of the UK featuring the cream of the Detroit label's stable of singers.

March 1965: Jeff Beck has his first press profile in DISC WEEKLY ...

MON 22ND
The Yardbirds are at BBC's Maida Vale Studio 4, 7.00–11.00 pm pre-recording instalments to be broadcast on BBC Light Programme's "Top Gear" on April 10. Brian Matthew is the host. They record the Eric Clapton arrangement of Snooky Pryor's *Someone To Love Me*, *I Ain't Got You*, *For Your Love*, *I'm Not Talking*, and *Steeled Blues*. Three of the five songs recorded are issued in 1991 on the CD *Yardbirds ... On Air*, and provide a glimpse of a guitarist playing assuredly with a great Telecaster tone, but only hinting at his full potential. The Maida Vale complex, counting five different studios, is situated in Delaware Road in London.

TUE 23RD
Burton's Ballroom, Uxbridge
In the afternoon, the Yardbirds appear on BBC Light's "Pop Inn", broadcast live between 1.00–1.55 pm from the Daily Mail Ideal Home Exhibition at the Olympia Conference Centre, where the BBC for the occasion has set up 'Studiolympia'. Keith Fordyce interviews the guests on the show, which combines live interviews with canned music. Afterwards the group heads westward out to Middlesex for the evening's show.

WED 24TH
The Yardbirds videotape a performance on TWW's (Television West and Wales) "Discs-A-Go-Go," compèred by Kent Walton. The location is TWW Centre, Bath Road in Bristol, and the teenage-styled show is described as a "musical comedy pop programme".

For Your Love is surely the band's offering for the show though probably in a live performance at least. This programme is aired the following Monday in most areas though delayed until the following Saturday in others.

THU 25TH
Astoria Ballroom, Oldham
The group drives back up north to Manchester for a repeat appearance on today's "Top Of The Pops" for the BBC (7–7.30 pm), again miming along to their fast rising hit *For Your Love*.

That same evening they play a date in nearby Oldham in Lancashire before heading back down to London.

FRI 26TH
Links Club, Borehamwood
The Yardbirds play this London venue, which is also variously known as the 'Lynx' or 'Links' Club.

SAT 27TH
Royal Hotel, Lowestoft
Jeff has his first feature in the music press when DISC WEEKLY publishes a story on him today, styled as his personal letter to the paper: "I have been very lucky – I appreciate that. Eric Clapton left and Jimmy Page, who is a tremendous guitarist, suggested that I replace him. And it seems very funny that it's happened at the express time the 'Birds have their first really big hit ... Apart from our sense of humour, we agree on one other very big thing. And that is that after work our time is our own ... I think that really is the system for being friendly and not arguing too much. Otherwise you spend all your time together, you begin to get to know each other too well and faults start coming out ... I know this sounds corny but just to end with I'd like to say that the thing that has thrilled me more than anything else is the way the boys seem to be pleased with what I do. Because more than anything I really want to be respected for my music. That's what counts to me," Beck wraps up the letter.

The Lowestoft show is with the support group the Statesmen.

DESIGN: HAMISH GRIMES

SUN 28TH
Crawdaddy Club, Richmond Athletic Association Club House, Richmond
Alternately Jeff's return to this cornerstone booking for the Yardbirds, or his actual debut here (► March 14).

MON 29TH
Marquee Club, London
The Yardbirds return for a night at the Marquee Club supported by the Mark Leeman Five. The pre-taped appearance on TWW's "Discs-A-Go-Go" is also transmitted on ITV (► March 24).

The Yardbirds are also guests on Radio London's "Teen Scene" (10.30–11.15 pm).

TUE 30TH
Capitol Theatre, Aberdeen, Scotland
The Yardbirds help out the Kinks who have cut short a tour of Scotland after Ray Davies collapsed from exhaustion a few days prior in Stirling. The Yardbirds step in for tonight's booking on short notice, flying up to Scotland for the occasion.

WED 31ST
The Yardbirds return to London.

APRIL

THU 1ST
For the third week in a row the Yardbirds are back at the BBC's Manchester facilities to mime *For Your Love* for the nation on tonight's "Top Of The Pops" (BBC 1 7.00 pm.) A scheduled double booking at the Carlton, Erdington and the Adelphi, West Bromwich is seemingly cancelled.

FRI 2ND
Dungeon Club, Nottingham
Interviewed in today's edition of NEW MUSICAL EXPRESS, drummer Jim McCarty boasts of the Yardbirds' new guitarist: "... Geoff [sic] gets so many weird sounds out of his guitar you'd think he's trained as an effects man. Cars hooting, chickens squawking ... he can imitate them all on that guitar."

Tonight also marks a return to "Ready, Steady, Go!" or rather "Ready, Steady Goes Live!" which is the new title of the show given because it is – from today – broadcast all-live (6.08–7.00 pm). In a dual effort to both satisfy the British Musicians Union (which is pressuring producers of programmes with musical entertainment to forgo having artists mime to records) and to make the show more exciting for both performers and viewers alike, this programme switches today from the standard lip-synch format to all 'live' in an attempt to distance itself from the more conservative approach of the BBC's "Top Of The Pops". The show would now originate from Rediffusion's Wembley Studio 1 and also be hosted by Cathy McGowan (dropping Keith Fordyce).

SAT 3RD
St. George's Ballroom, Hinckley
Support by the Staggerlees.

SUN 4TH
Ultra Club, Downs Hotel, Hassocks
In the afternoon the Yardbirds are heard on BBC Light Programme's "Top Gear" (► March 22), broadcast 4.00–5.00 pm. Later the group plays the Downs Hotel in West Sussex, where tonight's fee is a minimum £100 or 50% of the door, with the Shades as support group.

MON 5TH
Guildhall, Southampton
A pair of bongos – the same used to record *For Your Love* – plus a microphone are stolen from the group tonight. They are later retrieved by two girl fans, who in August are rewarded

April 1965: A-side of the new single is recorded in London ...

with a trip to London to visit the Yardbirds in the studio.

TUE 6TH
The Yardbirds pre-record "Ready–Steady–Radio" for Radio Luxembourg (a show routinely taped on Tuesdays), the actual broadcast is on April 11.

In light of the success of their chart-topping record, the Yardbirds form a limited company appropriately named 'Yardbirds Ltd.' with its business year effective as of this day. Jeff Beck is not a formal partner, however, but rather a salaried employee.

WED 7TH
The band flies at the BBC's expense up to its Manchester facility to pre-tape another appearance on "Top Of The Pops". Instead of appearing live as the show is broadcast, the BBC often allows bands to videotape performances which will be slated for an upcoming show depending on the chart position of the song. Often this arrangement is made too when charting bands would be off on tour and would not available for the Thursday broadcast from Manchester. In this instance, the BBC's broadcast files reveal that today's taping is ultimately not used on the programme this week or in subsequent weeks, possibly due to the failure of the song to hit the top spot in the official charts. This despite possible reporting of the Yardbirds scheduled inclusion on the shows as broadcast April 15 and 22 in the music press at the time.

THU 8TH
McIlroys Ballroom, Swindon

FRI 9TH
London Architectural Association, London
A busy day for the Yardbirds who pre-tape BBC's "Saturday Swings" at BBC location Piccadilly 1 in the afternoon, for an airing on April 17.

The set list for today's session is an interesting one, consisting of Chuck Berry's *Too Much Monkey Business*, Bo Diddley's *I'm A Man*, Willie Dixon's classic *Spoonful* plus the requisite *For Your Love*. According to BBC files, the session is further padded out with a song listed as *Runaround*. Tape evidence, in the form of a garbled, low-fidelity excerpt of the Yardbirds' performance (almost certainly from this broadcast) suggests however, that the band plays a variation on the blues standard *Bottle Up And Go*. It is perhaps an impromptu and somewhat improvised rendition which may be some sort of rewrite by the band (as was their tendency to do with blues material!) This 1940 classic by Delta bluesman Tommy McClennan and later by Josh White (whose version was available on LP in the UK in the early 60s) is at least the basis of this performance. There is nothing in the audible lyric to suggest it is anything other than an adaptation of *Bottle Up And Go* and is definitely not a version of the obscure Chuck Berry recording *Run Around*. To make matters worse, this recording has long been mis-labelled by tape collectors as *Five On Board*. All the same, this blues song epitomizes classic early Beck; a tough, wiry Fender sound which is wholly committed and convincing. Perhaps most startling is Beck's command of the slide, and his effortless, flowing improvisation. With even more time to fill, the session ends with the odd choice of the American slave ballad *Hush A Bye (All the Pretty Little Horses)* – essentially a Relf solo performance.

The band then moves on to appear on "Ready Steady Goes Live!", transmitted from Rediffusion's Wembley Studios facility (6.07 pm.) The long day will be rounded out by an evening appearance at a dance at the London Architectural Association in Bedford Square.

Lastly, today also marks the US release of *For Your Love*, identical to the UK single's coupling.

SAT 10TH
Corn Exchange, Bristol
Today is the air date for the Yardbirds on "Top Gear" (BBC Light, ▶ March 22). Also featured are the Supremes, the Temptations and Arthur Greenslade & the Gee Men.

SUN 11TH
Royal Star, Maidstone
The Yardbirds are also heard on Radio Luxembourg's "Ready–Steady–Radio" (at 9.30 pm, ▶ April 6) today.

MON 12TH
A scheduled performance at Manor House in Ipswich is seemingly cancelled and may be related to the need for time for further recording.

TUE 13TH
Town Hall, High Wycombe
Today, and certainly in other separate visits to Advision on New Bond Street around this time, a new single is taped in addition to some selections held aside for an upcoming EP. According to a contemporary press report (New Musical Express, April 23), two songs are specifically named as being recorded "last Tuesday" which allowing for the standard lag between the issuing of the press release and publication in the paper would place it on this Tuesday. Specifically named are Mose Allison's *I'm Not Talking* and *My Girl Sloopy*, originally recorded by US R&B group the Vibrations, both of which are cited for inclusion in the aforementioned upcoming EP. The latter title will prove to be a US chart-topper as *Hang On Sloopy* by US group the McCoys later in the year. It may well be that this session was targeted toward completing work on the EP with these two tracks either re-recorded from possibly the March 15 date or indeed were the first stabs at them. *I'm Not Talking* had at least been in the group's repertoire since their March 16 and 22 sessions for the BBC.

The Yardbirds are now also under great pressure to follow-up their initial success. In the fast-paced pop world of this era one had better have a successor to one's hit ready for release once the current success is showing any signs of losing its hold in the charts. For the Yardbirds it was thought best to stick with their winning composer, and accordingly, Graham Gouldman produces another custom number for them called *Heart Full of Soul*. Paul Samwell-Smith has been promoted to musical director for the session, so upright bass player Ron Prentice is hired in his place.

Most importantly, manager Gomelsky has detected an Eastern slant in the song's main riff and has booked an Indian sitar-player and tabla-player to perform on the record. However, the Indian musicians have trouble adjusting to the song's regular 4/4-meter and the engineer fails in getting a proper sound balance from the sitar. In what appears to be an early run-through of this sitar version (issued years later), reveals a rather weak sound and performance indeed. At some point in the proceedings according to numerous accounts, Jeff plugs in and plays the riff on his Telecaster guitar aided by a fuzz box borrowed from Jimmy Page. "Jimmy was actually present at the studio at the time, and I borrowed his [Roger] Mayer fuzz box to work out the idea. Then, when I went to record my part later, I used a Sola Sound Tone Bender, which was one of the first fuzz boxes available commercially." (Guitar World, October 1999). By implication of Jeff's using a different guitar effect "later" it seems that the final master version is done at a separate session, possibly

April 1965: The Yardbirds play the Ricky Tick Club in Windsor ...

April 20. This is supported by a short announcement published in the May issue of BEAT INSTRUMENTAL (on sale April 25) which reveals that the recording of *Heart Full of Soul* as it existed at this point specifically includes sitar (cautiously attributed to Chris Dreja!) and tabla implying that indeed the sitar version had initially been considered for release. This would give further weight to the idea that the fuzz guitar/final master version is done slightly later at a separate session (▸ April 20) perhaps once it was realized that Beck's idea would result in a much stronger recording.

Despite the earlier version ultimately not being used, the idea of a sitar and a tabla predates the Beatles' Indian flirtations by a full six months. It is not until October that the Beatles will use the sitar on their seminal recording *Norwegian Wood*. The Kinks also dabbles early on with the Indian sound with their recording of *See My Friends*. Though itself not issued until the end of July in England, it was in fact recorded around this same time, though again a sitar was not used but rather that instrument's distinctive drone was approximated on an acoustic 12 string guitar with a pick-up feeding back slightly and the signal heavily compressed on its way to tape.

Finally, according to the informative press statement by Giorgio Gomelsky, the Yardbirds are also working on an album to be called *A Yardbird View Of A Beat*, which will spotlight their interest in gospel and rhythm & blues. Despite this promising start, the album never materializes even following repeated attempts to do so later this year and into 1966.

After tonight's engagement in High Wycombe, a party is held to celebrate the success of *For Your Love*, currently topping the NEW MUSICAL EXPRESS single charts.

THU 15TH
Cook's Ferry Inn, Edmonton
With *For Your Love* riding high, the Yardbirds are thought to appear on BBC Television's "Top Of The Pops" (BBC 1, 7.30–8.00 pm) today, whose main attraction is the Beatles' new single *Ticket To Ride*, albeit in a pre-recorded insert. However, BBC files show no indication of the Yardbirds on this show. At night the band does another club date in Greater London.

FRI 16TH
Ricky Tick Club, Thames Hotel, Windsor
For the third consecutive Friday, the

"READY, STEADY, GO!", APRIL 1965

Yardbirds are again guests on the re-formatted "Ready, Steady Goes Live!" (6.07–7.00 pm). Other participants on tonight's show are the Kinks, Herman's Hermits, Adam Faith and the Roulettes and American soul songstress Doris Troy, while George Harrison and John Lennon are interviewed on the air to plug their hit *Ticket To Ride*. An impromptu jam for the finale mixes members of the show's lineup in a performance of Don & Dee Dee Ford's R&B chestnut *I Need Your Lovin'*.

In the evening the Yardbirds play the Ricky Tick out in Berkshire, which is – along with the Marquee and the Crawdaddy – another of their favourite London-area clubs. It would be this club's interior which would be exactly recreated for the Yardbirds' appearance in October 1966 in the feature film "Blowup".

SAT 17TH
Plaza Ballroom, Oswestry
In the morning the Yardbirds are heard on "Saturday Swings" on BBC Light Programme (10.00–12.00 am, ▸ April 9) – which today also star Rosemary Squires, Jerry Allen and his Trio and Mike Redway – while in the evening they play an Easter Saturday dance way out in Shropshire.

SUN 18TH
Community Centre, Southall
Originally booked for the Starlite Ballroom in Greenford but evidently not finalized.

MON 19TH
Marquee Dance Club, City Centre, Birmingham
Tonight's venue is erroneously listed in the national music press as the Corn Exchange. Although unlisted in the local advert for this show, tonight's support act is almost certainly the Birmingham band the Crawdad-dies as Dave Pegg later of Fairport Convention fame, recalls a memorable early support spot at this club with the Yardbirds.

TUE 20TH ✴
Some schedules show a repeat booking at the Grosvenor Ballroom, Aylesbury but this is not the case from local evidence. It is likely the re-recording of *Heart Full Of Soul* without the Indian musicians occurs at this time (▸ April 13). Regardless of the exact circumstances of its recording, the record's ultimate release is wisely timed to follow their current tour commitments so as to allow the band's availability for the next round of press, TV and radio obligations.

WED 21ST
Bromley Court Hotel, Bromley
A regular venue for bands of the day out in Kent.

THU 22ND
Lakeside Ballroom, Hendon
Another ballroom appearance in Greater London at night.

FRI 23RD
King's Court Hotel, London
Tonight's show is in the Bayswater section of London proper.

SAT 24TH
Corn Exchange, Chelmsford

SUN 25TH
Winter Gardens, Droitwich Spa
A return booking to the Community Centre, Southall is also listed in the local paper but is likely a mistake.

MON 26TH
Marquee Club, London
The Yardbirds are back with their regular monthly Monday spot and again with the Mark Leeman Five as support act.

April 1965: Bob Dylan begins his first tour of England, immortalized by D.A. Pennebaker in the film "Don't Look Back".

April and May 1965: The Yardbirds and the Kinks on UK package tour ...

TUE 27TH
Assembly Hall, Tunbridge Wells

WED 28TH
Fully entrenched in the rat-race of constant radio, TV and recording sessions plus press appointments, the Yardbirds are seemingly allowed a day off from concert performances, before they once again jump back on the treadmill for the next round once the new single is poised for release – after a solid month of tour dates up and down the length of England and Scotland. This was no extraordinary feat at the time however, where the demand from the market was insatiable and most of the Yardbirds' peers were involved in equally punishing itineraries in an effort to rake in the higher guarantees a band with a record high in the charts could command from promoters.

FRI 30TH
THE YARDBIRDS (WITH JEFF BECK): FIRST BRITISH TOUR
"The Kinks Show"
Adelphi Cinema, Slough
The group is at BBC's Playhouse Theatre from 10 o'clock onwards to rehearse and sound check before their on the air appearance on BBC Light Programme's "Joe Loss Pop Show" (broadcast 1.00–2.00 pm). They perform before a live audience two of the tracks from their forthcoming EP: *I'm Not Talking* and *I Ain't Done Wrong* plus, for good measure, the now instantly recognizable *For Your Love*. Later today also, the Yardbirds embark on their first full-length tour of Britain with Jeff Beck as their lead guitarist. The itinerary is a 21-date twice-nightly package tour (Mondays are off) presented by Arthur Howes, where the Yardbirds, dressed in their newly purchased mustard coloured suits, support headliners the Kinks and the American all-girl group Goldie & The Gingerbreads. The bill is rounded out with Mickey Finn, Jeff & Jon, Val McKenna plus the Riot Squad (with a teenaged John 'Mitch' Mitchell on drums).

There is a mild rivalry between the Kinks and the Yardbirds. But while the former have racked up three Top Ten hits they suffer from serious internal squabbles, whereas the Yardbirds are on a roll with their first hit and a new guitarist. After the debut show many of the groups party at popular West London's Cromwellian club in Knightsbridge (complete with an upstairs casino, the place stays open until 4 am) together with Lord Sutch and members from the Pretty Things and the Tremeloes.

Additionally, the Yardbirds are originally scheduled for the Ricky Tick Club at the Plaza Ballroom, Guildford, one of Rikki Farr's operations. It is unlikely that they are able to keep this booking as well following their two relatively early shows in Slough.

MAY

SAT 1ST
"The Kinks Show"
Granada Cinema, Walthamstow, London

SUN 2ND
"The Kinks Show"
Odeon Cinema, Lewisham, London

MON 3RD
Marquee Club, London
The Yardbirds, with the Mark Leeman Five, play their monthly Monday residence at the Marquee on their day off in the hectic Kinks itinerary.

TUE 4TH
"The Kinks Show"
Guildhall, Portsmouth

WED 5TH
With some sort of previous commitment to keep, the Yardbirds are replaced by the Rockin' Berries on the Kinks tour for the show tonight in Aldershot, although the Yardbirds name does appear in early adverts for the show. The Yardbirds presumably honour a previously contracted booking elsewhere.

THU 6TH
"The Kinks Show"
Granada Cinema, Kingston-on-Thames

FRI 7TH
"The Kinks Show"
Granada Cinema, East Ham, London
Unit 4 Plus 2 are a one-off addition to the tour tonight.

SAT 8TH
"The Kinks Show"
Gaumont Cinema, Hanley, Stoke-on-Trent
Whereas the Kinks and other members of the touring party indulge in an all-night jam session at the local club 'The Place' in Henley, the Yardbirds return to London to party at the Cromwellian and to celebrate the Cup Final where Liverpool FC won 2-1 over Leeds United.

SUN 9TH
"The Kinks Show"
Coventry Theatre, Coventry
Jeff is interviewed by Penny Valentine of Disc Weekly for a feature published May 15, where he shares his enthusiasm for the Kinks tour, telling anecdotes of mischief and fun. Clearly Jeff enjoys the adulation, the friendliness and the partying: "It's all in good fun!"

TUE 11TH
"The Kinks Show"
Odeon Cinema, Swindon

WED 12TH
"The Kinks Show"
Odeon Cinema, Southend

THU 13TH
"The Kinks Show"
Granada Cinema, Bedford

FRI 14TH
"The Kinks Show"
Granada Cinema, Tooting, London

SAT 15TH
"The Kinks Show"
Winter Gardens, Bournemouth

SUN 16TH
"The Kinks Show"
Gaumont Cinema, Ipswich

MON 17TH
Marquee Club, London
The Yardbirds return to the Marquee (7.30–11 pm) again on their night off

---

Set List/The Yardbirds

British package tour with the Kinks; spring '65

Too Much Monkey Business • I Ain't Done Wrong • I Ain't Got You • Five Long Years • For Your Love • I'm A Man

---

© May 12, 1965: Dylan records in London with John Mayall's Bluesbreakers with Eric Clapton but which produces no usable results.

May 1965: The Yardbirds leave the Kinks tour to play Scotland ...

in the 'Kinks Show' for a rare second Marquee booking in the same month.

TUE 18TH
"The Kinks Show"
Gaumont Cinema, Taunton

WED 19TH
"The Kinks Show"
Capitol Cinema, Cardiff, Wales
The tour is an eventful happening in true sixties fashion, as the Kinks pull out of their own tour tonight after a spectacular on-stage brawl between their drummer Mick Avory and lead guitarist Dave Davies one song into the show during the first house. Their continuous offstage bickering culminates in public when Avory hits Davies across the head with his hi-hat stand leaving the guitarist sprawled on the stage bleeding. Davies is later treated with 10 stitches. The Kinks are promptly replaced on the tour by upcoming teen-heart throbs the Walker Brothers.

THU 20TH
"The Kinks Show"
Gaumont Cinema, Wolverhampton
Jeff befriends the Walkers; three Americans living in England, and although masquerading as brothers, they are not related. Beck eventually buys a well-worn Fender Esquire guitar off John Walker (nee Maus) for £70 after their brief encounter on this tour. Jeff will use this guitar for recordings and live appearances.

FRI 21ST
THE YARDBIRDS:
FIRST SCOTTISH TOUR
Raith Ballroom, Kirkcaldy, Scotland
Whereas the Kinks/Walker Brothers package tour continues with three further concerts around England (Bolton (21st), Leeds (22nd), and finally in Derby (23rd)), the Yardbirds skip these last dates (the Hollies take their place) as they had already been booked to play a tour of Scotland, which starts tonight in Kirkcaldy with the Andy Ross Orchestra.

The original 10 day schedule has been altered and rearranged somewhat to allow the band to finish up in time to be back in London the following Monday to dig in on promotional work for their next single release.

SAT 22ND
City Hall, Perth, Scotland
"Dancing tonight! London's top group and no. 1 in the Hit Parade the colossal Yardbirds supported by the Couriers from Dundee 8–11.55 pm 7/6."

SUN 23RD
Top 10 Club, Palais, Dundee, Scotland
Tonight is a 7 pm show supported by Dundee's Poor Souls plus the Executives; and the final of the Miss Holiday Top Ten competition with 11 beautiful girls competing for £20 and a week at Butlin's Holiday Camp! Originally announced as at Plaza Ballroom in Stirling which is cancelled entirely.

MON 24TH
Assembly Rooms, Wick, Scotland
The band makes the long haul to the uppermost region of the Scottish Highlands for this one-off where they appear with the local favorites the Aktual Facts starting at 9.30 pm. The band also makes an in-store appearance at the Music Shop, signing autographs from 4–6 pm.

TUE 25TH
Locarno Ballroom, Montrose, Scotland
Tonight, the well-travelled Yardbirds are supported by Gary Summers & the Highlanders. 8.30 pm–1 am.

THU 27TH
Paisley Ice Rink, Glasgow, Scotland
Appearing also are Rob & the Clansmen, the Poets, the Beatstalkers, and the Boots starting at 7.30 pm. Originally scheduled for Barrowlands on the 31st, the Glasgow booking is switched to this band-jammed event instead.

FRI 28TH
Drill Hall, Dumfries, Scotland
Originally slated for Edinburgh which was moved to the 30th to nearby Newtongrange.

SAT 29TH
An unconfirmed venue and location, Scotland.

SUN 30TH
New Hall, Newtongrange, Scotland
Billed as one of a regular series of 'Border dances' the Yardbirds are one of two 'grand attractions' this weekend (besides Brian Poole & the Tremeloes) Admission is 7/6. Originally slated for Dundee, which is moved up a week to the 23rd. However it seems this marks the end of the Scottish tour after tonight's show.

MON 31ST
The band is back in London today for a day of recuperation. The media onslaught to help push the new single up the charts begins in earnest tomorrow. The originally announced version of the Scottish tour would have ended today at Barrowlands, Glasgow, however this last date seems to have been called off to allow the band to get back home to London a day earlier.

JUNE

TUE 1ST
A day devoted to the BBC. First the group appears live in an interview segment on "Pop Inn" (1.00–1.55 pm), broadcast from the Paris Cinema, a BBC studio on Lower Regent Street in London. Then the Yardbirds switch to BBC's Maida Vale 5 studio, to pre-record (between 4.30–6.30 pm.) both sides of the new single *Heart Full Of Soul/Steeled Blues* and a run-through of the Isley Brothers' *Respectable*, a holdover from the Yardbirds days with Eric Clapton; all to be transmitted on "Saturday Club" on June 5.

WED 2ND
Country Club, Mudeford
Back again at the BBC, this time the Playhouse Theatre, the Yardbirds record an instalment for 'The Beat Scene' segment of "The Joe Loss Pop Show" before the usual live audience this time reprising performances of *For Your Love* and *I Ain't Got You*, plus *Heart Full Of Soul*, to be transmitted on BBC Light initially on Friday June 11 but then rescheduled for July 2.

The day ends with a club date in Mudeford, Dorset.

FRI 4TH
Fender Club, Harrow, London
Another busy day, beginning with yet another BBC session, this one at their Maida Vale 4 studio for a pre-recording for the next week's Light Programme "Saturday Swings", transmitted on June 12. Five songs are taped, again featuring the A- and B-sides of the new single (*Heart Full Of Soul/Steeled Blues*) plus plus two tracks (*I'm Not Talking, I Ain't Done Wrong*) and yet two further reprises from the Clapton days, Bo Diddley's *Pretty Girl* and John Lee Hooker's *Louise*. The

May 25, 1965: Influential Blues singer/harpist Sonny Boy Williamson (aka Rice Miller), who toured with The Yardbirds in 1964, dies in Arkansas.

June 1965: Radio, TV and concert appearances to promote "Heart Full of Soul"...

latter is almost given a country flavour with Jeff's bright and twangy guitar solo, a clear distinction from the Clapton version.

The Yardbirds then move on to Rediffusion's Studio One at Wembley Park along with the Kinks (Dave Davies and Mick Avory now having reconciled their differences), the Rolling Stones and the French group les Surfs for tonight's simulcast edition of "Ready, Steady, Go!" (6.07–6.30 pm over the ITV network), which has reverted to its original title after a spell as "Ready, Steady Goes Live!"

The new Yardbirds single *Heart Full Of Soul* is released this Friday in Great Britain, while the American release is held back because *For Your Love* has not yet finished its chart run. The single marks Jeff's recording debut with the Yardbirds, and features his groundbreaking quasi-raga riff. Interestingly, the original pressings credit "The Yardbirds featuring Jeff 'Steel' Beck on the B-side, a nickname that obviously does not catch on! The song peaks at #2 in Britain during a nine week chart stay, and at #9 in the US, although not until September. In Britain the single is held off the top by the Byrds' *Mr. Tambourine Man* during two consecutive weeks in July. Funnily, some fans confuse the two groups, so at some shows the Yardbirds have requests for the Byrds' recent number one hit.

Tonight's booking is at the aptly named Fender Club in Harrow on the northwest edge of Greater London.

Single
THE YARDBIRDS
A: HEART FULL OF SOUL (Graham Gouldman)
B: STEELED BLUES (Beck/Relf)

Released Friday June 4, 1965 (UK Columbia DB 7594); July 19, 1965 (US Epic 9823)
Personnel is Jeff Beck (ldgtr), Keith Relf (hrmnca/bongos/vcls), Chris Dreja (rhygtr), Paul Samwell-Smith (bs) and Jim McCarty (drms); Ron Prentice plays bass on A-side
Recorded at Advision Studios, New Bond Street, London, April 20*, 1965 (A) and March 15*, 1965 (B)
Produced by Giorgio Gomelsky
Musical direction by Paul Samwell-Smith
Engineered by Roger Cameron
Highest Chart Position UK: #2
Highest Chart Position US: #9

SAT 5TH
Peterborough Palais, Peterborough
The whole group spends an hour at BBC's Paris Cinema (11.30 pm–12.30 pm) for an interview to be included on BBC's "The Top Ten Game," to be broadcast on June 8. Hosted by David Gell, the concept involves a studio audience equipped with push-buttons to pick their own top ten from the current hits and the best of the new releases. The group is also featured on BBC Light's "Saturday Club," presented by Brian Matthew (10 am to noon, ► June 1), which also features Marianne Faithful and the Moody Blues.

In the evening they appear in person in Peterborough.

SUN 6TH
Elm Park, Romford
Giorgio heads to New York this week to meet with Premier Talent Agency to plan the Yardbirds' first US tour which is announced in VARIETY (June 16) as running August 20–September 12. It will later be announced as a double billing with San Francisco's the Beau Brummels. This arrangement would replace the pencilled in booking made back in April for the Yardbirds to be included as part of a Dick Clark Caravan of Stars package show to criss-cross the US July 2–September 6 and feature a number of British acts. The cancellations, however, are felt back at home when summer bookings eventually prove to be sparser than usual due to attention focused on getting to the States.

MON 7TH
Country Club, Borley
Earlier schedules list tonight show as Bournemouth which is cancelled.

TUE 8TH
Marquee Club, London
One more time at the Marquee with the Mark Leeman Five. A booking at Burton's Ballroom, Uxbridge announced back in April is possibly a cancellation. Also the BBC transmits "The Top Ten Game" today (► June 5).

WED 9TH
An instalment for BBC Light Programme's "The Ken Dodd Show" is pre-recorded today for a transmission on Sunday June 20 with a repeat the following Wednesday, June 23. The group performs *Heart Full of Soul*.

THU 10TH
In the afternoon, the Yardbirds rehearse at the Marquee, which – together with the Crawdaddy Club – is being used as rehearsal space. Curtis Mayfield's *I've Been Trying* is worked out, and the group is also interviewed by Penny Valentine of DISC WEEKLY.

An announced booking at the Manor Lounge in Stockport, Cheshire is actually a booking by the Birds with young Ron Wood and another example of the periodic confusion in these similarly named acts (the Birds, the Byrds, and the Yardbirds).

FRI 11TH
Empress Ballroom, Winter Gardens, Blackpool
A reappearance on "Ready, Steady, Go!" (6.07–6.30 pm) today, and also a summery dance in Blackpool in Lancashire with the Hollies, the Ken Turner Band, the Johnny Wollaston Band, Bruce & the Spiders and Dene Hunter & the Newtones.

SAT 12TH
Stafford Rugby Club, Stafford
In the morning the Yardbirds can be heard on BBC Light Programme when "Saturday Swings" (10.00–12.00 am) is aired (► June 4), which also presents Acker Bilk's Paramount Jazz Band, the Silkie and Bobbie Britton.

At night, they play a barbecue in Staffordshire with Hipster Image and Alan Elsden & His Jazz Band.

SUN 13TH
The Yardbirds spend a Sunday afternoon miming *Heart Full Of Soul* at ABC-TV's Alpha Television Studio in Astor, Birmingham. The programme also includes Gene Pitney and Peter & Gordon, and is to be transmitted on the highly popular variety show "Thank Your Lucky Stars" on the following Saturday, June 19. Despite being transmitted across the ITV network, the show is hosted by Brian Matthew, who is best known for his BBC engagements.

MON 14TH
Parr Hall, Warrington
In addition to tonight's engagement in Lancashire, the group is also guests on Granada TV's "Scene At 6.30" likely taped earlier in the day at Granada's Manchester studio. The show is transmitted at – understandably – 6.30 pm and runs for half an hour.

TUE 15TH
Stamford Hall, Altrincham
The Yardbirds appear with local support group the Bumblies.

WED 16TH✱
After returning from their string of

June 1965: The Yardbirds open for the Beatles in Paris ...

northern dates and with the return of manager Gomelsky from a US trip, this is the likely time the Yardbirds make a promotional film in b&w (a 'pop promo' as it is called) to plug *For Your Love* on American television. To make it more visually exciting, they are dressed up in medieval costumes – Jeff as a cavalier – and the film is shot at the Ricky Tick in Windsor and then on a field outside. Gomelsky, who has recently been in the US on a trip with Herman's Hermits to do some research and planning for the Yardbirds' first US visit, puts his film background to good use to direct and produce the shooting. Although originally intended for the US market, it seems to go unaired at this time although this early pop promo is later aired on French TV on a Sunday lunchtime, giving the group a great boost in France. Reportedly, outtakes of this same footage are used to assemble a film to accompany the B-side *Got To Hurry* but is likely never aired.

THU 17TH
Pier Pavilion, Worthing

FRI 18TH
University of Birmingham, Birmingham

No doubt one of the traditional June Balls held at universities across Britain with the arrival of summer. Originally announced as Central Pier, Morecambe, which is rescheduled for July 28.

SAT 19TH
Starlight Room, Gliderdrome, Boston

Besides tonight's concert in Lincolnshire with the Yes 'n' No and the Essex, the Yardbirds can be seen via videotape plugging *Heart Full Of Soul* on "Thank Your Lucky Stars" (5.50–6.35 pm, ▶ June 13).

SUN 20TH
Palais Des Sports, Paris, France

Through his connections with Beatles manager Brian Epstein, Gomelsky secures this prestigious one-off spot as opening act (along with French acts les Pollux, Jean-Claude Germain, les Jets, Moustique, Evy and les Haricotes Rouges) for the first night of the Beatles' 1965 European tour. The group's original booking at the Crawdaddy tonight is dropped. There are two shows (at 3.00 and 9.00 pm respectively) in front of capacity audiences of 6,000 fans. (A live recording available on bootlegs is believed to be from Paris, with the Yardbirds doing *I Wish You Would*). When Jeff breaks a string on his guitar just before one of the shows, the Beatles' roadie Mal Evans helpfully lends him George Harrison's Gretsch guitar – tuned down a half-step which causes some frustration! The band briefly gets to meet the Beatles just prior to showtime.

The Paris visit marks Jeff's first concert appearance outside Great Britain, indeed his very first time abroad. The French record industry is using EPs as a standard rather than the more common single format, and the Yardbirds have just issued a successful EP adding the as-yet-unreleased *My Girl Sloopy* to the *Heart Full Of Soul/Steeled Blues* coupling (Riviera 231 099).

At home, British comedian Ken Dodd's regular BBC radio programme "The Ken Dodd Show" is broadcast today 2.30–3.00 pm featuring the Yardbirds as guests (▶ June 9).

MON 21ST
Just back from Paris, the Yardbirds pre-tape a radio appearance at BBC Aeolian Studio 2 today which consists of the newly worked up Curtis Mayfield song *I've Been Trying* (with a strong backing vocal arrangement), plus *Heart Full Of Soul* and *Berry's Boogie* (aka *Jeff's Boogie*) all to be broadcast on the penultimate edition of the popular BBC Light Programme "Top Gear" on June 26. The show was inaugurated by the Beatles barely a year earlier and has proved an unqualified success. (In 1967, the BBC re-launches the programme with John Peel as presenter.)

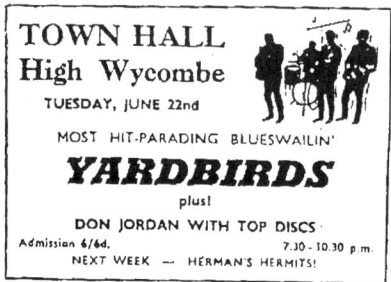

TUE 22ND
Town Hall, High Wycombe

WED 23RD
City Hall, Salisbury

Tonight's support act is the Troggs from Andover in one of their early appearances (7.45–11.45 pm).

THU 24TH
In late February the Yardbirds were booked to appear at the Kave Dwellers' Club first anniversary in Billingham on May 6, but obviously had to cancel as they were doing the Kinks package tour. Unfortunately, tonight's re-booking is again the victim of cancellation as both Beck – incidentally on his twenty-first birthday – and Samwell-Smith are bedridden with a stomach complaint picked up during their Paris visit.

FRI 25TH
Another cancellation – this time at Manchester's Oasis Club, although originally listed as Leeds University. Samwell-Smith explains to DISC WEEKLY: "We're all very tired now because we've been overworking. We've been eating irregularly and it's been ruining our stomachs." However, the group's booked spot on today's "Friday Spectacular" (Radio Luxembourg 10.00–11.00 pm, pre-recorded earlier this week) is broadcast.

SAT 26TH
Drill Hall, Scunthorpe

In the afternoon the Yardbirds, Doris Troy and West Five are heard as guests on "Top Gear" (at 4 pm, ▶ June 21). A date originally scheduled at Memorial Hall, Cleethorpes is cancelled probably due to their booking at a festival there the following month.

SUN 27TH
Crawdaddy Club, Richmond Athletic Association Club House, Richmond

Likely the final Yardbirds appearance here prior to the club's closing in July.

WED 30TH
Corn Exchange, Bristol

The Yardbirds appear with the Fanatics after earlier in the day doing TWW's "Discs-A-Go-Go" from Bristol in West England.

JULY

THU 1ST
Dreamland Ballroom, Margate

FRI 2ND
Palais, Wimbledon

"The Joe Loss Show" spotlights the Yardbirds today on 'The Beat Scene', the regular band feature within the show (▶ June 2).

SAT 3RD
The Whitehall, East Grinstead

The group is at BBC's London Playhouse Theatre between 2.00–3.00 pm, to record an instalment for tomorrow's edition of the popular "Easy Beat" programme. The band plays live before a teenage audience, treating them to performances of *I Ain't Done Wrong* and the obligatory *Heart Full Of Soul*. This show runs every Sunday from 10.30 to 11.30 am and is presented by David Symonds.

At night the band plays in nearby Sussex supported by the Roadrunners.

SUN 4TH
Starlite Ballroom, Greenford

Besides a ballroom date outside London, the Yardbirds are also the main attraction on today's "Easy Beat" (BBC Light, ▶ July 3). Also on the show are Lulu and Goldie & the Gingerbreads.

MON 5TH
Bath Pavilion, Bath

Epic Records issue the first Yardbirds album in the US this month, entitled *For Your Love* to capitalize on the hit single. Despite Beck's picture on the cover (confusingly seated at a piano!), he appears on only three songs; *I'm Not Talking*, *I Ain't Done Wrong*, and *My Girl Sloopy*. The rest of the album contains songs with Eric Clapton as the featured guitarist. The album makes it into the BILLBOARD Top [150] LPs some weeks later, where it peters out after reaching #96.

TUE 6TH
Marquee Club, London

The morning finds the Yardbirds reportedly pre-taping a "Ready–Steady–Radio" segment (Radio Luxembourg), broadcast on Sunday July 11 at 9.30 pm. The afternoon is likely spent pre-taping an insert on Rediffusion's "Ready, Steady, Go!" for broadcast on Friday. An interview done by Keith Altham at Rediffusion's Wembley Park studios in conjunction with the videotaping is published in this week's NEW MUSICAL EXPRESS (dated July 9). Here the group – in a 'very frank' question-time – surprisingly slags the "Ready, Steady, Go!" show, which after all has featured the Yardbirds extensively: "The show is cutting its own throat. It's nowhere as good as it used to be." At night, the group returns to the Marquee again.

THU 8TH

The Yardbirds mime *Heart Full Of Soul* (currently at #4 in the NEW MUSICAL EXPRESS charts) on "Top Of The Pops" (BBC, 7.30-8.00 pm) tonight. Interestingly tonight's show is broadcast from Studio 2 of the BBC Television Centre as the show has moved to London for the summer season.

FRI 9TH
Assembly Hall, Farnborough Technical College, Farnborough

First, the Yardbirds can be seen on "Ready, Steady, Go!" (6.07–6.30 pm)

SHAPES OF THINGS

A Yardstick To The Future

The importance and influence of the Yardbirds far exceed their record sales or number of hits. Their influence is reflected in styles as different as psychedelic 60s West Coast rock, glam-rock and latter-day heavy metal. They became synonymous with guitar virtuosity, at a time when guitar solos meant short, tightly-constructed breaks. Part of the fascination is of course the succeeding presence of three of British rock's most celebrated guitarists – Eric Clapton, Jeff Beck and Jimmy Page.

Of course the Yardbirds were a lot more than a guitar-centric band; both musically and lyrically they were innovators. Undoubtedly, the period with Jeff Beck was their peak commercially and artistically. Although Jeff lacked Clapton's assured fluency and graceful phrasing, he more than made up for this with a wide range of influences, less blues purism plus a willingness to experiment. In fact, he was anything but a purist. Where Clapton favoured a studied approach – albeit a very impressive one – Beck seemed equally influenced by Spike Jones as by B. B. King. Beck viewed the guitar as a mirror of a wide range of emotions, where humour and craziness were ingredients just as much as pain and heartbreak. More important than hiring skills, the Yardbirds inadvertently hired an attitude – a guitarist not afraid to go out on a tangent, ready to re-write the rule book. Beck also brought with him a flamboyant stage presence, playing the guitar behind his head or leaving it atop his amplifier crying with feedback.

He made his mark already with the EP recorded in March–April 1965, which featured a mini-portrait of the artist as a young guitarist. He utilised the wah-like effect created by fiddling with the tone control; *nobody* else did that, and the regular foot-operated wah-wah was at least two years away. The two guitar solos in *I'm Not Talking* were stupendous, the cool ascending guitar line in the second solo break was followed by Beck wiggling a totally off-the-wall note in the listener's face. Even the dated *My Girl Sloopy* had some Cliff Gallup-triplets buried within, while *I Ain't Done Wrong* was fully robust Chicago-style bottleneck guitar.

But more than anything, it was the singles that Jeff cut with the Yardbirds that made his reputation. The sandblasting lick in *Heart Full of Soul* was both simple and wonderfully effective. The riff that Jeff forged out of Paul Burlison's original octave jump in *The Train Kept A Rollin'* was a classic understanding of the power chord – a two note chord with shifting intervals. On *I'm A Man* it sounded like Jeff ran out of fretboard so he just bashed the guitar neck in a moment of pure inarticulate angst, creating sheets of sound with rapid-fire block chords – justifying the "steamroller chasing a chicken" cliché used to describe his playing. But the psychedelic milestone *Shapes Of Things* was a new benchmark in rock guitar playing, because of its outlandish, yet perfectly commercial, guitar solo. Here Jeff painted an astonishing sound picture which completely transcends mundane guitar solo clichés.

The so-called *Roger The Engineer* album from '66 benefitted from clean production, and displayed Jeff's guitar playing in full flower. It was incredible how the young Beck, not yet 22, fully understood the sonic vocabulary of the electric guitar. *The Nazz Are Blue* – a 14 bar blues no less – contained Jeff's pioneering use of feedback with a single note sustained and bent through a whole verse. The simple sing-along *I Can't Make Your Way* featured a sweet, singing violin tone, while *Over, Under, Sideways, Down* was propelled by a turbo-charged fiddle lick. On *Lost Woman* Jeff went toe to toe with Relf's harp, showing that never did his guitar sound more inspired when pushed by a vocalist or another lead instrumentalist. The amazing multi-tracked parts on *Jeff's Boogie* never cease to surprise. Atop Sam's thumping double-bassy boom and McCarty's easy-going swing, Beck overdubbed four–five guitar parts, using tones ranging from a needly Fender to a throaty Gibson, using harmonics, corkscrew rips, slide – and buried way down in the mix – what sounds like his own guttural vocal accompaniment.

Many who saw the Yardbirds live on a good night in the Beck-era claim their records pale in comparsion with their explosive and daring live shows, where songs would be bent and stretched and where the use of big, hypnotic, repetitive ensemble grooves were the key to the Yardbirds' "rave-ups".

Arguably, Jeff Beck was the very first Guitar Hero, who succeeded in being noticed for his extrovert, futuristic guitar playing and at the same time being a teen idol. Rock and roll has a long tradition for maverick guitar players, but Beck was the first who made a huge commercial impression without adjusting his approach – on the contrary, his style was the vital ingredient on the Yardbirds' hits. ∎

July 1965: The Yardbirds are excluded from "Thank Your Lucky Stars" ...

tonight, together with among others the Dave Clark Five, Goldie & the Gingerbreads, Ivy League and Lulu. The Yardbirds' insert is pre-recorded a few days previously (▶ July 6).

Afterwards the Yardbirds and the Sole-Tones appear in concert 8 pm–12 midnight in a show sponsored by the college's student union. One of Jeff's former employers, Kerry Rapid a.k.a. Alan Hope (from 1961) is part of the opening act. Hope, now fronting this rhythm & blues outfit, recalls years later how the evening ends abruptly after a massive fight breaks out on the dance floor.

SAT 10TH
Corn Exchange, Cambridge
Jeff is profiled in DISC WEEKLY (July 10) in Mike Ledgerwood's regular column 'The Honest Truth': "It's pretty marvelous how the kids have reacted. I can't get over it. I suppose I was pretty popular with the Tridents ... but not because of my looks. More because of the sounds I made, I think." Asked about which musicians he admires, Beck says: "Guitarists. Anybody's who's good. I can listen to any guitar music. Particularly blues or country and western ... I like people like the Miracles and the Impressions. If we go to America I'd like to meet Chet Atkins." Ledgerwood also asks Beck what he would do if he should do a number on his own: "Oh, I'm mad. I like making funny noises and getting abstract sounds. I'd like a big soul group with loads of saxes. A big fat sound so I can go really mad."

WED 14TH
Jeff attends a special 'Bastille Night Party' at the swish Scotch of St James discotheque in London's Westminster district. Newly opened, this place has already become a popular night-club, and tonight all of the Beatles with wives and dates minus Paul McCartney are here, plus Brian Jones, Eric Burdon, Gary Leeds (better known as Gary Walker, Jeff's chum from the Walker Brothers), Chas Chandler and many other celebrities.

Brian Auger's Trinity (with Mickey Waller on drums) provide the night's entertainment. Auger has a weekly residence here at the time and the club is the site of countless jam sessions.

THU 15TH
Winter Gardens, Great Yarmouth

FRI 16TH
Whaddon Football Ground, Cheltenham
A classic double bill as the Yardbirds are paired in concert with the Who.

SAT 17TH
Because of internal miscommunication, the Yardbirds fail to turn up for tonight's booking at the Birdcage Club at Kimbells Ballroom, Southsea, Portsmouth (reported erroneously in the music papers as located in Southampton). The club's promoter, Rikki Farr, threatens to ban the band from the string of clubs he books. The situation is resolved and the Yardbirds schedule a make-up show for Farr at the Savoy Ballroom on August 2.

THE YARDBIRDS
FOR YOUR LOVE
A1 FOR YOUR LOVE *(G. Gouldman)* **A2** I'M NOT TALKING *(M. Allison)* **A3** I AIN'T GOT YOU *(C. Carter)* **A4** PUTTY (IN YOUR HANDS) *(Rogers/Patton)* **A5** GOT TO HURRY *(O. Rasputin)* **A6** I AIN'T DONE WRONG *(Relf)*

B1 I WISH YOU WOULD *(B. B. Arnold)* **B2** A CERTAIN GIRL *(A. Neville)* **B3** SWEET MUSIC *(Lane/Cobbs/Bowie)* **B4** GOOD MORNING LITTLE SCHOOLGIRL *(Demarais)* **B5** MY GIRL SLOOPY *(Russell/Farrell)*

Released July 5, 1965 (US Epic LN 24167 mono/BN 16167 stereo)
Personnel is Eric Clapton (ldgtr except A2, A6, B5), Jeff Beck (ldgtr A2, A6, B5), Keith Relf (hrmnca/vcls), Chris Dreja (rhygtr), Paul Samwell-Smith (bs) and Jim McCarty (drms). Brian Auger (harpsichord), Denny Piercey (bongos) and unknown (upright bass) play on A1.
Recorded at Olympic Studios, Baker Street, London (A3, A4, A5, B1, B2, B3, B4); IBC Studios, 35 Portland Place, London (A1) and Advision Studios, New Bond Street, London (A2, A6, B5), between March 1964 and April 1965.
Produced by Giorgio Gomelsky
Musical direction by Paul Samwell-Smith (A1)
Highest Chart Position US: #96

SUN 18TH
Bad luck strikes again as the Yardbirds are 30 minutes late for the taping of "Lucky Stars Summer Spin" in Birmingham (to be transmitted next Saturday 24 July), resulting in the group being excluded from this important TV exposure. Commenting to NEW MUSICAL EXPRESS a few days later, Giorgio Gomelsky adds schoolmasterly: "I do not know why they were late, but we shall be holding an inquest on their return from Scotland. This is not the way to carry on."

MON 19TH
Majestic Ballroom, Newcastle
Today *Heart Full Of Soul* is available in the US. Tonight's show is at the Majestic, which is a part of the Top Rank Suite as given in some music papers.

WED 21ST
THE YARDBIRDS: SECOND SCOTTISH TOUR
Kinema Ballroom, Dunfirmline, Scotland
The Yardbirds pay a short return visit to Scotland with tonight's show 8 pm to midnight with a 4/– admission.

THU 22ND–SUN 25TH
The Yardbirds play further undocumented shows around in Scotland. A previously announced date for July 25 at Guildhall, Portsmouth as part of a series of Sunday shows by promoter Mervyn Conn is cancelled.

Also of note, on the 25th, the Crawdaddy Club in Richmond is closed down after two years because of increasingly unruly behaviour.

TUE 27TH ✱
Presumably, at the end of July, the Yardbirds squeeze in a recording session in their busy schedule, this time at Olympic Studios in its original location on Baker Street near Marble Arch, London with engineer Keith Grant. The recording in question is *Still I'm Sad*, a song co-written by Paul Samwell-Smith and Jim McCarty. Importantly, it is their first self-penned composition to venture outside the rhythm and blues structure of previous song writing attempts, as the song is inspired by medieval Gregorian chants. Besides the Yardbirds' singing, Giorgio Gomelsky adds his voice to the choir-like backing. The song's vocal arrangement is supposedly rehearsed by the group during visits to various gents' rooms while touring! On this occasion only the backing track is done and the song is finished later (▶ August 17).

August 1965: Jeff Beck's a sensation at the 5th National Jazz & Blues Festival ...

WED 28TH
Floral Hall, Morecambe
With the Peeps, 7 pm–1 am.

THU 29TH
Though reported to be back on BBC Television's weekly "Top Of The Pops" show tonight miming to *Heart Full Of Soul*, the BBC's programme as broadcast files do not indicate so.

FRI 30TH
Jeff Beck is ill, but despite this the Yardbirds appear at Studio One in Wembley in yet another segment of Rediffusion's "Ready, Steady, Go!" (6.00–7.00 pm). Reportedly, the group is plugging the new EP out next week and thought to have at least played *My Girl Sloopy* on this show. However, Jeff is unable to make tonight's club appearance at the Ricky Tick in Windsor.

NEW MUSICAL EXPRESS also reports today that more than 100,000 copies of *Heart Full Of Soul* were ordered at the CBS Records Convention in Miami, Florida held on July 16.

1965 EAST COAST FESTIVAL OF JAZZ & MODERN MUSIC — CLEETHORPES
JULY 30th, 7 p.m.–12, JULY 31st & AUG. 1st, 3 p.m.–12

16 STAR BANDS including (in programme order):
THE ANIMALS · MANFRED MANN · MIKE COTTON · ACKER BILK · THE YARDBIRDS · JOHNNY DANKWORTH ORCHESTRA · LONG JOHN BALDRY · GEORGIE FAME · TERRY LIGHTFOOT · KENNY BALL · SOUNDS INCORPORATED · BARRON KNIGHTS · GOLDIE and the Gingerbreads · IV / LEAGUE
Bookings from the Cleethorpes Corporation by the ROY TEMPEST ORGANISATION

SEASON TICKET covering all 3 days 30/-
Day Ticket Prices: July 30, 10/-, July 31 & Aug. 1, 12/6 each day
TICKETS and enquiries: Publicity Dept., Town Hall, CLEETHORPES
CAMPING SITE · LICENSED BARS · CATERING

SAT 31ST
"1965 East Coast Festival of Jazz & Modern Music"
Boating Lake Grounds, Cleethorpes
The Yardbirds appear on the second day of a three-day festival held in this coastal town in Lincolnshire. Among the many groups featured over the weekend are Sounds Incorporated with a teenage Tony Newman on drums. The Saturday lists Georgie Fame, Johnny Dankworth, Acker Bilk, Long John Baldry, Keith Conway & the Aristocrats plus the Yardbirds. Jeff is still not feeling well but makes the show anyway, and Keith Relf comments to the EVENING TELEGRAPH (August 2): "He shouldn't have gone on, but he insisted. He did a great performance. He was in a collapsible state before he went on."

AUGUST

SUN 1ST
An announced booking at the Odeon, Bournemouth, planned as another of Mervyn Conn's Sunday concerts is replaced by a stage adaption of "The Sound of Music" instead!

MON 2ND
Savoy Ballroom, Southsea, Portsmouth
The make-up date for the no-show at the Birdcage on July 17. Tonight's show is with the Klimaks.

THU 5TH
Assembly Hall, Worthing
Yet another BBC pre-recording, this time at Maida Vale 4, for an edition of "Saturday Swings" to be broadcast on August 14. The five songs recorded are Keith Relf's acoustic *Hushabye (All The Pretty Little Horses)*, *San-Ho-Zay* (attributed in BBC files as 'San Jose' and as composed by the Yardbirds, but almost certainly it is the Freddy King guitar instrumental and phonetically identical in title), *Heart Full Of Soul*, *I've Been Trying*, and lastly a brand new group composition called *Love Me Like I Love You*, which will never be officially released.

The Yardbirds then drive down to Worthing on the south coast for an evening performance.

FRI 6TH
"Fifth National Jazz & Blues Festival"
Richmond Athletic Association Grounds, Richmond
The annual National Jazz & Blues Festival is in its fifth year, and as usual presents both pop-groups as well as jazz names. The Friday night – dubbed 'Ready, Steady, Richmond!' – is set

EP
THE YARDBIRDS
FIVE YARDBIRDS
A: MY GIRL SLOOPY *(Russell-Farrell)*
B1: I'M NOT TALKING *(Mose Allison)*
B2: I AIN'T DONE WRONG *(Keith Relf)*

Released Friday August 6, 1965 (UK Columbia SEG 8421)
Personnel is Jeff Beck (ldgtr), Keith Relf (hrmnca/vcls), Chris Dreja (rhygtr), Paul Samwell-Smith (bs) and Jim McCarty (drms).
Recorded at Advision Studios, New Bond Street, London, March 15* and April 13, 1965
Produced by Giorgio Gomelsky
Highest Chart Position UK: #2

aside exclusively for pop, and the running order – from 7.30 until 10.30 – is the Mike Cotton Sound, the Moody Blues while the Who and the Yardbirds top the bill. Over the next two days further artists such as Georgie Fame, Manfred Mann, the Spencer Davis Group, and the Animals (backed by a full horn section for the occasion) perform. The festival is filmed by Brian Epstein's company Subafilms and the American company Selmur Productions. Edited parts are later shown on American television as part of a "Shindig Goes To London" special, with the Yardbirds performing *For Your Love* and *My Girl Sloopy*. The two-part special edition is transmitted in December, with the Yardbirds' part being aired in the second instalment on Thursday December 9 on ABC Network TV. The whole of Friday night – including the Yardbirds' performance – is also recorded with highlights being broadcast on Radio Luxembourg's "Ready–Steady–Radio" show, presumably already on August 8.

Before the festival, however, the Yardbirds do a BBC pre-recording at the Playhouse Theatre on Northumberland Avenue. Six songs are taped as part of a bank holiday special for Light Programme called "You Really Got ..." for transmission on August 30 provisionally sub-titled "Holiday Pop": *I Wish You Would*, *Love Me Like I Love You*, *For Your Love*, *Heart Full Of Soul*, *Too Much Monkey Business* and *I'm A Man* in addition to a group interview with host Denny Piercy (and bongo player on *For Your Love*!).

Today also finally sees the release of the *Five Yardbirds* EP in Britain, containing the three songs recorded in the spring not available elsewhere in Britain. In the separate EP chart which is published in RECORD MIRROR, the EP enjoys a long spell with a peak position at #2.

SAT 7TH
Oasis Club, Manchester
A make up date for the cancellation due to illness on June 25.

SUN 8TH
North Pier Pavilion, Blackpool
The Yardbirds visit another coastal town in a double show (6 and 8 am) with Dave Berry & the Cruisers, Billy Burden and local group the Hobos, which includes a young Glenn Cornick, later of Jethro Tull fame.

MON 9TH
The group travels to Manchester to pre-record an appearance on the Light

August 1, 1965: The Byrds arrive in London for a much publicised but critically disappointing 1st UK tour.

August 1965: The Yardbirds are filmed in London for US TV show "Shindig!"...

RICHMOND FESTIVAL. FACSIMILE FROM US TOURBOOK AUG '66

Programme's "The Beat Show". The BBC studio location in Hume, Manchester is confusingly also named the Playhouse Theatre, like its sister studio in London. "The Beat Show," lighter in content than the more teen-age-oriented shows like "Saturday Club," is transmitted on August 13, originally only for the Northern region but eventually broadcast nationally. The Yardbirds perform three songs this day: *Heart Full Of Soul, Love Me Like I Love You*, and *I Ain't Done Wrong*.

A 10-day Continental tour had been announced (DISC WEEKLY July 3) to begin today but is seemingly scrapped, especially as it coincides with the traditional European holiday season. Chris Dreja also finds time to get married this month.

TUE 10TH–WED 11TH
The Yardbirds, the Hollies, Georgie Fame, the Pretty Things, Lulu and others have been filmed over the past weeks (July 26-August 6) by a US TV team at Stage 3 at Twickenham Studios, London for inserts on the popular US TV show "Shindig!" The show is hosted by LA disc-jockey Jimmy O'Neill and directed and produced by Dean Whitmore. The Yardbirds perform *I Wish You Would, For Your Love, Heart Full Of Soul* and *I'm A Man*. The latter is a tour de force visual display of Jeff playing slide with his picking hand and ending with him unstrapping his Fender and putting it atop the amplifier while the guitar shrieks with feedback – an utterly groundbreaking performance which leaves a lasting impression on countless musicians and musicians-to-be once it is aired in the US. These four selections are inserted into various episodes of the programme throughout the autumn and winter season. *Heart Full Of Soul* and *For Your Love* are aired September 23, the epic performance of *I'm A Man* going out December 16 and finally *I Wish You Would* on December 23.

THU 12TH
The Yardbirds are on "The Beat Show" (8.00–9.00 am) today (▶ August 9) with programme regulars Barbara Kay and Trad Lads.

SAT 14TH
The Yardbirds, Acker Bilk & the Paramount Jazz Band, Johnnie Spence & his Orchestra and Rose Brennan and the Fourmost and can all be heard on BBC's "Saturday Swings" (10.00–12.00 am) today (▶ August 5).

SUN 15TH
The originally announced booking for this date at the Pier, Llandudno, Wales (the last of the Mervyn Conn's Sunday concerts) is cancelled.

TUE 17TH
According to a report of a recording session in BEAT INSTRUMENTAL attributable to this day based on a reference to the original scheduled departure for the US, the Yardbirds book studio time to complete recording their next single during a late night session at Advision Studios in London. It has been decided to record a third Graham Gouldman composition called *Evil Hearted You*. Also finished tonight is the Samwell-Smith/McCarty collaboration *Still I'm Sad* (which was begun at the end of July at Olympic Studios), and finally Keith Relf dubs an Italian vocal on *Heart Full Of Soul*'s original backing track – although this version is never released. Further studio evidence indicates that *Evil Hearted You* is entirely redone at a separate session at Advision on August 23 however.

WED 18TH✱
Probably on this day, Jeff Beck and Jimmy Page go to see Eric Clapton playing with John Mayall's Bluesbreakers at the Pontiac Club in Putney where Mayall has a Wednesday residence this month.

Page in his new role as staff producer for Immediate Records had also taken on Mayall's band for a shot at the singles chart with *I'm Your Witchdoctor* b/w *Telephone Blues* (issued October 22). During the course of the night, Jeff and Jimmy get up on stage, forming an impressive three guitar line-up of Clapton, Page and Beck! Peter Robinson, who sees several Yardbirds and Mayall shows during this era recounts how the three guitarists play a slow blues where Page goodhumouredly sneaks the opening riff of *Heart Full Of Soul* into his solo, and then gives Beck a two fingered gesture with one hand behind his back whilst keeping a long, sustained note with the other!

Of historic note, according to Page, he and Eric travel back to his home in Pangbourne that same night and the following day the two guitarists record a long blues jam onto a small 2-track which is later overdubbed and issued on a series of Immediate Records compilations.

THU 19TH
The long-anticipated US tour is due to start today, but is delayed at the eleventh hour because of confusing American union and Labor Department clearance rules which cannot be resolved in time. The original tour set to begin August 20 through September 12 is a series of dates in conjunction with California band the Beau Brummels. Cancelling out of this tour meant that an entirely new set of dates will have to be hastily arranged for the Yardbirds. Departure is reset first for August 23, then August 26 and then August 28, but these tentative start dates have to be dropped too.

MON 23RD
The band returns to Advision to recut *Evil Hearted You* following the earlier attempt on August 17.

LATE
With the various members of the band sitting around due to the endlessly delayed US tour, assorted side projects are undertaken at this time.

Paul Samwell-Smith and Giorgio Gomelsky co-produce Graham Gouldman's band the Mockingbirds. Presumably done at Olympic Studios, the Mockingbirds recordings (*You Stole My Love* b/w *Skit Skat*) are A&R'ed by Jimmy Page in his new capacity as staff producer for Immediate Records, the newly formed and highly publicized independent record label formed by Andrew Loog Oldham and Tony

August 14, 1965: Dylan's "Like A Rolling Stone" peaks at #2 in the BILLBOARD charts.

September 1965: The Yardbirds begin first US tour ...

Calder. (Immediate's debut singles are unleashed August 20.)

Another session held at this time is for an American singer, one Andy Anderson, for whom Jimmy Page had arranged a backing band which will reunite the rhythm section that once backed the legendary Cyril Davies in his heyday. The reformed All Stars, consisting of Cliff Barton (bass), Carlo Little (drums) and Nicky Hopkins (piano) are augmented by Jeff, who at this point finds himself with time on his hands. According to recollections by Little, the Anderson session – likely held at Olympic Studios – goes quickly and with time available at the end, a couple of instrumentals are casually put down on tape just for fun. However, in 1968, these tapes are exhumed, credited to Jeff Beck & the All Stars, and included in the sampler album *Anthology of British Blues/Blues Anytime* along with other archival findings.

Also around this same time, Jeff is reported to be involved in a session for singer-composer Chris Andrews, supposedly playing guitar on *Too Bad You Don't Want Me* b/w *Yesterday Man* (UK Decca/US Atco), released on September 17 in the UK. *Yesterday Man* becomes a sizeable hit, and is one of UK's top selling singles of 1965.

THU 26TH

Another scheduled departure date is put off two days as the band waits for a crucial clearance by the American Federation of Television and Radio Artists (AFTRA) which has been promised but which is not yet forthcoming. As a consequence, the initial bookings must all be cancelled. These include weekend shows pencilled in for Binghamton, New York (27) and Scranton, Pennsylvania (28) before heading to New York City (29) where the filming of "Hullabaloo" is set for the 30th–31st and it is hoped a clearance will come through in time to make a Saturday departure. An appearance on the "Ed Sullivan Show" is also mentioned at this time, but no set date is ever made official and this high-profile booking is never rescheduled.

FRI 27TH

The AFTRA clearance comes through late today which will finally allow the Yardbirds to appear on the scheduled season opener of "Hullabaloo" set for production on Monday–Tuesday next week, but arrangements cannot be finalised so late in the day and it will be too late to do so on Monday (30th), so it is decided to delay the start date of the tour once again until the following Thursday which will allow the band to make a pair of Stateside weekend bookings to start the tour rolling. "Hullabaloo" producer Gary Smith, sympathetic to the Yardbirds' cause, invites them to appear the week of September 13 when the next two episodes will be filmed.

Meanwhile in London, the Yardbirds are again last minute guests on Rediffusion's "Ready, Steady, Go!" (6.00–7.00 pm), along with among others Italy's Bobby Solo.

SAT 28TH

Today's booked flight on Aer Lingus E1 141 at 12.15 pm is also cancelled.

MON 30TH

The Yardbirds can be heard on the Bank Holiday BBC radio special "You Really Got ..." titled in honour of the Kinks, who also perform on the show (▶ August 6). Also featured are the Transatlantics and Kenny Lynch. The programme airs 10.00 am–12 noon.

SEPTEMBER

WED 1ST

An announced date for Philadelphia, Pennsylvania (likely the city's Convention Hall) is dropped pending the Yardbirds' shifted arrival date.

THU 2ND
THE YARDBIRDS: FIRST NORTH AMERICAN TOUR

Finally, it seems all arrangements are in order, enabling the Yardbirds to fly out today to New York City via Ireland for their eagerly anticipated first US tour. Owing to the oft-shifted arrangements, no grand welcoming for the band's arrival is waiting as is de riguer for visiting British pop stars. Their trip will ultimately turn into something of an anti-climax, although their mere presence on American soil is a huge accomplishment.

With *Heart Full Of Soul* steadily climbing upwards in the US charts – this week entering the upper twenties in CASH BOX – the Yardbirds enter the country with a 17-day H-2 visa. Giorgio Gomelsky travels with the band and because of the ad hoc nature of the tour with cancelled and re-scheduled dates, his talents as manager will prove valuable when handling problems with visas, union regulations and work permits. New York booking agency Premier Talent is responsible for arranging the itinerary, which will include live, radio and TV appearances while publicity is handled by Connie De Nave Public Relations. The band stays overnight in New York before travelling on to Oklahoma the following day. Blown out today is a tentative date for Louisville, Kentucky (likely at the State Fairgrounds).

FRI 3RD
Oklahoma State Fairgrounds Grandstand, Oklahoma City, Oklahoma

From New York, the Yardbirds fly on to the Midwest to pick up this initial date on their first US tour.

It is reported at the time that 1,500 witness their debut in the pouring rain though the actual attendance is characterized later as much less than that. The show is sponsored by the local but far-reaching 50,000 watt radio station KOMA which brings a stream of national chart acts to the area in this era.

SAT 4TH
The VIP Club, Jaycees Hall, Phoenix, Arizona

While the original schedule had the group set for Dallas, Texas today, this has fallen through. Instead a hastily arranged show is set for Phoenix which at least breaks up the roughly 1,000 miles westward drive to Los Angeles they have to make in a rented car. The ride across America's Southwest is no doubt exciting as they head out across the fabled Route 66 (made immortal by Bobby Troup's song of the same name) taking in the famous landmarks of Amarillo, Texas; Gallup, New Mexico and Flagstaff, Arizona.

Tonight's show in a local teen club pairs the Yardbirds with house band the Spiders whose lead singer is one Vincent Furnier who later adopts the more female and admittedly more successful name Alice Cooper. Indeed, Cooper later claims Keith Relf as one of his main influences and certainly the Spiders were thrilled to have one of their favorite British bands pull up in a rented car, plug in their guitars and play. As a somewhat warped tribute, the Spiders reportedly play a plethora of Yardbirds songs in their own set making it a bit awkward for the Yardbirds themselves to follow.

SUN 5TH

While the original plan calls for a show today in Houston, Texas this too has fallen through. Still bound by ground travel, the culture-shocked young Brits set out on another gruelling day and continue towards Los Angeles along Route 66. Unknowingly, the wayward entourage works

September 3, 1965: Dylan makes his West Coast electric debut to an enthusiastic crowd at the Hollywood Bowl.

September 1965: The Yardbirds arrive in Los Angeles ...

its way into downtown Los Angeles via the ghetto of Watts, which only a few weeks prior (August 11-15) had been shattered by destructive race riots requiring 1000s of National Guard troops to be brought in. Nevertheless, the sunny state is a revelation with its warm climate and exploding youth culture. All this makes for a great impression despite the distinctly rude welcome they receive upon arrival at their hotel on the Sunset Strip, where the management refuses to honour the booking because of the their long hair, forcing the humiliated band to make arrangements elsewhere.

MON 6TH

An American holiday (Labor Day) presumably gives the band a chance to soak in some California sun before digging in on their scheduled TV and radio work set for the following days.

In Canada, the exclusively compiled LP *Heart Full of Soul* (Capitol T-6139) is released today. Again a collection of both Beck and Clapton tunes, Jeff is heard on *My Girl Sloopy*, *I Ain't Done Wrong*, *I'm Not Talking*, *Heart Full Of Soul* and *Steeled Blues*.

TUE 7TH–WED 8TH

Continuing the band's unwelcome reception to LA, a key booking on ABC Network television's "Shindig!" out of Hollywood falls through due to lack of promised clearance. While this is a blow to the band's morale, there is possibly some consolation in the fact that inserts taped for the programme back in London in August can be aired and these are used instead on upcoming episodes which will provide important national exposure for the Yardbirds as they perform their two big hits. An actual in-person appearance however would be preferable as visiting bands were routinely given more numbers in a given episode over the single insert arrangement they ultimately had to settle for.

The group is able to do some promotion on local radio stations and in the press during their stay, including interview for various teen magazines such as FLIP, where, when asked a typically inane question how it feels to join an existing group, Jeff quips: "Better than joining a non-existing group!" Still the band suffers further insult when they are refused entry to Disneyland in Anaheim to do an on-location radio interview for the offenses of having British accents and long hair. The group's troubles with authorities prompts the LA-based radio station magazine THE BEAT to write an editorial in defense of the group arguing with justified incredulousness: "They were dressed neatly enough and their hair was combed, but that was not sufficient."

Giorgio Gomelsky has arranged a visit to RCA Studios in Hollywood during this week and according to his published recollections an early attempt at *I'm A Man* is done, although subsequently it is left to collect dust once the band cuts the definitive version later in the tour in Chicago. RCA had been suggested by the Rolling Stones who just a few months ago taped *Satisfaction* there. In fact, the Stones are back at RCA this very week recording *Get Off Of My Cloud* and other titles. As the Yardbirds had no express permission to record in the US, this and other studio visits were all arranged on the sly.

THU 9TH*

Another scheduled TV appearance – this time on Dick Clark's new weekday afternoon series "Where The Action Is" – is miraculously accomplished likely on this day, but is not used for broadcast at this time due to the recurring union clearance problems. This after-school music programme is shot on location primarily in the Los Angeles area with the artists typically surrounded by dancers and assorted teens. The regular house band, Paul Revere & the Raiders, have recently established themselves with their colourful Colonial military uniforms. It is recalled that on this show the Yardbirds are outfitted in American football gear as they lip-synch to *For Your Love*. This clip was evidently scheduled to be aired on the April 8, 1966 edition of the programme but dropped then too. This is also the likely timing of a photo opportunity where the band poses with an American high school football team.

Also while in Hollywood, the Yardbirds run into pop entrepreneur Kim Fowley, who hears of their problems and swiftly arranges for the band to play at a private party as a gesture of goodwill to counteract the litany of bureaucratic resistance and discourtesy they have experienced. The gathering is held in a huge house owned by Bob Markley's family, up in the Hollywood Hills. Markley is the son of a wealthy oil tycoon and also dabbles in music as a member of the West Coast Pop Art Experimental Band. The party attracts a reported crowd of 600(!), and the impressive list of people who wanders in during the night includes Peter & Gordon, Jackie De Shannon, Danny Hutton, members of the Byrds and even Phil Spector. More importantly, it is here that Jeff meets actress Mary Hughes, who will become his steady girlfriend for the next few years. The fair Miss Hughes has appeared in several lightweight bikini movies, the latest being "Dr. Goldfoot and the Bikini Machine".

A group called Brin Smythe provide music before the Yardbirds take the stage around midnight using the opening band's equipment (to cap their run of bad luck, the Yardbirds' 12-string acoustic guitar is broken). Louise Criscione of THE BEAT is on hand to report on the group's hour-long set, and is highly impressed: "Seriously, if you think you've heard all there is in the way of English groups – you haven't seen anything until you see the Yardbirds move and hear them wail! They didn't touch either one of their big American hits ... Instead they concentrated on long and fantastically good versions of such songs as *Smokestack Lightning* and *Hang On Sloopy* ... Standing out in the Yardbirds' instrumental line-up is the tremendous lead guitar of Jeff Beck. Talk about working a guitar – well, Jeff slaves his! He moves right up to the amplifier to catch the 'reverb' [sic] and produce that driving sound. The Yardbirds have used the Smythe's amplifiers and since Jeff's process of catching the 'reverb' sometimes results in blowing up the amplifier – was the owner of that particular amp scared!" At 3 o'clock in the morning the group conducts a transatlantic interview with Richard Green of RECORD MIRROR (September 18).

FRI 10TH

- **The Clearpool, Memphis, Tennessee**
- **Skateland Frayser, Memphis, Tennessee**

After California, the Yardbirds travel by plane to the Mid-South, to Memphis, a landmark American city known for its rich musical heritage. Part of the master plan is to record here under the guidance of Elvis Presley's original mentor and producer

---

Set List/The Yardbirds

First US tour September '65

The Train Kept A-Rollin' • I Ain't Done Wrong • For Your Love • My Girl Sloopy, • Heartful Of Soul • I'm A Man • Still I'm Sad • Smokestack Lightning • Here 'Tis • [blues number]

Sam Phillips, but so far contacting the elusive Mr. Phillips has failed. In any case, two performances have been arranged here by a local promoter. Presumably the early show of the night is at the Clearpool, an entertainment and swimming complex on Lamar Avenue out near the Memphis Airport which operates a very popular teen club on the ground floor. Upstairs is the country music bar, the Eagle's Nest, the site of some of the earliest public performances by Elvis Presley in 1954.

A roller rink an hour's drive across town on Millington Street in the northern section of the city known as Frayser is the confirmed second venue. Typically these shows went till later in the evening and local groups, including the Gants warm-up the all-ages crowd while the band makes its way clear across town.

SAT 11TH
Robinson Auditorium, Little Rock, Arkansas

Another impromptu booking due to the originally scheduled date in Atlanta (probably at Municipal Auditorium) falling through. The band drives by car from Memphis the 130 miles to Little Rock. In the pre-Interstate highway days this is a difficult 2 1/2 hour drive on a good day but as the inland remnants of Hurricane Betsy drop 3–5 inches of rain overnight in the area causing some severe flooding more than likely hampered the ride. Once in Little Rock they play on a bill with three local groups, the Gants, the Commotions and the Groupe. Attendance is sparse with about 400 people in the big hall, but the group reportedly delivers a strong performance nonetheless. Evidently still without even their own guitars they rely entirely on other band's equipment. McCarty and Relf and Gomelsky are also interviewed by writer Jack W. Hill for a story in the Arkansas Democrat. They eat prior to showtime at the Grady Manning Hotel after a failed attempt to gain entry at Shakey's Pizza Parlour where the band is refused service.

After the show the Yardbirds drive back to Memphis. Although the rain has ceased, the residual flooding makes it a difficult drive. (Gomelsky recalls later being harassed by some rednecks at the show and that they drove back right afterwards through the night and claims this to be the inspiration for *Shapes of Things* which is likely blurred with a similar drive from Iowa to Chicago in December.)

THE GOLDEN ROAD

Trailblazing Experiences

Although the Beatles instigated the so-called "British Invasion" with their arrival on the stage of the Ed Sullivan Show on February 9, 1964, the ensuing flood of similarly hopeful British rock 'n' roll acts ultimately was not so welcome by the authorities to the United States. Despite the the welcome response the British bands found with the teenage record buyers in the States, there developed a deep resentment by American artists who felt they were being displaced in the US charts by their British competition. Not only did record sales by US artists suffer, but also their ability to maintain concert bookings; both these factors were heavily impacted by the seeminly insatiable demand for British acts on record and in personal appearances.

American artists had long enjoyed open access to the British public for anyone who could justify a visit financially and clear the standard arrangements with British Immigration and the Musicians Union. In the US, arrangements for visiting British artists had been somewhat more complicated to begin with due to a complex web of immigration laws, labor laws and the presence of strong unions.

The process consisted of initially obtaining a visa to be allowed entry into the country. The US Department of Immigration issued either a visitor's visa – primarily aimed at tourist and simple business travel – or two further classes of visas where the intent was to perform work in some manner. Visiting performers could apply for and routinely qualify for an H-1 visa which was given to foreign "artists of unique distinction and merit". During 1964 many notable British acts toured the United States with these visas in hand, including the first tours by the Beatles, the Rolling Stones and the Animals. Toward the end of 1964 the US Department of Immigration changed its policy and stopped issuing H-1 visas to visiting rock 'n' roll acts, who by implication were no longer deemed to be "artists of unique merit and distinction."

Following this ruling, the US government would only issue H-2 visas to visiting rock 'n' rollers, which were far more restrictive. This clearly secondary class of visa required the holders to prove they were performing a job which no American was capable of doing. It was essentially designed to keep migrant workers from taking work away from willing US residents. And while under H-1 laws the applicant only needed a single work permit from the US Department of Labor in order to actually perform, under the H-2 laws the visiting performer now had to get individual permit approvals from the labor department in whatever city or state he or she wished to perform in. The onus of proof shifted to the performer or their manager to present a case to the officials via press clippings, chart showings or whatever to demonstrate that a local artist could not perform exactly the same job. At the same time it empowered local bureaucrats, who likely not knowing "one juvenile singer from another" (to cite Variety, June 16, 1965) were putting foreign visitors in random peril.

This ruling applied across the boards such that even the mighty Beatles were subject to this. However, the Beatles and the Stones were well-established by this point with well-organized businesses which were able to work their way through the web. The real effect was on up-and-coming British bands with maverick type management who might have a single record or two in the charts and wanted to break ground in America; bands like the Yardbirds, the Moody Blues and the Pretty Things faced very stiff resistance. Bands like the Zombies or the Nashville Teens were able to get into the country by restricting work to single extended bookings such as the Murray the K holiday show in New York, as the powerful disc-jockey was able to get a one-time clearance. For a cross-country tour the bureaucracy became prohibitive, and in 1965 the Searchers and others instead settled for package tours like Dick Clark's Caravan of Stars, where the mighty Clark organization was able to accomplish the necessary paperwork, but the tours were gruelling and showed almost no financial return.

One of the more notorious examples is that of the Kinks who briefly toured the US in the summer of '65. Initially they were to tour on a double-bill with the Moody Blues who were barred from appearing at the eleventh hour. The Kinks came anyways, rearranging the schedule somewhat, but the mercurial Kinks were unhappy with the arrangements and the cold reception by the show-biz establishment led to confrontations with promoters and union officials. In essence, the Kinks were blackballed by the influential unions who both advised and exerted influence at the Labor Department and Immigration as to who should get work. As a result, the Kinks did not tour the US again until 4 years later, effectively killing their US career.

It was into this atmosphere that the Yardbirds finally arrived in the US. ∎

September 1965: Memorable recording sessions in Memphis and Chicago...

SUN 12TH
The band returns to Memphis still hoping to contact Sam Phillips to book studio time at his legendary Sun Studio in Memphis. Unbeknownst perhaps to the band, Phillips' current studio is actually a different, more modern facility on Madison Avenue; his original Sun Studios at 706 Union Avenue having been closed in 1960 when the new studio was ready for business.

After a failed attempt to record at another local studio that afternoon instead, Gomelsky finally tracks Phillips down later this night upon his return from a fishing trip. Tempted by a reported cash offer of $600 for a session, Phillips finally obliges. At first suspicious of a gang of 'Limeys' playing rhythm & blues, Phillips warms to the Yardbirds as soon as he hears them play. Both *The Train Kept A-Rollin'* and Mike and Brian Hugg's *Mister You're A Better Man Than I* are taped during an intense late night session, which runs into the early hours of Monday morning. *The Train Kept A-Rollin'*, one of Jeff's all-time favourite songs as performed by the Rock And Roll Trio, was seemingly introduced to the group's repertoire this month.

MON 13TH
The Yardbirds fly back to New York City first thing this morning to film their scheduled appearance on "Hullabaloo" after their failure to have done so at the outset of the tour. As AFTRA have cleared this appearance, the band arrives thinking all is in order. However, this time it is the US Department of Labor who inexplicably reverses its original permission based on the convoluted logic that since they were ultimately replaced for the season opening show, they are not then unique, which had been the basis of their original request and therefore are now not eligible for clearance. The band is evidently present at rehearsals this day for an episode of "Hullabaloo" hosted by comedian Jerry Lewis (to be aired September 20). It is likely that this reversal of their clearance prompts manager Gomelsky to tackle the problem directly as he heads to Washington DC to straighten matters out on his own.

TUE 14TH
Gomelsky meets with officials at the British Embassy and together they present their case to the US Department of Labor which ultimately sympathises with the complex situation. Today, the Department of Labor formally reverses its stand on the work permits for the Yardbirds (according to VARIETY, September 15), which will allow them now to appear on the next episode of the show due to begin rehearsals the following day. The Yardbirds themselves kill time in New York awaiting their fate.

WED 15TH
With work permits from the US Department of Labor now in hand and having been slotted into an appearance on another "Hullabaloo" episode the band arrives on the set at NBC Studios in Rockefeller Center to begin rehearsals today. This episode which airs September 27 also includes Brenda Lee, the Animals and Peter & Gordon and is hosted by British actor David McCallum, currently enjoying fame in his role on the hit TV series "The Man From U.N.C.L.E.". The band gets so far as rehearsing a skit with McCallum but unfortunately the Yardbirds will ultimately not appear in this episode either. Rather they are rescheduled yet again by producer Gary Smith to film the following week which is evidently now possible as the Yardbirds have been granted a short extension on their visas. As this newly scheduled episode (with Frankie Avalon hosting) will not air until December 6, it is possible there is some other factor at work, possibly even that the airing of the "Shindig!" inserts (▶ August 10–11) dictated that there may be more appeal to have the group appear later rather than earlier. Indeed as it transpires when the band films its spot next week, they will be able to perform their freshly recorded next single (*I'm A Man*), neatly timed to air when the record will be in the charts.

THU 16TH
A scheduled concert tonight likely sponsored by WARM radio (Scranton-Wilkes-Barre) set for Scranton, Pennsylvania, possibly at the local CYO Hall is most likely cancelled especially if plans had originally been set to be taping the "Hullabaloo" appearance this evening. It is likely band members attend the post-filming party with the Animals and other "Hullabaloo" guests this evening instead.

FRI 17TH
The Rolling Stone, New York, New York
Today is devoted to press duties, slotting spots with various teen magazine writers for both morning and afternoon sessions. In one such interview for the magazine FLIP entitled 'The Yardbirds Want To Be Heard!' the band vents its frustrations about this tour: "First we had our arrangements stolen then our important 12 string guitar broke, then we were barred from "Shindig!", then we went into rehearsal for "Hullabaloo" only to be told we couldn't appear."

This is also probably the date of a photo shoot for the band which will be used for their next US LP cover and various promotional purposes.

This evening the Yardbirds attend and perform at an Epic Records reception and a 'bon voyage' party held in their honour at the Rolling Stone discotheque in Manhattan at 304 East 48th Street. The club is co-owned by well-known disc-jockey Scott Muni, and the house band is a group of transplanted Brits called the Mersey Lads. Following a set by the exiled Brits, the Yardbirds take the stage for a single hour long performance, borrowing the house band's amplification equipment and drum kit. Calamities abound as the show gets off to a shaky start when the PA system proves insufficient, then the drum stool Jim McCarty is borrowing collapses mid-song and finally Chris Dreja is forced to borrow Mersey Lad Gerry Clarke's prized 1955 Stratocaster when he breaks a string on his own guitar. Despite this, the Yardbirds turn in an impressive show in the end and this single essentially unadvertised show would be the Yardbirds' only New York performance for almost two years, and Jeff Beck's only performance here until his triumphant return in June 1968 with his own band.

SAT 18TH
Arie Crown Theater, Chicago, Illinois
Chicago, like Memphis, is known for its rich musical heritage and is a magnet for the Yardbirds.

Tonight is a classic British double-bill with the Yardbirds and the Hollies. Booked weeks in advance, this show originally also starred British cohorts the Animals who cancel out shortly prior to this date in order to fly to Los Angeles to record their next single there at RCA Studios. The Hollies fly in from London this very afternoon for a week of TV and concerts facing the same uncertainties with clearances and permits as the Yardbirds. Despite the typical lack of print evidence of the show in the local press, Graham Nash confirms that the concert goes ahead as planned in a phone call to the NEW MUSICAL EXPRESS two days later.

September 1965: The Byrds record their next US chart topper, "Turn, Turn, Turn" at Columbia Studios in Hollywood.

September 1965: The Yardbirds finally appear on "Hullabaloo" in New York ...

SUN 19TH
Though no documentation survives, this is almost certain the day of yet another recording session on American soil. This takes place when the Yardbirds enter Chicago's famed Chess Studios on South Michigan Avenue, home of countless classic blues recordings of many of their musical heroes. The arrangements have been made in advance by Gomelsky through the British National Jazz Federation. It is presumed to coincide with the band's concert here as they would have had to leave the country the following day according to the original schedule. According to legend, the Yardbirds' session comes immediately following one by Chess's Billy Stewart.

The band, assisted by engineer Ron Malo, record a song destined to be a Yardbird-classic: Bo Diddley's *I'm A Man*. Interestingly the original recording is more like their standard live performance in length and the single is edited down afterwards through a number of splices.

It is unclear if any other recordings were done today as Gomelsky later recalls that 5 hours had been booked to cut two songs and that the band finished early due to things going so well. While Gomelsky will maintain that *Shapes of Things* is the second song done this day, in retrospect contemporary evidence and clues point to the fact that it was not recorded now but rather at a later Chess session (▶ December 21–22).

Originally, today should have been the last date of the Yardbirds' first US tour. However Giorgio has by now managed to extend the visas for a few more days and gain the assurances they will be permitted to make the one TV show they are dead set on accomplishing, so the entourage flies back to New York probably tonight.

MON 20TH
In their fourth attempt, Giorgio Gomelsky finally manages to sort out the technicalities, allowing the Yardbirds to appear on "Hullabaloo". Today, the group rehearses the show at NBC Studios. This show's host – which revolves weekly – is teen crooner Frankie Avalon, and other guests include the Hollies, Nancy Sinatra and the Ronettes. Unlike routine episodes broadcast shortly after their taping, this show would not be aired until December 6 and its delay may be due to the fact that it was also one of the few episodes filmed in colour even though it would not survive in that form over the years.

TUE 21ST
Further rehearsals for "Hullabaloo" continue today with an early evening filming where the Yardbirds perform *I'm A Man* recorded in Chicago only days earlier and in fact still without its master vocal track. The instrumental backing track for the record is mimed to by the band while Keith Relf does a live vocal and accompanying harmonica part. Of note is the fact that, still under the watchful eye of network censors, the line "make love to you baby in an hour's time" is cleaned up to the more tepid "I'll kiss you baby in an hour's time".

The backing track is explosive and the segment staged in the show's mock discotheque – the Hullabaloo A Go Go – with the show's dancers engaged in a high-spirited cutting contest is a riveting sight to behold. The show itself is not transmitted until December 6 which benefits the Yardbirds as it allows time for the song to hit the airwaves and the charts first.

With the TV filming wrapped up, the later part of the evening is saved for the fourth and final recording session of the tour, at Columbia Studios with engineer Roy Halee, which goes from 10 pm until 4 am Wednesday morning. As time this week had originally been set aside for work on a studio LP in London, more recording is fit in as the Yardbirds clearly prefer the results they obtain in American studios over their British counterparts. Three existing backing tracks are worked on tonight; *The Train Kept A Rollin'*, *Mister You're A Better Man Than I* and *I'm A Man*, presumably adding, doubling or re-recording Keith Relf's vocals plus any final mixing or finishing touches. Lastly, an entirely new recording fittingly entitled *New York City Blues* is committed to tape. The song is actually a lyrical rewrite by Relf and Dreja of Eddie Boyd's blues classic *Five Long Years* and a concert staple of the Clapton-era Yardbirds. The dour performance could be considered the band's parting farewell to New York!

WED 22ND
Leaving New York today, the Yardbirds presumably fly on directly to their next commitment in Holland. Reflecting the last minute nature of this US tour extension, a pre-arranged booking on the British TV programme "Gadzooks – It's All Happening!" today is obviously cancelled.

THU 23RD
The Yardbirds are able to honour their Dutch television debut at NCRV Studios in Bussum, Holland, where they tape For Your Love for the teen programme "Tiener Magazine", to be broadcast on December 3.

Also on this very night the Yardbirds can be seen in the US on "Shindig!" on the ABC TV network, performing *Heart Full Of Soul* and *For Your Love* from the filming done in London (▶ August 10–11). Also featured on this edition of "Shindig!" are Jerry Lee Lewis and British rhythm & blues group the Pretty Things, plus – amazingly! – Raquel Welch singing *Dancing In The Streets*.

SAT 25TH
After their Dutch stop-over, the group finally returns to England. Interviewed at London Airport, Keith Relf tells the press in a predictable upbeat manner: "The tour was extremely successful" *(Heart Full Of Soul* peaks at #9 in the BILLBOARD chart this week.)

SUN 26TH
Back home again, the Yardbirds immediately commence promotional live, radio and TV dates for their new British single, beginning with a rehearsal and taping in Birmingham for "Thank Your Lucky Stars" (ABC-TV), to be broadcast Saturday October 2 at 5.50–6.35 pm. Brian Matthew has now retired from the show, and actor Jim Dale has taken his place as host.

MON 27TH
The Yardbirds tape an instalment of BBC Light's "Saturday Club," also to be broadcast on October 2. The session is held at BBC's Aeolian 1 studio, between 4.00–6.30 pm. Songs performed today are the double A-sided single *Evil Hearted You/Still I'm Sad* plus *My Girl Sloopy*, *The Train Kept A-Rollin'* and Freddy King's classic instrumental *The Stumble*, noted by BBC record keepers as 'Beck Stumbled'.

Further planned work early this week on their proposed studio LP is delayed.

TUE 28TH
Today, the group is in Manchester to tape "Scene At 6.30" on Granada TV, presumably aired later the same day.

WED 29TH
More television work, as the Yardbirds are in Bristol for a simulcast on TWW's "Discs A Go Go" (7.00–7.30 pm).

THU 30TH
Locarno Ballroom, Swindon

© September 1965: Eric Clapton and his new band the Glands arrive in Greece while on a short-lived break from his stint with John Mayall's Bluesbreakers.

October 1965: "Evil Hearted You"/"Still I'm Sad" new single in the UK ...

OCTOBER

FRI 1ST

The Yardbirds' new single *Evil Hearted You/Still I'm Sad* is released in Great Britain today. Because of favourable reactions from disc-jockeys and record pluggers, it is decided to promote and advertise the single as a double A-side. The record peaks at #3 (#2 in the MELODY MAKER charts); the group's third consecutive Top Three smash in Britain, and the last song in a trilogy of hits penned by Graham Gouldman, but it is the experimental – and self-penned – *Still I'm Sad* which is the stronger of the two sides. "Sounds like the doctors and dentists choir!" quips comedian Ken Dodd when he is played the song in MELODY MAKER's weekly 'Blind Date' column, where the guests are asked to comment on some of the week's new releases.

The Yardbirds also return to "Ready, Steady, Go!" tonight (incredibly, this is Jeff's tenth appearance on the show) along with the Searchers, Long John Baldry and visiting American folk trio Peter, Paul and Mary.

SAT 2ND
Drill Hall, Grantham

The Yardbirds are heard on the air today on BBC Light Programme's "Saturday Club" at 10 am (▶ September 27). Also appearing on the show – besides the Silkie, the Zombies and Bo Diddley – is the London-based Steam Packet; a coalition of Brian Auger's Trinity and the three-pronged vocal front-line of Rod Stewart, Long John Baldry and Julie Driscoll. The last (one of Gomelsky's protéges) has also worked as the Yardbirds' fan club secretary, a position later also held by Keith's sister Jane Relf until June '66. Incidentally, daddy Bill Relf is also employed by the group, as their trusted road manager.

Tonight's concert in Grantham, Lincolnshire is with support groups Maniax and Omruds.

MON 4TH

A pre-recording of BBC's "The Beat Show" is as usual done in Manchester's Playhouse Theatre, for transmission on October 7. Again the two sides of the new single are the main feature plus a reprise of *Heart Full Of Soul* for good measure.

WED 6TH
The Witch Doctor, Hastings

THU 7TH
Ricky Tick Club, Thames Hotel, Windsor

In the afternoon, the Yardbirds are guests on BBC Light Programme's "Beat Show" (transmitted at 1 pm, ▶ October 4). The day is rounded off with an appearance at the Ricky Tick.

FRI 8TH
Town Hall, Staines

The Monday October 18 instalment of the Light Programme's regular show "This Must Be The Place" is recorded today at Studio S2, Broadcasting House, London, with the Yardbirds as guests. It is definitely a hits-only rundown today with *Evil Hearted You*, *Still I'm Sad*, *For Your Love* and *Heart Full Of Soul*.

Tonight's show is in Surrey.

SAT 9TH
California Ballroom, Dunstable

Becoming almost regular employees of the BBC, the Yardbirds are back again for the third time this week, now at London's Playhouse Theatre, for tomorrow's edition of "Easy Beat" which strictly features the new two-sided hit.

Tonight's show in Dunstable is at 8 pm to midnight with local support.

SUN 10TH

The Yardbirds and the Everly Brothers are heard on David Symonds' radio show "Easy Beat" (10.00–11.30 am, ▶ October 9). For almost every day this week the Yardbirds have saturated the BBC airwaves, either pre-recording sessions for the 'Beeb' or being on the air on different radio shows.

MON 11TH
Majestic Ballroom, Rhyl, Wales

The exciting *I'm A Man* from the Chicago visit in September is rush-released as the new American single today. The A-side, a mainstay of their repertoire during the group's entire existence, has already been recorded previously with Eric Clapton on the *Five Live Yardbirds* album. This version, however, is in essence the Yardbirds' on stage rave-ups compressed to two and a half minutes complete with a speeded-up middle section where Beck runs riot during the ensemble solo. It peaks at #17 in the BILLBOARD Hot 100 chart during December.

TUE 12TH
Marquee Club, London

The Yardbirds make a return to the Marquee tonight billed as 'Welcome Back from the US'. The Mark Leeman Five, now actually minus Leeman who was tragically killed in an auto accident in June, play support.

WED 13TH ✱

Buddy Guy is in Britain as part of the Fourth American Folk-Blues Festival this month (which also stars Eddie Boyd and Big Mama Thornton plus others), and Giorgio Gomelsky hosts a

---

Single
THE YARDBIRDS

A: EVIL HEARTED YOU *(Graham Gouldman)*
B: STILL I' SAD *(Samwell-Smith/McCarty)*

Released Friday October 1, 1965 (UK Columbia DB 7706)
Personnel is Jeff Beck (ldgtr), Keith Relf (hrmnca/vcls), Chris Dreja (rhygtr), Paul Samwell-Smith (bs) and Jim McCarty (drms); Giorgio Gomelsky sings backing vocals on *Still I'm Sad*.
Recorded at Advision Studios, New Bond Street, London, August 23, 1965 (A) and Olympic Studios, Baker Street, London, July and August 17, 1965 (B)
Produced by Giorgio Gomelsky
Musical direction by Paul Samwell-Smith
Engineered by Roger Cameron and Gerald Chevin (Advision) and Keith Grant (Olympic).
Highest Chart Position UK: #3

Single
THE YARDBIRDS

A: I'M A MAN *(Ellas McDaniels)*
B: STILL I' SAD *(Samwell-Smith/McCarty)*

Released Monday October 11, 1965 (US Epic DB 9857)
Personnel is Jeff Beck (ldgtr), Keith Relf (hrmnca/vcls), Chris Dreja (rhygtr), Paul Samwell-Smith (bs) and Jim McCarty (drms); Giorgio Gomelsky (vcl on B)
Recorded at Chess Studio, 2120 South Michigan Avenue, Chicago, September 19, 1965 and Columbia Studios, New York, New York, September 21–22, 1965 (A) and at Olympic Studios, Baker Street, London, July 1965 and Advision Studios, New Bond Street, London, August 17, 1965 (B).
Produced by Giorgio Gomelsky
Engineered by Ron Malo (Chicago) and Roger Cameron/Keith Grant (London)
Highest Chart Position US: #17

October 1965: "I'm A Man" new single in the US ...

party in his honour which turns into a big jam-session before it is stopped by the police. Jeff Beck and Keith Relf both attend the celebration, and so do Brian Auger, Zoot Money, Steve Winwood and some of the Animals. The party is probably held mid-week, which is a rare breather in the Yardbirds' busy schedule and also an off day in the Blues Festival itinerary.

THU 14TH
Queen's Hall, Barnstaple

FRI 15TH
Guildhall, Axminster

SAT 16TH
Winter Gardens, Weston-super-Mare

MON 18TH
Trade Union Hall, Watford

Besides the Watford, Hertsfordshire booking, the Yardbirds – and Billy Fury – are also heard on BBC Light Programme's "This Must Be The Place" today (at 1 pm, ▶ October 8).

TUE 19TH
Town Hall, High Wycombe

WED 20TH
Town Hall, Stourbridge

THU 21ST
Winter Gardens, Cleethorpes

Unlike their previous devotion to regular "Top Of The Pops" appearances to promote their newest release, this spot today from the BBC TV Studios in Manchester for tonight's edition of "Top Of The Pops" (BBC 1, 7 pm) would be the Yardbirds sole showing for *Evil Hearted You/Still I'm Sad*. Afterwards the band heads north for the evening's show in Cleethorpes.

FRI 22ND
Marine Ballroom, Central Pier, Morecambe

Support by house regulars the Executives (with future NEW MUSICAL EXPRESS journalist Roy Carr) plus Harold Graham, organist!

SAT 23RD
Student Union, University of Leeds, Leeds

A student "hop" with Leeds favorites the Yardbirds plus the Detroits, Al Crossland, and the Unwanted Pregnancies. This would be the third time the Yardbirds played here to date. The UNION NEWS (October 22, 1965) enthuses: "The Yardbirds and the Who are the only two groups currently playing anything new, because these alone are not rehashing, essentially American styles." Of Beck, the paper observes: "Jeff's sheer prowess on guitar has opened new fields to the group ... [Beck] admires B.B. King, Buddy Guy, Spencer Davis ... but his style is devoid of external influences – in fact it epitomises the uniqueness of this outstanding group."

SUN 24TH
Oasis Club, Manchester

MON 25TH
Queen's Ballroom, Wolverhampton

TUE 26TH
Sherwood Rooms, Nottingham

FRI 29TH
The Yardbirds return to Rediffusion's "Ready, Steady, Go!" (6.08–7.00 pm) TV show tonight. Other guests on the show are Chris Andrews, the Ivy League and the Dave Clark Five.

SAT 30TH
Baths, Leyton

After the Leyton show, the band is involved in a row with promoter Roy Tempest who claims he has booked the group at the Zambesi Club in Hounslow tonight. Mr. Tempest – true to his name – fires a broadside at band and management in RECORD MIRROR: "More co-operation between the Yardbirds' management, who are completely and utterly ridiculous, and the Yardbirds, who have let down so many people they have become a joke, is needed."

SUN 31ST
Tonight is Halloween and Jeff is partying at London's Cromwellian club with, among others, the Animals' Eric Burdon and Chas Chandler, Jim McCarty, and drummer John "Twink" Alder and host of other celebrities. Beck is considered a natural member of SLAGS (Society of Looning Alcoholic Guitarists), a casual union of pub-loving musicians initiated by guitarist Andy Summers from Zoot Money's Big Roll Band, and which also counts Eric Clapton and Hilton Valentine among its members.

Of the Yardbirds, Jeff is the one who is most often observed at many of London's clubs, some of which – like the 3-story Cromwellian and the Scotch of St. James just off Piccadilly Circus – cater to the hip pop elite. Dave Davies, another notorious young reveller about town, later describes Beck as another "really obnoxious party-goer from this period".

•

Around October and November 1965, the Yardbirds are determined to finish an LP in time for Christmas. On several occasions management and the group attempt to put pressure on themselves by informing the music press about the forthcoming record. Originally begun in April, the album to be called *A Yardbird View Of A Beat*, now has the working title *The Yardbirds' Eye-view Of Beat* (also misinterpreted as *Yardbirds, I View* in one music paper). The long player is planned to include one side with five original numbers – one from each of the group (an idea which is returned to later but ultimately abandoned), while the other side would feature the recent recordings from their US visit; *The Train Kept A-Rollin'*, *Mister You're A Better Man Than Me*, *I'm A Man*, and *New York City Blues*. Samwell-Smith explains to DISC WEEKLY; "[the new album] will be out some time in November ... it will have some great rhythm and blues tracks on it which we recorded in Memphis," while MELODY MAKER reports "one side will contain original numbers, while the other side will be typical Yardbirds arrangements of classic numbers". Eventually the group runs out of time; the US tracks are released as single sides over the next six months, and album plans are postponed until early next year. However, neither the recent American single *I'm A Man* or the irresistible version of *The Train Kept A-Rollin'* will be honoured with a British release in this decade.

NOVEMBER

MON 1ST
Pavilion, Bath

TUE 2ND
Floral Hall, Gorleston

WED 3RD
Orchid Ballroom, Purley

Also today, the third quarterly meeting of directors of Yardbirds Ltd. is held at the Dreja home in Surbiton, Surrey. The Yardbirds minus Jeff are present in addition to Giorgio, Relf senior and Dreja senior who is chairman. While his bandmates increase their weekly salary to £52.10s, no formal mention is made of Jeff Beck's wages.

FRI 5TH
ABC Theatre, Cleethorpes

With tonight's booking, the Yardbirds briefly step in on short notice to re-

November 1965: UK Package tour with Manfred Mann...

place singer Billy Fury, who is starring in an on-going package tour with Herman's Hermits and Wayne Fontana.

SAT 6TH
Marcam Hall, March

In today's RECORD MIRROR, the Who's Pete Townshend lashes out at the Yardbirds new disc, *Still I'm Sad*: "That Yardbirds thing doesn't deserve to be a hit. The recording technique is no good. That idea of a Gregorian war chant is useless, who wants to know about that?" This prompts a sarcastic reply from Paul Samwell-Smith the following week: "Townshend ... made references to a Gregorian war chant, does he think that the Gregorians were a tribe of Indians?"

MON 8TH
Baths, Eltham, London

TUE 9TH
THE YARDBIRDS: SECOND CONTINENTAL TOUR
K-52, Frankfurt, West-Germany

The Yardbirds fly into West-Germany to undertake a short tour of Europe opening tonight in Frankfurt.

•

Two European-only albums, *For Your Love, Heart Full Of Soul & Others* (Ricordi International LIR 22-001) and *Our Own Sound* (Riviera 421 030) – for the Italian and French market respectively – are issued this month. Both albums feature a cross-section of Beck and Clapton selections already available elsewhere with the exception of two alternate Clapton-takes.

WED 10TH

The Yardbirds travel from Frankfurt to Munich.

THU 11TH

A press reception and interviews take place in Munich's Beer Cellars.

FRI 12TH
The Big Apple, Munich, Germany

Tonight's show at this large discotheque in Munich is reportedly recorded with a view to release it as a live album, a good idea which sadly never reaches fruition.

SAT 13TH AND SUN 14TH

After West Germany, the Yardbirds continue to Belgium with a high profile TV appearance in Brussels on "Adamoroso (The Adamo Show)" which is pre-taped for transmission on November 21. The group performs *Still I'm Sad* and *For Your Love*, both of which are staged in unusual settings with studio effects.

It is believed it is this appearance which is used the following spring as Belgium's entry into the Montreaux TV Festival. A TV date in Holland had also been mentioned to be set at this time but seems to have not occurred.

MON 15TH

A tentative concert at the Colston Hall in Bristol is ultimately cancelled.

TUE 16TH

Pre-recording an instalment on a BBC Christmas radio show at S2, Broadcasting House, London, today, the Yardbirds tape *Smokestack Lightning, Mister, You're A Better Man Than I, The Train Kept A-Rollin'* and *Still I'm Sad* for BBC Light Programme. These songs are featured on the BBC's "The Sound of Boxing Day", broadcast on December 27; a Christmas special which also stars the Hollies and the Ivy League. (It should be noted that the version of *Smokestack Lightning* recorded here has long been misdated by collectors to be of the Page-on-bass-era but this is patently not so.)

WED 17TH
Locarno Ballroom, Stevenage

A dress rehearsal for the upcoming 'Marquee Show' tour is also held today, besides a single live appearance in Hertsfordshire at night.

THU 18TH
THE YARDBIRDS:
SECOND BRITISH TOUR
"The Marquee Show"
ABC Cinema, Stockton

The Yardbirds share top-of-the-bill on this 16-date twice-nightly package tour with Manfred Mann, who are currently enjoying a hit with *If You Gotta Go, Go Now*, one of their many Bob Dylan interpretations. The tour is technically just a tour of England, as the itinerary does not cover Ireland, Wales nor Scotland. The schedule is typically tight with only two days off. The bill is rounded out by musical satirists the Scaffold (including Paul McCartney's brother, Mike McGear), pop brothers the Ryan Twins, the Mark Leeman Five, Gary Farr & the T-Bones plus the American husband-and-wife team Inez & Charlie Foxx. Eventually the last mysteriously fail to appear, and are hurriedly replaced by Goldie & the Gingerbreads, an American act who have taken up temporary residence in Great Britain. The Yardbirds have crossed paths with Goldie Zelkowitz (who some years later adopts the stage name Genya Ravan) and her Gingerbreads on several occasions including the Kinks Show earlier this year, and Beck is friendly with this all-girl group. In fact, sometime this month Jeff and Georgie Fame drop in on one of Goldie's recording sessions.

Album
THE YARDBIRDS
HAVING A RAVE UP WITH THE YARDBIRDS

A1 MISTER YOU'RE A BETTER MAN THAN I (*B. Hugg/M. Hugg*) **A2** EVIL HEARTED YOU (*Gouldman*) **A3** I'M A MAN (*E. McDaniels*) **A4** STILL I'M SAD (*Samwell-Smith/McCarty*) **A5** HEART FULL OF SOUL (*Gouldman*) **A6** THE TRAIN KEPT A-ROLLIN' (*Bradshaw/Mann/Kay*)

B1 SMOKESTACK LIGHTNING (*C. Burnett*) **B2** RESPECTABLE (*O. Isley/R. Isley/R. Isley*) **B3** I'M A MAN (*E. McDaniels*) **B4** HERE 'TIS (*E. McDaniels*)

Released November 29, 1965 (US Epic LN 24177 mono/BN 26177 stereo)
Personnel is Jeff Beck (ldgtr), Eric Clapton (ldgtr B1, B2, B4), Keith Relf (hrmnca/vcls), Chris Dreja (rhygtr), Paul Samwell-Smith (bs) and Jim McCarty (drms). Girorgio Gomelsky (vcls A4), Ron Prentice (dbl bs B1)
Recorded at Advision Studios, New Bond Street, London, April 20*, 1965 (A5), Olympic Studios, Baker Street, London and Advision Studios, New Bond Street, London, July and Auigust 17 and 23, 1965 (A2, A4), Sam Phillips Studios, 639 Madison Avenue, Memphis, Tennessee, September 12, 1965 (A1, A6), Chess Studios, 2120 South Michigan Avenue, Chicago, Illinois, September 19, 1965 (A3), Columbia Studios, New York, New York, September 21-22, 1965 (A1, A3, A6) and live at the Marquee Club, 90 Wardour Street, London, April 1964 (feat. Eric Clapton on guitar; B1, B2, B3, B4)
Produced by Giorgio Gomelsky
Engineered by Keith Grant (A4), Roger Cameron (A2, A4, A5), Sam Phillips (A1 and A6), Ron Malo (A3) and Philip Wood (B1, B2, B3, B4), Roy Halee (A1*, A3*, A6*)
Highest Chart Position US: #53

November 1965: "Having A Rave-Up With The Yardbirds" released in the US ...

The tour is jointly promoted by the George Cooper Organisation and Marquee Artistes (hence the name 'Marquee Show') and presented by Giorgio Gomelsky. Unfortunately, the tour is not a particularly big success, having less press coverage than usual, and the groups find themselves playing to half-filled halls on several dates.

FRI 19TH
"The Marquee Show"
ABC Cinema, Chesterfield

SAT 20TH
"The Marquee Show"
Gaumont Cinema, Derby

SUN 21ST
While an off night for the band on tour, tonight the Yardbirds' appearance on the Adamo Show is aired on the Belgian RTB channel at 8.30–9.30 pm (▶ November 13–14). Other guests include Francis Claude, the Morgan's, Rolly et Harry, les Ballets and Renée Lafontaine.

MON 22ND
"The Marquee Show"
Gaumont Cinema, Bradford
The Yardbirds miss the first of two shows after they are stranded in a blizzard with a punctured tire.

TUE 23RD
"The Marquee Show"
Ritz Cinema, Luton

WED 24TH
"The Marquee Show"
Ritz Theatre, Chatham

THU 25TH
"The Marquee Show"
ABC Cinema, Cambridge

FRI 26TH
"The Marquee Show"
ABC Cinema, Southampton

SAT 27TH
"The Marquee Show"
Granada Cinema, East Ham, London

SUN 28TH
"The Marquee Show"
Coventry Theatre, Coventry

MON 29TH
"The Marquee Show"
ABC Cinema, Northampton
Of interest at this Monday show, Manfred Mann features a new bass player, no less than Jack Bruce, whose credentials to date include Alexis Korner's Blues Incorporated, the Graham Bond Organization and briefly John Mayall's Bluesbreakers.

Also today, a second Yardbirds album – christened *Having a Rave Up With The Yardbirds* – is issued exclusively in the States, both to cash in on their recent hit single and also to tie in with the Yardbirds' upcoming North American tour to commence in a few weeks. Promotional copies likely went out the prior week. Like the group's first American album, this is another hodge-podge collection of single sides fleshed out with some old Clapton-era live tracks from *Five Live Yardbirds*. Jeff Beck plays on six out of ten selections, including the first official outings for *The Train Kept A-Rollin'* and *Mister You're A Better Man Than I*. The album makes US #53 and is considered by many fans to be one of the classic albums of the sixties rock era.

TUE 30TH
"The Marquee Show"
Guildhall, Portsmouth

DECEMBER

WED 1ST
Giorgio Gomelsky is still intent on breaking the Yardbirds into the Italian market, so today Keith Relf dubs an Italian vocal on the original backing track to *Still I'm Sad*, presumably at Advision in London. Just like the attempted Italiano-version of *Heart Full of Soul* recorded in August, this is never released either.

THU 2ND
"The Marquee Show"
Granada Cinema, Bedford

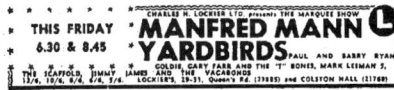

FRI 3RD
"The Marquee Show"
Colston Hall, Bristol
Way down on today's bill are also Jimmy James & the Vagabonds, featuring Phil Chen, a bassist who impresses Jeff enough to take note of his name for future use.

Today too, the Yardbirds are on the Dutch TV show "Tiener Magazine" (Channel-1 20.05–20.35, ▶ September 23).

SAT 4TH
"The Marquee Show"
ABC Cinema, Plymouth

SUN 5TH
"The Marquee Show"
ABC Cinema, Exeter
Originally billed for a Manchester appearance at the Palace Theatre, tonight's show is moved to Exeter.

MON 6TH
"The Marquee Show"
Adelphi Cinema, Slough
An extra and final date is added to the 'Marquee Show'.

Across the Atlantic, the Yardbirds are Frankie Avalon's guests on "Hullabaloo" where they are seen nationally performing a pulverizing rendition of the then freshly recorded single *I'm A Man* (▶ September 21).

WED 8TH
Radio Caroline Club Ball "Zowie 1"
New Brighton Tower Hall, New Brighton
The Yardbirds are top of the bill for a club ball for the pirate radio station Radio Caroline, which also stars the Four Pennies, the Mark Leeman Five, Paul & Barry Ryan, Brian Poole & the Tremeloes, the Honeycombs and Jimmy James & the Vagabonds to name a few. The 'Zowie 1' is a chaotic affair, where all the bands travel by train from London in the morning, and then have to make a wild dash back to the station after the show to catch the train home. A weary Paul Samwell-Smith complains to RECORD MIRROR: "You can quote me as saying that I never want to do another thing like this again."

THU 9TH
The American TV show "Shindig!" in a special two-part programme called "Shindig Goes To London" airs the second instalment from the Richmond Festival (▶ August 6), featuring a quintessential British Invasion line-up of the Yardbirds, the Who, Manfred Mann and the Graham Bond Organization (with Jack Bruce and Ginger Baker). The Yardbirds ferociously bang out *For Your Love* and *My Girl Sloopy*. This and the "Hullabaloo" TV show a few days earlier are a perfect set-up for the group's US tour set to begin the following day.

FRI 10TH
THE YARDBIRDS:
SECOND NORTH AMERICAN TOUR
The Yardbirds, accompanied by Giorgio Gomelsky, make the 9 hour flight to Chicago from London Airport arriving at 12.30 pm today to commence a six-week American tour. The date of departure had been resched-

December 3, 1965: The Beatles' 6th LP "Rubber Soul" is issued in the UK and again tops all LP charts.

December 1965: The Yardbirds commence second US tour ...

uled from December 15th and moved up to the 10th, forcing a cancellation of planned shows at St. George's Ballroom, Hinckley on the 11th, the Olympia in Paris, France with Chuck Berry on the 14th, and a BBC session for the following day.

Arriving in a snowy America, legend has it the Yardbirds are greeted at their hotel by the presence of an enormous basket of fruit courtesy of Epic Records, and the tour is thus affectionately dubbed 'The Fruit Tour' in Yardbirds lore.

This tour will again be plagued by trouble with the authorities, when the TV/radio union AFTRA restricts television appearances once again; the group is also victim of inappropriate and constantly shifting bookings by Premier Talent Agency. But it is at least a busy itinerary with live shows spread across the States, unlike their September visit which amounted to half a handful of obscure concerts.

Two road managers are employed for the tour, to handle the band's own equipment which will be used on many dates, depending on logistics. One of them is Ray Reneri who will in fact work for Jeff Beck in later years. And with Chicago as one of their main operating bases this tour, the band will have a much more satisfying experience this time around.

SAT 11TH
- Arie Crown Theater, Chicago, Illinois
- Rock River Roller Palace, Rockford, Illinois

In the afternoon, the Yardbirds take part in a big package show from 1 o'clock onwards with American acts the Lovin' Spoonful, the Turtles, the Buckinghams (a popular local Chicago group), the New Colony Six (who later record *Mister You're A Better Man Than I*), the Flock, Little Boy Blues, and the Fantastic Epics. The show is hosted by WLS deejay Art Roberts, and presented by Rock Productions. Afterwards the Yardbirds play a dance in nearby Rockford promoted by Thumbs Up Management (aka Marv and Tret Stewart) with support from Mickey They And Them from Wisconsin, 8–11.30 pm.

SUN 12TH
IMA Auditorium, Flint, Michigan
A second package show from 4 pm onwards with another slew of American acts; San Francisco's Beau Brummels, the Strangeloves (most known for their American almost-Top 10'er *I Want Candy*, a punkish pop tune), the Jones Boys, and finally local Flint group Terry & the Pack, who a few years down the line evolve into Grand Funk Railroad. The band likely travels the 200 miles back to Chicago after the show.

MON 13TH–TUE 14TH
Two days off in Chicago allows the band time to explore the nightclub scene where they take in performances by Muddy Waters and Howlin' Wolf. It's probably at this point that Giorgio with Jeff in tow visit Howlin' Wolf's club on the West Side where Jeff is invited onstage to jam with Wolf's Killing Floor Band featuring influential guitarist Hubert Sumlin. Jeff later recalls this as a "night I'll never forget" to BEAT INSTRUMENTAL: "when Giorgio went up to Howlin' Wolf and asked if I could have a blow – I nearly died!" Jeff adds: "I've told people like Eric Clapton and Jimmy Page about it, and they went green with envy!"

WED 15TH
Renfro's, Emporia, Kansas
Leaving Chicago by train today, the Yardbirds travel all day 600 miles into Kansas to play a large beer hall and dancing joint in the small town of Emporia, home of the State Teachers College. One of the regular bands at Renfro's, a local outfit of college students called the Out Group, have convinced the club owner to take a chance and book the Yardbirds into his place. Out Group guitarist Jack Trice recalls picking up the Yardbirds at the train station and ferrying the band around to their motel and the club. The band's Vox amps are driven from Chicago by Ray Reneri, although the Yardbirds will use the house band's PA equipment. This is a true club booking where the band is expected to fill out much of the evening. As the band later recalls it as a welcomed opportunity to stretch out like they did in their Crawdaddy Club heyday. The Yardbirds impress the college crowd mightily. After the show, Trice and members of local Kansas bands the Blue Things and the Red Dogs hang out with the Yardbirds until early morning. At some point while in Kansas, the group also buys a stash of cherry bombs (they are only legal in a very few States) for later indulgences in time honoured on-the-road pranks.

THU 16TH
The Yardbirds' epic live performance on film of *I'm A Man* is aired on tonight's episode of "Shindig!" (ABC Network TV 7.30–8.00 EST)(▶ August 10–11). Also appearing on this episode are the Pretty Things, Unit Four + 2, Vashti and Georgie Fame.

FRI 17TH
The Yardbirds reportedly play an end-of-semester concert at a high school in a small Mid-Western town. No further details are available, however the band would recall shortly later in an interview that they were impressed by the warmth and hospitality of the small town locals.

SAT 18TH
Danceland Ballroom, Cedar Rapids, Iowa
Supported by local group the R-Tistics, the Yardbirds play two shows at 8.30 pm and midnight for a $2 admission. This second floor dance hall in downtown Cedar Rapids was later demolished to make room for the modern Five Seasons Center.

SUN 19TH
Surf of the Four Seasons Ballroom, Clear Lake, Iowa
Billed as 'England's Fabulous Yardbirds', they play a dance from 8 pm until midnight. This ballroom was the site of Buddy Holly's very last concert before he, the Big Bopper and Richie Valens were killed in an airplane disaster in February 1959. The building still stands to this day.

An alternate series of tour dates initially planned and announced in the music press would have led the band westward and then south after these Iowa dates but all fall through leading to some last minute juggling of the itinerary as the tour is in progress. The scrapped dates are [City Auditorium] Denver, Colorado (22nd), [City Auditorium] Colorado Springs, Colorado (23rd), Pueblo, Colorado (24th), [Civic Auditorium] Albuquerque, New Mexico (25th) and [Municipal Auditorium] San Angelo, Texas (26th).

MON 20TH
The Yardbirds travel the 300-plus miles back to Chicago by car. This night the band holds a rehearsal in the back room of the Thumbs Up club in the Old Town section of Chicago to work up a basic arrangement for a new song for the following day's session at Chess. The song begins life purely as a musical set of ideas without lyrics.

TUE 21ST
A big day in Yardbirds history as this is almost certainly the day that *Shapes Of Things* is committed to tape at Chess Studios. The momentous occa-

December 1965: "Shapes of Things" recorded in Chicago ...

sion is recounted by Jeff himself years later to GUITAR WORLD (May 1999): "I remember there was mass hysteria in the studio when I did [the solo]. They weren't expecting it. It was just a weird mist coming from the East out of an amp. Giorgio was freaking out and dancing about like some tribal witch doctor." Following the recording of the backing track, Samwell-Smith and Relf both retire to separate bars to produce suitable lyrics to fit the exciting new backing track for a vocal dubbing session set for the following day.

To top off the day, Gomelsky has arranged a "blues party" this evening again in the back room at the Thumbs Up club. Invited and attending are Willie Dixon, Shakey Jake, James Cotton and Buddy Guy, the latter two join in on an informal jam session as the evening progresses and captured on film by Chicago fan and gal Cheryl Jennings.

WED 22ND

A real 'day off' in Chicago allows some of the band members to catch up on sleep. While Chris Dreja is interviewed for HIT PARADER magazine two members of the band are over "at the recording studio working on some cuts they had made" (Keith Relf and Paul Samwell-Smith for vocal dubs and initial mixing). The whole group is also interviewed by the two teenagers Andrea Michna and Barbera Wold. The girls want to know which English groups they like (Jeff: "The Beatles are No. 1 and always will be. I also like the Who and John Mayall's Bluesbreakers") and ditto American groups (Jeff: "Paul Butterfield Blues Band"). Beck also picks *I'm A Man* as his Yardbird fave and Chuck Berry as his biggest musical influence.

Later today the Yardbirds are interviewed for TEEN SCENE magazine and then heads to the airport for their flight to DC. The band will leave its coveted Vox amps behind in Chicago at this point as it is too costly to fly them around for the next block of shows and likely are not seen again until their LA dates. As they had done on the last tour, the band has to cobble together amps and equipment from opening bands.

THU 23RD
Alexandria Roller Rink, Alexandria, Virginia

For tonight's show the Yardbirds play support to the headlining Shangri-Las, a female trio from New York who have hit big with a string of classic teen anthems such as *Leader of the Pack* and *Give Him A Great Big Kiss*. Also on the bill a plethora of locals acts: the Hangmen, the Open Roads, the Plague and Joey Welz. The show starts at 8.30 pm and is sponsored by Jack Alix of WEAM radio in Washington. The Yardbirds are elated tonight as an estimated 4,500 teens attend. Meanwhile, the Yardbirds' filmed insert of *I Wish You Would* is aired on tonight's episode of "Shindig!" (ABC Network TV 7.30–8.00 EST) (▶ August 10–11) which the band members watch in their hotel room prior to their show this night.

FRI 24TH

The band flies to New York City for a day off before resuming the gruelling pace again. The Yardbirds are in town for the Christmas Eve celebration, partying at their hotel with fellow British popsters Peter & Gordon (who are themselves in town playing Murray The K's Christmas Show at the Brooklyn Fox Theatre). The fun culminates when Jim McCarty lets off a cherry bomb outside Gordon Waller's room, burning the carpet and blowing a hole in the door. Early rock star antics indeed! Earlier in the evening, members catch the Miller–Goldberg Blues Band at the popular discotheque, the Phone Booth on E. 55th. The Miller here is a young Steve Miller, later of solo fame.

SAT 25TH
The Peppermint Stick, Wheatfield, New York

Christmas day the band flies out of New York City via Mohawk Airlines to Buffalo in upstate New York where a winter storm has deposited a large amount of snow in the area. As it transpires the original booking at the Club Commodore in downtown Buffalo has been shifted to another club 20 miles outside the city due to a neighboring church which protests that a rock 'n' roll show on Christmas night is objectionable. The band is forced to drive through snow-filled roads to wend their way out to the obscure suburb of Wheatfield. The promoter has advertised that buses would run from downtown Buffalo out to Wheatfield and back in an effort to attract customers but legend has it that as few as 10 people attend, though with two shows scheduled this night (at 6 & 9 pm with local band the Rogues opening) one hopes this was not a combined total! This booking would become the cornerstone of Yardbirds lore of the absurdity of their touring experience in America.

SUN 26TH
Daniel's Den, Saginaw, Michigan

Sub-billed as 'Young Adult Club – The place where nice people meet'. Support by the Jay Hawkers.

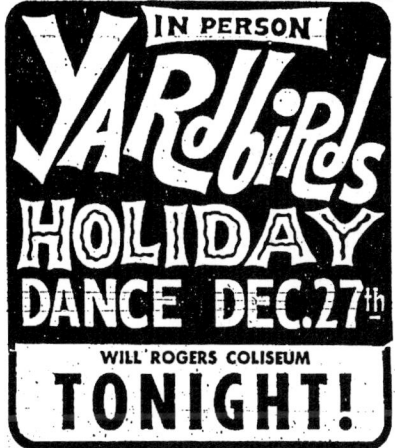

MON 27TH
Will Rogers Memorial Coliseum, Fort Worth, Texas

Another example of the group's gruelling schedules; from Michigan they fly south for a quick Texas appearance tonight before they fly back up north the following day to Pennsylvania. Opening acts include Mouse & the Traps from Tyler, Texas; local group Larry & the Blue Notes; the Bad Seeds from Corpus Christi, and almost certainly Scotty MacKay.

Tonight's appearance is originally slated to be one of four dates running December 26–30 but only this one is finalized, and again scrambling for last minute arrangements leads to more obscure bookings and nonsensical routings. The band also visits Dealey Plaza, the sight of the Kennedy assassination. (It can also be noted that the Yardbirds did not play the Astrodome in Houston at this time as stated in earlier histories of the band.)

Meanwhile at home, the British public can hear the Yardbirds (and the Seekers and Elkie Brooks) on "The Sound of Boxing Day" on BBC Light (10.00 am–noon, ▶ November 16).

⊙ December 22, 1965: The Byrds record a rejected first version of their raga-rock milestone "Eight Miles High" at RCA Studios in Hollywood.

December 1965: The Yardbirds and the Beach Boys on the same bill ...

TUE 28TH
"Christmas Shower of Stars"
Pittsburgh Civic Arena, Pittsburgh, Pennsylvania

An ambitious holiday presentation with the Four Seasons as the star attraction but also including Chuck Berry, Little Anthony & the Imperials, Sam the Sham & the Pharaohs, Simon & Garfunkel, Lou Christie, Mitch Ryder & the Detroit Wheels, Maxine Brown and the Thunderballs. As the Yardbirds are without their amplifiers, they ask some of the other acts on the bill to lend them theirs. When approaching Chuck Berry with their sights on his guitar amp, Berry proves to be his customary self and either refuses or insist they buy it! Attendance is 12,000 (Jeff's biggest audience yet) and one of the big draws tonight is Simon & Garfunkel, who have just climbed to BILLBOARD's #1 position with their debut *The Sounds of Silence*.

Mitch Ryder's drummer, Johnny Bee, has fond memories of encountering Jeff Beck on this show: "There'd be the Yardbirds with Jeff Beck playing B.B. King licks in the corridor backstage, and Jim McCarty (not the Yardbird-drummer's name-sake, this McCarty plays lead guitar with the Detroit Wheels) going 'Johnny, you gotta hear and watch this guy play guitar!'"

WED 29TH

The dizzying itinerary finds the band now flying off to San Francisco on the West Coast, where they at last have a well earned night off, sleeping until evening. While the band does not actually play Frisco until the following August, this encounter immediately pre-dates the emergence of the underground music scene. Future rock legend Bill Graham's bookings at the Fillmore Auditorium are just getting off the ground with single monthly shows beginning in November.

THU 30TH
• **Chico Teen Center, Silver Dollar Fairground, Chico, California**
• **Skateland, Marysville, California**

Two of the more obscure bookings on this tour find the Yardbirds in the relatively remote area of gold rush country in Northern California. No one from the tour party really seems to be sure where these shows are but arrangements are finally sorted out. However, as the New Year holiday begins early with many people off from work on Friday, the band gets caught in such horrible traffic that they miss their scheduled flight out of San Francisco to Sacramento. In desperation, the Yardbirds are forced to charter a pair of air-taxis directly to Chico.

So distraught is Jim McCarty at the absurdities of such arrangements that he briefly locks himself in a rest room at the airport in protest. Once coaxed aboard the flimsy looking aircraft, bad weather forces them to land in Sacramento requiring further travel by car arriving at the first show in Chico just in time to go on following an opening set by the local band the Heard. No sooner do they finish this show than they have to charge off to nearby Marysville for a second performance at the local roller rink.

FRI 31ST
• *"1966 New Year Spectacular"*
University of Puget Sound Field House, Tacoma, Washington
• **Evergreen Ballroom, Olympia, Washington***

Promoted by Pat O'Day and Dick Curtis, this New Year's Eve show all-star package show features an impressive line-up of the Yardbirds, Gary Lewis & the Playboys (with Jim Keltner on drums) and a quartet of California bands; the Beau Brummels, the Vejetables, the Mojo Men (featuring the unknown Sly Stone on keyboards), Alexys & the Third Generation plus bill-toppers the Beach Boys. Seats are $3, $4 and $5. In a rare review from this period the local Tacoma music critic offers some interesting insight into both the Yardbirds' performance and the prevailing attitudes of the time. "The Yardbirds of England really brought down the roof. They bounded on the stage following the brief, but comparatively restful lull at intermission. This reviewer sensed impending torture when they set up several huge amplifiers", writes Bruce Johnson in the TACOMA NEWS TRIBUNE. Jeff Beck is certainly making an impression: "The lead guitarist almost pierced the listeners' eardrums. He did things with that infernal guitar that seemed physically impossible. As this reviewer suffered, the real cool operator stabbed the neck of his guitar into the big amplifier and picked the strings with his left hand."

Drummer Dewey Martin (later of Buffalo Springfield) clearly recalls seeing the Yardbirds at this time while he was in this area himself as a member of Sir Raleigh & the Coupons. His recollection is seeing them at the Evergreen Ballroom in Olympia, not very far south from Tacoma. Advertisements for the Evergreen reveal no formal appearance by the Yardbirds at this time but a big New Year's Eve dance which ran from 9.30 pm until 3 am featuring local bands the Viceroys and the Statesmen could certainly have attracted performers from the 'Spectacular' package show (which would have wound up by 11 pm). Martin's vivid memory of seeing Jeff Beck & Co. in action here, is best explained by a likely impromtu performance by the Yardbirds in the early hours of the new year using available equipment onstage at the Evergreen.

•••

Amazingly, in less than ten months Jeff Beck has become nationally recognized. In a poll to pick the best instrumentalists of 1965 in the prestigious British magazine BEAT INSTRUMENTAL (1965 Gold Star Awards), he takes second place in the guitar category behind the Shadows' Hank Marvin, but ahead of George Harrison (3rd), Keith Richard (4th), Eric Clapton (6th), Pete Townshend (7th), Dave Davies (8th) and Jimmy Page (10th). Upon hearing the results, a pleasantly surprised Jeff tells BEAT INSTRUMENTAL: "I really can't believe it. I didn't think I'd been around long enough to finish very high." Jeff is subsequently portrayed in the January 1966 issue of the magazine to honour his high placing in the readers' poll. About the Yardbirds' future, Beck details eagerly: "We intend to dig out a lot of Gene Vincent material", singling out Vincent's *Cat Man* and *Red Blue Jeans And A Pony Tail* as possible additions to the group's repertoire.

•

1965 is indeed a very successful year for the Yardbirds. In the NEW MUSICAL EXPRESS yearly round-up in January '66, the Yardbirds place eighth in a table based on chart positions throughout the year, prompting the paper to comment: "[The Yardbirds] make the most remarkable jump of anyone in the upper bracket ... [They] are probably the most improved group in the country."

A fine testimonial to the addition of Jeff Beck into the band.

◢ 1966

JANUARY

SAT 1ST
"1966 New Year Spectacular"
Seattle Center Coliseum, Seattle, Washington

The Yardbirds' US tour continues into the new year today with a second appearance opening for the Beach Boys' extravaganza with the full line-up identical to the Tacoma show the previous evening.

SUN 2ND

As best can be determined, today is an off day for the band in Seattle to catch their breath before the busy schedule waiting for them in Los Angeles.

MON 3RD

Arriving at 4.30 am in the morning, the Yardbirds are in Los Angeles today to begin work on several pre-booked TV shows. Flying from Seattle they hit a severe snowstorm and are forced to skip a stop-over in Portland, Oregon en route. Upon their arrival in LA a photographer from the BEAT dutifully meets them in their exhausted state.

Tonight they tape "Shivaree", one of a multitude of teen music shows popular at the time. This takes place at local ABC Network affiliate KABC-TV Studios, Hollywood where it is broadcast locally the following Saturday and then syndicated nationally. Surrounded by a bevy of go-go dancers the the Yardbirds mime to *I'm A Man* and *Heart Full of Soul*.

The original plan is for the Yardbirds to tape a total of seven music programmes while in town but AFTRA again restricts their opportunities and imposes a limit of just three. The tapings of two further music variety shows "Where The Action Is" and "Hollywood A Go Go" plus the teenage soap opera "Never Too Young" are all victims of this union directive.

TUE 4TH

Presumably today, although undocumented, the Yardbirds appear on "9th Street West" hosted by Los Angeles disc jockey Sam Riddle and produced at KHJ-TV Studios in Los Angeles for broadcast on Channel 9 from 6–7 pm.

Later the Yardbirds are guests of honour at a press reception held at the Red Velvet Club in Hollywood, billed as an 'Epic Records/Pep Distributing Cocktail Clambake'. Later this night Kim Fowley – in a repeat from last year – throws another private party for the band, this time at his residence in the Hollywood Hills. Word spreads rapidly and the party attracts another big crowd; the VIP guest list includes members of the Byrds, Derek Taylor, Mary Travers and Dylan manager Albert Grossman, in addition to a slew of teenaged Hollywood celebrities. A reporter for THE BEAT is on hand to cover the impromptu party, and writes: "They simply plugged in their equipment, crawled over the heads of about 31 people to the balcony area – and from their little alcove in the corner let out some of the wildest sounding music heard in a long, long time." Those who in vain tried crashing the party settled for dancing outside once the Yardbirds began playing around midnight. Jeff is no doubt reunited with Mary Hughes by now too.

WED 5TH
The Hullabaloo, Hollywood, California

Tonight the Yardbirds begin a four-night residency at Dave Hull's Hullabaloo club on Sunset Strip. Originally built as the Earl Carroll Theater, the structure later becomes the club Moulin Rouge before being renamed the Hullabaloo only a month prior, hence the casual local reference sometimes to the Yardbirds having played at the Moulin Rouge.

Afforded a state-of-the-art sound system and the ability to play in the same club several nights in a row secures the group a perfect live sound, and the shows are a great success with packed houses every night with a capacity of 1,200. Indeed, even Beck himself fondly recalls this as one of the high point of his time in the Yardbirds with the band at the height of its powers.

KRLA BEAT reports: "When several members of the BEAT staff fell by the Hullabaloo night club where the Yardbirds were appearing in concert they found plaster from the exceptionally high ceiling raining down upon them during one of the numbers. No, the building wasn't falling apart – the Yardbirds were just tearing it apart!" The group is also interviewed by Gene Trindl for a later feature in TEEN SET, where Trindl describes their stage act: "During one number, Jeff sets his guitar on one note, puts it on the floor, walks over behind Sam's amplifier, and helps play the bass guitar. Three hands on one guitar – the result is something you just don't hear very often." The support these nights is the club's house band the Palace Guard – with a young Emitt Rhodes on drums.

THU 6TH
The Hullabaloo, Hollywood, California

The band's residency continues here. With no travelling involved and an early finish to their own shows, the band can take in some of the sights and do some club hopping after hours. One of the bands they encounter is an early incarnation of the Mothers (pre-'of Invention') who at the time includes guitarist Henry Vestine, later of Canned Heat fame.

FRI 7TH
The Hullabaloo, Hollywood, California

Originally listed in some early ads as a day off in the four-out-of-five day residency, the following day is actually the break in their stay which allows them to do a show in Sacramento.

Additionally, according to union files, the later part of the evening (from 11 pm) is spent recording just down the street from the Hullabaloo at Columbia Studios. Tape evidence shows that the main activity tonight is the doubling of Relf's vocal track on *Shapes Of Things* which it is decided needs more depth. Evidently the mix accomplished at Chess in Chicago is not re-doable. Accordingly Relf sings along to the Chess mix which is

Newsflash January 1966: Recording sessions in Hollywood and New York ...

blended into a new mix onto a new mono master tape (accounting for both a double tracked vocal master and a mistakenly released single-tracked vocal master). The session possibly includes some preliminary work on their Italian-only single *Questa Volta* which Relf associated years later with this studio as well.

SAT 8TH
Memorial Auditorium, Sacramento, California

The Yardbirds – referred to as "a lively group of London lyricists" in the SACRAMENTO UNION – share the stage with the Beau Brummels, the Lovin' Spoonful and the John Rosasco Quartet in Sacramento for a single show starting at 8.30 pm. The Yardbirds (advertised as 'Yardbyrds') fly up from Los Angeles on United flight 792 and arrive at Sacramento Municipal Airport at 3.05 pm. Meanwhile, back at the Hullabaloo, Dion & the Wanders fill in this open night.

Also today, "Shivaree" featuring the Yardbirds is aired in greater LA on Channel 7 KABC TV 7–7.30 pm PST (▶ January 3).

SUN 9TH
The Hullabaloo, Hollywood, California
The final night at the Hullabaloo.

MON 10TH
Today is another session, this time at the RCA Studios in Hollywood, where the Yardbirds are booked starting at 2 pm. Conflicting accounts imply this is both a rehearsal and/or mixing/mastering session. As it transpires the Yardbirds are set to represent Britain in the annual San Remo Festival in Italy upon their return from the States, and today they have a rehearsal with the show's musical director which seemingly accounts for their presence at RCA. The Yardbirds' entries will be *Questa Volta* and *Pafff...Bum*, both Italian pop songs. Confusingly, according to statements made shortly after this time by Samwell-Smith, RCA is where *Shapes Of Things* was "done"; perhaps only meaning "mastered". Samwell-Smith's recollection to RECORD MIRROR (February 26, 1966) is that he really liked the sounds they could get in this studio making reference to both *Shapes Of Things* and *Pafff...Bum*.

Tonight is the likely night that three of the Yardbirds get on stage with the Paul Butterfield Blues Band for an impromptu jam. The Butterfields are in residence with the Byrds January 6–16 at the Trip, a nearby club on Sunset Strip. According to a report in the NEW MUSICAL EXPRESS, local officials threaten the band members with immediate deportation for violating the conditions of their visa which (according to an over-zealous union representative) doesn't include jamming! (It is also possible this took place at the Hullabaloo where Monday nights were informal jam nights.)

TUE 11TH
Today is an unexpected off-day in LA. The band is originally scheduled to fly out for an appearance in Albany, Georgia but this date and likely a few others in the South including a foray into a studio in Nashville (either Bradley's Barn or RCA's Studio B) all fall through. Instead the band affords itself a free day in LA during which Jeff rents a Stingray to speed around in at his leisure.

Tonight however is almost certainly when the Yardbirds tape the last of their three allotted TV programmes, which is "The Lloyd Thaxton Show" at KCOP-TV Studios in Hollywood, first broadcast live locally then syndicated nationally on tape. The Yardbirds lip-synch to the just completed and as-yet-unreleased *Shapes Of Things* plus *For Your Love*. In syndication the earliest confirmable broadcast date is February 15th (two weeks in advance of the single's release in the US) with the song listed as *Shapes Of Things To Come*. Their performance of the song on this show is later released in 1997 on a bonus disc to the CD *Where The Action Is*. While only a lip-synching to the record, it is interesting because McCarty is playing along to it in the TV studio and also because host Thaxton, obviously never having heard the recording before, thinks the song is over after the guitar solo and begins his announcement: "All right! There they are ... the Yardbirds", only to utter "Oh no!" once the final verse begins. This audio momento displays both the unrehearsed and casual nature of the programme and the excitement of the first airing of this new recording.

WED 12TH–FRI 14TH
Under the revised schedule, after the Thaxton broadcast, the band flies back to New York which it will use as a temporary base of operation for the next week of the tour, primarily for further recording and press duties. At the top of the list is to submit the master of their newest recording *Shapes Of Things* to Epic Records as the follow-up to the successful *I'm A Man*.

SAT 15TH ✱
- **Eudowood Gardens, Baltimore, Maryland**
- **Annapolis National Guard Armory, Annapolis, Maryland**

A double booking which is either a remnant of their scheduled southern swing (to have started in Georgia on January 11) or this is simply booked on short notice to keep some income flowing. The Baltimore show is at a large facility on Putty Hill Avenue sponsored by local radio station WCAO and their charismatic deejay Kerby Scott and is reportedly packed. Owing to the last minute nature of the booking and the local newspaper's lack of coverage, no documentation of other acts on the bill exists. Later the band hurries over to neighboring Annapolis for a second show featuring the opening act Norman's Norts in a show sponsored by radio station WYRE. Arriving very late, this show includes impressive versions of *Heart Full Of Soul*, *I'm Not Talking*, *Smokestack Lightning* and an extended *I'm A Man*. Jeff's guitar cable falls out several times and he audibly complains at one point about "the stupid American equipment", again pointing to the band relying on the opening act's gear.

SUN 16TH
The group returns to New York.

MON 17TH–WED 19TH ✱
In New York for the week, the task at hand is to complete the recording of both sides of their Italian song entries. Attending these sessions is Italian A&R man from Ricordi Records International, Gianni Marchetti, who has flown in from Italy to New York to act as arranger and hurry the completed tapes back to Italy for rush-release on record. Done at Columbia Studios, *Questa Volta* and *Pafff...Bum*, the group's two entries in the San Remo Festival are completed. Whereas *Pafff...Bum* is translated into English, Keith Relf sings *Questa Volta* phonetically in Italian. Jeff is not fond of this song, in fact he dislikes it so much that Chris Dreja is persuaded to play lead. An uncredited piano-player – possibly Samwell-Smith – plays on *Pafff...Bum*. The group does not make any personal appearances in New York City now, but uses the town instead as a base for their other activities. At night the band goes clubbing.

THU 20TH ✱
Possible travel day back to Chicago where they will play two last shows before heading for Britain.

---

42   © Janaury 24-25, 1966: The Byrds re-record their next single "Eight Miles High" at their record company's insistence.

January 1966: The Yardbirds take part in disastrous song festival in San Remo ...

FRI 21ST
Valparaiso Armory, Valparaiso, Indiana
An obscure booking in this small town 45 miles southeast of Chicago. While Jeff arrives late, the show runs 8 pm to midnight with the band driving back to Chicago afterwards.

SAT 22ND
Aragon Ballroom, Chicago, Illinois
Chicago fans are treated with a quick return performance at this large ballroom, known a short while later as the Cheetah, where witnesses recall Jeff in full antic mode this night playing guitar behind his back and coaxing from his instrument his usual array of tricks. Again reflecting the ever-changing shape of this tour, the original routing called for this last date to be at the University of Lowell in Lowell, Massachusetts but like many other dates on this "book as you go" tour, it was never finalized.

SUN 23RD
After more than six weeks on tour in the States, the Yardbirds board a 6 pm flight to London, arriving back the following morning.

TUE 25TH✱
After catching up on lost sleep, the Yardbirds are fitted with their new dinner jackets for their upcoming San Remo visit designed by Chris Dreja prior to the US tour. Giorgio wastes no time in getting a press release out to the music papers to announce *Shapes Of Things* as the next single as duly noted in the national music papers later this week.

WED 26TH✱
The Yardbirds fly out to Nice and travel by bus along the Mediterranean Coast to San Remo in Italy.

THU 27TH
Preparations are held for the San Remo festival.

FRI 28TH
"The 16th Festival of Italian Songs"
Casino Municipale, San Remo, Italy
The Yardbirds compete in the big song festival on the Italian Riviera, just across the border from France. Giorgio Gomelsky's strategy is to get the group a foothold in the big South-European market, and an appearance at San Remo he believes will secure instant recognition. The festival is broadcast on Italian TV and linked to further Continental broadcasters (although not in Great Britain) to an audience of reportedly 125 million viewers. However, the contest is decidedly bland and plush (seats are about £25 each), and the musically outlandish Yardbirds are misfits. Besides national acts like Italy's Gigliola Cinquetti, some international stars like Americans Pat Boone, Gene Pitney and PJ Proby (who lives in Britain) also compete. The rules demand that invited guests – like the Yardbirds – must cover songs already entered in the contest by Italian artists. Not only that, the entries must be written by Italian composers. The festival is a two-day affair, and on the first night they do the trite *Questa Volta* (translating "This Time"), also performed by Italy's big star Bobby Solo. Whereas all the acts are accompanied by a 50-piece orchestra, the Yardbirds doggedly decide to play live as a five-piece, which make their performances sound rough and tame by comparison. Reportedly only one microphone is available to cover the whole band's sound from the stage.

SAT 29TH
"The 16th Festival of Italian Songs"
Casino Municipale, San Remo, Italy
On the second night of the competition the Yardbirds play *Pafff...Bum*, which is better received than *Questa Volta*; still neither of their entries make the final round. (The winners of the festival are Domenico Modugno and Gigliota Cinquetti with their version of *Do Come Ti Amo*). After the official concert tonight, Giorgio organizes a party and a jam-session with the Yardbirds in the bar at the hotel where they're staying, which proves to be the high point of their visit here and this unofficial performance is the one which would leave a lasting impression on festival goers in the end.

There also is some evidence, but undated, that the Yardbirds played a one-off club date in Milan (home base of Ricordi International, the Yardbirds' Italian label) around this time too. The show is with fellow Ricordi artist Lucio Dalla, a popular recording artist of the day and saxophonist who also recorded *Pafff...Bum*. Jeff later recalls: "[I]n the club we played, there was a group with an acoustic bass, a saxophone, no drummer and a guitarist doing *Giddy-Up-A-Ding-Dong*. That was Milan. And that was the sort of gigs we played, [because of our] completely hopeless management."

While Gomelsky envisioned this trip to Italy as an opportunity to break through the stale and stiff atmosphere in a country highly resistant to the emerging youth culture, the Yardbirds looked at it as one step too far in his trailblazing ethic. The band's attitude toward Gomelsky severely cools after this trip.

A single coupling *Questa Volta* with *Pafff...Bum* is released the following week in Italy only, plus on a compilation LP from the festival, *San Remo '66*.

SUN 30TH
Jeff and the band minus Jim McCarty fly back to London, while Giorgio, Jim plus roadies Bill and Terry take a few days to drive from Italy through the French countryside meeting up with the others slightly later in Paris.

FEBRUARY

THU 3RD
THE YARDBIRDS: FRENCH DATES
The Yardbirds visit Paris for a weekend of TV and live shows. The Yardbirds – or les Yardbirds as the French will have it – are very popular in France, and today is spent doing rehearsals and recording in Paris for a TV appearance likely on "Music Hall de France," broadcast on French Television ORTF-1 on February 12 (10.55).

FRI 4TH
Golf Drouot, Paris, France
The Yardbirds perform at this popular Parisian club tonight on the corner of Boulevard Montmartre and Rue Drouot in a special concert organized by the local Yardbirds fan club.

SAT 5TH
Palace de La Mutualité, Paris, France
The Yardbirds and fellow Brits the Moody Blues are supported by French

Single
THE YARDBIRDS
A: QUESTA VOLTA (Satti/Dinamo/Mogol)
B: PAFFF...BUM (Reverberi/Bardotti/Samwell-Smith)

Released February 1966 (Italian Ricordi SIR 20-010)
Personnel is Jeff Beck (ldgtr on B), Keith Relf (hrmnca/vcls), Chris Dreja (rhygtr, ldgtr on A), Paul Samwell-Smith (bs) and Jim McCarty (drms); unknown piano-player (poss. Samwell-Smith).
Recorded at CBS Studios, New York, New York, January 17–19✱, 1966
Arranged by Gianni Marchetti
Produced by Giorgio Gomelsky

January 30, 1966: The U.S. resumes its bombing of North Vietnam following failed holiday peace talks.

February 1966: Single "Shapes of Things" is released in the UK and the US ...

acts Ronnie Bird, Antoine and Vigon. Reportedly the concert is attended by 3,000 fans.

SUN 6TH
Today is an off-day for the band to relax and go club-hopping in Paris. In fact the whole of the next 10 days are official "off days" for everyone to recover before the release of the next single. Jeff flies back to London ahead of the others this night once he realizes he is catching a cold. The rest of the band will follow suit the next day, excepting Keith Relf, who stays behind to do his own visiting of the French countryside.

MON 7TH–WED 16TH
Official band holidays. Meanwhile back in the States the syndicated edition of "The Lloyd Thaxton Show" (▶ January 11) is broadcast nationally on February 15 and includes their debut of the new Yardbirds single.

THU 17TH
Deemed an official rehearsal day, the band gears back up for another round of intense activity to promote the new single due out in two weeks time.

FRI 18TH
The band returns to action with an appearance on Rediffusion TV's "Ready, Steady, Go!" (6.07–6.30 pm), transmitted live from Wembley Park Studios today with other guests including the Hollies and Tom Jones. Jeff, dressed in a new fringed suede jacket, plays his trusted Esquire guitar.

SAT 19TH
Baths Hall, Scunthorpe

SUN 20TH
A guest spot on ABC-TV's "Thank Your Lucky Stars" is pre-taped in Birmingham at Alpha Studios, Aston to be broadcast the following Saturday on the ITV Network. The band does a lip-synch performance to *Shapes Of Things*. This will be the band's last appearance on this show, which after a few failed alterations ends with a final transmission on June 12 of this year.

MON 21ST
A day set aside entirely for press interviews in London.

TUE 22ND
After a long absence from the Beeb, the Yardbirds return for an interview on BBC radio, broadcast live today from Paris Theatre in London, on "Pop Inn" (BBC Light, 1.00–2.00 pm).

THU 24TH
A formal press conference with the band is held today at the Europa Hotel, London, conveniently on the same day that Keith Relf marries April Liversidge at Paddington Registry Office.

FRI 25TH
Iron Curtain Club, St. Mary Cray, London

Today marks the British release of *Shapes Of Things* and causes some very positive reactions in the music press. "Great Beck guitar means a big, big Yardbirds hit" enthuses a MELODY MAKER headline: "Quite fantastic guitar ... Beck achieves a sitar effect on guitar and contributes much to the group's individual noise. The boys deserve full marks for coming up with something different." The single becomes the group's fourth consecutive British Top Three smash (it makes #3 in March), and importantly their first self-penned true A-side.

In the evening the Yardbirds play a club in London.

SAT 26TH
The Yardbirds are seen on ABC-TV's "Thank Your Lucky Stars" (5.50–6.35 pm, ▶ February 20). Also on tonight's edition are Tom Jones, Gene Pitney and Cliff Bennett & the Rebel Rousers.

SUN 27TH
The Yardbirds take part in an INECTO sponsored broadcast on Radio London at the Marquee. (Officially, the usually open-all-week Marquee is closed today). *Shapes Of Things* will actually make #1 in the 'Radio London Fabulous 40' play list.

MON 28TH
A "Saturday Club" insert is pre-recorded today at London's Playhouse Theatre, to be broadcast on Saturday March 5. The session is done between 4.00–6.30 pm and the five songs performed today are *Mister You're A Better Man Than I*, *Shapes Of Things*, Curtis Mayfield's ballad *I've Been Trying* and Elmore James' evergreen *Dust My Blues*, where Beck sounds uncannily like Eric Clapton and where he is also given a rare vocal spot. The session certainly features Jeff's new acquisition, a Gibson Les Paul guitar, which he has just bought at Selmer's music shop in Charing Cross for a reported £175. (All except *I've Been Trying* are released on *Yardbirds ... On Air* in 1991.)

The US single version of *Shapes Of Things* is released today with *I'm Not Talking* as the flip side. However, it is soon quietly withdrawn and reissued with *New York City Blues* as the new B-

---

Single
THE YARDBIRDS

A: SHAPES OF THINGS (Samwell-Smith/Relf/McCarty)
B: MISTER YOU'RE A BETTER MAN THAN I (Hugg/Hugg)

Released Friday February 25, 1966 (UK Columbia DB 7848)
Personnel is Jeff Beck (ldgtr), Keith Relf (vcls), Chris Dreja (rhygtr), Paul Samwell-Smith (bs) and Jim McCarty (drms).
Recorded at Chess Studios, 2120 South Michigan Avenue, Chicago, Illinois, December 21–22, 1965 plus Columbia Studios, Hollywood, California, January 7, 1966 (A) and Sam Phillips Studios, 639 Madison Avenue, Memphis, Tennessee, September 12, 1965 and and Columbia Studios, New York, New York, September 21–22, 1965 (B)
Produced by Giorgio Gomelsky
Engineered by Ron Malo (A) and Sam Phillips (B), Roy Halee (B*)
Highest Chart Position UK: #3

Single
THE YARDBIRDS

A: SHAPES OF THINGS (Samwell-Smith/Relf/McCarty)
B # 1: I'M NOT TALKING (Mose Allison)
B # 2: NEW YORK CITY BLUES (Relf/Dreja)

Released Monday February 28, 1966 (US Epic 9891) A + B version 1, then replaced March 28, 1966 (US Epic 10006) by A + B version 2
Personnel is Jeff Beck (ldgtr), Keith Relf (hrmnca/vcls), Chris Dreja (rhygtr), Paul Samwell-Smith (bs) and Jim McCarty (drms).
Recorded at Chess Studios, 2120 South Michigan Avenue, Chicago, Illinois, December 21–22, 1965 plus Columbia Studios, Hollywood, California, January 7, 1966 (A), Advision Studios, New Bond Street, London, April 13* 1965 (B #1) and Columbia Studios, New York, New York, September 21–22, 1965 (B #2)
Produced by Giorgio Gomelsky
Engineered by Ron Malo (A), Eddie Offord (B #1) and Roy Halee (B #2)
Highest Chart Position US: #11

© February 1966: Liverpool's Cavern Club – home of The Beatles – closes down.

March 1966: The Yardbirds videotape "Where The Action Is" in London ...

side a month later. Again it provides the group with a sizable hit when the song peaks at #11 in the charts.

MARCH

TUE 1ST
The Yardbirds guest on Rediffusion TV children's programme "Five O'clock Club" hosted by Muriel Young and Wally Whyton presumably lip-synching to the new single. This is transmitted live 5.00–5.24 pm. Also scheduled to appear are Unit Four Plus Two and singer Charles Dickens.

WED 2ND
Continuing the requisite TV spots, the Yardbirds head out to Bristol to appear on TWW's "Now!" transmitted live, though some regions delay broadcast until Saturday the 5th.

THU 3RD
Featured in MELODY MAKER (March 5) on sale today, Jeff praises Eric Clapton for his idealism and for "sticking to his guns". About his own prowess, he says: "A Marquee Club audience would spit me off stage if I played badly ... although at other times I just bash chords at audiences and they don't realize."

FRI 4TH
The Yardbirds make yet another return to Rediffusion TV's "Ready, Steady, Go!" (6.07–6.30 pm.) as last minute substitutes for a cancelling Spencer Davis Group. Also appearing are the Small Faces and David Bowie.

The band is originally booked to appear in Middleton outside Manchester but this is seemingly cancelled.

SAT 5TH
Corn Exchange, Cambridge
The Yardbirds are heard on "Saturday Club" with the Animals and Dave Berry & the Cruisers (10.00 am–noon, ► February 28) plus perform in Cambridgeshire in the evening.

SUN 6TH
A rare off-day in the group's calendar.

MON 7TH
Town Hall, Chatham

TUE 8TH
A rehearsal is scheduled today.

WED 9TH
Corn Exchange, Bristol
Supported by the Fanatics.

TUE 10TH
With *Shapes Of Things* at #13 in the MELODY MAKER charts and steadily climbing, the Yardbirds return to the BBC Television's hit parade "Top Of the Pops" (BBC 1; 7.30–8.00 pm). The host is Alan Freeman, and other acts on tonight's telecast include the Small Faces, the Kinks and the Walker Brothers.

FRI 11TH
Ricky Tick Club, Staines

SAT 12TH
St. George's Ballroom, Hinckley
The afternoon is spent at BBC's Paris Cinema for tomorrow's edition of "Easy Beat" where *Shapes Of Things* and *Mister You're A Better Man Than I* are committed to tape. Afterwards it is off to Hinckley in Leicestershire.

SUN 13TH
BBC Light's "Easy Beat" is broadcast 10.00–11.30 am (► March 12). Also on the show are the Bachelors.

MON 14TH
Pavilion, Bath

TUE 15TH
Marquee Club, London
The Yardbirds – supported by Liverpool group the Clayton Squares – make a triumphant return to the Marquee Club. This is their first appearance here in six months, and they break all box-office advance booking records. The Yardbirds' regular club appearances prove they are in the unique position of not being accused of selling out despite their many chart hits, unlike, say Manfred Mann, who forever seem chained to package tours and who were essentially abandoned by their original fans from their club-slogging days playing jazz and R&B.

This is also the likely date Eric Clapton, in one of his off-nights from John Mayall's Bluesbreakers, steps on stage to jam with Jeff and his old mates in the Yardbirds. A young Brian May (like McCarty and Samwell-Smith, a pupil from Hampton Grammar School) is in the audience, and has vivid memories of seeing Beck and Clapton on stage together: "I saw a gig at the Marquee ... and Eric Clapton came on and jammed at the end. That was pretty amazing."

Jeff at this time also develops a new technique, where he tunes one guitar to an open chord, puts it atop an amplifier and lets it feedback, while he accompanies this racket on another guitar.

WED 16TH
The Yardbirds are at Granada TV Centre to tape an appearance on "Scene At 6.30" broadcast later the same day (6.30–7.00 pm), miming to *Shapes Of Things* yet again.

THU 17TH
The group films insert segments for Dick Clark's US TV show "Where The Action Is" on location outside the Royal Albert Hall, Kensington, London. Songs lip-synched in the windy cold weather are *Shapes Of Things* and *The Train Kept A Rollin'* (broadcast programme #75/66, April 15) and *I Wish You Would* and *Mister You're A Better Man Than I* (broadcast programme #93/66, May 11). Several publicity pictures of the group are taken on this occasion standing on the stairs in front of the hall featuring Jeff with his new Gibson, bedecked in his fur coat purchased recently in Chicago. Other groups being filmed today and yesterday are the Small Faces, the Action, Them and the Who.

The same day the Yardbirds reportedly also appear in Southend for an appearance on the music quiz show "Pop The Question" for Southern Television.

FRI 18TH
A booking at the Top Rank Ballroom, Brighton appears to be cancelled.

SAT 19TH
Jigsaw Club, Manchester
Support by the Powerhouse Six.

SUN 20TH
An official off-day to recuperate.

MON 21ST
Queen's Ballroom, Wolverhampton
The Yardbirds and unnamed supporting group. 7.30–11.00 pm.

TUE 22ND
Winter Gardens, Malvern

WED 23RD
Majestic Ballroom, Leeds
Also a possible rehearsal according to the band's original date sheet, this may have been blown out as a previously unscheduled show in Leeds is added.

THU 24TH
Victoria Ballroom, Chesterfield
Originally slated for an appearance on "Top of the Pops", this does not occur today but rather the following week, nor evidently does the original booking at Streatham Ice Rink, London.

© March 4, 1966: John Lennon makes his controversial "Christianity will go. We're more popular than Jesus Christ right now" remarks to the Evening Standard

April 1966: Jeff collapses on stage in France...

SAT 26TH
Imperial Ballroom, Nelson
Plus the Mutineers and Gidion's Ways.

MON 28TH–WED 30TH*
A show booked at Town Hall, High Wycombe on Monday is reset for April 12, and a tentative date in Preston on March 29 is dropped. Also the scheduled taping of an interview for BBC World Service programme "Carnival" at Aeolian 1 Studios, London on March 29 set for broadcast May 21 is also evidently not done.

Instead it seems the Yardbirds enter Advision Studios in London for yet another attempt to finish the promised album *A Yardbird's Eye-View of Beat* (by now the slightly altered title) for which work had begun the previous October. The band is full of optimism and ambition, and Gomelsky enthusiastically explains to RECORD MIRROR that "we are writing a rock and roll symphony – this is part of the expansion of the group and pop music!" At these sessions only backing tracks are cut, a few of them re-recorded a couple of months later after the group has ousted Gomelsky.

The selections put down on tape are *Jeff's Blues* (an instrumental workout on which later becomes *The Nazz Are Blue*); *What Do You Want* (also vocal-less, this Bo Diddley-inspired slide guitar exercise is done again under the same name but with vocals added and a new arrangement), and *Pounds & Stomps* (an early rough instrumental version of *He's Always There*). Also recorded is a song first attempted back in the Clapton-era, Snooky Pryor's *Someone To Love Me* with Clapton's arrangement essentially maintained from the earlier try and later labeled by compilers as *Someone To Love Me Pt. 2*. It is believed that the mono backing tracks and later overdubbed vocal version of this song subsequently issued on various compilations are indeed Clapton-era recordings brought into the studio for the band to relearn with Beck. The flashier stereo version, recorded at this time with Beck, is much closer to its final form achieved with new lyrics as *Lost Woman*. Similarly, *Here 'Tis*, the stereo instrumental version, is from these sessions, while the mono vocal version (labeled *For RSG*) is again recorded much earlier and certainly a Clapton era-outtake. Similarly to *Someone To Love Me*, the band revisits this song instrumentally with the aim of rewriting it. A further three songs taped at these same sessions were never improved upon nor re-recorded; *Chris' Number*,

Crimson Curtain and *Like Jimmy Reed Again*; the latter a pedestrian blues workout and likely no more than a level-checking warm up by the band. Keith Relf is not present on tape at these sessions. Never intended as either finished or for general consumption, these outtakes are the property of Gomelsky, and have been repackaged many times subsequently.

The idea of individual solo projects is bandied about now, but it is only Keith Relf who manages to realize this idea with his version of Bob Lind's *Mr. Zero* (the orchestral backing track of which is taped this week, perhaps also explaining his absence from the Advision sessions). Paul Samwell-Smith is to record a Jackie De Shannon song *(Green Trees)*, while Chris Dreja and Jim McCarty are to join forces for a comedy record, and Jeff to cut an unspecified instrumental after first toying with the idea of recording George Gershwin's *Summertime*. Jeff explains to BEAT INSTRUMENTAL: "I was going to do [it] because I thought there had never been a really good version, but I ended up deciding it had been done too often." However, like the album, none of these projects get beyond press announcements.

THU 31ST
The first order of business for the day is a return to the BBC's Television Centre, London where the band appears on today's edition of "Top of The Pops" (7.30–8.00 pm) miming to *Shapes Of Things*. The Yardbirds (minus Samwell-Smith) then fly to Amsterdam en route to their appearance on a special edition of "Ready, Steady, Go!" in Paris. Paul instead travels straight to France tonight to meet with his wife-to-be, Rosemary Simon (a production assistant at "Ready, Steady, Go!") who is in Paris already with the show's producer Vicki Wickham.

It is also at some point around this time that, as a result of markedly growing dissatisfaction with Gomelsky's performance as manager, the subject of finding a new manager comes up and Wickham suggests Simon Napier-Bell, an ex-jazz musician and documentary film-maker who is about to have some chart success as co-lyricist for Dusty Springfield's *You Don't Have To Say You Love Me*. He is also taking on new clients in his new venture as a pop manager. As fate will have it, after this trip the Yardbirds are never quite the same again as a number of events unfold and erupt right up till Beck's departure at the end of the year.

APRIL

FRI 1ST
THE YARDBIRDS: EUROPEAN TOUR
La Locomotive Club, Paris, France
The Yardbirds, together with the Who, star in "Ready Steady Allez!", a special broadcast of the popular British TV show "Ready, Steady, Go!" Additionally the French artists Antoine, Hughes Aufrey, Eddy Mitchell and Mireille Mathieu participate. Bill Wyman and Brian Jones of the Rolling Stones are in the audience this night too. The day doesn't proceed without the usual problems as the rest of the Yardbirds and manager Giorgio Gomelsky miss their morning flight to Paris, and have to charter a private plane in order to make the 2 pm rehearsal. Shooting takes place at La Locomotive Club on Boulevard de Clichy and on location at Place Pigalle. The show is transmitted live from Paris to England with great difficulty, as the telephone connections between the two countries continually threaten to break down. The broadcast is followed by a full performance in the Locomotive by the Yardbirds and later all attend a party at Chez Castel, a perennial Paris hot spot. The Yardbirds are also interviewed by Jacques Barsamian from DISCO REVUE (May '66).

SAT 2ND
The venue and location are unconfirmed, but on this day another concert is held in the South of France.

SUN 3RD
L'Omnibus, Marseilles, France
'Les Yardbirds' then travel to Marseilles for a show with French group les Messengers from 3 o'clock onwards. But during the Yardbirds' performance, Jeff dramatically collapses on stage. He is admitted to hospital with suspected meningitis. Luckily it

April 1966: Simon Napier-Bell the new Yardbirds' manager ...

is a false alarm and is later reported to have only been a serious case of food poisoning. After a short hospital stay, a fatigued Jeff flies back to London separately to recuperate while the other four continue temporarily as a quartet.

MON 4TH
Despite Jeff's absence, the Yardbirds honour the rest of their European tour, travelling first to Switzerland where likely a TV appearance is scheduled though no details are available if it is done.

TUE 5TH
The group minus Jeff travel on to Bremen, Germany for a recording today on the pre-eminent monthly German pop TV-show "Beat Club". Although reports suggests they were filmed, evidence also shows that it was never broadcast and that the absence of Jeff Beck likely brought about its ultimate cancellation.

WED 6TH
The Yardbirds also honour their Danish Easter bookings, where they perform as a four-piece with Chris Dreja handling guitar duties and covering for Jeff. Originally the group's Continental tour was scheduled to include further concert dates in Belgium, but were likely cancelled in favour of playing more one-nighters at home. Anyway, some of the European bookings are re-scheduled for late May.

THU 7TH
Besides an appearance in Copenhagen at the K.B. Hallen, dubbed the 'Young People's Ball' with no less than ten other local groups on the bill, the Beck-less Yardbirds also play a show at Fyns Forum, Odense on Fyn today.

FRI 8TH ✱
Today's whereabouts are unclear. Originally it was suggested they would continue on to Belgium for another TV appearance but this does not seem to have happened. It is possible the band briefly goes on to Stockholm instead for promotional purposes, as photographs of a Beckless four-man Yardbirds from this period taken by a well-known Swedish photographer exist. In any event they appear to be back in London by this evening or the following day.

•

Several factors seem to come to a head upon their return to London: dissatisfied with Giorgio Gomelsky's work of late (especially the San Remo debacle) and the lack of tangible financial returns for the band, at Paul Samwell-Smith's urging, the Yardbirds finally decide to terminate their management contract with Gomelsky and go with Simon Napier-Bell as their new manager and producer. The band has a lawyer draw up papers to instigate the process. For his part, Gomelsky later states it was Jeff's dramatically growing unreliablity that made him lose patience and interest in the Yardbirds altogether. Indeed it seems that since the LA portion of the last US tour and episodes during this European trip, this crisis begins a series of medically-excused abandonments by Jeff, each of which escalates over the next seven months until his eventual departure from the band. It could also be easily argued that the delicate balance of the band's dynamics is severely altered in the events of this week, such that the Yardbirds' career will never fully recover from its effects. Interestingly, Gomelsky's initial response (before his ousting) to the Beck crisis had been to suggest that they instead find a keyboard player and shift the focus away from guitar. (Ironically Relf and McCarty would do just that in 1968–69 when they formed the piano-centered band Renaissance.)

SAT 9TH
It is presumed that tonight's concert at the Rhodes Centre in Bishop's Stortford is cancelled to avoid putting weight on Chris Dreja. While Dreja was able to get through a few short shows on the Continent, it would be another story with full-length headlining spots back in England. Meanwhile serious maneuverings take place behind the scenes with regard to the management situation.

SUN 10TH
The band is booked to play the Agincourt Ballroom in Camberley (originally announced as at the Town Hall in nearby Farnborough) and while advertised in the local paper the Friday prior, it is presumably cancelled.

MON 11TH
The four man Yardbirds hop back over the English Channel to tape a one-off TV appearance for the programme "Teen Scene" at the Concertgebouw in Haarlem, Holland, to be transmitted on April 13. This would be their second and final Dutch TV appearance. Keith Relf gives a short interview to Dutch pop paper HIT WEEK, saying they have to lip-synch their insert because Jeff has fallen ill. The four piece band honour tonight's booking as part of a festival called "Het Hartewens Festival" also held at the Concertgebouw. The festival consists mainly of classical music, however the Yardbirds and a local Dutch band the Jokers were added no doubt to appease local teens.

An initially announced date for Ipswich in England is never finalized.

TUE 12TH
In a surprise move to the press and public, it is made official that Giorgio Gomelsky's five-year contract with the Yardbirds has terminated before its due time. Gomelsky, who has previously been burned by the handshake deal he once made with the Rolling Stones, is smart enough to make the split profitable this time however. A settlement is reached, wherein Gomelsky keeps the rights to all the recordings (both released and unreleased) he has produced with the group, which will prove most beneficial in the future. The settlement between the ex-manager and the Yardbirds is not finalized until 1967 however. Gomelsky later says that the solution with agreeing on future royalties – instead of a management percentage until the contract expired – was indeed the group's own decision.

While the Yardbirds sign with Napier-Bell's company Nomis Productions (Simon spelled backwards) for management services, Marquee Artistes remains the group's booking agency for the time being and most of the concerts, club and ballroom dates already booked are fulfilled even though their busy schedule initially suffers from Jeff's absence. One of Napier-Bell's primary tasks is to negotiate a new recording contract for the group and after declining an offer from Philips' guaranteeing the group £33,000, he instead works out a new deal with their present company EMI/Columbia, and manages to secure the group their first ever advance payment.

Tonight's booking at High Wycombe's Town Hall is presumably rescheduled and set for May 10.

WED 13TH
Due to Jeff's illness, the group's pre-booked live simulcast on BBC Light's "Parade Of The Pops" today is called off and rescheduled for May 4, but the pre-taped guest spot on Dutch TV's "Teen Scene" (AVRO Channel 2 at 8.00–8.30 pm, ▶ April 11) is transmitted in Holland today – featuring the Yardbirds but minus Beck.

© April 15, 1966: The Rolling Stones newest LP "Aftermath" is issued in the UK.

May 1966: The Yardbirds appear in the annual NME Pollwinners Concert ...

SAT 16TH
Floral Hall, Southport
For tonight's performance up in Lancashire, Jeff has recovered sufficiently to rejoin the group and normal bookings resume. MELODY MAKER reports: "While in hospital it was discovered he also has tonsillitis and will have to go back to have his tonsils removed soon."

Beck's variable condition will prove persistent, and combined with his increasing unhappiness with his role in the band, he never seems to completely rebound physically and emotionally from this point onward.

SUN 17TH
Cosmopolitan Club, Carlisle

TUE 19TH AND WED 20TH
Wasting absolutely no time in his new role as manager, Napier-Bell has already booked the Yardbirds for two days at Advision Studios in London to record a follow-up single to *Shapes Of Things* and begin work again on their LP, as all of the backing tracks committed to tape at the end of March now belong to Giorgio Gomelsky and are therefore rendered unavailable for release by the band. Although threatened with cancellation because of Jeff's condition, the session goes ahead as planned and produces both sides of the their next single: *Over, Under Sideways Down/Jeff's Boogie*.

Also, to make it official, a letter dated March 19 is sent by Marquee Artistes to the BBC to state in writing that Gomelsky no longer represents the Yardbirds who are now managed by Nomis Productions.

THU 21ST
Pier Pavilion, Worthing
Tonight is originally booked for City Hall, Salisbury.

FRI 22ND
Palais, Wimbledon
The annual week-long Montreux TV Festival opens in Switzerland today. Oddly enough, the Belgian entry to the contest briefly features an insert with the Yardbirds and is likely the appearance filmed last fall for the Adamo Show (▶ November 13, 1965)

SAT 23RD
Student Union, University of Bristol, Bristol
This is a confirmed appearance at this location despite a typo in some published date sheets which erroneously cite 'University, Preston' which has no university at the time.

MON 25TH
Silver Blades Ice Rink, Birmingham

TUE 26TH
Town Hall, Crayford

WED 27TH
Locarno Ballroom, Stevenage

FRI 29TH
Manchester Technical College, Manchester
The Yardbirds' perform *Jeff's Boogie* on "Ready, Steady, Go!" (Rediffusion TV, 6.07–6.30 pm) today, Beck's signature instrumental piece soon to be released on a single, while singer Keith Relf gets a preview solo spot with his new single *Mr. Zero* due out in two weeks time.

In the evening they play a college date in Manchester, Lancashire.

SAT 30TH
California Ballroom, Dunstable

•

Jeff Beck and Keith Relf grace the cover of the May edition of Britain's top teen trend magazine RAVE on sale the last week of April.

MAY

SUN 1ST
"New Musical Express 1966 Poll Winners Concert"
Empire Pool, Wembley
The Yardbirds, along with many of their contemporaries such as the Walker Brothers, the Small Faces, the Who, not to mention the Rolling Stones and the Beatles (the last playing what will be their last ever proper British concert), take part in the annual New Musical Express Poll Winners Concert in London before a 10,000 strong audience with the show starting at 2 pm. The running order finds the Yardbirds on seventh, sandwiched between the Walker Brothers and the Seekers. Although Napier-Bell has issued a statement in advance to expect a new-look Yardbirds with new hair styles and stage suits, such was not the yet case as they were still wearing their old tan stage jackets though now sporting black slacks rather than the matching tan pants but with shaggy hair intact. The short-lived new look (with white silk suits) would arrive later in the month. The entire show (excepting tragically the Beatles and the Rolling Stones) is filmed by ABC Television, and broadcast regionally on the "Poll Winners Concert" programme on the two consecutive Sundays following. The Yardbirds are featured in Part 2 (May 15) performing strong versions of *The Train Kept A-Rollin'* and *Shapes Of Things*.

TUE 3RD
Marquee Club, London
A return to the Marquee, supported by the Clayton Squares, 7.30–11 pm.

WED 4TH
Top Rank Suite, Southampton
To make up for the cancelled "Parade Of The Pops" appearance on April 13 due to Jeff's illness, the group is re-booked for today's live broadcast hosted by Denny Piercy (1.00–1.50 pm), from BBC's Playhouse Theatre in London where *Shapes Of Things* and *Mister You're A Better Man Than I* are performed.

The band then heads south to the coast for an evening ballroom performance.

FRI 6TH
The Yardbirds pre-record another set of performances for the BBC today at their Piccadilly 1 studio, taping both sides of the new single *Over Under Sideways Down/Jeff's Boogie*, Elmore James' *The Sun Is Shining*, Slim Harpo's *Baby Scratch My Back*, *Shapes Of Things* and *Mister You're A Better Man Than I*, all broadcast on "Saturday Swings" on May 21. *Baby Scratch My Back*, neatly credited to Keith Relf, is renamed *Rack My Mind* when recorded by the group for their first studio album the next month. *The Sun Is Shining* is a strong Beck vocal showcase, with an electrifying slide guitar performance which perhaps no other British guitarist could match at the time.

SAT 7TH–MON 9TH
The Yardbirds are scheduled to visit Holland on the weekend for TV and radio appearances but cancel.

TUE 10TH
Town Hall, High Wycombe
Tonight's show is likely the make-up date for a twice-cancelled performance, the first being March 28 delayed for recording but it seems the re-scheduled date – April 12 – is then moved to tonight as Beck had been ill.

THU 12TH
Ritz Entertainments Club, Skewen, Wales
The band heads off to the outskirts of Swansea for a pair of Welsh dates this weekend. In Skewen it is a 'Members Only' show with the Eyes of Blue

May 1966: Jeff Beck and friends record "Beck's Bolero" ...

(some of whose members later turn up in Man) and the Iveys (for whom this is a very early concert date for this predecessor to Badfinger). The night is rounded out by the Miss Skewen Contest to choose an entrant for Miss Wales Competition. A second announced booking in Port Talbot seems to have been dropped.

REGAL BALLROOM
AMMANFORD
TONIGHT
THE YARDBIRDS
THE KING BEES
& THE BLUES ORGANISATION

FRI 13TH
Regal Ballroom, Ammanford, Wales
The second show in greater Swansea is booked with the Kingbees and the Blues Organization.

SAT 14TH
Pavilion Gardens Ballroom, Buxton

SUN 15TH
Birmingham Theatre, Birmingham
While the day is spent at a photo shoot, following tonight's show, the Yardbirds take another holiday to gear up for the next intensive push for the new single. Paul Samwell-Smith travels to Ireland and Keith Relf and wife head to Corsica. Jeff stays put at home enjoying life with his brand new pale blue Corvette Stingray and finally getting to his promised solo project.

MON 16TH AND TUE 17TH
These first few days off are almost definitely when time has been booked at IBC Studios in Portland Place for the recording of Jeff's promised solo single. Assembled by manager/producer Simon Napier-Bell, this was part of the continuing master plan to let individual members of the Yardbirds pursue their own solo projects. This would be an important musical side project for Jeff who by now is obviously feeling hemmed in by the Yardbirds. Beck has an impressive dream band featuring the cream of London's studio players consisting of his close friend Jimmy Page on electric 12-string guitar, John Paul Jones on electric bass and Nicky Hopkins on piano. But rather than the drum spot routinely going to a session drummer, it is saved for a moonlighting Keith Moon of the Who – Jeff's favourite group. Moon's participation is decidedly covert and he arrives at the studio incognito well aware his involvement will prove explosive if revealed. Moon's availability

is due to a conveniently timed break in the Who's schedule this week as well. The instrumental *Beck's Bolero*, loosely based on Maurice Ravel's *Bolero* and credited to Page (even though Beck later claims authorship) is recorded and finished. Jeff recalls to Keith Moon biographer Tony Fletcher in 1998: "That was a momentous recording session. It was two days. We had a half-baked song, Jimmy and I, we didn't have to play it more than once or twice before the others were on to it. There was not an ounce of work in it. We didn't deliberate, we just played it through. Everyone in the control room was aghast: 'These guys don't even need to rehearse.' We did four or five cuts and it just sounded and felt like we shouldn't go anywhere else. We should just get rehearsing and carry this band."

A planned vocal number is intended as a B-side for release in July but ultimately *Beck's Bolero* stays in the can for almost a year, eventually surfacing on the B-side of *Hi Ho Silver Lining* in March '67 (with a contractually mandated Mickie Most production credit to boot) and then another year later on Beck's debut album *Truth*.

FRI 20TH
Simon Napier-Bell flies to America to negotiate the next Yardbirds US tour.

SAT 21ST
The Yardbirds are heard in BBC Light's "Saturday Swings" (10.00–noon, ▶ May 6), with Danny Street, the Ian Cambell Folk Group, and Brian Fahey & His Orchestra. Meanwhile Keith Relf, who has now released *Mr. Zero*, appears on the panel on BBC TV's popular show "Juke Box Jury" in the evening.

SUN 22ND
While today is intended to be an appearance in Brussels followed by two days of TV and radio work on the 23rd and 24th, local union problems cause the cancellation of the latter. While it is reported in the British music press that the Yardbirds perform at the festival in Brussels on this day, in fact their appearance is delayed until the following Sunday, May 29 and the Yardbirds instead enjoy a few more days off before returning to their work schedule.

WED 25TH
Top Rank Suite, Doncaster
Back from their respective breaks, the band resumes its regular touring schedule today.

AMBITIOUS

Zeppelin Unledded

Hot on the heels of a combustive recording session in London, May 1966, a lot of behind-the-scenes activities took place nearly culminating in the formation of a band to be called Lead Zeppelin (note spelling!) – a name suggested by either Keith Moon or John Entwistle as a paraphrase of "going down like a lead balloon". Moon and Entwistle, both entertaining thoughts of leaving the Who at this time, were to be the rhythm section, while Beck and Page would play guitars. In fact, Moon temporarily did quit the Who following an onstage fight with Pete Townshend on May 20, after Moon and Entwistle had arrived late for their gig in Newbury. Townshend: "[Keith] had a row with me, I got angry and threw a guitar at him and he threw a drum at me! He hurt himself, lacerated his leg; at the time he was intending to join Jeff's group" (VIBRATIONS #8, 1968). A badly beat-up Moon however withdrew the threat when another drummer had deputized for him; making a comeback with the Who in Blackpool on May 28.

To round out the dream band, both Steve Winwood and Steve Marriott were considered and casually approached as singers, but nothing came of it – especially after Beck was told in no uncertain terms by the feared manager Don Arden not to even think of luring Steve Marriott away from his clients the Small Faces. The grand plan seemed to fall apart almost as quickly as it began and outside of a few teasing references in the music press, the whole idea was destined not to be. But this was certainly the blueprint for what did become Led Zeppelin two years later when Page assembled *his* dream band from the ashes of the crumbled Yardbirds in July/August 1968.

Quite amazingly at this same time in late May, Eric Clapton was hatching his own supergroup. Not wanting to jeopardize his own gig with John Mayall's Bluesbreakers, Clapton conspired quietly with Ginger Baker and Jack Bruce. However once those players actually assembled to play together during the first week of June, word quickly spilled out as revealed in MELODY MAKER's June 11th issue.

Had Jeff Beck's plan gelled, it certainly would have given Cream a run for its money in the early supergroup sweepstakes, but alas, it has become only a footnote in rock history. ■

© May 1966: Jimmy Hughes releases the single "Neighbor, Neighbor", which Jeff includes in his JBG#1 repertoire, is a minor US soul and pop hit.

May/June 1966: Album recording sessions at Advision ...

THU 26TH
Locarno Ballroom, Bristol
Initially set for a show in Bradford.

FRI 27TH
Bluesville Club, Manor House, London
The new single *Over Under Sideways Down* is released in Great Britain today. The A-side is based on a phrase by producer Napier-Bell coupled to an attempt by the band to modernize Bill Haley's *Rock Around The Clock*. The song has Beck playing bass guitar in addition to guitar. The B-side, *Jeff's Boogie*, has been Beck's instrumental showpiece as long as he has been with the Yardbirds, and is based directly on *Guitar Boogie* by Chuck Berry. Jeff spices up the song with humorous four-bar injections like the nursery rhyme *London Bridge Is Falling Down* and the theme from the movie *Alfie* – a recent Top Ten hit for Cilla Black. This will be the Yardbirds' last major hit; it makes UK Top Ten in June, and peaks in the US at #13 in July.

To coincide with the new single, the Yardbirds are at Studio One, Wembley Park as guests on tonight's "Ready, Steady, Go!" (Rediffusion TV, 6.07-6.34 pm), which also features Chris Andrews, the Animals plus star attraction the Rolling Stones – who have a twelve minute segment performing three songs including *Paint It, Black*.

Tonight is originally announced as a booking at the Mecca Gaiety Ballroom in Grimsby but later switches to a London venue instead.

THE YARDBIRDS
A: OVER UNDER SIDEWAYS DOWN (Dreja/McCarty/Beck/Relf/Samwell-Smith)
B: JEFF'S BOOGIE (Dreja/McCarty/Beck/Relf/Samwell-Smith)

Released Friday May 27, 1966 (UK Columbia DB 7928) and Wednesday June 8, 1966 (US Epic 10035)
Personnel is Jeff Beck (ldgtr, bs on A), Keith Relf (vcls), Chris Dreja (rhygtr), Paul Samwell-Smith (bs on B) and Jim McCarty (drms).
Recorded at Advision Studios, New Bond Street, London, April 19–20 1966.
Produced by Simon Napier-Bell
Engineered by Roger Cameron
Highest Chart Position UK: #10
Highest Chart Position US: #13

SAT 28TH
Dreamland Ballroom, Margate
Support tonight at this stylish Art Deco seaside theatre in Kent is the Profile.

SUN 29TH
"Wolu-City 2"
Kentucky Palace, Woluwe-St-Lambert, Belgium
The Yardbirds, advertised as a 'beat orchestra', headline in an evening of "folk song" with the Settlers and Ferre Grignard in this suburb of Brussels. It marks the band's Belgian concert debut at this week-long annual festival. Mysteriously it is reported in the NEW MUSICAL EXPRESS (May 28) that the Yardbirds had appeared at this site the previous Sunday. While a show featuring a number of acts mentioned in the review (the Frugal Sounds, the Settlers, and the Kruzade) did appear that day the headliner instead was French rocker Eddy Mitchell. The reviewer never actually sees the Yardbirds (!) but still manages to write: "It was impossible to really appreciate the brilliant instrumental work of the group", but adds reassuringly "it must be assumed that they played all their biggest successes of the moment. Anyway, the fans lapped them up."

MON 30TH
"Top Pop Festival"
Lincoln City Football Club, Sincil Bank
Back in England, the Yardbirds appear at this giant pop show at a football ground in Lincolnshire on Whitmonday, along with other top groups including the Kinks, the Small Faces, Georgie Fame, the Creation, Screaming Lord Sutch, the She Trinity and the Who. The festival runs from noon until 10.30 pm. Despite the impressive line-up in what might in retrospect be called one of the ultimate billings of classic 60s rock bands, attendance is far less than hoped for and the football club spends years recovering financially from the event. The Yardbirds are decked out for the occasion in their new all-white silk suits, a short-lived new image for the band, no doubt dictated by manager Napier-Bell.

TUE 31ST
The Yardbirds are at Advision Studios in London for a marathon five-day session (Tuesday till Saturday) to complete the bulk of recording their first proper studio long-player. The sessions are produced by Paul Samwell-Smith in conjunction with Napier-Bell. The usual recording method is for Dreja, Samwell-Smith, Relf, and McCarty to lay down the basic tracks – including writing most of the material in the studio – before bringing Jeff in fresh to overdub his guitars. Many of the earlier attempted songs are now resurrected and rerecorded. The group also finds room for an interview on BBC Light's "Pop Inn" today, broadcast live between 1.00– 1.55 pm.

JUNE

WED 1ST, THU 2ND, FRI 3RD
Recording sessions for the new album at Advision continue. Paul Samwell-Smith takes a break from recording sessions on Friday to speak his mind to MELODY MAKER: "... we have five days to do this LP, writing all the numbers ourselves. If we could only have the studio for a month it would be fantastic. Instead, we have to rush all over the world. Am I a bit disenchanted? Yes! We must have made around 600 personal appearances over the last two years. And, really that's enough! You aren't creating, just doing the rounds. And frankly it bores me stiff!" The group is also visited by RECORD MIRROR for a story (June 11).

Simon Napier-Bell, by now already losing patience with his new charges ("a miserable lot" is how he later quite brusquely described them), details the sessions in his funny memoir 'You Don't Have To Say You Love Me': "We struggled through it and it wasn't much fun ... On top of that they all argued with Jeff Beck. He was the stand-out talent in the group, a truly brilliant guitarist. But they didn't give him enough freedom to show off his talent ... In one number, Jeff was given a solo to play. The others talked about it like it was a gift on their part, a generous offer ... It was a blues number [*The Nazz Are Blue*] and Jeff's petulant reaction to their indulgent attitude was to stand there and play one long note right through the solo."

SAT 4TH
Middlesex Borough College, Isleworth
After wrapping up recording sessions at Advision, the Yardbirds resume their concert and dance schedule.

MON 6TH
Paul Samwell-Smith pre-records an interview with Brian Matthew at Kensington House, Shepherd's Bush for an upcoming edition of BBC Light's "Pop Profile".

May 26, 1966: Bob Dylan plays his infamous concert at the Albert Hall in London, backed by the Hawks (later the Band).

June 1966: Original member Paul Samwell-Smith quits the Yardbirds ...

WED 8TH
The Yardbirds lip-synch a performance of *Over Under Sideways Down* for the TV show "A Whole Scene Going" also broadcast this day (BBC-1, 6.30–7.30 pm). The band is attired in their short-lived new white silk suits for the occasion. This half-year old programme is being billed as a "new series reflecting the tastes and times of Britain's under-twenty-ones". Other special guests today are Indian sitar virtuoso Ravi Shankar (whom Beck and Relf ask questions from the audience) plus a three piece version of the Kinks (with bassist Pete Quaife missing due to a recent accident). The taping takes place at BBC Television Centre, Studio 2 in London. Also today is the official release date for the *Over Under Sideways Down/Jeff's Boogie* single in the United States.

THU 9TH
The day starts at 1.30 at the Paris Cinema where the group pre-tapes an appearance on "The Joe Loss Show" (BBC Light) for airing on July 1. Songs performed are *Over Under Sideways Down*, *Shapes Of Things*, and *Jeff's Boogie*. Jim McCarty later says that the Joe Loss Orchestra joins in on *Over Under Sideways Down*, but this is likely just a rehearsal prank and not used on the final broadcast. The Yardbirds move on to Television Center where they then appear on today's BBC Television's "Top Of The Pops" (7.30–8.00 pm) chart show again promoting *Over Under Sideways Down*. At this same time, the band videotapes a second, differently staged performance of the song for insertion in the following week's programme. After the taping is finished however, Keith Relf is taken ill with an attack of his recurring asthma and as a consequence tonight's booking at the Ram Jam Club in Brixton is cancelled.

FRI 10TH
Ricky Tick Club, Thames Hotel, Windsor
Relf is well enough again and the group carries on with its live engagements. While it had been announced in early May that the Yardbirds were tentatively booked for a unique one-off show at the huge Yankee Stadium held in New York today, their booking was never finalized. Billed as "Sound Blast '66" it features an all-star cast headed by the Beach Boys plus the Byrds, Ray Charles, the McCoys and Stevie Wonder.

SAT 11TH
"Blues Festival"
Zambesi Club, Hounslow
Talking to DISC WEEKLY today about his upcoming solo project, Jeff explains: "... it's sort of a bolero – very pulsating and exciting. I'm not going to swear on it, but I think it should go, it's so strong. You've never heard such a thrashing sound!" As for the B-side, Jeff reveals "I thought it would be great if we just had a two-and-half-minutes' silence with a bit at the end saying 'Well, that's it – goodnight.' That sort of idea sounds good at the time, but if you did it, it would sound corny". When the interview is printed the next week (June 18th edition), the paper even optimistically announces "Jeff's disc, as yet untitled, will be released in about seven weeks' time". Ultimately however, the single will not be released during his time with the Yardbirds. The reason for this has been suggested as resistance by the band itself which perhaps had a change of heart about the prospect of its actually being successful. If so, this likely contributes to Jeff's growing frustration and unhappiness as a Yardbird.

The group also pre-records a BBC appearance for tomorrow's "Easy Beat". The taping is done at the Paris Cinema and the songs performed are *Rack My Mind* and *Over Under Sideways Down*. The band then heads off for the evening's club date in Hounslow on the western reaches of Greater London.

SUN 12TH
Starlite Ballroom, Greenford
In the morning, the Yardbirds are heard on BBC Light's "Easy Beat" (10–11.30 pm, ▶ June 11) together with the Barron Knights. After finishing the last set in Greenford, Jeff talks to Richard Lennox of DISC AND MUSIC ECHO (the new name given to the recently merged DISC WEEKLY and the MUSIC ECHO) and together they go to the Cromwellian in Jeff's Corvette for a late night meal, and say hello to Chris Farlowe, Zoot Money and Jonathan King. The interview (published in the June 25th edition) describes a dispirited Beck, strangely claiming to Lennox: "I don't really care what I do – I wouldn't mind if they sent me to Vietnam."

MON 13TH
Gay Tower Ballroom, Birmingham

WED 15TH ✱
This is likely the date when the Yardbirds record a contribution to the US TV special "It's A Mod Mod World" for broadcast by New York's WABC-TV on August 13. On location in London, the group mimes to *Over Under Sideways Down*, and – surprisingly – the seldom performed *Turn Into Earth*, although the latter is done without Jeff Beck. This turns out to be the last appearance by Samwell-Smith on film with the Yardbirds.

THU 16TH
City Hall, Salisbury
The band's separate insert taped for tonight's "Top of The Pops" is aired, miming again to *Over Under Sideways Down* (▶ June 9) allowing for a less crowded schedule today. Also a news item in MELODY MAKER (June 18) on the newsstands this day reads 'Yardbird Beck Makes Solo Debut', confirming "guitarist Jeff Beck is recording a solo single which is scheduled for release at the end of July".

FRI 17TH
Corn Exchange, Newbury

SAT 18TH
"May Ball"
The Queen's College, Oxford University, Oxford
The Yardbirds plus the Hollies and the Deep are booked to play the annual graduation ball at the Queen's College at Oxford University today. During the Yardbirds' set, a drunken Keith Relf embarrasses Paul Samwell-Smith to the point where he decides to quit the group there and then, not surprising as he has been thinking of leaving for some time and expressing his views in public. Samwell-Smith, a crucial component of the Yardbirds as both bassist and musical director, intends to remain as producer for the group, although this arrangement does not work out in the end.

Coincidentally, Jimmy Page is in the audience at the May Ball together with Mama Cass Elliot of the Mamas & the Papas (who are holidaying in Britain and arrived on Sunday a week ago). Page, having driven to Oxford with his friend Jeff, surprisingly volunteers to cover for Samwell-Smith as a stand-in bassist in order that the band be able to fulfill their immediate engagements, evidently eager to escape from the lucrative but increasingly dull routine of his session schedule. Jimmy interestingly had never played the bass previously but is an accomplished enough musician to

---

TRIVIA TROVE: Artist Ruth Hindman wants to paint Jeff because his face "is like craggy summits and windy places" (MM, July 1965)

June 1966: Eric Clapton quits John Mayall's Bluesbreakers (he is replaced by Peter Green) to form Cream with Jack Bruce and Ginger Baker.

June 1966: Jimmy Page replaces Paul Samwell-Smith ...

make it work for the short run. Seizing Page's enthusiasm to enter the fold, the band subsequently asks him to join and fill the position permanently – finally accepting an offer made twice before during the Clapton-era!

•

With Samwell-Smith's sudden defection, the Yardbirds also lose their key connection to Simon Napier-Bell who was brought at Paul's recommendation. With Samwell-Smith absent it is not surprising that relations between management and band also continues its decline from this point onwards. Around this time, Napier-Bell signs on a new band, John's Children, to which he will devote increasing amounts of his energies.

SUN 19TH
The Yardbirds' engagement at the Ultra Club at the Downs Hotel in Hassocks, Sussex has to be cancelled after Samwell-Smith's abrupt departure. Reportedly Jeff Beck personally drives to the club to explain the necessity of the band's short-notice cancellation. Presumably the show goes on with the support act Four & Seven Eighths. Officially, "food poisoning" is the explanation given why the date is cancelled. Unofficially it is more likely just a case of one very bad hangover.

MON 20TH
Samwell-Smith's departure is officially announced in a press release today.

TUE 21ST
Marquee Club, London
After a quick rehearsal, the new line-up with Jimmy Page debuts at the Marquee tonight with the Clayton Squares once more in support. It is a nervous Page on bass, but right from the beginning the intention is to switch with Chris Dreja, so the latter can move to bass and Jimmy play dual lead with Jeff. This is Jeff's eleventh appearance at the Marquee since he joined the Yardbirds in March '65 and in fact will be the last for the Yardbirds in this incarnation.

WED 22ND
Jimmy Page fulfills outstanding studio engagements and immediately begins the requisite press duties in an effort to minimize the negative effects of the loss of an original group member.

THU 23RD
Mecca Palais, Ashton-under-Lyne
In today's DISC AND MUSIC ECHO's (dated June 25th) regular column 'Zooming Up The Charts', Jeff offers his opinions on some of the current songs in the singles chart, saving his praise for the Beatles *(Paperback Writer:* "their best yet ... it really makes me move when I hear it") and the Kinks *(Sunny Afternoon;* "lovely – great ... something about Ray Davies' writing fascinates me"). The following week it is Peter Noone of Herman's Hermits who guests in 'Zooming Up The Charts', who says of *Over Under Sideways Down:* "It's a shame the Yardbirds have no image because they would be the #1 group in England."

FRI 24TH
"June Ball '66"
University of Durham, Durham
Similar to the Oxford event the week before, the Yardbirds are back at another university for another traditional seasonal ball. Tonight's show has an impressive and varied line-up in addition to the Yardbirds: the Roulettes, the Action, Mandy Rice Davies, Ronnie Aldrich, the Checkmates, Graham Bond, Ken Colyer, Simba, plus the Outer Limits. Today, coincidentally on Jeff's twenty-second birthday, a NEW MUSICAL EXPRESS write-up reads 'Samwell-Smith Quits the Yardbirds'. The ex-bassist, who will pursue a successful career in production, explains: "I'm leaving because there was too much travelling involved."

SAT 25TH
Palais de Danse, Bury
Promoted by Jack Venet Enterprises, and "the sensational Yardbirds" are supported by Frankenstein & His Monsters plus the Sheffields.

SUN 26TH
Le Weekend Club, Paris, France
The new-look Yardbirds fly to France today for a pair of club and TV appearances, beginning with a performance at this popular Paris night spot.

MON 27TH
"Provins Rock Festival"
Provins, France
Moving to the outer regions of Paris, the band records an appearance on the site of a castle to be broadcast on the French TV show "Music Hall de France" on July 2. Also appearing are the Small Faces. Stills from the rehearsal for this show provide the earliest known live photos of the new look Yardbirds.

TUE 28TH
It is reported that the Yardbirds go into an undisclosed studio with the intention to record a new single during the "last days of June", according to DISC AND MUSIC ECHO (July 2), for their first recording session with Jimmy Page. Neither title nor release date is revealed, and no further documentation exists.

WED 29TH
Bromley Court Hotel, Bromley
The Yardbirds return to one of their regular venues in nearby Kent.

JULY

FRI 1ST
Chiselhurst Caves, Chiselhurst
The Yardbirds were originally pencilled in to open a US Dick Clark package tour today dubbed 'Where The Action Is' (after the name of his successful TV programme) and lasting the whole of July, on a bill set to feature the Young Rascals and the Knickerbockers. The Yardbirds' slot however is eventually cancelled, and a similar tour is set October/November instead.

The group is also on BBC's "Joe Loss Show" (1.00–2.00 pm, ▶ June 9).

SAT 2ND
Ram Jam Club, Brixton, London
Originally booked to appear in South Wales tonight, the Yardbirds play the Ram Jam Club in Brixton instead – likely to make up for the cancellation at the same club the previous month. Jimmy Page is also featured in both MELODY MAKER and DISC AND MUSIC ECHO write-ups dated today.

SUN 3RD
North Pier Pavilion, Blackpool
The Yardbirds fly up from London to play a summer Sunday concert at Blackpool's North Pier together with the Troggs, while Manfred Mann and Marty Wilde play the South Pier.

TUE 5TH
Winter Gardens, Malvern

THU 7TH
Town Hall, Elgin, Scotland
The Yardbirds head far north for a quick pair of live engagements in Scotland.

FRI 8TH
Raith Ballroom, Kirkcaldy, Scotland
In today's edition of NEW MUSICAL EXPRESS, Paul Samwell-Smith explains why he left the Yardbirds, and Jimmy Page why he joined. Giving a hint of

July 1966: The Yardbirds' first studio album is released ...

the future, Page explains to journalist Keith Altham: "Chris Dreja is learning bass at the moment, and it seems likely that I will take over on guitar at a later date." Altham concludes: "With Jeff and Jimmy in the same group, the Yardbirds have, with the exception of Eric Clapton, two of the most creative guitarists around the group scene today."

SAT 9TH
Bass Recreation Grounds, Derby

SUN 10TH
Pier Pavilion, Hastings

MON 11TH–TUE 12TH✱
During the early part of the week, the Yardbirds are reported to record a commercial for a new cosmetic at a London studio. This presumably would be for Yardley, a long-established London cosmetics firm. No further details have ever surfaced regarding this project however and no unaccounted for recordings by this five man version of the band is known, rendering this as possibly a case of premature reporting.

While this venture is unconfirmed, Napier-Bell does pursue this avenue of exposure for the band and the Yardbirds will, around this time, pose for a magazine campaign for a British perfume called Miss Disc as part of their promotional push for the next single.

WED 13TH
The Yardbirds are poised to be in Paris, France again today, although this visit probably is cancelled.

THU 14TH
Town Hall, Kidderminster

FRI 15TH
- Palais De Danse, Cowdenbeath, Scotland
- City Hall, Perth, Scotland

For the second weekend running the band heads up to Scotland, with tonight a double booking. The Cowdenbeath press promises: "The Yardbirds play for dancing this week 9 pm– 2 am", while in Perth the advert reads: "Two of the country's top groups, special engagement on short notice", as it also features Brian Poole & the Tremeloes plus the Undermined 9 pm–1 am.

Originally the Yardbirds were booked for a string of appearances in Ireland, including one set for tonight in Kilkenny, but is replaced with these last-minute bookings in Scotland instead. Seemingly Jeff will never perform in Ireland and this is as close as he would come.

The NEW MUSICAL EXPRESS's gossip column Tailpieces reports "rumours suggest two Yardbirds and two members of Who may combine for new group..." Although no specific names are mentioned, it's obvious the concerned ones are Jeff and Jimmy plus Keith Moon and John Entwistle. This is a slightly stale rumour by this point in time.

SAT 16TH
Ice Rink, Ayr, Scotland

The Yardbirds are supported tonight by Maureen & the Thunderbirds (7.30–10.30 pm).

AYR ICE RINK
SUMMER SKATING SESSIONS — Monday-Saturday — 10 a.m, 2.30 p.m, 7.30 p.m.
SATURDAY 16th JULY
7.30 p.m.–10.30 p.m.
Tickets 7/6
ADVANCE TICKETS ON SALE
THE YARDBIRDS
ably supported by
"MAUREEN AND THE THUNDERBIRDS"

SUN 17TH
Victoria Ballroom, Dunbar, Scotland

WED 20TH
Town Hall, Stourbridge

THU 21ST
Assembly Rooms, Worthing

FRI 22ND
Co-op Hall, Gravesend

While playing Gravesend in Kent tonight, the Yardbirds can also be seen on Rediffusion TV's "Ready, Steady, Go!" (7.00–7.30 pm) with Dave Dee, Dozy, Beaky, Mick & Tich, and Paul & Barry Ryan and others. Rehearsals are held 2.00–6.30 pm. On tonight's programme they feature two songs (Farewell, Lost Woman) from their new LP. This, Jeff's seventeenth documented appearance on the show in little over a year (and Jimmy Page's first with the group), will also be his and the Yardbirds last, as "Ready, Steady, Go!" is taken off the air in December.

More importantly, on this Friday the first proper Yardbirds album is released in Great Britain and Europe, just called *The Yardbirds*, although later referred to as *Roger The Engineer* because of the Chris Dreja cartoon of engineer Roger Cameron on the cover. Actually, this cartoon is something of Dreja trademark, which was nicknamed 'Faubus' when he drew a sketch of it for FLIP magazine as early as September the previous year.

The album is a mix of rhythm and blues, folk and pop songs (or "African, Hebrew and Chinese sounds" as Keith Relf quips to DISC AND MUSIC ECHO). It is a true piece of teamwork; all songs are credited to the group collectively, and while Dreja designed the cover, Jim McCarty supplied the liner notes and Paul Samwell-Smith is credited as musical director. (Interestingly, McCarty and Dreja are at the time working on a book of anecdotes about life with the Yardbirds – sort of their "solo project" within the group – which is planned for publication in the latter part of 1966. With the aid of writer John Platt, the book is actually completed and published, but not until 1983!) Jeff is given his own vocal showcase (*The Nazz Are Blue*), and is otherwise featured as the main soloist. The group has also expanded their

---

Album
THE YARDBIRDS
THE YARDBIRDS ("ROGER THE ENGINEER")
A1 LOST WOMAN **A2** OVER UNDER SIDEWAYS DOWN **A3** THE NAZZ ARE BLUE **A4** I CAN'T MAKE YOUR WAY **A5** RACK MY MIND **A6** FAREWELL

B1 HOT HOUSE OF OMAGARARSHID **B2** JEFF'S BOOGIE **B3** HE'S ALWAYS THERE **B4** TURN INTO EARTH **B5** WHAT DO YOU WANT? **B6** EVER SINCE THE WORLD BEGAN (all titles: Dreja/McCarty/Beck/Relf/Samwell-Smith)

Released Friday July 22, 1966 (UK Columbia SX/SCX 6063)
Personnel is Jeff Beck (ldgtr, bs on A2, vcls on A3), Keith Relf (hrmnca/vcls), Chris Dreja (rhygtr, pno, vcls on B1), Paul Samwell-Smith (bs, bckng vcls) and Jim McCarty (drms, bckng vcls). Mick (surname unknown) plays bass on some cuts.
Recorded at Advision Studios, New Bond Street, London, April 19–20, May 31, June 1–4, 1966
Produced by Simon Napier-Bell
Musical direction by Paul Samwell-Smith
Engineered by Roger Cameron
Highest Chart Position UK: #20

July 1966: Jeff Beck is ill; the Yardbirds cancel Windsor Jazz & Blues Festival ...

instrumentation including piano (by Chris Dreja on *Farewell)*, while Samwell-Smith claims anonymous bass-player Mick (from the group Triangle) plays bass on many of the songs with Samwell-Smith presumably at the controls. The album is a clear studio creation, and half of the songs will never be performed in public.

The record receives good reviews; NEW MUSICAL EXPRESS writes: "You'll find new things about this album each time you play it, which should keep you playing it often," and RECORD MIRROR reports: "[This] album shows how important Jeff Beck is to the group," while MELODY MAKER claims: "The overall result is an interesting and often exciting album." During an eight week chart stay, the long player peaks at #20 in RECORD RETAILER'S charts in Britain. Eric Clapton, however, scoffs at the album when interviewed for RECORD MIRROR by Richard Green in early August: "I just don't want to know. One of those numbers I gave to them two years ago and arranged and everything." (Clapton refers to Snooky Pryor's *Someone To Love Me,* which was first attempted by the Yardbirds in the studio back in the pre-Jeff Beck days, the surviving tapes of which were later erroneously attributed to Jeff Beck as *Someone To Love Me Pt 1.)* But Clapton does have a good word to say about Jeff: "Who do I rate as guitarists? Jeff Beck and John Mayall's new guitarist [Peter Green]."

The album is interestingly released in widely different stereo and mono mixes, where for example the mono album features an extended guitar solo on *Hot House of Omagararshid* which is not present on the stereo version likely indicating Jeff recorded the solo as the mono mix was being done.

SAT 23RD
Pavilion Gardens Ballroom, Buxton

MON 25TH
Bath Pavilion, Bath

TUE 26TH ✱
A studio session again has been booked to hopefully complete a new single and an EP prior to the Yardbirds' upcoming US tour. Under the direction of Simon Napier-Bell at least the song *Happenings Ten Years Time Ago* is recorded at IBC Studios. Session musician John Paul Jones replaces Jimmy Page on bass guitar for this date. This move was no doubt requested by Page himself who likely felt that, although he could play passable bass on stage, recognized that it was not his forte;

and for an all-important potential hit single, it would only be sensible to bring in a pro (and friend from his own session days) to cut this A-side. The bulk of the session evidently proceeds without Jeff either while he apparently overdubs the guitar solo at the very end or in a separate session after the backing track is completed with Page available to cut the distinctive rhythm guitar part.

•

The group also switches agency representation at this time when they sign with the powerful Harold Davison (whose stable also include the Animals) and leave Marquee Artistes.

WED 27TH
Despite an ill Jeff Beck who is suffering a relapse of his swollen tonsils, the band today tapes an appearance on Rolf Harris' children's TV show "Hey Presto – It's Rolf!" at the BBC's Television Theatre at 11 in the morning. This will be broadcast two days later on July 29 on BBC-1 together with the other musical guests Dave Dee, Dozy, Beaky, Mick and Tich. The Yardbirds interestingly perform *Rack My Mind* from their new LP rather than the usual recent hit single. But having postponed his tonsil-operation, Jeff is bed-stricken once more, causing cancellation of some of the Yardbirds' upcoming dates, and worse still, threatening the group's upcoming US tour.

THU 28TH
Tonight's booking at the Palace Theatre in Douglas off the upper west coast of England on the Isle of Man is cancelled because of Jeff's illness.

FRI 29TH
The group is seen on "Hey Presto – It's Rolf!" on BBC 1 (▶ July 27).

SAT 30TH
Today, as England triumphantly beats West Germany in the soccer World Cup final before a brim-filled Wembley Stadium, the Yardbirds cancel their headlining appearance on the second night of the prestigious Sixth National Jazz & Blues Festival (once again to have shared the stage with the Who) held at the Royal Windsor Racecourse, because Jeff is still too ill to perform. Keith Relf goes onstage to apologize for the group's enforced absence. Of particular note, the following night marks the sensational official debut performance by the newly-formed Cream, for the occasion billed as "Eric Clapton, Jack Bruce, Ginger Baker" (although actually they sneak in a warm-up date at Manchester's Twisted Wheel club on July 29).

AUGUST

MON 1ST
Stateside, Epic Records release their version of the *Yardbirds* album renamed *Over Under Sideways Down* to cash in on the group's latest hit and to coincide with the upcoming American tour. The album matches the British, except that two tracks – *The Nazz Are Blue* and *Rack My Mind* – are omitted, a standard American practice to save material for later releases and reduce the publisher fees per album. The long player peaks at US #52.

Album

THE YARDBIRDS
OVER UNDER SIDEWAYS DOWN

A1 LOST WOMAN **A2** OVER UNDER SIDEWAYS DOWN **A3** I CAN'T MAKE YOUR WAY
A4 FAREWELL **A5** HOT HOUSE OF OMAGARARSHID

B1 JEFF'S BOOGIE **B2** HE'S ALWAYS THERE **B3** TURN INTO EARTH **B4** WHAT DO YOU WANT?
B5 EVER SINCE THE WORLD BEGAN *(all titles: Dreja/McCarty/Beck/ Relf/Samwell-Smith)*

Released Monday August 1, 1966 (US Epic LN 24210 mono/BN 26210 stereo)
Personnel is Jeff Beck (ldgtr, bs on A2), Keith Relf (hrmnca/vcls), Chris Dreja (rhygtr, pno, vcls on A5), Paul Samwell-Smith (bs, bckng vcls) and Jim McCarty (drms, bckng vcls). Mick (surname unknown) plays bass on some cuts.
Recorded at Advision Studios, New Bond Street, London, April 19–20, May 31, June 1–4, 1966
Produced by Simon Napier-Bell
Musical direction by Paul Samwell-Smith
Engineered by Roger Cameron
Highest Chart Position US: #52

© July 29, 1966: It is reported that Bob Dylan is seriously hurt in a motorbike accident in Woodstock in upstate New York.

August 1966: The Yardbirds leave for third US tour ...

TUE 2ND

The Yardbirds, who should have left England today for their third North American tour, have to postpone the flight a couple of days because of Jeff's illness. The first three days of the visit were slated for TV, radio and press duties in New York to help plug their new LP before starting up the concerts appearances on Friday. Barring any TV, these promotional functions seem to have been tacked on to the end of the tour instead, stretching the return date from September 4th to the 10th. With Jeff still recuperating, it is decided instead to blow off these duties and give Jeff a few more days to resume his full health for the gruelling five weeks which lay ahead. Rather, in preparation for the tour Jeff and Jimmy spend time at Jimmy's place rehearsing for the eventual switch to the two lead guitar line-up. Jimmy Page confides to BEAT INSTRUMENTAL (September 1966): "We've learned a couple of Freddy King solos note by note, and when we play them in unison it sounds good. We'll be doing quite a lot of this sort of thing, playing in unison or in harmony." There is no evidence that this switch would be expected to happen until after this tour as the greater challenge lies on Chris Dreja's shoulders to make himself accomplished enough on bass guitar to allow such a change-over. Tellingly Jimmy brings only his bass guitar on the tour, leaving his guitar behind in England.

THU 4TH
THE YARDBIRDS:
THIRD NORTH AMERICAN TOUR

The Yardbirds fly out from London Airport at 11.55 am on Air Canada flight 857, even though Jeff is – in his own words – "still not 100 per cent fit". Because the United States is in the grip of an airline strike, they fly via Canada. At a press reception at the airport before departure, the group is photographed in typical sixties hip garb; Jeff wears a bolero hat, while Jimmy Page turns up with a bus conductor's ticket machine as part of his outfit. It had been speculated in the British music press that the new-look all white suits would be what American audiences would be seeing the band wear but evidently the band rebelled beforehand or the suits were merely rendered obsolete by Samwell-Smith's departure. Simon Napier-Bell and road manager Brian Conliffe accompany the band on the tour, and Napier-Bell initially has to hire a private DC3 plane to fly the group around the States because of the strike. As on previous tours, it is a mixed date sheet booked by Premier Talent Associates with the group visiting a seemingly random selection of teen clubs, ballrooms, amusement parks, state fairs, and lakeside resorts. The Yardbirds do not perform in New York City on this visit either, instead concentrating on concerts in the Midwest and on the West Coast.

The nature of the bookings on this tour reveal that management and/or the booking agency were somewhat at a loss when it came to exposing the Yardbirds in the States, often booking them into obscure and remote locations, a fact which was not lost on the band. Financially the tour is reported to bring in percentages at every single performance, expecting to leave the States with "$100,000 (before taxes)", this according to June Harris, the NEW MUSICAL EXPRESS' regular Stateside correspondent. It should, however, be noted that Ms. Harris is married to none other than Frank Barsalona of Premier Talent and it was certainly in her interest to put forth such optimistic figures! Whatever profits the group may have made were likely eaten up by the unanticipated and prohibitive costs caused by the air strike.

FRI 5TH
- **Dayton's Auditorium, Minneapolis, Minnesota**
- **Col Ballroom, Davenport, Iowa**

A double date in the Midwest kicks off the tour. The first two performances are on of the 8th floor of a large department store in downtown Minneapolis (at 1 and 3 pm) supported by local band the Escapades in an event sponsored by the local Teen Board–Varsity Board. The performance is preceded by a press conference presided upon by the Teen Board where the group is also interviewed by 14 year old fan Lana Doerr for DATEBOOK magazine. At night, the Yardbirds move on to neighboring Iowa and play a dance date in Davenport supported by local group the XLs.

SAT 6TH
Civic Opera House, Chicago, Illinois

"The Yardbirds bring their fuzzboxes, sitars and Gregorian chants to the Civic Opera House" promises a write-up in the CHICAGO TRIBUNE as the band returns to their favorite stomping ground from the previous US tours, though this would only be a one-night stopover. The Yardbirds perform at 8 pm with ticket prices ranging from $2.50 to $5.50, and the support acts are reportedly two local bands Konquerer Worm Blues Band and Red, White & Blues Band. Jon Paris, later a renowned bassist, recalls how the group opens the concert with *Shapes Of Things* behind the curtains to dramatic effect before the vocals come in when the curtains part.

SUN 7TH
Maple Lake Pavilion, Mentor, Minnesota

A truly remote booking in the upper lake region of Minnesota, attendance for this show is reportedly very sparse and populated mainly by local musicians from Fargo and lower Minnesota who travel upstate to see their musical heroes in action. Tonight's booking and those for the following week seem to be sub-contracted out to a local agent whose specialty is lakeside summer resort areas, a circuit somewhat of a holdover from the big band ballroom days.

MON 8TH
Detroit Lakes Pavilion, Detroit Lakes, Minnesota

Sponsored by KQWB radio in Fargo, North Dakota, the originally announced location of the show (Fargo) is moved, possibly due to the Beach Boys being booked in the Fargo Municipal Auditorium a few days after this. The Yardbirds' show is ultimately held in neighboring Detroit Lakes, Minnesota, 25 miles outside Fargo with local legends the Unbelievable Uglies opening. The Yardbirds arrive at Hecktor Airport and are picked up by members of one of the promoter's own bands, the Pawnbrokers, who ferry the British quintet to the local Holiday Inn in Moorhead outside Fargo. Keith Relf complains of throat trouble, but the show goes ahead despite this. The band's own equipment has yet to arrive and the Uglies provide their own gear for use by the Yardbirds. Former Ugly Dave Hoffman vividly recalls "They were very loud, very intense and very good!"

TUE 9TH
Roof Garden Ballroom, Arnolds Park, Iowa

A landmark amusement park in the Great Lakes region of Iowa, where the Yardbirds' appearance is part of a series of 'Record Stars' every Tuesday, with tonight's show also featuring the Dark Knights from nearby Storm Lake. It is reported in KRLA BEAT that as the group's equipment had failed to arrive due to delays caused by the air strike that a replacement set of Vox

August 1966: US tour include out-of-the-way lakeside resorts ...

amplifiers is flown in from Chicago for tonight's show – all expenses paid. The famous ballroom would be destroyed by a tornado two years later.

WED 10TH
Green's Pavilion, Lakeview Park, Manitou Beach, Michigan
Tonight's show is in Michigan at a summer resort formerly and familiarly known to the locals as Devil's Lake Pavilion. Detroit-area guitarist Cub Koda (later of Brownsville Station fame), is in attendance with a large percentage of the greater Detroit area's garage band guitarists to witness Jeff Beck in action. Another attendee of this show fondly recounts his brush with Jeff off-stage. Hoping to impress upon the guitarist how much of a fan he is of his musical prowess and not wanting to come off as just another autograph seeker, the young man approaches Jeff with the opening line "Uh excuse me, Mr. Beck, I don't want your autograph, I just wanted to say...", to which Jeff snaps back mid-sentence "then blow me!" and promptly walks away. Beck's reaction is likely a clear reflection of his state of mind, stranded in the middle of the vast US on a decidedly unglamorous and unprestigious tour.

FRI 12TH
- **Indiana Beach Ballroom, Monticello, Indiana**
- **Cold Spring Resort, Hamilton, Indiana**

The final lakeside bookings of the week is seemingly a double date, the first located on Lake Schaeffer with two shows scheduled 8.15 pm and 10.05 pm. They are still able to get to a second booking 90 miles away at Hamilton Lake through the magic of having a personal aircraft. Though no print evidence can be located to unequivocally reveal the show time, the son of the owner at the time does recall the vivid impression of the band turning up with loads of huge Vox amps in an era when bands usually only had small amps. Cold Spring Resort, another turn of the century ballroom, could handle about 2,000 dancers.

SAT 13TH
Checkmate Young Adult Club, Amarillo, Texas
The next leg of the tour is handled by Checkmate Productions out of Amarillo, run by local band leader and entrepreneur Ray Ruff who operates his own band the Checkmates and is tonight also opening another business venture with this new teen club. Ruff assures the AMARILLO TIMES that "parents are invited to come to the club anytime. We want them to know that this is the kind of place they are glad for their kids to go to". Support for tonight's show (8.30 pm until midnight) is a local Amarillo group funnily called the Page Boys. The Yardbirds arrive at Amarillo Air Terminal at 5 pm, and to whip up excitement, "a mystery Yardbird man will be at the airport and the first person to discover his identity will receive $20".

This leg of the tour is also subject to a number of cancellations and shuffling of dates as announced shows in Colorado and probably Lubbock, Texas are dropped entirely and some other dates moved around. The originally announced show for tonight, Cedar Rapids, Iowa, is evidently dropped too.

Also today, the TV-special "It's A Mod Mod World" is broadcast on WABC-TV in New York (▶ June 15).

SUN 14TH
4-H Building, State Fairgrounds, Great Falls, Montana
The luxury of having a DC-3 to ferry the band around the enormity of the States allows such far-fetched booking practices as tonight's show 1,200 miles straight north from Texas. While the original booking at the Lakeside Amusement Park in Denver this day had fallen through, the band does fly straight over the Colorado mountains, a reference which will be used in *Psycho Daisies* (the band's tribute to touring the US).

The Yardbirds fly into Great Falls about two hours before show time, and around 100 fans meet them at the airport. All the group members are fatigued after a rough flight from Amarillo, and not feeling well after a Mexican dinner the previous night! Jim McCarty vividly recalls the plane's rapid and steep ascent as quite rough on their stomachs.

One fan recalls the show as being in an old armory type building though not as crowded as he expected it would be for a famous British rock 'n' roll band who made the effort to play in remote Montana. The lasting impression standing directly in front of Jeff Beck, who along with the band is on a stage maybe three feet high, is how good they sounded – very much like their records. Jeff, dressed in his tassled leather shirt, easily impressed as the most memorable figure with his wild use of feedback and usual array of guitar tricks.

The show however comes to an abrupt halt when Jeff dramatically slings his guitar onto the stage and promptly exits heading toward the dressing room in disgust at either an equipment problem or a disagreement with Keith Relf. Relf proceeds to have scarcely concealed words with Jeff in the dressing room and Beck eventually comes around and performs the rest of the show without incident, as if nothing had happened. As Jeff himself would later admit he was prone to such tantrums on stage due to his unhappiness with the whole situation. Besides his usual abuse of his amplification equipment, there are conflicts with singer Relf too, who often finds himself in musical battle with the sheer volume of the guitar on stage, especially in this era before proper vocal monitors.

MON 15TH
Cotillion Ballroom, Wichita, Kansas
A late addition to the tour due to a few of the planned dates falling through, tonight's show in Kansas is with the Frantics as opening act – a band originally from Montana but recently transplanted to Santa Fe. The Yardbirds play two well-received shows at 8 and 10 pm for a 1,700 strong crowd, a dance sponsored by radio station KLEO and Checkmate Productions.

Jack Trice, who helped secure their last Kansas booking back in December, recalls it as a very exciting night though feeling the band had lost some of the magic he witnessed with the previous line-up nine months earlier. The group is also interviewed for a feature on the WICHITA BEACON's 'Youth Page' (August 19).

TUE 16TH
Likely a day off due to last minute shuffling of the schedule. A scheduled show in Lubbock, Texas seems not to have occurred.

WED 17TH ✳
J.P.'s Palace, Santa Fe, New Mexico
Another last minute addition to the itinerary finds the Yardbirds playing the area's premier venue, a 1,500 capacity teen club, named for owner John Philbin, who brings a number of

---

INDIANA BEACH
MONTICELLO, IND.
Friday, Aug. 12
YARDBIRDS
Show 8:15 and 10:05
Adm. $2.50
BIG TUES., THURS. and SAT. TEEN DANCES
3,000 Capacity
Parents Invited Free
NEW SUSPENSION BRIDGE & PARKING LOT OPEN

© August 12, 1966: The Beatles' final US tour begins today at the International Amphitheatre in Chicago.

August 1966: Jimmy Page fronts four-man Yardbirds when Beck becomes ill...

national acts through this area at the time. (The originally scheduled show at City Auditorium, Colorado Springs, Colorado is another casualty of itinerary shuffling.) No print sources have been located to confirm the exact date of this show but it is almost certainly today. The strain of travelling is beginning to show and Jeff has taken to abusing his equipment – mainly the amps – as the tour wears on. This date has been referred to in stories of Jeff's heavy-handed treatment of malfunctioning amps.

THU 18TH
Tulsa Assembly Center Exhibit Hall, Tulsa, Oklahoma
Tonight's show is sponsored by local radio station KELI with 1,984 attending. Keith Relf is plagued by a ravaged voice and Jim is forced to take over lead vocals and furthermore the group's Vox amps do not arrive in time for the show. A frustrated Simon Napier-Bell meanwhile, has imprisoned himself in a suite at the Hilton Hotel in Chicago, and in situations like this attempts to make arrangements for new equipment to be shipped out to wherever the group is playing as necessary. The review in the local press drily notes: "The sound was terrible, mostly because the Yardbirds lost their first-string amplification equipment on the flight here. But it was also awful because the Yardbirds' lead instrument is a harmonica."

FRI 19TH AND SAT 20TH
Wedgewood Amusement Park, Oklahoma City, Oklahoma
A return to Oklahoma City, site of the band's first US performance, finds the Yardbirds at the local amusement park, again presumably sponsored by local AM radio giant KOMA.

SUN 21ST
Thrift City on Speedway, Tucson, Arizona
The Yardbirds headline a show with the Five of Us, the Lewallen Brothers, the Showmen and the Bow Street Runners (not the English group, these Runners are an Arizona breed). The concert is sponsored by the Monterey Recreation Center and radio station KFIF and runs from 8 pm until 1 am.

This is possibly the location of the infamous and oft-repeated story where Jeff, in another fit of anger over a malfunctioning amp, literally kicks the offending piece of equipment out a window behind the stage of the club where it dangles perilously above the ground by its cord. The situation is evidently made worse due to the club's malfunctioning air-conditioning system which makes for unbearable conditions inside the sweaty, packed place. While Jeff attributes this story as having occurred in Phoenix which they evidently didn't play on this tour, nearby Tucson seems the likely locale, though Santa Fe has also been mentioned as the site of this incident.

MON 22ND
After the South and Midwest itinerary, the next leg of the tour moves on to the West Coast with a series of dates beginning in California, where Simon Napier-Bell conveniently joins back up with the group. The Yardbirds arrive in Los Angeles today where they are scheduled to tape an appearance on Dick Clark's TV show "Where The Action Is" in Hollywood, but which is another late cancellation, giving the band instead a well-deserved day's rest.

TUE 23RD
"Moonlight Cruise to Catalina"
Casino Ballroom, Avalon, Catalina Island, California
Finally back in California, Jeff reunites with Mary Hughes who comes with the group for a booking on Catalina Island on the coast off Los Angeles. This show also features the Danes, Mike Clifford, and Stanley & the Fendermen who first play for a dance on board the S.S. Catalina and then with the Yardbirds at the Casino Ballroom in the evening. In its heyday the massive dance floor situated under a spectacular Art Deco dome was the crown jewel of what was termed the ultimate resort on the West Coast during the golden era of Hollywood, and was also the site of legendary national broadcasts in the big band era.

This outing is presented by Bill Quarry's Teens 'n' Twenties and billed as their only LA appearance. All in all, reportedly a great night for the Yardbirds, who find the atmosphere reminiscent of the Eel Pie Island and which proves to be one of the tour's high spots.

WED 24TH
Today's original booking is in beautiful Monterey, California, presumably at the Monterey County Fairgrounds (site of the legendary festival held here the following June), which evidently is cancelled, allowing another off day for the band in Los Angeles.

THU 25TH
Although he had planned to have his tonsils removed upon the group's return to Britain, Jeff has been battling with throat problems since leaving England and upon arrival in San Francisco he decides his condition is serious enough to require immediate attention and decides to drop off the tour this day.

An alternate explanation offered years later by Jimmy Page to TROUSER PRESS (October 1977) is an equally interesting one: "... Beck showed me his tonsils, said he wasn't feeling well and was going to see a doctor. He left for LA where we were headed in two days time anyway. When we got there, though, we realized that whatever doctor he was claiming to see must have had his office in the Whiskey [à Go Go]. He was actually seeing his girlfriend and had just used the doctor bit as an excuse to cut out on us."

In either case, with a prestigious San Francisco debut to honour and a dozen further dates still to go, it is decided to continue on as a four-piece with Jimmy as guitarist instead of cancelling the remainder of the tour. In effect this action enforces the permanent instrument switch between Page and Dreja. With Jimmy using Jeff's Gibson guitar, the temporary four-man Yardbirds debut tonight at the Carousel Ballroom in San Francisco. Chris Dreja recalls: "It was really nerve-racking; I'd never picked up a bass before, and Jimmy wasn't really ready to roar off on lead but it worked OK."

The well-known Carousel, formerly the El Patio Ballroom, is situated on the second floor of a car dealership at the corner of Market and Van Ness. This location would later be taken over by Bill Graham in July of 1968 as the re-

September 1966: Jeff Beck recuperates in California while tour continues ...

placement site for his bookings at the Fillmore Auditorium. The Carousel would then become known as the Fillmore West.

In an era of no established national music press for rock 'n' roll in the US, short of a slew of monthly teen magazines, word of the comings and goings of personnel in the rock world was extremely slow. With this abdication, Beck re-establishes the pattern begun in Marseilles in April: a long series of concerts with disappointed fans showing up expecting to see Jeff Beck and instead being told an essentially unknown bass player will take his place. Although Page is a quick study and will usually win over the doubting crowds, there were perhaps understandably consistent reports of initial disappointment with fans during this period due to the lack of Jeff Beck's presence.

FRI 26TH
Like the previous evening, tonight's show at the Rollarena in San Leandro on the East Bay is also staged by promoter Bill Quarry as part of his Teens 'n' Twenties rock dances. On both nights the Yardbirds headline supported by local San Francisco groups Harbinger Complex, Peter Wheat & the Breadmen, and Just IV. Again Jeff Beck's stature with the fans is clearly evident as the poster promoting the two San Francisco concerts shows his name in bigger lettering than the rest of the band! Unfortunately, Jeff is not to be found onstage.

•

After Jeff's defection, the four-man Yardbirds continue to honour their August engagements on the West Coast, including a double booking just north of LA at Earl Warren Showgrounds, Santa Barbara and Ventura High School Auditorium (both August 27), but the next show in San Diego at the Convention Hall (August 28) is cancelled at 4 pm the same day without explanation (but rumoured to be due to poor ticket-sales which may have been understandable since there is confusion in the newspaper's listing as to the correct date of the show), with it being also announced as for August 29 – conflicting with a show in Pismo Beach.

MON 29TH
The British press is officially informed that Jeff Beck has undergone an emergency operation in San Francisco this past weekend and will miss the remainder of the US dates on this tour until he is fully recovered (NEW MUSICAL EXPRESS, September 2). Today is an unscheduled day off in Los Angeles, after the shuffling of the San Diego and Pismo Beach dates. The West Coast dates continue with San Jose Civic Auditorium (August 30) and possibly the rescheduled Pismo Beach (Rose Garden Ballroom) now likely on August 31.

SEPTEMBER

THU 1ST
While Jeff recuperates in LA with Mary Hughes, the Yardbirds carry on with a concert today at the Civic Auditorium in Stockton, California (originally slated for Santa Rosa). Keith Relf, interviewed on a transatlantic phone line from San Mateo today, explains to DISC AND MUSIC ECHO: "Jeff's missed about seven dates so far – but Jimmy has been doing great ... leaping all over the stage."

September 2 is an off day in San Francisco which allows Jim McCarty to take in a concert by Jefferson Airplane at the Fillmore Auditorium where he witnesses his first light show and all-around first psychedelic experience. The present tour continues with concerts at the Salem Armory-Auditorium, Salem, Oregon (September 3) and HIC Exhibition Hall, Honolulu, Hawaii (September 4). The group then returns to California for a poorly-attended concert as part of a series 'Summer At The Civic' at the Civic Auditorium in Santa Monica (September 7). Before the show the Yardbirds attend a party at the Troubadour hosted by Jordan Electronics, a company that will be the next provider of the band's amps. On this tour the Vox equipment is ultimately deemed too unreliable for the Yardbirds' purposes. The Jordan amps provide more volume and don't blow out as easily and the band will briefly endorse them. Although Beck actually is in LA, he does not appear at either the party or the concert. It can also be noted here that the Yardbirds did not play the Whiskey à Go Go at this or any time as has been suggested elsewhere.

On September 8, the four-man Yardbirds fly back to New York where for the two next days they seemingly have rescheduled most of the functions originally set at the start of this tour. Among the activities are press interviews and attending a party hosted by Epic Records, while Relf also records the vocal track to his next solo single *Shapes In My Mind*.

A one-off commercial for the corporate American food giant, General Foods' powdered milkshake concoction Great Shakes, loosely done to *Over Under Sideways Down*, is likely done in New York now, bashed out by the reduced Yardbirds at a local studio though Beck is noticeably absent from this recording.

The weekend brings two more big package show appearances; the Alexandria Roller Rink, Alexandria, Virginia (September 9) and finally the Baltimore Civic Center, Baltimore, Maryland (September 10), both without Jeff Beck and again much to the disappointment of his loyal fans in the region who had caught the Yardbirds in this area back on their previous US tour.

SAT 10TH
While the Beck-less Yardbirds perform a final US tour date in Baltimore, back in Europe, a Radio Luxembourg special from the US reportedly features the Yardbirds, likely an interview for the show "Don Moss On The American Side" broadcast at 8.30 pm today.

SUN 11TH
Keith Relf flies into London today, while the others await the expiration of their visas and spend some time in the States before leaving. A second night in Baltimore had originally been promoted for this day but was cancelled the night of the 10th due to slow ticket sales.

MON 12TH
In an effort to squash any fall-out from Jeff's absence, Napier-Bell issues a quick press release today (published in NEW MUSICAL EXPRESS, September 16) announcing that after his tonsil operation, Jeff has been released from a San Francisco hospital and is expected to record with the band next week. Furthermore the new single's A-side *Happenings Ten Years Time Ago* is already set, tentatively for September 30, and the next US tour is to run October 14 through November 27.

THU 15TH
Jeff is by now declared fully fit and flies directly from Los Angeles to Kennedy Airport in New York, where he meets up with Page, Dreja and McCarty for the flight home.

•

Around this time Jeff accepts an assignment as a regular columnist in the British magazine BEAT INSTRUMENTAL and submits his first 'Jeff Beck Column' (published in the October issue

August 29, 1966: At Candlestick Park in San Francisco, the Beatles make their last public performance ever.

September 1966: With Jeff well again, the Yardbirds tour UK with the Stones ...

on sale in the latter part of this month). Here he recalls his early years as a struggling guitarist. Jeff credits his influences as "... a combination of the rockers and Les Paul. But let's get something straight. I never copied the blokes I respected. I believe that straight copying is a great mistake".

TUE 20TH✷

The week prior to their upcoming UK tour supporting the Rolling Stones, the Yardbirds have booked studio time presumably at their usual haunt, Advision, as they have a new song they wish to record. The song is evidently a last minute inspiration and will be issued as the B-side of *Happenings Ten Years Time Ago* which is already announced. It is likely the recording of a new B-side at least contributes to the postponing of the single's release from September 30 until October 7 but even then inexplicably further delayed until October 21. *Psycho Daisies* is a light-hearted in-joke written collectively by the band expressly for Jeff to sing. The song name-drops major points on their last two American tours, mentioning stops in Pennsylvania, Michigan, Texas, Oregon, Iowa and their flight over the Colorado mountains, and last but not least Mary Hughes herself, about whom Jeff seems to take pleasure in singing.

In another strange twist of instrumentation, since this is seen as nothing more than a quickie B-side, Jimmy Page, who now is at a more proficient level of expertise and confident of his abilities, opts for the bass part, of course leaving Jeff to handle all the guitar chores. Apparently, Chris Dreja does not appear at all, making this a unique Yardbird-power-trio session; Beck, Page & McCarty!

LATE

The famed Italian director Michelangelo Antonioni is in London shooting a full length feature film about a young fashion photographer in 'Swinging London', starring David Hemmings and Vanessa Redgrave. The script calls for a group to perform in a club scene, and the director originally wants to use the Who because their auto-destructive stage shows perfectly symbolize 'Swinging London' to Antonioni. However, they are either unable or uninterested or too expensive. Actor David Hemmings had recently seen a band called Tomorrow at the Tiles club in London, and they have now been picked. (The group have just changed their name from the less hip 'In Crowd',

and includes future Yes man Steve Howe on guitar.) Tomorrow write two songs for the film *(Am I Glad To See You* and *Blowup)* and – as an indication of the suddenness of the change – have actually rehearsed on the set for a few days. As Antonioni wants to have auto-destruction as part of the script, a series of cheap hollow body guitars are ordered for Howe to smash up. Then, evidently in late September, Simon Napier-Bell has a chance encounter with Antonioni at the Scotch of St James; arranges to meet the director at London's Savoy Hotel a day or two later, and persuades him to engage the Yardbirds instead of Tomorrow, but only after Antonioni seeing them perform live.

FRI 23RD
THE YARDBIRDS: THIRD BRITISH TOUR
"Rolling Stones '66"
Royal Albert Hall, London

The Yardbirds, together with Ike & Tina Turner with the Kings of Rhythm Orchestra (including the Ikettes, Jimmy Thomas and Bobby John) with compere Long John Baldry, support the Rolling Stones on a standard two week tour of Great Britain promoted by agent Harold Davison. Also on the bill are Peter Jay & the New Jaywalkers with guitarist Terry Reid, who at one point during this tour rescues Beck's well-worn Fender Esquire guitar after a fall – without case – from the top of a heap in an equipment truck. The Yardbirds are third on the bill, and play a 15 minute set consisting of five of their most well-known hits. The opening night of the tour at London's Albert Hall today is a riotous success with 5,000 fans and many pop-celebrities in the audience, including Paul Samwell-Smith. An after-concert reception is held at London's Kensington Hotel, and the party is filmed for later broadcast on "Top Of The Pops".

As it turns out, this tour is the only chance for the British public to see Jeff Beck and Jimmy Page on dual lead guitars live as with the return of a healthy Beck to the fold, the double guitar concept is now instigated as the official line-up. Owing to the limited amount of onstage time, precious little real stretching out musically can be achieved yet. Reviewing the Yardbirds' performance on the opening night, Norrie Drummond of NEW MUSICAL EXPRESS writes: "The Yardbirds' act was an outrageous cacophony which completely drowned out Keith Relf's voice ... Perhaps if Jeff Beck cut out the gymnastics with his

SHORT BUSINESS

This Band Ain't Big Enough

It's only with hindsight that one can marvel at what a mighty group the Beck/Page-era Yardbirds could have been. Due to managerial mishaps and a general sense of chaos, this short-lived edition of the Yardbirds never got around to do more than three recordings, and only two feature the truly revolutionary concept of twin lead guitars.

Of course two guitars in a group had been utilized in pop for years, but always in a strict lead/rhythm set-up. Jeff's idea of two guitarists on lead, creating stereo effects, harmonizing and playing riffs in unison had not been attempted before. This concept predates the American West Coast sound exemplified by the Grateful Dead and Moby Grape, not to mention Wishbone Ash and middle-period Fleetwood Mac (in the UK) and the Allman Brothers' (in the US) twin guitars in the early seventies.

Only *Happenings Ten Years Time Ago* and *Stroll On* demonstrated what the Beck/Page dual lead guitars could do (their third Yardbird recording together, *Psycho Daisies*, had Jimmy on bass). The great *Happenings* contained one of Jeff's wildest psychedelic solos, but whereas that song was steeped in the sixties both sonically and lyrically, it is *Stroll On*, with its John Bonham-ish drum into and embryonic Zep-feel, which truly is a cornerstone of heavy metal. Both Page and Beck would regularly perform *Stroll On* (or rather *The Train Kept A-Rollin'* as the song was based on) in their later groups.

Besides the three Yardbirds songs with Beck/Page, this potentially awesome duo also recorded the thunderous instrumental *Beck's Bolero*, one of Jeff's perennial favourites. Powered by Jimmy Page's strong 12-stringed guitar plus the rhythm section of Keith Moon and John Paul Jones and fleshed out by Nicky Hopkins' piano, Jeff plays the quicksilvery melody before Moon goes berserk in an astonishing break leading the band into a glorious crescendo.

Unfortunately, Jeff would never collaborate long term with another guitarist after the break-up of the Yardbirds – only a few weeks with Ronnie Wood in '67 and some minimal contributions from Bob Tench in the latter-day Jeff Beck Group and then of course Jennifer Batten in 1998/1999. ■

September 21, 1966: The hitherto unknown Jimi Hendrix arrives in England with manager Chas Chandler.

October 1966: The Yardbirds participate in "Blowup" movie ...

guitar, the group might find some semblance of music!" After witnessing tonight's performance, Antonioni is convinced to forego the band he had initially chosen and opt for the Yardbirds instead. This will require a little shifting in the group's schedule as they are poised to leave on another US tour October 14. Accordingly, the Yardbirds push the tour back a week to October 20 shifting some initial dates to the end, which will allow them to be filmed the week prior to the new US start date. Once they have the official green light from Antonioni and MGM, the Yardbirds must produce a suitable song (and recording of it), ready in time for filming.

SAT 24TH
"Rolling Stones '66"
Odeon Theatre, Leeds
From today and till the end of the tour, the regular routine is two concerts each night.

SUN 25TH
"Rolling Stones '66"
Empire Theatre, Liverpool

WED 28TH
"Rolling Stones '66"
ABC Theatre, Ardwick, Manchester

THU 29TH
"Rolling Stones '66"
ABC Theatre, Stockton
Both the Yardbirds and the Rolling Stones drive the wrong way from Manchester to Stockton, with the result that both groups arrive 20 minutes late for the first house, causing a near riot. Peter Jay & the Jaywalkers and the Ike & Tina Turner Revue play additional sets to cover for the missing acts. BBC TV's "Top Of The Pops" (7.30–8.00 pm) is aired including the scenes shot at the post-Albert Hall party (► September 23).

FRI 30TH
"Rolling Stones '66"
Odeon Theatre, Glasgow, Scotland
The 'Rolling Stones '66' entourage briefly visits Scotland.

OCTOBER

SAT 1ST
"Rolling Stones '66"
City Hall, Newcastle-Upon-Tyne

SUN 2ND
"Rolling Stones '66"
Gaumont Theatre, Ipswich

MON 3RD–WED 5TH✱
With the Yardbirds cast as the pseudo group in Antonioni's new feature film, a soundtrack for their performance is needed and it is recorded early this week, at Sound Techniques studios in Chelsea, allowing enough time before filming is due to begin to ensure satisfactory tracks are available. Reportedly the Yardbirds offer five different choices including some original material and a workout of *Smokestack Lightning* which are all rejected by Antonioni who suggests their set opener *The Train Kept A-Rollin'* instead. To avoid copyright problems, the song is slightly rearranged – but the unmistakable riff is retained – and Keith Relf modifies the lyrics, first with the working title *You've Got To Stop*, then as *Stroll On*. The song features both Jeff Beck and Jimmy Page on lead guitars and captures this classic line-up on tape forever.

Also circa this time, Jeff writes and submits his second monthly 'Jeff Beck Column' in BEAT INSTRUMENTAL (November 1966) where he advises "copying is very wrong and lets you down badly when you are on stage. Audiences are very bright and can spot a phony a mile off".

THU 6TH
"Rolling Stones '66"
Odeon Theatre, Birmingham

FRI 7TH
"Rolling Stones '66"
Colston Hall, Bristol
Tonight the tour's compere, Long John Baldry, joins the Yardbirds onstage to sing an impromptu blues.

SAT 8TH
"Rolling Stones '66"
Capitol Theatre, Cardiff, Wales
The 'Rolling Stones '66' itinerary also includes a concert in Wales.

SUN 9TH
"Rolling Stones '66"
Gaumont Theatre, Southampton
Tonight is the last date of the Stones show, and the group honour everyone who has been on the tour with a bottle of Scotch. The Yardbirds receive a mere £2,300 for the tour, which split five ways amounts to £460 to each member for twelve nights of two shows (excepting the opening night), i.e. twenty pounds per performance per musician. Assuming all expenses are covered – which likely they were not – this serves to illustrate how poor the financial returns were for pop groups at this time. (Even the Rolling Stones' account for the tour shows a meager profit of £615.)

The Yardbirds, meanwhile, are plagued by persistent rumours of an imminent break-up in the wake of the Stones tour, as reported in both DISC AND MUSIC ECHO and MELODY MAKER – no doubt fueled by Beck's absence from the end of the last US tour. Relf explains to DISC: "We're not splitting – that's definite," while in MELODY MAKER (October 22), the group's spokesman hits back "... (we) keep hearing these rumours, but it's completely untrue that Keith is leaving the Yardbirds". An angry Keith adds a week later: "If they print this kind of rubbish then we are entitled to an answer and I hope we can put a stop to the rumours." Jeff Beck also causes a furor when he claims to Richard Green of RECORD MIRROR (October 15) that two girls had been paid to jump on-stage during the Rolling Stones' spot at the Royal Albert Hall. Stones manager Andrew Loog Oldham is furious and threatens to sue Simon Napier-Bell for libel, but the case is promptly forgotten.

MON 10TH
In the States, Connie DeNave Public Relations issues a press release announcing details of the Yardbirds' upcoming fourth US tour which will now run from October 20 through December 4.

TUE 11TH✱
Jeff Beck tapes an appearance on an unconfirmed British TV programme about the guitar, on which he evidently performs a solo version of his *Jeff's Boogie*. While the programme reportedly mostly features classical guitar, Beck's inclusion is both a tip of the hat to his unique talent as much as possibly a concession by the show's producers to somehow acknowledge the youth audience.

WED 12TH–FRI 14TH
The Yardbirds spend about three days at Elstree Film Studios, Borehamwood in North London, shooting their contribution to Michelangelo Antonioni's

---

Set List/The Yardbirds

Rolling Stones UK tour September/October '66

Train Kept A-Rollin' • Over Under Sideways Down • Shapes of Things • Heartful of Soul • For Your Love

---

October 7, 1966: Cream's shamelessly commercial debut single "Wrapping Paper" is issued in the UK.

October 1966: The Yardbirds start fourth US tour ...

feature thriller "Blowup". Here the director has completely reconstructed the Windsor Ricky Tick Club in the film studio for the Yardbirds' scene in the picture. The group mime to *Stroll On*, climaxing with Jeff smashing a cheap guitar against his amplifier before he puts a foot through the guitar body and then throws the guitar neck into the crowd. Although Jeff swears by solid body guitars, the guitar that is being used as a prop is in fact a hollow-body made to Steve Howe's specifications! During the filming, the Yardbirds have been put up in a hotel in the posh Knightsbridge section of London at MGM's expense to ensure that the band is all in one place for their pickup by coach each morning. Jimmy Page and Jeff Beck are also interviewed by American reporter Carol Gold for the US magazine TEEN SET (March 1967). After the final day of filming, the Yardbirds stage an impromptu concert on the set for the crew and extras.

WED 19TH

On the eve of their departure for the States, the Yardbirds pre-tape two separate performances of *Happenings Ten Years Time Ago* for BBC Television's chart show "Top Of The Pops", for possible use while the band is away on tour until early December. This is done at Lime Grove Studios, London. However the record does poorly in the charts and only one of the inserts is ultimately used, broadcast on Thursday November 17 during the single's peak in the charts.

THU 20TH
THE YARDBIRDS:
FOURTH NORTH AMERICAN TOUR

Today the Yardbirds leave for New York to begin their fourth US tour, but tellingly Simon Napier-Bell stays behind in England while a new American road manager, Henry Smith, comes on board to replace Brian Conliffe. After their arrival on TWA at 1.30 pm, the group stages their first proper New York press conference later in the afternoon at the Hotel Americana. A number of reporters from local radio and the teen press are present and the band are asked about their opinions on a variety of issues such as psychedelic music, the Beatles, Antonioni, and the mod scene in London. The five aptly describe their music as "progressive nervous tension". When asked about their musical aims, Jeff replies quite optimistically: "Basically we hope to keep playing on and on and on till we die." After the press conference, the group travels to Springfield, Massachusetts as a stop-over to their first concert date the next night.

Three independent dates precede the start of the Dick Clark Caravan tour, where again the Yardbirds will be reduced to banging out their hits in a twenty minute spot on stage each night. These three dates would in effect constitute the only three performances by the double lead guitarists where they were allowed to stretch out and realize some of the potential of this unique line-up.

FRI 21ST
The Comic Strip,
Worcester,
Massachusetts

Opening night of tour is at this small teen club in Worcester 30 miles west of Boston, where the ads warn "No slacks, please!" The Yardbirds are supported by local band the New Breed, and attendance is circa 400. Jeff is even interviewed by the local newspaper WORCESTER TELEGRAM & GAZETTE, which notes: "It seemed like a good scene [in the US] last time we were here. So we're back."

However all is not well as a very angry Jeff smashes his Jordan amp in frustration on stage mid-performance. Reviewer Ted Scourtis later writes (NEW ENGLAND SCENE, September 1968): "One of [Beck's] stacked Jordan amps was emitting static. Beck gave the amp a few shoves and when the amp didn't respond to coaxing, he rammed his guitar head first into the speaker, sending the amp flying, to land in about a hundred separate pieces. The look on [his] face was one of absolute hate!" This is maybe not so surprising when considering these transistorized amps were especially designed to avoid feedback and distortion! However it seems to set the tone for this tour, that right from the start it is obvious Jeff Beck is unhappy with the prospect of the coming six weeks on the road crisscrossing the vast American continent with no visible improvement in the performing conditions or locations since the last poorly booked US tour.

Also today the new Yardbirds single *Happenings Ten Years Time Ago* coupled with *Psycho Daisies* is finally released in Great Britain. The B-side, with its oblique reference to Mary Hughes, is a rare Jeff Beck lead vocal.

The British music press is slightly baffled; NEW MUSICAL EXPRESS (October 21) sums up: "Great Yardbirds – but what's it all about?" while MELODY MAKER (October 22) writes: "The unsubtle approach is exciting, and Jeff Beck's guitar swings along on a well constructed record." When Cat Stevens reviews the single a week later in MELODY MAKER (October 29), he opines: "Jeff Beck is a beautiful guitarist." All the same, the single fails after the group's previous British successes, and stalls at a disappointing #43 perhaps attributable to its delayed release after their British tour and to the unmistakable fact that the group is abandoning its British fans to concentrate on the American market.

SAT 22ND
Staples High School Auditorium,
Westport, Connecticut

The tour moves to this affluent commuter suburb of metropolitan New York City. That roadie Henry Smith is from this area and friendly with the local promoter no doubt accounts for this booking. The Yardbirds are supported by the Chain Reaction, a group from Yonkers, New York, featuring drummer Steve Tallarico who later

---

Single

THE YARDBIRDS
A: HAPPENINGS TEN YEARS TIME AGO *(Relf/McCarty/Beck/Page)*
B: PSYCHO DAISIES *(Relf/McCarty/Dreja/Beck/Page)*

Released Friday October 21, 1966 (UK Columbia DB 8024)
Personnel is Jeff Beck (ldgtr, rhygtr + vlcs on B), Keith Relf (vcls on A), Jimmy Page (ldgtr on A; bs on B) and Jim McCarty (drms); John Paul Jones plays bass on A
Recorded at IBC Studios, 35 Portland Place, London, July 26*, 1966 (A) and Advision Studios, New Bond Street, London, September 8*, 1966 (B).
Produced by Simon Napier-Bell
Highest Chart Position UK: #43

October 1966: The Yardbirds play the Fillmore in San Francisco ...

achieves fame when he swaps drumsticks for a microphone and adopts the stage name Steven Tyler. Tyler has vivid memories of the concert, and recalls in Stephen Davies' Aerosmith biography: "They did *The Train Kept A Rollin'* and it was just so heavy. They were just an un-fuckin'-believable band." Also present is photographer Linda Eastman who snaps pictures of tonight's show which is a single performance starting at 8.30 with tickets at $3. To make the concert on the opposite coast in California the following day, the Yardbirds fly westward early the following morning from New York.

SUN 23RD
Fillmore Auditorium, San Francisco, California

Billed as 'One Sunday Afternoon' (2 to 7 pm) and presented by promoter Bill Graham, the Yardbirds play the Fillmore supported by Country Joe & the Fish. This is perhaps the penultimate Yardbirds concert with Jeff Beck and by all accounts their performance is an impressive one in a city with a blossoming music scene of its own and a reasonably high standard of expectations for visiting performers.

In the somewhat trippy style of the day reviewer Ed Denson gives an interesting impressionistic account of the show (BERKELEY BARB, October 28): "Eleven amplifiers, eleven amplifiers, the Yardbirds have 11 amplifiers, Jesus Christ – the words seemed to spring from the air in the Fillmore last Sunday as the other groups on the afternoon show waited for the Yardbirds, the stars, and the amplifiers, and their equipment to arrive ... Standel advertises that 10 of theirs have the power to kill anyone standing in front of them ... [The Yardbirds'] first note reveals the meaning of the eleven amplifiers. The guitar has a power, a fullness of tone, a depth, that has not been often heard outside a recording studio. The sound moves out of the three amplifiers and possesses you, driving the normal impulses out of your nervous system and replacing them with music. But not a music that you've ever heard before. It has the textures and rhythms of Chicago blues, like almost all rock now, but as they play the bass player turns his body so that his instrument is facing the 27 square feet of amplifier and speakers that stand behind him, taller than he, and the feedback tones fill the room with a sound more powerful than anything before it, and touching more on what is happening, and then the lead guitarist goes into an incredible distorted run with notes and feedback blending into a beautiful new sound ... No other group has been as close to it as the Yardbirds – Beatles, Stones forget it. At the back of the hall it is too loud, muddy, much of it inaudible and the sound system has utterly failed to match the eleven amplifiers. Not a word can be heard.... I am convinced, I am converted, the Yardbirds are the best group in the world. It took a day to come down from that idea. After it was over I watched them leave, clear smiles on their faces and plane schedules on their minds, and I remembered what they had done to my favorite music, and how my mind ached with the glory of today [but] all the songs sounded the same ... They don't have the variety, or didn't choose to on stage that day. Like Butterfield they did one thing, and really well."

Perhaps in their one last great performance, a glimpse of the promise of this line-up of the band is realized this day. Greg Douglass, an aspiring guitarist who later plays with Steve Miller, also attends this show and equally impressed recalls: "It was just incredible. When I saw Jeff Beck it was like, 'Whoa, what's going on here?'" Page himself has said the dual line-up only yielded two or three successful performances and this seemed to be one of them. Despite the lack of a PA powerful enough to project an audible vocal over the wall of amplifiers, like Jeff Beck did in Los Angeles at the Hullabaloo the previous January, he and the Yardbirds as a band make a grand impression on a nascent music scene with this show. It is undeniable that the influence would seep in through local musicians in attendance. One might argue that this show and the recently recorded *Stroll On* could be considered the partial embodiment of what the band might have been, given the proper direction and opportunity.

It would be a year and a half to two years before both Beck and Page would fully realize their individual musical visions in their immediate post-Yardbirds bands (Jeff Beck Group and Led Zeppelin respectively). It was perhaps all the more frustrating for Jeff and the others to maybe glimpse the power of what the band could be, the potential of its future, and then in a matter of a few days later suffer the insult of once again being reduced to cranking out a few quick solos in a fifteen to twenty minute spot just playing the hits.

MON 24TH–WED 26TH

Following the San Francisco show, the Yardbirds fly to Los Angeles and over three days rehearse and tape a guest spot (possibly two) on the variety programme "The Milton Berle Show" at ABC Television Center in Los Angeles, where they mime to *Happenings Ten Years Time Ago*. As TV listings show the band scheduled on two separate programmes (November 11 and again on December 2 which was itself moved forward from December 9) it is not entirely certain if two separate appearances were taped or if only one was taped and bounced at the last moment from the November 11 programme and rescheduled ultimately for December 2.

During this time in LA the group also visits radio station KFWB to promote their new single, plus get time to stop in on the studio set at Columbia Pictures in Hollywood where the Monkees tape their TV show. While in LA, Jeff of course reunites once again with the fair Mary Hughes.

THU 27TH AND FRI 28TH

After their brief West Coast sojourn, the Yardbirds are booked into one of a series of Dick Clark's cross-country package tours. Designated "Caravan of Stars" Company #39, this unlikely setting for the group puts them on the same bill as Gary Lewis & the Playboys *(This Diamond Ring)*, Sam The Sham & the Pharaohs *(Wooly Bully)*, Bobby Hebb *(Sunny)*, 50s star Jimmy Clanton *(Just A Dream)* and fading teen-throb Brian Hyland (he who was *Sealed With A Kiss* and sang *Itsy Bitsy Teeny Weeny Little Polka Dot Bikini* and *Ginny Come Lately*) plus a duo called the Distant Cousins and a band the Jokers, who also function as back-up musicians for the solo acts on the tour. Lewis' Playboys include future Derek & the Dominos bassist Carl Radle, Tulsa-based guitarist Tommy Tripplehorn and drummer Jimmy Karstein. Memphis-based ex-Mar-Key Don Nix and friend of Lewis' (and future Beck producer) is also among the ranks, as is Jokers' guitarist Scotty McKay, who had already befriended the Yardbirds (and later will release a Yardbirds-inspired version of *The Train Kept A-Rollin'* as well as an obscure cover of *I Can't Make Your Way*).

The Yardbirds are the only British act on the bill. All the participants in Clark's caravan meet up in Los Angeles, and travel together by Greyhound bus heading toward Texas, a long 1,000 miles to the east and a two day bus ride away. Jeff, admittedly enamoured

October 1966: The Yardbirds' classic sound-alike hit "Psychotic Reaction" by the Count Five is in the US top 10.

October 1966: Jeff Beck walks out on the Yardbirds in Texas ...

of the sunny California lifestyle, happy to be reunited with Mary Hughes and already weary from the Yardbirds' constant travelling (not to mention his own mounting dissatisfaction within the group) certainly does not look forward to the tour and by all accounts is not a happy member of the entourage from the first moment.

The originally scheduled opening night at the Tri-State Fairgrounds Coliseum (October 28) is seemingly cancelled as everyone after the fact recalls Dallas as the opening night. No evidence of the Amarillo show actually occuring can be found.

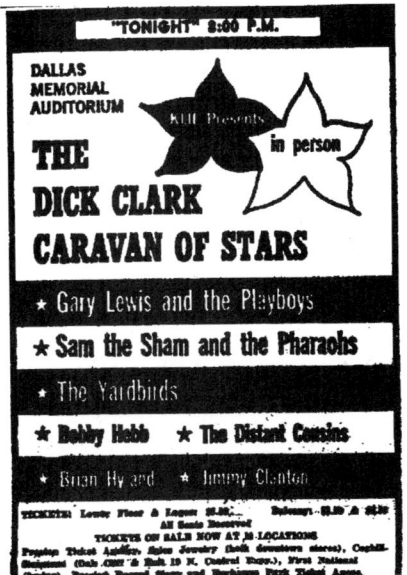

SAT 29TH
"Dick Clark's Caravan of Stars Show"
Dallas Memorial Auditorium, Dallas, Texas
Tonight is the opening date of the package tour and by one fan's account is a straight-ahead performance without incident on stage. There is only one show at 8 pm and due to the enormous distance to the show the following afternoon, the entourage presumably leaves soon afterwards without an opportunity to shower or get a proper night's sleep. But such are the typical conditions on these infamous Dick Clark bus tours. The company travels overnight the 500 or so miles to the nearly southern-most tip of Texas, in the heart of the Rio Grande Valley, very close to the Mexican border.

SUN 30TH
"Dick Clark's Caravan of Stars Show"
• **Harlingen Civic Auditorium, Harlingen, Texas**
• **Memorial Coliseum, Corpus Christi, Texas**
As best as can be determined, after an all-night slog in a crowded bus and straight to the venue, Jeff has had

RACK MY MIND

Turmoil In Texas

The exact details of Jeff's last dates with the Yardbirds have long been somewhat of a legendary "non-fact". Every time the tale is told, the story seems to change. Whether it be one month or thirty years later, each version of the story seems to contradict another. Here are some of the ways it has been told and how research can at least help narrow the often noticeable distance between fact and simple misstatement.

➤ **Jeff Beck** (BEAT INSTRUMENTAL, January 1967): "When we got to Dallas we did two spots ... and we had to hang around in between them because we weren't allowed to go back to the hotel. This meant we couldn't change, and so we played the second spot in the same sweaty clothes. It was all wrong. At the end of the second spot we were all pretty depressed; then someone said something to me which made me blow up. Hence the smashed guitar." This account, despite being written soon after the incident, misspeaks a few key facts. There was only an evening performance in Dallas, no matinee, and at best Jeff perhaps combines the Dallas show with the Harlingen show the following afternoon but nevertheless does not account for the completed evening show in Corpus Christi.

➤ **Jeff Beck** (*Beckology* CD booklet, 1991): "It was a Dick Clark tour: 600 mile a day jaunts in the bus ... I suppose it was mix and match but it was dreadful: there was no camaraderie. I stayed about two weeks. Then right in the middle of Kansas I felt like I'd die if I stayed another day." Interestingly, now the locale has become Kansas, which to add to the confusion, the tour *did* visit (on November 5 and 7). However, a published review reveals that Jeff was not present on November 2 (in Arkansas), so unless he left and briefly rejoined the tour, one would be forced to surmise that Texas and Kansas might be easily and innocently confused by a Brit. Also, it is worth noting here, a published review and an eyewitness account definitely confirm that Jeff was absolutely gone for good by November 8 (for a show in Iowa). The reference to "two weeks" is likely his referring to the start of the independent portion of the tour on October 20.

➤ **Chris Dreja** (Platt/Dreja/McCarty; THE YARDBIRDS, 1983): "Jeff walked off the tour. He did one show and quit." Dreja at best is referring to the Clark portion of the tour but his assessment of the number of shows Jeff did, seems at least two short.

➤ **Jim McCarty** (*Where The Action Is* CD booklet, 1991): "After the first night of the Clark tour, he lost his rag and smashed his guitar in the dressing room." Again a fellow Yardbird characterizes Jeff's departure as almost immediate.

➤ **Keith Relf** (*More Golden Eggs* LP, 1974): "It was over Mary [Hughes] that he left the Yardbirds ... cause we had to go back out on the road and he didn't want to leave Hollywood ... It was being on the road that got to Jeff. He didn't want to go out anymore. We stayed in Hollywood for a bit – it's a bit of a painful period to go over. It was during a Dick Clark tour, all right? – which is heavy enough anyway. We had a few days off and Jeff fell in love with Hollywood. ... We went out on the road and by the second day Jeff had had enough. So he flew back to Hollywood." Also likely a casual reference but it would place the Beck defection as the day after Dallas.

➤ **Don Nix,** (ROAD STORIES AND RECIPES, 1997) a Clark tour member, recounts that the incident occured in Brownsville, Texas (25 miles south of Harlingen) during the "first week" of the tour, where he reported that Beck stormed off stage mid-set after spitting at the audience and then locked himself in the dressing room backstage. Security had to be called to get into the room and when they finally got in, he had his prized guitar over his head ready to smash to bits. The Brownsville reference would seem to be a simple confusion with Harlingen as the latter is confirmed from the itinerary and no evidence exists of a show in the former. Accounting for the departure from LA on October 27 an abandonment on October 30 could easily be construed as during the first week.

➤ **Tommy Tripplehorn and Jimmy Karstein,** of Gary Lewis' Playboys, both recall the scene of the onstage incident as a matinee show, likely in Harlingen and both observed that Jeff was a time bomb waiting to explode that day. Their only variation is an insistence that the guitar was smashed onstage as they watched in shock from the wings, and an inkling the episode may have been slightly further into the tour.

Even allowing for a few accountable misspoken facts and a little blurring of the chronology, the sequence of events which seemingly transpired over this 24 hour period across three separate cities in Texas almost 35 years ago still does not quite exactly add up as neatly as they should. For the moment, however, an absolutely indisputable account of Jeff's final hours in the Yardbirds remains out of reach. ■

November 1966: "Happenings Ten Years Time Ago" released in the US ...

enough. Reportedly further upset by a long distance phone conversation backstage, it is a Jeff Beck near combustion point who joins the Yardbirds onstage for their matinee spot. It is now, according to some accounts of this day's complex series of events, that Jeff experiences one of his recurring equipment problems and in a repeat of previous onstage furies, smashes his amp to bits with his Les Paul, storms offstage and locks himself in the dressing room. When the band finally gets in to subdue him following their performance, he has his prized Les Paul over his head which he promptly smashes into pieces on the floor in the final act of his frustration. As Jimmy Page recalls (TROUSER PRESS, October 1977):"... in the dressing room, I walked in and Beck had his guitar up over his head, about to bring it down on Keith Relf's head. But he smashed it on the floor instead. Relf looked at him in total astonishment, and Beck said, 'Why did you make me do that?!!!'" It has been alternately and convincingly recounted by Playboys Tommy Tripplehorn and Jimmy Karstein that the onstage portion of the rampage includes the demise of the Les Paul as well.

After-the-fact, Jeff calmly explains in his regular BEAT INSTRUMENTAL column published two months later: "I have sad news to report ... I've smashed my Gibson Les Paul, and what is more, it wasn't an accident. I picked it up, swung it by the neck above my head, and smashed it on the floor. The neck came away and the pick-ups flew in two directions. Jimmy Page was horrified, but so was I when I realized what I'd done a bit later." He elaborates: "I had a reason at the time though, in fact, several reasons, and they were all good. I'm afraid it wasn't a good tour. We got the receptions OK, but the conditions were terrible. All the American groups with us on the bus played their guitars non-stop and they were always singing – can you imagine? Cooped up in a stuffy bus with everyone around you singing Beatle songs in an American accent. Then, when we stopped for meals, we were given about 1/4-hour instead of the proper time we needed. ... This starchy food was making me ill." Judging by this column, Jeff himself still considers his departure as temporary: "Now I'm hoping that we can stay on form through our long-awaited rest period."

> **TRIVIA TROVE**
> "What with an inflamed throat, inflamed brain and inflamed cock..."
> (Jeff to ROLLING STONE on why he quit The Yardbirds, 1972)

With the benefit of years of hindsight, Chris Dreja later summarizes the situation in the book he writes with Jim McCarty and John Platt: "Everything that had been going on for six months suddenly came to a head. Partly he was ill, partly he wanted to get back to LA to see Mary Hughes, and partly he hated the idea of this whole ghastly tour. ... We were faced with the decision of whether to continue the tour ourselves. It was Jimmy who persuaded us; he was still fresh and could take the strain. Also he was very professional and felt we should honour the contract." Dreja would also quite insightfully add: "I think Jeff was depressed a lot ... and emotionally he got his emotions out through his guitar and extreme amounts of semi-violence in terms of smashing up amps ... And in fact at times it was quite unpleasant because it wasn't part of the performance. It wasn't showmanship, it was just pure moody-having-a-fit! ... And that was embarrassing and stressful for everybody else to say the least!"

Assuming this scenario, the situation would have been contained enough for everybody to continue on to the 7.30 show in Corpus Christi, 125 miles up the Gulf Coast. Presumably realizing that Corpus Christi with its international airport is Jeff's gateway west, the troubled guitarist – it is now documented – in fact fulfills this further performance, implying either the use of a borrowed guitar or rather that the backstage smashing incident was somehow not until after this show. In any event, it does seem to have been decided by this evening that Jeff will exit the tour the following day. For tonight's show local rockers the Zachary Thaks are added to the bill. Indeed, this night the Yardbirds give a riveting guitar-driven performance which causes a lot of slackened jaws by local fans and aspiring musicians alike. But based on best available evidence, this sadly looks like Jeff's last show as a Yardbird.

MON 31ST
The Clark entourage travels further up the gulf coastline for two shows at the Municipal Auditorium in Beaumont, Texas with Jimmy Page taking over sole guitar duties for the duration of the tour. Jeff meanwhile is dropped off at Corpus Christi International Airport where, coincidentally, members of the Zachary Thaks (en route to Houston to record) encounter the wayward Jeff who agrees to have lunch with them, having been impressed by their set the night before. By evening Jeff is presumably back in LA back with Mary Hughes to bide his time until the dreaded tour is over.

NOVEMBER

The Clark tour carries on at Parrish Coliseum, Louisiana State University, Alexandria, Louisiana (November 1); Southern State College Field House, Magnolia, Arkansas (November 2); Decatur High School Auditorium, Decatur, Alabama (November 3).

FRI 4TH
Finally, the new single *Happenings Ten Years Time Ago* is released today in the States. Here the original British B-side is replaced with *The Nazz Are Blue* – the song title a word play on comedian Lord Buckley's nickname for Jesus – instantly making *Psycho Daisies* an obscure rarity to US fans. Incidentally, *The Nazz Are Blue* is one of the tracks left off the American *Over Under Sideways Down* album, and also

---

Set List/The Yardbirds

Dick Clark tour, Oct/Nov '66

Heart Full of Soul • Over Under Sideways Down • Shapes of Things • I'm A Man

---

Single
THE YARDBIRDS
A: HAPPENINGS TEN YEARS TIME AGO (Relf/McCarty/Beck/Page)
B: THE NAZZ ARE BLUE (Relf/McCarty/Dreja/Beck/Samwell-Smith)

Released Friday November 4, 1966 (US Epic 10094)
Personnel is Jeff Beck (ldgtr, vlcs on B), Keith Relf (vcls on A), Chris Dreja (rhygtr on B), Jimmy Page (ldgtr on A), Paul Samwell-Smith (bs on B)) and Jim McCarty (drms)
Recorded at IBC Studios, 35 Portland Place, London, July 26*,1966 (A) and at Advision Studios, New Bond Street, London, May 30–June 4, 1966. (B).
Produced by Simon Napier-Bell
Musical direction by Paul Samwell-Smith (B only)
Engineered by Roger Cameron (B)
Highest Chart Position US: #30

November 1966: After eighteen months, Jeff Beck quits the Yardbirds ...

another rare Beck vocal. It fares better than in Britain as it peaks at US #30 in the BILLBOARD charts.

The Clark tour moves on with the Yardbirds yet again minus their famous guitar-slinger in tow. Tonight's show is originally announced as at Barton Coliseum, Little Rock, Arkansas but this is evidently cancelled and presumably replaced with another at an unconfirmed location. The tour then continues on, visiting Memorial Building Auditorium, Kansas City, Kansas (November 5); Bartlesville Civic Center, Bartlesville, Oklahoma (matinee) and Tulsa Assembly Center Arena, Tulsa, Oklahoma (evening) (November 6); Chanute Auditorium, Chanute, Kansas (November 7); RKO Orpheum Theater, Davenport, Iowa (November 8); Memorial Field House, Indiana State University, Terre Haute, Indiana (November 9); Kiel Auditorium, St. Louis, Missouri (November 10).

FRI 11TH

The Yardbirds are scheduled to appear tonight on "The Milton Berle TV Show" (▶ October 24–26, 1966). Other guests are Jan Murray, Eddie Fisher, Irving Beson and acrobats(!) and the Amandia. Berle is attempting a television comeback with this programme, hoping to attract a new and younger audience since his television pioneering heyday in the 1950s.

Meanwhile, the Dick Clark tour soldiers on at Indiana Fairgrounds Coliseum, Indianapolis, Indiana (November 11); Akron Civic Theater, Akron, Ohio (matinee); Grover Center, Ohio University, Athens, Ohio (November 12); Baltimore Civic Center Arena, Baltimore, Maryland (November 13); Paintsville High School Gymnasium, Paintsville, Kentucky (November 14); Diddle Arena, University of Western Kentucky, Bowling Green, Kentucky (November 15); Memorial Gymnasium, Tennessee Technological University, Cookeville, Tennessee (November 16)

THU 17TH

Back in London, the Yardbirds are seen on tonight's "Top of The Pops" (BBC 1; 7.30-8.00 pm, ▶ October 19) as *Happenings Ten Years Time Ago* reaches its peak in the UK charts.

And in the US the Caravan of Stars is at the Field House, University of Tennessee, Martin, Tennessee tonight.

FRI 18TH

In today's edition, the NEW MUSICAL EXPRESS speculates that "Yardbirds Split Soon?" suggesting that both Jeff Beck and Jimmy Page will leave the group as soon as they return to London. The band is to re-group as Keith Relf & the Yardbirds.

Tonight's show (and the following two nights) of the Clark tour is a slight variation called 'Carnaby St. Fun Festival with Dick Clark and His Cavalcade of Mod Stars' held at Michigan State Fair Coliseum, Detroit, Michigan (2 shows daily November 18–20). This three day run also features a 'Mod Wedding' with the Velvet Underground & Nico; in a rare early concert appearance outside of their New York City base. The tour then continues on to Richmond Civic Hall, Richmond, Indiana (November 21); Pittsburgh Civic Arena, Pittsburgh, Pennsylvania (with added headliners Sonny & Cher, November 23). Tour headliners Gary Lewis & the Playboys drop out of the tour after Pittsburgh and are replaced for the remainder by Dino, Desi & Billy, taking in Raleigh County Armory, Beckley, West Virginia (matinee); Charleston Civic Center, Charleston, West Virginia (November 24, but for which the Yardbirds do not perform due to illness).

FRI 25TH

Reporting in today's NEW MUSICAL EXPRESS, New York correspondent June Harris explains: "Mental exhaustion is the reason behind the non-appearance of Jeff Beck on the current tour ... While sympathizing with Jeff's bad health, it came as no surprise to learn the news. He missed several dates on their last tour because of his throat condition and on their return to the U.S. for their current Dick Clark tour, his health seemed no more improved."

The tour plays tonight at the Memorial Coliseum, Winston-Salem, North Carolina but also without the Yardbirds due to illness. The Clark tour winds up, with the Yardbirds back among the ranks at Washington Coliseum, Washington, District of Columbia (November 26)(also with Little Anthony & the Imperials, 2 shows); and Cabell County Memorial Field House, Huntington, West Virginia (November 27). After a few days rest, the group then proceeds with a few selected independent dates in Ohio which Beck seemingly has every possibility to do.

MON 28TH

Persistent rumours of Jeff's leaving filter back to London. Confusion reigns at the home base about Jeff's whereabouts. A frustrated Napier-Bell informs MELODY MAKER: "I don't know anything. I've not heard anything. We haven't been told [Jeff] is leaving and he hasn't told us he is leaving." The four other Yardbirds cover for Jeff, as Keith Relf explains: "We've been hearing rumours too but I can assure you they are not true."

Jeff Beck himself remains in California for as long as his visa is valid. He recuperates, spends his days with Mary Hughes, relaxes and visits the clubs. While still in Los Angeles, Beck writes and submits his monthly columns for BEAT INSTRUMENTAL. In the column, Beck writes further about his dual lead guitar experiments with Jimmy Page and writes with no indication that his abandonment of the Clark tour would constitute dismissal from the band: "I got to see Barney Kessel at Shelley Manne's Mannhole ... personally speaking, I found that my technique was improving and that Jimmy and I were getting a much closer sound. We'd play separate solos and then, when we played together, we'd find that our ideas were running into each other. Each of us would play separate solos but, when one of us started a phrase the other would slide into it, so that in the end we got a sort of stereo-sound effect between the two guitars. Now I'm just hoping that we can stay on form through our long-awaited rest period."

TUE 29TH✱

Jeff Beck likely speaks with manager Simon Napier-Bell by phone prior to departure. The fact that he doesn't do any of the independent dates with the Yardbirds but rather returns directly to London, seems evidence that his fate is actually sealed at this point. With his health back and the Clark dates over it would not have been much of a stretch for him to re-join the band for the additional independent dates later this week.

WED 30TH

Jeff leaves from Los Angeles and returns to England rather than travelling to Ohio. In London, Simon Napier-Bell takes it upon himself to finally announce to the press that, yes, Beck is leaving the Yardbirds due to persistent ill health; Napier-Bell likely phones in this information as the papers go to press later this day and are on sale the next day (Thursday, though dated December 3) such that Jeff will arrive back in London with the announcement of his departure already in print!

December 1966: Tom Jones tops the UK charts for five weeks straight with "Green, Green Grass of Home".

December 1966: Jeff is awarded a 'Gold Star' in BEAT INSTRUMENTAL poll ...

DECEMBER

THU 1ST
Jeff Beck arrives back in London.

FRI 2ND
Originally slated for a transmission on December 9, the Yardbirds' second announced (although possibly only) appearance on the "Milton Berle Show" (ABC Network) is brought forward to this Friday, reportedly because of especially strong sales of the Yardbirds new single *Happenings Ten Years Time Ago* (► October 24–26, 1966). Berle's show tonight also features Liberace (!) and Dorothy Louden.

In person tonight, the Yardbirds are at the Union Ballroom, Baldwin-Wallace College, Berea, Ohio for a concert with local band the Choir, three-fourths of whom, with the addition of Eric Carmen, would later gain fame themselves as the Raspberries.

SAT 3RD
Despite Jeff's apparent falling out with the others in the group, for a time they half-expect him to come back – and vice versa. But now Jeff's leaving is at least conceded by management, as Simon Napier-Bell admits the news in a NEW MUSICAL EXPRESS story entitled "Yardbird Definitely Leaving Group". Rumours are also rife about Jimmy Page leaving too, with the band to continue with an organist.

SUN 4TH
Meanwhile, Jimmy, Jim, Chris and Keith finish the US tour with two shows at the Springbrook Gardens Teen Center in Lima, Ohio. Guitarist-cum-repairman Seymour Duncan attends this concert and disappointedly learns of Beck's absence, although he is allowed to view Jeff's Esquire for an up-close inspection.

MON 5TH
The four-man Yardbirds fly home.

TUE 6TH✸
Following their return to London, this is likely when a band meeting is called and Jeff is officially informed of the decision that the Yardbirds intend to carry on as a four-man unit without him. It is felt Jeff is clearly not physically capable to do the kind of road work the band feels necessary to maintain a career. Jeff is particularly disappointed as this means he will miss the upcoming Australian tour set for mid-January which he had been looking forward to. Despite the may-be justifiable circumstances of his dismissal, Jeff is obviously hurt and embittered by the firing and takes some time off to consider his future plans.

A press release is issued to the national music papers announcing Beck's official departure, which runs in this week's edition.

SUN 18TH
In New York today the movie "Blowup" debuts to strong reviews.

TUE 20TH
Today, Keith Relf and Paul Samwell-Smith represent the Yardbirds on the taping of the very last "Ready, Steady, Go!" fittingly retitled "Ready, Steady, Goes!", transmitted on December 23.

WED 21ST
After a strong recommendation by a female friend, Jeff goes to hear Jimi Hendrix at the club Blaises in Queen's Gate, London tonight. Hendrix, who arrived in England with ex-Animals bassist-turned-producer Chas Chandler just three months earlier, has already gained an awesome reputation as a guitarist. Fate dictates that Ron Wood and his girlfriend Krissie Findlay also are at Blaises tonight. Wood is still playing guitar with the remnants of the Birds – the very group that used to headline over the Tridents at the 100 Club – but is now looking for greener pastures.

THU 22ND
The Yardbirds' first – and fruitless – recording session without Jeff Beck is produced by Paul Samwell-Smith today but is never completed. And today's on sale edition of MELODY MAKER (dated December 24) also confirms Beck's defection, as Simon Napier-Bell further explains that "due to Jeff's ill-health on two American tours it has become obvious he is not up to intensive touring ... it was decided, reluctantly, that the Yardbirds would carry on as a four-piece, without him. We realize, of course, that Jeff has been an integral part of the group's sound".

Behind the scenes however some things move quickly on Jeff's behalf. In spite of Jeff's formal departure as a member of the Yardbirds, Napier-Bell maintains a piece of his professional relationship with Beck. Napier-Bell immediately begins negotiations of a deal with RAK Productions, headed by Mickie Most, with whom they will soon enter into an agreement whereby Beck will be signed to Mickie Most for record production purposes and Napier-Bell will co-manage Beck's affairs in conjunction with the management arm of RAK Productions headed by the formidable Peter Grant. A similar deal is negotiated in early January for the Yardbirds but with Napier-Bell selling off his entire management contract to Peter Grant with record production also going to Mickie Most. In effect Napier-Bell sells off his entire interest in the Yardbirds, leaving them contractually saddled with a record producer with whom no successful working rapport is ever achieved, effectively killing the Yardbirds' stature as an innovative recording act. On the plus side, Peter Grant will prove to be a financial boon to the Yardbirds, who will at least show profits from their touring activities until their demise 18 months later.

Allegedly, today also Ron Wood calls up Jeff to offer his services.

SUN 25TH
On Christmas day the Yardbirds head back to the States for the first time without Jeff as a member. Despite it being only a two week tour to capitalize on the Christmas holiday break, news travels extremely slowly in the teen music world at this point and people are still initially disappointed by the non-appearance of Jeff Beck at the assorted Midwest and Northeast shows the band does. But now it is a highly energized Yardbirds who accept the challenge of losing their star instrumentalist, determined with the talents of Jimmy Page to prove their continued viability as a concert attraction. Reports from shows on this tour are of a very impressive live band.

MON 26TH✸
A press release is issued and appears in the December 31 edition of NEW MUSICAL EXPRESS on sale this week confirming that Jeff Beck has signed a recording contract with independent record producer Mickie Most and that he will be jointly managed by Simon Napier-Bell and Most's management partner in RAK Productions, Peter Grant.

•

Although it's been a chaotic year and his days with the Yardbirds are ended, Jeff is voted number one in the 'Lead Guitarist' section in the annual readers' poll in BEAT INSTRUMENTAL ('1966 Gold Star Awards'), ahead of Hank Marvin (2nd – last year's winner) and Eric Clapton (3rd). The other nominees are George Harrison (4th), Steve Winwood (5th), Keith Richard (6th), Tony Hicks (7th), Steve Marriott (8th), Pete Townshend (9th) and Dave Davies (10th).

December 16, 1966: Cream's debut LP "Fresh Cream" & the Jimi Hendrix Experience's debut 45 "Hey Joe" are issued in the UK.

▶ 1967

JANUARY

As Jeff Beck later remembers it, early 1967 is a miserable time for him personally. After the whirlwind days with the Yardbirds, Jeff is essentially out of a job although he already has a contract with Mickie Most in his pocket. Furthermore, Simon Napier-Bell still considers Jeff star material despite his experiences with him in the Yardbirds. Another key figure who also gets involved is Mickie Most's partner Peter Grant, who will prove to be an efficient no-nonsense manager.

Since his return from California the previous December, Beck has had no place to live after the breakup with his wife Patricia (the couple shared a flat in Balham, London). Unexpected help comes from a road manager who used to work for the Misunderstood, who puts Jeff up in a place in London with singer Rick Brown. Brown has fronted the Misunderstood, an American band living in England, who disintegrate when most of them are deported back to the States at the end of 1966. (As a sidenote, this motley gang was heavily Yardbirds influenced, and also featured the novelty of a steel guitarist, Glenn R Campbell.) Another shock for Beck is seeing Jimi Hendrix on the London club scene, tearing up the rule book and playing flamboyant futuristic guitar.

After Christmas '66 Jeff Beck settles into a penthouse flat in the Banstead–Sutton area southwest of the capital. A typical bachelor pad on the eleventh floor, with a Union Jack for a table cloth, a Yardbirds poster on the wall and miniature car models on the mantelpiece, Jeff enjoys the relaxing surroundings outside the busy city life with his Chevrolet and his Afghan Hound. The dog is Kehm Karahn, but affectionately named Pudding, and it follows Jeff around just about everywhere.

Beck is prompted by dire finances to return to his guitar, and does a little unspecified session work, again on the recommendation of Jimmy Page. It is widely believed that it is Jeff who plays the lead guitar on *But She's Mine*, a Who-pastiche by John's Children – a group managed by Simon Napier-Bell – released in March 1967. The Children's main claim to fame is Marc Bolan, who admittedly joins after this non-hit.

Ron Wood and his mate from the Birds, bassist Kim Gardner, join up with Beck for informal jam sessions at this time, usually at Jeff's flat, with a vague idea of a musical collaboration. Jeff's ace up his sleeve is singer Rod Stewart, who he recognizes slumped in a corner one night at the Cromwellian. Already impressed by his unique voice, Jeff invites him to form a group. Stewart, the self-proclaimed 'Rod the Mod', has previously enjoyed modest success with the British soul-style revue Steam Packet and then the similarly designed Shotgun Express. The latter group makes their last appearance with Stewart on January 13.

MON 2ND
Jeff is reportedly a guest at Ian Stewart's wedding held at St Andrew's Church in Cheam, Surrey.

SUN 8TH
Mickie Most flies to New York to gather new material for his various acts.

THU 19TH
Jeff Beck and Mickie Most record their first session together at London's De Lane Lea studio. The song in question is freshly penned by the two Americans Scott English (lyrics) and Larry Weiss (music) and called *Hi-Ho Silver Lining*, which Mickie Most has picked up from a music publisher on his recent trip to New York. Without a permanent group, Jeff is accompanied by session musicians Clem Cattini and John Paul Jones on drums and bass respectively. Jones also scores a string arrangement which is then overdubbed.

Both Rod Stewart and Mickie Most sing backing vocals, while Most, who regards Beck as the commercial star attraction, persuades Jeff to sing the lead vocal himself.

TUE 24TH
Jimi Hendrix plays the Marquee. Guitarist Pete Banks in support band the Syn later recalls that Jeff Beck is in the audience.

LATE
Groping for ideas, Jeff decides to put together a quartet consisting of himself, Rod Stewart on vocals, legendary one-time Shadows bassist Terence "Jet" Harris and drummer Viv Prince (ex-the Pretty Things). Harris' credentials stretch back to the late Fifties when he backed the Most Brothers (with Mickie Most on vocals), and he also scored a huge post-Shadows hit with the instrumental *Diamonds* in February 1963 (which had Jimmy Page on guitar in one of his first studio sessions). Prince, on the other hand, is the archetypical British 'looner', known for both his off-stage antics as well as his wild drumming.

This strangely conceived 'supergroup' briefly makes the gossip column in RECORD MIRROR before breaking up after just a few try-outs in a rehearsal place on Goodge Street in London.

FRI 27TH
Today sees the release in Great Britain of an EP of four previously released Yardbirds songs. The EP is titled after their '66 hit *Over Under Sideways Down*.

SUN 29TH
Jeff, along with much of Swinging London's in-crowd (John Lennon, Paul McCartney, Eric Clapton, Jack Bruce and Steve Marriott to name a few), attends a much celebrated show at London's stately Saville Theatre on Shaftesbury Avenue to hear Jimi Hendrix and the Who.

•

Jeff uses his regular column in BEAT INSTRUMENTAL (February) this month to vent his frustrations about the Yardbirds: "As you must have heard by now, I've left the Yardbirds. I can't say I'm sorry and, in fact, now I can't think why I didn't do it sooner." He elaborates: "... there's a great deal of information which I couldn't really pass on. It concerns all sorts of things like money, ungratefulness, sheer stupidity and thoughtlessness." Jeff places the fault squarely on the others: "You see, I was never really fully accepted into the group and when things got a little rough, as they did on the last American tour, most of the moans were directed at me."

FEBRUARY

EARLY ✱
Jeff Beck does what is probably his first interview since the break-up of

Newsflash March 1967: Jeff Beck is a fiasco at Finsbury Park Astoria ...

the Yardbirds, later published in the April edition of HIT PARADER, America's hippest teen/music magazine in the pre-rock press era. Tellingly, Beck shows off the guitar which was smashed in Texas the previous autumn: "This is where the Yardbirds career ended for me." Eager to make a clean break from his past, Jeff dismisses the Yardbirds as a "pointless group", and has this to say on his plans for a new group: "... I'm prepared to work hard [and] I'm entitled to make a joke of it. If I can't make a joke of it, I don't want to do it." Jeff adds, which in view of the coming months happenings proves astonishingly correct: "There's nothing I hate more than standing on stage playing my latest disc. I hate the thing that it stands for. I want to do something more than that." The interview is written by the magazine's British correspondent Valerie Wilmer, herself an eager blues fan whose house has been a temporary home for numerous visiting American blues legends.

MID *

After the attempted Harris/Prince group breaks up, Jeff takes some time off and holidays on the Continent this month. Meanwhile Peter Grant books him on a month-long package tour of Great Britain supporting Roy Orbison and the Small Faces, to coincide with the release of his first single.

MON 20TH

The soundtrack from *Blowup* is released in the US today, with the

LEFT TO RIGHT: RAY COOK, JEFF BECK AND RON WOOD AT STUDIO 19 LONDON FACSIMILE FROM BEAT INSTRUMENTAL APRIL 1967.

Yardbirds playing *Stroll On*. Otherwise, the soundtrack features incidental music by Herbie Hancock. (The LP will be issued in the UK on April 7.)

LATE

Peter Grant tracks down Beck in Belgium, and upon his return to London, Jeff hurriedly puts together a new band with Rod Stewart. With short notice to have a band ready for the Roy Orbison tour, Beck ropes in Ron Wood and asks him to play bass, while Jeff's old pal from the Tridents, Ray Cook is installed on drums.

Ron Wood, an able guitarist, explains to MELODY MAKER at the end of February: "... I don't mind playing bass with Jeff. He's a very good blues guitarist and I expect we will be playing blues – with a difference." This new un-named quartet then rehearses at Studio 19 on Gerrard Street, London, to prepare for their live debut, less than a week away.

Lastly, this month Jeff Beck signs a solo contract with Columbia Records, the very same EMI subsidiary that he was contracted to while with the Yardbirds. For the next two years all of Jeff's records will be released on Columbia in Great Britain and on Epic Records in the United States.

•

This month marks the end of Jeff Beck's monthly contributions to BEAT INSTRUMENTAL (March 1967), and he uses the opportunity to shed some light on an exciting future: "I'll be taking the main part in a couple of group films. Don't get me wrong, they are not going to take the form of 'British Monkees' productions. They'll go out as 'B' films. They are not being made with TV in mind. From the film group I'm hoping to form a new group for live performances. I think the very best way to publicise a group is through films. We could go and do the long slog round the well-known ballrooms, being paid next-to-nothing for appearances – but that's not the way I want do to it."

However, within weeks of writing this Jeff will be back on the treadmill – playing ballrooms and probably "being paid next-to-nothing".

MARCH

FRI 3RD
Astoria Theatre, Finsbury Park, London
The barely week-old band Jeff Beck has put together make a disastrous debut on the first night of a full-scale package tour of Great Britain compered by Ray Cameron and starring the Ryan Twins, the Small Faces and headliner Roy Orbison. Sonny Childe & the TNT, the Robb Storme Group and the Settlers round out the bill as opening acts. Backstage visitors include Krissie Findlay, Kim Gardner and Rod Stewart's old friend Mickey Waller.

What may have been considered to be an easy victory by Jeff turns into a full farce as Beck's ragged and under-rehearsed performance culminates in booing during the second show when an amplifier malfunctions, reportedly sabotaged by a Small Faces roadie.

The press is unmerciful in their reviews of the show the following week. MELODY MAKER (March 11) devotes the front page to the story, writing under the headline 'Beck Leaves Tour – Disastrous Debut': "The group were obviously under-rehearsed and in the first house on opening night Jeff walked off stage when the power failed. Rod Stewart attempted to salvage what remained of the act. In the second house they played badly and created a very poor impression. It was a sad occasion and an object lesson on relying too heavily on past reputations." Chris Welch sprinkles further salt in the wound in the review inside the same issue: "Jeff Beck's new group presented a quite extraordinary performance. It was obvious they had not rehearsed sufficiently, and Jeff seemed to have difficulty even playing a good solo." Mike Ledgerwood in DISC AND MUSIC ECHO (March 11) notes how "Jeff Beck looked unhappy and sounded diabolical. It's hard to believe he is a guitarist praised to the heavens for his talent. Audience reaction to his solo debut must have more than disheartened him", while Richard Green in RECORD MIRROR (March 11) claims "Jeff Beck's act was full of sound gimmick and a stack of

---

Album
"BLOW-UP" THE ORIGINAL SOUNDTRACK ALBUM
B1 THE YARDBIRDS: STROLL ON (Relf/Beck/Page/Dreja)
[Other music written and performed by Herbie Hancock]

Released Friday April 7, 1967 (UK MGM C 8039 mono/CS 8039 stereo) and Monday February 20, 1967 (US MGM E-4447 mono/ES-4447 stereo)
Personnel is Jeff Beck (ldgtr), Keith Relf (vcls), Jimmy Page (ldgtr), Chris Dreja (bs) and Jim McCarty (drms).
Recorded at Sound Techniques, Chelsea, London, October 3-5*, 1966
Produced by the Yardbirds
Engineered by John Woods (poss.)
Highest Chart Position UK: –
Highest Chart Position US: –

Ⓒ March 1967: Steve Winwood, just out of the Spencer Davis Group, forms new group Traffic with Dave Mason, Chris Wood and Jim Capaldi.

March 1967: Mickey Waller joins Beck's group on drums ...

noise and excitement", although unkind voices say that Green was not even in the theatre for Jeff's performance.

SAT 4TH
After last night's debacle, Beck withdraws from the tour with immediate effect; tonight's concert in Exeter goes ahead without him. His place is taken by ex-Ikettes singer Pat (or P. P.) Arnold, who joins the tour on Tuesday 7.

Jeff tries to justify his actions when he explains to DISC AND MUSIC ECHO today (published March 11): "A lot of reasons contributed to me calling off the tour. All these things seemed to come to a head on the opening night. It's not worth appearing on a bill starring names such as Roy Orbison and Small Faces. Frankly, I would never tour with such artists again ... I'd rather top on a ballroom tour." True enough, as the era of the package tour draws to a close, Jeff will never again tour under such conditions.

SUN 5TH
Saville Theatre, London
Despite his catastrophic appearance at the Finsbury Park Astoria just two days earlier, Jeff is reportedly a last minute addition to tonight's 'Sunday At The Saville' show. Here he supports New Orleans rhythm and blues-singer Lee Dorsey along with up and coming psychedelic stars Pink Floyd.

MON 6TH
Badly bruised by heavy criticism and lack of rehearsals, Jeff and his group temporarily retire from live performances to sort things out.

Ray Cook is unceremoniously fired from the group and is immediately replaced by Mickey Waller, beginning a confusing period where drummers come and go. Waller is an old acquaintance of Stewart, and has previously drummed with Marty Wilde & the Wild Cats, Cyril Davies' All-Stars, Georgie Fame & the Blue Flames, Brian Auger's Trinity and Steam Packet.

TUE 7TH
Jeff Beck and group make their first live recordings for BBC Radio at the Playhouse Theatre (between 4.30–7.00 pm), London, under the direction of producer Bill Bebb. Mystery surrounds who exactly appears on this session. The BBC files credit Beck, Stewart and Wood obviously, but also Ray Cook, who already presumably is replaced by Mickey Waller. As Jeff explains to presenter Brian Matthew that he has added a couple of members, there is a chance that Ron Wood is actually on rhythm guitar – which is featured prominently on this session – plus an unknown bass player. Anyway, Jeff Beck tapes what is essentially his group's short set-list: The shuffle *Let Me Love You Baby* (actually introduced as *Let Me Have You Baby*, a Buddy Guy number); *Stone Crazy* (also by Buddy Guy, where Rod and Jeff sing a pair of verses each); Howlin' Wolf's *I Ain't Superstitious;* the new single *Hi Ho Silver Lining*, and finally the Temptations' *(I Know) I'm Losing You*. The five numbers are transmitted March 18 on "Saturday Club".

Brian Matthew asks Jeff to catch up on the story since he left the Yardbirds: "I was very, very ill, and I kept hanging them up with excuses, I'll be better, I'll be better, but there was no way I could carry on, so they had to carry on without me. So that left me without a job. And then I wanted to play again, so I got a band together, and I got a demand to do a tour with the Small Faces." Brian Matthew wants to know how long notice Jeff got? "About a week altogether ... but the musicians weren't powerful enough. So I've completely re-formed the group. I've got a couple of new members, so it sounds better now."

FRI 10TH
Hi Ho Silver Lining, which is set for release today, is delayed because of technical difficulties.

SUN 12TH
In today's SUNDAY MIRROR, a British tabloid paper, Jeff offers outspoken details to Jack Bentley on his groupie experiences: "I had to get away before I became a sex maniac." He also gives the readers some useful geographical advice: "Derby and Nottingham are good scenes. In those areas girls will follow groups within a fifty-mile radius and the message is always the same – have sex, will travel. The West Country is pretty useless, so it's a favourite to take a girl with you when going to Exeter or Plymouth." In the States, the girls are apparently even more crazed: "At a hotel in Cedar Rapids I went to my room one night and found the hotel receptionist waiting in my bed. She did not even know whose room she had gone to. As long as it was a pop musician's she did not care."

MID
Chris Welch interviews a defensive Jeff for a feature published in MELODY MAKER (March 25). Jeff explains: "I hadn't played for three months, and I was on holiday in Brussels when I got a phone call from my manager Peter Grant. He told me he had squeezed me on the Small Faces tour. As I couldn't go on and do a Donovan I had to get a group together. I just made a mistake and I feel I'm entitled to make one mistake. People who like music and know I've got Rod Stewart and Mickey Waller with me will know I have a good group now. I challenge any group to compete with us in a group battle!"

Not only that, Welch has even interviewed unfortunate drummer Ray Cook's mother(!). In the story, Mrs. Winifred Cook tells Welch: "Ray has had such a raw deal. Now he faces a very grim future with no job and a very heavy debt incurred by a new drum kit costing £400 which he was told he would need for the new group. ... I can't understand why Jeff should do this to Ray. We've known him a long time ... [and] Jeff was a friend of the family. Ray had his nineteenth birthday the day after the tour opened. What a marvellous birthday present. I don't know how or where he'll pick up again." (Cook will in fact briefly hook up with Jet Harris and then return to Sands, the Kent group he quit to play with Jeff.)

SAT 18TH
Jeff Beck is heard on BBC Light Programme's "Saturday Club", broadcast between 10.00 am and noon (▶ March 7). Funnily enough, the music press announce the booking as 'The Jeff Beck Trio'. The other main attractions on today's show are Zoot Money's Big Roll Band and the Mindbenders.

THE PAVILION WORTHING

Thursday, March 23rd

You've seen him in the YARDBIRDS — now see

The Jeff Beck Group

ADMISSION: 5/-
7.30 to 10.45 p.m.

THU 23RD
Pavilion, Worthing
By all accounts, this is the very first live appearance by Beck's restructured band, and for the first time billed properly as 'The Jeff Beck Group', with

March 1967: Single "Hi Ho Silver Lining" is released in the UK ...

Mickey Waller on drums plus Ron Wood on bass, Rod Stewart on vocals and of course Jeff himself.

FRI 24TH

Jeff's first solo single *Hi Ho Silver Lining* is released in Great Britain. *Beck's Bolero* from the spring of '66 is dusted off and put on the B-side. Strangely, RECORD MIRROR reports the B-side to be an instrumental called *Knee Jerk*, maybe a working title for the bolero, which – despite having been in the can for nearly a year – has so far not been named nor heard by the general public. The single enters the Top Thirty during April, and during a 14 week run it peaks at #14.

The critics agree on the song's commercial value, and NEW MUSICAL EXPRESS (March 25) comments "A worth-while solo-vocal debut from the ex-Yardbird. He dual-tracks in uninhibited style, belting in a harsh drawl which I think the girls will find strangely appealing ... It builds to a whistleable happy-go-lucky chorus that's a real blues-chaser", while RECORD MIRROR (March 25) declares: "I'm sure this is a hit song – and I'm pretty sure this is a hit treatment by the new solo figure on the scene."

The flip side is also reviewed; "[a] virtuoso (and noisy) guitar instrumental" attests RECORD MIRROR, while NEW MUSICAL EXPRESS points out how

AD FOR HI HO SILVER LINING IN THE STATES.

the song is "a showcase for Jeff's prowess as a guitarist. A number he wrote himself, and he certainly pulls out all the technical and psychedelic tricks." *Beck's Bolero* causes many raised eyebrows in the guitar crowd, and Jimi Hendrix for one is prompted to exclaim "Beautiful guitar!" to Keith Altham of NEW MUSICAL EXPRESS in early April. DISC AND MUSIC ECHO's 'Scene' column adds at the end of April: "Jimi Hendrix thinks Jeff Beck is Britain's best guitarist." And across the Atlantic a young Duane Allman finds "it [is] the hottest thing he has ever heard", according to his then bandmate Paul Hornsby, directly inspiring Allman to take up slide guitar.

Beck's *Hi Ho Silver Lining* causes a small controversy because of another version released simultaneously by Decca group the Attack (with guitarist David O'List, soon to join the Nice). Whereas Jeff's single is a resounding smash, the Attack's version fails. Although a sizeable hit, the song is unrepresentative of Jeff's present musical ideas. It is eventually re-released several times in Great Britain, and the sing-along nature of the song makes it a repeated hit, much to Jeff's chagrin.

SAT 25TH

DISC AND MUSIC ECHO prints two letters proving Jeff has loyal fans; Janice Palmer from Warley proclaims "What a disappointment – Jeff Beck backing out of the Orbison/Faces tour. After this shock I want to sell two tickets at the Coventry Theatre on Sunday, March 26. They are 15/– each, four rows from the front", while Valerie Johnson of Barrowford demands Jeff to "get back on the scene now!".

SUN 26TH✱

Jeff leaves London and escapes to California for a two-week break to visit Mary Hughes. He also uses the opportunity to do a bit of publicity in a couple of teen magazines, in an attempt to put right the stories that went around after his defection from the Yardbirds. Jeff furthermore buys clothes (including an expensive wolverene fur coat which he takes to wearing constantly), albums (the majority of which is Little Richard stuff) and checks out the burgeoning West Coast music scene, and one night is spent seeing Iron Butterfly at the Galaxy Club on Sunset Strip.

With Jeff's group temporarily on hold, Mickey Waller takes up another offer to join the Walker Brothers' regular backing group, the Quotations, in time for a big package tour starring the unlikely combination of pop singer Engelbert Humperdinck and Jimi Hendrix, from March 31 onwards.

APRIL

MON 3RD

Hi Ho Silver Lining is issued in the US, incidentally on the same day as the Yardbirds' first post-Beck record, *Little Games*, and the two singles are given adjacent catalogue numbers. *Hi Ho* never gets beyond the 'Bubbling Under' section in BILLBOARD, making #131 on May 20 before peaking at #123 the following week and then disappearing without setting the charts further afire. (*Little Games* fares better, peaking at #51, but will be the Yardbirds last significant chart success.)

SUN 9TH✱

Jeff returns from his brief holiday break in California in the early morning hours.

MON 10TH✱

Regrouping for rehearsals, Jeff's band now features bassist Dave Ambrose, which frees Ron Wood to play second guitar, while Rod Coombes is reportedly on drums. Ambrose is another old Stewart acquaintance from Shotgun Express. This new five-man line-up rehearse at the Granada in Kennington, gearing up for Jeff's stage return proper.

While rehearsing in Kennington this week, Keith Altham interviews Jeff for NEW MUSICAL EXPRESS's regular 'New To The Charts' column (April 15). Jeff freely admits the absurdity of the situation he finds himself in: "I'm delighted the single is in the charts,

---

Single

JEFF BECK
A: HI HO SILVER LINING (*English/Weiss*)
B: BECK'S BOLERO (*Page*)

Released Friday March 24, 1967 (UK Columbia DB 8151), Monday April 3, 1967 (US Epic 5-10157)
Personnel is Jeff Beck (ldgtr, ldvcls), Mickie Most and Rod Stewart (backing vcls), John Paul Jones (bs and string arrangements) and Clem Cattini (drms) (A); Jeff Beck (ldgtr), Jimmy Page (12 strng gtr), Nicky Hopkins (pno), John Paul Jones (bs) and Keith Moon (drms) (B).
Recorded at De Lane Lea Studios, 129 Kingsway, London, January 19, 1967 (A) and IBC Studios, Portland Place, May 16–17*, 1966 (B).
Produced by Mickie Most (A) and Jimmy Page (B)
Musical direction by John Paul Jones (A)
Engineered by Dave Siddle (prob.)(A) and Glyn Johns (B)
Highest Chart Position UK: #14
Highest Chart Position US: #123

April 1967: Rod Coombes replaces Mickey Waller on drums ---

but the singing is an embarrassment to me. It's even more of a joke when you realise I left the Yardbirds to concentrate on guitar work, and we have a really great vocalist like Rod Stewart in my group, who does nearly all the vocals on stage." In parting Jeff tells the NME readers: "We've got a great group together now and I'm hoping to be able to communicate with my own material for the very first time." According to Altham, Jeff and the group are also working on a guitar concerto to "take up one side of their first LP".

The grand idea of a 'guitar concerto' is mentioned in the press a couple of times during 1967, but it is uncertain if it is only a novelty served to the press or if indeed any serious work is being done on this. Mickie Most could certainly be capable of dreaming up something like this, but the concerto never gets beyond the drawing board.

Jeff Beck has by now secured full cooperation from Mickie Most and Peter Grant. Simon Napier-Bell however has lost all interest in Beck and instead directs his attention towards John's Children, so Grant buys out his share in their dual Beck involvment. Grant and Most have set up RAK Management in a fancy office at 155 Oxford Street, and an agreement with NEMS Enterprises to book the Jeff Beck Group is in the works. To complicate matters, Rod Stewart has a separate contract with John Rowlands and Geoff Wright, so an agreement to allow him to perform and record with Jeff is worked out, while the rest of the members are left to fend for themselves and negotiate their own salaries. Besides not being the best foundation to build team spirit, Ronnie Wood later claims he was not even on a retainer at this time but was paid per performance.

TUE 11TH
Marquee Club, London
The Jeff Beck Group, now consisting of Jeff Beck and Ron Wood on guitars,

WHERE WERE YOU

The Most of Beck

Mickie Most spent 1967 trying to consolidate Jeff Beck a position as a pop star – "the Engelbert Humperdinck of the Guitar" – while many of Jeff's contemporaries cultivated a serious image as 'album artistes' and explored the new progressive and psychedelic music scene. Jeff was certainly hand-cuffed by his producer's limited visions, but, then again, he was totally dependent on a catalyst to get his career going and Mickie Most merely followed what was considered sound advice at the time. The problem with Jeff was that although he was the de facto band leader, he neither wrote songs nor considered himself a vocalist – both essential assets if you wanted to be a pop star in the sixties. In his time with the Yardbirds Jeff brilliantly managed to combine innovative guitar playing within a commercial framework, but in 1967 he developed two parallel courses – one as a pure blues-based guitarist and another as an utterly commercial hit artist, but never again did he combine the two with such natural flair as he had in the Yardbirds.

Hi Ho Silver Lining was a charming artifact of the sixties with its super catchy chorus and slightly out of sync double-tracked guitar solo, but Jeff's two next singles didn't much improve matters: The power pop of *Tallyman* was at odds with hippydom and flower power, while the Euro-schmaltz of *Love Is Blue* was plain bewildering. In fact, fans who had followed his career since the Yardbirds could certainly accuse Jeff of having completely lost it. The goodies were tucked away on the B-sides; the fabulous *Beck's Bolero*, a rollicking *Rock My Plimsoul*, and *I've Been Drinking*, with its fuzzboxed guitar solo that stung like a bee.

Throughout 1967 the Jeff Beck Group were somewhat schizophrenic, torn between lightweight pop and heavy blues rock. A problem was the lack of a proper group image. The Jeff Beck Group failed insofar as they missed the air of mysticism that was a crucial ingredient to build the group as a brand name. On many occasions the band was simply billed as 'Jeff Beck' (but to be fair, Rod was often credited as a featured attraction), and all records between 1967 and 1969 would be credited to Jeff Beck only. He also handled all press relations and publicity. With all attention focused on Jeff, this also relegated the other band members – even a potential front man as lead vocalist Rod Stewart – to mere anonymous sidemen in the public view. Beck was thrown in at the deep end as band leader, a situation the 23-year old guitarist was ill-suited to handle, a skill which was desperately needed in a group consisting of a 'star' and his hired hands. Personnel-wise, the group was a shambles, and only Jeff and Rod survived the various permutations. Ron Wood quit and rejoined the group on two occasions, while at least six drummers passed through its ranks. Neither Tony Newman, Mickey Waller nor Ron Wood have few if any good memories of the Beck Group.

It was a pity that the talent in the group was not encouraged more. Rod Stewart and Ron Wood became a prolific songwriting team in the seventies, yet little was done to nurture them during their time with the Jeff Beck Group. And Britain's premier piano player, Nicky Hopkins, never realised his full potential with Beck.

The year 1967 left Jeff behind, while both Jimi Hendrix and Eric Clapton got a headstart on the American market and the new, adult rock audience. There were three big missed opportunities for Jeff Beck that year: Firstly, it was the "guitar concerto" which was mentioned to the press on a couple of occasions, which could have been the germ of what Jeff eventually did on *Blow By Blow*. Secondly, there was a definitive plan to record a live album, which, if properly done, should have been a classic of British blues. Thirdly, Jeff was briefly in line for the Monterey Festival on June 16–18 but nothing came of it, although it could be argued that he would have found it hard to compete with the onslaught of both the Who and Jimi Hendrix in their prime. ■

Dave Ambrose on bass, Rod Stewart on vocals and likely Rod Coombes on drums make their 'West End Premiere' at the Marquee Club. Support act is Wynder K. Frog.

Happily, the Marquee booking restores Jeff's reputation. He recounts to RECORD MIRROR shortly afterwards: "I pulled in, with the boys, 1,000 at the Marquee ... and we were able to put matters right." Ron Wood's house guest Jon Lord (the keyboard player who later finds fame with Deep Purple) attends the concert and finds this line-up more impressive than the eventual one-guitar set-up. However,

© April 1967: Jimi Hendrix causes havoc on UK package tour with Cat Stevens/Walker Brothers/Engelbert Humperdinck, often setting his guitar on fire.

April 1967: And then Aynsley Dunbar replaces Rod Coombes on drums ...

an irate fan from Sunbury complains to MELODY MAKER: "When Jeff Beck left the Yardbirds why didn't he go literally solo? ... He completely drowned out the other instrumentalists and the great Rod Stewart practically burst a blood vessel trying to make himself heard."

THU 13TH
Assembly Hall, Worthing
The ad in the Sussex newspaper bills the group as 'The Jeff Beck Sound'.

SAT 15TH
St. George's Ballroom, Hinckley
'Jeff Beck and his Group featuring Rod Stuart' reads the advertisement in the HINCKLEY TIMES.

MON 17TH
Upon hearing the news that *Hi Ho Silver Lining* has entered the charts, Beck tells DISC AND MUSIC ECHO today: "I'm delighted. This is really one in the eye for those who knocked me down."

Today also, *The Yardbirds' Greatest Hits* is issued in the United States, containing eight Beck contributions out of ten selections. The album peaks at #27, the only Yardbirds album to make BILLBOARD Top Fifty despite their many Top Twenty single entries. Eventually, it will sell 250,000 copies. Despite Beck's departure, this LP goes a long way toward solidifying his reputation in the States with the record buying public. Intentionally or not, Epic do not include a photo of the band on the cover, thereby avoiding the reality that a key member has left.

MID
Rod Coombes' short stay with the Jeff Beck Group is already up when he is replaced by Liverpudlian Aynsley Dunbar in mid-April, who will pro-

BECK, WOOD, STEWART, DUNBAR. EMI PRESS PHOTO

vide stabilization in the group for some months. Dunbar previously drummed with the Mojos and then John Mayall's Bluesbreakers (with Peter Green), where his place is briefly taken by Mickey Waller. The proficient Dunbar has already gained a reputation as one of Britain's top drummers, not least because of his live work with the Bluesbreakers. (Dunbar is also featured on the yet-to-be released monumental *A Hard Road* album by John Mayall.)

Around the same time, bassist Dave Ambrose quits to join first a short-lived group put together by Cat Stevens (which funnily enough again sees Mickey Waller behind the drums!) before moving on to the revised Brian Auger's Trinity with Julie Driscoll. With Ambrose gone, Ronnie Wood switches back to bass guitar, returning the group to a quartet.

In an interview with Peter Jones of RECORD MIRROR (April 29, 1967) conducted at this time, Jeff describes Dunbar as "fantastic. He has this strange technique. It's like the rhythm of the chain-gang workers in the deep Southern States in America. That sort of thing. Could be very good". Jeff also explains his musical policy: "I never do anything twice as far as my guitar playing goes, so I'm sure it'll be the same for my singing. ... But the point is this: *Hi Ho* was aimed at the people who don't know me. It's different from the stuff I've done before – it's just a commercial record."

FRI 21ST
Market Hall, St. Albans
This performance, besides being Aynsley Dunbar's presumed first show with the Jeff Beck Group, marks a return to regular one-nighters for Beck, although his touring schedules will not be as punishing as in the days of the Yardbirds.

SAT 22ND
Westbrook Hall, Bradford Technical College, Bradford
A Student Union dance.

SUN 23RD
Beachcomber Club, Nottingham

MON 24TH
Jeff signs a long-term agency deal with NEMS Enterprise today, the company founded by Beatles manager Brian Epstein. The following day, NEMS duly informs the BBC that the company is appointed by Beck as his regular booking agent.

TUE 25TH
Winter Gardens, Malvern
The Malvern show is a big success. Jeff explains to MELODY MAKER a few days later: "We played at Malvern recently and there were magnificent scenes. The kids went berserk."

THU 27TH
Jeff appears on BBC Television's weekly "Top Of The Pops" (7.30–8.00 pm) to mime *Hi Ho Silver Lining*, videotaped at BBC Television Centre in Lime Grove, London. Other acts on tonight are the Who (plugging *Pictures of Lily*), Lulu, the Warm Sounds, Sandie Shaw and Tom Jones. Jeff is also interviewed by the Dutch pop paper MUZIEK EXPRES today (July '67).

FRI 28TH
Upper Cut Club, Forest Gate, London
Jeff returns to London for tonight's engagement (8.0–11.45 pm) at this popular nightclub owned by British champion boxer Billy Walker. (A recent attraction here has been Jimi Hendrix.) Support act is the Warren Davis Monday Band.

SAT 29TH
Royal Links Pavilion, Cromer
Billed as 'The Greatest Guitarist in this Country' no less, Jeff Beck headlines a ballroom date in Norfolk, with the

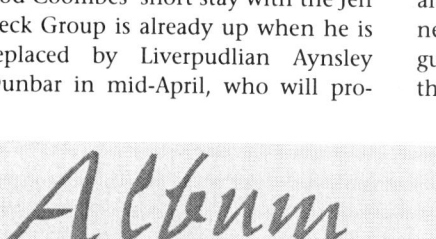

THE YARDBIRDS
THE YARDBIRDS' GREATEST HITS
A1 SHAPES OF THINGS (Samwell-Smith/Relf/McCarty) **A2** STILL I'M SAD (Samwell-Smith/McCarty) **A3** NEW YORK CITY BLUES (Relf/Dreja) **A4** FOR YOUR LOVE (Gouldman) **A5** OVER UNDER SIDEWAYS DOWN (Dreja/McCarty/Relf/Beck/Samwell-Smith)

B1 I'M A MAN (McDaniels) **B2** HAPPENINGS TEN YEARS TIME AGO (Relf/McCarty/Beck/Page) **B3** HEART FULL OF SOUL (Gouldman) **B4** SMOKESTACK LIGHTNING (C. Burnett) **B5** I'M NOT TALKING (M. Allison)

Released Monday April 17, 1967 (US Epic LN 24246 mono/BN 26246 stereo)
Personnel is Jeff Beck (ldgtr except Eric Clapton: ldgtr on A4, B4) + others
Highest Chart Position US: #27

April 13, 1967: The Rolling Stones play behind the Iron Curtain in Warsaw, Poland.

May 1967: Jeff Beck slated to appear at "NME Poll Winners Concert" ...

Marmalade and local group the Feel For Soul. The night ends in a big bloodstained brawl after a fight breaks out in the audience.

MAY

MON 1ST ✱
Still struggling to comprehend the logic behind *Hi Ho Silver Lining,* Jeff explains to MELODY MAKER for a feature published at the end of the week (May 6): "Mickie Most will kill me for saying this, but although the song is good, it isn't worthy of being a number one. It's just not me – and I'd rather *Bolero* was at number one." Otherwise, Jeff is very pleased with the present situation: "We've got a knockout group now, and we are going down tremendously well. ... We've got enough numbers off for an hour and we do two half-hours."

On the subject of *Hi Ho Silver Lining,* Jeff enlarges to DISC AND MUSIC ECHO (May 20): "First, I don't like the song. It was made before I got my present group together, and is nothing like our stage act. In fact, I get very embarrassed when I have to play *Hi Ho* on stage, and tend to try to ignore it." Of his new group's stage act, Jeff says: "People may get fed up with looking at us on stage. We just smile and play. We wear what we like, and don't burn our guitars or smash up our drums."

TUE 2ND
Jeff Beck does an on-the-air interview for BBC Light's "Pop Inn" radio show (1.00–2.00 pm) today, transmitted from the Paris Cinema.

Afterwards, Beck, Wood and Stewart (without Dunbar) go to nearby St. James Park for a photo session with Mike James to be published in the US magazine TEEN SET. Despite the summery weather, Jeff is dressed in his beloved fur coat. Carol Gold, who writes the piece for TEEN SET, has dinner at Jeff's flat afterwards.

THU 4TH
Jeff Beck and photographer Nicholas Wright visit manager Kenneth Pitt, in an attempt to interest Pitt in Beck as a professional model. This odd change of course proves short-lived, and as it turns out Pitt – who at the time also manages David Bowie – is not interested anyway. All the same, some of the pictures taken by Wright are used for publicity purposes in the following months.

Jeff then spends the evening at the Finsbury Park Astoria, seeing the Beach Boys on their second UK visit.

SAT 6TH
Public Hall, Heacham near Hunstanton

SUN 7TH
• **"NME Poll Winners Concert", Empire Pool, Wembley**
• **Starlite Ballroom, Greenford**

With *Hi Ho Silver Lining* nesting at #17 in the NEW MUSICAL EXPRESS' singles charts this week, Jeff Beck is a late addition to this annual celebration of pop music, which attracts 10,000 fans to the Empire Pool. Among the many names taking part are the Beach Boys, Cream, Spencer Davis Group, Georgie Fame, Paul Jones, Lulu, the Move, the Small Faces, Dusty Springfield, Cat Stevens, the Troggs and Steve Winwood (who recently left Spencer Davis and has yet to unveil Traffic. Winwood chooses to do one number alone with a piano.) However, it is unclear if Jeff indeed does appear on the show despite the pre-press announcements; he is not mentioned in the review of the show, and NEW MUSICAL EXPRESS's 'Tailpieces' column reports rather cryptically that it was "impossible to meet Jeff Beck's demands" backstage at the Poll Concert.

Jeff Beck is also booked to appear at the Starlite in Greenford with support act Sean Buckley.

MON 8TH
The Carlo Ponti production "Blowup" is premiered in Cannes, France at the annual film festival today. The Yardbirds, but not Jeff Beck, are in Cannes to attend the gala. The film has a short sequence with the group miming *Stroll On* and Jeff thrashing a guitar, but it attracts more attention for a few seconds showing a girl in the nude.

The film goes on general release on the ABC circuit in Great Britain on Sunday May 14.

TUE 9TH
Beachcomber Club, Nottingham

The Jeff Beck Group intensify their gigging schedule, as they commence a string of club and ballroom dates around Great Britain in May. Tonight they are billed as 'Jeff Beck plus the Rod Stewart Show', and the Beachcomber also tempts patrons with a special raffle for tickets to the Monkees' upcoming London concerts.

WED 10TH
The Jeff Beck Group spend the afternoon at BBC's Television Theatre in Shepherds Bush, London, videotaping a "Top Of The Pops" appearance for transmission the following night, which ultimately is rejected for reasons unknown. Besides chatting with Jimi Hendrix and Noel Redding, who are also on the set, Jeff is interviewed by Keith Altham.

TRIVIA TROVE: Jeff collects children's books and his particular favorite is "Thomas The Tank Engine." (Jeff in NME, May 1967)

Altham begins the feature in NEW MUSICAL EXPRESS (May 27) thus: "Jeff Beck gets a somewhat perverse satisfaction from having a 'wicked' reputation in the pop business. At his best, he is a talented, guitar-perfectionist with a pleasant, conversational manner", before continuing almost prophetically: "At his worst, he's an obstinate, uncompromising character who avoids doing things he dislikes by the simple expedient of walking out on them" – words that still ring true more than thirty years later. Altham then uses Beck's clothes (a £400 fur coat, a pair of faded jeans and a pair of basketball boots from Marks and Spencers) as an analogy to describe the contradictory nature of Jeff Beck.

Of his current position as a hit maker, Jeff himself has this to say: "... *Hi Ho Silver Lining* may be a bum record for Jeff Beck, but it's been good in other ways. It's in direct opposition to all that publicity I got about being a fantastic guitarist only concerned with my music. I don't want to be put in one bag or labelled." On Jimi Hendrix, he observes with clever insight: "Look at Hendrix! Isn't he a card? He's the governor. Jimi's only trouble will come about when he wants to get off the nail he has hung himself on. The public will want something different, and Jimi has so established himself in one bag that he'll find it difficult to get anyone to accept him in another."

Jeff also reveals that he hopes to visit the Monterey Pop Festival in California in June. Another personal ambition is – of all things – to appear in "smutty 'B' films!". Neither idea is realised.

THU 11TH
Yesterday's insert for tonight's "Top Of The Pops" is not aired after all.

FRI 12TH
"Two Day Light Show"
Roundhouse, Chalk Farm, London

Originally booked for an appearance in High Wycombe, which is presum-

May 1967: A live album by the Jeff Beck Group is rumoured ...

> **ROUNDHOUSE**
> CHALK FARM ROAD, N.W.1
> **TWO-DAY LIGHT SHOW**
> THIS FRIDAY, 12th MAY, 9 p.m.—2 a.m.
> **JEFF BECK GROUP**
> THIS SATURDAY, 13th MAY, 9 p.m.—2 a.m.
> **SIMON DUPREE**
> AND THE BIG SOUND
> Supporting Groups on both nights.
> WINSTONS FUMBS & THE SAM
> GOPAL INDIAN BLEND.
> 10/- at door. Late licensed bar

ably cancelled to allow Jeff instead to appear at the Roundhouse tonight for a late night show (9 pm–2 am), supported by Winston Fumbs and the Sam Gopal Indian Blend.

SAT 13TH
Drill Hall, Kingston-upon-Thames

MON 15TH
Blue Opera Club, Feathers Hotel, Ealing
Before playing Ealing in the evening, the Jeff Beck Group appear live today on the BBC Light pop show "Monday, Monday" (1.00–1.50 pm), transmitted from the Playhouse Theatre on Northumberland Avenue. The show is as usual presented by Dave Cash, and also appearing are Guy Darrell, the Gibsons and Mike Mercado, 'The Singing Monk'! A sound check is held earlier in the day. Three selections are featured; *Let Me Love You*, *All Night Long* and *Hi Ho Silver Lining*. The intriguingly named *All Night Long* is highly likely just the first recorded version of what will become the group's anthem, *Rock My Plimsoul*.

TUE 16TH
Chinese R & B Club, Corn Exchange, Bristol
Rod is again billed as 'Rod Stuart' in the local press.

WED 17TH
Jeff Beck flies alone to Holland to make an appearance on the Dutch TV show "Moef-Ga-Ga" to be transmitted on Saturday May 20. Jeff mimes *Hi Ho Silver Lining* from AVRO-TV's Studio A in Hilversum, and is also briefly interviewed for a feature published in the Dutch pop paper HITWEEK (May 27).

THU 18TH
Still plugging *Hi Ho Silver Lining*, Jeff Beck appears on BBC Television's weekly "Top Of The Pops" (7.30–8.00 pm) today, transmitted live from BBC's Lime Grove studios. Jeff is helped out by the resident 'Top Of The Pops' Orchestra' and even three female vocalists; Gloria George, Barbara Moore and Margaret Stredder.

Mickie Most, the faithful dog Pudding plus an unnamed female American publicist are also in tow. For the occasion BEAT INSTRUMENTAL is on hand to do a feature on Beck (published June 1967), talking about his choice of guitars and amplifiers.

FRI 19TH
Victoria Hall, Selkirk, Scotland
The Jeff Beck Group's first trip out of England, albeit only to Scotland, is billed as 'Border Dancing' with local band the Galvanters opening.

SAT 20TH
Market Assembly Hall, Carlisle
Today, too, *Hi Ho Silver Lining* is on Dutch TV "Moef-Ga-Ga" (▶ May 17).

TUE 23RD
Jeff Beck is filmed today for an interview on BBC 2 TV's "Man Alive", a newly introduced weekly documentary programme which focuses on people and the situations which shape their lives. Jeff appears in a programme about groupies (subtitled 'The Ravers') which is transmitted on June 28. The insert is filmed at the RAK offices on Oxford Street.

THU 25TH
University of Liverpool, Liverpool

SAT 27TH
Shoreline Club, Bognor Regis
NEW MUSICAL EXPRESS reports today: "Jeff Beck's first solo LP is likely to be recorded live before an audience of about 250 of his fans. His recording manager Mickie Most is currently looking for a suitable venue for the session. The album, complete with audience reaction, is being planned for late summer release by Columbia." This potential Great Lost Live Album of course never sees the light of day, and was probably not recorded.

•

A dozen or so songs make up Jeff's stage act in the summer of 1967, these being: A funky Elmore James shuffle called *Talk To Me Baby* (aka *I Can't Hold Out* or *Telephone Blues*); Albert King's Stax hit from the previous year, *Oh Pretty Woman*; two Buddy Guy numbers – the slow *Stone Crazy* and the fast *Let Me Love You, Baby*; B. B. King's *Sweet Little Angel* (also recorded by Earl Hooker, King cut the original in 1956 but Jeff likely got his version from B. B.'s classic 1965 album *Live At The Regal*); Jeff and Rod's adaption of another B. B. King song – *Rock Me, Baby* – as the perennial favourite *Rock My Plimsoul*; Howlin' Wolf's menacing *I Ain't Superstitious* (written by Willie Dixon); and two blues songs of obscure origin, a tough shuffle called *Bye, Bye, Baby, Bye, Bye*; and a slow blues known as *I Think I'll Be Leaving This Morning* or plain *This Morning* (an early ancestor of *Blues de Luxe*).

However, the Jeff Beck Group were not on a strict blues diet, as they also did the old Drifters' single *Some Kinda Wonderful* (written by Gerry Goffin and Carole King and a US #32 in 1961); the Four Tops' *Loving You Is Sweeter Than Ever* (a fair-sized US hit co-penned by Stevie Wonder that fared better in the UK than the US with a #21 placing in September 1966); the Temptations' *(I Know I'm) Losing You* (a Tamla Top Ten Stateside and a UK Top Twenty in January this year) and Jimmy Hughes' powerful *Neighbour, Neighbour* (a minor US pop/R&B hit from June '66). And of course Jeff does *Hi Ho Silver Lining*. Oddly enough, *Beck's Bolero* seems not to be part of the set list yet, possibly because it was hard to recreate Jimmy Page's crucial rhythm guitar part in an instrumental trio format. Only *Jeff's Boogie* is retained from the Yardbirds' repertoire, although the group will of course later revive *Shapes Of Things*.

Many of these songs remain staples of the live set until the group's demise in 1969. The soul covers are left out by 1968, and *Oh Pretty Woman* is also dropped along the line, maybe because John Mayall's Bluesbreakers (with Mick Taylor) release a popular version of the song later in the year.

SUN 28TH
The Tabernacle, Stockport

WED 31ST
Orford Cellar, Norwich

> **Set List/Jeff Beck Group**
>
> *British club and ballroom dates; summer 1967*
>
> Talk To Me Baby • Oh Pretty Woman • Stone Crazy • Let Me Love You, Baby • Sweet Little Angel • Rock My Plimsoul • I Ain't Superstitious • Bye, Bye, Baby, Bye, Bye • This Morning • Some Kinda Wonderful • (I Know I'm) Losing You • Loving You Is Sweeter Than Ever • Neighbour, Neighbour • Jeff's Boogie • Hi Ho Silver Lining • Tallyman

July 1967: Jeff Beck, John Mayall and Cream at Saville Theatre ...

JUNE

EARLY *
The Jeff Beck Group record at De Lane Lea Studios in London with Mickie Most producing. The group commits two songs to tape for an upcoming single; a brand new Graham Gouldman composition called *Tallyman*, plus Jeff and Rod's re-arrangement of B.B. King's *Rock Me Baby* as *Rock My Plimsoul*. The latter is credited to 'Jeffrey Rod' and published by Enquiry Music, a company that will have publishing rights to all original songs by the Jeff Beck Group over the next two years.

THU 1ST
Jeff and singer Lulu (another of Mickie Most's signings) are among the pop celebrities to attend a London reception for visiting American group the Turtles.

FRI 2ND
Civic Hall, Solihull
A big presentation in Solihull tonight has Jeff Beck appearing with the Barron Knights, Wayne Fontana, the Monopoly, Diane Ferraz & the Checkmates and the Exception plus disc jockey Doc Holliday.

SAT 3RD
Burton's Ballroom, Uxbridge
In a roundup in DISC AND MUSIC ECHO under the headline 'Was it worth the long wait or should we just take *Sgt Pepper* with a pinch of salt?', some of the top names in the pop business are asked about their impressions of the brand new Beatles album. Just about all (Pete Townshend, Eric Burdon, Mike Leander, Chris Denning, Simon Dee, Ray Davies, and the Tremeloes' Alan Blakely) are unanimous in their praise, while Jeff has the only dissident opinion: "I haven't heard the record and have no intention of doing so. It's not my type of music at all, so I'm not interested."

Jeff also gets to review *Tallyman* in RAVE's (July 1967) 'Whether Chart': "It's basically a hit song, but after the last one, I don't know what it'll do. That was pretty bad record. It was like giving someone a lousy car to win a race with – well I got a lousy song to prove myself with."

SUN 4TH *
Jeff Beck, Pete Townshend and John's Children are among the guests at visiting US singer Mitch Ryder's farewell party in London.

TUE 6TH
Marquee Club, London
Supported by the Nite People, Jeff and his group make a return to the Marquee.

WED 7TH
Caravelle Club, Birmingham Airport Viewing Lounge, Birmingham

WED 14TH
Floral Hall, Gorleston
The Floral Hall has the previous week promoted the Attack, and will also stage concerts by the Bee Gees and Cream later in the month.

Rod Stewart is again given separate billing in the local ad. St. Willie Cool School is the opening act.

FRI 16TH
Hexagon Restaurant, Colchester
The full bill for the the University of Essex's 'Grand Going Down Ball' (held at the Hexagon which is decked out to look like Hell) are the Nashville Teens, the Sound, the Truncles, the Jeff Beck Group and the Attack. So perhaps the public got to hear *Hi Ho Silver Lining* played twice tonight!

SAT 17TH
Palace Theatre, Douglas, Isle of Man
Isle of Man, in the Irish Sea, is as close as the Jeff Beck Group will ever get to Ireland. Also appearing tonight – and indeed for the whole week – is Sounds Incorporated, but now with a new drummer instead of the experienced Tony Newman, who has recently been standing in for an ill Bobby Elliot in the Hollies.

MON 19TH
Cook's Ferry Inn, Edmonton

SUN 25TH
Midnight City, Birmingham

WED 28TH
"Even the women who wept when Valentino died might find it hard to grasp what it means to be a raver. Today the girls who follow the pop groups start young – and once started there is no stopping them. They come from every kind of background. The only things they share in common are their youth and their idols ... a world where the social pattern their parents thought entirely natural has been turned on its head and the girls have become the hunters, the boys the hunted" runs the blurb in RADIO TIMES about today's BBC 2 TV show "Man Alive" (8.05–8.35 pm), where Jeff appears in an interview sequence to give his views on the groupie scene (► May 23), certainly a follow-up to his frisky comments to the SUNDAY MIRROR in March.

JULY

SAT 1ST
The Pier, Colwyn Bay, Wales

```
SAVILLE
TEM 4011
BRIAN EPSTEIN PRESENTS
THIS SUNDAY, 2nd JULY
6.00 & 8.30 p.m.
CREAM
JEFF BECK GROUP
JOHN MAYALL'S
BLUESBREAKERS
Resident Compere: RICK DANE
Tickets 20/-, 15/-, 10/-, 6/-
```

SUN 2ND
The Saville Theatre, London
Brian Epstein presents Cream supported by the Jeff Beck Group, John Mayall's Bluesbreakers and Jimmy Powell & the Dimensions in two performances (at 6.00 and 8.30 pm) as part of the weekly 'Sunday At The Saville' series. For the occasion Jeff, dressed in hat and fur coat, plays without shoes. On a couple of songs Jeff uses Ron's electric twelve-string guitar tuned down a whole step to create a particularly big sound.

The four groups on the bill are incestuously related; both Eric Clapton and Jack Bruce of Cream have been apprentices of John Mayall's Bluesbreakers, and so has Jeff's drummer Aynsley Dunbar. Mayall's drummer now, Keef Hartley, used to play with Ron Wood's brother Art. Rod Stewart was once the harmonica player in Jimmy Powell's band, while of course both Jeff and Eric were guitarists in the Yardbirds at one time.

The reviews of the show spend their paragraphs on Cream, but Penny Valentine in DISC AND MUSIC ECHO (July 8) notes: "A bit more togetherness would have helped Jeff Beck. Playing a lot better than he ever did with the Yardbirds, in his green floppy hat and fur coat with a nice drummer. But the rest of the group ought to organise themselves and realise that an audience is worthy of more professionalism." Nick Jones in MELODY MAKER (July 8) dismisses the Beck

July 1967: Single "Tallyman" released in the UK ...

group as "... also playing yesterday's blues only a bit louder and with even less finesse than the grand Mayall". Jones' sums up Cream's encore number as "... *I'm So Glad* freaking into a four guitar feedback finale", which indicates that all the guitarists on the bill (Clapton, Beck, Mick Taylor plus perhaps Jimmy Powell's guitarist) appear on stage for a closing jam.

Afterwards, Jeff goes to the Speakeasy on Margaret Street. This club, which opened in January, has quickly become the place where musicians hang out and socialize. Tonight is a big night out, because also present at the Speakeasy (where the Toys perform, before heading for oblivion) are Mike Nesmith and Mickey Dolenz of the Monkees, George Harrison, Lulu, Spencer Davis, Pete Townshend (who also was in the audience for the Saville show) and Keith Moon.

MON 3RD

England is in the throes of 'Monkee-mania', and impressario Vic Lewis throws a big celebration party for the Monkees at the Speakeasy after their wildly successful three sold out appearances at the Wembley Stadium. The impressive guest list includes Paul McCartney, George and Patti Harrison, John Lennon, Lulu, Eric Clapton, Dusty Springfield, members of Procol Harum, Mickey Dolenz and Peter Tork from the Monkees – plus Jeff.

TUE 4TH

The Jeff Beck Group record a session at BBC's Playhouse Theatre with producer Bill Bebb to be broadcast on "Saturday Club" on July 8. Faithful renditions of *Tallyman* and *Rock My Plimsoul* are put on tape, along with the otherwise unreleased *This Morning*, largely a vehicle for Jeff's blues guitar before Rod Stewart comes in for a few lines at the very end. For this session, the group is paid £30.

FRI 7TH
Skyline Ballroom, Hull

Besides tonight's appearance in Hull, Yorkshire, Jeff's new single *Tallyman* is released today in Great Britain to fine reviews. On *Tallyman*, Jeff and Rod sing two-part harmony, with Jeff on a powerful slide guitar break. The flip side *Rock My Plimsoul* has a three chorus solo and also features a nice effect where Jeff plays behind the nut of the guitar. RECORD MIRROR finds *Tallyman* "... a beat opus dedicated to the debt-collecting gentry. Excellent guitar moments and the voice comes through well, too. Very exciting, I thought, mid-way especially"; in DISC AND MUSIC ECHO, Penny Valentine enthuses "I like this! I didn't like *Hi Ho* one bit and this is so much better sung, recorded and produced that it must do well. Jeff's guitar does high pitched moans and it's a record that makes you listen right from the opening. Nice."; the headline in NEW MUSICAL EXPRESS simply reads "Better Beck!", while Chris Welch in MELODY MAKER praises "Jeff's guitar is sounding more 'human' every day". In the same issue Graham Nash of the Hollies is a guest in the paper's 'Blind Date' column and thinks "... it gets pretty good as it goes on. [Jeff] hasn't got the ability to sing, but he's getting there. I just wish he'd stop spending so much time commiserating himself and get down to some really hard work. That's what he needs man." (All reviews dated July 15.)

The single is again credited to just 'Jeff Beck', even though the whole group plays on both selections. The record peaks at a disappointing #30 during a three-week stay in the British charts during August.

SAT 8TH
Supreme Ballroom, Ramsgate

Jeff Beck is on the BBC Light Programme's "Saturday Club" (▶July 4) this morning, promoting the new single *Tallyman*. Other guests on the show are Pinkerton's Colours and Kenny Ball's Jazzmen.

At night, the Jeff Beck Group play at the seaside resort Ramsgate on England's east coast.

SUN 9TH
Starlite Ballroom, Greenford

FRI 14TH

Jeff Beck is at the BBC to do two interviews today for BBC Transcription Service (later BBC Worldwide). At 11.30 am he is at Studio S2, at BBC Broadcasting House to be used in the overseas programme "Top Of The Pops" (no. 141). Not to be confused with the popular television show of the same name, this is a different, specially made programme for BBC's overseas subscribers, and will usually feature previously recorded BBC live music sessions linked together with these specially made interviews. (Programme no. 141 is set for the week of August 11, 1967.) Afterwards Beck does an interview for the Transcription Series' "The Young Scene" (no. 13), recorded at BBC's Bush House studio.

SAT 15TH
"Summer Rave"
Town Hall, Torquay

Another coastal resort, another summer show, with the Jeff Beck Group supported by the Sabres and the Insexts.

•

About mid-July, Aynsley Dunbar forms his own group, the Retaliation, announcing his imminent departure from the Jeff Beck Group. However, he will fulfill outstanding engagements until August.

SUN 16TH

Jeff Beck, John Walker and Mickie Most all make personal appearances – but do not perform – at Ipswich Stadium, Foxall Heath, Ipswich, Suffolk, today as part of a Radio London sponsored two-day fair.

SAT 22ND
Starlight Room, Gliderdrome, Boston

Supporting the Beck Group tonight are the Equals (a group led by Eddy Grant), Motown Trinity and Ray Bones.

Also today, reader John Secombe of Slough ponders in DISC AND MUSIC ECHO's 'Pop The Question' column: "Is Jeff Beck releasing an LP soon?" "No plans for an album at the moment" is the reply, so obviously the proposed live album has been buried.

SUN 23RD
Blenheim Park, Woodstock

Manfred Mann plus the Jeff Beck Group, P. P. Arnold & 'her' Nice and Simon Dupree & the Big Sound all appear at this special Sunday concert by Blenheim Palace in Oxfordshire, once the home of Winston Churchill. The

Single
JEFF BECK
A: TALLYMAN (Gouldman)
B: ROCK MY PLIMSOUL (Jeffrey Rod)

Released Friday July 7, 1967 (UK Columbia DB 8227) and Monday August 14, 1967 (US Epic 10218)
Personnel is Jeff Beck (ldgtr, ldvcls on A), Rod Stewart (vcls on B), Ronnie Wood (bs) and Aynsley Dunbar (drms)
Recorded at De Lane Lea Studios, 129 Kingsway, London, London, May/June 1967.
Produced by Mickie Most
Engineered by Dave Siddle (prob.)
Highest Chart Position UK: #30
Highest Chart Position US: –

August 1967: Jeff Beck is at the 7th National Jazz & Blues Festival ...

> **THIS SUNDAY, JULY 23rd**
> **BLENHEIM PARK, WOODSTOCK, OXON.**
> ADRIAN HOPKINS PRESENTS FOR THE ST. JOHN AMBULANCE APPEAL YEAR
> **MANFRED MANN**
> **JEFF BECK GROUP**
> **P. P. ARNOLD & her NICE**
> SIMON DUPREE & the BIG SOUND
> GATES OPEN 2.30 p.m.
> SHOW COMMENCES 4.0 p.m.   ADMISSION **10/-**

concert is held as a benefit for the St. John Ambulance Appeal, and admission is set at 10 shillings.

SUN 30TH
Town Hall, Truro

AUGUST

TUE 1ST–WED 2ND

An interesting news item in BILLBOARD (August 12) throws unexpected light on Beck's extracurricular activities: "Jeff Beck replaced an ailing Syd Barrett when the Pink Floyd flew to Germany for a TV date." In fact, two TV shows have been booked; one in Hamburg ("Music For Young People") and one in Bremen ("Beat Club"). Despite this announcement no further documentation of this trip exists, and other sources claim Pink Floyd cancel the trip, although this has not been proven conclusively either. But the sight of Jeff Beck playing along to *See Emily Play* (the Floyd's present #8 UK hit) would be riveting!

Lending strength to this possibilty, Jeff in fact travels to West Germany to do some promotional work without his group at this time.

SUN 13TH
"7th National Jazz & Blues Festival"
Royal Windsor Racecourse, Windsor

The annual three-day Windsor festival features a very impressive line-up of jazz, pop and blues groups, most of them British. Aynsley Dunbar debuts his new group the Retaliation on Saturday the 12th on a bill topped by Pink Floyd (who eventually pull out because of leader Syd Barrett's nervous exhaustion) and Arthur Brown.

Sunday night (from 7.00–11.30 pm) is headlined by Cream and also debuts Peter Green's Fleetwood Mac plus, in alphabetical order, P. P. Arnold & the Nice, Jeff Beck, Blossom Toes, Chicken Shack, Denny Laine, John Mayall's Bluesbreakers and Pentangle. Attendance is in the region of 7,000, and – as NEW MUSICAL EXPRESS points out in their backstage report – while Clapton arrives with a beautiful long legged lady by his side, Beck arrives with Pudding in tow.

GOT THE FEELING

The Singing Beck

Despite always considering himself a guitarist first and foremost, Jeff Beck has sung lead vocal on the occasional song in just about every group in which he has been a member. Jeff has an easily recognizable and characteristic voice. For a short spell in early 1967, Mickie Most found his voice more unique than his guitar playing!

In the sixties it was customary to spotlight other members of a group than the lead singer with a vocal number, so one of the songs demo'ed by the Tridents was the group composition *Wandering Man Blues*, sung by Jeff in his customary dour tones.

While with the Yardbirds, Beck usually sang some blues songs live and on radio broadcasts, like the fine *The Sun Is Shining* and the Elmore James standard *Dust My Blues*. On record he sang his pet project *The Nazz Are Blue*, which prompted some critics to compare his voice favourably with Steve Winwood's. Jeff also willingly did the autobiographical B-side *Psycho Daisies*, because his then girlfriend Mary Hughes was mentioned in the lyrics. Finally, he was also responsible for the cockney'd spoken passages in *Happenings Ten Years Time Ago*.

When Jeff teamed with Mickie Most in 1967, commercial considerations forced him to sing lead on a couple of single sides; *Hi Ho Silver Lining* and *Tallyman*, both of which were big hits. But although Jeff did, out of sheer necessity, share some vocal duties with Rod Stewart in the first Beck group, he kept his mouth firmly shut when singer Bobby Tench fronted the second edition of the Jeff Beck Group in the years 1971–72, except when they very briefly performed *Superstition* as an encore in the summer of '72. Jeff had already sung the song when it was originally recorded at Electric Lady a few weeks previously.

In Beck, Bogert & Appice however, Jeff was brought forward to sing the powerful *Black Cat Moan*, and his voice proves some relaxation amidst the whining of Carmine Appice. The lead vocal was certainly shared with Jeff to lift some of the vocal duties off Appice's shoulders.

Jeff Beck began fronting all-instrumental groups from 1975 onwards, but he was still known to shout the encore *Going Down* as late as 1981. When Nile Rodgers was brought in to produce the *Flash* album in the eighties, he did a Mickie Most and persuaded Jeff to sing on a couple of songs. Besides mumbling some gibberish on *A Day In The House* on *Guitar Shop* in 1989, the last song featuring Jeff singing was the single *Wild Thing* in 1986. And then he typically processed his voice electronically beyond recognition.

Due to neighbours' complaints the volume is kept down, to the point were MELODY MAKER's Chris Welch reports (August 19): "Hosts of guitarists like Peter Green, Eric Clapton, Jeff Beck, David O'List and others had their sound reduced to a near pathetic level." Welch sums up Jeff's performance in one sentence: "Jeff Beck suffered from loss of volume but played well." Derek Boltwood from RECORD MIRROR (August 19) is more helpful: "Jeff Beck was in great form, and the

> **Set List/Jeff Beck Group**
>
> *Seventh National Jazz & Blues Festival, Windsor, August 13, '67*
>
> Some Kinda Wonderful • Talk To Me Baby • (I Think I'll Be Leaving) This Morning • Rock My Plimsoul • Hi Ho Silver Lining

group gave a very enjoyable performance. They're a formidable combination, with Jeff's guitar work – too much – Rod's voice and Ron's body (I should explain – Ron, the bass guitarist, appeared on stage stripped to the waist, and dressed as a Red Indian, complete with feathers!)"

🔊 A rough audience tape survives from the Windsor festival, beginning with an excellent version of *Some Kind Of Wonderful* (with Stewart borrowing a few lines from Solomon Burke's *Everybody Needs Somebody To Love*), followed by the fat, monstrous Elmore James boogie *Talk To Me Baby* (with a magnificent Stewart vocal above Beck's greasy slide guitar, both driven by a rock steady Dunbar shuffle), and a slow blues with Rod singing the immortal lines about what happened when he woke up this morning. Eric Clapton often described his vision of Cream as "Buddy Guy with a rhythm section" (before he under-

---

August 14, 1967: After three weeks at #1, "Light My Fire" by the Doors drops down the US singles charts.

August 1967: Mickey Waller is back on drums in the Jeff Beck Group ...

stood they were a different animal altogether), and that is precisely what the Beck Group sound like tonight.

This is also Aynsley Dunbar's last performance with the Jeff Beck Group. Dunbar, who has been important to the group's creativity and musical direction, is replaced by the returning Mickey Waller. The group rent rehearsal space at Studio 19 in Gerrard Street, London around this time, to welcome Waller back in.

MID *

Jeff does a bit of press promotion in August. He explains his musical concept to Derek Boltwood of RECORD MIRROR (August 26) thus: "What I want to do – what I'm trying to do – is to produce the white equivalent of coloured music. I really hate white music ... When you take good white records, and there are some, for example *Whiter Shade Of Pale* and *Groovin'*, the reason they're good is because they sound coloured." Jeff elaborates: "I've studied negro music – by listening to it a lot. And I have records of coloured musicians dating from the nineteen-twenties right up to the present time. ... What I try to do is get the same feeling in my playing – not just an imitation of the coloured sound – but real soul ... But I'm a bit hung up now, because I've worked hard at trying to get the sound I want, and now I'm almost there. I feel as if I've been dropped. Hendrix and Clapton have reached the same point as I have – and they've been accepted. But so many things went wrong at the beginning of my career –

including the release of *Hi Ho Silver Lining*. That was a terrible record."

Beck is not particularly fond of *Tallyman* either, as proved by an interview in BEAT INSTRUMENTAL also from this time (published September 1967): "I made the record and sort of closed my eyes. I just didn't think it could be a hit. It wasn't a really good follow up to *Silver Lining*." More interestingly, Jeff mentions in passing the next planned single: "The whole thing is a bit frustrating, really, because I have just heard the demo of the number we'll do as the next single. A great slow and solid number. It's not even recorded yet. The writer is completely unknown." This mysterious song is never heard by the public, however, and was perhaps not recorded either. Describing his musical dreams, Jeff mentions both "co-produce with Phil Spector" and "... sit in with Ray Charles on a session with the Raelettes as he did on the Milt Jackson album. Failing this, then, the Ike & Tina Turner Show."

MON 14TH

Tallyman is released in the United States, but is scantly promoted and as a consequence sinks without a trace.

SAT 19TH
California Ballroom, Dunstable

After the appearance at the Windsor festival, Jeff's group resumes playing one-nighters around Britain again, tonight at Dunstable in Bedfordshire – with the Washington D.C.'s and the Sneakers – from 8 pm until midnight. This presumably is Mickey Waller's debut back with the group.

SUN 20TH
Starlite Ballroom, Greenford

The Jeff Beck Group make their third appearance this year at the place where the ads promise 'modern low lightning' and a 'knockout atmosphere'.

THU 24TH
Assembly Hall, Worthing

According to Noel Redding's diaries, Jeff Beck is backstage at the BBC Television Centre in Shepherd's Bush, as Jimi Hendrix Experience mime *The Burning Of The Midnight Lamp* for tonight's "Top Of The Pops". Also on the programme is Alan Price. However, official BBC records show that Beck himself is not booked for the show.

In the evening, Jeff, Rod, Ron and Mickey play a concert in Worthing again inexplicably billed as 'The Jeff Beck Sound'.

SAT 26TH
Toft's*, Folkestone

After playing Folkestone in Kent tonight, Jeff goes to the Speakeasy to party and to hear Dantalion's Chariot, a psychedelized version of Zoot Money's Big Roll Band. Also hanging out at the Speakeasy this night are Brian Jones, Jimi Hendrix and members of the Nice.

SUN 27TH

Jeff is at the Speakeasy again tonight relaxing with Hendrix, Keith West and Alan Price. During the evening, Hendrix gets on stage to jam with Fairport Convention.

MON 28TH
"Festival of the Flower Children"
Woburn Abbey Park, Woburn

This three-day festival, clearly named in the spirit of The Summer of Love and arranged 'by kind permission of His Grace, the Duke of Bedford' promises non-stop music for 72 hours from Saturday 26th at 2.30 pm until 11 pm on Monday 28th. The groups play during the daytime, alternating with records and tapes in the night time. Among the many acts set for the festival are the Kinks, the Small Faces, Eric Burdon & the Animals, the Bee Gees, Alan Price and the Marmalade. The Jeff Beck Group appear on the last day of the festival.

The festival is not without accidents; the audience has been handed free sparklers and in a careless moment a canopy catches fire and Keith West and Tomorrow (featuring Steve Howe on guitar, Junior Woods on bass and John 'Twink' Alder on drums), who had just started playing, have to cut their set short.

SEPTEMBER

SAT 2ND
New Century Hall, Manchester

SUN 3RD
The Tabernacle*, Stockport

TUE 5TH
Winter Gardens, Malvern

THU 7TH
Eric Burdon weds model Angela King this afternoon, and Jeff attends both the ceremony at Caxton Hall Registry Office and the reception held at the Speakeasy. For the latter, members of the Animals and the Hollies plus Chris Farlowe and Madeleine Bell also show up.

FRI 8TH
Town Hall, Rugby
Billed as a 'Flower Power Lovin' night, the Jeff Beck Group appear with the Kleek and the Future for a late night dance (9 pm–1 am).

SAT 9TH
Nautilus Club, Lowestoft
'Guitar Heroes' being the order of the day, MELODY MAKER runs a profile of Britain's top guitarists under the headline "The Magnificent Seven". Jeff Beck is described as "the enigma of the Seven. At one time his style was clearly cut and he was hailed as one the best blues guitarists. But then he went through periods of change in an attempt to create a style that owed nothing to Clapton and was more commercially acceptable on the pop front. ... But Jeff is still a fine guitarist and made a huge name for himself while playing exciting music with the Yardbirds ... He has considerable speed and ideas on guitar and it remains to be seen how he will develop." (The six others profiled are Eric Clapton, Peter Green, Jimi Hendrix, Jimmy Page, Pete Townshend and Steve Winwood.)

Today's club appearance is at the self-proclaimed 'East Anglia's premier big beat centre and discotheque', with the Soul Concern.

TUE 12TH*
Jeff Beck meets Frank Zappa at the Speakeasy. Zappa, who arrived in England the previous day, is in London to play a concert at the Royal Albert Hall later in the week. Beck and Zappa, reportedly together with Jimi Hendrix, also visit Keith West and Tomorrow a couple of days later.

THU 14TH
Jeff Beck and Rod Stewart – but not the rest of the group – are at AVRO-TV's Studio 1 in Hilversum, Holland to appear on "Moef Ga Ga" to promote *Tallyman*, which is broadcast on September 29.

FRI 15TH
Brittania Rowing Club, Nottingham

SAT 16TH
Sports Centre, Bracknell
A teenage dance with the Soul Bucket and the Jeff Beck Group.

SUN 17TH
Chertsey

FRI 22ND
Queens Rink Ballroom, Hartlepool
With the Tony King Sound and disc jockey Billy Vann.

SAT 23RD
Jeff Beck, Jimi Hendrix and members of the Hollies spend the evening at the Royal Albert Hall, where the Mothers of Invention make their much ballyhooed British debut. Zappa has even secured accompaniment by members of the London Philharmonic Orchestra.

MON 25TH
Cooks Ferry Inn*, Edmonton, London

TUE 26TH
Marquee Club, London
Supported by the Time Box (with guitar prodigy Ollie Halsall), Jeff Beck is the main attraction at the Marquee this week.

A live tape of eleven songs is reported to be from this night at the Marquee and portrays the Beck Group as a rough-hewn blues band with Jeff's ferocious guitar constantly on the edge. Where many of his '67 colleagues strive to forge a smooth sound, Beck seems intent on throwing aesthetics out the window in favour of a pure yet dirty tone. The poor guitar twists and turns in Beck's hands, squeezed to uncontrolled feedback, as he bends the strings in either big swooping lines or in sudden outbursts of energy. People who see Jeff around this time also says he cut out the showboating he did with the Yardbirds (playing the guitar behind his back and above his head etc.), and restricts himself to standing still, legs apart, body thrust forward with the occasional facial expression.

Firmly rooted in the British blues boom, the set is strong on 12-bars, and features several driving boogie shuffles with wild guitar solos; *Rock My Plimsoul*, *Talk To Me Baby*, and *Bye Bye, Baby, Bye Bye* are all cut from the same cloth. Rod urges Jeff to 'play the blues!' in *Talk To Me Baby*, and Jeff replies with quoting the melody from *The Bridge Over The River Kwai!*; a good example of Beck's not-so-serious attitude to blues puritanism. There is also an intense slow blues, *(I Think I'll Be Leaving) This Morning*. However, much of the adventerous, psychedelic style he pioneered with the Yardbirds is laid to rest, the only moment occurs during the guitar solo in *I'm Losing You*, where Beck dabbles with orientalisms. During the crowd pleaser *Jeff's Boogie*, the licks ripple from his guitar in a blur. Jeff has yet to expand his boogie to include an unaccompanied segment, but the trick with accelerating the tempo halfway is used effectively.

Throughout, Rod Stewart sings with great feeling and Ron Wood's lean and driving bass is the strong foundation for Jeff Beck to go where he pleases, while Mickey Waller combines looseness and punch behind the drums.

FRI 29TH
• Dartford
• UFO, Roundhouse, Chalk Farm, London

The Jeff Beck Group have two bookings today; the first being in Dartford southeast of London, and the second less than twenty miles across town at the UFO, the capital's most popular

October 1967: Jeff sees Vanilla Fudge in concert in London ...

underground club that still depends on bigger acts like Jeff Beck to break even.

Also tonight, *Tallyman* is televised on Dutch TV show "Moef-Ga-Ga" (▶ September 14).

SAT 30TH
St. George's Ballroom, Hinckley

UNDATED
Possibly it is this month that Jeff does a rare session appearance, when he adds some bluesy guitar runs to John Walker's *I See Love In You*, which is put on the B-side of Walker's single *If I Promise* (UK Phillips, released October 20, 1967). This ex-Walker Brother is in fact the very same John Maus that Jeff bought his well-worn Fender Esquire from, back in his Yardbirds days.

OCTOBER

SUN 1ST
American singer/guitarist Tim Rose is an added attraction at tonight's 'Sunday At The Saville' concert – which otherwise stars the Incredible String Band and Pink Floyd – and seeing Rose perform tonight, both Jeff and Rod are inspired to cover his folksy standard *Morning Dew*, which becomes a staple of Beck's live act for many years.

TUE 3RD
Ron Wood, going AWOL from Jeff's group and playing guitar, sits in with the Crazy World of Arthur Brown for a BBC Radio One session to be broadcast on the 8th.

Kim Gardner also tempts Wood with good work and better wages with the Creation this autumn, where Gardner is presently the bassist. The Creation have caused a small sensation with their live appearances complete with auto-destruction and action-painting, but despite their two Top 50 singles in the UK (*How Does It Feel To Feel* and *Painter Man*), they haven't quite made it. Their main asset, guitarist Eddie Phillips, is about to quit and Gardner wants to reel Wood in.

WED 4TH
A Wednesday that turns out to be a key date in Jeff's diary. Visiting New York quartet Vanilla Fudge are a last minute addition to a concert at Finsbury Park Astoria headlined by Tomorrow, Traffic and the Young Rascals. Presently in the British charts with their '45 rpm-at-33 rpm' version of the Supremes' *You Keep Me Hangin' On*, Vanilla Fudge, in their double breasted jackets mix gospel-tinged harmony vocals and a sprinkling of Wagner with their R&B roots.

Jeff is in the audience, and is very impressed by the Fudge, and particularly their rhythm section of bassist Tim Bogert and drummer Carmine Appice.

THU 5TH
Jeff drops in on a Jimi Hendrix Experience recording session at Olympic Studios in London. Also around are Dave Mason from Traffic and members of the Move. The Experience are recording tracks for their second album, eventually named after the Hendrix composition *Bold As Love*.

FRI 6TH
Top Rank Suite, Swansea, Wales

Jeff Beck Group support the Bee Gees, who presently have a big hit with *Massachusetts*. Also on the bill are the Koo Koo Bird Bicycle Band, Soul Society, the Power Stop and Kartune plus disc jockey Les Savill.

SAT 7TH
The Refectory, University of Leeds, Leeds

Jeff Beck with T. D. Backus & the Powerhouse and the Fendermen play from 7.30 until 11.30 pm.

MON 9TH
Three selections are being pre-recorded by the Jeff Beck Group today (*Rock My Plimsoul*, *Let Me Love You*, and the rare *Walking By The Railings*) for the newly inaugurated BBC Radio One. The BBC premiered the redefined network on September 30. Radio One's new vigorous format replaces the rather sedate Light Programme in response to the popularity of pirate radio.

The recording takes place at Paris Cinema in London, and will be broadcast on the daily "David Symonds Show", October 16–20; which runs Monday until Friday at 5.33–7.30 pm.

FRI 13TH
Gent, Belgium

The Jeff Beck Group cross the British Channel for their first visit to the Continent.

SAT 14TH
University of Reading, Reading

After the lightning trip to Belgium, Jeff and the group are back in Britain for further one-nighters, tonight in Reading. Simon Dupree & the Big Sound – another group in the NEMS stable – are also on the bill.

Perhaps as an in-joke on Jeff and his dog Pudding, RECORD MIRROR's gossip column 'The Face' cryptically notes today: "First release from the Pudding Chair Sometime featuring the Peking Omnibus Company will be a rock 'n' roll number, with Jeff Beck on guitar ..."

SUN 15TH
Wooden Bridge Hotel, Guildford

According to the advertisement in the SURREY ADVERTISER AND COUNTRY TIMES, Jeff Beck is to "open the Bridge" together with the Switch.

MON 16TH
Rock My Plimsoul is transmitted on the "David Symonds Show" on BBC Radio One (▶ October 9).

THU 19TH
Jeff hears Vanilla Fudge again, when they play the Speakeasy after a jaunt around the Continent. Also at 'the Speak' tonight are Peter Frampton, Eric Clapton, P. P. Arnold and Alan Price. Apparently, Jeff Beck, Tim Bogert and Carmine Appice are introduced for the first time, and an unconfirmed report even says an impromptu jam is attempted.

Let Me Love You is featured today on "The David Symonds Show" (▶ October 9).

FRI 20TH
The Jeff Beck Group's *Walking By The Railings*, presumably a self-penned variation on Elmore James' *Talk To Me, Baby* and otherwise never officially released by Beck, is broadcast today in the last edition of this week's "The David Symonds Show" (▶ October 9).

SAT 21ST
University of Southampton, Southampton

THU 26TH
The Speakeasy, London

Jeff Beck is performing at the Speakeasy for a change, after being a guest

December 1967: Jeff Beck a possible Pink Floyd ...

here on numerous occasions this year. During the night, well-known British trad jazz trombonist Chris Barber comes on stage and joins the Beck Group for a jam.

FRI 27TH
Assembly Rooms, Tamworth
Support act is the Parchment People plus disc jockey Mickey Dunne and the Go-Go Dancers.

SUN 29TH
Kirklevington Country Club, Kirklevington

MON 30TH
Coventry

NOVEMBER

WED 1ST
The Jeff Beck Group record an extensive five-song session for popular BBC Radio One deejay John Peel with producer Bev Phillips. The well-known Peel is an ardent advocate of the burgeoning British progressive rock movement, and will regularly play Jeff Beck records on his shows.

Put down on tape today are *I Ain't Superstitious*, *Beck's Bolero* (with Beck himself likely providing the rhythm guitar part although Rod Stewart will later learn it for stage use), *Loving You Is Sweeter Than Ever*, *You Shook Me* (subtitled *Tales of Mickey Waller* because of the drum solo) and finally the otherwise unreleased *You'll Never Get To Heaven (If You Break My Heart)*; a mostly-instrumental version of a Burt Bacharach/Hal David song, which Jeff likely never performs live. *You Shook Me*, on the other hand, becomes a centre piece in Beck's repertoire. Originally one of the songs by Muddy Waters recorded with Earl Hooker's band at Chess in 1961–62, and eventually issued in the UK on an EP on Pye International in September 1963.

The recording takes place at BBC's Maida Vale 4 studio in London, and all selections are transmitted on November 5.

FRI 3RD
Poole College, Poole
A student night billed as 'Poole College Social Dance'.

SAT 4TH
University of Exeter*, Exeter

SUN 5TH
John Peel presents Jeff's group on his regular BBC Radio One "Top Gear" show this Sunday (broadcast between 2.00–5.00 pm, ▶ November 1). Peel's other guests in today's programme are Pink Floyd, Denny Laine & the Electric String Band and the American soul duo James & Bobby Purify.

FRI 10TH
Beachcomber Club*, Nottingham

SAT 11TH
Matlock Bath Pavilion*, Matlock

THU 16TH
Club-Au-Go-Go, Newcastle

SAT 18TH
Lanchester Technical College*, Coventry

SAT 25TH
Haverfordwest, Wales

THU 30TH
City Hall, Salisbury

DECEMBER

FRI 1ST
University of Cardiff*, Cardiff, Wales

SAT 2ND
Gaiety Ballroom, Romsey

TUE 5TH AND THU 7TH
The Jeff Beck Group record two sessions at EMI Studios on Abbey Road, taping the obscure ballad *I've Been Drinking* plus possibly other titles for future use. To flesh out the sound, pianist Nicky Hopkins and singer Madeleine Bell are added in the studio. It is actually unclear if Ron Wood is present at all, as Jeff doubles on bass guitar on *I've Been Drinking*.

Surprisingly, the sessions are not held at De Lane Lea, Mickie Most's declared favourite London studio. But Jeff had told BEAT INSTRUMENTAL in August that he was keen to try out EMI's Abbey Road studios, so likely this change of environment was his idea.

FRI 8TH
University of Birmingham*, Birmingham

SAT 9TH
Kingston Technical College*, Kingston-Upon-Thames, London

MON 11TH
Slough College, Slough

TUE 12TH
Marquee Club, London
Jeff's fourth and last engagement at the Marquee this year.

THU 14TH
Sussex University, Brighton

FRI 15TH
North East London Polytechnic*, Walthamstow, London

SAT 16TH
The Wellington Club, East Dereham
The Wellington is a much visited club where every sixties group worth its salt plays.

> St. John Ambulance Brigade County of Oxford Appeal Year, 1967
> **SATURDAY, DECEMBER 23rd**
> Town Hall, Oxford   8 p.m. till 11.45 p.m.
> **JEFF BECK GROUP**
> **THE TEN YEARS AFTER**
> and Bicester's prize-winning group
> **ADRIANS PEOPLE**
> Tickets 10/- each from Taphouses or at the door

SAT 23RD
Town Hall, Oxford
Promoted by St. John Ambulance Brigade County of Oxford Appeal Year 1967 (who also staged the benefit at Blenheim Palace in July). Jeff Beck shares the stage for the first of many times with Ten Years After, starring fleet-fingered Alvin Lee.

•

In the annual BEAT INSTRUMENTAL Readers' Poll for 1967 (published February 1968), Jeff is displaced to number four (after Eric Clapton, Jimi Hendrix and Hank Marvin), after his triumphant victory the previous year. Below follows Peter Green, George Harrison, Pete Townshend and Alvin Lee, but Jimmy Page is conspicious by his absence in the poll.

Lo and behold, Jeff's first year as a solo artist has been a success where he has ably sustained a lot of the popularity he attracted in the Yardbirds. Still, with two hit singles and an impressive 90 or so live appearances to his credit, Jeff Beck's reputation as a guitarist is disputed, and he needs to take stock of the future.

•

In late 1967, Pink Floyd again briefly but seriously consider Jeff Beck as replacement to the increasingly erratic Syd Barrett. In the end, the remaining Floyds decide that "he [Jeff] would be too expensive and couldn't sing", and settle on the little known David Gilmour instead.

December 7, 1967: The Beatles' Apple shop in London is opened to the public.

1968

JANUARY

SAT 27TH
Norwich

After a month's layoff, the Jeff Beck Group get back together again for their first live appearance in the new year. Ron Wood has used the layoff to rehearse with the Creation, playing lead guitar, and even recording several sessions with that group. Fed up with his position as hired hand in the Beck Group, Ron considers quitting Jeff's band altogether to join the Creation, who are a big draw on the Continent, playing to big crowds and for good money to boot.

UNDATED*

Jeff Beck is invited to a special recording session for singer Paul Jones. For the occasion, producer Peter Asher (ex-one half of Peter & Gordon) and arranger Mike Vickers (like Jones, an ex-Manfred Mann) have assembled a stellar line-up of Jeff Beck on guitar, Paul Samwell-Smith on bass, Nicky Hopkins on piano and the novelty of Paul McCartney playing drums. A song called *The Dog Presides* is recorded, and released as the B-side of Jones's version of a Bee Gees song, *And The Sun Will Shine* single (UK Columbia). Although not documented, the session is likely held at EMI's Abbey Road Studios in early 1968. Even if Jeff is prominent on the B-side, there is some uncertainty about his contribution, if any, to the A-side. The single is released on March 8, 1968.

FEBRUARY

SAT 3RD
Egham

MON 5TH

Although session details are not available, it is believed that today is when Jeff Beck records – at Mickie Most's behest – an instrumental version of *Love Is Blue* at De Lane Lea. The song is originally *L'Amour Est Bleu,* and was Luxembourg's entry (sung by Vicky Leandros) in the European Song Contest the previous year. Surprisingly only coming in fourth, it still remains one of the few melodies from the annual contest to become an evergreen. The catchy melody inspires cover versions by a wide variety of easy-listening artists.

FOR VALENTINE'S DAY YOU STILL HAVE TIME TO SEND JEFF BECK LOVE IS BLUE INSTEAD OF A CARD

This is actually a true solo recording by Jeff as none of his regular group plays at the session. A rush job, as Jeff explains to NEW MUSICAL EXPRESS a few weeks later: "I heard it on Wednesday, got the demo on a Friday, cut it in three takes on a Sunday [Monday], and it was out the next Friday."

Session musicians, including a whole orchestra, a female choir and a harpsichord in addition to bass and drums (the latter reportedly by Clem Cattini) are supplied by Mickie Most.

FRI 9TH
Britannia Rowing Club*, Nottingham

THU 15TH

Jeff Beck is at the BBC to do two interviews today for Radio One. First he is contracted to appear at Studio B9 at BBC's Broadcasting House for "Scene And Heard", chatting with Johnny Moran, which presumably is not aired until Saturday (February 17, between 6.30–7.30 pm). Then Jeff is interviewed by Barry Alldis for a live sequence on another new programme, "Late Night Extra", which is transmitted simultaneously on Radio 1 and 2 between 10.00 pm and midnight this Thursday. Jeff's new single *Love Is Blue* is also played on record.

FRI 16TH

Love Is Blue is released today, the last song of a trilogy of attempts by Mickie Most at turning Beck into a conventional pop star.

The single is met with bewilderment by many of Jeff's fans and a lukewarm reception by the press. Chris Welch in MELODY MAKER (February 17) writes: "One of these utterly simple but unbeatably commercial tunes ... being feverishly covered by everybody in Britain from Ted Heath to our Jeffery. Beck's version sounds the most likely to hit with a vocal chorus, strings, and a few bars of note-bending."

Beck's version has to compete with Frenchman Paul Mauriat's single, but Jeff still peaks at #23 in the British charts during a seven week stay. Additionally, the song is a medium-sized hit on the Continent, racking up healthy sales in Scandinavia. (Mauriat's *Love Is Blue* scores a US chart-topper this month. Jeff's version, on the other hand, is not released in the US.)

As the song climbs the charts during March, Jeff duly includes the tune in his live shows for some time.

SAT 17TH
Hammersmith, London

TUE 20TH
Marquee Club, London

The Jeff Beck Group are booked for a return to the Marquee Club, supported by the Nite People.

LATE*

Jeff Beck is interviewed by RECORD MIRROR, DISC AND MUSIC ECHO (both March 2) and NEW MUSICAL EXPRESS (March 9) at the end of February to promote *Love Is Blue*.

"As far as I'm concerned the wild sound of Jimi Hendrix and the Cream is finished. The latest albums by both of these groups [*Axis Bold As Love* and

Single

JEFF BECK
A: LOVE IS BLUE
(Andre Popp/Pierre Cour)
B: I'VE BEEN DRINKING *(Mercer/Tauber)*

Released Friday February 16, 1968 (UK Columbia DB 8359)
Personnel is Jeff Beck (ld gtr) + session musicians (drms, bs, harpsichord, strings and vocals) (A); Jeff Beck (gtr, bs), Rod Stewart (ldvcls), Mickey Waller (drms), Nicky Hopkins (pno) and Madeleine Bell (back vcls) (B)
Recorded at De Lane Lea Studios, 129 Kingsway, London, February 5, 1968 (A) and EMI Studios, 3 Abbey Road, London, December 5 and 7, 1967 (B).
Produced by Mickie Most
Engineered by Dave Siddle/Martin Birch
Highest Chart Position UK: #23

© February 15, 1968: Chicago blues harpist Little Walter is stabbed to death in a Chicago street fight.

Newsflash March 1968: Single "Love Is Blue" a hit in Europe ...

Disraeli Gears] were not at all sensational – nothing new in them!" is Jeff's opening salvo in DISC AND MUSIC ECHO, in an attempt to justify why he has recorded *Love Is Blue*: "It wasn't a deliberate change. Mickie Most, my recording manager, found the song and suggested I do it. We rushed into the studio and the whole thing was finished in a couple of days", before adding half-heartedly "and the fantastic thing is I really like the melody."

To Derek Boltwood in RECORD MIRROR, Jeff explains that *Love Is Blue* is an attempt to broaden horizons: "But the thing is that my aim now is to give guitar concerts – using a large orchestra to back me. Just as a singer gives a concert, I'd like to do the same thing with my guitar. And I think that releasing a record like *Love Is Blue* is a step in that direction." Reassuringly, Beck adds: "I'll still carry on with the group. In fact, we've just changed our name to Jeff Beck's Million Dollar Bash – and we've started using a rock 'n' roll pianist as well. So that scene will obviously carry on for a while – it's just that I'll release solo discs as well." The piano player may be Nicky Hopkins – who did perform on the flip side *I've Been Drinking* – and who indeed joins Beck's group later in the year. But neither the guitar orchestra nor the name change is realized.

For the NEW MUSICAL EXPRESS item, a frustrated Beck is interviewed by Richard Green at a transport café in Fulham. Like the other interviewers, Green portrays a guitarist with an image problem – blues or strings? Beck is a contradictory character, as he claims he wants to concentrate solely on colleges and universities rather than ballrooms ("[the] audiences are so much better"), while at the same time he promotes *Love Is Blue*, exactly the type of hit that will push him straight back to the ballrooms. Jeff laments: "What do the fans want from me?" "I don't know what to do at the moment," he goes on, "I know blues is my scene, but everybody's doing it." He reserves his praise for the Who ("The only group with a real image of their own ... I'd love to play with them. The guitarist is fantastic") and Eric Clapton: "The greatest blues guitarist in the country and always will be", adding: "I don't know why he's grown his hair like that way, he doesn't need it. The short crew cut, Levis with paint on them and sneakers were always his scene." Beck also gives telling insight into Mickie Most's strategy: "I'd like to make an LP, but Mickie doesn't think it's time. He doesn't want to spend a lot of money on an album until we've decided what we're going to do."

MARCH

SAT 2ND
University of Manchester*, Manchester

SUN 3RD
Rotterdam, Holland
The Jeff Beck Group undertake another quick visit abroad, this time across the channel to Holland.

FRI 8TH
Dartford

SAT 9TH
Middle Earth, Covent Garden, London
"I adore the song *Love Is Blue* but Jeff Beck's version does nothing to enchance it. ... Jeff Beck should stick to raving pop, he's much more suited to it", thinks reader Linda Rookes in today's NEW MUSICAL EXPRESS.

Tonight, Jeff Beck plays the hippest club in London at the moment (situated in Covent Garden) with Fusion and Tyrannosaurus Rex, the duo featuring Marc Bolan.

FRI 15TH
Plaza Ballroom*, Oswestry, Wales

SAT 16TH
Co-op Hall, Chesham
Also with the Tender Trap.

SUN 17TH
Cat Ballou, Grantham
Supporting Jeff's group tonight are the Rats, the pride of Hull featuring guitarist Mick Ronson. The Rats secretly tape Jeff's set, and it gives Ronson – who is a huge Beck fan – instant access to all the songs that later wind up on the Beck Group's first LP.

MID✱
Right before an unspecified non-BBC television appearance, Jeff is interviewed by Pete Goodman for a feature published in BEAT INSTRUMENTAL (April 1968), where he has to defend his recent statement in DISC AND MUSIC ECHO about Jimi Hendrix and Cream being outdated: "I was put down over that story. I just didn't say that. What I said was that if they didn't look after their public in this country they might lose their tremendous popularity. The actual sounds, the music, they make, are fantastic, but they must keep it up all the time – in front of their fans." On his apparent change of style, Jeff adds: "I don't want to be a sort of Engelbert Humperdinck of the guitar, but I'd like to have the sort of successful career that Engelbert and the Shadows enjoy." "Obviously, it was a bit of a worry coming out with a version of *Love Is Blue* in the face of so many opposing versions, including the American number one. But I felt it was a great song and melody and I felt it called for this quieter sort of treatment." Beck adds hastily: "Not me at first hearing, but it's the sort of thing that grows on you." Jeff's Afghan Hound is also portrayed: "Pudding is a born guitarist. The only trouble is that the mean pooch chews up the neck of any guitar I give him!"

Jeff also does a profile in DISC AND MUSIC ECHO (March 23), which runs as the paper's regular 'Me' column, and Jeff gives Steve Webbe a quick overview of his likes, dislikes, thoughts and ambitions. As hobbies Jeff lists "Pale blue Chevrolet Stingray and black '32 Ford", while politics "infuriates me. I have no power in that scene, my views don't mean anything". Eating and drinking tastes run to pilaf, curry, steaks and rosé wine, while ambitions are restricted to "produce successful singles, considers LPs just a necessity" besides "marrying a rich widow"! Jeff also vents his frustration on his ex-mates in the Yardbirds: "They ought to look back and think about the old magic ... when a group's doing that badly [as the Yardbirds now] it's just punchupsville."

Jeff also reviews the week's chart singles in DISC AND MUSIC ECHO (dated March 30, where his version of *Love Is Blue* is at #29 down from the previous week's #25). According to Beck, chart-topper Tom Jones (*Delilah*) is "good – a great powerful voice", while Cliff Richard's *Congratulations* "goes right under my foot". He also gives top marks to both Lulu and Cilla Black. As for *Lady Madonna*, Beck comments diplomatically "I wouldn't like to pass judgement on the Beatles!"

At this time, too, Jeff and his constant companion Pudding leave their penthouse apartment in Sutton behind, and move to Chelsea, where Beck's round-the-corner neighbours include Who manager Chris Stamp and Dusty Springfield.

© March 28, 1968: The Yardbirds begin the 8th and final North American tour which will last ten weeks.

April 1968: First European tour by the Jeff Beck Group ...

TUE 19TH✶
Jeff, TV personality Simon Dee and deejay Duncan Johnson appear at a special London fashion show this week dubbed 'Love Is Blue'.

WED 20TH
A day in the studio according to Waller's diary, which marks the debut session for Beck's first album, and it is reportedly a new, re-arranged *Shapes of Things* which is put on tape first.

Meanwhile, across the Atlantic in Los Angeles, California, Jeff's ex-missus Mary Hughes is arrested along with Eric Clapton and members of Buffalo Springfield in a well-documented drug raid.

THU 21ST
In a letter, Jeff informs the BBC that he has signed a contract with the Ellis–Wright Booking Agency Ltd., and is no longer tied to NEMS. (Terry Ellis and Chris Wright also manage Jethro Tull and Ten Years After.)

FRI 22ND
Northeast London Technical College, Walthamstow

SAT 23RD
Wilton Hall, Bletchley
'The Fabulous Jeff Beck Group' with unspecified support band tonight.

SUN 24TH
Britannia Rowing Club✶, Nottingham

WED 27TH
The student union at University of East Anglia in Norwich has provisionally booked a 'End Of Term Dance' today to star Jeff Beck plus the Pretty Things, but Beck cancels out.

SAT 30TH
College of Technology, Wolverhampton
In today's DISC AND MUSIC ECHO, a fan reassures readers "Jeff Beck might have changed his recording style for *Love Is Blue*, but when I saw him last week his blues was still sensational. ... True, Clapton is Britain's best blues guitarist, but Jeff Beck still comes a close second!"

The Wolverhampton show is originally advertised as a Yardbirds appearance, but they cancel (to tour the US), and in their place Jeff takes over the booking.

•

When an offer to join a well-paid tour of Spain and Germany with the Creation comes up, Ron Wood temporarily quits the Jeff Beck Group.

The new bassist in the Beck Group is John "Junior" Woods from the recently defunct Tomorrow. Woods also has a side project together with Tomorrow's eccentric drummer Twink called the Aquarian Age. It is not clear exactly when Woods comes in and Wood goes out, but Junior is definitely at several UK shows before the upcoming Continental tour in April.

APRIL

MON 1ST
Winter Gardens, Cleethorpes

THU 4TH
Glen Ballroom, Llanelli, Wales

FRI 5TH
Garrison Theatre, Bicester

SAT 6TH
New York correspondent June Harris in NEW MUSICAL EXPRESS reports that Peter Grant "feels the time is ready for Jeff Beck to come in [to the States] with a four-piece group". The tour opening is scheduled for May 30.

SUN 7TH
Black Prince Hotel, Bexley

MON 8TH
Pavilion, Bath

TUE 9TH
Marquee Club, London
Opening for the Jeff Beck Group is the New Nadir, featuring New Zealander guitarist Doug Jerebine (also known as Doug Blake), whom Beck finds impressive enough to note his name for future reference.

THU 11TH
Assembly Hall, Worthing
A return to Worthing sees Jeff, Rod, Junior and Mickey again billed as 'The Jeff Beck Sound'.

SUN 14TH✶
THE JEFF BECK GROUP: FIRST EUROPEAN TOUR
Starting a Continental tour, the Jeff Beck Group briefly visit Zurich but only to make an appearance on a local TV show, likely "Hits A Go Go" on SRG-TV.

Love Is Blue is a fair Euro-hit and bassist Junior Woods is now on board. The set list relies much on the basic Beck repertoire of the previous year, but Tim Rose's *Morning Dew* is introduced by now and of course *Love Is Blue* is played too.

MON 15TH
Hotel Drei Könige, Chur, Switzerland
The first live show of a three week Continental tour takes place this Easter Monday in Switzerland. Support tonight is les Hirondelles. The Swiss part of the itinerary is promoted by Rolf Armisegger.

TUE 16TH
Kursaal, Lucerne, Switzerland
Three local bands play support before the Beck Group enter the stage at 10 pm. Playing to a full house, Jeff serves up favourites like *Hi Ho Silver Lining*, *Talk To Me Baby*, *Morning Dew* and *I Ain't Superstitious*. "On the right; Jeff B., long black locks. But he didn't need the looks. He is a sensation in himself. He found new guitar techniques, unknown tone colours. With vibrating fingertips he played virtuously ... The guitar was held diagonally above his head ... Old primitive rhythms were borne out of this chaos. Jeff Beck: A roundabout to the blues?" writes the LUZERNES NEUE NACHRICHTER the following day.

WED 17TH
Africana Music-Club, St Gallen, Switzerland

FRI 19TH✶
Arriving in Copenhagen, Jeff holds a press conference, and the reporter from EKSTRABLADET (April 20) notes: "... *Love Is Blue* is not exactly [Beck's] cup of tea, even if he – either of old habit or to be courteous to his manager – mumbles something about that he really likes it, needs it commercially and wants to smash his image as a blues guitarist par excellence." As for a debut album, Jeff explains: "Now we have sort of straightened out our musical aims, and have begun writing our own stuff. The first number on the LP is already in the can, so we're getting there."

SAT 20TH
• **Brøndby Pop Club, Copenhagen, Denmark**
• **Parken, Trelleborg, Sweden**
The Jeff Beck Group actually make two personal appearances today, one in Copenhagen, Denmark, on a bill with Ten Years After, Sweden's Tages and local group the Baronets, before they cross the sound to the south-coast of Sweden. Here, in Trelleborg,

TRIVIA TROVE: In 1968 Jimi Hendrix gives his Bassett puppy dog "Ethel Floon" to Jeff, after she has outgrown Jimi's London flat.

© April 4, 1968: Martin Luther King is assassinated in Memphis, Tennessee.

May 1968: Jeff Beck play Paris for the first time since 1966 ...

the group commences a show at 11 pm (supported by Swedish groups the Hounds and Short Back & Sides) in one of Sweden's many 'folkparks'. *Love Is Blue* is presently at #5 in the Swedish hit parade. Arne Worsøe is promoting the Scandinavian leg of the European tour. No reports exist from Trelleborg, but the Brøndby show is not a particular hit with the critics.

SUN 21ST
- Pop-Puk, Copenhagen, Denmark
- Fjordvilla, Roskilde, Denmark

Jeff Beck has previously been booked to headline the last day of an 'Easter Pop Week' in Hilversum, Holland together with Dutch group Penny Wise today, but this is then cancelled to allow Beck to play further Scandinavian concerts.

Today is another double-date, this time in two towns barely 15 miles apart in Denmark. The return to Copenhagen finds Jeff Beck again on a bill with Ten Years After and the Tages (7–11 pm), before Beck and the Tages move on to Roskilde for an evening concert.

WED 24TH
Cue Club, Gothenburg, Sweden

Support by the Outsiders. For Jeff's return to Sweden, he has to play on a borrowed guitar – probably due to an equipment mix-up – and Gösta Hanson in GÖTEBORGS-TIDNINGEN (April 25) is not impressed at all: "It is sad when your old idols fail to deliver ... Jeff Beck played quite uninterestedly through a selection of numbers and generally the quartet sounded rather bland. Occasionally he dusted off his virtuoso guitar technique, but it could not save the overall impression. A catastrophic lack of stage presence spoiled the evening." However, some of the damage is redeemed by an encore: "A Muddy Waters-thing and a blues finally brought out some feeling in Beck's playing." Still, Hanson sums up: "Jeff has a big following. I am sad to say that I cannot count myself amongst them anymore."

The other big Gothenburg paper, GÖTEBORGS-POSTEN, is not impressed either: "Jeff has a lazy, heavy tone in his guitar and picks out many funny sounds. Sometimes it sounded like a air alarm. Sometimes like a big dog. Sometimes brittle and acidic. But this combination of young, white musicians and blues are not ideal, with the possible exception of John Mayall. The singer in Jeff Beck's band had misunderstood his task. To sing the blues is not to scream and moan."

THU 25TH
- Uddevalla, Sweden
- Gyllene Cirkeln, Stockholm, Sweden

Two further live appearances in Sweden today; the first in Uddevalla north of Gothenburg, and then 220 miles to the east in Stockholm.

The Stockholm show is a rough, almost careless, run-through of the usual numbers, plus a rendition of *Love Is Blue* which is played off-handedly, as if Jeff does not really want to do it. *Morning Dew* is a shambles, and *I Ain't Superstitious* fails to ignite any sparks. There are some good moments during *Jeff's Boogie*, and *Oh Pretty Woman* is cocksure and tough, but overall the show lacks any real excitement. Also, Junior Woods keeps a much lower profile than the forceful guitaristic bass approach by Ron Wood, thereby reducing the needed push from behind.

FRI 26TH
Rigoletto, Jönköping, Sweden

Support by the Shakers.

SAT 27TH
Kristinehamn, Sweden

SUN 28TH
Le Carousel, Copenhagen, Denmark

The Jeff Beck Group make a return to Denmark after the dismal show in Copenhagen the previous Saturday. Arne Worsøe explains to EKSTRABLADET (April 27) that as Jeff felt his Copenhagen shows were not up to standard and the week in Sweden had done the group good, Beck wants to make a return booking to make up for the previous week's disappointing Danish shows. After Denmark, the group likely returns home before dashing off again for a weekend in Paris.

MAY

SAT 4TH
Point Gamma, L'Ecole Polytechnique, Palaiseau, France

France is a Beck stronghold since the Yardbird days and this is his first return in two years. Jeff is booked to play a college in Greater Paris tonight on a big presentation with les Swingle Singers, jazz trumpeter Bill Coleman and a host of other French artists, just at a time when Paris is in the middle of severe student riots. Several publicity photos are taken in Paris, the only official photos of Junior Woods with the Beck Group that exist.

SUN 5TH
Paris, France

A second show in Paris at an unconfirmed venue.

FRI 10TH
Victoria and Bull Pub, Dartford

SAT 11TH
Bradford

SUN 12TH
Country Club, Kirklevington

TUE 14TH, WED 15TH, THU 16TH

For three days, the Jeff Beck Group record their first long player at EMI's Abbey Road studios, St. John's Wood, with Mickie Most. In fact, much of the time Most is not present as he is also engaged in a Donovan recording session at Olympic Studios over in Barnes. Many of the songs chosen for the album are part of the group's stage act and do not require much rehearsing or polishing. In fact one of the songs, *Blues de Luxe*, has canned applause added during the mixing to give the impression that it is recorded live. A similar process to the recording of *Roger The Engineer* is used again: after taping backing tracks, Jeff plugs in his guitar and overdubs solos, fills, intros and outros. Experimenting with sounds, Jeff's amplifier is put in a closed cupboard with a microphone outside to achieve a muffled, fat tone. An inspired re-make of the Yardbirds' *Shapes Of Things* is also preserved on tape, slowed down and much heavier than the original. This also marks Jeff's debut on the wah-wah.

The undecided Ron Wood is back on bass for these sessions, although he is still committed to the Creation. Two old friends of the group, Nicky Hopkins and John Paul Jones, are also around to add piano and organ to some songs.

May 1968: Recording sessions at Abbey Road for first Jeff Beck Group album ...

SAT 18TH
Winter Gardens, Weston-super-Mare
Ken Birch Band and the In-Mates Trio support the Beck Group.

MON 20TH
Ron Wood signs up with the Creation again for a short tour of Germany and Holland; but by early June the Creation (now on their last legs) play a final concert at the John Lewis Store on Oxford Street, London, of all places.

SAT 25TH
Another Jeff Beck recording session, likely mixing and putting the finishing touch to the forthcoming album. Rod's version of *Ol' Man River*, which features Jeff on bass, may well be recorded today.

TUE 28TH
Original opening date for Beck's American tour, which is then delayed until mid-June, perhaps because the Yardbirds are still touring the States and presumably Peter Grant wants to use the same road crew.

WED 29TH
EMI files show that the otherwise unissued song *Long Blues* is logged today, presumably an outtake from the EMI sessions.

UNDATED
In the spring of '68, Jeff is reportedly involved in a production of a Yorkshire group called Smoke, who the previous year scored a minor hit with *My Friend Jack*. How this comes about is unclear, but Beck is credited as co-producer with Dave Mason. A single, the charming psychedelic waltz *Utterly Simple* written by Mason for Traffic, is released on July 12, 1968, but then withdrawn.

JUNE

SUN 2ND
Coventry

FRI 7TH
"Bluesville '68", Manor House, London

EARLY
The Jeff Beck Group spend their time up till departure for their American visit honing their live act. But with 130-odd concerts under their belt, the group is well primed and groomed for their all-important American debut. America is also tempting Ron Wood, who exchanges guitar for bass and rejoins Jeff. Basically, two repertoires are worked out; one for when they play support to bigger acts, and a longer set for club dates or headlining dates.

The group's set list is tightly centered on the blues-rock material and conveniently avoiding European hits like *Tallyman* and *Love Is Blue*, but *Hi Ho Silver Lining* is inexplicably retained – a song Jeff has disowned almost since it was recorded. The Motown material is also dropped. *You Shook Me* and *Let Me Love You* serve as the standard two-fisted opening medley. Three slow blues songs are featured on a revolving basis; *The Sun Is Shining* (also a showcase for Jeff's slide guitar), *Sweet Black Angel*, and another tune lifted from B. B. King's *Live At The Regal* album, *It's My Own Fault*. Some important additions are now made to the play list. Rod Stewart dons a rhythm guitar to allow *Beck's Bolero* to be performed. *Shapes Of Things*, recently recorded for the first album, is included, perhaps too, because it will be recognized by the American audiences. Finally, a brand new instrumental christened *Mother's Old Rice Pudding* is debuted on this tour. This long, loose, unwieldy beast will be in a permanent state of flux until recorded next spring, but will invariably feature some of Jeff's most adventurous playing.

THU 13TH✷
The Jeff Beck Group leave for the United States. They meet Jimmy Page and Peter Grant in New York – Page tired from what will be the Yardbirds' last US tour, which wound up in Alabama on June 5.

FRI 14TH
THE JEFF BECK GROUP:
FIRST NORTH AMERICAN TOUR
Fillmore East, New York, New York
Jeff Beck, Rod Stewart, Ron Wood and Mickey Waller make their New York debut when they and Buzzy Linhart's Seventh Sons support the Grateful Dead at Bill Graham's Fillmore East theatre for two shows a night (8 and 11.30 pm). Despite being a veteran of four US tours with the Yardbirds, Jeff has yet to play a properly advertised concert in New York other than an essentially promotional performance at a discotheque in September 1965.

Incredibly, Jeff's group receives a standing ovation when they appear onstage at the Fillmore, although a stage frightened Rod Stewart sings the opening song from the wings. As soon as the crowd warms to their brand of bluesy rock, they seemingly can do no

wrong. With a stroke, Jeff and Rod are an overnight sensation. The four musicians are an arresting visual sight, too: A bespectacled Waller seated behind a small drum kit; Stewart in tight corduroy jeans and sunglasses; a young Ron Wood with rooster haircut; and a shirtless Jeff with braces [suspenders], a stack of amps and a low-hung Les Paul – a sight that will inspire legions of guitarists.

As no new Jeff Beck material has been released in the States since the scarcely available *Tallyman* the previous year, Jeff's reputation rests solely on his Yardbirds days, but a crucial added factor is the receptive American audiences. As in the Yardbirds' days, it is Frank Barsalona and Premier Talent who book the dates, and the tour is characterised by the exciting bills and the extravagantly designed posters, where the Jeff Beck Group share the stage with many of the top performers; not only in rock, but also in jazz and blues. In the almost two years since Jeff last toured the States, a big change has occured, largely because a sympathetic network of psychedelic ballrooms has grown up and concert promotion is becoming a well-oiled business. Compared to the stressful US itineraries of '65 and '66, this tour looks more like a holiday, with a combination of residencies in several towns and many days off.

Rumours have it that Jimmy Page is backstage for Beck's New York debut, keenly observing the reaction Jeff receives.

SAT 15TH
Fillmore East, New York, New York
The respected music critic Robert Shelton writes an ecstatic review of the previous night's concert in THE NEW YORK TIMES today: "They were standing and cheering for a new British pop group last night at the Fillmore East. The American debut of the Jeff Beck Group promises much heated enthusiasm for the quartet in its six-week American tour. Mr. Beck is

---

© May 24, 1968: The Rolling Stones return to their rock roots with the UK release of their new single and instant classic "Jumpin' Jack Flash".

JEFF BECK GROUP CHEERED IN DEBUT

British Pop Singers Delight Fillmore East Audience

a young Londoner who distinguished himself for a year and a half as the lead guitarist of the Yardbirds. He was seen, if not really heard, in a sequence of the film "Blow-Up" and had generally earned a reputation as a highly polished and adroit blues guitarist. He and his band deal in the blues mainly, but with an urgency and sweep that is quite hard to resist. The group's principal format is the interaction of Mr. Beck's wild and visionary guitar against the hoarse and insistent shouting of Rod Stewart, with gutsy backing on drums and bass. Their dialogues were lean and laconic, the verbal ping pong of a musical Pinter play. The climaxes were primal, bringing the 'big beat' of the English rock school forward. But there were whimsy and invention and modernist games thrown in, in *Beck's Boogie* [sic] and variations on *Bolero*. All told, an auspicious beginning for an excting group." Shelton concludes: "The British group upstaged, for one listener, at least, the featured performers, the Grateful Dead of San Francisco."

THE VILLAGE VOICE (June 20) comments: "The Jeff Beck Group caused something like a mild furor last weekend at the Fillmore East. Arriving without a fanfare of advance publicity, their full-grown English hard-rock, driving and together, caught everyone off-guard. ... The audience cheered and shouted and would hardly let them off, even when lead singer Rod Stewart pleaded for his voice, which was going. If their debut ... is any indication (it is), they're going to be one of the hottest groups around."

June Harris (the Mrs. Frank Barsalona!), telephones her impressions to NEW MUSICAL EXPRESS (June 29): "The greatest thing happened in New York last Friday. On his first performance in this country, Jeff Beck became a star. Even in his Yardbird heyday, when Jeff toured America with a few hits under his belt, he didn't get the standing ovation he and his present group received in the middle of their performance ... America has never seen a team like Jeff Beck and Rod Stewart. The only possible description of their two-fold dynamite would be to suggest it's like watching the brilliance of Jim Morrison teamed with Eric Clapton. ... Rod Stewart far surpasses one hundred per cent of the lead singers who have been passing through New York of late."

Taking advantage of the good press, Peter Grant xeroxes the reviews and sends them to promoters across the US. Grant also ensures that the crucial network of FM radio stations receive advance tapes of Jeff's coming album. This promotional tape contains (in sequence) *Rock My Plimsoul, Ol' Man River, Shapes of Things,* an edit of *You Shook Me, Morning Dew, Let Me Love You, Greensleeves* and *I Ain't Superstitious.*

SUN 16TH
"Daytop Under The Stars"
Daytop Village, Staten Island, New York

A four-day festival held on Staten Island just south of Manhattan with a mixed line-up of primarily folk and jazz artists. The Jeff Beck Group as such are not billed, but as Sunday headliners the Grateful Dead have to go back to San Francisco, Beck is added as a last-minute replacement. However, Rod Stewart's voice is shot after the Fillmore nights, but Jimi Hendrix steps in for a surprise appearance. Hendrix has no rhythm section, so Ron Wood and Mickey Waller ably back him before Jeff joins halfway through the show. Annie Fisher from THE VILLAGE VOICE (June 20) notes: "The group that ended up playing was composed of Beck, Ron Wood and Michael Waller, his bass player and drummer. ... At Daytop [Hendrix] improvised first with Wood and Waller, then Beck wandered onstage, and they jammed long and loose, feeling each other out, bringing off a few really remarkable moments, finally breaking into *Foxy Lady* to finish it off. Dynamite!"

In Cleveland a few days later, Jeff enthuses on the phone to DISC AND MUSIC ECHO: "I'm not really in favour of jamming. But I heard three numbers and just stood there aghast – and then I had to play. So I leapt onstage and we all jammed together. Jimi was fantastic, and it sounded as though they approved of my guitar playing!"

TUE 18TH, WED 19TH, THU 20TH, FRI 21ST, SAT 22ND
The Scene, New York, New York

While New York City is drenched in continual downpours, the Jeff Beck Group hold court for five nights at the popular nightclub Steve Paul's Scene, supported by Kenny Rankin and the Boston group Earth Opera. Uniquely, the American club and ballroom scene allow groups to play residencies – i.e. several nights in a row – making for a relaxed atmosphere, well-rested musicians and a good sound. The Scene at West 46th Street and 8th Avenue has become a very popular spot attracting the unlikely combination of New York jet-setters, visiting musicians and the hippie community, although Beck later said that he felt the club too cramped.

Reportedly, for every single of Beck's nights at the Scene, Jimi Hendrix drops by for a blow. Hendrix is in New York recording his third album to be titled in honour of his studio in-the-works, Electric Lady. On June 18, Eric Clapton – coming off a gruelling four month American tour with Cream – wanders in, and the crowd is treated to the unique sight of Clapton, Hendrix and Beck on the same stage. Another night, Buddy Miles sits in on drums. On one occasion, guitarist Mick Cox of Hendrix-protégés Eire Apparent, witnesses how Hendrix on bass and Beck on guitar play *I Ain't Superstitious:* "It's one of those [songs] that has a break of two seconds. As it came to the break they threw each others' guitars. Beck caught the bass and [Jimi] caught the guitar and they carried straight on into the song. People weren't even noticing that you know!" Another recollection is about a jam with Hendrix on bass guitar behind a three-pronged guitar frontline of Alvin Lee, Buddy Miles (a drummer yes, but now with a guitar around his neck) and Jeff Beck performing *Good Morning Little Schoolgirl, Hey Joe,* and *Wild Thing.* On June 22, Larry Coryell and Alvin Lee again jam with Hendrix, although it is not documented if Jeff also joins in. (Interestingly, no accounts of this busy week in New York include Jimmy Page, who presumably has flown back to England by now to ponder the future.)

WED 26TH, THU 27TH, FRI 28TH, SAT 29TH
Boston Tea Party, Boston, Massachusetts

The Boston Tea Party, situated on Berkeley Street, is a converted Kingdom Hall with a capacity of 750, and is rapidly becoming one of the most popular rock clubs on the East Coast. Working closely together with local radio station WBCN (with among others disc jockey 'the Woofa Goofa' aka Peter Wolf), the Tea Party will

June 1968: Jeff Beck to Disc: "It's like a great big birthday surprise!"

soon thrive on the new underground scene. In fact, the Jeff Beck Group are the first full weekend booking of a prominent British act at the club. Despite the station already airing tracks from Beck's as-yet-unreleased album, the Wednesday night is slow, so the band goes to the 'BCN studio the following day on a late afternoon show for an interview to help whip up excitement for the remaining nights, though word of mouth about this hot band mostly does the trick.

The powerful local agent Don Law later remembers the attitude-difference between English bands and the West Coast groups: "Jeff Beck ... he had Rod Stewart and Ronnie Wood. And he was chewing them out! 'You wankers! We gotta play this thing better than we're playing it – these people came to hear the record ...' Really chewing them out. You'd never hear that from a West Coast band."

The Friday show is reviewed by Ted Scourtis of NEW ENGLAND SCENE (September 1968), who writes on Beck: "Perhaps the most striking quality in Beck – in addition to his skill – is his stage appearance. Unlike Clapton who rarely changes an expression, Beck constantly involves the audience. When the audience was asked to sing (and didn't), Beck involved the listeners by having them clap a rhythm. He then proceeded to use the audience as a drum, working guitar phrases and runs around the tempo. He laughs and defies the image of the tough, esoteric rock musician whose only source of meaning and pleasure comes from music." Scourtis also gives special praise to Ron Wood: "He is a bass player who possesses a completely personal style. His bass lines often sound like lead lines, contrasting with Beck's playing, but at the same time weaving a web ... and held the entire sound together."

In the audience this weekend is 17-year old Joe Perry (later of Aerosmith fame), who recounts his impressions of seeing Beck: "On one of these weekends, I saw the Jeff Beck Group ... I'm down in front, watching Jeff in total awe. No one who was there ever forgot those early Jeff Beck shows."

JULY

FRI 5TH AND SAT 6TH
Grande Ballroom, Detroit, Michigan
The two nights in Detroit find the Jeff Beck Group as headliners supported by a quartet of local groups; Faith, plus Charging Rhino of Soul (on Friday) and Gold, plus Frost (on Saturday). Originally booked for Dearborn University, the shows are moved to Detroit's popular Grande Ballroom on the west-side, run by promoter Russ Gibb. Although Detroit audiences are tough by reputation, Jeff describes the two nights in Detroit as "... outrageous. Everyone was really enjoying themselves, and there were about 30 or 40 people grooving along on stage."

SUN 7TH
5th Dimension Club, Ann Arbor, Michigan
While Jeff Beck continues his triumphant American tour with a show in Ann Arbor (a hip college town with a strong blues scene), across the Atlantic in Luton, England, the Yardbirds play their very final concert today. With this behind him, Jimmy Page actively begins to recruit new members for a revamped line-up.

TUE 9TH, WED 10TH, THU 11TH
La Cave, Cleveland, Ohio
Jeff conducts transatlantic phone interviews with both DISC AND MUSIC ECHO and RECORD MIRROR (July 20) while in Cleveland. He explains to Derek Boltwood of RECORD MIRROR: "It's amazing and overwhelming, and very different from our annual gig at the Nottingham Rowing Club. I only came over to America to do some shopping really and I was in New York and it started to rain – so I went into the Fillmore to take shelter. The next thing I knew I was up on stage. Incredible. But seriously, it was very breathtaking to go down so well on our debut. We spent a long time planning our American tour, getting things just right – and it was worth it. Even so we didn't expect the sort of reception we're getting – it's unbelievable. ... what knocks me out is that a lot of the audiences over here still remember me from the Yardbirds ... we're enjoying ourselves immensely at the moment."

To DISC AND MUSIC ECHO Jeff exclaims "it's like a great big birthday party surprise! [Indeed, Jeff turned 24 on June 24, likely celebrating in New York.] It's the original group I had a year ago, I've had several changes since then and finally changed back. It's their first trip over here and they're doing very well – I'm very proud of them."

FRI 12TH AND SAT 13TH
The Catacombs, Houston, Texas

WED 17TH
LuAnne's, Dallas, Texas

A well-recorded live tape of unknown origin from one of the club appearances on this American tour has come to light, and displays the Jeff Beck Group at their brilliant best. An appreciative but very quiet audience greets the band. "It's like a library in here" Jeff mutters between songs. After the standard opening medley *You Shook Me* and *Let Me Love You*, the group kicks into *Talk To Me Baby*; a swaggering, strutting delight, with Jeff smoothly weaving a dazzling three chorus slide-and-finger solo, ranging in tone from dirty Elmore James to a deep, resonant cello. *Jeff's Boogie* is now featured as a key piece with Beck quoting the distinctive riff from Matt "Guitar" Murphy's *Steppin' Out*, pulling out his own *Over Under Sideways Down* signature riff, plus the assorted ragbag of Cliff Gallup, Les Paul and Scotty Moore licks. Jeff then stretches the middle into a long unaccompanied section, incorporating a familiar banjo tune – the theme song from *The Beverly Hillbillies* – borrowed from Flatt & Scruggs. "Clap your hands!" intones Jeff before they play a funky, tongue-in-cheek version of *Hi Ho Silver Lining*. Actually, this works just beautifully, and serves a function as a Lovin' Spoonful-ish breather between the otherwise blues-based songs.

The second set begins with Stewart on rhythm guitar for *Beck's Bolero*, before a tight *Oh Pretty Woman* is performed. The show also previews a brand new composition: "This is one called *Mother's Old Rice Pudding*," says Rod, and Jeff continues: "This next number has never been heard before, 'cause we've never played it. And we're gonna jam, so, you know, groove along." At this stage, the tune is very different to the one that eventually is recorded next spring, the

---

Set List/Jeff Beck Group

US tour June/July '68, club date

First set
You Shook Me • Let Me Love You • Talk To Me, Baby • Jeff's Boogie • Sweet Little Angel • Shapes of Things • Hi Ho Silver Lining

Second set
Beck's Bolero • Rock My Plimsoul • Oh Pretty Woman • Morning Dew • Rice Pudding • The Sun Is Shining • I Ain't Superstitious

---

July 1968: The Small Faces top the UK album charts with "Ogden's Nut Gone Flake" for four weeks.

July 1968: Jeff Beck Group play six nights at the Fillmore West ...

only similarity being no vocals. Tonight's version is a psychedelic tour de force; a long, rambling but constantly inventive and highly charged jam, with Beck, Wood and Waller chasing each other to new heights. Waller (introduced as "a five foot stick of dynamite") also has a short solo. Still, Jeff's playing is always focused and to the point, avoiding the twenty minute excursions so in vogue at the time.

In both sets, a little nifty uptempo riff is used to segue into a slow blues; *Sweet Little Angel* in the first set, and *The Sun Is Shining* in the second set. Actually, it is the same segue that Jeff will later record as *Livin' Alone* on the Beck, Bogert & Appice album.

THU 18TH

Arriving in San Francisco, Jeff and Rod catch Janis Joplin's impressive show at the Fillmore West tonight. In fact, so impressive, it scares Stewart to the point of confidence-loss.

FRI 19TH, SAT 20TH, SUN 21ST
Fillmore West, San Francisco, California

This weekend the Jeff Beck Group and Siegel-Schwall Band support Sly & the Family Stone, incidentally one of Jeff's favourite American groups. Reportedly, one of the Fillmore sets is taped for an undocumented local FM broadcast. Promoter Bill Graham has in fact, just two weeks earlier, moved his operation into the Carousel Ballroom at Market and Van Ness from the original Fillmore Auditorium (where Jeff performed with the Yardbirds in October 1966), and will adapt the moniker 'Fillmore West' for his premier West Coast theatre.

On the Friday, Jeff is contracted to do a transatlantic chat with Johnny Moran for BBC Radio One's "Scene And Heard", for transmission the following day (6.32–7.30 pm), with a repeat on Monday July 22.

TUE 23RD, WED 24TH, THU 25TH
Fillmore West, San Francisco, California

The Jeff Beck Group play further three nights at promoter Bill Graham's Fill-

Set List/Jeff Beck Group

Fillmore West, July 23–25 '68

You Shook Me • Let Me Love You • Morning Dew • Jeff's Boogie • The Sun Is Shining/Blues de Luxe • Hi Ho Silver Lining

ALL SHOOK UP

Truth Or Consequences

June 14, 1968 became a turning point in Jeff Beck's career. That night he stepped off stage in New York after a tumultuous reception, having won the audience and the critics over. During the previous year, Beck seemed to have lost momentum, reaching a low point with *Love Is Blue* in the spring of 1968, and Mickie Most's pop-oriented career decisions had nearly cost Beck his professional reputation – but now he was back with a vengeance. Most's partner, Peter Grant, played an important role in getting the Jeff Beck Group to America, where the receptive audiences accepted Jeff Beck with open arms.

The *Truth* album was an electrifying experience – right from *Shapes of Things* which jumpstarts side one, until Mickey Waller's drum rumblings which end side two. The key to the group's successful blues-rock hybrid was the interplay between Beck's guitar and Stewart's voice. On the whole the Jeff Beck Group toned down the eclecticism and psychedelia of the Yardbirds, and the maverick rockabilly influence was gone in favour of a refined blues-rock sound. Or as music writer Mark Michaels so succinctly would put it: "Beck played less like Les Paul on the Les Paul guitar than he did on the Telecaster". *Rock My Plimsoul* was the blueprint for not only the Jeff Beck Group but also for much white blues-rock which came in the wake of *Truth*: An old blues song (in this case B.B. King's sensous and swinging *Rock Me Baby*) was sped up and performed slightly heavy-handed with emphasis on the guitar riff, and here with Rod's hoarse croak replacing King's big-voiced delivery.

The wah-wah pedal became an expressive tool under Jeff's foot. He of course saw the humourous quality of the pedal by recreating dogs barking and cats meowing on *I Ain't Superstitious*. The excellent *Blues de Luxe* paired Jeff's Buddy Guy-flirtations with Nicky Hopkins' Johnnie Johnson-styled piano figures. There was also room for some non-blues pieces, like the wistful version of Tim Rose's *Morning Dew*, the charmingly clumsy *Greensleeves*, and an evocative interpretation of *Ol' Man River*.

Although *Truth* was a blues-rock milestone, the group members sorely lacked songwriting skills. Oddly enough, amidst their disintegration, the situation was partly rectified on the Jeff Beck Group's second album, *Beck-Ola*, which did include some decent self-penned material such as the minor classic *Plynth* and the brash *Spanish Boots* (watch out for Tony Newman's thrilling drum break!). The most ambitious number was the meandering *Rice Pudding*, which was a roller-coaster ride through moments of brilliance and the abyss of confusion.

By now Jeff had switched from the smoothness of a Les Paul to the cutting urgency of a Stratocaster, perfectly reflecting the chaos within his group. The wah-wah had more or less gone, but slide guitar dominated Jeff's playing more than before. Unfortunately, the album short-changed the public with only seven tracks and less than 30 minutes of playing time. On the whole, *Beck-Ola* is generally accepted as inferior to *Truth*, but it nevertheless boasts some of the rawest playing by a sixties band – particularly on the two demented Presley covers *Jailhouse Rock* and *All Shook Up*, where Jeff and his group sound like they literally break up in the studio.

For a few months in late 1968, the Jeff Beck Group were up there tugging at the crown of Cream and Hendrix. But in 1969 the pressures became too heavy, and the Jeff Beck Group did not manage to sustain the excitement and instead fizzled out. ∎

more venue in San Francisco, this time sandwiched between Mint Tattoo and headliners Moby Grape.

The trade magazine AMUSEMENT BUSINESS notes: "The Jeff Beck Group received standing ovations two consecutive nights ... from 2,500 audiences each night, in accord with a generally enthusiastic reception during their entire run [at the Fillmore]." Peter Thompson reviews one of Beck's Fillmore West concerts in THE STANFORD DAILY (August 6): "Beck is among the most versatile of rock guitarists, able to go from bottleneck interpretations of *Bolero* to the good-timey *Hi Ho Silver Lining* to a fifteen minute totally improvised display of just how well a young white boy can play his own blues."

[⊙⊙] A short tape, barely half an hour from one of the Moby Grape shows, unfolds with *You Shook Me/Let Me Love You* highlighted by a superb and fluid Beck solo and the trademark voice/guitar interplay at its very best.

July 1968: "Truth" is released in the US ...

Beck then seemingly switches to a Fender for the remainder of the set, beginning with *Morning Dew,* an exercise in light and shade, where quiet passages suddenly burst to life when Jeff steps on the wah-wah. A lucid and loose-limbed *Jeff's Boogie* is brimming with wild ideas, before the slow blues *The Sun Is Shining* (with Rod also quoting from *Blues de Luxe*) makes its entrance. Finally, Jeff winds up proceedings with a tongue-in-cheek *Hi Ho Silver Lining.*

FRI 26TH AND SAT 27TH
Shrine Exposition Hall, Los Angeles, California

After a week at the Fillmore in San Francisco, Jeff's group moves south for two nights at Los Angeles' big Shrine Expo Hall supporting Pink Floyd and Blue Cheer. The two shows draw 6,500 attendees.

The Jeff Beck Group are sandwiched between Pink Floyd and the California-based Blue Cheer. The reviewer from LA FREE PRESS observes that what he "hadn't counted on was that the Jeff Beck Group ... would put both Pink Floyd and Blue Cheer to shame."

MON 29TH

To captalize on the their recent concert success in the US, the first album by the Jeff Beck Group is rush-released today. Called *Truth,* it will not be released in Great Britain until October.

Some of the group's earlier recordings have been re-recorded for the album, including *Rock My Plimsoul* and *Beck's Bolero.* While the first is actually used (replacing the single version with Aynsley Dunbar from the previous year), a presumably re-recorded attempt at *Beck's Bolero* is dropped from the album, because, as Jeff explains in the witty liner notes "we couldn't improve on it". Another song, *You Shook Me,* bears the legend "last note of song is my guitar being sick – well so would you be if I smashed your guts for 2.28."

Again the recording only credits 'Jeff Beck', while the album is in fact a product of the Jeff Beck Group. The girl depicted on the cover is Jeff's new girlfriend Celia Hammond.

The album is warmly received in the States, and Al Kooper in ROLLING STONE (September 28) hails it as the current equivalent to the John Mayall/Eric Clapton album, although he confesses he was dubious after seeing the group at the Scene in June: "It was an unnerving experience to hear the Beck group. I had to leave after three numbers. The band was blowing changes, the bass player was losing time, Beck was uncomfortably and bitingly over-volumed ... It didn't make a hell of a lot of sense to me." *Truth* is an entirely different kettle of fish, according to Kooper: "This album is quite another matter ... a classic in much the same way the Clapton–Mayall album is," summing up: "As a group they swing like mad on this record. It remains to be seen what will happen to them in person. I hope the public is honest enough to make them work out." Jeff later sneers about Kooper: "He's a real big head – that's my opinion of him anyway; from the articles of his I've read, he talks out of the back of his arse. But he came to see us play and said 'Sorry ... now I've seen you, it all ties up. I admit I was wrong'. But I didn't care. I'd rather he had stuck to his guns than crawl."

While in California, Jeff is interviewed by John Sharkey for a feature in GUITAR PLAYER (October 1968). Describing the difference between the Yardbirds and his present group, Jeff uses this analogy: "... it is like giving a little child a piece of ground to play in, a huge 20-mile field, and say 'play'. He has all the space to play and he'll probably just sit down and do nothing. You know what I mean? But when you are restricted you want to get out. When I was with the Yardbirds, I was restricted so badly that I used to be like a naughty boy and play all these weird things all the time. Now, I've got my own band and it's like being in my own field, there's so much to do that it is really difficult." When asked to give the readers a hint as to the direction he will be taking, Jeff, always the opportunist, explains: "It's making noises people want to hear."

Album
JEFF BECK [GROUP]
TRUTH

A1 SHAPES OF THINGS *(Samwell-Smith/Relf/McCarty)* **A2** LET ME LOVE YOU *(Jeffery Rod)* **A3** MORNING DEW *(Bonnie Dobson/Tim Rose)* **A4** YOU SHOOK ME *(Willie Dixon)* **A5** OL' MAN RIVER *(Jerome Kern/Oscar Hammerstein II)*

B1 GREENSLEEVES *(Trad.)* **B2** ROCK MY PLIMSOUL *(Jeffery Rod)* **B3** BECK'S BOLERO *(Jimmy Page)* **B4** BLUES DE LUXE *(Jeffery Rod)* **B5** I AIN'T SUPERSTITIOUS *(Willie Dixon)*

Released Monday July 29, 1968 (US Epic PE 26413) Friday October 4, 1968 (UK Columbia SCX 6293)
Personnel is Jeff Beck (ldgtr, pdl stl gtr on A1, ac gtr on B1, bs on A5), Rod Stewart (vcls), Ron Wood (bs except A5, B1 and B3), Mickey Waller (drms except B1 and B3). Nicky Hopkins (pno on A3, B3, B4 and poss A4), John Paul Jones (hmnd org on A5 and poss A4, bs on B3), Jimmy Page (12 string gtr on B3), Keith Moon (drms on B3 credited as "You Know Who"), unknown (bagpipes on A3)
Recorded at EMI Studios, 3 Abbey Road, St John's Wood, London, April 20, May 14–16 & 25, 1968 and IBC Studios, Portland Place, London, May 16–17*, 1966 (B3).
Produced by Mickie Most, Jimmy Page (B3)
Arranged by Jeff Beck
Engineered by Ken Scott (all except B3) and Glyn Johns (B3)
Highest Chart Position US: #15
Highest Chart Position UK: –

AUGUST

FRI 2ND AND SAT 3RD
Shrine Exposition Hall, Los Angeles, California

Another two dates at LA's Shrine auditorium round off a tremendously successful American tour. The Jeff Beck Group share the bill with blues great Albert King (also on the bill over the weekend are Charles Lloyd, Big Mama Thornton and Steve Miller Band), which Jeff considers another high point of the tour.

While in Los Angeles, the group stays at the Continental Hyatt House (or the 'Riot House' according to rock mythology), where American record producer Lou Reizner bumps into Rod Stewart after seeing him at the Shrine. Two months later Reizner signs him to Mercury Records and leads him on to eventual superstardom.

SUN 4TH ✱
The group flies home to London.

August 1968: Jeff Beck Group play the 8th National Jazz & Blues Festival ...

SAT 10TH
"8th National Jazz & Blues Festival"
Kempton Park Racecourse, Sunbury
Back in Britain again, Jeff Beck returns to this annual festival marking his fourth appearance here in all. The festival site has now moved to Sunbury, and the three-day affair begins on Friday with Jerry Lee Lewis as the main attraction.

After the jazz programme at noon, the pop and rock groups come on stage from 7.00–11.30 pm. In alphabetical order the festival today presents Ginger Baker (and surprise guest Eric Clapton), Jeff Beck, Arthur Brown, Joe Cocker, Deep Purple, the Nice, the Nite People, Ten Years After, and Tyrannosaurus Rex. A confident Jeff Beck Group have the added one-off attraction of Nicky Hopkins. In his review, Keith Altham of NEW MUSICAL EXPRESS points out that "... there is no doubt that this group have come back from the States with a harder sound and a much more together act – particularly enjoyable is the vocal/guitar play between Beck and Stewart."

MON 12TH
Today's on-sale edition of AMUSEMENT BUSINESS (dated August 17) reports on how Beck's second weekend at the Shrine gathered a crowd of 5,000, and that the four nights combined there grossed $35,000. Excitingly, the paper also runs this news item: "London session bassist John Paul Jones and vocalist Robert Plante [sic] have been asked by Jimmy Page to join his new Yardbirds"; the first printed evidence that Peter Grant is already getting behind his other ex-Yardbird client.

THU 15TH
Contracted to do a short interview for BBC Radio 1, Jeff Beck talks to Keith Altham for transmission on "Scene And Heard" two days later, August 17 (6.32–7.30 pm), with the obligatory repeat on Monday August 19. *Shapes Of Things* is also played on record.

SAT 24TH
Truth enters the American charts at #163 today, and after selling around 150,000 copies it will peak at #15.

SEPTEMBER

FRI 6TH
"Bluesville '68", Manor House, London
'First club date after fantastic US tour!' trumpets the advertisement.

SAT 14TH
Norwich
DISC AND MUSIC ECHO explains in today's edition how piano player Nicky Hopkins will debut with the Jeff Beck Group in Sweden at end of the month. This proves to be a bit premature, as Hopkins will not join until a few days into the American tour in October.

MON 16TH
A single combining *Ol' Man River* with *Blues de Luxe* is scheduled for issue in the States today, even given a catalogue number (Epic 5-10390) but then cancelled. Still, this odd coupling is released on the Continent, including France.

TUE 17TH
The Jeff Beck Group are at 201 Piccadilly, Studio 1, London to pre-record an appearance on John Peel's "Top Gear". Under the guidance of producer Bernie Andrews, they tape *You Shook Me*, *Shapes of Things*, *Sweet Little Angel*, the new group instrumental *Mother's Old Rice Pudding* (now rearranged as a funky wah-wah number with a James Brown groove plus a long bass solo) and *Rock My Plimsoul*. The first four selections are broadcast a week-and-a-half later on September 29, while *Rock My Plimsoul* is held back until November 3.

Additionally, the version of the blues *Sweet Little Angel* is added to a transcription disc programme for overseas consumption entitled "Progressive Pop".

WED 18TH
A recording session is booked today. Futher details are not known, but the only real new addition to the group's repertoire is *Mother's Old Rice Pudding*, so that may have been attempted.

MON 23RD
The Jeff Beck Group are booked to pre-record an appearance on BBC Radio One's "Stuart Henry Show" today, with a broadcast date pencilled in for Sunday September 29. Beck's appearance is then cancelled and renewed for Sunday October 6, but this is cancelled again and the contract is not reissued.

SUN 29TH
The Jeff Beck Group and Joni Mitchell are the main guests on "Top Gear" (BBC Radio One 3.00–5.00 pm, ▶ September 17). Also on today's programme are Fairport Convention and Ten Years After.

MON 30TH
THE JEFF BECK GROUP: SECOND SCANDINAVIAN TOUR
Stockholm, Sweden
The Jeff Beck Group commence a short Scandinavian tour, beginning with concerts in Sweden's capital, Stockholm, as part of a nine-day 'British week', which sees other prominent UK artists like Paul Jones and Chris Farlowe also appearing.

Jethro Tull, who are about to release their debut album in a few weeks, play support on the stretch of Scandinavian dates.

OCTOBER

TUE 1ST, WED 2ND, THU 3RD
Stockholm, Sweden
Three further engagements believed to be in the Stockholm area. Jeff is also interviewed on Sveriges Radio P3 by Ulf Elving. Asked to pick a personal favourite, Jeff chooses *Rock My Plimsoul*.

On Wednesday, the Jeff Beck Group attend the gala opening of Stockholm's new discotheque Dang Dang in the company of Paul Jones and Bibi Johns. Jeff apparently also appears at Stockholm's Konserthuset on Thursday night.

FRI 4TH
Rigoletto, Jönköping, Sweden
Finally, today also sees the release of the *Truth* album in Great Britain, with identical song sequence and cover as the American version. Despite the great success in the US, the album does not chart in the UK. Reviewers in England are for the most part impressed however. RECORD MIRROR (November 30) enthusiastically reports "... and the basic truth of the album is that it is extremely good, varied and musicianly", while DISC AND MUSIC ECHO (December 7) awards the record four stars for 'an outstanding LP' and recommends it for a Christmas present. The only sour review is in NEW MUSICAL EXPRESS (November 30), where Allan Evans writes "... although competent, the whole LP lacks atmosphere and becomes mildly boring".

Beck's return to Jönköping (where he played in April), now supported by local group Seductions, is a great success according to JÖNKÖPINGS-POSTEN, which devotes its front-page to the concert: "The local public rewarded the boys with a big applause when they stepped off the stage after the concert."

October 1968: Jeff Beck Group begins second US tour in Chicago ...

THE JEFF BECK GROUP IN JÖNKÖPING, SWEDEN. FACSIMILE FROM JÖNKÖPINGSPOSTEN, OCTOBER 5, 1968

SAT 5TH
Brøndby Popclub, Copenhagen, Denmark

On a bill with Jethro Tull and Danish group the Baronets, the Jeff Beck Group produce a particularly uninspired show according to Carsten Grolin in EKSTRABLADET (October 7): "There is of course the possibility that Jeff and his group simply had an off-day on Saturday. But is seems clear that Beck has undergone a fundamental change ... His musical policy has been strangely erratic and seems to be influenced by what his manager's idea of commercial success is, rather than a personal conviction ... It is understandable that such an insecure person accepts the devotion he has met in the USA. But it is sad that such a talented and sensitive guitarist should waste his energies on a cold and incoherent technical show-off." Grolin's observations are correct enough; afterwards a frustrated Beck trashes his hotel room.

Grolin also reviews *Truth*, which he, however, gives top marks: "[The Jeff Beck Group] deliver a handful of unforgettable gems, where everything falls in place, working beautifully and vibrantly." *Truth* is issued in Europe concurrently with the British release, and Jean-Nöel Coghe in BEST (February 1969) – who dubs Beck "l'enfant terrible" – also gives the album a glowing recommendation.

SUN 6TH

'Jeff Beck's Plane Stopped By Police' screams the headline in the Danish EKSTRABLADET. Two club appearances (to be held at the Star Club in Copenhagen and at the Fjordvilla in Roskilde respectively) with Jethro Tull and the Norwegian group the Beatnicks are dramatically cancelled when the Beck Group – with the gross from the Scandinavian concerts already in their pockets – simply flee from their hotel bill at noon and book a flight back home. The group is arrested at the airport before take-off, and Jeff's manager is detained until matters are cleared. A disturbed Arne Worsøe, Jeff's Scandinavian tour promoter, explains: "I know Jeff Beck has big personal problems right now, where after three years he has broken through in the States ... If Beck had explained his situation to me, I would have cancelled the Sunday concerts even if it would have put me in an awkward position ... I spoke with him late Saturday night, and he was very disappointed by his performances, but intent on taking revenge on Sunday."

THU 10TH ✱

Together with tour managers Richard Cole and Pete Sanders, Beck, Stewart, Wood and Waller fly out to the States.

FRI 11TH
THE JEFF BECK GROUP:
SECOND NORTH AMERICAN TOUR
'Lectric Theater, Chicago, Illinois

The Jeff Beck Group commence their second American jaunt in Chicago today, a natural stop-over for Beck but one which was not included in his summer tour. Going out as the headlining act, originally the Chicago stop was to be a three-day residence, with support from Pacific Gas & Electric, Fever Tree and Rotary Connection (the last only on the 12th).

The aspiring guitarist-cum-salesman Rick Nielsen (who later finds his fame with Cheap Trick) catches tonight's concert, and going backstage afterwards sees a roadie accidently dropping Jeff's beloved sanded-down Les Paul so the neck comes apart. Nielsen recounts: "So I went backstage, and said 'Hey, you don't know me, but I've got a lot of guitars, and if you'd like I'll give you my number.'"

With the Les Paul broken, Jeff switches to an old beat-up Fender guitar kept as back-up. Although the Les Paul is eventually repaired and put to use again, it does seem likely that Jeff, for a few shows, depends on hired equipment.

SAT 12TH
Alma College, Alma, Michigan

SUN 13TH
Mentor Hullaballoo, Mentor, Ohio

Jeff Beck appears for two shows at 3 and 7.30 pm at this club just outside Cleveland, emceed by WKYC deejay Chuck Dunaway. Two Ohio groups complete the bill: Munx and Cyrus Erie, the latter includes future Raspberry singer-guitarist Eric Carmen. THE CLEVELAND PRESS writes that *Truth* has been Cleveland's fastest-selling album.

FRI 18TH AND SAT 19TH
Fillmore East, New York, New York

Also on the bill for the Fillmore shows are Tim Buckley and Albert King. Two performances a day at the 2,700-seat Fillmore bring a gross total of an impressive $33,000.

The Fillmore concerts also mark Nicky Hopkins' official debut in the Jeff Beck Group. The pianist who has played with Jeff on several occasions both in the studio and on stage, has a formidable reputation, having also worked with the Beatles (on *Revolution*), the Rolling Stones (lately on *Beggars' Banquet*), the Kinks, the Who and countless others, and it is a coup to have him in the group. With Hopkins onboard the set is slightly re-arranged, and his piano showcase is an instrumental version of the Carole King/Gerry Goffin ballad *(You Make Me Feel Like A) Natural Woman. Hi Ho Silver Lining* and *Oh Pretty Woman* are dropped altogether, but otherwise the repertoire contains no surprises.

During the group's visit to Bill Graham's Fillmore East, the Jeff Beck Group are filmed miming to *Shapes of Things*. Billed as "Welcome To The Fillmore", it is unclear if it is used as a broadcast; but it is probably intended as a promotional TV clip.

October 4, 1968: Cream's final US tour begins in Oakland, California.

October 1968: Nicky Hopkins joins Beck's group ...

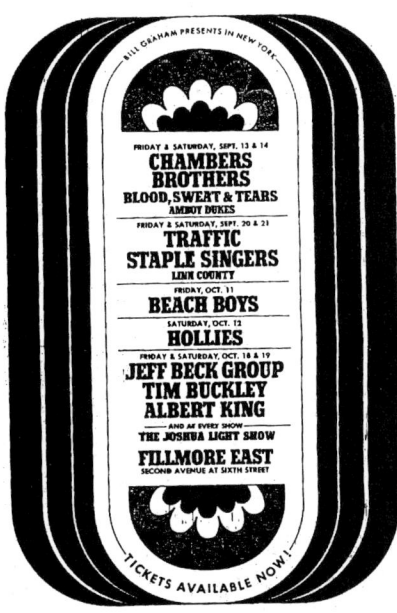

Pat Costello, who is Jeff's publicity contact, secures Beck an interview while in New York with David Walley and Patricia Kennely, which runs as cover story in JAZZ & POP in June 1969. A 'serious' interview, Jeff and the two journalists engage themselves in long discussions on music, quite different from the ususal pop magazine fare. Jeff confesses a liking for jazz ("Charles Lloyd. I just saw him in concert; way out, you know") and classical music, and when asked about musicians he admires, he surprisingly names British cellist Jaqueline Du Pre and opera singer Kathleen Farrier. Beck muses: "She's [Farrier] dead now ... It takes someone to die before they come to life. Instantly when she died, right, it was on the television. So when I die, I'll probably get like a one-inch column in the DAILY WORKER, you know. 'Pop Guitar Player Dies. Age 24. Foul playing was not suspected.'" The interview ends with a long talk about Jeff's conversion to vegetarianism: "I've only been one for six months, though", whereupon David Walley replies "You're looking pretty good", to which Beck shoots back "Well, my girlfriend in England has been one for seven years, and *she* looks pretty good!" Beck cannot praise Nicky Hopkins (who he has much enthusiasm for working with) enough: "I really truly must be one of the luckiest guys, I mean, to have Nicky in the group. He's going to help write songs and put them down in a true musical way, which I can't put over to the others. It's going to be an entirely different group, I think."

SUN 20TH
Alexandria Roller Rink, Alexandria, Virginia
Returning to the venue he visited with the Yardbirds in December 1965, Jeff Beck opens for Janis Joplin and Big Brother & the Holding Company. Promoted by DCS Productions, the show pulls 6,000 fans with a gross of $26,000.

MON 21ST
Peter Grant and Mickie Most meet up with Jeff at the Waldorf Astoria in New York City. Most has come to the States to see some of his acts perform, including Jeff, Donovan (on October 25) and singer-guitarist Terry Reid.

TUE 22ND, WED 23RD, THU 24TH
Boston Tea Party, Boston, Massachusetts
The Jeff Beck Group return to the Tea Party for three nights supported by Kensington Market and Earth Opera.

Mickie Most is present on the Tuesday, and is convinced of Jeff's American success. He recounts to NEW MUSICAL EXPRESS: "It looked as if the Marquee had been planted in Boston!"

Writing on Wednesday's show, Richard T. Schmidt in the [Boston College] HEIGHTS comments: "I guess it doesn't matter what they looked like except that Jeff Beck looked like a skinny guy who has been lifting weights for about a year. ... Jeff Beck surprised me. He was clean and happy. He really likes playing the guitar, and he likes sounds. He finds a note he likes and follows it until it comes back to the song. He builds sounds into waves and stands next to the amp so he can feel it. He smiles. He laughs. He plays the guitar well. And I like that." And reviewing the following night, Steve Grant in THE [MIT] TECH (November 1) writes: "Last Thursday night the best rock guitarist in the world showed his stuff here in town ... Beck says and

Set List/Jeff Beck Group

Boston Tea Party, Oct 22 '68

Talk To Me Baby • Jeff's Boogie • Blues de Luxe • Rock My Plimsoul • (You Make Me Feel Like A) Natural Woman • Shapes of Things • Rice Pudding • I Ain't Superstious

Boston Tea Party, Oct 23 '68

You Shook Me • Morning Dew • Sweet Little Angel • Rock My Plimsoul • (You Make Me Feel Like A) Natural Woman • Shapes of Things • Beck's Bolero • Rice Pudding • Bye Boston

---

IT DOESN'T REALLY MATTER

The Chicken And The Egg

Much has been written about the similarities between the Jeff Beck Group and Led Zeppelin. Not only did both bands spring from the Yardbirds and sported identical line-ups based on the interplay between a vocalist and a guitarist backed by a fierce rhythm-section, but their respective debut albums were conceptually alike – right down to the unfortunate doubling of Willie Dixon's *You Shook Me*.

Otherwise both albums contained a strong blues influence, an acoustic piece each, a touch of folk and some original songs. When it came to borrowing blues tunes and tailoring them for their own use, the Jeff Beck Group were no better than what Led Zeppelin have been accused of. Then again, it may be argued that the Yardbirds started this dubious trend; many of their songs were lifted from blues originals.

Truth was released in the United States in August 1968, six months before Led Zeppelin's debut, and caused a controversy between Beck and Page because of *You Shook Me*. Although Jimmy Page has vaguely claimed that he had not heard Jeff's version, in hindsight that does not seem likely – it is practically impossible to think how Jimmy could *not* have heard Beck play and perform *You Shook Me* before Led Zeppelin both recorded and released their debut album. Robert Plant has suggested it was probably just an unfortunate coincidence, and as Jeff later readily admitted: "They [Led Zeppelin] had a better package." The irony was of course that Led Zeppelin broke through while the Jeff Beck Group just broke up. ■

does more things on a Gibson guitar than can easily be believed."

🔊 A high point of the first night is a further extended *Mother's Old Rice Pudding*, which is even more sprawling now that Hopkins has come aboard. Not as coherent and funky as the version done for BBC Radio One in September, now it is basically a Hendrix-y wah-wah workout with long drum and bass solos. But very nice, too, to hear Ron Wood kick in the riff from *Satisfaction* during his bass solo, a tune he invariably will be

November 1968: Jimmy Page joins Jeff Beck on stage in Miami ...

well acquainted with later on! A storming *Jeff's Boogie* follows and shows off Beck's encyclopedic knowledge of guitar styles, be it jazzy chords, rockabilly finger picking, country runs or blues bends. *Blues de Luxe* is beautiful and Beck's intro solo on *Rock My Plimsoul* is positively hair raising.

The second night is nowhere as good as the previous. The over-all impression is of a looser and more untogether group; strangely enough Nicky Hopkins' piano offsets the finely tuned balance between Beck and Stewart and the rhythm section. Jeff seems also to fight with his guitar, presumably a back-up Fender, and is slightly out of tune when he strains for the painfully high notes. *Rock My Plimsoul* is dedicated by Rod to "our favourite deejay here, Peter Wolf", and swings along just fine with Nicky Hopkins playing brilliant blues piano like only he knows. Next up is a rather unneccesary version of *Natural Woman*, performed instrumentally, with Hopkins to the fore. *Shapes of Things* is also quite tame, and *Beck's Bolero* – with Hopkins recreating his original piano part – is played very close to the recorded version. Before the finale – a slow *Goodbye Boston* blues – the group mauls *Mother's Old Rice Pudding*, which is not even close to last night's version.

FRI 25TH AND SAT 26TH
Electric Factory, Philadelphia, Pennsylvania

Sharing the stage with the Beck Group in Philadelphia are fellow Brits Ten Years After and US group the American Dream. Mickie Most also attends the second concert at the Electric Factory. On Saturday, Jeff buys several guitars from Rick Nielsen and another Chicago tradesman, including a Les Paul sunburst for $350. This beautiful tiger-striped Gibson is immediately put to use, and will remain Jeff's main stage guitar until it is stolen along with Ron Wood's Telecaster bass sometime the following year. The much-abused sanded down Les Paul is retired for the time being but later given a major overhaul.

SUN 27ND
Rock Pile, Toronto, Canada

Beck visits Canada's top rock club today and Ritchie Yorke of TORONTO GLOBE AND MAIL (October 28) interviews Jeff ("Beck was sporting yellow canvas boots, a silver chain around his stomach rather than holding up trousers, and – get this – blond-tipped hair") and reviews the concert: "On stage, Beck worked with bass, piano and drums ... His guitar playing; performed with great mastery, was sharp, prudent and biting enough to cut through ice. He was a guitar contortionist – moaning, groaning, dragging out blue notes the way an oil drill shrieks through rock to find a pocket of fluid ... Beck is probably one of the three finest white blues guitarists today. The fact that almost 2,000 young Torontonians turned out to worship at this successful new rock shrine shows he may soon be joining Eric Clapton as one of the blues guitar gods of the sixties."

Because of an equipment hitch, the first of two houses has to be cancelled, and the second show does not start until 10 o'clock. According to Yorke, Beck's managers demand full fee despite the forced cancellation, and as Yorke drily notes, "the group got its way".

THU 31ST

Back in New York City again – in the wake of a Buddy Miles concert at the Fillmore East – the Jeff Beck Group play a short, unadvertised set at a benefit in aid of the children of Biafra. Several other big name groups in town today also appear at this little-documented event, and Jeff and Rick Zehringer (later Derringer) of the McCoys join in on the final jam.

•

The LPs *Blues Anytime Volumes 1 & 2* are released this month in the UK on Immediate Records. They contain the two songs *Chuckles* and *Steelin'*, credited to Jeff Beck and the All Stars, from way back in 1965. These have been re-packaged endlessly on albums such as *Anthology of British Blues* (Immediate), *Guitar Boogie* (RCA) and *White Boy Blues* (Compleat).

Interestingly, the albums also contain four songs by Santa Barbara Machine Head, a one-off studio project with Ron Wood, Jon Lord, Kim Gardner and Twink, recorded just prior to Wood joining Beck.

NOVEMBER

FRI 1ST, SAT 2ND, SUN 3RD
Grande Ballroom, Detroit, Michigan

For three consecutive nights, the Jeff Beck Group headline while various local groups like Toad (on Friday), McKennon Mendelssohn Mainline (replacing original choice, Dogfox, on Saturday) and Joyful Wisdom (on Sunday) play support at the Grande.

Meanwhile, home in Britain *Rock My Plimsoul* is broadcast on the 3rd on John Peel's "Top Gear" radio show (► September 17).

MON 4TH✱

Back in New York City again, Jeff attends Terry Reid's debut performances at the Scene. (Reid has a residency here November 4th–20th).

TUE 5TH

A performance at the Music Hall, Kansas City, Missouri, is reportedly cancelled, although advertised in the papers on the day of the show.

FRI 8TH
Music Hall, Houston, Texas

SAT 9TH
McFarlin Auditorium, Southern Methodist University, Dallas, Texas

SUN 10TH
Oklahoma City, Oklahoma

Originally booked for Independence Auditorium, Baton Rouge, Louisiana, tonight is replaced with an Oklahoma show at short notice.

MON 11TH–THU 14TH✱

With a few days off, Jeff Beck apparently returns to New York, where he meets up with Peter Grant, who is in town with Jimmy Page. Grant and Page deliver the master tapes of the first Led Zeppelin album to Atlantic Records, with whom they just signed.

FRI 15TH AND SAT 16TH
Thee Image, Miami, Florida

Peter Grant, Jimmy Page and Jeff Beck fly down to Florida, where Beck's group are booked to play a weekend at Miami's top rock spot. Grant recalls how his imposing appearance comes

November 26, 1968: Cream play their farewell concert at the Royal Albert Hall.

December 1968: Jeff Beck Group headline four nights at the Fillmore West ...

in handy when Beck and Page are taunted by some sailors: "... there was this time when some sailors were having a go at Jimmy and Jeff. The three of us were flying down to Miami, and I turn around and hear these blokes. One of 'em looked like a little touch, so I lifted him up under the arm and said 'OK what's your trouble Popeye?'" According to Richard Cole, Page even joins Beck on stage for a jam on the Friday – the first time the two have shared the stage since October 1966 – before Jimmy jumps on a plane back to England in time for a Led Zeppelin college gig in Manchester on Saturday night!

FRI 22ND AND SAT 23RD
The Grand, Cleveland, Ohio

Not to be confused with Detroit's Grand*e* Ballroom, Cleveland's Grand is a less-illustrious venue, where Beck is supported by the Wild Yama Rama Chuck Band for the Friday night, while Detroit's own MC5 share the bill for the Saturday spot. Originally, the Friday was scheduled for Memorial Auditorium, Burlington, Vermont.

WED 27ND
Eagles Auditorium, Seattle, Washington

FRI 29TH AND SAT 30TH
Shrine Exposition Hall, Los Angeles, California

The Jeff Beck Group alternate with fellow Brit-groups the Moody Blues and Ten Years After (plus the local Outlaw Blues Band) on two different stages to provide continuous music. A 7,000-strong crowd each night guarantees new attendance records for the two nights at the Shrine. A lengthy review by Michael Etchison in LOS ANGELES HERALD-EXAMINER (December 3) is used in full as an advertisement in MELODY MAKER on January 4, 1969. Under the headline 'Enthusiasm For Beck Justified', Etchison writes: "Saturday night they were received with wild enthusiasm, and justifiably. Playing the usual blues oriented rock, Beck is as good as almost anyone, as searing solos in *Let Me Love You Baby* and *Rock My Plimsoul* showed. Outside that style, there is no one who can touch him. In his showpiece, *Beck's Boogie* [sic], he played not only straight rock and 1940s-style boogie but also some Les Paul and Earl Scruggs."

After one of the Shrine shows, Beck, Nicky Hopkins and Rod Stewart record three songs with Frank Zappa (behind the console) and his protégés the GTOs in a late-night session. The GTOs ('Girls Together Outrageously') count notorious groupie Pamela DesBarres among their ranks. Three weird songs are put on tape; *Eureka Springs Garbage Lady, Captain Fat Theresa Shoes* and *Shock Treatment,* and all are issued on the GTOs album *Permanent Damage* (US Straight Records) on December 8, 1969.

DECEMBER

TUE 3RD
The TV special "Elvis" airs on NBC TV, and features Elvis Presley in portions of the show backed by Scotty Moore, Charlie Hodge and D.J. Fontana. The show revitalizes his career, and features *All Shook Up* and *Jailhouse Rock* plus a slew of other classics. In all probability Beck and band watch this on their day off in LA.

THU 5TH, FRI 6TH, SAT 7TH, SUN 8TH
Fillmore West, San Francisco, California

The Jeff Beck Group finish their second US tour when they headline four nights running at the Fillmore West. For the first two nights, Spirit and Sweet Linda Tillery provide support, while Divine and Sweetwater open the shows on the latter two.

The group flies up from Los Angeles on the Thursday. During the whole San Francisco stay, photographer Baron Wolman – working on an assignment for EYE magazine (and published in the April 1969 edition) – documents both the group's hotel life and the Fillmore concerts. The group shares a couple of rooms at the Continental Lodge motel: "The next four days [the motel] was home, the television set was their hearth – tube on but sound off. That left them free to fiddle with guitars and rap, and at the same time scan the screen." Wolman also details how Jeff buys a hot-rod for $2,500. Jeff is also interviewed by HIT PARADER (July 1969).

Financially as well as critically the tour has been a tremendous success and marks the high point of the Jeff Beck Group's turbulent life.

MON 9TH
Beck, Stewart, Hopkins, Wood and Waller plus Pete Sanders board a London bound flight at 10 am.

TUE 10TH–THU 12TH
Back in London, Nicky Hopkins partakes in "The Rolling Stones Rock & Roll Circus" filming at InterTel's Stonebridge Park Studios in Wembley.

MON 16TH
The Jeff Beck Group are originally billed to appear tonight at the Pavilion in Bath. However, they pull out at the last minute and their replacement are none other than Led Zeppelin.

SAT 21ST
Middle Earth, The Roundhouse, London

The Jeff Beck Group play a one-off pre-Christmas show in London supported by Blond On Blond and Turnstile.

THU 26TH
To cash in on Jeff's recent US triumph, Peter Grant has provisionally booked Jeff Beck on a further selection of American dates slotted in for the Christmas season, to open today in Denver with Vanilla Fudge. But Beck is tired, so Peter Grant has already decided to send out another of his clients, Led Zeppelin, on *their* first US tour.

FRI 27TH
Two club dates before New Year's Eve are reportedly cancelled, the first today at the Hornsey Wood Tavern in London. The second is on Sunday, December 29th, at Mothers Club in Birmingham.

•

In their yearly round-up, ROLLING STONE awards Jeff and his band a very special trophy: "The Jeff Beck Group was the best thing from England this year, with the exception of Traffic. Deluged by British blues bands, they said it with a rock and roll difference, a good record characterized by new sounds, and a respectable tour ... Anyway, Jeff Beck went around the country without his shirt on – maybe it's warm – and set that style in his publicity pictures, so to Jeff, the Annual Robert Christgau Erect Left Nipple Award."

•

In the annual BEAT INSTRUMENTAL Readers' Poll for 1968, Jeff is again rated as number four, while Rod Stewart, Nicky Hopkins, Ron Wood and Mickey Waller are all represented in their respective sections.

▽ 1969

JANUARY

TUE 14TH
Marquee Club, London
A packed Marquee greets the Jeff Beck Group on their sole January booking, where Andromeda are the support act.

Reviewing the concert in MELODY MAKER (January 25), Chris Welch writes: "Jeff Beck's band blew a solid set ... last week to a packed house and proved why they have been so successful in America. Jeff himself was in good form, and after a shaky start, when some of the amplification was switched off, Nicky Hopkins' piano came through loud and clear and gave the band a highly distinctive sound. Jeff blew some nice blues and shone on his flag waving piece *Beck's Boogie* [sic] ... Rod Stewart, a most underrated singer, leapt and sang with his usual enthusiasm and great spirits, while Ronnie Wood used his bass intelligently. Mickey Waller is a fine drummer ... the band as a unit are often a little rough, but are happily different and unpretentious and once they get up a head of steam can blow many a group off stage." In fact, Jeff will never perform at the Marquee officially again. Since 1965, Beck has played here about two dozen times.

FRI 24TH
Jeff joins Noel Redding for a jam at the Speakeasy.

LATE
Beck – who a year earlier told DISC AND MUSIC ECHO how he loved to cook himself pilaf, curry and steaks – has become a vegetarian, so when Chris Welch conducts an interview in late January for MELODY MAKER (February 1), it of course takes place at a veggie restaurant in London.

Beck's new found financial rewards also allow him and his girlfriend Celia Hammond to move to a 500 year-old cottage in Egerton, Kent, about fifty miles southeast of London. The house is surrounded by woodlands and tall trees, and will soon be furnished with antiques and worn remnants from older days, plus Celia and Jeff's 18 cats and 2 dogs.

Talking about the receptive hippie audiences in the US, Jeff quips: "The underground scene is really big in the States. Here it only means Mile End tube station." Beck furthermore gladly confesses: "... we're all lazy bastards, I'll admit ... The band has been rusty because we haven't been playing much recently."

MON 27TH
Pivotal San Francisco group Moby Grape arrive in England for a tour, and borrow Beck's amps.

FEBRUARY

SAT 1ST
An unconfirmed news item says the Jeff Beck Group are booked to appear at the Lanchester College Arts Festival in Coventry today, but no actual confirmation of the fact can be found.

Excitingly, according to Go (February 21), the group has completed a new single: *All Shook Up/Throw Down A Line*, which sadly is not released.

WED 5TH
Toby Jug, Tolworth
Playing almost on home turf in Tolworth, Surrey, Jeff's father is present to hear his son perform: "He doesn't play round here so often, so I've not heard him very much. But I've got all his records." Beck junior is also interviewed for an article in BEAT INSTRUMENTAL (March 1969).

EARLY
As it turns out, the Toby Jug gig on the 5th turns out the be the final appearance by the present Jeff Beck Group. Claiming their playing has deteriorated, Jeff fires the rhythm section of Mickey Waller and Ron Wood on the eve of the group's third American tour. Actually, it is a bit more complex than that. According to legend it is Jeff and Nicky who have put this scheme together; Beck allegedly wants to get rid of Wood and Hopkins ditto of Waller.

MON 10TH
Epic' 'Memory Lane' Series re-releases *Hi Ho Silver Lining* b/w *Beck's Bolero* in the US.

TUE 11TH
As Ron Wood celebrates his girlfriend Krissie's 21st birthday, Peter Grant calls and casually tells him his services will not be needed for the upcoming American tour; Mickey Waller presumably receives a similar phone call. Waller and Wood loosely form a group right away with Leigh Stephens, the former Blue Cheer frontman who has settled in the UK and is known by Waller and Wood from last year's American tour.

Beck's new drummer is Tony Newman, who Jeff calls up out of the blue asking if he's available, because he remembers his heavy back beat from when Newman drummed in Sounds Incorporated. Newman is very experienced, having toured extensively with Sounds Incorporated (including supporting the Beatles on an American tour), and is presently doing sessions for Cliff Richard and the like.

On bass Jeff strangely enough hires another guitarist, New Zealander Doug Jerebine, who impressed Beck so much when he supported the Beck group at the Marquee the previous April. Jerebine has now taken to using the stage name Doug Blake.

•

The need to break in the new members results in the cancellation of five engagements of the group's coming North American tour, which are rescheduled for later dates. These being a weekend at the Fillmore East in New York City (February 14–15), which has been on the cards since Christmas, originally to also feature the Small Faces and Johnny Winter (interestingly, Beck topping over the Small Faces would be unthinkable in Britain. Anyway, the Faces also cancel out and in the end Sam And Dave, Chuck Berry and Savoy Brown top this weekend at the Fillmore); State University of New York, Stony Brook, New York (February 16) with Mountain and Jethro Tull; Kinetic Playground, Chicago, Illinois (February 21) with Savoy Brown and Mother Earth and Kiel Auditorium, St. Louis, Missouri (February 22) with Procol Harum. Premier Talent sets about rescheduling dates to make up for the cancelleations.

FRI 14TH
The Canadian agencies Richard Flohil Productions and Concept Associates had attempted to organize a concert planned for today at Toronto's Massey Hall, promising the Jimi Hendrix Experience, Eric Clapton, Mike Bloomfield and the Jeff Beck Group, but this airy project proves unmanageable.

Newsflash February 1969: Tony Newman replaces Mickey Waller on drums ...

THU 27TH✻
Beck, Stewart, Hopkins, Blake and Newman plus Pete Sanders fly out to the States.

FRI 28TH
There is some confusion whether tonight's concert at Worcester Memorial Auditorium, Massachusetts actually does take place (with Jethro Tull and Mountain and intended as the date for resuming the tour). While an advertisement appears in the local newspaper this same day, seemingly the show is cancelled at the eleventh hour after Beck's arrival from England.

Ron Wood in England. Now in a position to negotiate his wage, he accepts and gets on the first plane out. Wood himself later remembers his demand as a stupefying £2,000 per gig (or roughly $5,600); hardly likely as this was more than what the group sometimes grossed in a single performance.

Mickey Waller, of course, does not return to Jeff's group. Instead he immerses himself in several projects this spring; a news item says he is to fly to the States to record an album with Galt McDermott (who wrote the *Hair* musical); then he joins Steamhammer for a spell; drums briefly with Brian Jones' post-Stones attempt, before he forms Silver Metre with guitarist Leigh Stephens.

MARCH

SAT 1ST
THE JEFF BECK GROUP: THIRD NORTH AMERICAN TOUR
Alexandria Roller Rink, Alexandria, Virginia

With an it'll-be-alright-on-the-night-attitude, the Jeff Beck Group open their 3rd North American tour today in Virginia (on the edge of greater Washington DC) with two shows, supported by Jethro Tull.

Not much is known about this ill-fated tour, but presumably the set list is kept more or less identical to the last US tour in October–December '68, relying on songs from *Truth* plus a selection of blues covers and the inevitable crowd pleaser *Jeff's Boogie*. For this tour the group is occasionally equipped with Rickenbacker Transonic amps, the result of an endorsement deal set up by Peter Grant who also briefly furnishes his other clients, Led Zeppelin, with these cumbersome transistor amps.

SUN 2ND
Douglas Blake proves totally unsuitable and is fired after the previous night in Alexandria. As a result, tonight's concert at Boston's Symphony Hall – again with Jethro Tull – is also cancelled. With a series of engagements already lined up and a small fortune in tour receipts at stake, a frantic transatlantic call is made to

TUE 4TH
EMI files show that the otherwise unissued song *Blues Title* is logged today, perhaps a trial recording with Newman and Blake done during February.

FRI 7TH
- **State University of New York, Stony Brook, New York**
- **Island Garden Arena, West Hempstead, New York**

A double date on Long Island marks Ron Wood's return to the fold. The Stony Brook college concert is rescheduled from mid-February and the group also performs a single show in West Hempstead with Savoy Brown and Mountain at 8.00 pm the same evening.

SAT 8TH
The Grand, Cleveland, Ohio
Support are provided by the two local groups Cast and Midnight Shift.

SUN 9TH
Electric Theatre, Toronto, Canada
A brief visit to Canada with support by Toronto band Meat.

FRI 14TH AND SAT 15TH
Kinetic Playground, Chicago, Illinois
Jeff Beck plays two nights at Chicago's main psychedelic ballroom – supported by Sweetwater and Van Morrison – to make up for the cancelled concerts in February.

SUN 16TH
Baltimore Civic Center, Baltimore, Maryland
The Jeff Beck Group appear in a major concert with B.B. King, Canned Heat plus local Maryland group King Solomon's Minds.

MON 17TH
Between tour dates, the Jeff Beck Group go out on the town in New York to see Jerry Lee Lewis today at the popular nightclub, the Scene. Many stars turn out for Lewis' first New York appearance in a long time, including Jimi Hendrix and members of Vanilla Fudge.

FRI 21ST AND SAT 22ND
Grande Ballroom, Detroit, Michigan
Supported by Sweetwater and Dick Rabbit, the Jeff Beck Group headline for two nights running in Detroit.

By now, Jeff feels the tour is a struggle, and it is decided to cancel at the first possible opportunity, which Beck also tells Russ Gibb in an interview at Detroit radio station WKNR on the Saturday: "That's the next thing we're gonna do, we're going home on Monday!" Jeff explains to Gibb that he's anxious to get back to England in order to record a new album.

SUN 23RD
The Minneapolis Labor Temple, Minneapolis, Minnesota
Supported by Zarathustra and Spider John Koerner & Willy Murphy for one show at 7 pm, this proves to be the last date of the tour as Beck has decided to cut the trip short and return to England.

ⓒ March 1, 1969: The Doors appear in concert in Miami during which Jim Morrison is alleged to have exposed himself for which he is later arrested.

March 1969: Jeff Beck cancels rest of US tour to record new album in London ...

MON 24TH
The Jeff Beck Group return to Britain in disarray. Nicky Hopkins would later comment on Jeff's behaviour: "We'd wake up one morning in the States and find he'd left the night before and was in England. It was just ridiculous. He blew so many chances."

At a press conference in Minneapolis, Jeff formally announces the cancellation of the remaining dates of the chaotic US tour, primarily so the group can return to England to compose and record a new album. The rest of the tour, with an estimated loss of a quarter million dollars in gross receipts, is cancelled and the official reason given is a collapse on the part of Beck. Besides the assumed money loss, this also comes hot on the heels of Jeff's recent cancellations when he was unable to put together a band for the start of the tour. All in all, this damages his reputation a lot and many – not only promoters but his fans, too – come to think of Jeff as unreliable.

•

The following dates are cancelled: Thee Image, Miami, Florida (March 28–30), Palm Springs Pop Festival, San Diego, California (April 2), Seattle Center Arena, Seattle, Washington (April 3), Agradome, Vancouver, Canada (April 4), Coliseum, Spokane, Washington (April 5), Fillmore West, San Francisco, California (April 10–13), The Haze, Riverside, California (April 18), Convention Center, Anaheim, California (April 19), Santa Clara Fairgrounds, San Jose, California (April 20), Southern Methodist University, Dallas, Texas (April 26) and Continental Ballroom, Houston, Texas (April 27). Funnily enough, Jeff's one-time drummer Aynsley Dunbar and his Retaliation were booked as support act for four nights at the Fillmore West.

APRIL

EARLY TO MID
Rod Stewart and Ron Wood are handed the job with coming up with suitable material for the new Jeff Beck album. Never having written together before, the two huddle together in a flat to compose songs. The irony that Ron Wood is given this responsibility – who just two short months earlier had been sacked for having deteriorated – likely escapes Jeff.

SAT 12TH
MELODY MAKER, citing a spokesman for the Beck Group, reports: "There has been a genuine health problem. We know this is a usual excuse but in Jeff's case this is true. He will be resting for a while and then he hopes to get an album, and possibly a single, together in the next few weeks."

MON 14TH–THU 17TH✱
After a couple of weeks rest, the Jeff Beck Group record tracks for a new album in London. The basic sessions, reportedly finished in just four days, are held at De Lane Lea in Kingsway. However, morale is low and only a few new songs are prepared, and Nicky Hopkins is busy recording with the Rolling Stones over at Olympic at every opportunity.

Mother's Old Rice Pudding, which has featured in the group's set nearly a year and now equipped with a strong guitar hook, is finally recorded. To make up for lack of their own material, two old Presley songs, *All Shook Up* and *Jailhouse Rock*, are recorded on the spot in the studio. For these sessions Jeff plays an old Fender Stratocaster.

While recording at De Lane Lea, Swedish Television (STV-2) films a documentary about Mickie Most. The programme – broadcast in Sweden in late 1969 and then in Norway (NRK-TV) in early 1970 – features brief clips of the group recording *Plynth* and then Beck alone doing guitar overdubs on *Mother's Old Rice Pudding*.

MON 21TH–THU 24ST✱
After the inital sessions, it is believed another four days are set aside for overdubbing and mixing to finish the new album. Besides recording, Jeff's group also rehearses a new stage act for their upcoming American tour, introducing the new material.

FRI 25TH
The Lyceum, London
The Jeff Beck Group headline one of the regular 'Midnight Court' Friday concerts held at the Lyceum. Support acts are Caravan, Al Stewart, Ron Geesin and the Edgar Broughton Band. The show runs from 12.30 until dawn, and the ads proclaim 'Last London appearance before going to the States'. Apparently, the Jeff Beck Group have been added as a last-minute attraction to boost ticket-sales, as the advertisement for the concert the previous week showed Al Stewart as bill-topper.

In the audience are Ian McLagan, Kenny Jones and Ronnie Lane from the Small Faces. Ian McLagan recounts in his book 'All The Rage': "It was a great band and a fantastic night, and though Rod didn't command the stage with Beck ... I could hardly take my eyes off him. He was so flash! But Nicky really blew my mind that night. Hunched over the piano at one side of the stage, not even looking at his hands, his fingers were all over the place ... He made it look so easy, but he had no ego ..."

As fate will have it, this will be Jeff's last live apperance in England for almost three years. Interestingly, Jeff seemingly only plays three concerts in England this year – the Marquee in January plus Tolworth in February and then the Lyceum tonight – although he manages to undertake three separate US tours!

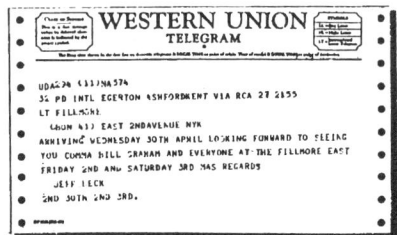

WED 30TH
The Jeff Beck Group fly out to New York today.

MAY

FRI 2ND AND SAT 3RD
THE JEFF BECK GROUP:
FOURTH NORTH AMERICAN TOUR
Fillmore East, New York, New York
A short American tour opens in New York with Joe Cocker & the Grease Band and NRBQ on the bill. Actually, these concerts were originally the two final dates in the long spring tour which broke off in late March.

"The Jeff Beck Group, slightly changed from its last visit, also provided some great music, but that had been expected. Vocalist Rod Stewart was apparently suffering from overstrained cords, and the excitement was slightly dampened, but the rest of the group, especially pianist Nicky Hopkins, took up the slack nicely ... A double helping of Elvis, *All Shook Up* and *Jailhouse Rock*, marked a departure for the group ... but the heaviest credit must go to the encore, *Beck's Boogie* [sic]" writes CASH BOX (May 17) in its review, but the greatest praise is reserved for Joe Cocker.

Rod Stewart recalls in 1972 how it was to follow Joe Cocker on stage, just a few months shy of Cocker's breakthrough appearance at Woodstock:

May 1969: The Who's ambitious and influential 'rock opera' "Tommy" is released.

May 1969: The Jeff Beck Group record with Donovan ...

"... I was shit-scared of following him onstage once. He was under us on the bill ... and it scared the living daylights out of me!" Actually, for one of the shows, Cocker makes a guest appearance with the Jeff Beck Group during their set.

Backstage following one of the Fillmore shows, Jeff is interviewed by William Higbie of MONTCLARION (May 21): "We're spending 10 days in New York, then we're going home to cut our third album. The second is the most important and after it's released, we'll sort of sit back and relax," Jeff tells of the future.

This is also likely the occasion when Jeff details his listening habits for HIT PARADER's regular column 'My Favorite Records' (July 1969). Beck lists a wide variety of artists ranging from Brahms, Bach and Beethoven via well-known classical cellist Jaqueline Du Pre to Janis Joplin and Stevie Wonder ("[his] vocal timing is sensational"). Jeff says: "I own thousand of albums and particular favorites don't come to mind", and concludes "let's just say I like music in general."

For this short tour, the Jeff Beck Group have reworked their stage act and premier many of the tracks from their forthcoming album. These include the two Elvis covers *All Shook Up* and *Jailhouse Rock* plus the group material *Plynth*, *Rice Pudding* (now omitting the 'Mother's Old' part of its title) and *Spanish Boots* – the latter complete with a bass solo. Otherwise old favourites like *Shapes Of Things*, *Jeff's Boogie*, *Let Me Love You* and *I Ain't Superstitious* (usually also Newman's drum spot) are kept in the act.

TUE 6TH, WED 7TH, THU 8TH
Boston Tea Party, Boston, Massachusetts
A return to the Boston Tea Party for a three night residence, together with the Nice. While in Boston, Jeff purchases an extreme-looking sports car for £1,000 which costs him a further £400 to ship back to England.

Bob Gross reviews the Wednesday concert in MIT's paper THE TECH (May 13), and he is not merciful: "Jeff Beck is dead. Perhaps it's better to say he's dying ... Jeff Beck could be fantastic if he wanted to. Listen to *Jeff's Boogie*, *Happenings Ten Years Time Ago* and other early Yardbirds material. Presently, however, he's on a big ego trip, and it's too bad ... A good way to point out some of the group's faults is to compare the Beck group with Led Zeppelin. The latter has interesting material and arrangements whereas the former's are fairly stock ... After having seen all three graduates of the famous 'Yardbirds School for Lead Guitarists', I've concluded that Jimmy Page is the most interesting, Clapton the most proficient musically, and Beck the dullest (in his present state)."

The Tuesday night is a comparatively rough affair, but opens well enough with the new *Plynth (Water Down The Drain)*, which has all the hallmarks of being a Beck Group classic. The new Presley interpretations are both featured, but leave no particular impression. *Blues de Luxe*, clocking in at nearly ten minutes, is competent, but the group does not seem to muster any great enthusiasm for the rest of the set. For an encore they come back to do a rattling *Jeff's Boogie*.

Wednesday night is an improvement, and gets off with a potent version of *All Shook Up*, underpinned by churning bass and driving drums. Apparently, Hopkins' acoustic piano from the previous night has broken down, so he uses an electric piano instead, which distorts nicely and works well within the overall sound, although it obviously hampers Hopkins, which is likely the reason Nicky's featured number *Blues de Luxe* is dropped tonight. *Rice Pudding* is long and meandering, and ignites a few sparks. "Is there anything anbody'd like to hear?" Jeff asks the crowd, which prompts a flood of replies, before Jeff launches into a storming *Rock My Plimsoul*. A forgotten gem in Jeff's song book, *Spanish Boots*, follows and ends with a trebly bass solo. On the last number, *I Ain't Superstitious*, Jeff involves the audience in a long call, clap-and-response sequence before Newman's rather routine drum solo, which signals the end of the concert. After a few minutes the group gets on stage to encore with *Shapes of Things*.

FRI 9TH
Woolsey Hall, Yale University, New Haven, Connecticut
Two shows tonight at the 2,000 capacity Woolsey Hall round off the short East Coast tour. Reportedly, Beck cuts the first show down to about 30 minutes because opening band Rhinoceros overrun their schedule.

SUN 11TH✱
The group returns to London.

FRI 16TH AND SAT 17TH✱
On a weekend in May, Mickie Most teams the Jeff Beck Group with another of his clients, singer and songwriter Donovan. Hastily arranged, Most has booked Advision Studios, and has to rent a guitar ("any old Fender will do") for Jeff, as his equipment is still locked up in the group's van. In a spirited six-hour session at least five songs are completed. These are *Goo Goo Barabajagal*, *Trudy (Bed With Me)*, *Suffer Little Children*, *Homesickness* and *Stromberg Twins*. The last – a song about carburettors! – is written as a homage to Jeff. Another title, *From Here On, Your Guess Is As Good As Mine*, is also presumably recorded. Madeleine Bell and Lesley Duncan overdub backing vocals later.

Although scant pre-planning has been done; Donovan apparently writes parts of the songs on the spot in the studio, the recording is a great success. Donovan himself remembers it as the most extraordinary session he ever did. As Jeff later explains to DISC AND MUSIC ECHO "sometimes these things work and sometimes they don't – but this session just burst out in flames!" To NEW MUSICAL EXPRESS in August he elaborates: "I mean, *Goo Goo Barabajagal* – let's be fair! A song with a title like that isn't something you sit at home planning for six months."

FRI 16TH
EMI files show that the otherwise unissued song *From Here On, Your Guess Is As Good As Mine* (with Donovan) is logged today.

SAT 17TH
EMI files show that *Stromberg Twins* is logged today.

SAT 31ST
EMI files show that the otherwise unissued song *Suffer Little Children* (with Donovan) is logged today.

JUNE

MON 2ND
Today sees the release of the new single *Plynth (Water Down The Drain)* b/w the Presley song *Jailhouse Rock* as

---

Set List/Jeff Beck Group

Boston Tea Party, May 6 '69

Plynth • All Shook Up • Let Me Love You • Rice Pudding • Blues de Luxe • Rock My Plimsoul • Spanish Boots • Jailhouse Rock • Shapes of Things • Jeff's Boogie

---

June 28, 1969: Led Zeppelin headline the Bath Festival in England, attended by 12,000 fans.

June 1969: Nicky Hopkins quits the Jeff Beck Group ...

a taster for the American market, where it sinks without a trace. (The single is not issued in England.)

WED 4TH
On this very day, Nicky Hopkins quits the group after an argument. Whereas Wood, whose musical sights are already wandering, will stay loyal to Beck at least through the upcoming US tour, Hopkins' leaving is definite, reducing the group to a quartet once again. Reminiscing about the Jeff Beck Group in 1973, Hopkins sums up: "We could have made it so big. Every opportunity was there and we blew it by constantly cancelling out tours ... I left on – I don't know why I remember it – June 4, 1969."

The frustrated Nicky Hopkins – who recently has recorded with Jefferson Airplane (for their *Volunteers* album) – spends the rest of the month recording with the Rolling Stones at Olympic (including *Let It Bleed*). He eventually moves to California permanently, where he briefly works as auxiliary pianist for Steve Miller, before joining Quicksilver Messenger Service full time in the late summer.

FRI 6TH
In the NEW MUSICAL EXPRESS today, Ron Wood is reported to be joining the Small Faces as guitarist, replacing Steve Marriott: "No definite date has been set, but Ron has been rehearsing with the group recently."

This day should also mark yet another return for the Beck Group to the Marquee, supported by Steamhammer (with Mickey Waller on drums!), but by all accounts it is a last minute cancellation – again.

•

The Jeff Beck Group are on the verge of collapsing, although more work is lined up in the States later this summer. Nicky Hopkins is gone, and a disgruntled Ron Wood – eager to play guitar instead of bass – has already hooked up loosely with the remnants of the Small Faces (soon to drop the 'Small') at the end of May. Having just lost front man Steve Marriott, the Small Faces rehearse at the Rolling Stones' rehearsal space in Bermondsey, South London. Meanwhile, Rod Stewart records his first solo album at Landsdowne Studio in Notting Hill and Morgan Studios in Willesden. The album, which will be issued in February next year, features both Mickey Waller and Ron Wood, but Jeff has not been asked to contribute.

Sometime in June, both Wood and Stewart play at Cambridge University with an expanded Small Faces – for the occasion billed as Quiet Melon – including Ron's brother, Art, plus bassist Kim Gardner.

As for the Jeff Beck Group, it is mainly Tony Newman who is keen to keep the band going, as Jeff has lost enthusiasm too.

EARLY ✱
It is believed that it is this month that Jeff briefly helps out British eccentric rocker Screaming Lord Sutch for his big league debut *Lord Sutch & Heavy Friends*, which is released on Atlantic Records in the States in February 1970 (and May in Great Britain). Whereas most of the album is recorded in Los Angeles ealier in the year with a stellar line-up including Jimmy Page, John Bonham and Noel Redding, the one track with Beck – *Gutty Guitar* – sounds suspiciously like a leftover from the mid-sixties. Actually, the song features Nicky Hopkins, Carlo Little and Ricky Brown. The details behind the session remain in the dark, but a distinct possibility is that Beck adds a new guitar track this month on an old backing track.

MID
In mid-June Jeff attends a housewarming jam at ex-Jimi Hendrix Experience bassist Noel Redding's new home in Ashford, Kent.

THU 26TH
Donovan and the Jeff Beck Group – Beck, Stewart, Wood and Newman – are assigned to pre-record an appearance on BBC-TV's "Top Of The Pops" to mime *Goo Goo Barabajagal* today, done at the BBC Television Centre, Lime Grove, London. The insert is likely aired on July 24.

FRI 27TH
This Friday, the joint Donovan/Jeff Beck Group single *Goo Goo Barabajagal* is issued in England. Nick Logan in NEW MUSICAL EXPRESS (June 29) gives the song a glowing review, exclaiming "everything else this week fades into insignificance against this gem of a record ... This totally compelling, marvellous little single is the kind of song from which pop standards are made. But though it's Donovan's song, the importance of the Beck Group's contribution cannot be understated."

The single is a big hit on both sides of the Atlantic, and marks both Donovan and Jeff's last flirtations with the single charts. In the UK it peaks at #12, while in the States it tops at a respectable #36 in early September.

MON 30TH
To coincide with the forthcoming American tour, the second Jeff Beck Group album, *Beck-Ola Cosa Nostra*, is issued in America (the British release is held back until September). The record is usually just referred to as *Beck-Ola*, which is a nickname Peter Grant has given Jeff. All songs stem from the same sessions in April, and portrays a rougher and harder sounding group. Although the record label once again credits Jeff Beck, a proper Jeff Beck Group credit does appear on the back of the record sleeve.

Except for the two Elvis Presley rave-ups *Jailhouse Rock* and *All Shook Up*, all the material is penned by members of the band. The instrumental *Girl From Mill Valley* (reportedly a paen to the girlfriend of David Freiberg, the

JEFF BECK [GROUP]
A: PLYNTH (Water Down The Drain) (Hopkins/Stewart/Wood)
B: JAILHOUSE ROCK (Leiber/Stoller)

Released Monday June 2, 1969 (US Epic 5-10484)
Personnel is Jeff Beck (ldgtr), Rod Stewart (ldvcls), Ron Wood (bs), Tony Newman (drms), Nicky Hopkins (pno).
Recorded at De Lane Lea, 129 Kingsway, London, April 14–17*, 1969
Produced by Mickie Most
Engineered by Martin Birch
Highest Chart Position US: –

DONOVAN & THE JEFF BECK GROUP
A: GOO GOO BARABAJAGAL (LOVE IS HOT) (Leitch)
B: TRUDY (BED WITH ME) (Leitch)

Released Friday June 27, 1969 (UK Pye 17778), Monday July 21, 1969 (US Epic 10501)
Personnel is Donovan (ac gtr, vcls), Jeff Beck (ldgtr), Rod Stewart (backvcls), Ron Wood (bs), Tony Newman (drms), Nicky Hopkins (pno); Madeleine Bell and Lesley Duncan sing backup vocals on A
Recorded: Advision Studios, New Bond Street, London, May 16–17*, 1969
Produced by Mickie Most
Highest Chart Position UK: #12
Highest Chart Position US: #36

July 1969: The Jeff Beck Group play the Newport Jazz Festival ...

bassist in Quicksilver Messenger Service) is a Nicky Hopkins showcase, and barely features guitar. The cover art is a famous painting by surrealist René Magritte called 'La Chambre d'Ecoute' (translating 'The Listening Room'). In the liner notes, Jeff writes rather wearily "today, with all the hard competition in the music business, it's almost impossible to come up with anything totally original. So we haven't." Still, the album is a hit in the States where it climbs to #15 (matching *Truth's* peak position), and when issued in England a bit later it creeps into the Top Forty at #39.

The album is well-received, as shown by the review by Ben Gerson in ROLLING STONE (August 9): "This is a brilliant album, dense in texture, full of physical and nervous energy, equally appealing to mind and body. There is a guiding intelligence which enables these five excellent, assertive musicians to work with and not against each other. The group benefits from the addition of Nicky Hopkins, the most perfect of rock pianists (although his playing is sometimes overshadowed by the electrical sturm und drang around him ...), Ron Wood's very prominent bass provides the rhythmic background of the album, and Tony Newman's drumming is solid and wonderfully varied ... Beck himself, of course, is the star. His playing doesn't quite have the excellence and logic of Clapton, but his ideas are unsurpassed. Outside of Jorma [Kaukonen] of the Airplane, Beck plays the most unpredictable guitar lines in rock, yet manages to combine them with a heavy blues feeling."

Jeff also talks to DISC AND MUSIC ECHO today (published in the July 5 edition), to promote the joint Donovan/Beck Group single: "... Donovan's very easy to work with. He just walked into the studio, picked up a guitar and strummed the song while we joined in and wailed behind him."

JULY

TUE 1ST
Although the Jeff Beck Group are in a shambles and reportedly have agreed to disband soon, they reassemble for a final selection of lucrative summer concerts in the States. Jeff's prestigious appearance at the Newport Jazz Festival has been pencilled in since February, and to promote the new album more dates with several festivals have been added, mainly on the East Coast and in the Midwest.

Back to a quartet, the Jeff Beck Group with Pete Sanders fly into New York today. Peter Grant's American partner, lawyer Steve Weiss, is in charge of business. Weiss argues as this is just a promotional tour, payments will be held down, which of course does not improve the already strained relations within the band.

WED 2ND
THE JEFF BECK GROUP:
FIFTH NORTH AMERICAN TOUR
Aerodome, Schenectady, New York
An inauspicious tour opening takes place in a small city in upstate New York, a show which Tony Newman later recalls as truly awful.

After Hopkins' departure, the live set has been slightly trimmed and rearranged. *You Shook Me* is brought back again, while *The Hangman's Knee* is added from the new album, and both *Plynth* and *Spanish Boots* are dropped, but there are no surprising song selections otherwise.

THU 3RD
Fillmore East, New York, New York
Support by Jethro Tull plus Soft White Underbelly, an American group that later evolves into Blue Öyster Cult.

FRI 4TH
"16th Annual Newport Jazz Festival"
Festival Field, Newport, Rhode Island
The Jeff Beck Group are one of the big draws on the second of four nights at the annual Newport Jazz Festival, and together with Blood, Sweat & Tears, Roland Kirk, Steve Marcus, Ten Years After and Jethro Tull, Beck appears on this unique presentation billed as 'An Evening of Jazz-Rock'. Attendance is a record-breaking 24,000.

The Newport festival is usually reserved for only jazz and blues, and this year marks the first and last time regular rock groups will be invited to take part. The festival is not without problems as thousands of rock fans unexpectedly invade the town – nearly forcing the organisers to cancel Led Zeppelin's Sunday performance until Peter Grant intervenes – but the promoters still reckon the festival is a success. However, the scheduled US debut of Blind Faith at the same site the following weekend is cancelled as this time the city has had enough of unruly rock audiences.

SAT 5TH
"New York Pop Festival"
Downing Stadium, Randalls Island, New York
Billed to appear at this festival are Michigan group Grand Funk Railroad (soon to release their debut album on Capitol), Steppenwolf, John Sebastian and Jethro Tull – plus Jeff Beck.

MON 6TH–THU 10TH✱
While staying in New York in-between tour dates, Jeff receives a call at his hotel from ex-Yardbird roadie Bruce Wayne at the beginning of July. Wayne now works with Vanilla Fudge, and their guitarist Vinnie Martell falls sick during a recording session. In a flash of inspiration, Wayne invites Jeff to participate, and together with the three remaining Vanillas (Tim Bogert, Carmine Appice and Mark Stein), he records a 'Things Go Better With Coke' jingle. He is duly paid for the session, and the jingle – which exists

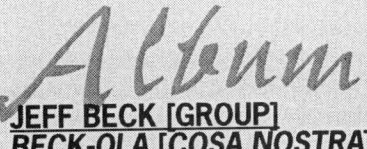

JEFF BECK [GROUP]
BECK-OLA [COSA NOSTRA]
A1 ALL SHOOK UP (Presley/Blackwell) **A2** SPANISH BOOTS (Beck/Stewart/Wood)
A3 GIRL FROM MILL VALLEY (Hopkins) **A4** JAILHOUSE ROCK (Leiber/Stoller)

B1 PLYNTH (WATER DOWN THE DRAIN) (Hopkins/Stewart/Wood) **B2** THE HANGMAN'S KNEE (Hopkins/Stewart/Wood) **B3** RICE PUDDING (Hopkins/Newman/Wood)

Released Monday June 30, 1969 (US Epic BN 26478) and Friday September 5, 1969 (UK Columbia SCX 6351)
Personnel is Jeff Beck (ldgtr), Rod Stewart (vcls), Ron Wood (bs), Nicky Hopkins (pno) and Tony Newman (drms).
Recorded at De Lane Lea, 129 Kingsway, Holborn, London, April 14–17*, 21–24*, 1969.
Produced by Mickie Most
Engineered by Martin Birch
Highest Chart Position US: #15
Highest Chart Position UK: #39

© July 3, 1969: Brian Jones is found dead in his pool; two days later the Rolling Stones debut guitarist Mick Taylor at a giant free concert in London's Hyde Park.

July 1969: Jeff Beck records with Vanilla Fudge in New York ...

in at least four different versions – is used on US radio stations during late 1969. Jeff of course has kept an eye on the group since he saw their impressive London debut nearly two years ago. Jeff and Tim and Carmine immediately find common ground, and decide to play together again as soon as the opportunity arises.

Beck later tells how John Bonham, Jimmy Page and he would listen to Vanilla Fudge's *Near The Beginning* (the group's February '69 live album) with its pivotal performance of *Shotgun:* "One night John Bonham, Pagey and myself were sitting around listening to albums when someone put on the Fudge's *Near The Beginning* album. When it came to the *Shotgun* track it was a revelation, particularly Carmine's drumming. I just knew I had to work with that rhythm section."

SINGER BOWL JULY 13, 1969. FROM LEFT: TONY NEWMAN, JIMMY PAGE, RIC LEE. FACSIMILE FROM GO

FRI 11TH
"1st Spectrum Summer Music Festival"
The Spectrum, Philadelphia, Pennsylvania
The Spectrum festival is a two-day affair, and today features Sly & The Family Stone, the Mothers of Invention and three British groups: Savoy Brown, Ten Years After and the Jeff Beck Group (the next day Led Zeppelin are billed to appear). Despite the strong bill, the show is poorly attended, with about 3,500 ticket-holders of a possible 16,000 capacity.

SAT 12TH
"Pop At Laurel Festival"
Laurel Race Course, Laurel, Maryland
Situated on the outer edge of Washington, D.C., Laurel is the sister festival to the 'Spectrum Pop Festival', where all the acts just swap days. The Guess Who are also added to the bill. This concert does not go without incident either, as fans break down the fencing and set fire to chairs. Carl Bernstein in THE WASHINGTON POST (July 14) dismisses all the British guitarists at the festival as "fretboard acrobats".

SUN 13TH
"The Singer Bowl Music Festival"
Singer Bowl, Flushing Meadow Park, Flushing, New York
This fateful day at the Singer Bowl in Queens is a well-documented legend, where the Edwin Hawkins Singers, Ten Years After and the Jeff Beck Group support headliners Vanilla Fudge. Jeff later recalls to Steven Rosen in the 'Beck Book': "It was one of these riotous sorts of day, everyone's energy level was 100 % and we were throwing things at each other on stage. I threw a mug of orange juice at Alvin Lee and it stuck all over his guitar. It was just one of those animal things. Three English groups at the same place has to add up to trouble."

Not appearing, but also hanging around are members of Led Zeppelin and Jethro Tull. A jolly John Bonham makes an unscheduled and impromptu appearance during *Rice Pudding*, after having made a general nuisance of himself. For the encore of *Jailhouse Rock*, Jeff, Rod, Ron and Tony take the stage with an impromptu big band also featuring Jimmy Page, Robert Plant, Jethro Tull bassist Glenn Cornick and Ric Lee, the drummer in Ten Years After, plus Carmine. The four drummers on stage share one kit but have a floor tom each, enjoying themselves and making a nice racket! The wild night ends when Bonham strips off his clothes and is arrested by the police. Eric Clapton is supposedly also hanging about, having played Madison Square Garden the night before with Blind Faith.

The Jeff Beck Group's brilliant show steals the thunder from bill-toppers Vanilla Fudge completely, and Tim Bogert later says he hands in his notice to Fudge-manager Phil Basile tonight, but promises to honour outstanding engagements. Meeting backstage, Jeff, Tim and Carmine again lay plans for a mutual future.

MON 14TH
"Schaefer Music Festival Series"
Wolman Memorial Rink, Central Park, New York, New York
Part of the summer long Schaefer Music Festival, with two shows at 7 and 9.30 pm supported by Orpheus. It is believed that Jeff briefly performs *The Star-Spangled Banner* as part of the group's set (likely during the stretched out middle-part of *Jeff's Boogie)*, four weeks before Jimi Hendrix will immortalize the anthem at Woodstock in a full-scale version.

Seeing as this tour is more than a promotional jaunt, Stewart, Wood and Newman feel they are being badly paid, and demand cash upfront before tonight's concert. Each then receive a considerable sum.

FRI 18TH
Pirate's Cove, Pirate's World Amusement Park, Dania, Florida
Jeff Beck fly south for the first of two nights at Pirate's World, an amusement park close to the Everglades. Due to delays at Kennedy Airport in New York, the group arrives late and goes on stage at 10.15 and because of the park's curfew at eleven o'clock, Jeff plays for barely half an hour.

"Jeff's guitar was 'heavy', as always. Which means that it was loud. Singer Rod Stewart sounded like Rod Stewart, an Englishman trying to sing blues and not really succeeding even when he sounded good. The group never actually got it together. They sounded hollow and flat, probably a result of Beck's physical condition after a full day flying. One of the best moments of the concert came with *You Shook Me*, a song from Beck's first album and a song which the audience had obviously sat in the rain to hear. They ended their set ... with *Jailhouse Rock*, a song which no one had heard them do, and which they did fantastically", runs part of the review in the MIAMI HURRICANE (August 8).

SAT 19TH
Pirate's Cove, Pirate's World Amusement Park, Dania, Florida
Confusingly, the Jeff Beck Group are also advertised to appear at Kennedy Stadium in Bridgeport, Connecticut today. However, they definitely remain in Flordia, where their second night in Dania is a success according to the MIAMI HURRICANE: "[E]veryone said that the ... performance was dynamite, that everything came together and grooved perfectly, and that the Jeff Beck Group vindicated themselves perfectly".

July 20, 1969: US astronauts Neil Armstrong, Edwin 'Buzz' Aldrin & Michael Collins land on the moon.

July 1969: Donovan and Jeff Beck are on "Top of The Pops"...

MON 21ST
"Mountain Rock Festival"
Tamarack Lodge, Ellenville, New York
Staged by Triple C Promotions, 'The Mountain Rock Festival' runs four to five Mondays in July–August. The Jeff Beck Group plus Borealis play the second Monday. Tony Newman remembers well this place in the Catskills Mountains region, where there's a bit of a riot after the concert and claims the incident in part caused problems for the band with the American Federation of Musicians.

Today is also the US release date for *Goo Goo Barabajagal*.

TUE 22ND
Commodore Ballroom, Lowell, Massachusetts
The band continues its rapid disintegration with an unglamorous booking 25 miles north of Boston where legend has it that the band members are reduced to openly bickering onstage.

THU 24TH
Today, likely, is when the pre-recorded performance with Donovan and Jeff Beck Group miming *Goo Goo Barabajagal* is aired on "Top Of The Pops" (7.30–8.00 pm, ▶ June 26), making this occasion Beck's last appearance on this British pop institution.

FRI 25TH
Tonight's scheduled performance by the Jeff Beck Group at the Grande Ballroom in Detroit (the first of three nights) is cancelled and Procol Harum gamely step in on short notice.

SAT 26TH
Grande Ballroom, Detroit, Michigan
This chaotic weekend in Detroit is believed to be the very end of the Jeff Beck Group. After cancelling the previous night, Jeff Beck at least honours tonight's booking. Originally a triple booking (Friday–Sunday), the Sunday show is initially dropped because Beck is scheduled to appear at the Midwest Rock Festival in Wisconsin on July 27. Confusingly – or perhaps not considering the conditions of this tour! – the Wisconsin appearance is ultimately called off and Beck seemingly intends to play a second night at the Grande on the Sunday, which is also scrapped.

At 4.30 in the afternoon Beck is interviewed by Russ Gibb on radio station WKNR, discussing *Beck-Ola*, the Donovan single, a new Terry Reid single, Nicky Hopkins' absence, Jeff's hot rods and a new album: "I have ideas, but only in my head."

Tim Bogert and Carmine Appice are also said to be in Detroit this weekend, and – realizing the need for a frontman for his projected Fudge union – Jeff wants to keep Rod Stewart as singer, so the four meet up for a talk at the hotel.

This summer Jeff Beck is followed around the States by Led Zeppelin like a shadow, a shadow that grows longer and stronger every day. Now the two groups even sport identical lineups again as Nicky Hopkins is gone, and they both do *You Shook Me*. While Beck & Co still blast out *Shapes Of Things*, Led Zeppelin usually kick their sets off with *The Train Kept A-Rollin'*. The seeds for a pared down group is certainly sown in Beck's mind this summer – albeit with Bogert and Appice replacing Wood and Newman.

Within days of their eventual dissolution, the Beck group nevertheless put on a tremendous performance tonight, which blasts off with *All Shook Up*, followed by the double punched salvo *You Shook Me/Let Me Love You*, with all the Beck–Stewart call and response magic fully intact. *Hangman's Knee* is a treat; loopy and heavy with an excellent Stewart vocal and with a perfect rolling guitar riff that works much better here than on the recorded version. Beck then pours all his soul into a slow blues where Stewart ad libs on how he wishes it would rain, and Jeff touches the stratosphere with his ethereal guitar playing. *Rice Pudding*, too, is formidable; Beck, Wood and Newman feeling each other out and producing passages of great excitement. For the night's two last numbers, Beck switches to a Stratocaster on an unhinged *Rock My Plimsoul*, where he works the wang bar furiously, before curtain call is signalled with *Shapes of Things*. "See you tomorrow!" Jeff mutters, yet the Sunday night is called off after all.

Oddly enough, so close to a break up, at least tonight the group sounds like it has rekindled the fire from the first American tour a year earlier. Generally, the Jeff Beck Group play very focused, even at the most psychedelic of times; Jeff keeps his

Set List/Jeff Beck Group

Grande Ballroom, July 26 1969

All Shook Up • You Shook Me • Let Me Love You • The Hangman's Knee • Blues de Luxe • Rice Pudding • Morning Dew • Jeff's Boogie • Rock My Plimsoul • Shapes of Things

---

AIR BLOWER

Beeb Pop A Beck

Jeff Beck recorded several radio sessions exclusively for the BBC in the years 1965–1972, firstly with the Yardbirds and later fronting his own groups. Often ridiculed for their conservative musical policy and a staff of white-coated gentlemen with little understanding of rock, truth reveals that the BBC were indeed willing to provide an opportunity for artists to test material in a less-than-serious environment, or to perform songs that had improved vastly after countless nights on the road, or to just have a lark in the studio.

While a good amount of the BBC sessions Beck did with the Yardbirds have been legitimately issued in the 90s, less is known about the BBC recordings he did with his own group. Besides doing the obvious hits and album tracks, several hidden gems can be found which never made their way to the Beck Group's records. Top of the pile is an astounding version of Dionne Warwicke's *You'll Never Get To Heaven*, also the fine Tamla-cover *Loving You Is Sweeter Than Ever* (both from November 1967), and a slow guitar blues called *This Morning* (from July 1967).

The last session the original Jeff Beck Group did for the BBC, in September 1968, features a storming *Shapes of Things* with Beck injecting a stirring guitar figure at the opening of the second solo, and a cocksure *Rock My Plimsoul*, where he plays a glorious bum note in the solo which he then resolves beautifully. There is also a funkified *Mother's Old Rice Pudding* with a crisp wah-wah guitar – very different from the recorded version – but tighter and with a trebly bass solo.

The Jeff Beck Group II also did some recordings for the BBC, the best of which certainly was the oft-bootlegged appearance on "In Concert" in July 1972. Performing more or less their regular set in front of a small audience, the programme captured Beck and band in a good mood. Close-miked and very dynamic, the listener feels like he is sitting right between Jeff's amplifier and Cozy's drums. A highlight is the wonderful *Ain't No Sunshine*, well-suited to Bobby Tench's voice and with a sensitive guitar solo.

Some of the sessions from the BBC vaults have been released officially in the CD-age, and hopefully the time will soon come for a definitive *Beck At The BBC* compilation. ∎

August 1969: The Jeff Beck Group break up before Woodstock appearance ...

solos to a max of three or four choruses, and with the possible exception of *Rice Pudding,* the group never ventures into the Great Unknown as do many of their contemporaries, who excel in lengthy and thus often boring guitar, bass and drum solos.

SUN 27TH

Rescheduled to play a second night at the Grande, instead local bands fill-in as Beck is ultimately a no-show at the last minute despite his statement at the end of the Saturday night show. This is in addition to his earlier canceling out of a prominent festival booking for this same date at the three day happening 'Midwest Rock Festival' in West Allis, Wisconsin. This event begins on Friday topped by a strong performance by Led Zeppelin, and continues with Blind Faith headlining the following night. Had Jeff been able to play the Sunday as originally billed (but who cancels, as do Zephyr, Jim Schwall, Jethro Tull and MC5!), this event would then have boasted the three original Yardbirds guitarists!

Although more appearances are lined up, the Jeff Beck Group are coming apart at the seams. Jeff is caught between the strong-willed Steve Weiss and Peter Grant (who in effect run the band) on one hand, and his bandmates on the other. At the end, Beck is not on speaking terms with the others, but with the Bogert and Appice possibilities looming on the horizon, he does not seem to care either way.

Tony Newman recalls how the poor payment becomes a big problem, and Ron Wood has this to say in his biography: "... Tony Newman started the uprising. Jeff didn't really have a lot to do with it, it was Tony against the management ...."

Rod Stewart, who has received unequivocal signals about a future with Bogert and Appice ("[It] could have been an immaculate group, a world-class group" he is known to have said), is unsure of what to do. Despite the uncomfortable relationship with Beck, Stewart still has affection for him, as confirmed by later interviews, such as in ZIGZAG (May/June 1971): "I wasn't really knocked out by the things the Fudge were doing at the time, though Carmine and Timmy were two incredibly nice guys. When a group breaks up, the usual line to come out with is 'we couldn't have gone any further musically.' Well, that's a lot of bollocks – me and Beck could've played together for years and still come up with nice stuff."

AUGUST

Seemingly following the Detroit debacle, the group hastily returns to England and the rest of the tour is cancelled. A two-night stand at the Kinetic Playground, Chicago, with Terry Reid and the Blues Image (replacing Fleetwood Mac) on August 1–2 is not fulfilled as best as can be determined, even though Beck is advertised right up to the day of the show. Further cancelled dates are the Rock Pile, Toronto (August 9), 'The Woodstock Music & Arts Fair', Bethel, New York (August 17) and 'The Montreal Pop Festival' (August 22).

The posters for Woodstock were distributed in July, and the original running order for Sunday August 17 promised the Jeff Beck Group along with the Band, Blood, Sweat & Tears, Joe Cocker, Crosby, Stills & Nash, Johnny Winter, Ten Years After, Iron Butterfly, and headliner Jimi Hendrix.

A year later, when Woodstock and especially the movie documenting the event has become a widespread success, Rod Stewart explains in NEW MUSICAL EXPRESS: "We'd been doing two festivals a week there at the time and we just thought 'Oh another festival.' We blew it because we must have made the film – we were bigger than Cocker at the time. This must be one of the biggest regrets of my life – and Beck's." However, it later proves to be a blessing in disguise, as a spot in the movie could have chained both Beck and Stewart to the sixties forever – much like, say, Ten Years After, who never escaped the shadow of Woodstock.

MON 4TH

EMI files show that the otherwise unissued song *Gospel Title* is logged today. No further details are known.

EARLY–LATE

Back in England, Jeff sets about promoting both the Donovan collaboration and *Beck-Ola,* soon to receive a domestic release. He is interviewed for features in NEW MUSICAL EXPRESS (held at the RAK office), ZIGZAG, RECORD MIRROR, and BEAT INSTRUMENTAL.

In NEW MUSICAL EXPRESS (August 16), Jeff informs Alan Smith: "We're disbanding very shortly. Ronnie Woods [sic] is leaving because he wants to play lead instead of bass, and I wish him the best of luck." Jeff reassuringly adds "there are no bad vibes or anything like with most groups", adding: "We made the decision after our second-to-last tour of the States.

We were all exhausted, the group had seen America, and they've seen enough of it." About the future, Jeff details how he has secured "two name faces to join the group. They're going to be news when they happen, and if I only had the griff on it, if I only had it signed and sealed, I'd tell you. But until then I'm afraid it's all shtum. You see, both these name faces are under recording contracts at the moment, so they've got to be careful."

The ZIGZAG (#5, September 1969) interview is conducted in mid-August, and the new British underground rock magazine also puts Beck on its cover. Jeff talks at great lengths about his career, influences and future plans to ZIGZAG's Pete Frame and Mac Garry. Again the two unnamed "bass[ist] and drummer over from the States" are mentioned, and when asked whom Beck is keeping from the old group, he replies: "Possibly Rod. Nicky's left, Ronnie's gone to what's left of the Small Faces to replace Steve Marriott. Tony'll probably do session work." Of Stewart, Jeff says: "Well, I could see his potential. People used to just get the impression he was camp. But I saw beyond that. He's not camp anyway – campish maybe, but I really dug his gritty voice, which is why I asked him to join me." And of his recording manager, Jeff maintains: "Mickie Most, let me tell you, all he wants to do is make hit records, and all I want to do is play my music. When *Love Is Blue* was recorded, he was unbelievably hard to work with, he really let me know who was boss. But when he went to the States and saw us play, and realised just how huge the market was, he did a big swallow." Although America has proven highly important to his success, Jeff will not move: "I don't mind working there, but it's such a long way. I certainly couldn't ever live there – it's bad enough just visiting for a few weeks, let alone buy-

© September 13, 1969: The Plastic Ono Band, including Eric Clapton on guitar, make a surprise live appearance in Toronto.

November 1969: Jeff Beck seriously hurt in car accident ...

ing a house and living in the middle of all that rubbish."

"Why throw away a successful formula?" RECORD MIRROR (September 6) ironically asks, referring to the fact that Jeff has just disbanded his group while a brand new album is released and *Goo Goo Barabajagal* is high in the charts. Jeff tells Ian Middleton: "Now I'm looking for a good singer [indicating that Stewart is not part of his scheme anymore] but the trouble is there's a terrible shortage of them ... the step I'm taking with the new group is so drastic, I can't really think of the outcome." Again Jeff refuses to disclose their names, but the piece concludes with "if you're wondering who the mystery musicians are, try an each way bet on the Vanilla Fudge!" Middleton furthermore has talked to Tony Newman: "Jeff's group has always been unstable, ever since I joined it. There were always undercurrents going on and disputes happening all the time ... in the eight months I was with the group we rehearsed about twice which is ridiculous."

Jeff Beck – with Mickie Most – lastly talks to BEAT INSTRUMENTAL (December '69), explaining: "You see I don't project any image to fall back on, and make me remembered. My guitar playing is my image."

•

A determined Beck keeps in touch with Bogert and Appice, but there is a series of business contracts that have to be cleared before the union can take place, so Jeff has to remain silent for the time being. Vanilla Fudge has touring commitments, including a trip to England in late September.

Ron Wood meanwhile is happily entangled with the Faces, while Rod Stewart has already signed a solo deal and has lost interest in Beck and bows out. Tony Newman later cuts a pair of LPs with May Blitz before resuming a a career as session drummer.

SAT 23RD–SUN 24TH

A provisional appearance by the Jeff Beck Group at Belgium's Bilzen Festival this weekend is also scrapped.

Interestingly, Jeff Beck is also briefly in line for the Isle of Wight festival (August 29–31; this year starring Bob Dylan) and – along with Woodstock – a mind-boggling culmination of missed Jeff Beck Group opportunities this summer. Talking to RECORD MIRROR three years later, Jeff explains: "We blew out the Dylan Isle of Wight because I knew we wouldn't be ready for it. Dylan can control all that – there's magic coming out of him."

SEPTEMBER

FRI 5TH

Beck-Ola is issued in Great Britain today. RECORD MIRROR (August 30) awards the album four of a possible five stars: "Micky [sic] Most produced it, which means to say that the sound is well-defined, clear, effective and primitive – in the nicest possible sense. Beck's guitar work is exceptionally original of its kind." MELODY MAKER's (September 13) review of the album enthuses: "Plenty of no-nonsense guitar, much yelling vocals, and singularly violent percussion." A fortnight earlier in the same paper, the week's 'Blind Date' guest, guitarist Peter Frampton, comments upon hearing selections from the album: "I'm not too keen on Jeff's guitar playing. Not on *Jailhouse Rock*, anyway. He's played some stuff that has been amazing."

SAT 13TH

MELODY MAKER's 'Raver' column reports: "Jeff Beck adding Carmine Appic [sic] and Tim Bogert of Vanilla Fudge to his group."

SAT 20TH

MELODY MAKER news item says Vanilla Fudge are to make a sole London appearance, then fly to Montreux and Paris before finally disbanding.

TUE 23RD

Vanilla Fudge arrive in London to commence a short promotional tour. Bogert and Appice of course spend much time with Jeff conspiring about the future.

FRI 26TH

Vanilla Fudge play the Marquee. MELODY MAKER's Richard Williams reviews the show: "I've a feeling that they committed suicide at exactly the right time."

OCTOBER

Appice and Bogert have meanwhile found an American singer, Rusty Day from Detroit, once front man of Ted Nugent's group the Amboy Dukes. Although Jeff is sceptical about leaving England, the other three want Jeff to temporarily settle on Long Island to get the new group going. Jeff and Peter Grant book a flight to the States in early November, to finalise arrangements.

SAT 4TH

EMI files show that the otherwise unissued song *Instrumental* is logged today. Although specific details are not known, an intriguing possibility is that this may be an early studio attempt by Beck, Bogert and Appice.

SAT 25TH

DISC AND MUSIC ECHO confirms the rumour that Rod Stewart has joined the Faces, too, who now commence work on their first album, which will include a re-recording of *Plynth* as *Around The Plynth*.

NOVEMBER

SUN 2ND

In the early morning hours, Jeff crashes one of his hot rods, a 1923 A-Ford, outside Maidstone, Kent, when a tire blows and his car skids into a small Morris. The owner of the Morris breaks his knee, while Beck is thrown out of his car and is rushed to Royal West Kent Hospital in Maidstone, seriously injured. He is placed in intensive care, suffering from concussion, a broken nose and tooth, suspected broken pelvis and facial lacerations, and for a short time there is a fear that he might be paralyzed for the rest of his life.

MON 3RD

Jeff and Peter Grant's flight to the States is naturally cancelled.

SAT 8TH

A spokesman for Peter Grant states in today's MELODY MAKER "It is likely that Beck will be in hospital for three months." As a result of the accident, all of Jeff's activities including the Bogert and Appice project have to be postponed.

Eventually, Jeff's stay in hospital is kept comparatively brief. After a few days in intensive care he is transferred to a private room, before he is discharged at the end of the month. He spends the next months recovering in Egerton. Besides the bodily injuries, Jeff will suffer headaches for a long time as a result of the accident.

DECEMBER

MON 3RD

NEW MUSICAL EXPRESS reports today: "Jeff Beck now discharged from hospital and convalescing at home."

© December 6, 1969: The Rolling Stones stage a disastrous free festival at the Altamont Speedway in California, hampered by drug abuse and violence.

1970

JANUARY

FRI 9TH
On a night out during his convalescence, Jeff is present at Led Zeppelin's triumphant Friday night at London's Royal Albert Hall, incidentally on Jimmy Page's 26th birthday.

"The only time I've seen them, they were great. It was just after my accident – I didn't have a band and everything was in a state, and I went down to the Albert Hall. I was sitting up at the balcony, just amazed at what was going on down on stage. And me without a band" Jeff recalls vividly in 1972 of his old pal's enormously successful new group.

SUN 25TH
Beck attends the debut of Jack Bruce's new band – featuring Mitch Mitchell, Larry Coryell and organist Mike Mandel – at the Lyceum, London today. It is Bruce's first live venture since the demise of Cream.

MON 26TH
Jeff Beck and Noel Redding have formed a temporary liaison at the end of January. Conveniently, Redding's house in Ashford, Kent is a short distance from Jeff's home. And Redding is at a loose end as Hendrix has just put together his Band Of Gypsies.

Redding tells NEW MUSICAL EXPRESS today that he and Beck have "done some recording together" (actually only home tapes at best), but today Noel – who still feels obligated to his old boss Jimi Hendrix – flies to New York City to join up with Hendrix again, and the Beck/Redding partnership never reaches fruition beyond casual jams.

FEBRUARY

EARLY
Jeff flies to New York City, supposedly on the invitation of American producer Earle Doud.

TUE 3RD, WED 4TH, THU 5TH
For three hectic days a giant jam session takes place in New York City, involving scores of American and British musicians. The sessions are organized by producer Earle Doud (whose reputation rests on several American satire albums), and are taped with the Record Plant's mobile unit at a hall in the Madison Square Garden complex.

With a core line-up of local New Yorkers Stu Woods (bass guitar) and Moogy Klingman (keyboards) plus one-time Janis Joplin drummer Roy Markowitz, Jeff records four selections which eventually find their way onto a finished album; Lee Dorsey's *Working In The Coalmine;* two run-of-the-mill blues jams credited to Klingman called *Cherrypicker* and *Big City Woman* (the latter sung by Tommy Cosgrove), and finally a version of the Meters' *Cissy Strut.* On the last Todd Rundgren shares guitar duties with Jeff, and it also features a brass section (including members of Blood, Sweat & Tears), suggesting a later overdub session. On the whole, Jeff sounds rusty and is not helped by the uninspired backing. However, as things turn out, this will be the only officially released example of his guitar playing this year.

Other musicians who happen to be in New York and appear at the recordings include Eric Clapton, Dr. John, Keith Emerson, Mitch Mitchell, Buzzy Feiten, Linda Ronstadt and Delaney Bramlett.

Rumours of the sessions circulate for a long time, but a release is held back because Doud is unable to obtain the necessary clearances from the many record companies involved. The tapes are then given to the head of Charisma Records, Tony Stratton-Smith, who attempts to release the album as early as June 1970, but he also runs into record company opposition. After negotiations, Stratton-Smith finally manages to issue the sessions as the double album *Music From Free Creek* in May 1973. Jeff Beck is then credited as 'A.N. Other' because of contractual reasons, while Eric Clapton is masquerading as 'King Cool'. Another three years later, the album is repackaged as a single disc under its intended original title, *Summit Meeting,* but this time without A. N. Other's contributions.

MARCH

SUN 1ST
Jeff finds no less than four of his old employees on the same stage when he attends another Lyceum Sunday concert, tonight starring the Faces (with Ron Wood and Rod Stewart), Silver Metre (with Mickey Waller) and Brian Auger's Trinity (with Dave Ambrose on bass).

EARLY
Having had to back out of the project with Bogert and Appice, Jeff decides to recruit members for a new group, and a provisional debut date is advertised for early April at Birmingham's Town Hall (as announced in MELODY MAKER, March 7), promoted by the local club Mothers in conjunction with Peter Grant. Although Beck has done some tentative work with Noel Redding, Redding is over in New York and Los Angeles tied up with Hendrix plus doing some recordings on his own. So with the assistance of his old road manager Pete Sanders, Jeff wants to begin from scratch with a new band; first and foremost he decides he needs a good drummer.

In Birmingham, Jeff finds no less than two potential drummers. One is Malcolm Poole, who is playing with Marsha Hunt, and who very briefly considered for the drum spot in Led Zeppelin two years previously. However, Poole declines, and instead forms Warhorse a few months later – featuring a guitarist peculiarly named Jedd Peck!

With Poole out of the picture, Beck and Peter Grant organize an audition at a rehearsal room in Hampstead later in March. This attracts the attention of Cozy Powell, another Birmingham boy. Beck takes an instant liking to Powell's attitude, and hires him – and his giant red double-bass drumkit – on the spot. Besides music, Powell also shares Beck's passion for cars.

Powell's credentials include time with several Birmingham groups; the Sorcerers and then the Ace Kefford Stand, fronted by ex-Move bassist Chris 'Ace' Kefford, which eventually evolves into Big Bertha, a short-lived group including brothers Dave and Dennis Ball.

APRIL

Jeff Beck and Cozy Powell rehearse, and often use the hospitable Noel

Newsflash May 1970: Jeff and Cozy Powell record at Tamla Motown ...

Redding's music room at his Ashford home to practice and audition a long line of possible bassists. (Redding himself will be in the States until June.)

Powell introduces Beck to Big Bertha's bass player Dennis Ball, and this trio briefly try out at a rehearsal place in London. Encouraged, Jeff then invites Ball down to Egerton and further rehearsals at Redding's place, before Ball returns to Birmingham – without any job.

Another short-lived group during these spring months consists of Beck, Powell, Chris 'Ace' Kefford and Nic Potter. Although he used to serve as bassist in the Move, Kefford is brought in as singer, while bassist Potter once played with Van Der Graaf Generator. However, this promising constellation never gets off the ground. Jeff also expresses interest in working with pedal steel guitarist B. J. Cole of British country-rockers Cochise, although this does not amount to anything either.

Funnily enough, one singer who also intends to audition for Beck is American Steven Tallarico aka Tyler. Tyler is a friend of Henry 'The Horse' Smith, ex-Yardbirds roadie and friend of both Jimmy Page and Beck, and he suggests Tyler makes a tape and send to Beck. A tape is recorded, but it is never submitted.

SAT 11TH

EMI files show that the otherwise unissued Jeff Beck recording *No Title* is logged today, further documentation does not exist, but it is likely a studio test by one of these early line-ups.

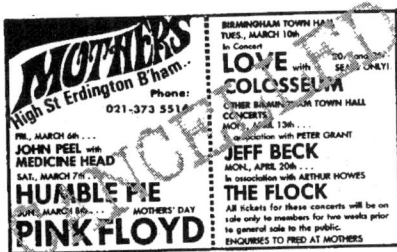

MON 13TH

Jeff Beck's planned return to the stage at Birmingham's Town Hall is cancelled as Jeff and Cozy are unable to secure a complete band.

LATE

Jeff turns up to see Screaming Lord Sutch perform at the Speakeasy one night at the end of April, and so do Mick Jagger, Keith Richards, BBC radio deejay Johnnie Walker plus Ahmet and Neshui Ertegun of Atlantic (Sutch's current label).

MAY

In May, MELODY MAKER's Royston Eldridge conducts the first comprehensive interview with Jeff Beck since the car accident the previous year. The interview, held in Hyde Park and published in the May 23 edition, details the demise of the Jeff Beck Group, the accident, the failed Vanilla Fudge union and the future. It will be Beck's only major interview the whole year.

Jeff begins with bringing the readers up to date: "When [the Jeff Beck Group] split I planned to have three months off work. I'd been working hard for nearly two years, and I'd come to the end of what I felt was the first chapter of my career. I had to decide what I wanted to do. The others wanted to do their own bit, they weren't happy, and we'd just come to the end of a phase of music that we were involved in. I didn't know musically what I wanted to do. ... I had a phone call from Timmy and Carmine from Vanilla Fudge – I'd met them before and I'd played with them. I always fancied myself as a bit of a lunatic but I couldn't stand the pace with these two, charging around all day, looning everywhere! We spent an evening together talking and I was so proud that they were soon to be my bass player and drummer. ... all we had to find was a singer. They had a guy in mind which would have meant three Americans and me the only English person. That sounds okay on paper but I'm very hard to get on with. Not moody, but I need friends rather than business colleagues."

On the car accident: "It was really depressing in hospital. I had a private room but I was so depressed. ... they only let me out provided I lay in bed. Music really wasn't that important then, any degree of noise gave me terrible headaches."

About his new find, Cozy Powell, Jeff enthuses: "[At the audition] there were a lot of anaemic little drummers and then there was Cosy [sic] screaming away, a tremendous drummer with lots of bite."

The interview also reveals Jeff and Cozy's forthcoming visit to Detroit's Motown studios to record an album.

Still in search of a suitable bassist, Jeff confirms: "We've had about 118 bass players up for auditions. We pick them up at the station, give them an hour or so, and take them back to the station. There's no one so far, I'd be kidding myself and them if I said it was ... I would have liked to have got Greg Reeves playing bass in the group. He was a Motown session man before he joined Crosby, Stills, Nash & Young; they beat me to him." In truth, Reeves has this very month been forced to quit Crosby, Stills, Nash & Young as a result of ego clashes and internal squabbles.

SUN 10TH

Screaming Lord Sutch plays London's Lyceum with sundry 'Heavy Friends' which are said to include Jeff Beck, Carlo Little, Nick Simper and Matthew Fisher among others. In any event, Beck does not join Sutch on stage tonight, but Sutch uses his ex-colleagues' names blatantly to promote his new album *Lord Sutch & Heavy Friends* and accompanying touring: "[But] I'll have some real heavy names with me ... I will start from the top down, really heavy people. With all these groups splitting and supergroups forming and then splitting, there are lots of really great players available for gigs like this – top talent too."

FRI 16TH

Tim Bogert and Carmine Appice, who are used to being on the road and working intensively, have given up waiting on Jeff and have formed a new group called Cactus. Together with singer Rusty Day they have added guitarist Jim McCarty (not to be confused with one-time Yardbirds' drummer of the same name) from Mitch Ryder's Detroit Wheels and the Buddy Miles Express. The new group makes a high profile debut at Temple University, Philadelphia, Pennsylvania, today, supporting the Steve Miller Band, Grateful Dead and headliner Jimi Hendrix.

MID

The relatively unknown American singer Chris Moon flies in from New York to try out for Beck and Powell. Mickie Most hopes he can bring Moon with him back to the States for the upcoming Motown sessions. But Moon is deemed unsuitable, and nothing more is heard of him.

SAT 23RD

Jeff Beck, Mickey Waller, David O'List, Nick Simper, Viv Stanhall, Keith Moon and Spencer Davis are all hoped for as surprise guests at Lord Sutch & Heavy Friends' performance at the Hollywood Music Festival in Newcastle. None of the promised star names appear, and the 'Friends' who back Sutch are indeed a nameless

© May 1970: Emerson, Lake & Palmer are formed out of the remnants of the Nice, King Crimson, and Atomic Rooster.

August 1970: Jeff Beck and Elton John team up briefly ...

bunch "who couldn't really get into anything musically satisfying", according to NEW MUSICAL EXPRESS.

On the coming Tamla Motown excursion, Mickie Most in DISC AND MUSIC ECHO today exclaims: "It's a fantastic thrill for me to record at Motown, and I've great hopes for the album. Jeff is bound to have some influence on the Tamla musicians, and – who knows – I may even record Mary Hopkin there!"

FRI 29TH

Jeff Beck, Cozy Powell, and Mickie Most fly to Detroit, Michigan, today to record an album's worth of songs at the famed Motown studios on 2648 West Grand Boulevard.

JUNE

MON 1ST–WED 10TH✱

Beck, Powell and Most intend to record a set of instrumentals featuring Jeff and Cozy backed by the regular Motown house musicians, including backing singers, brass section, percussionist 'Bongo' Eddie Brown and, last but not least, famed bassist James Jamerson. The occasion is also unique because this is the first time anyone outside the Motown system has been allowed to rent the facility and record here.

However, not enough pre-planning has been done, and where Jeff and Cozy rely on feel and head arrangements, the studio musicians claim they need written scores. The mood in the studio is not good – there's tension between Most and the black staff on one hand, and between Beck and Powell and the studio musicians on the other.

Despite this, half a dozen songs are committed to tape, including *Reach Out, I'll Be There* (a Holland–Dozier–Holland composition that was a US #1 for the Four Tops in 1966); *(I Know) I'm Losing You* (the Temptations song that Rod Stewart used to sing in Beck's group in '67); *I Can't Give Back The Love I Feel For You* (written by Nicholas Ashford and Valerie Simpson for Syreeta Wright), *Just Like You Never Loved Me*, and *Don't Give A Hoot*. It was also hoped that Smokey Robinson should contribute new material to the album, but instead Motown staff writers Pam Sawyer and Joe Hinton compose some songs exclusively for the project. In truth, Sawyer and Hinton are two of Motown's less successful writers; they have penned a couple of hits for Junior Walker & The All-Stars, while Pam Sawyer also shares a credit in the Supremes' 1968 number one *Love Child*.

While in Detroit, Mickie Most – always looking for new talent – discovers a young Suzi Quatro playing with her sisters in a group called Cradle at the city's Hideout Club, and signs her to his newly formed RAK Records label (a venture that also involves Peter Grant).

MID

Jeff Beck, Cozy Powell, and Mickie Most return to England.

JULY

WED 15TH

EMI files show that three otherwise unissued songs are logged today; all tracks from the Motown sessions to be mixed and declared finished. These are *Just Like You Never Loved Me, I Can't Give Back The Love I Feel For You* and *Don't Give A Hoot*, the latter neatly summing up Jeff's own feelings on the whole Motown project.

SAT 18TH

'Coming Soon: Jeff Beck's New Tamla Motown Sound' promises a headline in today's MELODY MAKER. The paper has interviewed Mickie Most, who explains the motivation behind the Motown sessions: "We went to the States with the intention of making something other than the old blues group thing, and the best source of material in the world is Motown." "Tamla have the best rhythm sections in the world. They have a couple of bass players who are completely out of sight ...", claims Most, adding: "we also used brass and some of their singers, but I didn't use the strings because that would possibly be taking Jeff too far away from what he is." As for the future, "Jeff's putting a new band together at the moment with Cosy [sic] on drums, and he'll tell them all to play like the stuff we've just recorded."

Eventually, the tapes from Motown are deemed to be of sub-par quality by both Jeff Beck and Mickie Most. When Epic Records sign Jeff Beck to a recording contract the following year, they secure the Detroit recordings as part of the hand-over deal with Mickie Most – to bar RAK from releasing them – and they remain forever buried in the vaults of CBS–Epic.

AUGUST

EARLY

In an attempt to get back into action, Jeff rehearses with the still largely unknown Elton John at Camden Town Hall in London. John has made one album the previous year and is just about to release his second, eponymous album, but any chart success has so far eluded him.

Urged by a fleeting business associate, Jeff watches one of Elton's appearances at the Speakeasy and is suitably impressed. The two then meet at the Revolution Club on Bruton Street, Mayfair, before rehearsals get under way. The news at least prompts a reader in RECORD MIRROR to celebrate: "I've just heard that Jeff Beck is joining Elton John ... and yet everyone is still grousing about the lack of originality in modern music." However, within a week the partnership falls apart. Beck dislikes John's drummer Nigel Olsson and bassist Dee Murray, and wants to have Cozy Powell in, together with another bassist. John's manager Dick James advises Elton to go it alone anyway, promising – quite rightly – a breakthrough in the States soon.

Elton John reveals the facts behind this interesting linkup for the first time to ZIGZAG (November 1972), and expresses doubt in retrospect: "I'd always said I'd never mention this, but when Jeff Beck came to talk to me after I'd done a set at the Speakeasy one night, he said he'd really like to join the band. Well, I obviously wasn't going to let an offer like that go by, but at the same time I was a bit worried that he may try to turn us into a wailing guitar group, which I was always against. Anyway we set up rehearsals and I just couldn't believe how well Jeff fitted into the band, he was so good. ... I've got no malice against [Beck], in fact I think he's really a great guy, besides being an incredible guitarist."

Talking to NEW MUSICAL EXPRESS in 1974, Elton John takes up the story again: "He's a really nice guy, though, We nearly worked together, actually rehearsed for a week at Camden Town Hall. He actually approached us and asked to join ... We had rehearsals which went just fine, but he wanted to chuck out my bassist and drummer and things would've disintegrated and I would've ended up as Jeff Beck's pianist. He said 'Seeing as I got a big name in the States, I'll take 90 per cent and you and the rest of the lads

 August 26–30, 1970: The Isle of Wight festival is topped by what turns out to be Jimi Hendrix' last ever British concert appearance.

December 1970: Yardbirds re-union stalled ...

can have 10 per cent between you', and that put us off a little bit."

The 90/10 per cent deal may be a slight exaggeration, as Elton's producer Gus Dudgeon clarifies in 1972: "And at one point, Jeff Beck offered to join the group. It nearly came to something ... The reason it didn't come off was entirely due to the fact that Jeff's representatives were ridiculous when it came to the money side of it. Jeff *asked* to join the band and then they wanted Elton to receive less than a quarter of the over-all profit. It was all very flattering, but we're glad it didn't come off in the end ... If we'd have got Jeff, it wouldn't have been Elton John or Jeff Beck, it would be really peculiar."

Reminiscing about this odd union, Jeff Beck recalls to John Tobler in 1984: "So we went for a rehearsal ... but I turned up late and he gave me a terrible roasting, which made me think it wasn't such a good idea ... here I was, playing lead guitar for a band that was already complete, because Elton didn't want to change his rhythm section. I thought the next thing would be that he'd have me wearing a tie or something ..."

Scarcely a fortnight later, Elton John performs his first concert on American soil on August 25, playing the Troubador in Los Angeles, getting rave reviews and consequently heading off to stardom.

THU 27TH
The annual Isle of Wight festival has been extended to five days to allow several additions to the bill to appear. This Thursday features Tony Joe White backed by just Cozy Powell, while late at night (actually on the morning of the 28th) Cactus make their British debut in front of a wet and cold crowd.

To make ends meet awaiting the outcome of his and Jeff's new group, Powell does several sessions for Mickie Most's RAK label including albums by CCS, Duncan Browne and Hot Chocolate. He is also asked to join Uriah Heep but declines.

SEPTEMBER

SUN 6TH
After their Isle of Wight appearance, Cactus step in to replace the Doors on a European trek, beginning with the Montreux Festival on August 31 and lasting until a concert at the Olympia in Paris on September 14. They also make a quick return to London today. Jeff is presumably duly present when Cactus appear at London's Lyceum on a bill with Hawkwind and Amazing Blondel.

FRI 18TH
Jimi Hendrix dies in London, and his ex-manager Chas Chandler notes in his eulogy in RECORD MIRROR two weeks later: "What's more, [Hendrix] showed the way to a new style of pop music. Half the groups who made it owed something to Jimi. Now, I suppose, it is up to Jeff Beck and Eric Clapton to teach the world, but Jimi was there first."

OCTOBER

Jeff's musical career is threatening to grind to a complete halt this autumn, to the point where RECORD MIRROR's weekly gossip column 'The Face' this month worriedly asks "What's happening to Jeff Beck?"

The answer would be 'Not much'. In the autumn of 1970, Beck still keeps up his regular bashes with Noel Redding, now sometimes with drummer Les Sampson, but otherwise Jeff lives life at a leisurely pace, and spends the time tinkering with his cars in Egerton. Occasionally he is observed at London night spots like the Speakeasy, still with a broken tooth. Cozy Powell is still around, but has to find other means of income until Beck decides what to do.

NOVEMBER

SAT 21ST
A news item runs in DISC AND MUSIC ECHO (dated today), saying the Yardbirds are to re-form for a one-off concert at London's Roundhouse on December 13. The item also mentions that negotiations for the group's three original guitarists; Eric Clapton, Jeff Beck and Jimmy Page to appear, are under way.

DECEMBER

THU 3RD
Cozy Powell, together with the Ball boys Dave and Dennis, plays Frankfurt's Zoom Club today with a hastily re-formed Big Bertha on one of the stops of a short German tour.

I GOTTA HAVE A SONG

Panic in Detroit

Jeff Beck's visit to Motown in the summer of 1970 was by all accounts a total cultural collision. Berry Gordy's Tamla Motown empire was a much more closed-circuit organization than, say, Atlantic Records, which had a much more open attitude to white rock.

Apparently not enough had been prepared when Mickie Most, Beck and Cozy Powell came into the studio. They expected to be met with open arms and a team of musicians who were game to jam. Instead, they were scorned by the reguar session musicians, who teasingly asked them: "Where are your songs?" And when Benny Benjamin's drum set was carried out to give way for Powell's massive kit, bassist James Jamerson reportedly told Jeff: "You want the Motown sound? You just took it out!"

Beck himself offered this assessment the following year: "Yes we went, but I wasn't ready, musically I wasn't ready, and it was a terribly disorganised trip. The reason was that I wanted to incorporate my sound, my guitar style, with the Motown backing which could have been quite good but it was a miserable flop."

Still, the trip did fulfill Jeff's dream to play with the influential Jamerson. Mickie Most many years later described the sessions thus to John Tobler: "That was unbelieveable, ten fantastic days of doing nothing yet doing everything."

None of the about half a dozen recordings have ever been officially released, although a selection was considered for inclusion on the 3 CD retrospective *Beckology* in 1991. ∎

SUN 13TH
The briefly rumoured Yardbirds reunion late this year has been given a tentative date at a 'Space Party' to be held at London's Roundhouse this Sunday. Reportedly, Jeff is keen on the idea, and the plan also falls in neatly with Keith Relf and Jim McCarty's recent departure from their group Renaissance. However, it is Keith Relf who backs out in the end, although it is likely that neither Page or Clapton would have agreed.

The 'Space Party' goes ahead anyway, starring Hawkwind, the Pretty Things, Alexis Korner, Peter Green (in one of his very few '70's solo performances in the post-Fleetwood Mac years) and Pink Fairies.

◀ 1971

FEBRUARY

Jeff and Cozy finally find a suitable bassist in Clive Chaman this month, an English Trinidadian whom Cozy bumped into at a casual jam session. Talking to SOUNDS in April, Jeff explains his relief: "The bass player came about the right moment, before I had a nervous breakdown. I'd rehearsed, I don't know, maybe thirty or forty, which is a lot. What happened was that Cozy met one of his friends who said if you're still looking for a bass player, I've got just the boy ... we heard him, and that was it. He was the best player, the nearest, you know, to what I had in mind."

Chaman has played in the group Flare with his namesake Stanley Chaman, a group that has held down a weekly residency at Upstairs At Ronnie's the previous spring. Indeed, Flare play what is perhaps their last gig here on Wednesday February 3rd. Just before teaming up with Cozy and Jeff, Chaman briefly rehearses with Cat Stevens with a view to form a backing group for touring purposes.

With a complete rhythm section behind him, Jeff begins rehearsals in earnest. A suitable singer remains the main problem, briefly solved when Brian Short – who also was in Flare – is brought in.

In desperation, Jeff and Cozy are known to have flown to the United States and visit Macon, Georgia, to check out potential singers. By all accounts, the trip is a waste of time and the twosome return home empty-handed.

LATE

Jeff guests in the regular blindfold test 'Blind Date' in MELODY MAKER (March 6), commenting on an admittedly rather dull cross selection of this week's releases. Jeff passes judgement on songs by artists as diverse as Bix Beiderbecke, the Supremes and Captain Beefheart. "There's nothing here I really like", Jeff sums up.

The session takes place at the RAK offices on Oxford Street. After the 'Blind Date' spot, Jeff meets Jimmy Page and Robert Plant, who have also dropped by RAK.

MARCH

FRI 26TH

A single by the obscure studio-only band Holy Smoke is released today, featuring Jim McCarty, Jeff Beck and singer Danny Street. The ex-Yardbirds drummer has been offered a one-off deal by his music publisher B. Feldman & Co. to record the McCarty-composition *If You've Got A Lot To Give*, originally written for Dave Clark. McCarty organizes the session (believed to have been taped earlier this year), and the group name Holy Smoke is thought up on the spot.

APRIL

EARLY

After a short time as a trio, Clive Chaman suggests a piano friend of his to fill out the new group; Max Middleton, a well-schooled pianist with classical background, who is another refugee from Flare. In fact, a piano player has already been on Jeff's mind. It is apparently around 1970/'71 when he approaches Roy Young, who for years has fronted his own band with a Jerry Lee Lewis-meets-Little Richard piano style, but a partnership with Young is never realized. About Middleton, Jeff enthuses to SOUNDS: "Max, yeah, he was a really good find. Apparently he is one of those guys who plays all day long, practice, practice, practice, and he's got years of classical music training. And he wants to throw it all away and play with me!"

The wheels are now set in motion to make a proper comeback. Business-wise, Jeff is still contracted to Mickie Most and Peter Grant, who work out a new recording deal and begin planning Jeff's return to the stage with some try-out concerts in West Germany in mid-summer. However, a new figure appears on the scene at this time. He is Ernest Chapman, who will soon play an integral role in Jeff's future career.

MID

Brian Short is ousted after a brief time, and Scotsman Alex Ligertwood is quickly added as vocalist to complete a new Jeff Beck Group (henceforth referred here to as 'Jeff Beck Group II'). Ligertwood has been recommended to audition for Beck by Maggie Bell (singer with Stone The Crows, another Peter Grant signing), and has wide experience from local Glasgow groups the Quintones and the Senate (using the alias Alex Jackson). The latter band was a popular club attraction who often toured with visiting American soul stars like Ben E. King. Lastly, he has spent some time in Italy with a group of relocated Englishmen called the Primitives.

In mid-April rehearsals then get under way at the Country Club in Hampstead, before moving on to a disused dancehall in Wood Green, London.

ROLLING STONE correspondent Chris Hodenfield attends the practice runs in both Hampstead and Wood Green and describes the music as "'heavy', sure, but not glue-sniffing heavy, it's mostly thudding Romilar action" (ROLLING STONE, June 24). On the future, Jeff sums up bluntly to Hodenfield: "This time I have to make it work. There's no room to fuck about, really."

LATE

Towards the end of April, the newly formed group begins tentative recording sessions at Island Studios on Basing Street in London. Besides working on self-penned material (including an embryonic *Situation* with lyrics by Ligertwood), other songs are tried out including a rearranged version of *Morning Dew*, the Stevie Wonder tune *Show Me Where There's Music* plus a Ben E. King original called *Ain't As Sweet As You*. Helping the newly assembled group out is American producer Jimmy Miller, whose track record includes his work for Traffic and the Rolling Stones.

On the fourth day in the studio, Jeff is interviewed by Royston Eldridge of SOUNDS, for a cover story dated May 1. Although not heralded as such, this interview signals Jeff's comeback after a year out of the public eye. Talking about new material, an apprehensive Jeff explains: "A few riffs, you know. I don't write songs, I just write the guitar parts ... There's still a lack of direction when it comes to lyrics ... I hope that we'll have enough original material so we don't have to use anyone else's on the album." In parting, Jeff is asked about which other guitarists he listens to? "They all bring me down. Neil Young

Newsflash May 1971: Ernest Chapman becomes Jeff's new manager ...

I like, he's got a very good band, and John Williams and George Benson I like too."

MAY

EARLY
After a week of recording at Island, things come to a head with the RAK management. Jeff is dissatisfied with the new recording contract being drawn up and decides to take matters into his own hands and flies to New York to negotiate a deal with CBS directly. Jeff's actions understandably upset Mickie Most and Peter Grant, and they in turn confiscate the tapes from the Island sessions which come to an abrupt halt, causing further friction in an already tense relationship. By now Ernest Chapman asserts his influence in full, and begins to untangle Beck from the RAK management.

SUN 15TH
Jeff is at the Crystal Palace Bowl today, seeing the Faces, Pink Floyd and US visitors Mountain. Afterwards, Jeff talks to guitarist Leslie West, who he remembers from when an early incarnation of Mountain opened for him in New York in March 1969.

JUNE

FRI 18TH
Starline Records, a budget line in the EMI empire, releases *Remember ... The Yardbirds* today, a compilation of their biggest hits. Ultimately, the Yardbirds will become one of the most repackaged sixties groups, but this collection – split evenly between six Beck and six Clapton performances (but no Page-era songs) – serves its function to awaken interest in the Yardbirds once again.

JUNE/JULY

Jeff's comeback threatens to fall apart as he terminates his business association with Peter Grant and Mickie Most.

Ernest Chapman is appointed Jeff's personal manager, and a limited company named Equator Management Services is established to handle Jeff's affairs, while an offshoot company to handle music publishing – Equator Music – is also set up. The company operates from Chapman's offices at 2 Goodwins Court, St. Martin's Lane in the heart of London. The settlement between Equator and RAK includes a return of the Island tapes which have been kept under lock and key.

A recording deal is struck with the new UK CBS subsidiary Epic. 'New' in the sense that although the Epic label has figured as a well-known company in America, the label has only now debuted in Britain this year with an initial release by Argent on January 22. Essentially it is the same label Jeff recorded for with both the original Jeff Beck Group and the Yardbirds. The contract is for 10 albums, and the deal is otherwise believed to include a much better-than-average advance.

Amidst the upheaval in the management camp, word come back from CBS president Clive Davis that Epic is not satisfied with the vocals on the material recorded so far. Ernest Chapman is given the task to fire Alex Ligertwood. (Who goes on to join Brian Auger's Oblivion Express and later becomes a mainstay of Santana).

The new singer is Bobby Tench. He has been a member of Gass, a group whose origins stretch back on the London club scene to the mid-sixties. Tench and Gass have made an album for Polydor the previous year, with a guest appearance by Peter Green. Incidentally, Tench is also a proficient guitarist, an instrument he barely uses while working with Jeff Beck. Gass also functioned as the pit orchestra in Jack Good's rock musical *Catch My Soul*. This bastardisation of Shakespeare's *Othello* – starring P. J. Proby, P. P. Arnold and Lance Le Gault – has been a box-office hit at London's Roundhouse. In February the production moved to the Prince of Wales Theatre in the West End, and Gass used the opportunity to bow out to return to the club scene. Like Flare, Gass are also regulars at Ronnie Scott's first floor establishment 'Upstairs', and they play here on May 25–27, maybe their last engagement before Tench quits and the group dissolves.

Finally with a stable line-up but with a deadline for new product looming, the revitalized Jeff Beck Group II return to Island again this summer to finish their first album. Ligertwood's vocals on the original tapes are erased, and Bobby Tench is given short notice to come up with new sets of lyrics, and add his vocals before mixing – all in a few weeks. Jimmy Miller is dropped along the way so Beck fills the producer's seat himself, a decision he later regrets.

HE'S ALWAYS THERE

The Importance of Being Ernest

During the summer of 1971 Ernest Chapman became Jeff Beck's personal manager. A British lawyer with seemingly scant background in show business, Chapman was hired in the first place to help Beck untwine himself from the RAK management, before he took over full responsibilty of Jeff's career. Neither Grant nor Most can have been particularly sad at the loss of their client – since November '69 he has done precious little to further his own career.

Jeff's previous managers – Giorgio Gomelsky, Simon Napier-Bell and the Mickie Most/Peter Grant partnership – all combined creative flair and promotional stuntmanship with the job of recording producer. Ernest Chapman, however, represented a new breed of manager, where a knowledge of business, accounting and law were the greatest assets. Indeed, Chapman has remained Beck's manager to this very day. From a creative viewpoint Jeff in fact managed himself from now on, although Chapman certainly acted as counsellor.

Ernest Chapman, later abetted by right hand man Ralph Baker, has successfully established Jeff Beck as one of the most respected rock guitarists ever. ∎

The new management's first task is to organize a return to the stage with a European tour in the autumn while Beck's group prepare themselves.

AUGUST

JEFF BECK GROUP II: FIRST EUROPEAN TOUR
SUN 22ND
"Ruis-Rockfestival"
Runsala-parken, Turku, Finland
Jeff Beck's reported live comeback after two years takes place in Finland as the Sunday attraction of this three-day festival on a bill with Fairport Convention, the Finnish group Tasavallan Presidentii and the Swedish bands Fläsket Brinner and Cumulus. Indeed this is Jeff's first appearance in Finland and certainly chosen as a convenient low-key venue. The Finnish newspaper HELSINGIN SANOMAT notes in

July 3, 1971: The Doors' lead singer, Jim Morrison, dies in Paris, France.

August 1971: Jeff Beck returns to the stage on festivals in Europe ...

its review of the show: "The audience had high hopes of Jeff Beck's performance. Generally this guitar virtuoso wasn't upstaged by any of the bands in this year's Ruisrock." (Other acts appearing over the weekend include the Kinks and Canned Heat.)

"AHOY POP FESTIVAL", ROTTERDAM, HOLLAND, SEPTEMBER 11, 1971

SEPTEMBER

SUN 11TH
"Ahoy' Pop Festival"
Ahoy' Hal, Rotterdam, Holland
The Jeff Beck Group II continue with further appearances in Europe to test their live appeal before an American tour the next month.

The Rotterdam event is a two-day affair, and the Sunday programme in full features Fairport Convention, Reality, Gypsy, The Everly Brothers, Jeff Beck, Seatrain and finally Osibisa. (Saturday has Soft Machine, Colosseum, Help Yourself, Incredible String Band and more.) Attendance is expected at around 8,000. ALGEMEER DAGBLAD notes that long breaks between the artists and too few people in the big, cavernous sports hall spoils the festival: "Pop-show in Ahoy' muzikaal mislukt." But Jeff Beck, resplendent in plaid shirt and braces and his well-worn Stratocaster with a broken pick-guard, is barely mentioned in the review of the show.

Beck is also interviewed by Willem Hoos for the Dutch pop paper MUZIEKKRANT OOR, parts of which are used in an extensive Yardbirds article the following year (August 30, 1972).

UNDATED
Arosa, Switzerland
The Jeff Beck Group II play at a Swiss ski resort, not far from Chur.

☺ Uncharacteristically, Jeff's guitar is out of tune at times and he's playing sloppily tonight, marring both *Jody* – which simply falls apart – and a brand new song called *Ice Cream Cakes*. Otherwise, the musicianship is faultless; Cozy Powell plays with fire and conviction, Bob Tench sings well, Max Middleton's distorted electric piano crackles and sparkles while Clive Chaman thuds and growls on the bass. The show's highpoint is a chunky version of Freddie King's *Going Down*, which rocks fine.

OCTOBER

MON 4TH
A major concert to be staged at Glasgow's Electric Garden today promises a bill to include not only the new Jeff Beck Group – in what would be their British debut – but also Curved Air, Rory Gallagher, Slade, Humble Pie, Supertramp, Skid Row and Beggars Opera.

For reasons unknown, this ambitious concert is cancelled, and Jeff's British comeback is delayed until next year.

SAT 16TH
Zoom Club, Frankfurt, West Germany
Beck's new group also pays a visit to Germany for some live dates, including Frankfurt's Zoom Club. British promoter Rikki Farr, who attends the German concerts, later exclaims to NEW MUSICAL EXPRESS: "I saw the Beck outfit in action in West Germany and can promise audiences [in Britain] that they are in for a real treat."

MON 25TH
Rough And Ready, the first album by the Jeff Beck Group II, is released Stateside to coincide with a US tour. The LP features purely original material, with Beck credited as composer of six of the seven songs, although he freely admits it has been a co-operative effort with everybody in the group contributing. It is understood that Beck gets the publishing rights, while the group members are paid a flat fee in return for their songwriting contributions. In the long run, this of course serves Beck well, as the album will remain a steady, albeit minor seller.

The cover depicts the five musicians in simple black & white portraits, with Powell looking uncannily like Beck. Musically the album is a departure from the previous Beck Group, with an emphasis on harmonically more complex songs and a slight funk/Motown influence. Middleton has contributed the all-instrumental, jazz-inflected *Raynes Park Blues* (the actual park is in London, just south of Wimbledon), while Brian Short – the singer who once sang in Chaman and Middleton's group Flare – shares a co-credit with Jeff for *Jody*.

Accompanied by full page ads in BILLBOARD and ROLLING STONE, Jeff's comeback album is eagerly awaited in the States. The ROLLING STONE review (November 25) notes: "Beck is back, and in pretty good shape too." Jeff's strong following secures a #46 chart position in the USA.

TUE 26TH ✱
The Jeff Beck Group II arrive in the States for a whirlwind 16-day tour. The visit has already been re-sched-

---

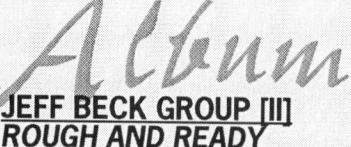

Album
JEFF BECK GROUP [II]
ROUGH AND READY

A1 GOT THE FEELING (BECK) **A2** SITUATION (BECK) **A3** SHORT BUSINESS (BECK) **A4** MAX'S TUNE (RAYNES PARK BLUES) (MIDDLETON)

B1 I'VE BEEN USED (BECK) **B2** NEW WAYS/TRAIN TRAIN (BECK) **B3** JODY (BECK/SHORT)

Released Monday October 25, 1971 (US Epic KE 30973) and Friday January 7, 1972 (UK Epic 64619) A quadrophonic version is released in the United States in February 1972 (US Epic EQ 30973)
Personnel is Jeff Beck (gtrs), Bobby Tench (vcls), Max Middleton (pno, el pno), Clive Chaman (bs), Cozy Powell (drms).
Recorded at Island Studios, 8–10 Basing Street, London, April–July 1971.
Produced by Jeff Beck
Engineered by Phil Brown
Highest Chart Position US: #46
Highest Chart Position UK: –

Ⓒ August 1, 1971: George Harrison stages the "Concert For Bangla Desh" at Madison Square Garden in New York City.

October 1971: Jeff Beck begins his first US tour in two years ...

uled, as tentative dates for Providence, Rhode Island (October 17) and Boston, Massachusetts (October 19) have been cancelled.

THU 28TH
JEFF BECK GROUP II:
FIRST NORTH AMERICAN TOUR
TraveLodge, Phoenix, Arizona

The Jeff Beck Group II make their highly anticipated American debut with two shows (7.00 and 10.30 pm) in Phoenix.

Jeff now plays a Fender Stratocaster exclusively, having retired the Gibson Les Pauls. The set list consists of four songs from the group's first album and a new number, *Ice Cream Cakes*. Furthermore a pair of cover songs are performed; Bob Dylan's *Tonight I'll Be Staying Here With You* and Freddie King's *Going Down*. Only three old favourites will be recognizable to the audiences, these being an obligatory *Jeff's Boogie* plus two songs from *Truth*; a re-styled version of *Morning Dew* including a fast middle passage (which will eventually evolve into the instrumental *Jizz Whizz* over the next two years) and a slow, funky version of *I Ain't Superstitious*.

> **POP MUSIC**
> **JEFF BECK GROUP,**
> **Flash Cadillac, Long**
> **Beach Auditorium, 8 p.m.**

FRI 29TH
Long Beach Auditorium, Long Beach, California

Rock and roll revivalists Flash Cadillac & the Continental Kids support the Beck Group for one show at 8 pm. Not surprisingly, guitar players in particular are drawn to Jeff's comeback tour. One is guitarist Ed King, once of the Strawberry Alarm Clock, who is among tonight's 3,600-strong crowd.

The review IN CASH BOX (November 13) notes: "Well, Beck is back, and those looking for comparsions came out in droves ... Even though some of the material remains, vocalist Bob Tench is enough of his own man to be judged as such ... Beck apologized for the group's performance, stating that he felt the audience to be the victims of 'an enourmous rip off'. Most, including myself, were so happy to see him back and that, for once, the legendary terrible L.A. concert sound didn't really matter."

Although Jeff feels jittery at facing the stern West Coast crowds, tonight *Jeff's Boogie* plows along like a steam train with Beck pulling out all stops, licks either flying by at lightning speed or crashlanding in a torrent of feedback. Although he is usually prone to slip in musical jokes during *Jeff's Boogie*, the set is otherwise kept straight-faced and serious. It is all the more surprising when Jeff, of all things, briefly dusts off his old finger picking excercise, the Chet Atkins tune *Trambone!*

SAT 30TH
Winterland, San Francisco, California

The Winterland, a 5,400 capacity disused skating arena, is Bill Graham's alternate facility to his Fillmore West for larger presentations. Opening acts for Beck's one night in San Francisco are Nazgul and Billy Preston.

The local reviews differ. Conrad Silvert in ARTSTRA (November 5) is not pleased: "Beck looked intimidated by the famously superhip San Francisco audience. He never once looked the people in the face (Jimi Hendrix used to weave his spirit into a cosmic fuck with the crowd through his guitar), but Beck seemed neurotically twisted to stage left looking at his hands except for an occasional jump around towards his band, when he acted as if he were gettin' it on when all he was really doing was appealing for help. He was much too much the superstar that night but couldn't fulfill the role, and the band couldn't disguise it. It was frustrating, embarrassing, and a shame, because no doubt they must make music sometimes." On the other hand, THE STANFORD DAILY (November 4) is only positive: "Beck and his sidemen ... soon gave the audience everything they wanted with an eclectic selection that included material from both the old and new Jeff Beck Group ... It is an indication of Beck's musicianship that he is able to so clearly dominate such a talented group of artists ... He controls every aspect of his group's performance – hearing everything – and so cueing his sidemen while still managing to make the renowned guitar dominate the scene ... The return of one of rock's finest guitarists on this tour and on the new album is considerable cause for rejoicing. Beck's back."

The Frisco concert is solid and well-played, although the new songs sit uneasily along covers and old favourites. A high point is the rarely performed *Show Me Where There's Music* – with a long prelude where Jeff plays some patently absurd guitar. As yet the new material is not familiar turf, but the whole performance is greeted enthusiastically by the usually jaded West Coast crowd. "We're going to take the liberty of stealing a tune, as everybody does. It's a lovely tune, and it goes something like this!", Jeff says before he puts on a slide and counts off *Tonight I'll Be Staying Here With You*. The perennial *Jeff's Boogie* repeats the unaccompanied free-form middle section from 1968/1969 where Jeff indulges in various flights of fantasy, including quoting the *Beverly Hillbillies* theme, the slightly corny aside he will invariably stick into the song for another two years. *I Ain't Superstitious* is done as languid cocktail jazz, and lacks the vitality of the original Beck recording. Max Middleton excels at acoustic and electric piano, blending well with Beck's needly Strat tones. But Cozy Powell is the stand-out player, extremely powerful and tight, welding the band together in a funky, functional whole.

SUN 31ST
Swing Auditorium, San Bernardino, California

A Halloween concert with the American Indian band Redbone.

NOVEMBER

TUE 2ND
True to his word, Jeff takes a day off on the second anniversary of his car accident, having promised himself never to venture out on this date.

THU 4TH
A show at the Music Hall in Cincinnati, Ohio is pencilled in for today but is ultimately never finalized.

FRI 5 AND SAT 6TH
Academy of Music, New York, New York

The Jeff Beck Group II make their Big Apple debut supported by Bill Wyman-protégés Tucky Buzzard and Redbone (Ernest Chapman is their UK agent). The Howard Stein-promoted concerts are sold-out in advance, and the audience includes Rick Derringer, Steve Paul, Cactus and Clive Davis.

Set List/Jeff Beck Group II

Academy of Music, Nov 5/6, '71

Going Down • Ice Cream Cakes
• Tonight I'll Be Staying Here With You
• Jeff's Boogie • Jody • Morning Dew
• I Ain't Superstitious • New Ways/
Train Train • Got The Feeling •
Situation (Encore)

November 1971: Jeff Beck plays New York to sell-out crowds ...

Beck is also interviewed by Beverly Magid for a feature in CIRCUS (February 1972).

The late Saturday show – there are two shows each night – is a big success with the group playing into the early hours of Sunday morning. The set is devoid of lengthy solos, instead giving room for short and tight breaks. Max Middleton opens the show with a short prelude of boogie piano mixed with classical flourishes before *Going Down* blasts off, while Cozy Powell has brief spots in both *Jody* and *Got The Feeling*. The simple yet catchy middle riff in *New Ways/Train, Train* is used by Jeff to encourage a singalong. A cheerful Beck tells the audience: "I tell you what. I think I've got me about one of the best rock 'n' roll groups in the country!"

Correspondent Chuck Pulin, who covers the concert for SOUNDS (November 20), writes: "... Beck himself, who proved he hasn't lost his fine guitar style and drive, showing easily that he is still one of the top guitarists on either side of the Atlantic."

MON 8TH
Music Hall, Boston, Massachusetts
"As Beck fired along with the group, its collective sound was exciting. The evening really belonged to Beck who dazzled the audience with brilliant guitar work. Beck is the great improviser. His riffs flow easily from blues to bluegrass, from chirping birdcalls, to mean and gritty rock. Beck is a master of idioms and imagination. The combination is effortless for Beck, as he gravitates from passion to humor", comments Charles Giuliano in the BOSTON HERALD the following day. The college paper THE TECH (November 16) praises the musicianship but blames the crowd: "Unfortunately, the audience was very cold, with hardly anyone getting into the excellent music." Redbone play support.

According to legend, Jeff is holed up in his hotel room with two bodyguards as there is a threat on his life. Idling his time in front of the TV, Jeff accidentally comes across a programme on the PBS channel, "The Best Unknown Guitarist In The World", showcasing the largely unknown Washington DC-based guitarist Roy Buchanan, which impresses him greatly.

Jeff has felt tremendous pressure on this tour which results in isolation and headaches – the latter attributed to post-effects from to his car accident two years ago.

WED 10TH✱
The Jeff Beck Group II fly home.

SAT 27TH
Like Glasgow in October, tonight is another tentative UK booking (at Manchester University with 9.30 Fly) which is then cancelled. Obviously there was an intention to do some home dates at the end of this year.

DECEMBER

In early December, the Jeff Beck Group II reconvene and begin pre-production for their second album at the Rolling Stones' rehearsal studio on 47 Bermondsey Street in South East London. Studio time has been booked in the States with Stax guitar-legend Steve Cropper producing, no less. A return to the British stage is also being prepared for early 1972.

Dick Meadows of SOUNDS and Chris Welch of MELODY MAKER attend the rehearsals for some press coverage to tie in with the planned British tour.

JEFF BECK GROUP [II]
A: GOT THE FEELING (Beck)
B: SITUATION (Beck)

Released Monday December 6, 1971 (US Epic 5-10814); Friday January 7, 1972 (UK Epic EPC 7720)
Personnel as on *Rough And Ready*.
Recorded at Island Studios, 8–10 Basing Street, London, April–July 1971.
Produced by Jeff Beck
Engineered by Phil Brown
Highest Chart Position US: –
Highest Chart Position UK: –

The SOUNDS article (December 18) is headlined 'Beck Breaks Silence!', and Jeff sums up his present position as "I just want to be a member of the band. That is all I have ever wanted to be with any band, a lead guitarist." Cozy Powell enthuses "we have found more direction now. I think the band has improved 100% since the beginning." Asked about Jimmy Page, Jeff says: "His acoustic work frightens me sometimes, it is so good. Then I played *Led Zeppelin II* and it didn't do anything for me, his electric guitar playing that is."

In MELODY MAKER (January 1, 1972) Jeff already dismisses the *Rough And Ready* album with "I liked it when we first recorded it. I don't now", but hopes "the second one will be more listenable. The material will be less fiddly." He continues: "I am never happy! You've got to be conditioned not to be too satisfied. A lot of people who know me from the Yardbirds days know that I'm a totally different person on stage from on records. I can loosen up on live appearances."

MON 6TH
Got The Feeling is released as a single today in the States, going nowhere.

TUE 14TH
The Jeff Beck Group II tape three songs for BBC Radio One with producer John Muir. The recording is done at Studio T1, Kensington House, Shepherd's Bush, London. *Going Down* and *Got The Feeling*, will be broadcast on January 14, 1972 on John Peel's "Sounds Of The Seventies", while the last track, *Ice Cream Cakes*, will be held back until February 11, 1972 (on the same programme). *Going Down* will also be repeated almost a year later on BBC Radio One's "Sequence" on Friday January 12, 1973.

UNDATED
Although Beck is now committed to his own comeback, a strange link-up with singer Curtis Mayfield is on the drawing board sometime late in 1971.

Not much is known about this brief encounter, but Beck allows this much when interviewed by Nick Kent in November 1972: "Mayfield wanted me to play guitar in his band and as I was at a loose end and respected the music he'd been playing in the Impressions, I agreed. There was all sorts of hassles from the start and finally when I got together with Mayfield, I found I couldn't get on with him. He was into this thing about black and white ... so it all came to nothing."

October 29, 1971: Duane Allman is killed in a motorcycle accident in Macon, Georgia.

1972

JANUARY

MON 3RD–FRI 14TH✱

For the two first weeks of the new year, the Jeff Beck Group II return to the United States to record their second album in Memphis, Tennessee with guitarist Steve Cropper producing. The sessions are not held at the legendary Stax studios as hoped, but rather at TMI (Trans-Maximus Incorporated) Sound Studios, a new studio partly owned by Cropper.

Some of the songs recorded are already featured in the group's stage act, like the self-penned *Ice Cream Cakes* (inspired by the Ben E. King song *Ain't As Sweet As You* which Alex Ligertwood introduced to the group the previous spring). But whereas the previous album consisted of all original material, five cover songs are taped, including a re-make of one of Jeff and Cozy's Motown experiments, *I Can't Give Back The Love I Feel For You*. Other songs are obviously written in the studio, including the Steve Cropper/Jeff Beck collaboration *Sugarcane*.

The sessions are not totally smooth; after an argument with Beck in the studio, Cozy Powell smashes his right hand through a wall in frustration and fractures two fingers. Luckily, this happens on literally the very final day in the studio, so all of Powell's drum tracks are done.

With the recording sessions completed, Steve Cropper throws a party in honour of Beck and group. Among the guests are songwriter Don Nix, who applauds Jeff's version of *Going Down*, a song which Nix wrote for Freddie King the previous year. Nix, who used to play baritone sax in Cropper's old group the Mar-Keys, incidentally was also a member of the touring party on the fateful Dick Clark tour in October/November 1966 when Jeff left the Yardbirds for good.

A couple of months later, Jeff runs into Don Nix again in England via their mutual acquaintance Isaac Tigrett.

FRI 7TH

The single *Got The Feeling* – with identical flipside as the already released American version – is issued in Great Britain today. Concurrently *Rough And Ready* is also released in Europe, and Chris Welch's preview in MELODY MAKER (December 4, 1971) shares a view later echoed by several critics: "It's not a sensational album, but solid and packs plenty of action." Roy Carr (NEW MUSICAL EXPRESS, January 15) comments: "As with lot of albums currently competing for our attention, [the album] falls into that trap whereby the performance far exceeds that of the material, a pity but nonetheless true," but points out how "Beck hasn't lost any of his fire as he rips off solo after solo of flashy confidence."

DISC AND MUSIC ECHO and SOUNDS both run reviews on January 15, 1972. Although the title suggests a raw approach to DISC's Andrew Tyler, "... little is left to chance. It's free and loose but always under control", while an excited Billy Walker of SOUNDS concludes "... believe me if they come up with a better one it's going to be a monster." RECORD MIRROR's Valerie Mabbs (January 22) finds the album "a generally nice collection of sounds".

Derek Johnson, writing on the single *Got The Feeling* in NEW MUSICAL EXPRESS, claims "an excellent disc combining a strong commercial element with an altogether more progressive approach," while David Hughes in DISC AND MUSIC ECHO notes a mild Chicago influence: "... the mood and tempo changes, and you remain hooked till the end".

The album is also met with anticipation in France, where Patrice Michel of EXTRA is suitably impressed ("il est trop bon!") while Guillaume Rapin devotes a whole page feature on Beck in the fortnightly POP MUSIC SUPERHEBDO (December 16, 1971), tracing his career from 1965 till the new album.

FRI 14TH

John Peel presents the Jeff Beck Group II on his radio show "Sounds Of The Seventies" (BBC Radio One, 10.00 pm–midnight). Two pre-recorded selections are broadcast, *Going Down* and *Got The Feeling* (▶ December 14, 1971). Tonight's programme is completed by Medicine Head (incidentally one of the most recorded bands by the BBC in the early 70's), Barclay James Harvest and Arthur Brown's Kingdom Come.

SUN 16TH✱

The Jeff Beck Group II return to England, where Cozy Powell's hand injury forces him to immediately consult a physician in London and delay rehearsals for the group's upcoming British tour.

MON 17TH

Despite Cozy Powell's recent accident, today Rikki Farr of Buffalo Promotions eagerly announces a Jeff Beck tour of Britain to begin at the Polytechnic, Bristol on January 31. The tour concentrates solely on university and college venues, and after Bristol the group is to visit Kent University, Canterbury (February 1), Guildhall, Southampton (arranged by Southampton University, February 3), University of Worcester, Worcester (February 5), Sussex University, Brighton (February 9), College of Printing, London (February 11), Lanchester Polytechnic, Coventry (February 12), University of Lancaster, Lancaster (February 18) and finally a club date at London's Roundhouse on the 20th of February.

SAT 22ND

Based on Farr's announcement, the front page of SOUNDS today optimistically trumpets 'Beck – Tour On!'.

However, Cozy Powell has been ordered to four weeks rest by a London specialist, and after briefly considering asking Mitch Mitchell to act as stand-in drummer, the whole tour is postponed and the concerts rescheduled for March.

THU 27TH

Jeff is at the Speakeasy to hear Curtis Mayfield tonight, a show he later claims was one of his favourite live gigs all year, along with a Sha Na Na show later in the year.

SAT 29TH

The UK music press reports that Jeff's British tour to commence two days later in Bristol is cancelled because of Powell's injury. A rather lame made-up story of a power failure in Memphis with Powell falling down some stairs in the ensuing confusion, is served to the press as explanation of the injury. A new date sheet is immediately finalised by Buffalo Concert Promotions in association with Equator Management.

Ⓒ January 20, 1972: Pink Floyd debut their ambitious new work "Dark Side of the Moon" at the opening night of a UK tour in Brighton.

Newsflash February 1972: Jeff Beck Group II make their British debut ...

FEBRUARY

FRI 11TH
A leftover from the pre-Christmas session at BBC (▶ December 14, 1971), *Ice Cream Cakes,* is broadcast on John Peel's "Sounds Of The Seventies" (BBC Radio One, 10 pm till midnight). Other acts on Peel's show tonight are Keef Hartley, Mike Maran and Third Ear Band.

SAT 19TH
In today's NEW MUSICAL EXPRESS, the regular Thrills column teasingly asks: "Who is looking after Beck's publicity? NME had a strange call the other day from a lawyer at Lincoln's Inn to arrange an interview for Jeff." When enquiring if the caller has an intercom phone that allows one to hold a conversation from across the room, the publicist replies: "Yes. As a matter of fact, I'm in the bog!"

MARCH

WED 1ST
THE JEFF BECK GROUP II:
FIRST BRITISH TOUR
University of Manchester, Manchester
Jeff Beck makes his comeback on a British stage, his first live appearance in England since April 25, 1969 – almost three years earlier. Support act on all dates is Heaven, a horn-driven eight-piece group managed by Rikki Farr.

The set list is more or less identical to the American tour the previous autumn, with a rearranged version of Carl Perkins' rockabilly number *Glad All Over* and the Bill Withers' ballad *Ain't No Sunshine* being the only notable additions.

Tonight's tour opening is – along with tomorrow's concert in Sheffield – viewed as try-outs before the London concert on the 3rd. However, writes Penny Bosworth in MELODY MAKER (March 11), "the audience doesn't mind being guinea pigs," describing the start as "Jeff being nervously phallic with his guitar, it didn't seem if the music was going anywhere ... But once the barrier against returning to the stage again had been conquered, good sounds started to come out!" Called back for an encore, Jeff exclaims: "Thank you! We needed this gig."

THU 2ND
Student Union, University of Sheffield, Sheffield

FRI 3RD
London College of Printing, London
Tony Stewart of NEW MUSICAL EXPRESS (March 11) gives a vivid description of Jeff's return to a London stage, where "security was tuff-as-Fort Knox" according to one source: "The house record was broken, and between the time Heaven left the stage, and the Beck Group appeared there was an electric excitement of anticipation. The place stank, people close up together, anxiously scanning the stage for the guitar God. Guys and chicks stumbled onto the bar top; the chitter chatter hissed through the auditorium." Still, Stewart is not convinced: "Rock, Beck and his band of untogether lads, can do. Subtle? No way" he comments, continuing "... Beck I should point out was good, but working within the format of his group, it didn't really take off and get to any great heights ... The Jeff Beck Group doesn't cook that well, believe me. In fact the whole concert was a bit of an anti-climax."

SAT 4TH
Bristol Polytechnic, Bristol

WED 8TH
Sussex University, Brighton

FRI 10TH
University of Lancaster, Lancaster

SAT 11TH
Refectory, University of Leeds, Leeds

TUE 14TH
University of Southampton, Southampton

THU 16TH
Kent University, Canterbury
Originally booked for Liverpool University, tonight's show is then moved to Canterbury.

FRI 17TH
South Parade Pier, Southsea, Portsmouth
A MELODY MAKER reader witnessing tonight's show is awestruck: "Beck's recent concert ... was literally out of this world as an exhibition of sheer guitar wizardry. Yes, I have seen Jimmy Page, Clapton, Alvin Lee et al. But at Southsea, Beck beat the lot hands down. People walked out of the hall hardly believing what they had seen. I have yet to hear a guitarist who can coax a more incredible variety of sounds from his instrument. Beck's guitar pounded, screamed and soothed. There wasn't a single cliché in his playing, and for sheer speed he's better than he's ever been."

SAT 18TH
Waltham Forest Technical College, Waltham Forest, London

SUN 19TH
"Implosion"
Roundhouse, Chalk Farm, London
For today's 'Implosion' Sunday concert at the Roundhouse, running from 3.30–11.00 pm, the bill has been extended to also feature Trees and Stud.

Karl Dallas, MELODY MAKER (March 25) writes: "The audience erupted into paroxysms of joy. The vocalist wasn't much, the piano was nearly inaudible, but it didn't really matter because we had come to hear Jeff ...", before summing up: "[He] is quite the most ridiculously extravagant virtuoso on the guitar we have ever had, flashier than Hendrix, less confined by the boundaries than Clapton, more extrovert than Bloomfield, technically brilliant but not afraid to stop the band and retune his instrument half-way through a number ... a showman, a musician, a rock and roller."

LATE
In a two-part interview with Tony Stewart of NEW MUSICAL EXPRESS (dated

March 1972: Jeff Beck appears on "Beat Club" TV show in Germany ...

THE SECOND JEFF BECK GROUP... FACSIMILE FROM BEST, FEBRUARY 1973

April 8 and 15) conducted at Ernest Chapman's office in London, Jeff confides: "I don't have enough to say as a solo artist. In other words I couldn't sit on a stool with an electric guitar or any other guitar and entertain anyone for more than about half an hour. But it's not what I'd like to do anyway. I'd just like to sit back and play how I feel." Jeff is customarily blunt about the group's recent album: "The songs as songs are garbage, there's no two ways about it. They just don't mean anything." Characterizing his new band, Beck says: "... it's rather like having an Erroll Garner with a rock 'n' roll guitarist. And a funk drummer." Pressed on the subject of songwriting credits, Jeff gladly admits "nobody's any less the writer than the next man [in the band]." Questioned about an all-instrumental format, Beck observes: "I feel if I formed an instrumental group I'd play all I'd got to say in the first couple of tracks, unless someone wrote me a lot of tunes." In the second part, Stewart asks Beck: "How stable will this band be?" Ever the honest one, Jeff remarks: "I don't know. It could be I'll kick them out all next week."

Cozy Powell, Max Middleton and Clive Chaman are interviewed by Martin Hayman of SOUNDS (March 25), but without Beck.

SAT 25TH

The Jeff Beck Group II fly to Germany to videotape their only known TV appearance. The show in question is the popular "Beat Club", simulcast live from Radio Bremen's TV studios, Bremen, West Germany between 3.15–4.00 pm. Interestingly enough, the as-yet-unreleased instrumental *Definitely Maybe* is taped instead of a vocal number – in fact, singer Bobby Tench does not even appear on the show. Through the use of split-screen studio effects, a sullen-looking Jeff is shown playing all three guitar parts simultaneously on his well-worn Stratocaster.

APRIL

THU 6TH✱
JEFF BECK GROUP II:
FIRST GERMAN TOUR
After their British tour, Jeff's group begins a short tour of Germany, again supported by Heaven.

Sa., 8. April, 20.00 Uhr
Kongroßhalle — Mosso
The legendary
Jeff Beck
& his group
+ Heaven
In concert

FRI 7TH
Musikhalle, Hamburg, West Germany

SAT 8TH
Kongresshalle, Frankfurt, West Germany

MON 10TH
Oetker-Halle, Bielefeld, West Germany

WED 12TH
Killesberg, Stuttgart, West Germany

THU 13TH
Cirkus-Krone-Bau, Munich, West Germany

UNDATED
Offenburg, West Germany
After tonight's concert, Jeff talks to Bruno Eucat for an interview published in the French magazine EXTRA (June 1972).

MAY

MON 1ST
The second album by the Jeff Beck Group II, just entitled *Jeff Beck Group* is released in the US today to coincide with an upcoming American tour. The album is usually referred to as the *Orange Album* because of the fruit inexplicably pictured on the cheap looking cover. The collection is split between four self-penned compositions and five covers. *I Can't Give Back The Love I Feel For You* and *Show Me Where There's Music* are recorded in a Stax-meets-Motown style. Two staples from their live act for the last six months, Bob Dylan's *Tonight I'll Be Staying Here With You* and Freddie King's potent *Going Down*, are also included along with a modernized version of the rockabilly number *Glad All Over*. The original material is more riff-based and lacks the harmonic sophistication of the previous album. To add colour, backing singers are added on some songs, seemingly as an afterthought in the mixdown process. Surprisingly, no single is culled from the album.

Unfortunately, John Mendelsohn in ROLLING STONE (June 8) dismisses the album out of hand: "This album, and the group in general, is usually terrific when Beck's guitar-playing is in the spotlight. When either Bob Tench's vocals or Max Middleton's usually pleasant but seldom arresting and never-smoothly-integrated jazz piano are basking therein, Jeff Beck Group's music is mostly just dull – commonplace and predictable ... One might reasonably have expected Steve Cropper, as producer, to have nudged the group into a mellifluous Stax groove – whence Beck's sudden outbursts of outrage might have been nirvana itself – but no such good fortune. Truth be told, the record doesn't even sound – in the basic sense – appreciably better than *Rough And Ready*."

Still, one bad review doesn't stop the record from peaking at an impressive #19 in early July.

WED 3RD✱
The Jeff Beck Group II fly to New York to begin a 15-date North American tour. The tour does not include any West Coast stops, instead concentrating on the East Coast and the Midwest with a solitary date in the South.

THU 4TH
JEFF BECK GROUP II:
SECOND NORTH AMERICAN TOUR
Long Island Arena, Commack, New York
For the American tour the set list is changed slightly around. Both *Jody* and *Ain't No Sunshine* are dropped –

April 15, 1972: Neil Young returns to the top of the UK album charts with "Harvest", which has already been a US chart topper.

April 1972: Jeff Beck Group II begin their second US tour ...

the former never to be performed again – while *Ice Cream Cakes* is promoted to set-opener, displacing *Going Down* to later in the set. The old Carl Perkins' number *Glad All Over* is retained from the UK jaunt, and this tour also introduces *Definitely Maybe* to American audiences, with Bobby Tench usually duplicating the harmony guitar parts from the recorded version. The only surprise is a revival of *Plynth* from *Beck-Ola*, which is inserted halfway into the *New Ways/Train Train* medley.

FRI 5TH
Carnegie Hall, New York, New York
Two Howard Stein-promoted sellout shows (8 and 11 pm) at the prestigious Carnegie Hall mark a triumphant Beck return to New York City. Support act is Looking Glass, a group that soon will score a US chart-topper with *Brandy (You're A Fine Girl)*. The shows gross $32.000.

"Beck, in the forefront of rock and blues-rock musicians since his days with the Yardbirds, supplied his own critique with thumbs up or thumbs down gestures after selections by the Epic Records combo. Most of the times were thumbs up. His unit is a good one ... but the show was Beck's guitar work, which, when it works, pales most of rock's other lead guitarists", writes the show-biz magazine VARIETY (May 10) after the concert.

"The newest pastime at New York concerts is throwing balloons around", reports CIRCUS (May 1972), commenting: "Beck had a field day when several landed onstage. Without missing one note, he stomped on them all."

SAT 6TH
Allen Theatre Cleveland, Ohio
Promoted by Belkin Productions, tonight's show goes ahead at 8.30 pm.

SUN 7TH
Cobo Hall, Detroit, Michigan
Presented by Bob Bageris and radio station WRIF, tonight's triple bill at the big Cobo Hall also features Free – who are in the midst of a chaotic comeback tour of the States hampered by guitarist Paul Kossoff's drug abuse – and Stevie Wonder. Jeff expresses a strong interest in working with the Motown prodigy, and the seeds for a Beck/Wonder union are now sown.

Clive Chaman later recalls how Wonder's opening set is so powerful that Beck's performance is deliberately delayed an hour – due to "technical problems" – to calm down the crowd.

MON 8TH
Massey Hall, Toronto, Ontario, Canada
The tour takes in a stopover in Toronto, Beck's first concert in Canada since March 1969. Presented by Martin Onrot, tickets range from $6.00 to $3.50 and Looking Glass play support again.

WED 10TH
Riverside Theater, Milwaukee, Wisconsin
Two shows at 7 and 10 pm with the Siegal-Schwall Band.

THU 11TH
O'Hara Arena, Dayton, Ohio

FRI 12TH
Tonight's concert to be held at the Capitol Plaza in Frankfort, Kentucky, is cancelled on short notice for reasons unknown, with the public being offered a refund for tickets.

SAT 13TH
McCormick Place, Arie Crown Theatre, Chicago
"By the time the Jeff Beck Group took off on their second encore Saturday night at Arie Crown, Beck and his bassist had taken off their shirts as well. So maybe there was some honest sweat going on there, but for the most part what was coming off behind the footlights didn't seem that hot", writes Lynn Van Matre in the CHICAGO TRIBUNE (May 15) of tonight's concert. "Beck's guitar can sizzle electrically or simmer melodically. But as far as projecting any kind of real feeling, things remained as medium cool as television and about as spontaneous." A sentiment also echoed by MELODY MAKER'S Chicago correspondent Al Rudis (June 10): "They seem to be missing soul, and their set felt as cold as ice. Jeff's flashy guitar stirred up the audience, but there was little real music played. More's the pity for all the musicians appear to be excellent. Max Middleton, especially, plays some fine piano, and Bob Tench has a powerful, dramatic voice. But Bob was forced to constantly push and scream, and it seemed as if all the musicians were there merely to fill in between the guitar solos."

Live tapes actually prove this to be a fair concert, with the group offering a strong version of *Ice Cream Cakes* with an exemplary funky guitar/electric piano conversation. *Going Down* explodes when the band comes in after Middleton's piano-rhapsodizing and is highlighted by a sterling

Album

JEFF BECK GROUP [II]
JEFF BECK GROUP [THE ORANGE ALBUM]
A1 ICE CREAM CAKES (BECK) **A2** GLAD ALL OVER (SCHROEDER/TEPPER/BENNETT; ARR. BECK) **A3** TONIGHT I'LL BE STAYING HERE WITH YOU (BOB DYLAN) **A4** SUGAR CANE (BECK/CROPPER) **A5** I CAN'T GIVE BACK THE LOVE I FEEL FOR YOU (ASHFORD/SIMPSON/B. HOLLAND)

B1 GOING DOWN (DON NIX) **B2** I GOT TO HAVE A SONG (SHOW ME WHERE THERE'S MUSIC) (WONDER/HUNTER/HARDAWAY/RISER) **B3** HIGHWAYS (BECK) **B4** DEFINITELY MAYBE (BECK)

Released Monday May 1, 1972 (US Epic KE 31331) and Friday June 9, 1972 (UK Epic 64899) A quadrophonic version is released in the United States in August 1972 (US Epic EQ 31331)
Personnel is Jeff Beck (gtrs, elctrc sitar), Bobby Tench (vcls), Max Middleton (pno, el pno), Clive Chaman (bs), Cozy Powell (drms). Uncredited back-up singers appear on A4 and B2.
Recorded at TMI Sound Studios, Memphis, Tennessee, January 1972.
Produced by Stephen L. Cropper
Engineered by Ronnie Capone
Highest Chart Position US: #19
Highest Chart Position UK: –

May 1972: Stevie Wonder and Jeff Beck record "Superstition" ...

Beck solo. *Glad All Over* also works well with a dynamic coda with Bob Tench's vocal against Middleton's clavinet and Beck's guitar.

SUN 14TH

Another unexplained cancellation, this time at the Armory in Minneapolis, Minnesota, where Beck's group should headline supported by Tranquility in a Howard Stein presentation.

WED 17TH
Palace Theatre, Waterbury, Connecticut

Support by Todd Rundgren, who tours in support of the double album *Something/Anything*.

🎵 The Jeff Beck Group II play a fine set capped by two encores. *Ice Cream Cakes* proves an able attention-grabber as the the opening song, with Jeff's bluesy, mournful guitar lines. To enhance his keyboard sound, Middleton now often uses a wah-wah either on the electric piano or the clavinet and the brittle, trebly sound perfectly complements the guitar. As is customary, Beck evolves the middle section of *Jeff's Boogie* in a stream-of-consciousness blend of screaming blues bends, machine-gun pull-offs and a snatch of bluegrass. *Definitely Maybe* is simply beautiful, where Beck's use of the slide reminds one of a violinist with a wide vibrato. A tip of the hat to Beck's past, *Plynth* is put in service halfway into *New Ways/Train Train*. Always a great rocker, *Plynth* does not translate well by this Group. Even more awkward is *Let Me Love You*; instead of keeping the tune's original shuffle rhythm, it is now played with a stiff, quasi-funky feel and absolutely refuses to move forward.

After the concert, Beck is interviewed by Jon Tiven for NEW HAVEN ROCK PRESS, where Jeff vaguely hints at the future: "... we're going to work on a single. Nobody knows what's going to come out of it."

Set List/Jeff Beck Group II

Palace Theater, Waterbury, May 17 '72

Ice Cream Cakes • Morning Dew • Going Down • Tonight I'll Be Staying Here With You • Glad All Over • Definitely Maybe • Jeff's Boogie • Situation • New Ways/Plynth/Train Train • Let Me Love You • Got The Feeling

---

THU 18TH
Aquarius (Orpheum) Theater, Boston, Massachusetts

After staying overnight in Waterbury, the group travels collectively to Boston today for two shows at 7 and 10 pm.

FRI 19TH
The Spectrum, Philadelphia, Pennsylvania

A highpoint of the tour is tonight's sold-out concert at the 10,000-seat Spectrum, again with Todd Rundgren plus the Fabulous Rhinestones.

SAT 20TH
Pirate's World, Dania, Florida

A confusing situation today, as Jeff is billed to appear in two different cities in different states but at the same time! Although the ST. LOUIS DISPATCH runs an advertisement promising Beck and Malo (a group led by Carlos Santana's brother Jorge) tonight at St. Louis, Missouri's Kiel Auditorium at 8.00 pm, it is a simultaneously booked appearance in Dania, Florida, which goes ahead. The Pirate's World show with Richard Gerstein and A New Day Ahead attracts a crowd of 5,100 for a total gross of $25,000.

SUN 21ST
Mid-South Coliseum, Memphis, Tennessee

Supported by Malo, tonight's concert marks the end of a successful American tour. A return to the States is already being booked, including a concert in Gaelic Park, New York City in early August.

MON 22ND

Jeff Beck Group II are originally booked for a huge festival in Germany today (a three-day Whitsun affair dubbed 'Second British Rock Meeting' and held on a peninsula along the Rhine River near Mannheim), but cancel, perhaps due to the opportunity to record with Beck's idol Stevie Wonder in New York.

Beck has expressed interest in working together with Wonder, and Ernest Chapman and Epic Records have arranged a session at the famed Electric Lady Studios. The Motown star is there around-the-clock recording his new album and preparing a mammoth two-month US tour supporting the Rolling Stones to commence on the 4th of June.

TUE 23RD, WED 24TH, THU 25TH ✱

The Jeff Beck Group II are in New York City to record with Stevie Wonder. The purpose of the visit is to tape a single, considered a wise move as no suitable 45 was extracted from the *Jeff Beck Group* album. Over the course of three consecutive nights, about four basic songs are put down by Wonder and the Beck band. A pepped-up Wonder contributes lyrics made up on the spot.

One of the songs they do is *Maybe Your Baby*, a new Wonder composition which Jeff wants to use for the projected single. However, Wonder is not too keen to give the song away. Instead he comes up with the brilliant *Superstition* (or rather *Don't Be Superstitious* as it is briefly called) – a lick inspired by Jeff fiddling behind the drums one day in the studio. Beck, who later describes it as "the riff of the century", immediately senses the song's strong commercial potential and is intent on recording it as a new single. A version is duly recorded by Stevie Wonder and Beck's group. The original idea is actually to share the credit and release the song on a single jointly credited to 'Jeff Beck and Stevie Wonder'. Running out of time, it is decided to return to Electric Lady at the first opportunity to do vocal overdubs and mixing.

In return for *Superstition*, Jeff adds guitar to some songs for Stevie's album in the works, including *Looking For Another Pure Love*. Wonder also offers Jeff another song at these sessions called *Thelonius*, which Beck eventually will record two years later.

Electric Lady is bursting with activity these summer weeks, and also around are the J. Geils Band and – fatefully – Cactus, who by chance are recording *their* new album for summer release. Funnily enough, Cactus are now fronted by British singer Pete French, who knows Powell well from the Birmingham group Big Bertha.

Intrigued by the possibility of working with Tim Bogert and Carmine Appice, Jeff wastes little time in planning a future collaboration with the Cactus rhythm section.

Jeff's overtures to Bogert and Ap-

May 20, 1972: Marc Bolan and T. Rex makes their fourth UK #1 single with "Metal Guru".

June 1972: BBC Radio One "In Concert" features Jeff Beck Group II ...

pice don't go unnoticed by his present group, and Clive Chaman loses his temper one day in the studio and in the ensuing row with Beck decides to leave. The following day Chaman and Ernest Chapman settle matters in a separation contract.

JUNE

Back home in England, Jeff is enlisted to play guitar for an album by actor and singer Murray Head. The sessions take place at London's Island Studios.

Head, whose main claim to fame is his role as Judas on the highly successful *Jesus Christ Superstar* album the previous year, is working on a projected LP. Other musicians employed include Cozy Powell and Clive Chaman, plus Wings' guitarist Henry McCullough. Ultimately, Jeff's contributions never make it to the finished article *(Nigel Lived)*, but Jeff will play guitar for Murray Head later on.

FRI 9TH ✱

The Jeff Beck Group album is released in Great Britain this month. An ecstatic Chris Welch in MELODY MAKER (June 3) gushes: "... this is the boldest Beck guitar we have heard for a long time. His style might not be to everybody's tastes. It sounds almost sardonic at times, but distinctly personal, almost as if he is talking and chattering through the pickups. Beck's skill at timing and cliff-hanging suspense at the tail end of phrases is brilliant and his backing licks are almost as interesting ... Great stuff!"

On the other hand, Tony Stewart's lukewarm caption 'Beck Doesn't Make It' in NEW MUSICAL EXPRESS (July 1) cites Bob Tench as the main downfall of a sprawling collection of songs. Billy Walker of SOUNDS (June 10) finds the album "not up to the standard of *Rough And Ready*, and a slight letdown after a highly promising start." Rob Mackie of RECORD MIRROR (June 17, 1972) is not impressed either, dismissing side one of the record as "[giving] no clue that you're listening to the band led by one of Britain's best-ever guitarists."

Charles Shaar Murray (Oz #43, July 1972) offers a different slant: "Jeff Beck is the subject of many unprintable anecdotes centering around his groupies and fellow musicians. After about three bars of his performance on *Highways*, you know they are all true. Anyone who'd play that is clearly capable of stopping at nothing."

DISC, oddly enough, chooses to review the record twice! In their first review (June 17) the album is merely certified three stars (meaning 'Good'), while three weeks later Pete Erskine gives it a top rating of four stars (meaning 'Outstanding'), and defends the product: "Unfairly, this album seems to have endured a lot of heavy slagging. ... The band play as a tight unit, the sound is full and mellow; but for those of you who still like early Beck sounds, there's that too, on side two with *Going Down*".

WED 21ST ✱

Jeff catches New York rock 'n' roll satirists Sha Na Na at the Speakeasy tonight. Also around is Keith Moon, who takes on Sha Na Na as his personal protégés.

THU 29TH

Deputising for Roy Wood's Electric Light Orchestra on short notice, Jeff Beck Group II record a session for BBC Radio One's "In Concert" programme. As the name implies, the idea behind the weekly series is to showcase a group in a natural live surrounding, recorded in front of an audience. This takes place at the 400-seat Paris Cinema in London today, to be broadcast on Saturday July 8. The small theatre has an intimate atmosphere where every instrument comes across crystal clear, with the volume kept down but with ample room for dynamics.

In running order, Jeff Beck Group II perform *Ice Cream Cakes, Morning Dew, Going Down, Definitely Maybe* (with Bob Tench on second guitar), *New Ways/Train Train*, Bill Withers' *Ain't No Sunshine, Got The Feeling* and *Let Me Love You*. A ninth selection is also recorded – a version of *Tonight I'll Be Staying Here With You* (done after *Definitely Maybe* in the show) – but it is edited out of the syndicated version of the broadcast.

The programme is hosted by Mike Harding, and after *Ain't No Sunshine* he relates a long story about seeing an unhappy Beck in a seedy ballroom five-six years ago up in Scotland. "Are you happier now?" Harding wants to know, to which Beck shoots back: "No!" Beck the reluctant bandleader opens his mouth just once more when he talks to the audience halfway during the last number: "I must be out of mind but I'd like you to sing along with this thing. What you got to do is to sing 'let me love you baby' after Bobby sings it. Just follow, follow whatever Bob sings and uh, we should have a bloody great disaster."

JULY

SAT 1ST–SUN 2ND ✱

Seemingly, Jeff Beck and Max Middleton return alone to New York City and Electric Lady Studios this weekend to finish *Superstition*. Stevie Wonder is away on the Rolling Stones tour, so the sessions are done by Wonder's regular production team Bob Margouleff and Malcolm Cecil.

Jeff has rounded up Carmine Appice and Tim Bogert for the occasion, and Jeff handles lead vocal himself on some takes, while others feature a young good-looking singer named Kim Milford. Ernest Chapman has discovered Milford playing the role of Jesus in a staging of 'Jesus Christ Superstar' in Washington – a production that Chapman has business interests in. Milford also has experience in the little-known Eclipse, a band that sprang out of Genya Ravan's Ten Wheel Drive.

The basic backing track from May with Wonder's keyboards is used, with Appice replacing Powell's drums. SOUNDS' US correspondent Chuck Pulin comments teasingly: *"Don't Be Superstitious* [sic] is a good hardrocker with Jeff doing a bit of blues wailing. We won't tell you more about the track, just keep your ears open and look out for it." Along with *Superstition*, other songs are put down on tape including an embryonic and studio-written *Lose Myself With You* – actually Jeff Beck and Rod Stewart's old Buddy Guy-adaptation *Let Me Love You* twice removed!

Besides rehearsing, business deals are finalised to fulfill a forthcoming union between Beck and his old comrades. Although Jeff has a singer and a rhythm section back home in Britain, he is now fully set on finally getting his dream band together.

Bogert and Appice are still committed to Cactus at the moment, although that group is in a state of flux anyways, as ex-Iron Butterfly guitarist Mike Pinera has literally joined this week – just to be told that Bogert and Appice have other plans! Still, Cactus live on the road and return to an itinerary that includes dates booked right through July and August.

SAT 8TH

Jeff Beck Group II are Mike Harding's guests in BBC Radio One's "In Concert" tonight at 6.30–7.30 pm (► June 29).

The programme also features a segment with the Third Ear Band.

120

Ⓒ June 3, 1972: The Rolling Stones begin their first North American tour since 1969.

Blowup

The Nightshift

Jeff Beck and Brian Wiles at the
4th National Jazz & Blues Festival
in Richmond, August 7, 1964

GERRY CLARKE

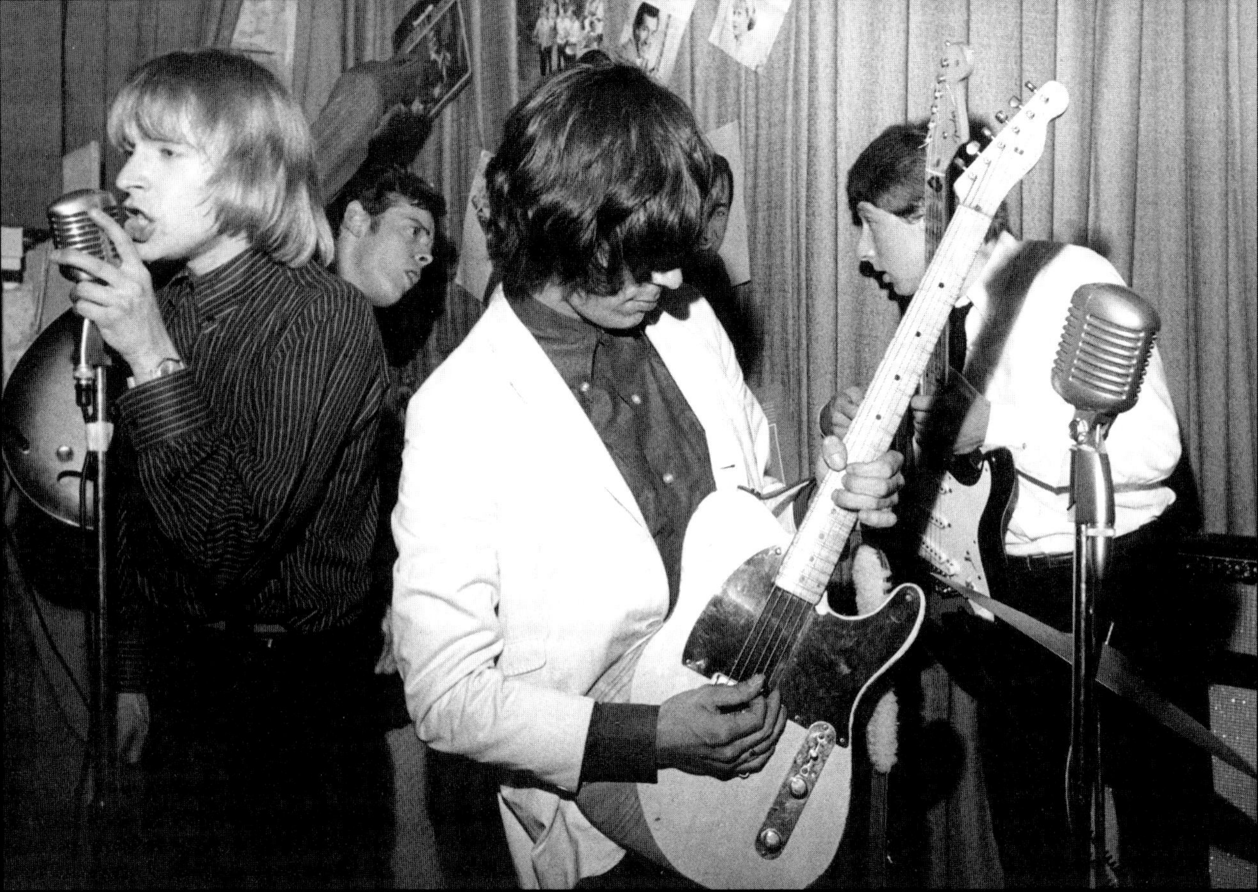

Above The Yardbirds at the Rolling Stone discotheque in New York, September 17, 1965 **Right** Jeff Beck at Palais des Sports, Paris, June 20, 1965 **Below, right** Beck and McCarty in Wichita, Kansas, August 15, 1965 **Below, left** A dapper Beck in paisley shirt in London circa summer 1967.

JOHN LEWIS STORE/COURTESY ANNETTE CARSON

MARTI HERRING

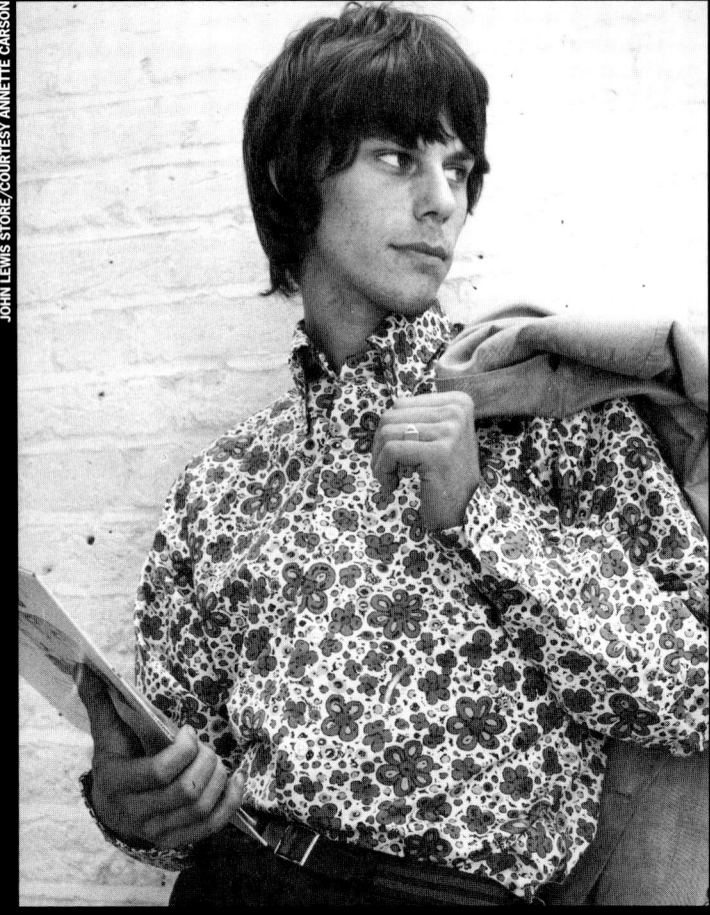

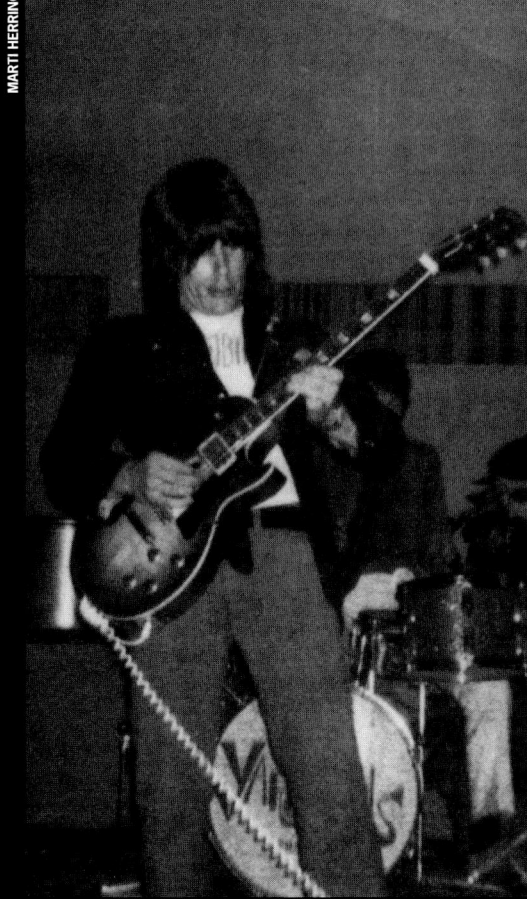

Vive les Yardbirds!

Blowup

The Rolling Stone discotheque, New York City, September 17, 1965

JOHN PINTO

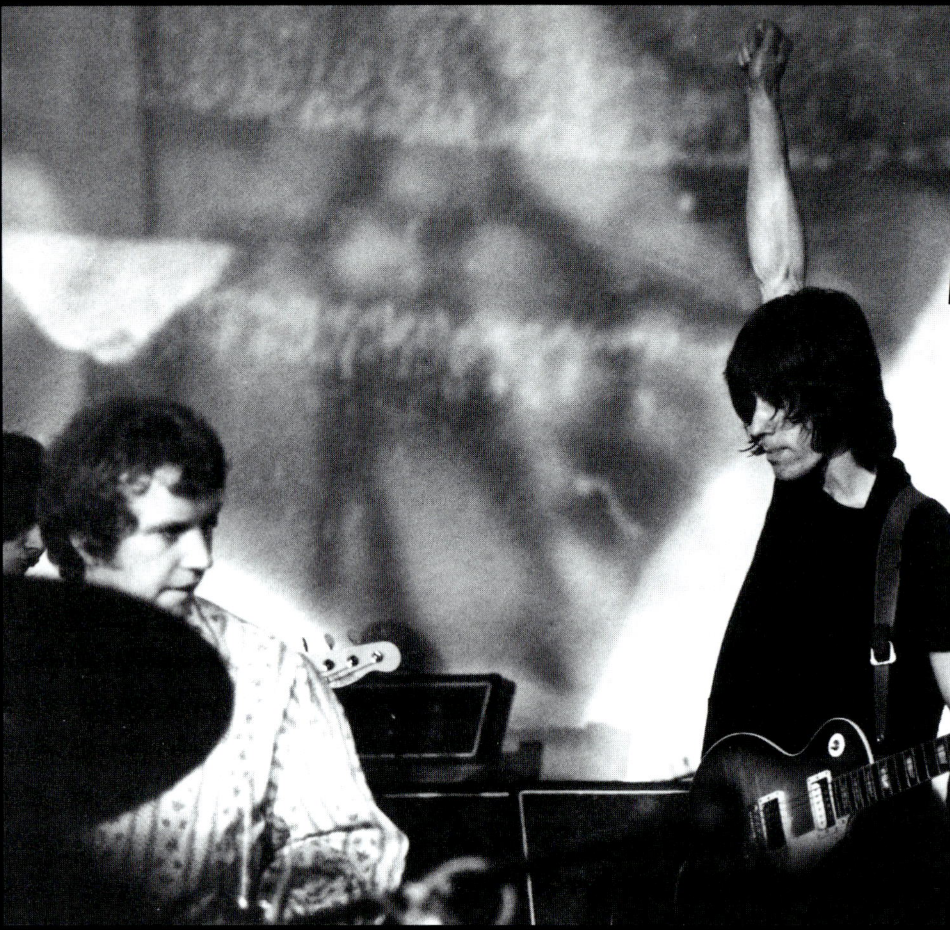

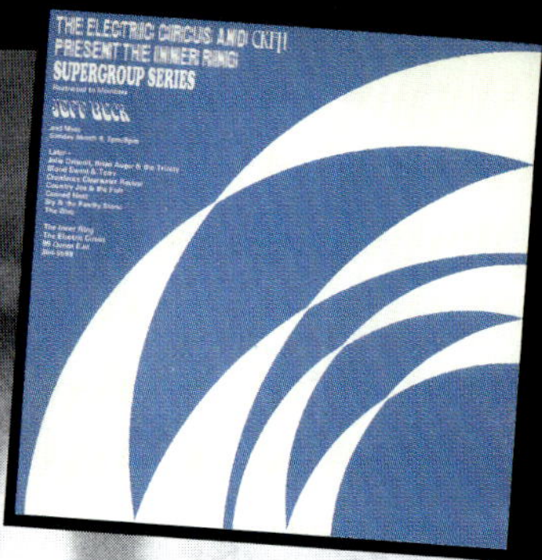

Above With Tony Newman; Electric Theater, Toronto, March 9, 1969 **Right** The Jeff Beck Group with (l to r) John Junior Woods, Rod Stewart, Mickey Waller and Jeff **Below** Jeff Beck at the Boston Tea Party in May 6–8, 1969.

DONALD MCCLELLAN

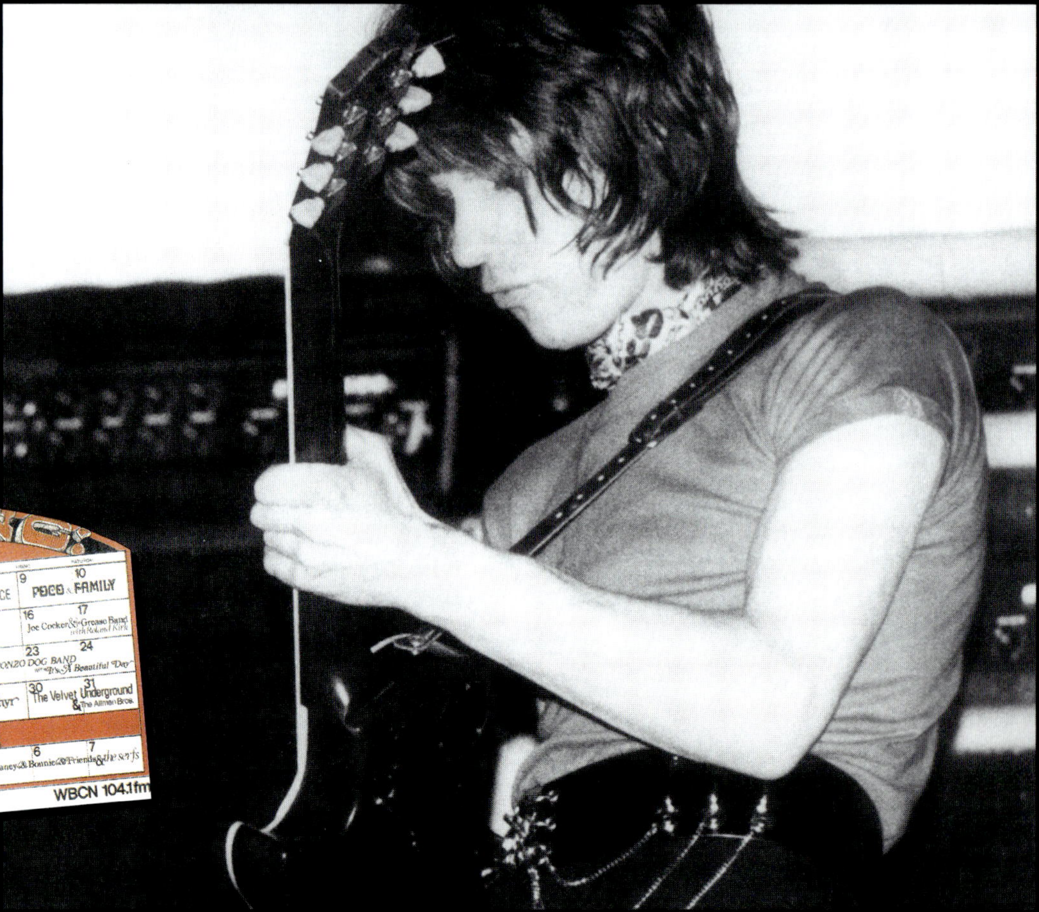

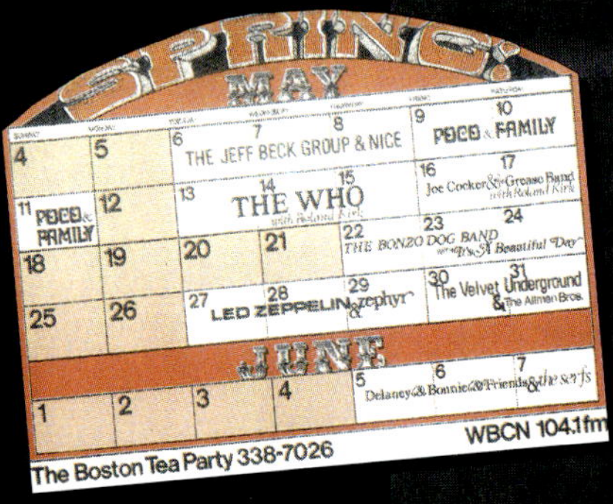

JOHN ABRAHMS

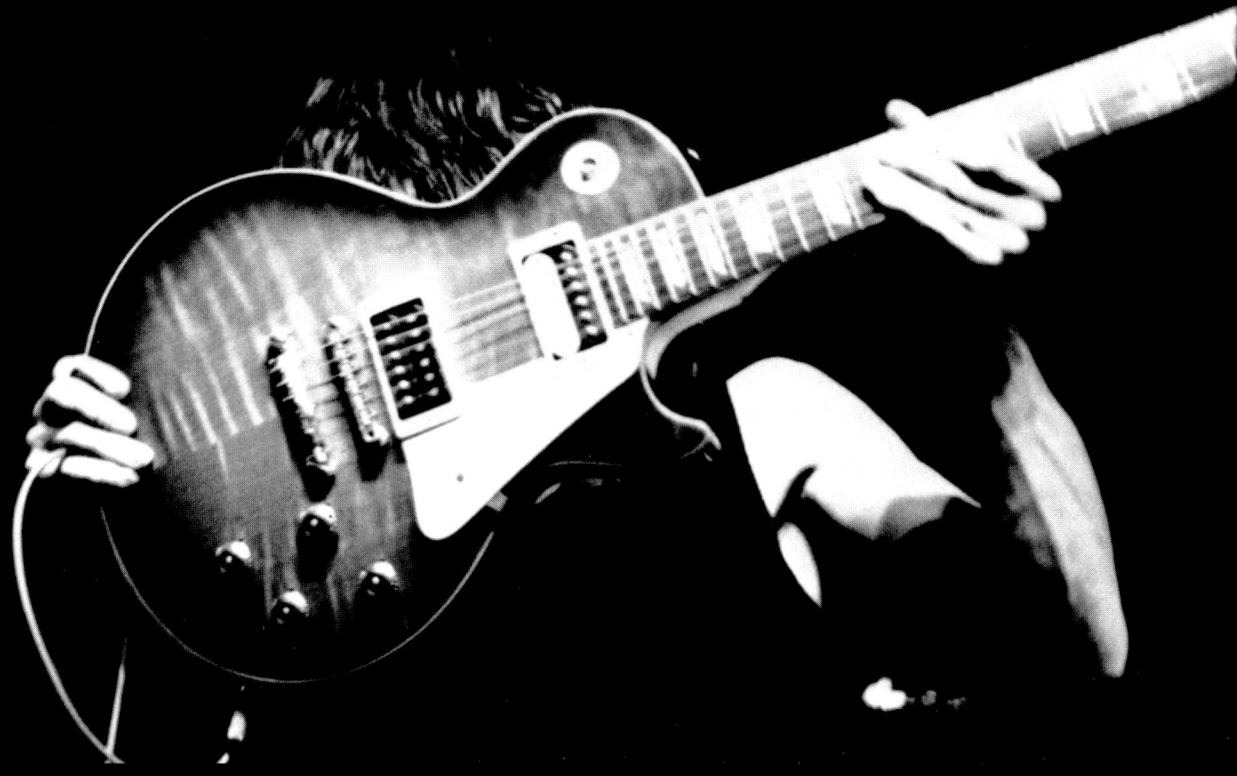

Above A night at the Fillmore West, December 5–8, 1968 **Below** Jamming with Buddy Guy at the Thumb's Up club, Chicago, December 21, 1965

CHERYL JENNINGS

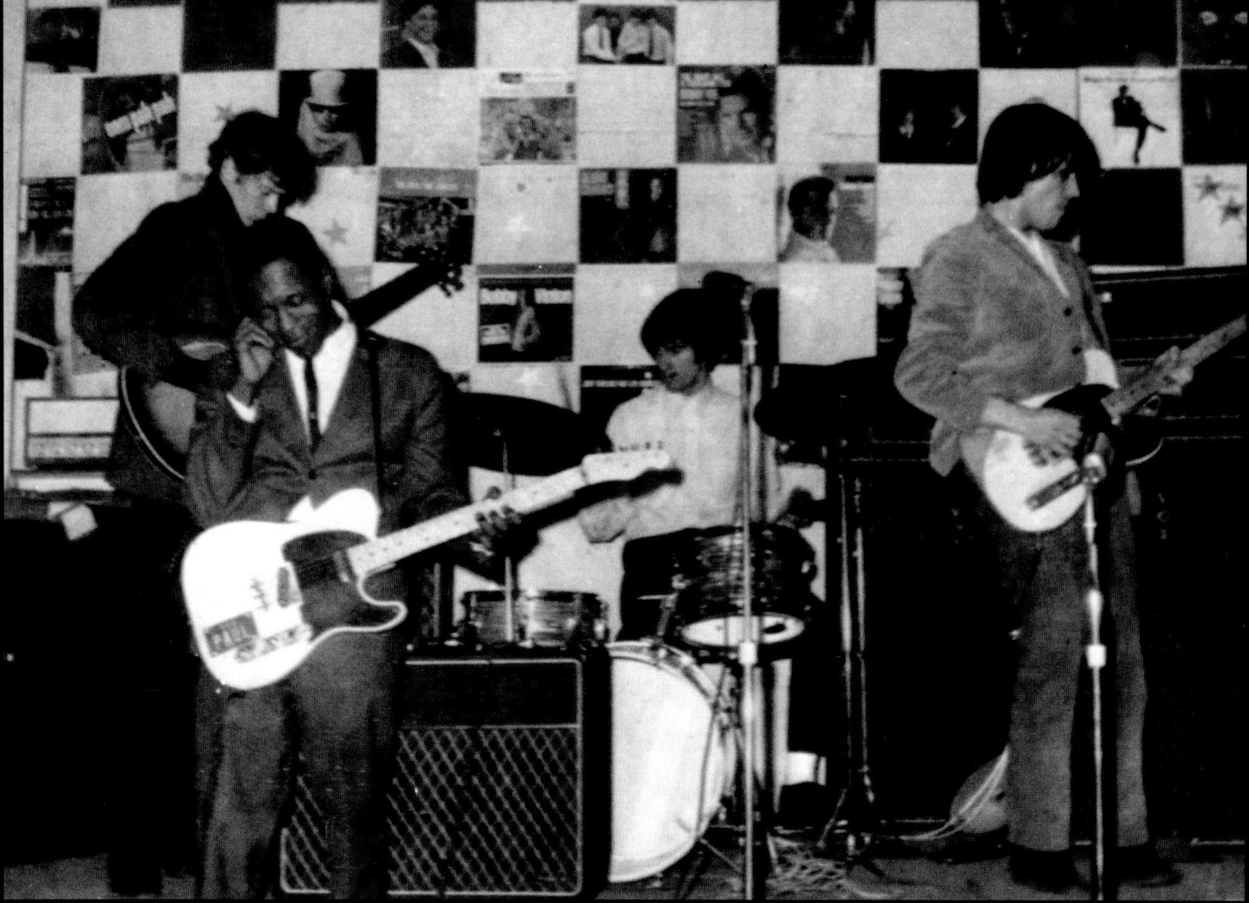

US tour November/December 1968 • **Above left and right** Jeff and Mickey Waller at the Shrine, Los Angeles, November 29–30 **Below right** At the Fillmore West, San Francisco, December 5–8 **Below left** Jeffrey Rod at Southern Methodist University, Dallas, Texas, November 9

R. E. BARNES

JOHN ROBERTS

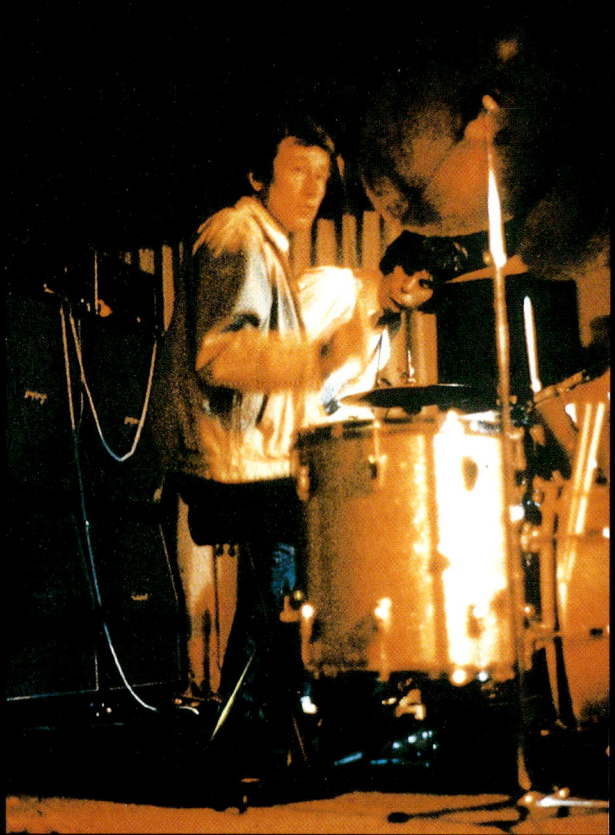

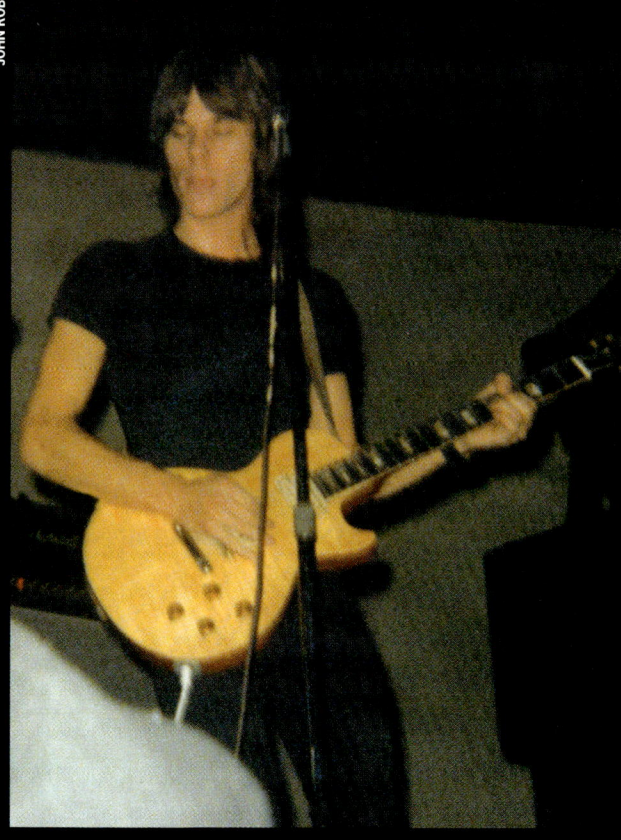

Above left Mickey Waller and Jeff Beck at LuAnne's, July 17, 1968 **Above left** Jeff Beck at the 'Lectric Theater, Chicago, October 11, 1968. After this concert, Jeff's Les Paul guitar was damaged seriously **Below** The Jeff Beck Group at Southern Methodist University, Dallas, Texas, November 9, 1968

R. E. BARNES

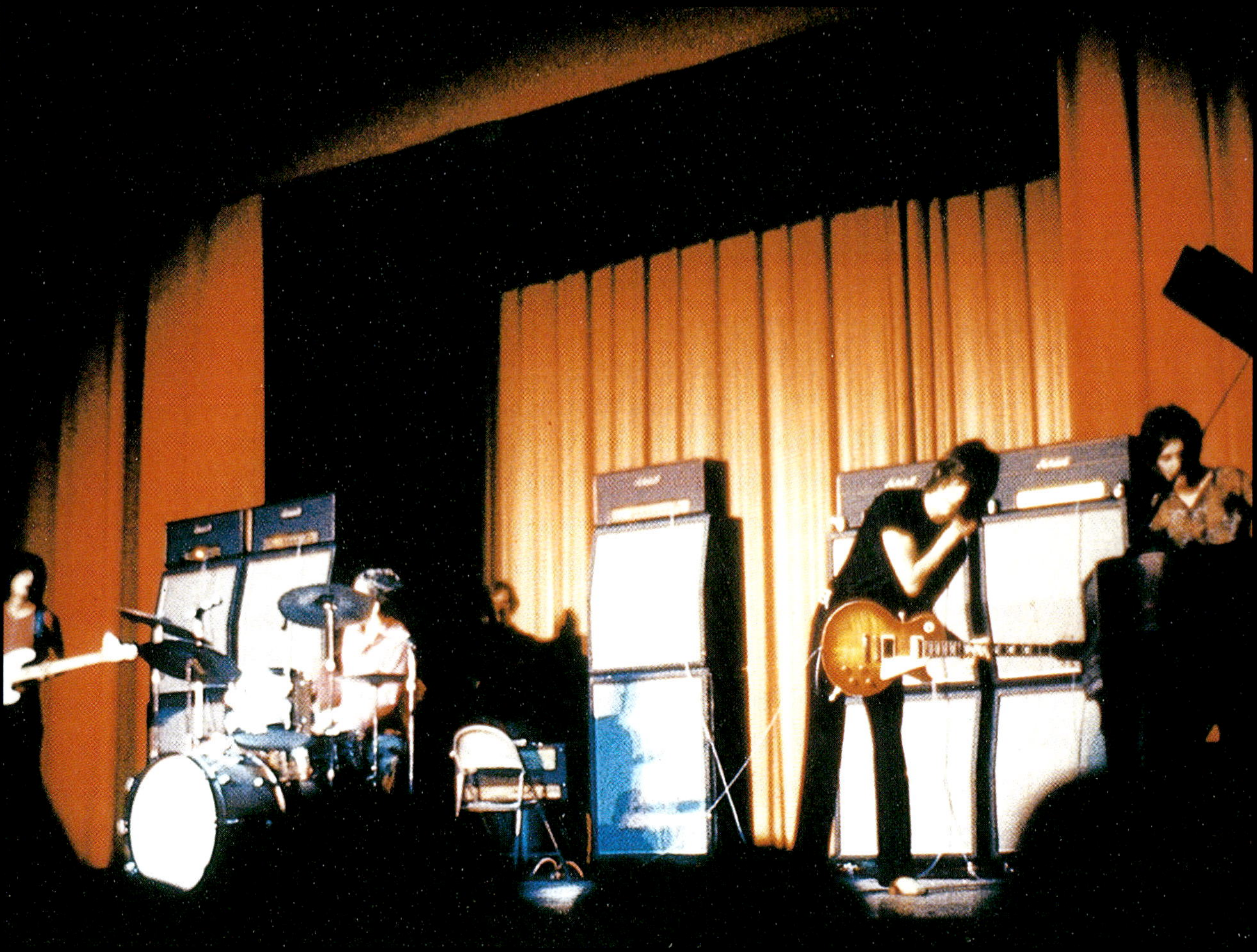

Fillmore West, San Francisco, July 1968

Above left "Ahoy' Pop Festival", Rotterdam, Holland, September 11, 1971 **Above right** Rotterdam, Holland, October 2, 1972 **Right and below** Aquarius Theater, Boston, October 24, 1972

Above left "Blow By Blow" tour at the Regis College, Denver, Colorado, June 7, 1975
Above right Beck at Colorado Springs, August 1972 **Below left** Beck with a Les Paul Special, Detroit, November 7, 1972

The Felt Forum, New York City, April 9–10, 1973

Blowup

Above Jeff Beck, Bobby Tench and Tim Bogert at the Hollywood Palladium, August 15, 1972 **Below right** "Blow By Blow" tour at the Regis College, Denver, Colorado, June 7, 1975 **Below left** Beck and voice bag at the Hollywood Palladium, May 3, 1973

July 1972: Jeff Beck Group II play their last British dates ...

SUN 9TH
**THE JEFF BECK GROUP II:
FIRST EUROPEAN TOUR**
"Wurzburg Giant Pop Festival"
Wurzburg, West Germany

Despite his flirtations with Bogert and Appice, Jeff is already committed to play a short European tour in July.

Duly, Jeff Beck Group II come together for a Sunday appearance at this two-day festival in West Germany. Other British acts on the bill are Joe Cocker, Alexis Korner, King Crimson, Juicy Lucy, Hardin & York and Status Quo.

Possibly a few further undocumented concerts are undertaken in Europe before the Jeff Beck Group II finish with a trio of UK dates.

FRI 14TH
Top Rank Suite, Birmingham

Three British dates in July promoted by Farr Knight Theatres Ltd. in association with Equator mark the end of the Jeff Beck Group II, as Beck has decided to break up the band as soon as the tour is over. For this short British jaunt, Home play support. An encore of Stevie Wonder's *Superstition* – sung by Jeff – is the only new addition to the group's live set, but *Ain't No Sunshine* is revived again while *Glad All Over* is dropped.

John Bonham and Robert Plant (both Birmingham boys by the way) attend tonight's show, Jeff's first return to the capital of the Midlands since December 1967. Playing to a full house, the eager crowd "seemed to expect Winter, Gallagher, Page and Clapton rolled into one", according to Robert Brinton in DISC (July 22): "The set opened abysmally with *Somebody Like You* [actually *Ice Cream Cakes*], gaping holes in the sound ... The second number, *Morning Dew*, was even worse, totally tired ... Sensibly, Beck increased the pace of the next one and the band began to pull together ... [They] began to hit it with Dylan's *Tonight I'll Be Staying Here With You,* followed by a very extended version of *Life's A Never Ending Road* [actually *Got The Feeling*] – easily their best number. ... *Let Me Love You* broke all the ice and everyone went wild. The band encored with *Superstition* ... to resounding applause and calls for 'more'." In SOUNDS (July 22), Howard Fielding is not particularly excited: "The criticism really is not so much of Beck's playing, but that the rest of the band is wasted. Bob Tench is a fine singer, and Max Middleton, on electric piano, deserves far more of the spotlight, which sadly seemed forever glued in a tiny circle around the magic fingers."

However, Tony Stewart in NEW MUSICAL EXPRESS (July 22), a stern critic of Jeff's present group, is impressed by tonight's show: "All five guys in the Beck group cramped to the left of the stage. Beck, himself, leaned at an angle and spurted out those licks. For the first time the whole band seemed to fuse into a funky unit. ... At last I think I've sussed what the band are attempting to do. Working within a blues framework, they are leaving room for improvisation, and taking the music one step on and into the realms of jazz. This has not been so obvious before, but on Friday it certainly got across."

WED 19TH
Top Rank Suite, Southampton

NEW WAYS

Rough, Ready, Go!

In 1971, out of necessity, Jeff Beck finally assembled a group to enable him to record and go back on the road. In his two-year absence, Beck's status had attained myth-like proportions in the States. He could hardly do wrong on his return to the American stage at the end of 1971. Cozy Powell later told interviewers that he had never seen such adulation in his entire career.

So the second incarnation of the Jeff Beck Group represented a more workmanlike period for Beck, but this group was underrated, although it provoked both love and loathing among Beck fans. The group was powered by the superb rhythm section of Clive Chaman and Cozy Powell, who were able to be funky, heavy or both. Especially Cozy Powell proved inspirational to Jeff and it was no coincidence that it was his lone drums which kicked off both *Rough And Ready* and the *Orange Album*. Robert Tench was a fine singer although he came in for a lot of flak in the music press. The group's greatest asset besides Jeff was undoubtedly Max Middleton. A pianist schooled in classics, theory and jazz, he was something else entirely from Nicky Hopkins' straight-ahead Chicago blues piano. Middleton took his cues from the new breed of jazz musicians such as Herbie Hancock and Bill Evans, and excelled at either a grand piano or a Fender Rhodes – and occasionally a twangy clavinet with an outboard wah-wah attached – which perfectly shadowed Jeff's trebly Stratocaster.

Rough And Ready was an admirable but not totally successful attempt at making a modern rock album. There was not a blues, a shuffle or a boogie in sight, but a series of more rhythmically and harmonically complex structures. All the same, the songs lacked strong melodies and tended to blur together. The music was fittingly described as "heavy metal Motown" and hinted at Beck's coming jazz flirtations, but missed the fury and unpredictable guitar playing of previous albums. However, side one is a joy from start to finish, and side two – with the exception of the dull *I've Been Used* – is good with a cool medley called *New Ways/Train Train* (a sparring match between Jeff and Cozy), and the noteworthy *Jody*, with a fluid guitar break and a proper melody. Throughout, solos were kept in rein, and the opening track *Got The Feeling* has Max Middleton asserting himself with a subdued Beck not waking up until the fade-out. It is not until track two, *Situation*, that the guitar is in command with an archetypical twisted Beck solo.

The successor, the *Orange Album*, lacked the cohesion of *Rough And Ready*. The album relied heavily on cover songs, including the nifty neo-rockabilly *Glad All Over*. The group worked up two Motown-goes-Memphis songs, *I Can't Give Back The Love I Feel For You* and *Show Me Where There's Music*, and Jeff turned *Going Down* (also covered by J J Cale and Freddie King) into a minor rock and roll classic with a sloppy yet fully inspired guitar performance. One can easily perceive Beck's frustration with the limitations of the regular rock guitar vocabulary as he unbuttons the straitjacket, bangs the tremolo arm and uses every inch of the guitar neck.

The original material, however, was not particularly strong. *Ice Cream Cakes* evolved into a perfect live number which did not come across on the record. Both the throwaway Beck/Cropper collaboration *Sugar Cane* and the inconsequential *Highways* sound like studio creations, although the latter is saved when Jeff briefly dusts off his blues licks in a ferocious opening salvo.

It is the instrumentals from this period that point to the future. *Rough And Ready's* jazzy, evocative *Raynes Park Blues*, the mighty guitar orchestrations in *I Can't Give Back The Love I Feel For You* and, in particular, the almost Morricone-waltz *Definitely Maybe*, which also became a hugely popular live number. ∎

July 9, 1972: Paul McCartney's Wings make their official live debut at the Théâtre Antique, Châteauvallon, France.

July 1972: Tim Bogert and Carmine Appice finally team up with Beck ...

ROUNDHOUSE CHALK FARM
SUNDAY, JULY 23 3.30-11.30
The Farr & Knight Theatre Co.
in association with Equator presents

JEFF BECK GROUP
HOME
THIRSTY TOO
COCKNEY REBEL
D.J. JERRY FLOYD
Advance tickets now on sale at Roundhouse Box Office, 267 1251

SUN 23RD
Roundhouse, Chalk Farm, London
Wearing a Gene Vincent & the Blue Caps T-shirt with a white Stratocaster around his neck, Jeff Beck welcomes his fans to the very last concert by the Jeff Beck Group II. In addition to Home, the bill also features Thirsty Too plus Steve Harley and Cockney Rebel. Attendance is huge, indeed big enough to break the previous box office record held by the Rolling Stones here. Ritchie Blackmore, who is home between two Deep Purple US tours, is in the audience.

Despite the group's imminent split, it is a powerful show. Andrew Means in MELODY MAKER (July 29) recounts: "The distinction between stars and mortals is so obvious at such times that it hardly needs comment. Stars are expected to be great, are greeted as great and act out the part till the last note of the inevitable encore ... And Beck is a showman. Watch him heave the axe across his body in customary giant phallus fashion ... All the while Cozy Powell is thundering on his drums ... At the beginning of *Morning Dew*, while Bob Tench is snarling out those familiar opening lines, Powell slams out the beat on the side drum, hits a cymbal and cuts it dead with his hand giving the rhythm an edge most drummers would never touch." A view also shared by Charles Webster in RECORD MIRROR (July 29) – "Cozy Powell on drums was quite amazing" – but who otherwise finds the show uninspiring: "Beck is back, but to be quite honest, does anybody care?"

Wittily kicking off *Jeff's Boogie* at funeral pace, Jeff cheerfully addresses the crowd: "This is definitely *the* very last time I'll be playing this tune!" Rather an overstatement, as this popular show-stopper will be retained for at least another year. For the encore, Jeff explains a new number: "I'd like to do a ... I can't sing for shit, but I'll sing a little bit. A tune by Stevie Wonder called *Superstition*." Anticipating a version of the *Truth* classic *I Ain't Superstitious*, the crowd breaks into a big applause, so Jeff hastily adds: "No no no – it's got an 'n' at the end!"

MON 24TH
The Jeff Beck Group II are defunct. Beck's management issues a press statement, declaring: "The fusion of the musical styles of the various members has been successful within the terms of the individual musicians but didn't feel it had led to the creation of a new musical style with the strength they had originally sought."

Funnily enough, Cozy Powell will renew his relationship with Mickie Most, creating a huge hit with *Dance With The Devil* in late 1973. Powell and Beck will remain friendly, and basking in the light of success with *Dance With The Devil*, Cozy notes of his previous boss: "For me, Jeff Beck at his best is incredible, there's no one to touch him today." Powell becomes an in-demand drummer enjoying spells with Ritchie Blackmore's Rainbow, Whitesnake and Black Sabbath, and fitting nicely into the one-album coalition Emerson, Lake & Powell.

Clive Chaman returns to session-work, while Bob Tench will work with, among others, Chapman–Whitney Streetwalkers, Humble Pie and Van Morrison in later years.

TUE 25TH
With the Jeff Beck Group II barely in the grave, Jeff and Max reportedly meet with Kim Milford, Tim Bogert and Carmine Appice – who all have just flown in from the States – at Jeff's Egerton home. In fact, Bogert and Appice have just left Cactus members Duane Hitchings and Pete French stranded somewhere in Texas. Hectic rehearsals then get underway to prepare for an American tour to commence in a few short days.

WED 26TH–THU 27TH
The new group moves operations to the Rolling Stones rehearsal rooms in Bermondsey, where they spend around three days intensely practising a new stage act.

FRI 28TH
NEW MUSICAL EXPRESS is given exclusive rights for the story of the new band (edition dated August 5), and Danny Holloway visits the Bermondsey rehearsals: "This is what Beck has

FACSIMILE FROM NEW MUSICAL EXPRESS, AUGUST 5, 1972

been waiting for for so long. His dream band. Get the idea?" Jeff explains his motives thus: "The thing is: we've never played what the people wanted to hear in America. They expect vicious, violent rock and roll. That's what I'm known for, but I was avoiding all that in the previous band. I was trying to play subtle rock and roll. That stuff was more suitable for clubs, not big stages. This new group will play much heavier music."

Robert and Dave Ellis take several pictures of the new band rehearsing, then outside on the street and then in a nearby pub – actually the only press pictures that exist of this group.

Curiously, Danny Holloway does not question the name for this newly assembled band, which will retain the moniker 'Jeff Beck Group' for the time being.

SUN 30TH✱
After wrapping up rehearsals, the new group flies to States for a seventeen-date tour in nineteen days.

AUGUST

TUE 1ST
JEFF BECK GROUP II, MARK II:
FIRST NORTH AMERICAN TOUR
Stanley Theatre, Pittsburgh, Pennsylvania

Due to sparse rehearsals, the basic set list from the Tench/Chaman/Powell-era is stripped down and retained, beefed up with a medley of the reworked *Plynth* married to Junior Walker's *Shotgun* (also popularized by Vanilla Fudge). Kim Milford is represented with an original number called *Over The Hill*. The set also features Bogert's bass showcase from his Cac-

August 1972: Short-lived new quintet begin a new American tour ...

tus days, *Oleo,* and Appice is also given a lengthy drum solo in the *Shotgun/Plynth* medley.

🔊 Tonight's show understandably has an air of nervousness, but the new group plays ably considering their short time together. Beck in particular is nothing short of spectacular, injecting *Ice Cream Cakes* with a wild intensity. He also plays a flowing, well-constructed solo during the *Plynth* medley, and spurred on up by his new rhythm section he delivers a fiery slide/fret solo in the last number, *Got The Feeling*. The poignant *Definitely Maybe* never sounded better, with a heartfelt guitar. Kim Milford's *Over The Hill* is a fair rock number, which rides out on a strong guitar hook. Milford's voice is fine, too, but it is his stage appearance which seemingly causes an embarrassment. Max Middleton has a very subdued role, however, and besides his usual opening tinklings on *Going Down* (which is reinstated as the set-opener) he is rendered almost inaudible the rest of the night, although he manages to be heard in the softer parts like *Definitely Maybe*. *Let Me Love You* is interesting as the song is already being rebuilt with a new melody on top, which eventually becomes *Lose Myself With You* a few months later when new lyrics are written. Carmine Appice tries to encourage the audience when the sing-along section of *New Ways/Train, Train* fails to arouse the crowd: "Come on, all you people can't be on Reds, I mean, I know it!"

WED 2ND
Gaelic Park, New York, New York
Along with Flash, Argent and New York heavy metalurgists Blue Öyster Cult, Jeff Beck tops the bill at an open-air festival in this huge park in the Bronx. After Argent's set, the long wait for Jeff Beck begins. Although his band is backstage, Jeff is nowhere to be seen. The restless crowd – triggered also by impending rain in the cool night – responds with booing and bottle throwing. Finally, at 10.45 and 15 minutes before curfew, Jeff arrives and the group takes the stage for a brief set before the crowd of 7,000.

NEW MUSICAL EXPRESS's US correspondent Lisa Robinson writes (August 12): "We had waited an hour and 20 minutes, and at that point, my friend and I split. Witnesses report that because of Beck's unexplained and undisciplined tardiness and because of the curfew on Gaelic Park, the Jeff Beck Group gave their tired and disgruntled yet anticipating audience a mere 30 minutes of questionable pleasure." One eyewitness says it is Bogert's bass solo in *Oleo* which provokes a shower of empty beer cans.

Stephen Garber in the Queens College paper NEWSBEAT (August 8): "Beck was good but not great, and although he is a remarkable guitarist I was left indifferent ... maybe one day Jeff Beck will come down off his throne and show up on time and really begin to show the world what a great performer he really is!" Later in the same paper (October 3), Alan Gellerman offers his impressions of the concert when he writes a summary on New York's summer of music '72: "... I had started to leave when Beck staggered into the park with a few groupies looking for the stage. Spaced-out as he was, I don't know how he ever managed to get on stage, let alone play, but play he did ..." But then Gellerman also describes Blue Öyster Cult's opening set as a "mellow-folk sound"!

Music writer Jon Tiven is also backstage, and with alarming accuracy and foresight reports in the NEW HAVEN ROCK PRESS (September 1972): "Max's presence seems as if it's a mere courtesy, the talented pianist looking about as satisfied as a kangaroo in a bullpen. The new singer, bedecked in blue and silver tin foil, has a terrible voice and stage presence unbefitting of anyone with even an iota of cranial capacity."

THU 3RD
An off and/or travel day.

FRI 4TH
Curtis Hixon Hall, Tampa, Florida
Presented by HBS Productions for one show at 7.30 pm, Jeff is supported by Argent and Poco, the latter replacing original choice It's A Beautiful Day.

SAT 5TH
Orlando Sports Stadium, Orlando, Florida
Beck headlines over Argent and It's A Beautiful Day: "The dream of every groupie, Jeff Beck, really held everyone's interest ... The Jeff Beck Group did some older numbers and some

cuts off his [sic] new album. The group was called back for two encores and the people still wanted more" is about the extent of the review of the Orlando concert in local paper THE WATCHER (August 11–24).

SUN 6TH
Music Hall, Houston, Texas
"Save a few flashes of expertise (particularly the break in *Got The Feeling*), Beck was disappointingly adequate. In an effort to let the other members of his quintet shine ... Beck stayed and played in the shadows during the hour I saw him before deadline. The group's tune *Down, Down, Down* [*Going Down*] was harsh and the sound unbalanced. The harshness was later fixed, but not the annoying lack of togetherness," writes Eric Gebber in the HOUSTON POST (August 7) after the show, where British boogie rockers Foghat play support.

MON 7TH
Majestic Theater, Dallas, Texas
With Foghat again. Originally announced at Dallas Memorial Auditorium with Ramatam, but both venue and billing are changed.

TUE 8TH
Arie Crown Theater, Chicago, Illinois
In an incident recalling Doug Blake's short stint in the old Jeff Beck Group in the winter of '69, Milford is fired tonight after just a handful of concerts. It was hoped that his pretty looks would boost the group's image, but he proves to be a major problem onstage. Tonight – with Blue Öyster Cult and Argent – is probably Milford's last appearance with the group. A back-up is already secured, as Bobby Tench is flown in as replacement much to the relief of everyone involved.

WED 9TH
Community Center, Tucson, Arizona
Reports point to yesterday in Chicago as being Kim Milford's exit from the group, while Bobby Tench's debut by all accounts is the following night in California. So there is some confusion as to the actual line-up tonight.

Set List/Jeff Beck Group II

Stanley Theater, Pittsburgh, August 1 '72 (with Kim Milford)

Going Down • Ice Cream Cakes • Over The Hill/Plynth/Shotgun/Plynth • Definitely Maybe • Oleo • New Ways/Train, Train • Let Me Love You (Lose Myself With You) • Got The Feeling

---

© August 5, 1972: The London Rock Festival attracts 50,000 people to see MC5, Wizzard, Jerry Lee Lewis, Chuck Berry and Little Richard and many more.

August 1972: Kim Milford is fired, Bob Tench returns ...

THU 10TH
Commmunity Concourse Convention Hall, San Diego, California
Bobby Tench's first appearance on the tour, where Jeff shares the stage with Edgar Winter (whose guitarist is Ronnie Montrose), plus singer/songwriter Judee Sill.

The set list is slightly rearranged, both to accommodate Tench and to include more numbers. *Superstition* is brought into the set, and so is a new medley comprising Dylan's *Tonight I'll Be Staying Here With You* coupled with Curtis Mayfield's gospel-tinged *People Get Ready* (once a staple of Vanilla Fudge's stage act and sung by Carmine Appice). For good measure, both *Jeff's Boogie* and *Morning Dew* are also tacked on as encores.

Jeff, who likes to travel by car whenever the touring schedule permits, is stopped twice for going 130 mph on a San Diego to Los Angeles jaunt.

FRI 11TH
Swing Auditorium, San Bernadino, California
Promoted by Concert Associates, tonight's show with Foghat and Edgar Winter grosses $22,500 from a 4,700-strong crowd.

🎙 Jeff is in a good mood as he asks the crowd: "Listen to this one, see if you can recognize it!" Jeff then teasingly plays a few bluesy runs on the guitar. "Does anybody recognize that one?" When the crowd roars in approval, Jeff mutters "you are all liars, 'cause I've never played it before!" The group then proceeds to play a version of *Tonight I'll Be Staying Here With You* with Bogert and Appice harmonizing perfectly. When Jeff plays a whacky fill with the slide, Tench cannot help but stop singing and start laughing. The Dylan tune then segues into *People Get Ready*, with Carmine conducting a three-part angelic choir with Tench and Bogert.

SAT 12TH
Civic Auditorium, San Jose, California
Jeff Beck shares the stage with Edgar Winter again tonight.

SUN 13TH
Hollywood Palladium, Los Angeles, California
"The reckless deification of lead guitarists has subsided a bit since the 'Eric Clapton is God' days, but there's always Jeff Beck around to keep the joke alive" begins a particularly savage review by Richard Cromelin in the LOS ANGELES TIMES (August 15) of the prestigious Palladium concert. "His group's lugubrious Sunday night Palladium performance, while eliciting the automatic accolades that his star status demands, was certainly one of the more boring excercises in unredeemed heavy-handedness this city has seen in some time. A new lead singer had been promised, but it seems he got the boot a few weeks ago and so there, to the dismay of many, was Bob Tench again, growling and rasping in his offensive parody of rock-blues vocalizing ... [Beck] is content to blast out endless series of leaden riffs and hopeless little psychedelic runs while running through some palsied theatrics that would be worthwhile only if they included smashing Tench senseless or setting him on fire."

Once again the revised Jeff Beck Group headline on an all-British show with Foghat and Argent. A considerably kinder review in NEW MUSICAL EXPRESS (September 16) reports how "it was Jeff's concert though, and everyone in the house knew it. Jeff and his new band had the crowd eating out of their hands", right from *Going Down*.

While staying in Los Angeles, Jeff is interviewed by Paul Bernstein at Los Angeles' Continental Hyatt House, where Beck stays. The interview runs as a cover story in ROLLING STONE (#85, October 26). Bernstein questions Beck on his relationship to both Rod Stewart ("He's a pop star and I'm a rock & roll guitarist. We're absolutely not in the same room, you know. He's in a different room altogether") and Jimmy Page ("We don't see each other at all now"). Asked about his songwriting (which admittedly is not Beck's forte), Beck explains: "I just mumble a lot of words while I'm getting a riff off. It's garbage, all garbage. It's a good excuse for me to sort of lay back for awhile and then go back when they've finished things."

Already sensing a problem with his new group, Jeff considers they are "more or less acceptable as a stage-act,

---

Set List/Jeff Beck Group II

Swing Audit., San Bernardino, August 11 '72 (with Bob Tench)

Going Down • Superstition • Tonight I'll Be Staying Here With You/People Get Ready • New Ways/Train Train • Definitely Maybe • Plynth/Shotgun • Got The Feeling • Let Me Love You • Jeff's Boogie • Morning Dew

---

but material-wise we have to stop and think, get to work."

MON 14TH
Berkeley Community Theater, Berkeley, California
Argent provide support for the five last dates of the tour.

TUE 15TH
Civic Auditorium, Albuquerque, New Mexico
Jeff Beck's very first visit to Albuquerque, with tickets at $4.50 and $3.75.

WED 16TH
City Auditorium, Colorado Springs, Colorado
Two shows at 7 and 10 pm.

FRI 18TH
Paramount Northwest Theater, Portland, Oregon
Foghat are added to the Argent–Jeff Beck bill today and tomorrow.

SAT 19TH
Paramount Northwest Theater, Seattle, Washington
Two shows at 7 pm and 10.30 pm for what is the last date of the tour.

LATE
Jeff returns to England.

SEPTEMBER

EARLY
During the recent US tour it has been decided to reduce the group to a power trio consisting of just Jeff, Tim and Carmine. Bob Tench, whose place has only been temporary anyway, leaves as does Max Middleton who eventually will work together with Beck at a later stage. Instead of finding a new singer/frontman, Carmine Appice will handle the main vocal chores, with both Bogert and to a lesser degree Beck supplying harmonies and the occasional lead vocal.

The obvious group name 'Beck, Bogert & Appice' is chosen not only because it rolls nicely off the tongue, but also to secure billing to everyone involved, thereby making the band a trio of equals. This arrangement spells equality both artistically and financially. All the same, the trio will still be billed as 'Jeff Beck Group' for another few weeks.

Beck, Bogert & Appice will be jointly managed by Ernest Chapman and Tim and Carmine's manager Phil Basile, while lawyer Steve Weiss will

September 1972: World debut of new trio Beck, Bogert & Appice ...

also represent the group. The Anglo-American union is a practical challenge, as Jeff has no intention of leaving England, and Bogert and Appice regard their home base as Long Island – all rather complicated when the group shall rehearse, record or otherwise get together.

SAT 9TH

Today's SOUNDS trumpets: 'Beck's Band Debut!' Plunging headlong into live work, the new band is added to a London festival next Saturday.

MON 11TH–FRI 15TH✹

After their short post-tour break and with a European tour already on the books, the three-some get together in England for a week's practice before they make their official debut. Rehearsals are split between London and an old cottage in South Molton, Devonshire, 'getting it together in the country' as the cliché goes.

Besides fine-tuning their existing set list, three brand new songs are worked up for their live act: *Why Should I Care*, penned by Ray Kennedy – a friend of Bogert and Appice – plus the group compositions *Lady* and *Livin' Alone*. Significantly, all three numbers will become centrepieces of the group's repertoire.

SAT 16TH
BECK, BOGERT & APPICE: FIRST EUROPEAN TOUR
"Rock At The Oval"
Kennington Oval Cricket Ground, London

Still billed as 'Jeff Beck Group', the first live appearance by Beck, Bogert & Appice is at one of the many open-air rock festivals in Great Britain this summer. Frank Zappa, Linda Lewis and Hawkwind head today's bill promoted by Ark Concert Presentations in co-operation with Rikki Farr, while the new trio are credited as 'Special Guests'. Popular Radio Luxembourg disc-jockey Kid Jensen is compere. In a pre-concert blurb, Charles Shaar Murray (in today's NEW MUSICAL EXPRESS) advises you to "drag your weary ass over to the Oval and fill your head with some of the most astounding, imaginative, staggering and just plain enjoyable music ever to come out of an electric guitar. If you hear what sounds like a steamroller chasing a chicken through a traffic jam with a brass band playing nearby, fret not – it'll only be Jeff Beck warming up."

The running order of the festival has been changed right up till stage-time, and the show opens with Quiver, followed by Sam Apple Pie, Biggles (fronted by Rikki's brother Gary Farr) and Welsh group Man. "So far, so good", notes Nick Kent of NEW MUSICAL EXPRESS (September 23) in his review, "but all the aforementioned bands were strictly second division propositions and this is not what the crowd, who were by then a little cold to be openly indignant, wanted." Sporting a green & yellow striped woolen sweater, a white jacket, a mosaic cross around his neck and a white Fender Stratocaster (an oft-seen image of Beck from the early seventies), Jeff and his new companions come on to a wild reception – "one prime kick-arse hot-lick combo par excellence", to cite Kent. Michael Oldfield in MELODY MAKER (September 23) also attributes the first real excitement of the day to Jeff's new group: "Beck looked very happy with his new two sidemen, ripping off chords in rip-roaring style, sending sparks around the stadium that must have warmed many a soul." Steve Peacock of SOUNDS (September 23) writes how "Jeff Beck surprised me: He's never been one of my guitar heroes, but the new trio, with Carmine Appice and Tim Bogert, played some very nice, upfront rock and roll ... they came on like an ace rock band and when they got into full flight they were remarkably good."

According to themselves, Beck, Bogert and Appice are scared rigid, but after a reassuring standing ovation, they come back for an encore of *Jeff's Boogie*. They play a stripped down forty-five minute set, and Stevie Wonder's *Superstition* is introduced as set opener – a position the song will hold for almost the trio's entire career. Otherwise the set includes the old Beck standards *Plynth* and *Let Me Love You*, the newly acquired cover song *People Get Ready*, the first airing of *Livin' Alone*, plus *Shotgun*, which is also Tim Bogert's showpiece on the bass guitar.

MON 18TH✹

After the Oval show, Appice flies back to the States for a brief visit home, while Beck and Bogert do some publicity and interviews, including features by Chris Welch of MELODY MAKER and Martin Hayman of SOUNDS (both dated September 30, 1972). In SOUNDS, Beck explains why he took such a liking to Vanilla Fudge: "Their version of *Shotgun* was really near to me in style, and I thought 'Christ, these guys can really play'. I wouldn't have associated my style with the grand, showy stuff, the stick-twirling and the harmonies, that had nothing to do with me whatsoever, but when I heard *Near The Beginning*, that changed my mind. I remember John Bonham of Led Zeppelin sitting around totally flabbergasted at the drums."

If one is to believe Tim Bogert in MELODY MAKER, the material is coming together nicely: "We've written all the tunes except one written for us by a dude from L.A. As soon as I heard it, I thought instant smash, if we can record that properly it'll be a hit." (The song in question is Ray Kennedy's *Why Should I Care*.)

THU 21ST–FRI 22ND✹

At the end of the week the trio reunite in London again for further rehearsals.

SAT 23RD
"The Great Caledonian Express"
Grangemouth, Falkirk, Scotland

Now officially known as Beck, Bogert & Appice (although the pre-show ads proclaim 'Jeff Beck Group'), the trio appears at this star-studded festival in Scotland with an expected draw of 40,000 spectators. In any event, less than 12,000 turn up and the festival is plagued by long delays and

September 9, 1972: BBC TV's "The Old Grey Whistle Test" is premiered today.

September 1972: Beck, Bogert & Appice play Europe ...

ANTWERP, BELGIUM. FACSIMILE FROM POP MUSIC, OCTOBER 19, 1972

PA problems, forcing compere John Peel to use canned music to fill the extended gaps between bands.

Organised by the Great Western Festivals in conjunction with the Town Council, among the day's attractions are Beggars Opera, Average White Band, the Everly Brothers, Status Quo, comedian Billy Connolly and folk rock quintet Steeleye Span, while both Uriah Heep and the Electric Light Orchestra fail to appear. Beck, Bogert & Appice go on at 11.30 pm as the next-to-last group (Lindisfarne top the bill), and although the audience has by now dwindled to a mere 2,000 spectators, they steal the show outright according to Charles Shaar Murray of NEW MUSICAL EXPRESS (September 30): "My friends, they were amazing. This band are just so good that I was spellbound. The all-time killer was the encore *Jeff's Boogie*. I watched Beck's set in the company of Tim Hart and Rick Kemp from Steeleye and during *Jeff's Boogie*, Kemp's jaw was dropping lower and lower with every bar. It's incredible that anybody could not only have such a bizarre imagination, but also the technique to execute it so brilliantly. Mr. Beck, I humbly salute you. The day was yours."

MON 25TH–FRI 29TH✻
Bogert and Appice remain in England awaiting the new group's upcoming European tour.

BECK, BOGERT & APPICE: FIRST CONTINENTAL TOUR
SAT 30TH
Concertgebouw, Amsterdam, Holland
Beck, Bogert & Appice commence

their first full-fledged tour as a three-piece in Europe. Clive Coulson, a veteran of several Led Zeppelin tours, joins the entourage as roadie.

The set list contains the usual selection of Beck and Fudge songs, plus the three new songs – *Livin' Alone*, *Lady* and *Why Should I Care* – worked up in recent rehearsals.

OCTOBER

SUN 1ST
Arena Hall, Deurne, Antwerp, Belgium
About 1,000 people turn up for Beck, Bogert & Appice's concert with Focus in Antwerp tonight. Three flags are draped behind the band; a Union Jack and two Stars & Stripes, which effectively will be the only stage presentation the group will ever use in their entire career.

After the concert, Jeff is interviewed by Jean-Noël Coghe for the French POP MUSIC (October 19), where Beck excuses the old repertoire (Coghe mentions *Morning Dew* and *Let Me Love You*), because it is his first time performing in Antwerp.

The reviewer does not complain however, and describes a "Beck en super forme, discret, poli, affable ... un immense respect pour l'enfant terrible."

MON 2ND✻
Grote Zaal, DeDoelen, Rotterdam, Holland
Lou Reed plays support to Beck, Bogert & Appice tonight. Barend Toot in MUZIEKKRANT OOR (October 11) slags the show: "And then Jeff Beck. First we had to wait for him to get his guitar at the Hilton Hotel at Schiphol [the Dutch airport]. What I always ask myself when I hear such things, is 'Why does the guy even play music?' ... In place of enthusiasm was the type of monomaniac heavy ego-tripping ... Beck may as well apply for the slot as heavy guitarist in Uriah Heep. Jimmy Page he will never be." Constant Meijers in ALOHA (October 1972) is also unimpressed, and writes under the headline 'Deepfreeze Versus Terror-rock': "I wonder if Beck changes groups so he can still play the same old repertoire. ... It is high time Jeff takes his talent and really gets down to work."

In the crowd enjoying themselves are a couple of members of the Dutch band Golden Earring.

TUE 3RD
Cirkus-Krone-Bau, Munich, West Germany
The tour moves on to West Germany.

WED 4TH
Messehalle, Nuremberg, West Germany

THU 5TH✻
Killesberg✻, Stuttgart, West Germany

FRI 6TH
Musikhalle, Hamburg, West Germany
Dave Stuart from NEW MUSICAL EXPRESS (October 14) catches the Hamburg concert and is totally won over: "When the house lights went down we were asked to welcome Jeff Beck on guitar, Tim Bogert on bass and Carmine Appice on drums. The throngs responded warmly and for their time and money they were treated to just about the best example of modern rock music I have ever witnessed ... the band's first number left an unsuspecting audience open-mouthed and visibly shocked into silence. When all was over and the audience finally admitted defeat, realising they were shouting in vain, I overheard someone comment that this could be the real follow up to Cream. I disagree. For my money they are already superior in every way."

Tucky Buzzard are also on tonight's bill.

SAT 7TH
Niedersachsenhalle, Hanover, West Germany
Billed as 'Hot Rock Night', this dramatic show in Hanover also features Beggars Opera, Livin' Blues, Karthago, Wind and Kraan, beginning at 6.30

© September 16, 1972: Slade ends their two weeks at the top of the UK singles charts with "Mama Weer All Crazee Now"

October 1972: A riot breaks out in Hanover during Beck concert ...

pm with tickets priced at 10 Deutsche Marks. A restless and unruly crowd erupts in a politically inspired riot during Beck, Bogert & Appice's set. It is the presence of the American flag – used as a backdrop onstage – which causes unrest in the crowd. The group's custom built PA system sustains considerable damage while Carmine Appice's drumkit is smashed to smithereens. The damage is valued at £4,000, and results in several cancellations in the upcoming itinerary. According to Beck, who recounts the story to Disc's Robert Brinton later on, "about 100 fanatics began to chant. Then one person threw a bottle onstage. After that it was hell – so we just blew the thing."

It is not so simple according to manager Brian Adams of Beggars Opera, also on tonight's bill: "With regard to the Jeff Beck/Hanover concert where the poor Mr Beck had the unfortunate experience of having his equipment smashed, I would like to point out one small thing in favour of a few thousand German fans. There was no trouble whatsoever until Beck decided after three or four numbers not to continue his show. His reasons for this seemed to be that he was not happy with certain parts of the crowd, what appeared to be lack of audience response so it seems he decided not to bother playing on." Tucky Buzzard, also on the bill at Hanover but unable to appear, place the fault on Beck's roadcrew: "No way could you blame the two thousand strong German audience for their disgust. The true cause of the riot was not caused by any lack of musical content as far as Jeff or his band were concerned, but by the stupid behaviour of his management and road crew, who attempted to act as superstars; dismantling Jeff's gear at least four times, threatening that if any other act came near the stage three hours before or two hours after that, Jeff would not appear ... Disgusted by the behaviour of Beck's management and crew, we refused to finish the tour with him and flew home."

On the lighter side, today, NEW MUSICAL EXPRESS publishes a musicians' poll, where 'the world's leading guitarists pick the world's leading guitarist'. A series of noted players nominate their three most highly rated contemporaries. Not surprisingly, Jimi Hendrix emerges as the triumphant winner followed by Eric Clapton and John McLaughlin while Jeff Beck – 'the comeback king' – notches up fourth position.

Some rate Beck at number one (Mick Box of Uriah Heep, Alice Cooper's guitarist Glen Buxton, Ron Hales of Snake Eye, Geoff Sharkey of Sammy, and, surprisingly, Syd Barrett), while a series of players regard him as good enough to merit either a second or third place.

Jeff himself, when posed the same question, cites Jimi Hendrix, Roy Buchanan and James Burton as his top 3 choices.

SUN 8TH
Jahrhunderthalle, Frankfurt, West Germany

Despite a damaged PA system and drumkit, Beck, Bogert & Appice (supported tonight by Irish group Thin Lizzy) manage to honour their engagement in Frankfurt on borrowed equipment. But it is decided to cancel the group's imminent visit to Switzerland and France, which would take in concerts in Basel (Tuesday 10), Zurich (Wednesday 11), Bern (Friday 13) and Mulhouse (Saturday 14).

MON 9TH–FRI 13TH✱

The cancelled Swiss–French concerts enable the trio to undertake more rehearsals in England in preparation of their showcase appearance in London and the following American tour.

Interestingly, Beck, Bogert & Appice also go into CBS Studios in London this or possibly the following week to record a single, according to NEW MUSICAL EXPRESS's weekly 'Around The Studios' column. No further details from the recording session are furnished, but before leaving on their upcoming American tour, DISC – in a Jeff Beck interview – reports that Ray Kennedy's Why Should I Care About You is the band's new single.

The trio may also have tried to re-record Superstition, which has been considered the perfect single all along. Although an almost finished version is already done in New York, there is a dispute because Electric Lady is asking for a huge payment before freeing the tapes.

SAT 14TH

Jeff Beck is to appear on today's "Scene And Heard" (BBC Radio One, 6.30–7.30 pm), but the original contract is cancelled due to its gone missing in the post(!), but is likely renewed with date of transmission as stated.

SUN 15TH
Sundown, Mile End, London

With new gear flown in to Britain for today's concert, Beck, Bogert & Appice round off their European itinerary with a concert at this newly opened venue. Using no warm-up acts, the trio hits the stage at 8 pm.

The three enormous flags used as a backdrop symbolize the Anglo–American union. The banners are, in fact, so large that Ernest Chapman later boasts about the "biggest flags

Ⓒ October 16, 1972: In a press release, Creedence Clearwater Revival announce their break-up.

October 1972: Beck, Bogert & Appice play London to rave reviews ...

the flagmakers have made since the coronation of George VI. They didn't think it was a serious order at first!"

After the first encore, *Jeff's Boogie*, the three musicians indulge in a friendly custard-pie throwing contest, before being called back for a second encore.

Beck's stature in England is rising dramatically at this time, as shown in Michael Oldfield's unconditional appraisal of tonight's London concert (MELODY MAKER, October 21): "It's difficult to describe the guitar playing of Jeff Beck ... And with the reception given Beck and his new band with co-members Carmine Appice and Tim Bogert at Mile End on Sunday night it looks like he's got himself a super-group of the status of Cream and Led Zep. It's no understatement to describe Jeff Beck as a wizard of the guitar; his high-speed playing looks so easy, yet it's obviously the result of years of hard work. One of his trademarks is playing a few bars so fast that it's just one wall of sound that's coming out, then holding a note for a couple of second, before tearing back again ... the band have got so tight it almost hurts to listen to them. Appice is one of the heaviest drummers in rock: He never hits anything if he can thump it ... [Bogert] got a chance to solo too – and he played bass like Beck plays lead – dynamite. ... When this band returns from the USA they're going to need the Empire Pool-Wembley to fit everyone in."

Martin Hayman of SOUNDS (October 21) finds Beck, Bogert & Appice "one helluva band. The trio format seems to suit them exactly and they gave a tremendous display of power and dynamics ... the most impressive thing about [the group] is that whilst very loud and 'heavy', they still retain a funky feel which so many of the heavy-metal bands fail to do. The combination of Bogert and Appice must take a lot of credit for helping Jeff out there."

MON 16TH

Shooting of the movie "That'll Be The Day" starring David Essex and Ringo Starr begins today on the Isle of Wight. The script calls for an imaginary 50's rock group – the Stormy Tempest – and CASHBOX reports that it will comprise big rock names like Pete Townshend, Keith Moon, Jack Bruce, Eric Clapton and Jeff Beck. In the end, only Keith Moon joins the cast, and certainly not Jeff, who is too busy touring and recording to join the ensemble.

TUE 17TH ✱

As will be customary during the next eighteen months, the group temporarily go their own ways with Bogert and Appice returning to the States and Jeff staying home in Egerton.

WED 18TH ✱

Before leaving on yet another US tour, Jeff invites writer Nick Kent and photographer Pennie Smith to his Egerton home for an extensive interview, published in NEW MUSICAL EXPRESS in two parts (dated October 28 and November 4).

Tracing his career from the Tridents onwards, Beck talks about his different groups and his guitar contemporaries Jimmy Page and Led Zeppelin ("I'm unsure how I feel about them, mainly because I don't like their records, but the only time I've seen them [January 9, 1970] they were great"), Alvin Lee ("this fixed image of being, like, the James Dean of the electric guitar") and Eric Clapton ("even when he's not on form he's better than anybody else around"). Asked if he's aware of the mystique surrounding his own person, Beck shrugs: "I can't imagine that at all."

In the relaxed setting of his own 500-year old home, Beck for once sounds cheerful when he admits "all I can say is that I'm really happy. This is the best band I've ever been a part of – the dream band, if you like. It's more comfortable than the Yardbirds or the two last bands." The house is populated with 29 cats and dogs, all waifs and strays saved from extinction by his girlfriend Celia, who is an eager animal rights activist. (Donovan wrote *Celia Of The Seals* about her, a tribute to her efforts for the animal rights cause.)

Robert Brinton of DISC (November 4) also meets a content and reflective Jeff at his house: "This is the biggest kick for me, the other was joining the Yardbirds ... For the first time in as long as I can remember the excitement is back, now I know I'm really doing what I want to again. In the past I've always worked against other people, but now I've learned to work with them – not only with other members of a band but management too." Always nostalgic about his Yardbirds days, Jeff wonders aloud "there's been talk of us re-forming in some form for the odd gig. I wouldn't mind doing it just for the nostalgia and a good laugh. But who should be the guitarist? That's the awkward thing – me, Jimmy or Eric?"

Beck also breaks the news that the trio will record at Chess in Chicago as soon as their upcoming American tour is over, the very same studio Jeff recorded in with the Yardbirds.

Also paying Jeff a visit at Egerton this month is Herve Muller from the French music magazine BEST, for a lengthy feature published in February 1973. Muller is accompanied by photographer Barry Plummer. Again, Beck is in a retrospective mood, commenting on his career from the earliest days in detail. Interestingly, too, Jeff says lyricist Pete Brown has been approached to contribute to the original material Beck, Bogert & Appice has gathered up: "I love *Politician* and some of the other songs by Cream. There is an idea to do something with Pete Brown." Beck also, for the first time, acknowledges the influence of John McLaughlin's Mahavishnu Orchestra: "What he is doing is fantastic. In a way, he gives me a reason to keep striving. It is encouraging to see guys like him have some success."

THU 19TH ✱

Jeff flies out to Florida for Beck, Bogert & Appice's first concert tour of the United States.

FRI 20TH
BECK, BOGERT & APPICE:
FIRST NORTH AMERICAN TOUR
Sportatorium, Hollywood, Florida

The first American tour by Beck, Bogert & Appice starts tonight with an itinerary that crisscrosses the East Coast and the Midwest. No Canadian, West Coast or California dates are included this time around. The tour covers mostly medium-sized halls with a 4,000–8,000 seat capacity, and the group does good business at the box office.

Seemingly, the set list is kept identical to the recent European tour, and runs on an average of one hour to seventy-five minutes. Many of the songs which relied on keyboards to come across, are dropped because they are ill-suited to a basic three-piece group. Jeff has no lead vocals, but sings some harmony vocals, like on *Tonight I'll Be Staying Here With You* and *People Get Ready*. Confusingly, Jeff claims he plays a piece on Spanish guitar on this tour, which is patently untrue. "It gives the other two a break and adds a bit of colour," Jeff says jokingly in RECORD MIRROR.

But the first night of the tour is no big success according to Jeff: "We only had one bad gig and that was in

October 1972: Jeff Beck is on the cover of ROLLING STONE ...

Miami where the CBS people became a real pain in the arse by trying to record the gig live and keeping the audience waiting while they set up the gear." The bill is completed by Blue Öyster Cult, Foghat and Ursa Major, and the HBS Productions promoted concert grosses $27,000.

To cash in on the resurgence of interest in Jeff Beck at the moment, Mickie Most re-issues *Hi Ho Silver Lining* today. The Europe-only maxi-single couples the old sing-along with its original B-side *Beck's Bolero* plus a bonus cut, *Rock My Plimsoul*. Jeff is not amused, and issues a press statement making it clear that this disc is no way representative of the way he plays today. "No one has consulted me about its release and I shall not be performing it on stage", comments Beck tersely. Jeff's stance spurs the obvious readers' letter in NEW MUSICAL EXPRESS: "Seeing that [Beck] doesn't want anything to do with this record, surely he will not accept the royalties from it?", followed by a suggestion by the reader to forward the royalties to his own address! All the same, the single charts right away and during an eleven week run peaks at a surprisingly strong #17, nearly matching the #14 position it reached when originally a hit five years before.

SAT 21ST
Jacksonville Raceway, Jacksonville, Florida

The American tour has its strange moments, as Jeff recalls to RECORD MIRROR a month later: "One time we played at a dragstrip, and the stage hadn't arrived in time. We ended up playing on orange boxes. There were about 6,000 [people] there, and I've seen rain, but this was unbelieveable, torrential rain, and still there were well over half of them staying to the end in the open."

JEFF BECK
A: HI HO SILVER LINING *(Scott English/Larry Weiss)*
B1: BECK'S BOLERO *(Jimmy Page)*
B2: ROCK MY PLIMSOUL *(Jeffrey Rod)*

Released Friday October 20, 1972 (RAK Replay 3) (UK only)
Personnel as on original single released March 24, 1967 (A, B1) and album version released October 4, 1968 (B2)
Highest Chart Position UK: #17

SUN 22ND
Coliseum, Greensboro, North Carolina

The brass-laden Mom's Apple Pie play support along with the James Gang, who recently lost their front man Joe Walsh and now features Domenic Troiano on guitar.

TUE 24TH
Aquarius (Orpheum) Theater, Boston, Massachusetts

Originally booked for Lowe's State Theater, Syracuse in New York today, this Don Law-promoted concert switches to a sell-out in Boston with Black Oak Arkansas, raking in $31,000 on gate receipts. Silly onstage pranks end with Beck laying on his back on the stage, before he rises up to plant a custard pie squarely in Appice's face.

Catherine Skidmore from the university newspaper MASSMEDIA (October 30) is very impressed with Appice's voice ("much better than Beck's ex-singer, Bob Tench") and Bogert ("a great stage personality"). And of Beck she writes: "Those in the audience who attended the concert out of curiosity went away, for the most part, confirmed Beck fanatics. Those who went in as Beck freaks left with their minds blown apart. Jeff Beck is quite possibly the greatest rock guitarist in the world. I know there are a lot of people who still fight for Clapton and for Hendrix. But those who do have probably not heard a live rendition of *Jeff's Boogie* or *Let Me Love You*. Jeff Beck is a genius in a time of no-talent hype. He can do anything with a guitar – anything. He is equally adept at blues and rock, he works wonders on slide and his vibrato is incredible. He has also been known to hit notes no one ever knew existed."

WED 25TH
Palace Theater, Providence, Rhode Island

Another sell-out, with Foghat opening the bill.

THU 26TH
Tower Theater, Upper Darby, Pennsylvania

"Carmine Appice, Tim Bogert and Mister Jeff ... Beck!" is the evening's breathless introduction – actually there are two shows at 7.30 and 10.30 pm – and the French ROCK & FOLK (February, 1973) magazine is on hand to review the concert in suburban Philadelphia: "White Stratocaster, open shirted, he immediately seizes the show ... They play hard, very hard. Carmine rocks his two big bass

drums, 'wam-bam thank you mam', this is a rock and roll show for sure ... [Beck] has the hall in the palm of his hand. It is good to have the great guitarist back after a long spell." The set includes a surprise rock and roll medley of Little Richard's *Jenny, Jenny* and Carl Perkins' *Blue Suede Shoes*.

Also, a portrait of Jeff Beck by Herbie Green graces the front cover of ROLLING STONE dated this day. The interview, by Paul Bernstein, was conducted in Los Angeles in late August during the previous American tour.

FRI 27TH
Capitol Theater, Passaic, New Jersey

Texas singer Boz Scaggs opens tonight's two concerts, which gross $27,218 at the 3,000-seat Capitol Theater. The concert is presented by John Scher and Al Hayward.

SAT 28TH
Physical Fitness Center, Hofstra University, Hempstead, New York

Foghat is again the opening act: "At least they haven't been trying to upstage us as a few of the other groups we've been playing with on this tour. These guys just come on and do a nicely balanced act, then leave the rest up to us," Beck comments.

The Hofstra concert is a fairly loose, relaxed affair, and opens strongly with *Superstition*. Sung by Bogert with Appice helping out on the chorus, the song is now close to the version that will eventually make it to vinyl, with Carmine's hi-hat lick installed. The group original *Livin' Alone* is a very basic boogie with a little opening riff Beck used in the Rod Stewart days. The most complex number is *Lady*, which has a strong Who-resemblance in the middle passages, although the lyrics are not shattering-

October 1972: Beck, Bogert & Appice on first American tour ...

ly original. Overall, the ensemble playing is occasionally sloppy (like the missed key change in *People Get Ready)*, and the *Plynth/Shotgun* medley meanders aimlessly. Curiously, *Let Me Love You* is not done like the revamped version with Kim Milford which basically was a new song called *Lose Myself With You*. Rather, it now stays true to the original from *Truth*. The song features a nice three-way discussion between Jeff, Tim and Carmine to spur the audience into participating in the standard sing-along refrain. The final number is a great *Jeff's Boogie* where Jeff utilises the tremolo arm Hendrix-style combined with howling feedback. The free-form section is full of brief quotes; Beck alone juggling chimes and jazzy 7-9th chords and the usual Cliff Gallup lightning triplets, even adding the riff to the Who's *A Legal Matter* into the mêlée. The song then segues into a slow blues interlude before Beck returns to the theme – all in all about eight minutes of guitar brilliance. Beck, Bogert & Appice are then called back for an encore, where they perform an inconsequential *Why Should I Care*. Throughout the show, the sound is very basic; Jeff uses just a Stratocaster with a boosted amp, his fingers, a pick and slide and a generous helping of knob-twiddling, but no wah-wah, fuzz or other pedal effects. The three are pretty rough compared to the Max Middleton-period Beck Group. Suffice to say, they will polish their act in the following months. Still, the concert has a definitive playfulness which shows the group enjoying being on stage.

SUN 29TH
Clark Gymnasium, Rochester Institute of Technology, Rochester, New York
"Any new cracks in the Clark Gym wall can be attributed to Jeff Beck. The sheer power of his performance there ... attested to the fact that he is a rock guitarist second only to Eric Clapton; and in the world of rock and roll, that is like comparing Christ to God ... Jeff Beck is phenomenal. He is a guitarist who can jump from an ear-splitting wail to a soft, emotional blues riff so smoothly that the notes just drip from the air," comments Scott MacLeod in the RIT paper REPORTER (November 3). However, the conditions are appaling according to the paper; promoter Somer Productions have sold too many tickets, resulting in "extremely uncomfortable seating for everyone." As a consequence, there's an almost two hour delay between Foghat and Beck.

A syndicated version of the BBC "In Concert" show (▶ June 29) is aired throughout the US this week under the series title "The BBC Presents".

MON 30TH
Century Theater, Buffalo, New York
Another Foghat–Beck, Bogert & Appice bill. Lorna Doone in the RECORD (November 14, 1972) typifies the reception Beck gets on much of this tour: "Listening to Jeff Beck's guitar, could really send chills up and down your spine. Loud, with a lot of feedback (but not a lot of noise), the guitar was displayed with every technique imaginable. This included several tunes done extremely well on a slide guitar."

TUE 31ST
DAR Constitution Hall, Washington, D.C.
Tonight's one show at 7.30 pm is with Afro-rock group Osibisa, who earn an encore for their efforts.

•

Stevie Wonder's album *Talking Book* is issued in the United States this October (it will not be released in Great Britain until January 1973) and contains *Looking For Another Pure Love*, with Jeff and Buzzy Feiten trading guitar licks. A month later, Wonder is pressurized by Motown to pull *Superstition* as a teaser from the album, despite having promised Jeff the song. The single tops the BILLBOARD Hot 100 in January 1973 for one week, effectively killing Jeff's attempts to have a hit single with the same song.

The Wonder-hit and Beck's non-hit causes some mild controversy between the two in the music press. When Beck accuses Stevie for "screwing up" in CIRCUS, Wonder later correctly counters in ROLLING STONE: "My understanding was that Jeff would be releasing *Superstition* long before I was going to finish my album; I was late giving [Motown] *Talking Book*. Jeff recorded *Superstition* in July, so I thought it would be out."

NOVEMBER

WED 1ST✱
While Bogert and Appice collapse in their hotel rooms on an off day in the schedule, Jeff motorbikes around Nassau County on Long Island.

FRI 3RD
Pirate's Cove, Pirate's World Amusement Park, Dania, Florida
A return to the Miami-area amusement park where Jeff played for the first time in the summer of 1969. Promoted by HBS Concert with a potential $40,000 gross.

SAT 4TH
Civic Coliseum, Knoxville, Tennessee
Supported by Ramatam (a new group involving drummer Mitch Mitchell and female guitarist April Lawton), Beck, Bogert & Appice play Knoxville, Tennessee, one of several out-of-the-way towns this tour visits.

TUE 7TH
Ford Auditorium, Detroit, Michigan
Two shows at 7.30 and 11.30 pm, supported by Ursa Major.

While in Detroit, Jeff is interviewed on transatlantic phone by SOUNDS' Ray Telford (November 18). With four more concerts to go, a pleased Beck tells Telford: "The tour has been really good for us in many different ways, people here are really getting off on what we're doing and that kind of reaction has really spurred us on and given us a lot more confidence than we had when we first went on the road. As I've said the group's got the groove I wanted to get into originally. It took us one or two gigs, though, but now it's there it's getting better all the time."

Set List/BBA

Hofstra University, Hempstead, October 28 '72

Superstition • Livin' Alone • Tonight I'll Be Staying Here With You/People Get Ready • Lady • Morning Dew (with drum solo) • Plynth/Shotgun (with bass solo) • Let Me Love You • Jeff's Boogie • Why Should I Care (encore)

◉ November 11, 1972: Allman Brothers Band bassist Berry Oakley is killed in a motorcycle accident eerily like Duane Allman's death the previous year.

December 1972: Recording sessions at Chess in Chicago ...

WED 8TH
North Illinois University Fieldhouse, DeKalb, Illinois
The music trade magazine AMUSEMENT BUSINESS reports tonight's concert is sold out with a moderate $15,000 gross.

FRI 10TH
Barton Coliseum, Little Rock, Arkansas

SAT 11TH
The Warehouse, New Orleans, Louisiana
The New Orleans concert is all sold out. The Warehouse, on Tchoupitoulas Street, is a popular Southern stop for touring groups.

SUN 12TH
Today, Beck, Bogert & Appice are originally scheduled to play a concert in Atlanta, Georgia, which is eventually cancelled.

It has been a successful but tiring tour, and Beck reckons that road fever catches them by the end: "... I was so tired, I didn't know where I was going. We got on really well together, but when you've been on the road in different motels, there have to be a few weirdities, and there were. Tim pulled the sink off the wall one day because there was no water. That's the way it affects you after 15 days on the road. He's a very highly strung person, but onstage, he really plays his ass off."

MON 13TH–FRI 17TH✱
Apparently, Beck, Bogert & Appice spend a week on pre-production for their upcoming album – likely in the New York area – hot on the heels of their American tour.

The famous Chess Studios in Chicago has been booked after a suggestion by Beck, because he has been impressed by the records – and in particular their drum sound – made at the studio over the years, and perhaps sarcastically cites the obscure *Here Comes The Judge* by Pigmeat Markham as a prime example. Of course Jeff also has good memories of the times the Yardbirds recorded there. Unfortunately, the original Chess site on South Michigan Avenue has in effect been closed down, but will be re-opened in December to accommodate Beck, Bogert & Appice.

SAT 18TH✱
Jeff returns home before regrouping with his drummer and bassist in Chicago next month.

DECEMBER

EARLY
Jeff Beck is interviewed by Robin Mackie of RECORD MIRROR and Bill Phillips of NEW MUSICAL EXPRESS (both dated December 23, 1972). The interviews are conducted at Ernest Chapman's London offices.

Writes RECORD MIRROR: "... Jeff's break, when we had a chat, was only a brief sojourn in the motherland before setting off again for the States before Christmas – for a week's recording in Chicago to finish off the album. At the moment, there are four numbers down, and half an album rehearsed." The pressure to come up with the goods worries Jeff: "I'll be terrified. If this folds, it's the gas station in Arizona."

NEW MUSICAL EXPRESS also prints a report on an expectant and enthusiastic Jeff: "This first album is crucial to me. Because it not only has to live up to the expectations of all the critics who have been so enthusisastic about our concerts – it has to live up to our expectations, because we know how good it should be." Material is a problem, not improved by a group living either side of the Atlantic, and the solution is "doing a lot on planes. When the atmosphere is thin and you get drunk easily, the ideas come rolling onto the tape". Pete Brown had originally been approached to write some lyrics for the album, but in the end his contributions amount to nothing.

A rumour circulating at the time suggests Free vocalist Paul Rodgers should join the trio. This is emphatically denied by Jeff: "He'd better not – there's no room!"

Jeff is also interviewed by the Dutch music paper MUZIEKKRANT OOR, for a lengthy piece not published until an edition dated March 28, 1973. For the first time, Jeff mentions the instrumental *Jizz Whizz* (or *Whiz-jiz*, as OOR will have it) – actually the tricky middle part of *Morning Dew* which has been part of the set for a year. Beck describes it as "an instrumental to take the place of *Jeff's Boogie*, thank Christ!"

MON 11TH–FRI 22ND✱
A little more than seven years after his first visit to Chicago in September 1965, Jeff returns to record his first album with Tim Bogert and Carmine Appice at Chess Studios from mid-December onwards.

However, the halcyon days when Chess was a pulsating centre of blues music are long gone. Conditions are far from ideal, with studio machinery breaking down amidst a general sense of decay. Some of the studio equipment has already been dismantled, and the studio is ill-suited to recording. Although the drums sound satisfactory, getting a proper bass sound first proves troublesome, then hopeless. To avoid the bass leaking, Bogert is put in a glass cubicle by himself, which causes the interplay to suffer. Despite this, half an album's worth of songs are quickly committed to tape during the Chicago stay.

The following five songs are thought to be recorded at Chess: A version of Stevie Wonder's *Superstition*; Ray Kennedy's *Why Should I Care*; an inspired choice of Curtis Mayfield's *I'm So Proud*; plus the two group compositions *Livin' Alone* and *Lose Myself With You*. The last actually picks up the thread from the re-arranged version of *Let Me Love You* introduced while Kim Milford was briefly in the band.

In fact, four of the five tracks (the ballad *I'm So Proud* being the exception) are notable for being broken in on the road over the last three months, and therefore relatively easy to transfer to tape.

SAT 16TH
Jeff takes time off from recording as he goes to see folksinger Eric Anderson, Mott The Hoople and country-rockers the New Riders Of The Purple Sage in a show at Chicago's Auditorium Theater.

The time in Chicago also has other happy moments, including a dinner with blues great Albert King, who is also stopping by Chess.

LATE
Carmine Appice's family in Brooklyn host a pre-Christmas dinner for the band and the managers.

As 1972 draws to a close and the group splits for the Christmas season, Jeff Beck can look back on his busiest touring year since the days of the Yardbirds: three separate American tours, a full-scale British tour and several scattered dates on the European Continent, tallying around 80 concerts – besides recording and releasing an album, doing sessions with Stevie Wonder and half-finishing another album at Chess!

Plus, naturally, changing horses in mid-course; dumping his old band and recruiting and trimming his dream band with Tim Bogert and Carmine Appice.

◎ December 9, 1972: "Tommy" as performed by London Symphony Orchestra is staged at the Rainbow, with guests Rod Stewart, Stevie Winwood and others.

△ 1973

JANUARY

TUE 2ND✱
Jeff returns to America to complete recording the first album by Beck, Bogert & Appice. The work done at Chess so far is not satisfactory, and it is decided to bring in an outside view. A last minute call is made to Don Nix who is quickly appointed producer by the trio. This is Beck's idea, who of course briefly got to meet him at the Steve Cropper sessions in Memphis the previous January. Nix meets up with Jeff, Tim and Carmine at Chicago's O'Hare Airport. As the trio are bereft of any cash, Nix has to pay running expenses out of his own pocket for the next couple of days, including hiring cars, purchasing plane tickets to Los Angeles and putting the group up in a hotel.

WED 3RD–FR 5TH✱
With Don Nix aboard, sessions at Chess are briefly wound up, before the trio move operation to Village Recorders in Los Angeles.

MON 8TH–FRI 19TH✱
Beck, Bogert & Appice's first album is finished in Los Angeles. But Don Nix takes an almost instant dislike to Bogert and Appice, and although he enjoys Beck's company, he is an odd choice of a producer. Nix supplies two original songs in a rough cassette format, the bluesy *Black Cat Moan* and the gospel-tinged *Sweet, Sweet Surrender*. Also recorded is the group composition *Lady*. Additional overdubs to the Chess tracks are done at Village Recorders including harmony vocals, which Bogert and Appice excel at. Some of Tim and Carmine's friends are rounded up to contribute both as composers and as musicians. Their former bandmates in Cactus, Pete French and Duane Hitchings, provide lyrics and keyboards respectively on a pair of songs, while singer Danny Hutton and keyboardist Jim Greenspoon from Three Dog Night appear on one track. Carmine has also already done a song solo at a studio on Long Island, *Oh To Love You*, which he brings with him more or less finished, and Jeff just overdubs a lead.

BBA-LOGO DESIGN BY KELVIN HUGHES

Nix and Beck spend the nights on the town, and after a high spirited evening at the Roxy, the two return to the studio where Nix coaxes Beck into singing the lead vocals on *Black Cat Moan*. He (Nix) later describes this late night session as the only enjoyable occasion of the whole Beck, Bogert & Appice experience.

MON 22TH–FRI 26TH✱
After the sessions are wrapped up the trio go their own ways, while Don Nix travels back to Memphis, Tennessee to mix the album at Ardent Studio with John Fry. Nix is not particularly pleased with the results, claiming in his autobiography 'Road Stories And Recipes' that "no matter how hard we tried, there was not enough tape to make a decent single, much less an album".

SAT 27TH✱
Don Nix flies to New York with the finished tape under his arm and plays it for Bogert and Appice. Apparently, a bit of fixing is done at Ultrasonic Sound in New York, but Bogert and Appice are well pleased with the results.

Nix, however, is met with no understanding when he asks for his expenses to be reimbursed, and the whole experience leaves him with a bitter taste in the mouth. Interviewed by John Tobler in ZIGZAG (#35) later this year, Nix recounts: "I did Beck, Bogert & Appice. I don't know how I got the job, but I'd sure have liked to get out of it. Beck asked me. ... I just did it on his word, in January. I went out to Chicago – we did it in Chicago and Los Angeles, and I took it to Memphis and mixed it ... it was pretty good, except for Bogert and Appice. I didn't like the Vanilla Fudge much, and I don't like them either. ... I took the album to Memphis and mixed it, I get up to New York, I give them the master – 'Perfect', a lot of hand slapping, that shit, you know, 'Great, thank you', then their lawyer comes around, Steve Weiss, and I asked him if I could get paid. He says, 'Wait a minute, do you have a contract?' I said no, and he said 'You're fucked'."

SUN 28TH✱
Bogert and Appice fly into London and are installed in a temporary flat owned by Ernest Chapman in Redcliff Square, Earl's Court.

Various matters are attended to at the end of January. Upon Bogert and Appice's arrival, Jeff and Carmine do press interviews with Charles Shaar Murray of NEW MUSICAL EXPRESS (February 10) and Robin Mackie of RECORD MIRROR (February 17) at the group's headquarters in Earl's Court. Bogert, sleeping off his jet-lag, skips these interviews. Murray, who picks the headline 'Rock 'n' Roll Vandals' to describe the band, lets Beck trace the origins of the power trio back to when Vanilla Fudge played London's Speakeasy in October 1967: "You were all sort of bubblegum, with the Fudge. You had the double-breasted jackets and the short haircuts ... I was knocked out because the concert was flawless, and I couldn't believe the music coming out of those guys." Beck also gives insight into his motivation for playing the guitar: "With most day jobs, or regular jobs, you can usually force someone to do the job. But with a musician you just won't. You won't make me play, that's for sure. I don't care if there were contracts binding me or putting me in jail. If the penalty was jail I wouldn't care."

One of these evenings Carmine Appice drops by Olympic Studios in Barnes to chat amiably with Cozy Powell, who is putting together a new group to be produced by Felix Pappalardi. There he unexpectedly also interrupts a session by West, Bruce & Laing, another group of Anglo-Americans, featuring Jack Bruce (who promptly and unceremoniously asks Appice to leave) and ex-Mountain men Leslie West and Corky Laing.

In January too, Jeff does some final overdubs at an unspecified London studio. These include the guitar solo on Carmine's *Oh To Love You*, which Beck wishes to redo after hearing Denny Dias' electric sitar solo on Steely Dan's *Do It Again*.

Don Nix also arrives in London: "So I came to England, and I called up Ernest Chapman ... I'd like to get at least my expense money out of them, because it cost me money to do this album. He said 'I'll go along with

Newsflash January 1973: Beck, Bogert & Appice prepare first full-scale UK tour ...

whatever New York says. I said 'Does that mean you're not going to pay me?, and he said 'Yes'. ... It cost me thirteen hundred dollars to cut a top ten album ... So those are the guys who really make it bad in the whole music business, you know, that you hear about, those who are like that. And they'll probably send some guys after me to break my leg, but fuck 'em, they'll have to catch me first, and I can run!" (Nix is eventually paid for his expenses.)

SUN 28TH–TUE 30TH✱

Warming up for their British tour, Beck, Bogert & Appice practice for three days, culminating in a final rehearsal held in a deserted Rainbow Theatre in London. Chris Welch from MELODY MAKER is on hand to do a story on the band (February 10). Beck, Bogert & Appice run through their set twice, adjusting ensemble passages and trying out new equipment. "They get on stage, and play from heart and soul. Wrists ache, fingernails tear and feet stomp. And it's the most convincing and exciting three-piece that I've seen since the days of Cream and the Hendrix Experience", writes Welch. Tim Bogert sums up the attraction of the threesome thus: "Mainly we appeal to people who like loud, raunchy, goodtime music. We're a raunchy band and we aim to get people turned on. What the hell. They've paid their four bucks. Let them kick it out."

For the British tour, the set list is slightly rearranged to give space to some of the recently recorded songs. The medley *Tonight I'll Be Staying Here With You/People Get Ready* is skipped in favour of another ballad, *I'm So Proud; Sweet, Sweet Surrender* tailends *Morning Dew* (the latter also spotlights Appice's drum solo), while *Black Cat Moan* is sandwiched between *Lose Myself With You* (the fourth and last newcomer to the set) and *Why Should I Care*.

Equipment-wise new investments have also been made; Carmine Appice has attached a wah-wah to his snare-drum and bought a fifty-inch gong, used to dramatic effect every night to introduce opening number *Superstition*. Jeff also unveils an old blackish Gibson Les Paul to replace the trusted Stratocasters he has used exclusively on stage since 1971. The Les Paul will remain Jeff's preferred stage-guitar for the next three years.

The tour advertisements also debut the striking Beck, Bogert & Appice-logo.

WHY SHOULD I CARE?

Strange Interlude

Beck, Bogert & Appice represented a strange chapter in Beck's career. Whereas Jeff's earlier groups had been somewhat unplanned and haphazardly put together, the union with Bogert and Appice was a carefully calculated career move. And just like Mickie Most's attempt at turning Jeff into a pop singer in 1967, this calculated attempt at forming something of a supergroup did not work either – perhaps precicely because it was *not* chancy, the very opposite of the unpredictability which is Beck.

Jeff Beck first saw Vanilla Fudge in London in 1967, and was immediately taken with their powerful rhythm section of bassist Tim Bogert and drummer Carmine Appice. In the summer of 1969, when Jeff shared some live dates with the ailing Fudge, he wanted to re-form his quartet by simply substituting Bogert and Appice for Wood and Newman, while keeping Rod Stewart at the helm. But Stewart decided to jump ship, and while the remaining three laid plans for the future, Jeff crashed his car and was temporarily out of the game.

Then, in the summer of 1972, the opportunity to work together arose again when they bumped into each other at Electric Lady Studios in New York. Since 1969, Led Zeppelin's rise had continued at its astronomical rate, and Beck's master plan was now to make a jump to the big league to help fill the seemingly unlimited demand for high-energy rock 'n' roll – particularly in the United States. (Jeff had of course not forgotten John Bonham's enthusiastic endorsement of Carmine Appice either.) Indeed, Beck's original vision called for a Zep-like formation: guitar–bass–drums plus a barechested singer. Thankfully, the obvious Zep-comparisons were avoided as this concept did not reach fruition when Kim Milford proved unsuitable. Instead, it was decided to keep the group as a threesome, whose grand strategy was to be the power trio to end all power trios.

The motivation was also, admittedly, a genuine desire to play together. For the first time in his career, Beck found himself in a situation where artistically as well as financially he and his partners were equals. But Beck, Bogert & Appice were never a group in the proper sense of the word, they were rather a project involving three people divided by the Atlantic Ocean. Despite their democratic billing, the trio never managed to project a true unity. They also had trouble coming up with original material, and whereas the Jeff Beck Group II had expanded Jeff's musicial visions, Beck, Bogert & Appice were a step back to a straight blues-rock format.

The trio's only studio album *Jeff Beck, Tim Bogert, Carmine Appice* has become the most dated in Jeff's back catalogue. The production was flat as a pancake, and pointed the attention to the trio's two problem areas: songs and vocals. Five out of nine tracks were covers, and not counting Appice's ballad *Oh To Love You*, the group compositions *Lady*, *Lose Myself With You* and *Livin' Alone* were simple guitar riffs turned into not-so-good songs. Throughout, the weak vocals just served to highlight the banal lyrics. The album's saving grace was the death rattling version of *Superstition*. Also, *Black Cat Moan* was splendid, where Jeff's vocals functioned well, although towards the end the rhythm section had a tendency to clutter the basic groove to the point of annoyance.

It was only onstage that Jeff, Tim and Carmine came to life. Whereas many of the trio's contemporaries excelled in stretched-out jams with ever-changing set-lists (notably Led Zeppelin's electrifying live experiences which could run up to three hours), Beck, Bogert & Appice did the opposite: a fast paced hour-long set rooted in soul revue schtick with quick segues and a touch of blue-eyed harmony vocals atop a crunching, munching heavy rock beat. The noisy concert document *Live In Japan* album was a good case in point: Although again the production was disappointing and not really doing justice to the group's live sound, Carmine Appice's agressive drumming gave the music a sharp edge, and with no relief available from a keyboardist, the trio setting gave the guitarist all the space to solo he could ever wish for. The thunderous live boogie shuffle *Blues de Luxe/BBA Boogie* (later released on *Beckology*) is great, despite being excessive, and it contains some of Jeff's most tortured, desperate playing ever.

Jeff was aware of the trio's limitations regarding material, vocals and their geographical separation – facts he acknowledged right from the start. The longer the group stuck together, the more obvious the problems became. From being Beck's dream band, by the spring of 1974 it was Bickering, Boredom & Apathy.

Never again would Jeff play within the tight framework of a blues-rock group nor for that matter, would he ever join a permanent, closely defined rock band. ∎

ⓒ January 13, 1973: David Bowie's single "The Jean Genie", actually a Yardbirds-go-Bo Diddley adaptation of "I'm A Man", hits UK #1.

February 1973: Beck, Bogert & Appice play London-area concerts ...

WED 31ST
Stevie Wonder briefly visits London on a three-day promotional stint, which once again sparks rumours of a Beck–Wonder collaboration.

FEBRUARY

THU 1ST
BECK, BOGERT & APPICE:
FIRST BRITISH TOUR
Queensway Civic Hall, Dunstable

Beck, Bogert & Appice embark on their first proper full-scale British tour tonight, supported by Flash, a group fronted by ex-Yes guitarist Pete Banks. Like the UK tour the previous spring, the date sheet concentrates on the university circuit with the occasional rock venue, but Beck, Bogert & Appice are certainly a much bigger draw than the Jeff Beck Group II. The tour opening is accompanied by much hoopla in the music press, typified by Charles Shaar Murray's ravings in NEW MUSICAL EXRESS (February 3): "And on lead guitar, Public Guitar Hero number one, the Pharaoh of the Phretboard, the Wazoo of the wah-wah, the Boss of the bent-note, the Sultan of the Stratocaster, the Rajah of Raunch, the one and only Mr. Jeff Beck." The stage backdrop with the three flags is naturally kept, while occasionally Tom & Jerry and Donald Duck cartoons are screened during the interval while the group's equipment is being set up.

Martin Hayman of SOUNDS spends the afternoon with the group at Redcliff Square for an interview (February 10 and 17). Here they all watch "Top Of The Pops" where Stevie Wonder plugs *his* version of *Superstition*, soon to enter the UK charts.

Greeted by a delighted crowd, Beck, Bogert & Appice play a good set, resulting in two encores where they have to revive *People Get Ready* plus a titleless boogie. Although Tim Bogert confides "I thought it sucked" to SOUNDS afterwards, Hayman is impressed by "... Appice's fantastic drumming, huge slabs of sounds laid down with a metronomic backbeat. Bogert's bass is fast and clipped, and he handles it unlike any other I can think of off-hand ... As a trio it is entirely convincing."

MELODY MAKER's nicely named Graham Punter is more sceptical in his review (February 10): "Playing against a backcloth of Stars and Stripes and the Union Jack, before a capacity crowd which demanded two encores, is no mean way to start your first tour of Britain. But it wasn't enough to convince me that Beck, Bogert & Appice will emerge during 1973 as a supergroup. At Dunstable they tried so desperately hard to prove that they were – and I suspect that was their downfall. ... On the rare occasions they turned the boxes down, they proved that not only could they sing, but more important – sing well together. The result was reminiscent of the Everly Brothers with the added advantage of a fuller sounds in support. The fault of the band lay in trying to show-off all their talents at once, to an extent where confusion replaced fluency."

FRI 2ND
Student Union, University of Reading, Reading

SAT 3RD
Great Hall, Imperial College, London

After two concerts in the provinces, Beck, Bogert & Appice play their first London concert – fully sold out – since October of last year. There is a long wait after Flash finish their set. Beck is dressed simply in jeans and an 'Oz Obscenity' T-shirt, "looking absurdly young and scrawnier than ever" according to Nick Kent in NEW MUSICAL EXPRESS (February 10): "At his best, Beck plays his guitar like Evel Knievel rides a motorcycle: moving at a breakneck speed, pulling any number of bizarre stunts, throwing in the most absurd riffs, playing tricks with the rhythms and somehow holding the whole show together." On the whole, Kent is disappointed by tonight's concert, however: "The band seem to have no set policy once they start a number, and while spontaneity sometimes can produce the greatest high-energy music, it more often than not leads to an aimlessness which becomes frustrating to listen to." Kent dismisses Bogert's bass solo as "horrendous ... needs cutting down drastically", with Beck himself only "producing a series of fiery fretboard doodlings which never seemed to connect properly". All in all, "a mediocre gig by a fine, fine band".

Kent's colleague Charles Shaar Murray, also present, is totally overwhelmed: "They just righteously tear it up. I don't think there's been a three-instrument band with this much class since the golden days of Cream and Hendrix, and even the Zep would have a hard time cutting BBA."

Lastly, Andrew Tyler of DISC (February 17): "... Beck, a brilliant if inconsistent musician, has at last found a pair of solid, unflappable teammates ... There's much talk about the trio taking over where Cream left off and although comparsions of this sort indicate the sort of skills an audience can except – that's about as far as the line should be extended. Bogert and Appice communicate in a way few, if any, other rock rhythm sections can, and Beck is the perfect counterpoint. He'll play a line then toss out a couple of weird chords for B & A to pounce and munch on and when they are in need of some more Beck senses it. And they sense his needs and are ready to chop and scramble tempoes to keep him interested. ... One small complaint. The set badly needs revising and will undoubtly receive an overhaul following the release of the new album."

MON 5TH
Inexplicably, Epic in the United States decides to re-release *Hi Ho Silver Lining*, oddly enough coupled with *Definitely Maybe*, for the American market. The single was a non-hit when originally released in America in 1967, and this re-release does nothing to rectify the situation.

Today is also likely the occasion when Carmine Appice is interviewed by Andrew Tyler for a story in DISC, while Jeff Beck is interviewed by Andrew Furnival for a whole page in TIME OUT (February 16–22). Besides talking about the impression Jimi

Single
JEFF BECK [GROUP I & II]
A: HI HO SILVER LINING *(Scott English/Larry Weiss)*
B: DEFINITELY MAYBE *(Beck)*

Released Monday February 5, 1973 (US Epic 10938)
Personnel as on original single released March 24, 1967 (A) and album version released Monday May 1, 1972 (B)
Highest Chart Position US: –

February 1973: Single "Black Cat Moan" released in the UK ...

Hendrix left on him and the importance of the Yardbirds, Jeff for once touches other subjects than his music: "I don't smoke pot. It probably looks like it, but I don't. I used to drink on tour. I was getting through a bottle of vodka a day, more than that because on the plane they dish out the drinks liberally and when they bring me a drink they'll bring me two doubles. As it gets to about 5 o'clock in the evening, you start getting excited about the show and you have a drink and you calm down and that wears off and you have another one and it goes on and on until you are just about to go on, then you down half a bottle and start getting really pissed." On money: "Financially I'm very wealthy and I don't have to worry about that. You know if I was really worried about making every penny that I could, I'd be there now and I'd be playing every little toilet from one coast to another, but I'm not interested in that. I've got enough to see me through a good many years. I don't live in luxury. It's luxury for me but not for other people."

TUE 6TH
Heavy Steam Machine, Hanley, Stoke-on-Trent

WED 7TH
Student Union, University of Liverpool, Liverpool

THU 8TH
Loughborough University of Technology, Loughborough

FRI 9TH
Student Union, Newcastle Polytechnic, Newcastle
The northern-most concert on the itinerary, as no appearance across the border in Scotland has been booked.

SAT 10TH
Student Union, University of Leeds, Leeds

SUN 11TH
The Hardrock, Manchester

MON 12TH
Top Rank Suite, Swansea, Wales
The first of two visits to Wales on this tour.

WED 14TH
Oxford Polytechnic, Oxford
Also today, one of Jeff's custom-built Ford model A hot rods is on display at a big car show at Crystal Palace, London.

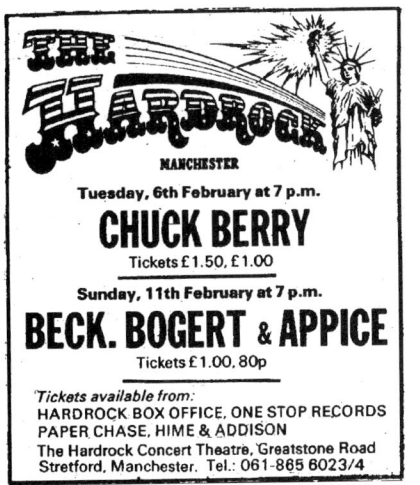

THU 15TH
The group's announced concert at the Hard Rock in Bournemouth tonight is called off by the venue's management due to adverse weather conditions.

As the tour draws to a close, Carmine Appice is also plagued by an infected arm, which is held in check by daily treatments, so no cancellations are neccessary.

FRI 16TH
Sundown, Edmonton, London
A return to London for a concert at one of the capital's three different Sundown venues, where Rod Stewart is in the audience cheering the group on. However, Beck is dissatisfied with the performance and gives it the thumbs-down to Charles Shaar Murray. The exuberant Murray himself is highly enthusiastic, summing up in NEW MUSICAL EXPRESS (February 24): "They flew my friends, they came screaming out of the sun to land right in the middle of your pleasure centres giving you just the right rush. Just high-energy guitar-trio rock de-bloody-luxe ... they just kept on burning, never letting up for a second. Even when they seem to be just jamming, the heat is always on, the level of concentration always high and little miracles just keep happening." Another of Beck's eager fans, Chris Welch of MELODY MAKER (February 24), starts his review with a simple "Amazing!" Welch elaborates: "There have been one or two rock concerts in the last decade. But Beck, Bogert & Appice's performance was one that will be remembered, when we all have gone to Great PA System in the Sky."

For the encore medley of *Plynth/Shotgun/People Get Ready*, the trio arrive on stage in style in one of Beck's hot rods shrouded in dry ice and smoke!

Also today, Beck, Bogert & Appice's first single, *Black Cat Moan*, is released in Great Britain. The review in NEW MUSICAL EXPRESS makes a point of the "tearing riff and Beck's vocals [which] are surprisingly good", but "it's lost its impact on record and I think the mediocre production could have a lot to do with it," while MELODY MAKER finds it "a very familiar riff and the whole affair is a bit diasappointing." John Peel, reviewing the single in DISC, is genuinely surprised: "Hey lawdy mama, what a treat! Cuts through the morass of weedy and degenerate snivelling we are asked to endure in the name of music with a power and aggression that would do credit to Liverpool F.C. themselves!" (All reviews February 24)

Despite Beck's recent return to the singles charts with the re-release of *Hi Ho Silver Lining*, the new single finds little favour among the record-buying public.

SAT 17TH
Originally slated for an appearance at the South Parade Pier in Southsea, Portsmouth today, this booking is later withdrawn from the itinerary.

SUN 18TH
Top Rank Suite, Cardiff
A Sunday concert with a return to Wales marks the end of Beck, Bogert & Appice's first UK tour proper.

TUE 20TH
Le Bataclan, Paris, France
Beck, Bogert & Appice are in Paris to make one of their rare TV appearances, when they perform on the French show "Pop Deux" (ORTF TV). Whereas Bogert and Appice fly over from London to Orly, Beck has hired a taxi-plane to shuttle him across the Channel in the afternoon. Jeff arrives at Le Bataclan on Boulevard Voltaire

Single
BECK, BOGERT & APPICE
A: BLACK CAT MOAN (Don Nix)
B: LIVIN' ALONE (Beck/Bogert/Appice)

Released Friday February 16, 1972 (UK Epic EPC 1251)
Personnel as on album Jeff Beck, Tim Bogert, Carmine Appice.
Recorded at Village Recorders, Los Angeles (A) and Chess Studios, 2120 South Michigan Avenue, Chicago, Illinois, (B), December 1972 and January 1973.
Produced by Don Nix and the Boys
Highest Chart Position UK –

February 17, 1973: Alice Cooper's "School's Out" is chosen as 'Best 1972 single' in Disc Music Poll Awards 1973.

February 1973: Beck, Bogert & Appice appear on live television in Paris ...

BOGERT AND BECK AT LE BATACLAN, PARIS, FEB 20. FACSIMILE FROM EXTRA, APRIL 1973.

at 4 pm, where the trio's equipment is already set up. At 6.25 pm the taping begins in front of an enthusiastic audience of 2,000 fans, where Beck, Bogert & Appice basically run through a shortened live set including *Superstition, I'm So Proud, Morning Dew,* and *Black Cat Moan*. The show is transmitted later in the month, presumably on Saturday February 24.

Although not a regular concert, this is Jeff's first live performance in Paris since May 1968.

The event runs as cover stories in France's three biggest pop magazines, MAXIPOP, EXTRA and BEST, and Jacques Le Blanc of MAXIPOP (February 27) writes excitedly: "Wow! What a superb surprise!"

LATE
After the Paris trip, Beck, Bogert & Appice take a month-long rest. While Beck retires to his Egerton estate, Bogert and Appice return to the States. A US tour is slightly delayed from its proposed mid-March start.

MARCH

MID
Before going back to America for another tour, Jeff does some interviews with the British music press to plug the group's forthcoming debut album, including Ray Telford of SOUNDS and Charles Shaar Murray of NEW MUSICAL EXPRESS (both dated March 31).

A recurring discussion centers around the lack of proper material in the group. "Rock music really reached a creative high three years ago with Hendrix and Cream", Jeff reflects in SOUNDS, "I don't say I'll pack it in but I've been playing for eight years and I reckon it's time I had some real action but the only way that's going to happen is if I get the right material." And in NEW MUSICAL EXPRESS Beck puts it bluntly: "As for memorable tunes, there aren't any – I know that. We need tunes ... I'm not proud. I'm not trying to say we're good writers. As writers, we stink. We're going to have to do something about that." For the service of NEW MUSICAL EXPRESS's readers, Jeff then gives a track-by-track commentary of the new album.

The music press agrees that Beck, Bogert & Appice would be ideal for recording a live album, but Jeff is sceptical: "[B]ecause if it's to be successful it really needs to capture the magic ... That means good mixing and a very sensitive production." In fact, Beck suggests recording a live EP of four numbers, but the idea is never realised.

LATE
After their month-long rest, Beck, Bogert & Appice get together in the States at the end of March for an extended US tour. The tour is split in two to allow a ten-day breather in the hectic schedule.

MON 26TH
To coincide with the opening of Beck, Bogert & Appice's mammoth North American tour, their first album – simply entitled *Jeff Beck, Tim Bogert, Carmine Appice* – is issued in the States today slightly ahead of the British release. The cover just depicts the group logo on a brown-clothy background. The album seeks to match the power of heavy metal with soulful vocals, but musically it is a step backwards from the more adventurous Jeff Beck Group II-period.

The reviews are generally favourable, but most agree on the lack of a punchy production. Ray Telford in SOUNDS (April 7) correctly point out how "of the nine titles less than half were written by the group – an unusual situation enough in these times of totally self-sufficient rock bands, though there's little doubt that there is a definitive spark of originality in a few of the Bogert/Appice compositions. In many ways BBA's first album

---

Album
BECK, BOGERT & APPICE
JEFF BECK, TIM BOGERT, CARMINE APPICE

A1 BLACK CAT MOAN (DON NIX) **A2** LADY (BECK/BOGERT/APPICE/HITCHINGS/FRENCH) **A3** OH TO LOVE YOU (BECK/BOGERT/APPICE) **A4** SUPERSTITION (STEVIE WONDER)

B1 SWEET SWEET SURRENDER (DON NIX) **B2** WHY SHOULD I CARE (RAY KENNEDY) **B3** LOSE MYSELF WITH YOU (BECK/BOGERT/APPICE/FRENCH) **B4** LIVIN' ALONE (BECK/BOGERT/APPICE) **B5** I'M SO PROUD (CURTIS MAYFIELD)

Released Monday March 26, 1973 (US Epic KE 32140) and Friday April 6, 1973 (UK Epic 65455) A quadrophonic version is released in the United States in August 1973 (US Epic EQ 32140)
Personnel is Jeff Beck (gtrs, ac gtr on B1, ldvcls on A1, hrmny vcls), Tim Bogert (bs, ldvcls on A4, B2, hrmny vlcs), Carmine Appice (dms, ldvcls, hrmny vcls) + Danny Hutton (bck vcls on B1), Duane Hitchings (pno, mellotron on A3), Jim Greenspoon (pno on B1)
Recorded at Chess Studios, 2120 South Michigan Avenue, Chicago, Illinois; Village Studios, Los Angeles, California (A1), Electric Lady and Ultrasonic Studios, New York, New York and unspecified studio locations in London; December 1972 and January 1973
Produced by Don Nix and the Boys
Engineered by Baker Bigsby, Gary Starr, Mike Colchamiro, John Fry (remix engineer)
Highest Chart Position US: #12
Highest Chart Position UK: #28

March 1973: Beck, Bogert & Appice's first album released ...

is a disappointment for Beck has yet to come up with a record to match his and this band's stage brilliance." Chris Welch of MELODY MAKER (April 14) loves the album, praising "Jeff – the great white hope of British guitarists. He can never lay back with these guys [Bogert and Appice] around. The result is a shot of pure stimulant into the arm of rock". Pete Erskine is equally over the moon in SOUNDS (April 14): "Totally unbelieveable; a superb album." The only apprehensive UK report is published in RECORD MIRROR (April 21): "... this summit meeting of a trio has a lot to live up to, and I'm not sure that this album does. Beck, who used to be the rudest guitar player of them all, seems to suffer from periodic bouts of good taste in such classy company, and despite flashes of his old absurd genius and undoubted virtuosity from all, better songs and a bolder approach would have been very welcome."

James Isaacs of ROLLING STONE (May 10) is frustrated by Beck's low profile: "When I put a Beck side on, I want to be shaken, rattled and rolled. I want him to wring the fucking guitar's neck! There is barely enough of the patented Beck flash here to satisfy the appetite." And GUITAR PLAYER (September 1973) finds the record "all in all ... quite good", where Beck "shows flair and a great deal of energy wah-wah-ing, chopping, whining and gurgling his way through four group originals and five borrowed numbers." The French ROCK & FOLK magazine (June 1973) thinks the album is "bizarre, but with honest, joyful playing" and singles out *"Livin' Alone,* perfect 'Jeff Beck tempo', a pure joy which recalls Beck on *Truth."*

The album scores a welcome US #12 and – on the strength of recent British tours and strong media coverage – UK #28. It is also a fair success on the Continent; in France, for example, the record peaks at #5 during August.

WED 28TH
BECK, BOGERT & APPICE:
SECOND NORTH AMERICAN TOUR:
FIRST LEG
Music Hall, Boston, Massachusetts

Beck, Bogert & Appice's high-profile North American tour opens in Boston on the East Coast, and will carry through twenty-some dates until Hawaii in mid-May. There are two shows tonight, and the box office grosses $45,000 of a $51,000 potential. The group's entourage is now expanded to include Allan Dutton, who is Jeff's personal roadie and guitar tech – who will maintain a relationship with Beck right up till the 90's.

Support act for the whole tour will be Wet Willie ("a silly name but a great band", Jeff quips). Hailing from Macon, Georgia, they are fronted by singer Jimmy Hall who also will work with Beck years later.

For this tour Jeff unveils the voice bag, a novelty device which allows him to 'speak' through the guitar. This will be used to great effect every night after Carmine's gong-crash to signal the show's kick-off amidst dry ice and smoke.

With Beck, Bogert & Appice in their prime, the set list is streamlined to about an hour and ten minutes, because, as Jeff puts it to SOUNDS before the tour: "We don't have to play long sets because we can get straight into a set without having to feel our way into it. Yeah, I reckon people get their money's worth at our gigs." In-between-song chatting is kept to a very minimum. The performances are tight and the song sequence very rarely varies from night to night, although ample room is left for improvisations in the three individual showcases: Bogert in *Lose Myself With You,* Appice on *Morning Dew* and Beck's during *Black Cat Moan.*

The group's new album is featured in extensio (bar Appice's studio-only *Oh To Love You*). To keep the fans happy, the well-worn medley of *Plynth* and *Shotgun* is retained. *Going Down* is also reintroduced for the first time since the American tour in August the previous year. A series of snatches from their collective back catalogue is also used to spice up the set list. The Cactus riff *Oleo* is sometimes brought out, and Jeff's vocal number *Black Cat Moan* will typically segue into a few bars of *Train Kept A-Rollin'* before moving from *Blues de Luxe* via *You Shook Me* to *Jeff's Boogie,* while in *Shotgun* Jeff and Tim usually whip out the *Heart Full of Soul*-riff in

Set List/BBA

US tour March–May '73

Superstition • Livin' Alone • I'm So Proud • Lady • Morning Dew (drum solo) • Sweet Sweet Surrender • Lose Myself With You (bass solo) • Black Cat Moan (medley incl. You Shook Me and Blues de Luxe) • Why Should I Care • Plynth/ Shotgun/Jeff's Boogie • Going Down/Oleo/Boogie

I'M NOT TALKING

The Electric Larynx

For the big-league American tour in the spring of 1973, Jeff introduced a voice bag – or talk box – as part of his sonic arsenal. The effect consisted of a small bag which Beck slung over the shoulder and a tube stuck in his mouth which drove a small speaker, and this combination allowed Jeff to modulate the guitar sound vocally. The origin of the effect stretches back to the forties, but it was briefly produced commercially in 1970 by Kustom, and it is believed that Jeff had one of the very first models. He picked up on the effect after hearing guitarist Mike Pinera.

Sounding like a cross between a strangulated comic book-hero and a visitor from outer space, many could not make head nor tails of the voice bag; "Beck singing through an airbag" suggested ROLLING STONE helpfully. Jeff would use it to startling effect live in call-and-response sequences with Carmine Appice. "Put your hands together!" the drummer would urge the audience, and Jeff would repeat the request modulated by the voice bag.

Although prominently featured on Beck, Bogert & Appice's *Live in Japan* album, the general record-buying public did not get to hear Jeff play it before the *Blow By Blow* album in 1975, especially *She's A Woman.* But by then several other guitarists had picked up on the effect, most notably Joe Walsh (on *Rocky Mountain Way* from mid '73) and Peter Frampton, whose platinum-success *Comes Alive* in '76 made the bag a household name. Consequently, after the *Wired*-tour in 1976 Jeff thankfully retired the voice bag. ∎

unison at breakneck speed. Jeff occasionally also teases the crowd with a few bars of the easily recognizable *I Ain't Superstitious*-riff whenever the mood catches him.

"It's the same formula you see at a Tamla Motown show where they come on with a medley and it's so beautifully arranged, you feel like you've heard all the numbers. I give 'em a taste of a number, then go onto another trip," Jeff explains to MELODY MAKER's Chris Welch in mid-April.

THU 29TH
Lowe's State Theater, Syracuse, New York

March 17, 1973: The banjo instrumental "Dueling Banjos" from the hit movie "Deliverance" is a surprise US #1.

March 1973: Big league American tour commences in Boston ...

FRI 30TH
Capitol Theater, Passaic, New Jersey
Originally set for Cherry Hill Arena in Cherry Hill, New Jersey, tonight's concert is switched to Passaic, where the attendance is just above three-quarter.

SAT 31ST
Georgetown University, Washington, D.C.
"Beck, a British guitarist and former member of the influential Yardbirds, helped define the role of the lead guitar and style that would be known as hard rock or heavy, metallic rock. Saturday, though, Beck did little other than repeat the same devices he initiated five years ago. The screaming, choked lines, the bird stutters, the rapidly ascending riffs and scales all sounded trite and stale ... In fact, BBA's basic problem was a lack of any apparent muscial direction. Instead of attempting to achieve some new musical style ... the band seemed content merely to blend aspects of Vanilla Fudge, Cream, and the Yardbirds into a new conglomeration", comments Tom Zito in WASHINGTON POST (April 2) of tonight's show.

Still, the trio have sold out the 4,150 capacity hall.

APRIL

SUN 1ST
Palace Theater, Albany, New York

MON 2ND
Veterans Memorial Auditorium, Columbus, Ohio

TUE 3RD
Kiel Auditorium, St. Louis, Missouri

WED 4TH
International Amphitheater, Chicago, Illinois
Telecaster-blaster Roy Buchanan is the added one-off attraction for tonight's concert.

THU 5TH
Minneapolis Armory, Minneapolis, Minnesota

FRI 6TH
Indiana Fairgrounds Coliseum, Indianapolis, Indiana
Black Oak Arkansas and REO Speedwagon are boosting the bill tonight.

•

Keen to follow-up last year's success with the re-issued *Hi Ho Silver Lining* and to cash in on the general interest in not only Jeff Beck but also Rod Stewart at this time, Mickie Most has combed the vaults to come up with another maxi-single featuring *I've Been Drinking* as the selling point. The song was previously tucked away on the B-side of Beck's *Love Is Blue* single in early 1968. The flipside consists of two tracks off *Truth;* Tim Rose's *Morning Dew* and Jeff's acoustic rendition of the traditional *Greensleeves*. To leave no doubts about the Beck–Stewart connection, RAK credits the maxi-single to 'Jeff Beck Group featuring Rod Stewart'. During a six week run, it peaks at a surprisingly strong #27 in the British singles charts, ironically easily outclassing Beck, Bogert & Appice's new single.

SAT 7TH
Community War Memorial, Rochester, New York

SUN 8TH
Cobo Hall, Detroit, Michigan
Tonight's performance is hot with the group breathing fire. The talk box-infested *Superstition* is not only funky but also swings. The bass and drums then bear down on *Livin' Alone* like a steam hammer, while the guitar coughs, spits and sputters. *I'm So Proud* follows with Beck and Bogert chiming in on sweet harmony vocals behind Appice. At the end Jeff scrapes his pick along the bottom E-string, before he kicks in the opening chords to *Lady*. Appice's vicious drum spot halfway into *Morning Dew* sounds like it threatens to engulf the whole auditorium. In *Sweet, Sweet Surrender* Jeff plays a hair-raising solo break, and Bogert displays lyricism in the nimble almost-jazzy first half of his showcase *Lose Myself With You* (which also includes a segment of *Let Me Love You*),

---

Single
JEFF BECK GROUP FEAT. ROD STEWART
A: I'VE BEEN DRINKING *(Tauber/Mercer)*
B1: MORNING DEW *(Tim Rose)*
B2: GREENSLEEVES *(trad. arr.)*

Released Friday April 6, 1972 (UK RAK Replay 4)
Personnel as on original single released Friday February 9, 1968 (A) and album version released Friday October 4, 1968 (B1, B2)
Highest Chart Position UK: #27

---

before he soars off like a spindizzy jet engine. Not only is Jeff's guitar on splendid form tonight, his vocal on *Black Cat Moan* is utterly convincing. During the coda of the next-to-last song, *Why Should I Care,* Jeff unearths the old *Rice Pudding*-riff. Then, with a greeting to 'the Boogie Capital of the World', Appice kicks off a medley of *Plynth* and *Shotgun,* where Beck in quick succession quotes *Heart Full of Soul,* the Beatles' *I Feel Fine* and his own guitar solo on the Yardbirds' version of *Too Much Monkey Business*, before pulling out absolutely all stops on a brief *Jeff's Boogie* culminating in the usual bluegrass rave-up. Finally, the trio then come back for a cool John Lee Hooker-style boogie. On a night like this, Beck, Bogert & Appice's raunchy, unsubtle approach is invincible.

MON 9TH AND TUE 10TH
Felt Forum, New York, New York
Beck, Bogert & Appice play two consecutive nights to jam-packed crowds – which "smelled like the Planet of the Apes" according to Linda Solomon in NEW MUSICAL EXPRESS (April 21) – at New York's prestigious Felt Forum, a 4,500-seat capacity auditorium located within the Madison Square Garden complex (the concerts gross $45,000 of a $58,000 potential). Solomon is not overtly amused however, finding the band "extremely competent with no outstanding surprises – just good, solid music ... They could trim some of their excess bass and drum solos and tighten up their rather nice vocal harmonies, and they'd be right up there with the best of the current crop." Local New York rag THE EXPRESS reports: "Jeff Beck Group [sic] was back in New York recently at the Felt Forum, and, as always, it was a pleasure to watch the king of British rock. Beck has adapted, much better that I thought he'd be able, to playing in a three piece band ... One of my major concerns about Beck's participation in a three piece unit is that he would have to play, play, play and have no time to be tasteful, but the boy wonder manages to do both."

Chuck Pulin, SOUNDS' (April 28) New York correspondent, remembers Beck's sad, last apperance in New York the previous summer at Gaelic Park, and for one is happy to report that the group's Forum performances were "not a drop of fat, just lean hard rock, blues and boogie".

That the New York concerts are an event is also evident from Lenny

April 21: Led Zeppelin's fifth album, "Houses of the Holy", peaks at UK #1 for a solitary week.

April 1973: After a break, tour resumes on American West Coast ...

Kaye's review in ROLLING STONE (May 10): "Backed by the blood and thunder of ex-Vanilla Fudge and Cactus members Tim Bogert and Carmine Appice, [Jeff Beck] strode back into the spotlight on this early leg of a 28-city tour with some of the hardest guitar-spinning he's laid out in a long while, re-establishing contact with his intensely loyal legion of fans while galvanizing those who came to see an instant replay of the familiar Cactus boogie." Kaye also praises the rhythm section: "Bogert especially is top-notch, matching Beck howl for howl." During the finale on Monday night, Beck plays his guitar with a blue comb a fan has tossed on stage.

The three stay at the city's plush Essex House hotel, where Lenny Kaye is granted an interview, later published in CRAWDADDY (August 1973). Beck typically downplays the Felt Forum shows ("I don't think we played too well last night"), and offers a simple musical philosophy: "The message is fun. Just kiss it off with a bit of fun."

WED 11TH
Syria Mosque, Pittsburgh, Pennsylvania

THU 12TH
John Carroll University, University Heights, Ohio
One show at 8 pm promoted by WMMS & Belkin Productions in University Heights outside Cleveland.

FRI 13TH
Concert Bowl, Maple Leaf Gardens, Toronto, Ontario, Canada
The tour also includes a sole visit to Canada, where Paul Butterfield's Better Days – featuring Amos Garrett – are added to boost the bill.

SAT 14TH
Providence Civic Center, Providence, Rhode Island
Although not a sell-out (70 % attendance with a box-office count totalling $39,000), tonight's show is acclaimed in the local press.

SUN 15TH
Field House, University of New Hampshire, Durham, New Hampshire
A last minute addition to the end of this leg of the tour. Originally set for the university's Snively Arena, the show is then moved to the gym because the arena does not have sufficient electrical power. This causes a couple of hours delay, forcing local added attraction Mad Angel to cancel, and Beck, Bogert & Appice do not go on until past midnight. The show is a huge success, according to reports in the University papers THE LOG (by Joe Coutore, May 1) and THE NEW HAMPSHIRE (by Tom Huhn and Dave Ganley, April 17). Coutore: "They walked off after almost two full hours, with cries to come back ... when Beck walked back on, I thought I would go deaf, although I was hollering myself. BBA rolled into *Plynth* and *Beck's Boogie* [sic] smiling widely." Huhn and Ganley go one better with their almost blushingly panegyric descriptions: "... The trio performed their art in such a relaxing manner as to reflect the maturity and intelligence of music. The music world has been blessed by [BBA], with an intelligence which one would only expect to find in Stravinsky's *Rite of Spring*. The element of intellectuality and maturity is the glue which cements the facets of their musical genius together. Raw spontaneity radiated through the intensity of the musical maturity. This may seem to be a paradox: calculated, developed rationale vs. raw spontaneity; but these seemingly opposing forces melt together ... they extend each other in such a way as to reveal the totality, the oneness of the music."

MON 16TH ✱
Palace Theater, Waterbury, Connecticut
Beck, Bogert & Appice round off the first leg of the tour tonight with a concert added late to the initial itinerary.

•

At some point during the US tour, Jeff Beck and Stevie Wonder get in touch, both to clear the air around the *Superstition* debacle, but also to discuss further collaboration. Beck is forever worried about his new group's lack of good songs and thinks Wonder's tune smith talents are a good solution.

Jeff explains to Robert Brinton of DISC: "We have discussed it, and he seems to be interested but I suppose it is really a matter of him finding the time. He's the one though, I can't really think of anyone else. See, I do feel the band needs a writer because I don't want to impose my own taste too strongly. Maybe it'll work out with Stevie." To CREEM (August 1973) Jeff adds hopefully: "We've got the thing with Stevie sorted out. He told me that he didn't want *Superstition* out as a single, 'cause that was originally written for us. But he says he'll write another song for us, and it should be tremendous. He's an incredible songwriter."

MID

In mid-April the promised tour break allows Jeff to go back to Egerton for some rest, while Bogert and Appice stay behind in the States. While at home, Jeff keeps himself busy with flying lessons, doing publicity and – most surprisingly – recording tracks for a planned solo album.

Because he lost his driving licence for speeding earlier in the year, Jeff has decided to try his hand at piloting. It is a passion he shares with Keith Emerson, and both Beck and Emerson are seen taking flying lessons in Sussex.

Jeff also spends a day in London doing interviews for Disc and MELODY MAKER (both dated May 5). At the Equator office in St. Martin's Lane, Jeff confides to DISC's Robert Brinton about his solo album: "I'll be writing all the material and playing all the instruments. I don't intend there to be any hurry because I want to record it at my leisure, just to put it out without any fuss – then hope people will like and accept it. Everyone seems to get trapped into doing one kind of thing and I want the album to show there's a lot more influences than some would imagine. I mean I am able to play almost any style, for instance Les Paul and Mary Ford were a big influence in the early days from a technical point of view. There might be a bit of bluegrass. Basically it'll give me the chance to get a lot out of my system." But Jeff also makes it a point of how much he thrives in Beck, Bogert & Appice: "I am just glad, that's all. Glad that it's happened and everything is going right."

The recordings for Jeff's solo project are done at the newly opened Escape Studios, an operation run by brothers Ted and Richard Roffery. The studio is situated in a converted barn in the Smarden–Egerton area of Kent, just a short distance from Beck's house. Jeff will spend much time at this studio over the next few years.

The MELODY MAKER interview is conducted in an Indian restaurant off Charing Cross Road, accompanied by guitarist Dave Ball of Cozy Powell's new group. Jeff is pleased with the tour, and credits the Mahavishnu Orchestra for educating the audiences in the States: "[they] are really listening now and the Mahavishnu have played a great part in getting 'em by the short and curlies."

Jeff also remembers the good old days in a special article to commemorate the Marquee's 15th anniversary. "I played the Marquee several times,

May 1973: Beck, Bogert & Appice end West Coast dates in Hawaii ...

and I loved it. When you played there it was like everybody was friends and you never had to worry. Every time I was in town, I'd be there to hear other bands. I used to like it most when they had a group from America, and the greatest night was when Buddy Guy played." Asked whether he would play the Marquee again, Jeff replies: "Why not? I'd rather play two nights there, than one in some places. I'd gladly do it. The money wouldn't make any difference."

LATE
Jeff Beck flies to the American West Coast to resume the tour.

The exact date is unclear, but Beck, Bogert & Appice videotape an appearance on the "In Concert" rock-show to be televised by ABC-TV on June 8. The recording is likely done before a special invited audience in the Los Angeles area in late April. The group performs fine versions of *Superstition* (Beck with tube in mouth) and *Morning Dew*; on the actual transmission the latter fades out with the credits rolling during Appice's drum solo. Besides a brief spot in a quasi-documentary called "The Trouble With Rock", the ABC-TV show is the only TV appearance by Beck, Bogert & Appice in the USA.

THU 26TH
BECK, BOGERT & APPICE:
SECOND NORTH AMERICAN TOUR:
SECOND LEG
Seattle Center Arena, Seattle, Washington

Beck, Bogert & Appice begin the second leg of their North American tour, which will concentrate exclusively on the West Coast and a solitary date in Hawaii. Tonight's concert is fully sold out, and Steely Dan is on the bill sandwiched between the regular opening act Wet Willie and Beck, Bogert & Appice.

FRI 27TH
Paramount Northwest Theater, Portland, Oregon

SAT 28TH AND SUN 29TH
Winterland, San Francisco, California

"Beck, Bogert & Appice hit the Winterland and had the packed audience on their feet from the opening number, *Superstition*. They played a set which teetered on the edge of greatness – but didn't quite make it all the way. After careful thought my own verdict is that despite the incredible virtuosity of the trio, personally I'd rather have had an hour of Beck alone", opines NEW MUSICAL EXPRESS's (May 19) US correspondent Larry Vilaubi. The crowd is satisfied though; an encore is followed by a five-minute standing ovation.

Black Oak Arkansas are also on the bill at Winterland.

MAY

TUE 1ST
San Jose Civic Auditorium, San Jose, California

WED 2ND
Robertson Gymnasium, University of California, Santa Barbara, California
Tower Of Power are added to tonight's concert.

THU 3RD
Hollywood Palladium, Los Angeles, California

Again with Tower of Power, this showcase concert is a near sell-out. Dennis Hunt in the LOS ANGELES TIMES (May 5) has a more balanced view than his colleague Richard Cromelin, who wrote an especially scathing review when Beck played the Palladium last August: "Many hard rock groups use excessive volume to mask their deficiencies. But this group need no such camouflage. It was refreshing to hear hard rock played with imagination and at a sensible volume. Their music was teeming with the kind of fascinating patterns, shifts and interchanges that are rarely heard in hard rock. Their finest number was their first – Stevie Wonder's majestic *Superstition*. I expected them to maul it somewhat, but they handled it gingerly and reverently."

Los Angeles is now temporarily besieged by UK musicians on tour. In town this week are Fairport Convention, Black Sabbath, Status Quo, Wishbone Ash, Humble Pie, Deep Purple, Rory Gallagher, Slade and Steeleye Span! Eric Burdon attends the Palladium concert in the company of NEW MUSICAL EXPRESS's Douglas Jones, who writes: "The band started off like they were going to rip the place apart, but in the end it wasn't one of their best sets. Brilliant musicians they are, but both Appice and Bogert seemed too anxious to prove solo dexterity at the wrong moments, and the set sagged. However, Beck proved conclusively why he is such an inspiration to so many guitarists."

For the last number, the crowd is rewarded with *Why Should I Care* where for once Beck, Bogert & Appice allow a guest on stage as Ray Kennedy comes on to share the lead vocals with Carmine. The trio then come back for an encore to play *Going Down* and the usual John Lee Hooker-inspired boogie.

FRI 4TH ✶
While in Los Angeles, Jeff also talks to Steve Rosen for features published in SOUNDS (July 7) and LOS ANGELES FREE PRESS (two parts; Deccember 7 and 14), plus a cover story in the prestigious GUITAR PLAYER (December 1973). Confusingly, the latter interview is also reprinted wholesale in the British BEAT INSTRUMENTAL as late as August 1976, credited to Rosen's alter ego Charles Stevenson. These interviews also form the basis for Rosen's Japanese-only book on Jeff Beck, published in 1978.

When Rosen wants to know if Beck, Bogert & Appice were formed to compete with Led Zeppelin, Beck counters: "There's no one that can compete with them. Once they've been elevated and sort of blown up to even half the size they are now, that was enough; no one could even get near them. Because the image becomes stronger than the music and then the music comes up to the level of the image and then you're off, you're on a home run. And therefore there's no way unless it happens to us which it won't because I've been 'round too long." Indeed, Led Zeppelin begin a US tour this very day at Braves Stadium in Atlanta, Georgia, playing before an utterly incredible 50,000 people for a quarter million dollars take at the box office.

The interviews touch on several other subjects, including his meeting with Jimmy Page ("I was most impressed with this guy; he used to play really fiery sort of fast stuff"), Jimi Hendrix ("It was kind of hard to grapple with that fucker") and his many groups past and present.

In parting, Beck tells Rosen in the GUITAR PLAYER story: "If the press would give me a chance I might come

May 5, 1973: David Bowie's "Aladdin Sane" follows the Faces' "Ooh La La" at the top of the UK album charts.

May 1973: Beck, Bogert & Appice tour Japan ...

up with something new. They might not realize it, but I play from emotion. I've never consciously tried to be flash. Emotion rules everything I do."

Also today, Charisma releases *Music From Free Creek* in Great Britain, a double album of songs from the 'super session' back in February 1970 which involved Jeff Beck and many others.

SAT 5TH
Sports Arena, San Diego, California
Besides playing San Diego tonight, Jeff reputedly also manages to travel the 80-odd miles to catch the end of Humble Pie's concert at the Forum in Los Angeles.

SUN 6TH
Long Beach Arena, Long Beach, California
Attendance at Long Beach is 7,320, resulting in a $36,549 gross.

TUE 8TH
Honolulu International Center Concert Hall, Honolulu, Hawaii
The highly successful North American tour ends in Hawaii today, the perfect starting point for Beck, Bogert & Appice's Far East foray.

"The show opened with a single blue spotlight shining on the large gong. A few minutes passed, and the group casually strolled on stage. Appice climbed behind his drums, hit the gong one time, smoke rose from below him, and Beck and Bogert led into *Superstition*, the Stevie Wonder song. From then on it was pure energy, from a group which is really all here, except for one thing – they desperately need a vocalist. Carmine, who handles most of the vocals, is a fine drummer, but he's got a voice that resembles something from a Grand Funk record. Bogert is a little worse, and Beck, well, he shouldn't even be allowed to have a mike in front of him", is Hank McMonigle's view in SUNBUMS (May 1973). Robert Knight, who later becomes friendly with Beck, is on hand to take photographs. Leon and Malia open the two shows in the HIC hall.

WED 9TH–THU 10TH
An Australian visit this May has been on the cards since early this year, but is at some point abandoned. Instead Beck, Bogert & Appice have some days off on the beach in Hawaii.

FRI 11TH
The group leaves Hawaii on a 4.00 pm flight for Japan.

SAT 12TH
BECK, BOGERT & APPICE: FIRST JAPANESE TOUR
Beck, Bogert & Appice arrive on flight JAL-001 from Hawaii at Haneda airport, Tokyo, at 7.25 pm local time. The three then check into the city's Takanawa Prince Hotel.

This is Jeff's first visit to Japan, but he has enjoyed a very good standing here for several years: When Beck's profile was at an all-time low in England and America in early 1971, he still topped the popularity stakes for 'Best Guitarist' (with Eric Clapton and Jimmy Page) in the Japanese pop magazine MUSIC LIFE.

SUN 13TH
A day for shopping and sight-seeing.

MON 14TH
Nippon Budokan Hall, Tokyo, Japan
After a soundcheck at 2.00 pm, Beck, Bogert & Appice go on stage at 6.30 pm without a support act.

As this is Beck's first appearance in Japan, the Tokyo-audience is treated to an expanded set tonight including a resurrection of the old Dylan/Mayfield medley *Tonight I'll Be Staying Here With You* and *People Get Ready*. A rousing version of *Jeff's Boogie* is also performed, which is kept tight and brief like on the recent American tour with no extended middle part for Jeff to improvise. The ecstatic Japanese crowd is awarded with two encores after the final song (*Why Should I Care*); first *Plynth/Shotgun* plus *Going Down*, before the trio reappears to play *Oleo* coupled with the usual boogie-antics – today highlighted by a brief *Train Kept A-Rollin'* with even a full verse sung by Carmine. All in all,

the show clocks in at close to 110 minutes, quite unusual for Beck, Bogert & Appice, who usually keep their sets to a mere 70–75 minutes.

TUE 15TH
A day set aside for publicity.

WED 16TH
Shi-Kokaido, Nagoya, Japan
At noon Beck, Bogert & Appice leave Tokyo on the Superexpress Hikari 35 and travel to Nagoya. Here the group checks in at the International Hotel Nagoya. Tonight's concert begins at 6.30 pm, and again there is no support act.

THU 17TH
Another day with travelling. At 1.03 pm the trio boards the Superexpress Hikari 33 and travels to Osaka, where they stay at the Royal Hotel.

FRI 18TH
Koseinenkin Hall, Osaka, Japan
After an afternoon off, Beck, Bogert & Appice play the first of two nights at the Koseinenkin Hall, commencing at 7.00 pm. Both concerts in Osaka are recorded by engineers Kenicki Handa and Tomoo Suzuki for a live album to be released exclusively for the Japanese market some months later.

SAT 19TH
Koseinenkin Hall, Osaka, Japan
The concerts in Japan show Beck, Bogert & Appice perhaps at their peak, still enjoying it and playing well to enthusiastic audiences. "We flattened Japan; they loved it", Jeff says matter-of-factly years later.

Carmine Appice's sense of theatrics causes pandemonium: at the end of the drum solo, with the kit shrouded in smoke, he quietly slips off the stool while a pre-recorded tape with a drum track is filtered through the PA. When the smoke clears, the drums keep playing with Appice gone!

SUN 20TH
Beck, Bogert & Appice go their separate ways again for a three week rest. In the afternoon Tim and Carmine board JAL-006 at Haneda for New York, while Jeff takes flight JAL-443 back to London.

Japan has been an unqualified success, and Jeff will return here many times in later years to perform for a loyal fan following.

MON 28TH
Inexplicably, Epic in the States decides to release *I'm So Proud* backed

---

Single
BECK, BOGERT & APPICE
A: I'M SO PROUD (*Curtis Mayfield*)
B: OH TO LOVE YOU (*Beck/Bogert/Appice*)

Released May 28, 1973 (US Epic 10998)
Personnel as on album *Jeff Beck, Tim Bogert, Carmine Appice*.
Recorded at Chess Studios, 2120 South Michigan Avenue, Chicago, Illinois, (A), December 1972 and Village Recorders, Los Angeles, January 1973 + unknown studio, December 1972 (B)
Produced by Don Nix and the Boys
Highest Chart Position US: –

May 28, 1973: Founding member Ronnie Lane quits the Faces. He emerges a few months later with his own group Slim Chance.

July 1973: Jeff Beck joins David Bowie on stage in London ...

with *Oh To Love You* today, two weeks after Beck, Bogert & Appice have finished their biggest tour of America yet. Although the *Jeff Beck, Tim Bogert, Carmine Appice* album is still riding high in the American charts (at #22 in CASHBOX this week), but with no support from a tour, the single goes nowhere.

JUNE

FRI 8TH
BECK, BOGERT & APPICE:
SECOND EUROPEAN TOUR
Musikhalle, Hamburg, West Germany
Beck, Bogert & Appice reunite for some concerts in Europe which will also cover the annual rock festival circuit on the Continent. Well-oiled from the American and Japanese tours in the spring, the trio seemingly plays tonight's warm-up concert without further rehearsals despite having had three weeks off. Anyway, the set list for the European jaunt is basically a repeat from Japan, so the Bob Dylan/Curtis Mayfield medley is included again.

Meanwhile in the States, Beck, Bogert & Appice are featured in a pre-taping on "In Concert" on ABC Network TV tonight (11.30–1 am, ▶ late April). John Kay (ex-Steppenwolf singer and frontman), Grass Roots, T Rex and Johnny Nash are also on the programme.

SAT 9TH
"1. Summer Rock Festival"
Waldbühne, West Berlin,
West Germany
After Hamburg, Beck, Bogert & Appice play two festivals as part of the Whitsun holiday, where all the acts just swap days. Some of the names appearing over the weekend include Thin Lizzy, Nazareth, Chicken Shack, Family, Golden Earring, the Groundhogs, Uriah Heep, McKendree Spring from the States, and the Dutch group Long Tall Ernie. Attendance is 6,000.

Strangely enough, Beck, Bogart & Appice's powerful music and live act directly cause the break-up of the popular British rock band Family. Their drummer Rob Townsend recounts to MOJO in August 1996: "We played a festival in West Germany, and had to follow Beck, Bogert & Appice, who were absolutely stunning. The set knocked everybody sideways. We said that we once had played with that passion and that fire and we weren't doing it now. Perhaps it's time we called it a day ... Mind you, the next night the billing was changed and we had to follow them, and we blew the arse off them."

SUN 10TH
"1. Summer Rock Festival"
Radrennbahn, Frankfurt,
West Germany
The second day of the German Whitsun festival, where the ten groups who yesterday performed in Berlin all play Frankfurt today, at a huge bike-racing-track, which attracts a crowd of 12,000 at a 20 Deutsche Marks admission. Beck, Bogert & Appice are the highest paid act of the festival, and appear for a fee of 15,000 DM (roughly £3,000 or about $8,500).

MON 11TH
"Pink Pop Festival"
Voetballstadion, Burgermeester
Damenssportpark, Geleen, Holland
Beck, Bogert & Appice fly on to Holland to appear in front of 30,000 people at the fourth annual 'Pink Pop Festival' in Holland. Besides Alquin (a Dutch group who steals the show according to the local press), the otherwise heavily-British bill runs thus: Stealer's Wheel (incidentally now with Jeff's old drummer Rod Coombes!), Fairport Convention, Colin Blunstone, Wishbone Ash and finally Beck, Bogert & Appice. Constant Meijers, covering the festival in MUZIEKKRANT OOR (June 20), finds BBA uneven and lacking in structure despite a strong opening *(Superstition)* but with too long drum and bass solos. But Jeff's show-stopper never fails to deliver: "That Beck is the best guitarist, was proved loudly in *Jeff's Boogie*, with which he ended his performance."

TUE 12TH–WED 13TH
Beck and band arrive in Paris in time to see John McLaughlin's Mahavishnu Orchestra playing at the Olympia on the Wednesday. Jeff and Carmine spend some time socializing with the Mahavishnu members, and Beck gets to meet Jan Hammer, the group's Czech-American keyboard player.

THU 14TH
Olympia Theatre, Paris, France
In the afternoon before the show, Jeff and Carmine (Tim Bogert chooses to sleep) speak to Claude-Alvarez Pereyre of ROCK & FOLK (August 1973). Much of the talk centres around John McLaughlin. Asked what he thinks of the Mahavishnu Orchestra, Jeff replies: "It is very good, the technique. It is the least 'dancable' music that exists! To listen to, to watch – wow! That's fantastic." Pereyre wants to know if the group will begin working on a new album after the tour? "No, I will rest. I have been invited to a concert by David Bowie, where I'll go," replies Jeff. "As musician?" Pereyre wants to know. "No, as a spectator," assures Beck.

BEST (August 1973) runs a review of Beck & Co's Olympia concert: "They enter in the dark ... Just a voice, alone, that syncopates the words 'top-ti-ta-ta-tip-ta-ta' and the guitar springs into action on the intro to *Superstition*. A crash, then under the spotlights: Jeff Beck, Tim Bogert and Carmine Appice have begun their concert at the Olympia." The reporter, Christian Lebrun, is disappointed by the repeat of the basic set list from the Bataclan show in February. "Beck, Bogert & Appice play with a high standard but without strong material they do not reach the sublime which their collective talent would suggest. Difficulties with the compositions? Too much confidence in the jams, in the improvisation? There is a problem with Beck, Bogert & Appice." Alain Wais in EXTRA (August 1973): "The music of BBA is the forceful music of a group who radiates energy without reserves ... At last a real hard rock group whose only strength lies in its music."

The Olympia concert is also recorded for a broadcast (date unknown) on the French radio show "Musicorama" (Europe 1).

SAT 16TH
Beck, Bogert & Appice's European tour should culminate today as one of the headliners at the summery 'Garden Party' in London. The 'garden parties' in Crystal Palace Park have been an annual occurence for a couple of years, but this year promoter Michael Alfandry has run into trouble with local residents, who have complained of excessive noise. Although permission has been granted by the Greater London Council Parks Department months previously, complaints from residents were raised in mid-May, resulting in today's cancellation. An al-

July 1973: Beck abruptly leaves US tour forcing cancellation of dates ...

ternative venue is being sought out, but with little time to go it is decided to call it off. Ultimately, later in June, a public hearing is held, and Alfandry is then allowed to stage a concert at the Crystal Park in September.

A pity as today's concert is also set to feature Focus, John McLaughlin's Mahavishnu Orchestra, Ten Years After, and John Sebastian besides Beck, Bogert & Appice. With Jeff back in England and a cancellation, Bogert and Appice fly home.

JULY

TUE 3RD

Jeff Beck joins David Bowie & the Spiders From Mars onstage at the Hammersmith Odeon in London. He is cajoled on stage by Bowie as a gesture to the Spiders' guitarist Mick Ronson, who is an ardent Beck fan. In fact, the two have become well-acquainted lately, going round to each others' houses. Jeff comes on towards the end of the show for a jam on Bowie's *The Jean Genie* (which actually is a rewrite of the Yardbirds' version of Bo Diddley's *I'm A Man!*), which includes a brief snippet of the old Beatles' hit *Love Me Do*. Then Bowie leads the collective ensemble into Chuck Berry's classic *Around And Around*. After trading solos with Ronson, Jeff pulls out the voice bag cheered on by a grinning Bowie.

David Bowie is now at the zenith of his commercial career, and this concert attains legend-status because Bowie announces the retirement of his alter-ego Ziggy Stardust after the last encore tonight. The whole concert is filmed for posterity by D.A. Pennebaker, later televised as "Bowie '73" in the States on October 25, 1974.

Beck also attends the post-show party held at the Cafe Royal on Regent Street, where he ends up at the same table as Bowie, Mick Jagger and Lou Reed. Also attending the party (whose guestlist resembles one of the many early sixties nights-on-the-town Jeff enjoyed) are Lulu, Paul McCartney, Ringo Starr and Keith Moon, while Dr. John provides the music.

Interestingly, immediately after the burial of Ziggy Stardust, David Bowie travels to France to record a personal tribute to the Swinging Sixties. The resulting album, *Pin-Ups*, will contain two Yardbirds associated songs; *I Wish You Would* and a remake of *Shapes of Things*.

TUE 10TH ✱

Jeff Beck flies to the American East Coast to begin a hastily-arranged tour with Bogert and Appice. Whereas the spring tour was both well-planned and well-publicized, the coming North American tour is put together very quickly and consequently receives little if any pre-tour publicity.

WED 11TH
BECK, BOGERT & APPICE: THIRD NORTH AMERICAN TOUR
The Spectrum, Philadelphia, Pennsylvania

A short Stateside tour commences today, visiting points on the East Coast and the South not covered on the massive spring tour. New Orleans' own Dr. John, the so called Night Tripper, is 'special guest' on this tour. Excitingly, Dr. John is also briefly involved as a lyricist in the pre-planning stages of the trio's upcoming album, but unfortunately this amounts to nothing.

A reason for this tour is surely also the demand from the lucrative US market, where the *Jeff Beck, Tim Bogert, Carmine Appice* album this week is at #27 in the CASHBOX charts. Manager Phil Basile's idea of a successful rock group is based on touring and yet more touring, a simple strategy with which the road-tested Bogert and Appice find no problem. Indeed, today's sold-out concert grosses an impressive $110,000, possibly the biggest take at the box office the trio will ever do. Despite the strong sales, all is not well within the BBA-camp, and Beck particularly is getting weary and restless.

Travelling with the band is Clive Coulson. This American tour also marks the arrival of Ralph Baker, who is employed by the British P.A. company the group uses on this tour. A while later Baker is hired by Ernest Chapman as his assistant and right hand man, a position he holds to this very day.

THU 12TH
Charlotte Park Centre, Charlotte, North Carolina

FRI 13TH
Curtis Hixon Hall, Tampa, Florida

SAT 14TH
Speedway Sportatorium, Hollywood, Florida

"Rock 'n' roll may be subject to stylistic fads at any moment, ranging from reggae to Elizabethan pop, but Saturday night at the Hollywood Sportatorium outside Miami, Jeff Beck proved once again that the guitar is still king ... Beck, Bogert & Appice moved the Sportatorium crowd with a relentless serving of hard rock, played with a professionalism befitting the group. ... Their set began with Stevie Wonder's *Superstition* and a Beck guitar-vocal that can only be categorized as bizarre. Having seen him play the guitar behind his back, and having watched the late Jimi Hendrix pick out guitar solos with his mouth, I thought the range of unusual approaches had just about been exhausted. But, no, there Beck was, with a plastic tube running from mouth to guitar frets, singing through his contraption, producing an effect that was eerie, and that proved again how wrong you can be," writes R. J. Dewhurst in MIAMI HERALD two days later.

SUN 15TH
Merriweather Post Pavillion, Columbia, Maryland

The box office gross suffers from a concert being promoted only two week in advance, according to the music trade-paper AMUSEMENT BUSINESS. Tonight's potential is $48,000 at this outdoor venue that has a 14,000-capacity, but Beck, Bogert & Appice and Dr. John's performance only grosses $35,700.

MON 16TH
Municipal Auditorium, Atlanta, Georgia

Although this is no less than Jeff Beck's fifteenth tour of the United States since 1965, this is his first performance in Atlanta – a point not missed by the ad in today's paper which trumpets 'First Time In Atlanta!' As it

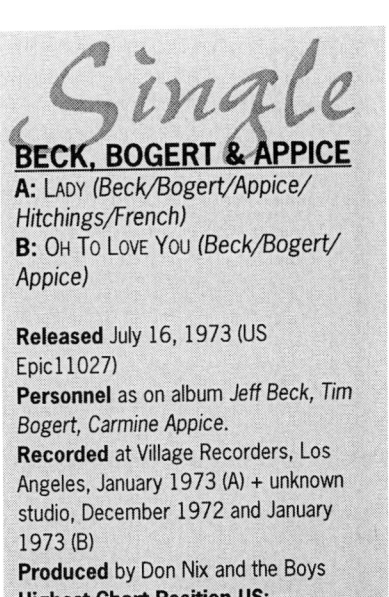

Single
BECK, BOGERT & APPICE
A: LADY *(Beck/Bogert/Appice/ Hitchings/French)*
B: OH TO LOVE YOU *(Beck/Bogert/ Appice)*

Released July 16, 1973 (US Epic 11027)
Personnel as on album *Jeff Beck, Tim Bogert, Carmine Appice*.
Recorded at Village Recorders, Los Angeles, January 1973 (A) + unknown studio, December 1972 and January 1973 (B)
Produced by Don Nix and the Boys
Highest Chart Position US: –

© July 15, 1973: Ray Davies announces he will leave the Kinks while onstage at London's White City Festival, although he will return to the band weeks later.

July 1973: London concert cancelled after Bogert's motorbike accident ...

turns out, not only is this Jeff's first time in Atlanta but it is also his last concert of the present tour.

Perhaps realizing that *Superstition* would not stand a chance after Stevie Wonder's momentous hit earlier in the year, Epic instead releases *Lady* today as the second single from the LP. (Despite contrary claims, *Superstition* is not released in the States. It was, however, issued in Japan in May.)

TUE 17TH ✱

Abruptly, Jeff Beck decides to jump ship and return home, even if the tour is not finished. The reasons for Jeff's decision remain unclear; in MELODY MAKER later in July, Carmine Appice offers an unelaborated excuse about Jeff being summoned home by personal trouble. Bogert and Appice are dumbfounded by Beck's departure, and further concerts are cancelled as a result of Jeff's vanishing act. These are Civic Center, Houston, Texas (July 19), Municipal Auditorium, San Antonio, Texas (July 20) State Fair Coliseum, Dallas, Texas (July 21) and Convention Center Complex, Denver, Colorado (July 24) – likely the final scheduled date of the tour.

THU 19TH

Stopping over in New York on his way home, Jeff Beck reputedly attends the second of the Mahavishnu Orchestra's two days in Central Park. Carmine Appice has apparently come to New York, too, and is with Jeff today. This concert will be a real eye-opener for Jeff, where he sees for himself how complex, high energy instrumental music can indeed cross over to the general public.

SUN 22ND

Tim Bogert is involved in a motorbike accident today, suffering a broken foot and ankle, which confines him to bed for two weeks: "I slid off the bike at forty miles an hour on the beach at Long Island. I went flying through the air swearing all the profanities I ever knew."

MON 23RD

Bogert and Appice have booked a flight to London today, to enable the trio to do some rehearsals before their headlining appearance in London on Sunday 29, but with Tim in bed, Carmine flies over alone.

SUN 29TH

A 10-day long 'London Music Festival' is held at the Alexandra Palace between July 27th and August 5th, and Beck, Bogert & Appice are booked as today's star attraction. The Ally Pally bill is rounded out by Back Door, Beckett and Earth & Fire. However, due to the recent injuries sustained by Bogert, the trio is forced to withdraw. The concert goes ahead as planned anyway, with Silverhead and Flash filling in for Beck, Bogert & Appice at short notice.

MON 30TH

With cancelled dates both in the States and in England, rumours spread of a break-up in Beck, Bogert & Appice. To put matters right, Appice talks with MELODY MAKER today and the paper reports on August 4: "People say Beck is back to his old tricks again because we cancelled some gigs in the States, but it is not really like that at all. They are telling stories that Beck, Bogert & Appice have broken up, but that's a load of crap. We are still together." Appice even informs MELODY MAKER that he and Beck will do some test recordings with a stand-in bassplayer, and says half-jokingly that they hope to work with Mickie Most on their next album, because Most got such a good guitar sound on *Truth* and *Beck-Ola*.

AUGUST

With Bogert convalescing and the group's immediate plans put on hold, Carmine Appice also collapses while in Wisconsin in mid-August and is rushed to hospital suffering from pneumonia.

With two-thirds of his group confined to bed, Jeff remains at home. Turning his attention elsewhere, he is assigned as producer for a newly formed trio called Upp, who record their first album at Escape Studios this month. Upp is made up of two members from the progressive rock group Clark-Hutchinson; Andi Clark (keyboards) and Stephen Amazing (bass) plus drummer Jim Copley (ex-Spreadeagle). Their music is described as symphonic soul funk, and Jeff adds healthy doses of guitar to their album in the works.

Jeff further partakes in sessions for American jazz-cum-blues electric saxophonist Eddie Harris, who records an album with a series of British musicians at Morgan Studios in Willesden, including Ian Paice, Steve Winwood, Rick Grech, Carl Palmer and Yes-men Chris Squire and Alan White. Beck is particularly pleased to work together with Albert Lee, a British country-style guitarist he rates highly. The sessions strech over two weeks into early September, and Jeff plays guitar on the tracks *He's An Island Man* and *I've Tried Everything* on the album *Eddie Harris In The UK* (UK Atlantic/US Atco), released spring 1974.

It is believed too that Jeff's unusually vigorous activity as studio guitarist this month also covers a session for the obscure American singer Dorian Passante. Passante, once of New York group Sweet Dirt, arrived in London the previous month to form a group to be called Zero. Talking to MELODY MAKER in July, Passante says: "Sweet Dirt were rivals to New York Dolls ... David Bowie was interested in some of their songs ... It seems like England is three years ahead of New York. Just as Bowie is breaking over there, he's retiring here. I'm looking for a record deal and I'll be forming a band as soon as I get settled in."

Little is known about the actual sessions other than that Beck plays on at least a song called *Inside Looking Out* and possibly another title called *Destination Nowhere*. Finally, in 1977, the album *Dorian Passante Zero* (US Amerama) is released including Jeff's contributions.

MON 13TH

The BBC "In Concert" appearance (► June 29, 1972) is syndicated in major markets throughout the US as "The BBC Presents".

TUE 14TH

Chris Spedding and the Sharks play the Marquee, and Jeff is at the bar.

SAT 25TH

Jeff hangs around backstage at the annual Reading Festival (which has replaced the old National Jazz & Blues Festival in Richmond), while Rod Stewart & the Faces are among the many groups who appear on stage. Also in the backstage area are Eric Clapton, Donovan, George Harrison, Peter Frampton and Keith Moon.

•

Although Jeff Beck and Keith Moon never were close friends, Jeff enjoys Moon's company: "[I]f he was in the Speak, you knew it was worth going, even if it was a long way off." Interviewed by Tony Fletcher for the Keith Moon biography 'Dear Boy' in 1997, Jeff remembers a particular crazy weekend spent at Moon's house Tara in the autumn of 1973. The weekend begins at the Speakeasy, where Moon tries to sell Beck a useless

Ⓜ August 23-25, 1973: This year's Reading Festival stars among others Traffic, Focus, Eric Burdon – and the Faces.

September 1973: Beck, Bogert & Appice a success at Crystal Palace ...

hot-rod, "a disaster on wheels". Beck is then invited to stay the weekend at Tara, which involves sight-seeing, drinking, talking and chauffeuring Keith and a girlfriend around Staines in a white Rolls Royce Corniche culminating in a near-crash in a roundabout. Being with Keith Moon could be an exhausting experience, too, as Jeff explains: "The jokes were coming out like rain, and I was thinking 'I have to remember this line', because he doesn't even know how funny it is. But thinking 'I don't know how much more of that I could withstand', because after you've laughed for half an hour you don't have any other form of expression. My jaws were aching ... it was pretty intense."

SEPTEMBER

SAT 1ST

A short three-date US tour by Beck, Bogert & Appice over the popular Labor Day weekend – set to commence with a festival appearance today in Benton, Tennessee – is optimistically announced despite Appice's illness. However, 'The Midwest Monster Peace Jubilee and Musical Festival' – which tentatively has also booked Black Oak Arkansas, Canned Heat, Dr. John and Edgar Winter among others – proves hopelessly unrealistic and is never staged and the two other proposed US concerts by Beck, Bogert & Appice also fall through.

MON 3RD–FRI 14TH✴

For the first time since the curtailed American tour in mid-July, Beck, Bogert & Appice get together again. Although the trio were on the brink of collapsing six weeks ago, it is decided to give it another go. While they have been apart all three have had the opportunity to get involved in other projects – Beck doing sessions while the bassist and the drummer have recorded an album with Jan Akkerman at Atlantic in New York – when they reconvene in London in the beginning of September. Here they enter Apple Studios at 2 Savile Row, to begin work on a second album, and helping the group out is engineer John Mills. At a relaxed tempo, the band tape at least three songs at Apple and also spend time simply rehearsing for upcoming concerts, including the Crystal Palace happening in mid-September.

Three of the selections taped are the ballad *Got To Find My Woman* (featuring lyrics by Carmine Appice), the Staple Singers' tune *Missing Word* (aka *Prayin'*) and finally the key-piece *Jizz Whizz*; an instrumental showcase that actually is an extension of the middle-section of *Morning Dew* with origins stretching back to the Max Middleton-era Beck Group.

Studio time is also used to invite the music press, and Charles Shaar Murray portrays the group for a story in NEW MUSICAL EXPRESS (September 29). Of *Jizz Whizz*, Beck points out to Murray: "Basically, we're known for playing rather than specific songs, so we felt that doing an instrumental would allow people to hear what they want to hear – us playing."

At this stage, they are producing themselves. Different producers have been considered including Rick Derringer, Mick Ronson and Jeffrey Haskell (who has worked with both Cactus and the J. Geils Band), but because of conflicting interests and schedules, none of the applicants work out.

SAT 15TH
"Celebration Garden Party"
Crystal Palace Bowl, London

After the cancelled summer concert at the Crystal Palace in June, this MELODY MAKER-sponsored event is rescheduled for today. The final bill – which has been changed right up until a week before the concert – finally features, in running order, Golden Earring, Back Door, Tony Joe White, Beck, Bogert & Appice, Lou Reed and James Taylor with the Section.

While the concert attracts more than 15,000 people, the general feeling in the music press is one of anticlimax. However, Beck, Bogert & Appice manage a strong performance, and it is Jeff Beck who steals the cover of MELODY MAKER (September 22) the following week under the caption

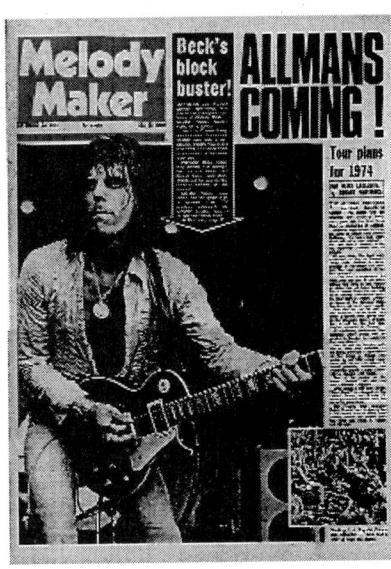

'Beck's Block Buster!' MELODY MAKER reports: "And there was Beck, open-necked blue shirt knotted at the navel, looking cocky, as the licks flipped out ... A good portion of the crowd had obviously come to see this band alone." Pete Erskine of SOUNDS (September 22) seconds this opinion, writing: "Beck really appears to be confident and at ease. His playing was sharp and dazzling and his vocals – channeled by way one of those vocal wah-wah attachments – were quite filthy sounding." NEW MUSICAL EXPRESS' (September 22) Nick Kent notes "Beck, Bogert & Appice ... arguably stole the show. Nothing really creative went down but we were all treated to a grandiose demonstration of advanced rock 'n' roll." The praise is not unanimous however, as DISC'S (September 22) reviewer sums up "generally while they weren't dreadful, they were not particularly good." Their setlist, devoid of any surprises, includes the for-the-occasion-only encore *Crystal Palace Boogie*.

MON 17TH–FRI 21ST✴

After a fortnight at Apple Studios, Beck, Bogert & Appice shift operation to De Lane Lea's no. 2 studio in Wembley, where Chris Welch of MELODY MAKER is on hand to comment on the sessions and for an interview (September 29). The previous weeks' attempts at Apple have not proved satisfactory and the tapes are being salvaged with overdubs and new mixes. Two of the songs being worked on at De Lane Lea are *Jizz Whizz* and *Got To Find My Woman*. A version of the latter finds the first recorded example of Jeff with his voice bag contraption. The bag is still a novelty, not having been used on record by many guitarists to date, barring a few scattered examples. Besides the

September 19, 1973: Country-rock singer/songwriter Gram Parsons dies in Joshua Tree, California.

October 1973: Recording sessions in London for second BBA album ...

basic guitar–bass–drums, Max Middleton is on hand to tinkle piano on an unspecified track.

FRI 21ST
The Japan-only *Beck, Bogert & Appice Live in Japan* is released today. A concert souvenir assembled from the two nights at Osaka in May this year, the album is a faithful presentation of their stage act if rather flatly produced and lacking the ambience of a real live concert. Somewhat confusingly, the resulting double album is not sequenced as the regular live shows.

The running order is as follows: (Side one:) *Superstition, Lose Myself With You, Jeff's Boogie,* (Side two:) *Going Down, Boogie, Morning Dew;* (Side three:) *Sweet, Sweet Surrender, Livin' Alone, I'm So Proud;* (Side four:) *Black Cat Moan, Why Should I Care, Plynth/Shotgun.* Although not one of their top-notch shows, there are several guitar high points: A lyrical solo in *Sweet, Sweet Surrender* rich on harmonic pinches, a startling slide performance on *Livin' Alone* atop Appice's busy drumming, a roof-raising *Jeff's Boogie,* and a brilliant solo on the closing number *Why Should I Care,* where Jeff Beck fuses regular blues phrases with Django Reinhardt-style half-tone runs culminating in a tremolo-effect created by flipping the pick-up switch rapidly on/off. (The record is never issued commercially in other markets and has only been available in the US and Europe as a Japanese import.)

SAT 22ND AND SUN 23RD
Beck, Bogert & Appice are poised to appear at a two-day '3rd British Rock Meeting' festival at Sandreenbahn Altrip, Ludwigshafen, in West Germany along with Pink Floyd, Frank Zappa And the Mothers of Invention, Lou Reed, Wishbone Ash, Genesis, the Sensational Alex Harvey Band, Back Door and the Electric Light Orchestra. However, this ambitious festival never gets off the ground.

MON 24TH–FRI 28TH✻
Next, sessions continue at Escape Studios in Kent, conveniently just a hop, skip and jump down from Jeff's Egerton home. Recordings include further refinements of *Jizz Whizz*. Pete Erskine of SOUNDS visits the group for a feature here (dated September 29).

SAT 29TH
Beck, Bogert & Appice are voted 'Brightest Hope' in the 'International Section' of MELODY MAKER's annual 'Pop Poll'. Despite this strong showing, Beck does not make the list of the top-ten guitarists in the same poll.

OCTOBER

MON 1ST✻
Jeff Beck, Tim Bogert and Carmine Appice attend MELODY MAKER's 1973 Pop Poll Party held at the Global Village, a club by the Strand in London.

Succumbing to an instant bout of stage fright (likely embarassment by being voted a 'bright hope' after almost ten years in the music business!), Jeff lets Tim and Carmine accept the award on behalf of the trio. The usual array of stars and music-biz folks show up at the ceremony, including Ahmet Ertegun, George Melly (who is also the show's compère), Robert Plant, Rick Wakeman, Jan Akkerman, and Maggie Bell.

TUE 2ND–FRI 12TH✻
During the two first weeks of October, Beck, Bogert & Appice patiently keep up work on their new album. It is now decided to call in experienced engineer Andy Johns to come in with a fresh pair of ears. According to NEW MUSICAL EXPRESS, the early October sessions find the group briefly returning to De Lane Lea besides rounding things up at Escape.

Beck, Bogert & Appice have now roughly finished a whole album, with about ten tracks in the can. Besides *Jizz Whizz, Got To Find My Woman* and *Missing Word* (aka *Prayin'*), the sessions yield the group composition *Solid Lifter* (another instrumental based on a simple ascending chord progression), the funky *Satisfied* (complete with female backing vocals), *All In Your Mind, Laughalong* (aka *Laughin' Lady* or *Song For Lovely Ladies,* this is a soulful ballad with Tim Bogert on double bass), *Get Ready Your Lovemaker's Comin' Home* (reputedly penned by Gloria Jones), and finally *Living Life Backwards* (an old Piblokto! song written by Pete Brown, Jim Mullen and Roger Bunn). Again, material is the recurring problem, with melodies and lyrics being scrounged from different sources. Lyricist Pete Brown supplies words for a group composition called *Getting Somewhere, Getting Nowhere,* which does not get beyond the demo stage. Singer Pete French, who received a writing credit on the group's first album, is also roped in to assist with lyrics. Seemingly, Jeff's protégés in Upp are also contributing to the sessions in an unspecified role.

No one is satisfied with the resulting tapes, and in the latter half of October the group decides to take another month-long break. The three weeks spent recording at Escape have proved especially troublesome, and looking back on the sessions a month-and-a-half later, Tim Bogert jokes: "We couldn't have cut a Troggs track and made it sound like anything, Tommy James & the Shondells could've cut us apart!" Although the intention is to get away from the city and record in a rural setting, the attraction of the countryside soon loses its impact on Bogert in particular. To relieve their boredom, the trio spend time "wrecking Corvettes and Jaguar E-types" according to CIRCUS. With this, further recordings are curtailed and Beck, Bogert & Appice take one of their customary breaks.

Talking to RECORD & RADIO MIRROR's John Beattie (October 13), Jeff explains: "[The new album] is in the very early stages at the moment, we've been to three different studios partly because of the unavailability of time and partly because of the failure to get a particular sound." Despite their recent setback and surviving an almost-split, Jeff now confidently enthuses: "I believe that this band has more potential, we have the ability to knock off things that we wouldn't have done in other groups. Our stuff is pretty filthy and violent on stage, but not offensively violent, just dynamic."

•

While winding up sessions with his own band, Jeff also plays guitar for Michael Fennelly at CBS Studios on Whitfield Street, London this month. Fennelly, an American who used to play with the groups Millenium and Crabby Appleton, is in Britain to record an album produced by Argent sideman Chris White. Beck plays guitar on *Watch Yourself, Shine A Light, Touch My Soul* and *Give Me Your Money,* that wind up on Fennelly's June 1974 album *Lane Changer* (UK Epic/US Epic). In fact, Beck also sings uncredited backing vocals on *Touch My Soul*.

Furthermore, Jeff is also marginally involved in sessions for an album by Hummingbird, the group featuring his old ex-sidemen Max Middleton, Clive Chaman and Bobby Tench. The group is completed by guitarist Bernie Holland and drummer Conrad Isadore. Their eponymous album *Hummingbird* (UK A&M/US A&M) is cut at Island during September–October (although it got underway as early as mid-July at Apple and CBS) and released in July, 1974.

November 1973: Beck, Bogert & Appice on tour in France and Belgium ...

MON 15TH
Jeff conducts a telephone interview with the Japanese trade magazine MUSIC LIFE, for a short feature published in the magazine's December issue, discussing Andy Johns' involvement with the new album.

NOVEMBER

MID*
Beck, Bogert & Appice reconvene for a short tour of the Continent, their first proper tour since July.

WED 21ST
BECK, BOGERT & APPICE:
THIRD CONTINENTAL TOUR
Salle de Fêtes, Fâches-Thumesnil, Lille, France

Fâches-Thumesnil is a small town about 5 miles from Lille in the north of France and is the opening night of the Continental tour, which effectively will only cover France and a single date in Belgium, and is viewed as a warm-up for a full-scale British tour in the new year and a chance for Beck, Bogert & Appice to get their chops back together before further studio visits. No reports on the repertoire exist from this little-documented tour.

Ralph Baker has now joined Beck's entourage full-time.

THU 22ND
Tonight's booked appearance at L'Théâtre Du Châtelet in Paris is cancelled at the very last moment because of "dangerous malfunction in the house electrical system", to cite a spokesman for the tour. After the French band Triangle have finished their set, Beck, Bogert & Appice's equipment is rigged but nothing further happens. Finally, at almost 11 pm, it is Ralph Baker who is given the unfortunate task of calling off the concert after Beck and his cohorts refuse to go on. The impatient audience nearly riots, but a confrontation is avoided at the last minute.

Commenting on the cancellation in an editorial in ROCK & FOLK, journalist Herve Muller puts the blame on the theatre management, and understands Jeff's fear of unsafe equipment, reminding his readers of Stone The Crows' guitarist Les Harvey's accidental death on stage the previous year due to a faulty microphone.

FRI 23RD
Palais des Sports, Besançon, France
Tim Bogert uses this gig as a prime example on how the special Beck, Bogert & Appice synergy works: "We had to drive 400 and odd miles in rotten traffic in France to get to Bordeaux and by the time I got to the gig it was time to walk on stage I just had so much nervous energy inside me ... we went out and the band screamed."

SUN 25TH
Forest National, Brussels, Belgium

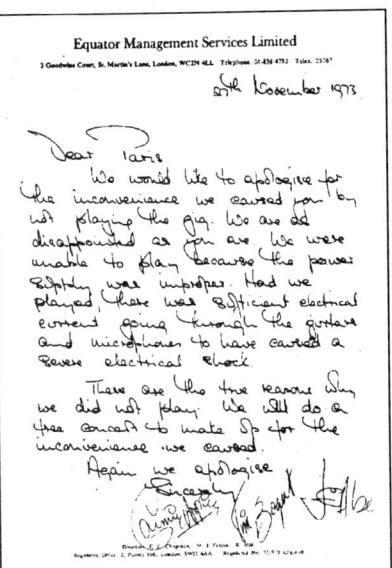

TUE 27TH
Palais D'Hiver, Lyon*, France
The exact location of tonight's venue is unconfirmed, but is belived to be in Lyon.

Plagued by a bad reputation in the aftermath of their cancelled Paris concert, Jeff, Tim And Carmine hastily write a 'we're sorry'-letter, which is printed in EXTRA (February 1974). Furthermore, on behalf of the group, Bogert and Appice write a letter of apology to France's leading music magazine ROCK & FOLK, published in January 1974, promising a make-up concert in France in the very near future.

THU 29TH
By Thanksgiving, the threesome go their own ways, with Bogert and Appice returning to the States and Beck to England.

DECEMBER

EARLY*
At the beginning of December, Beck, Bogert & Appice regroup again for a quick week's rehearsing and recording preparations at Beck's place in Egerton. Andy Johns has by now suggested hiring Jimmy Miller as producer, well-known for his work with Traffic and the Rolling Stones. Actually, Miller and Beck have crossed paths before as he also was on hand for the trial sessions for *Rough And Ready* in April 1971.

MON 10TH–FRI 21ST*
From the middle of December right up till Christmas, Beck, Bogert & Appice record and rehearse at another CBS facility, this one at 73 New Bond Street in London. Jimmy Miller and Andy Johns are employed in the control-room.

The sessions run smoothly at first, as confirmed by a pleased Tim Bogert in the SOUNDS 'Talk-In', published December 29: "[Miller and Johns] are good, really good. They're getting the sound I wish we'd had on our first album." Still, even if they get "more done in eight days at CBS than three weeks at Escape" to cite MELODY MAKER, but despite Bogert's enthusiasm, Beck is not totally comfortable with Jimmy Miller, finding the producer's role as too passive.

•

A Jeff Beck interview, conducted by Steve Rosen in Los Angeles in June, runs as cover story of the December edition of GUITAR PLAYER magazine – the first of five times, amazingly spread over a period of twenty years. A testimony to Beck's status as a guitarist. (Later cover stories appear in October 1980, November 1985, February 1990 and finally April 1993.)

CHRISTMAS
Beck, Bogert & Appice take a Yuletide break, with Bogert and Appice customarily going home to the States while Jeff stays put in England.

Around Christmas, Jeff Ward from MELODY MAKER talks to Beck for a story printed in the paper's January 5, 1974 edition. Ward has definitely understood the Beck persona: "Two questions then. One ... has he really 'cooked his own goose' as he himself suggests? Answer: In a sense, yes, because though as a person he's mellowed a little he still acts on impulse. But then that's what he's all about and it's that impetuosity that chases him into moments of grandiose creativity. Two, will BBA be his crowning achievement? Answer: Unlikely. For one gets the impression Jeff, as dear to our hearts as he is, will never find his feet, will probably always be searching for the lost chord, caught between the public's appetite for sensation and his own relatively undefined aspiration towards good music."

1974

JANUARY

THU 3RD

To promote the upcoming British tour, Jeff is interviewed by Rob Mackie of SOUNDS today at a pub in Leicester Square. The feature is published in the January 12th issue. Talk centres around the upcoming tour and the new album, and Jeff observes: "I've never really done anything good on record, what I have in mind and what goes down on tape are totally different things. Recording is worse than Hollywood ever was, really unnatural. I'm learning things about it all the time, but I'm not sure I enjoy it." Jeff also describes the future of Beck, Bogert & Appice as "this group could either go on for a very long time or die out very quickly".

TUE 8TH
BECK, BOGERT & APPICE: SECOND BRITISH TOUR

Beck, Bogert & Appice have to delay the opening of their British tour, which should start today in Glasgow, when Appice goes down with flu after a tooth operation in New York and is ordered to stay in bed for another few days.

The tour ads optimistically proclaim: "Beck, Bogert & Appice second album *(BBA Two)* in shops soon!" Despite a rush for the deadline, the album never materializes.

WED 9TH

Tonight's concert in Edinburgh is also cancelled because of Appice's indisposition. The two Scottish dates are rescheduled for late January.

THU 10TH
City Hall, Newcastle

Finally, Beck, Bogert & Appice are reunited and embark on their second full scale tour of Great Britain to a disappointing three-quarter full house in Newcastle. Support act for the whole tour is Upp.

A totally revised set is also presented with half the act featuring as-yet-unreleased songs from the album-in-the-works, peppered with certain old favourites. New songs in the repertoire are the fiery set-opener *Satisfied*, *Laughalong, All In Your Mind, Solid Lifter* (as the first section of a medley also including *Jizz Whizz* and Appice's drum extravaganza), *Missing Word* and *Get Ready Your Lovemaker's Coming Home*. *Jizz Whizz* is also more developed and complex than the insert earlier used during *Morning Dew*. Retained from last year are only *Livin' Alone, Superstition* and *Lady* while the final number is a loose medley of *Blues de Luxe* and *You Shook Me* (the only nod to the past) plus Appice's spur-of-the-moment boogie antics, as tonight's *Newcastle Boogie*. The latter culminates in Carmine's audience participation routine "Gimmie a B, gimmie an O etc" until the whole crowd bellows 'Bollocks!' in unison. The bass solo is chucked out, and significantly, *Jeff's Boogie* is finally retired after being Beck's showcase for almost a decade.

Jeff has no vocal duties on this tour, concentrating solely on the guitar. For the first time he adds a phase shifter to his arsenal, creating a huge organ-like sound. The voice bag is retained too, but its use is somewhat restricted.

"Of course, each member's individual virtuosity goes without saying. But as for the man they had all come to see – well, Jeff Beck showed that all the speed, mood and technique are still there. It was a delight to see a guitarist in the true sense – there's no denying that Beck is one of the best. The audience hardly moved all night. Mouths open, they were too busy watching a master at work", writes Keith Ging of MELODY MAKER (January 19) in his review from the Newcastle concert.

Set List/BBA

Free Trade Hall, Manchester, January 11 '74

Satisfied • Livin' Alone • Laughalong • All In Your Mind • Solid Lifter/Jizz Whizz • Morning Dew • Prayin' • Superstition • Lady • Get Ready Your Lovemaker's Coming Home • Manchester Boogie • Blues de Luxe/You Shook Me

---

FRI 11TH
Free Trade Hall, Manchester

Like the previous night, a far from full house greets Beck, Bogert & Appice. "Critics who describe Beck as flash have I'm afraid got the wrong man. The exhibitionist of the three is Tim Bogert who goofed aimlessly about in a particularly distracting way" comments David Clark in SOUNDS (January 19) of the Manchester show. "For most of the time Jeff Beck stood back, a sullen taut figure shaded by a dark purple spot. ... Alternating between great sinewy slabs of sounds and lancing riffs, he proved, once again, that when he's doing the spade work, the rest will follow. These highlights were regrettably too few and I still have doubts about the viability of such a basically confusing band," the reviewer writes in parting.

Appice greets the crowd with a "Well alright! Here's a thing from the new album!", as Beck quickly peels off both some two-hands-on-the-fretboard-playing and a countrified run before settling into the comfortable funky 7/9-chord groove of *Satisfied*. The dumb-but-great *Livin' Alone* follows, one of only three old BBA songs played tonight (the two others being *Lady* and *Superstition*, not counting the regular boogie show closer, tonight of course a *Manchester Boogie*). The new numbers work well, but some of their own material comes over as too weak, primarily the instrumental *Solid Lifter,* a tension-building spiral chord progression that awaits a release that is only partly fulfilled with the new, extended *Jizz Whizz*. Appice's drum solo is unusually brief lasting a mere minute or two. With a full-throated sound and a touch of phasing, Jeff achieves a nice Hammond-sound on *Laughin' Lady*. *All In Your Mind* kicks ferociously – built on the formula of earlier BBA-songs like *Lady* and *Livin' Alone:* A hefty double-time intro riff, before the tempo is halved for a regular heavy funk feel, and then back to double-time with Bogert's bass gnawing away but a perfect example of the trio's synchronicity. The Staple Singers' *Prayin'* is excellent, with two very different guitar solos drenched in a cool funk pulse. And the Manchester crowd gets as gospel as it can be when they answer Appice's call for prayer. *Superstition* is slightly slower and hence heavier than before, with a dynamic call-and-response section by Jeff, alternating the voice bag with straight guitar. The night ends with the regular uptempo boogie, which segues into a slow blues

Newsflash January 1974: Beck, Bogert & Appice on tour in the UK ...

featuring Jeff garbling *You Shook Me* through his voice bag.

Comparing this performance with, say, live tapes from Beck, Bogert & Appice's first tentative steps in October/November 1972, they have matured a lot. The vocals are not necessarily better nor is the material, but the coherent emphasis on funk suits the group well. This concert is proof that Beck, Bogert & Appice indeed were developing a new direction which was never allowed to reach fruition.

SAT 12TH
Refectory, University of Leeds, Leeds

SUN 13TH
De Montfort Hall, Leicester

MON 14TH
Civic Hall, Wolverhampton

WED 16TH
The Dome, Brighton

The always dependable Charles Shaar Murray from NEW MUSICAL EXPRESS (January 26) is on hand to review the Brighton concert: "They tell me that Brighton Dome is still standing. Age hath not tarnished its lustre, nor Jeff Beck, Tim Bogert and Carmine Appice demolished it by playing rock and roll in it. It simply seemed that way at the time, when these three respected gentlemen exploded all over the place, aided by nothing but a guitar, a Fender bass, and singularly large drum kit and a rather menacing looking P.A. system." Murray sums up his impressions: "... they were quite ridiculously marvellous, and I can't recall when I last heard so much rock and roll coming from three people."

THU 17TH
Top Rank Suite, Cardiff, Wales

SAT 19TH
University of Lancaster, Lancaster

SUN 20TH
Empire Theatre, Liverpool

TUE 22ND
City Hall, Sheffield

Today's concert features rabble rousing versions of *Livin' Alone* and *All In Your Mind*. The latter with the tempo change, where the trio effortlessly break up the pulse and Jeff burns intensely on a long sequence. *Superstition* is savage, too, with Jeff tearing up the fretboard with ultra-wide bends and furious harmonics, giving a taste of the music he will be playing in a year or two from now.

WED 23RD
Town Hall, Birmingham

THU 24TH
Colston Hall, Bristol

FRI 25TH
Guildhall, Portsmouth

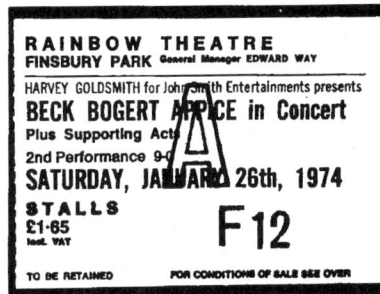

SAT 26TH
Rainbow Theatre, Finsbury Park, London

The tour's original culmination is at London's most prestigious rock venue at this time; in fact the Rainbow Theatre is a refurnished Finsbury Park Astoria – the very same location as Jeff's troublesome comeback concert in March 1967.

Because of ticket demand, an extra show is added at 6 o'clock, and it is this concert which is recorded in its entity for broadcast on the syndicated US radio show "Rock Around The World" on September 9 of this year. Of these recordings, the medley *You Shook Me/ BBA Boogie* is officially released on the retrospective CD-set *Beckology* in November 1991. This potpourri is especially potent tonight. Actually Beck, Bogert & Appice's one excessive moment (the version on *Beckology* runs for sixteen minutes), but every second is justified as Jeff wrenches some otherwordly sounds out of his guitar against the thunder and lightning of Tim and Carmine.

But by now, Jeff's patience with Tim Bogert in particular has grown thin, and the group is no longer a co-operative effort. The easygoing Appice, on the other hand, acts as mediator between a moody Beck and a temperamental Bogert. It is also Appice who introduces Jeff to Billy Cobham's seminal *Spectrum* album, featuring Tommy Bolin on guitar and Jan Hammer on keyboards, which is constantly being played when travelling on this tour.

"Dynamite wasn't the name for the introduction – it was so good. Beck prowled, slammed and half-heartedly swung his arm in arcs above

THE FINAL PIECE

Unfinished Business

For several months in late 1973 and early 1974 Jeff Beck, Tim Bogert and Carmine Appice struggled with recording their second album, which ultimately never saw the light of day, although it was even advertised as BBA 2 when the group toured Great Britain in January 1974.

It is of course not fair to judge the trio by the unfinished tapes in circulation among collectors. Their exact origin are not known, but it is believed they stem from the sessions at Escape Studios in September 1973.

The tapes contain nine different tracks. The best are the fast-paced funk-influenced songs like *Prayin'*, *Satisfied*, *Get Ready Your Lovemaker's Coming Home* and *All In Your Mind*. The latter features a break-stop rhythm, similar to what they had earlier done on both *Livin' Alone* and *Lady*. (A trait which can be traced to Yardbirds songs like *For Your Love* and *Shapes of Things*.) The weakest tracks are a pair of ballads, which suffers from Appice's rough vocals. Odd song out is *Livin' Life Backwards*, which bears a passing resemblance to the Yardbirds' experimental side. Most interesting is *Jizz Whizz*, a complex number which had developed from being a middle section in *Morning Dew* to a full blown jazzy rocker.

Oddly enough, even if the quality of the material had not improved particularly, the group come on as much more unified with a coherent vision, progressing towards a more refined funk-metal sound. ∎

his head and Bogert forced so much from his bass, that at times he lost control of his lower limbs and his left leg kicked and jerked involuntarily. ... I thought they had greatly improved since the Crystal Palace gig last September. One new space thing had me worried though [*Solid Lifter*]. The guitar was off-key and wailing painfully – but the frightening thing was that the introduction seemed to go right through the end. The beat kept on increasing until lo, the falling of one of the flags seemed to be part of a tactical plan which heralded a drum solo. For once a drum solo brought blessed relief", writes Hugh Kyle in DISC (February 2), the only major pop paper who runs a review of the Rainbow show. "The encore had Beck

January 23, 1974: Stevie Wonder performs at the Rainbow Theatre in London.

February 1974: BBA European tour cancelled ...

back in the old slow blues world of Mayall/Yardbirds which coupled with an up tempo *Rainbow Boogie* to produce some of the best lightning guitar picking, bashing and pelvic thrusts I've ever seen."

MON 28TH
Apollo Theatre, Glasgow, Scotland
The first of two rescheduled concerts from early January. Despite a group being on the verge of falling apart, the Glasgow concert is a success with the band being called back for two encores. NEW MUSICAL EXPRESS (February 9) honours Appice "who injected that spark of humanity and gave what would have been just a technically competent gig the atmosphere it needed." The reviewer, Stuart Hoggard, writes of Beck that he "stood almost immobile as his fingers ran over the fret board of his guitar, making the whole process of playing seem so bloody easy." In the audience tonight is Roxy Music's drummer Paul Thompson. A sour note: While the trio is on stage, Appice's hotel room is broken into by thieves.

TUE 29TH
Caley Cinema, Edinburgh, Scotland
Tonight's concert in Edinburgh's 1,400-seat Caley Cinema will eventually mark the very last live performance by Beck, Bogert & Appice.

Immediately after the British tour, Bogert splits for the States. Apparently, Appice stays behind a little longer, involving himself in post-production work on the second album at Island Studios in London.

With a string of dates in Germany and Italy already lined up plus some American concerts in March in the cards, the trio plans to get together again soon.

•

During the whole of January, hectic work is kept up on the group's second album first at CBS and then at Island, for the most part mixing and editing, which is done by the regular studio staff. Because of the ongoing oil crisis, CBS has reduced activities to a three-day week, while at Island a generator is used to keep up work.

UNDATED
During late January/early February, Beck adds a guitar solo to an album by Badger, a quintet fronted by ex-Yes keyboardman Tony Kaye and also featuring Jackie Lomax, Phil Pilnick, Roy Dyke and Jeff's old friend Kim Gardner. Their album is recorded at Allen Toussaint's Seasaint Studio in New Orleans around Christmas 1973, but Jeff's contributions on the title cut *White Lady* (UK Epic/US Epic) are overdubbed at a London studio. The album is released spring '74.

FEBRUARY

FRI 1ST–FRI 15TH✱
In the first two weeks of February, work is still kept up on Beck, Bogert & Appice's second album at Island on Basing Street, in an attempt to meet deadlines for new product. It is believed that Jeff and Carmine are marginally involved in this process, as work by now is purely post-production which requires just studio operators. Interestingly, Stevie Wonder is also recording at Island the first week of February (thanks to Jim Capaldi, who gave Wonder his pre-booked studio time).

TUE 5TH
Jeff Beck is invited to choose a selection of his favourite records – a dozen to be precise – in the weekly BBC Radio One programme "My Top Twelve". The accompanying interview is pre-recorded today at a BBC studio, and Beck picks twelve records spanning almost two decades (from Les Paul and Mary Ford's *The World Is Waiting For The Sunrise* to Billy Cobham's *Spectrum*) and ranging in style from rockabilly (Carl Perkins' *Matchbox*) to jazz rock (Frank Zappa's *Peaches En Regalia* from the 1970 album *Hot Rats*) to funk via Sly and the Family Stone's clarion call *I Want To Take You Higher*. The records are predominantly black, be it Stevie Wonder (*Superwoman* from *Music Of My Mind*, one of Beck's all time favourite albums), Diana Ross (*Ain't No Mountain High Enough* from her first album sans the Supremes), James Brown (the minimalist funk of *Hot Pants*) or Marvin Gaye (the beautiful *What's Going On*). Beck pays tribute to Jimi Hendrix by picking the often overlooked *Hey Joe* B-side *Stone Free* from 1966, and there is an obligatory Booker T & The MGs song, *Slim Jenkins' Place*. Interestingly, Jeff selects only one British group, and that is of course the Who and *My Generation*. More surprisingly, Jeff decides not to pick either a Gene Vincent record or Earl Hooker and Muddy Waters doing *You Shook Me*, or anything else which could be classified as blues. The programme is bookended by the regular theme music, Wynder K. Frog's version of *Willie and the Hand Jive*. The show is broadcast on Sunday March 10.

Jeff Beck is also interviewed by Brian Matthew for BBC Transcription Service's "Pop Profile" programme for foreign use. The show consists of a selection of old Beck tracks interspersed with talk. Jeff still has faith in his present band, and chats eagerly about the trio's upcoming touring plans of Germany, Italy, US, Australia and Japan this spring.

SAT 9TH
NEW MUSICAL EXPRESS's regular 'Thrills' column has discovered Bobby Tench playing back-up guitar for Joe Jammer at the Speakeasy, and Jammer comments "now you know why Beck got rid of him. He made Beck look shit".

WED 13TH
Beck, Bogert & Appice are set to begin a European tour today, which is cancelled at the eleventh hour. The tour would have covered five West German dates (starting today at the Stadthalle, Offenbach; Deutsches Museum, Munich (Thursday 14), Oberschwabenhalle, Ravensburg (Friday 15), Friedrich-Ebert-Halle, Ludwigshafen (Saturday 16) and Grugahalle, Essen (Sunday 17); the last three dates as part of a festival called "Pop-Carnival" along with four other groups). The tour would then continue with four concerts in Italy until the end of February. The official explanation for the cancellations is union strikes in West Germany and a

---

Jeff's Top 12

Asked to pick out a selection of his twelve favourites for BBC in February 1974, Jeff chose the following:

1. Sly & Family Stone: I Want To Take You Higher
2. Les Paul & Mary Ford: The World Is Waiting For The Sunrise
3. Frank Zappa: Peaches En Regalia
4. Stevie Wonder: Superwoman
5. Jimi Hendrix Experience: Stone Free
6. Billy Cobham: Spectrum
7. Diana Ross: Ain't No Mountain High Enough
8. Booker T & the MGs: Slim Jenkins' Place
9. The Who: My Generation
10. Carl Perkins: Matchbox
11. James Brown: Hot Pants
12. Marvin Gaye: What's Going On

April 1974: Beck, Bogert & Appice break up for good ...

newly-imposed rock ban on several big Italian venues.

When the European dates are cancelled, Appice also flies home awaiting the future of the band. He and Bogert keep in touch, and are interviewed by Ellen Mandell for a feature published in the April issue of CIRCUS.

THU 14TH

Jeff attends Roy Harper's high-profiled 'Valentine Day's Massacre' at the Rainbow Theatre tonight. Harper's all-star band for the occasion features Max Middleton, Ronnie Lane, John Bonham (on acoustic guitar no less), Keith Moon and Jimmy Page.

SAT 16TH

Following the previous week's piece on Bobby Tench, NEW MUSICAL EXPRESS corners him one night to ask him about his time with Jeff. Hoping for some juicy revelations, Tench merely sums up his time with Jeff with "I learned a lot from Jeff – both playing and attitude".

MON 25TH

Jeff participates in a session for British poet Pete Brown in London today, adding guitar to a song called *Spend My Night In Armour*. It is recorded for a planned single, but will not be released until a Pete Brown compilation in 1987; *Before Singing Lessons 1969–1977* (Decal). Also appearing on the same session are Jack Bruce (Brown's songwriting partner), Max Middleton and drummer Tony Fernandez.

Indeed Jeff should have been in the States today, as Beck, Bogert & Appice have been booked as a star attraction at an annual Mardi Gras Festival in New Orleans, Louisiana. Here they were billed to appear alongside Leon Russell, War and Dr. John, but with the trio's future uncertain, the trip is cancelled.

MARCH

RADIO AND TV

RADIO 1 8.30 a.m. "Junior Choice" with Wally Whyton; 10.0 Jeff Beck selects "My Top 12", introduced by Brian Matthew; 11.0 Dave Lee Travis; 1 p.m. Jimmy Savile with "The Double Top Ten Show"; 3.0 "The Story of Pop" (repeat of yesterday's broadcast); 4.0 "Solid Gold Sixty" with Tom Browne; 7.0-7.30

SUN 10TH

Jeff Beck makes a rare personal appearance on BBC Radio One today – albeit prerecorded – on the show "My Top 12", 10.00–11.00 pm (▶ February 5). This weekly programme is hosted by Brian Matthew, the very same BBC announcer who regularly introduced Jeff Beck on radio and television almost a decade ago.

SUN 17TH

Across the Atlantic, at the Nassau Coliseum on Long Island, Tim Bogert and Carmine Appice get on stage with Deep Purple during their encore number tonight.

APRIL

MON 1ST–FRI 12TH ✱

Carmine Appice telephones Jeff Beck in London and tempts him with a possible collaboration with Sly Stone, one of Jeff's idols.

Jeff flies to Sausalito, California to hang out with Bogert, Appice and Stone for about two weeks and record at the Record Plant, but the aborted sessions prove to be unusually fruitless, with no usable material recorded. The trouble seems to be Stone himself, who is too spaced out to engage in this project. "You'd have to have been in my shoes to have realised what kind of state that guy was in. He needed a whole entourage of people to help him around," Jeff explains to SOUNDS in 1975. This doomed salvage operation is not reported officially and warrants only a slight notice in NEW MUSICAL EXPRESS' 'Teazers' column. Just like the short Jeff Beck/Curtis Mayfield union in 1971, Jeff's Englishness is at odds with black culture. Speaking about the incident to John Tobler years later, Jeff recounts: "I went out to Sausalito and saw the bay and a few boats, counted a few bricks in the Holiday Inn wall, but nothing much happened, except that I wasted two weeks and realized I wasn't a Negro, and didn't want to be part of all that black power thing".

This is the final attempt by Jeff, Tim and Carmine to keep the group together, before they once again drift apart – this time forever.

SAT 13TH

Eyewitnesses say Jeff attends a concert at the Winterland in San Francisco, just across the bay from Sausalito. Tonight's triple-bill consists of Mott The Hoople, Bachman Turner Overdrive and up-and-coming Boston group Aerosmith.

LATE ✱

Carmine Appice, Don Ellis (Epic A&R man) and Ernest Chapman meet up in Toronto of all places to do a last evaluation of the doomed second Beck, Bogert & Appice album. It is decided to shelve the whole project for the time being. On the way home from Canada, Appice runs into producer Shadow Morton at the airport, and together they plan a Vanilla Fudge reunion.

SAT 27TH

The first bulletin on a possible breakup of Beck, Bogert & Appice is reported in today's MELODY MAKER. A spokesman for CBS explains: "They don't seem to be a real working unit anymore. And we don't think they're going to be together much longer." The spokesman however hopes Beck will travel to the States to conclude the as-yet-unfinished *BBA II*.

No comments are forthcoming from the group themselves, but according to the report, Bogert and Appice have approached Leslie West for a possible union.

MAY

SUN 5TH

Backstage after a Robin Trower and King Crimson concert at the Felt Forum in New York, Tim Bogert confirms the dissolution of Beck, Bogert & Appice to NEW MUSICAL EXPRESS' Steve Clarke.

SAT 18TH

"Bogert Says: BBA Finished" reads the headline in NEW MUSICAL EXPRESS, dated today. The report continues: "Rumours concerning an imminent split in BBA, which have been rife for several weeks, were confirmed by bassist Tim Bogert."

Robin Trower is asked to replace Jeff, but Trower, who is very successful with his own trio, does not wish to be tied down.

The report concludes: "No comment was available either from Beck or his manager, whose whereabouts are at present unknown to his publicist".

SAT 25TH

MELODY MAKER also reports on the break-up of Beck, Bogert & Appice today. Still no official reason is given for the split, and a spokesman for Jeff Beck merely states that it is "hoped to issue a statement next week".

•

After the breakup of Beck, Bogert & Appice, Tim Bogert moves to Califor-

---

© April 6, 1974: 'California Jam' festival draws 200,000 people to hear Emerson, Lake & Palmer, Black Sabbath, Deep Purple and others.

June 1974: Recording sessions for first solo album at Escape ...

nia and sets up a band called Pieces which lasts a couple of years – albeit never recording. Afterwards Bogert moves to England for a year, joining Boxer to record the album *Absolutely*. Interestingly, previous incarnations of this group included both Tony Newman and Bob Tench!

LATE

At the end of May, Jeff is at a party in Portobello Road thrown by London celebrity Sally Payne. Late at night, an impromptu 'million dollar quartet' ends up jamming the night away. The four are Ron Wood, Rod Stewart, Mick Jagger and of course Jeff Beck. The racket disturbs neighbours, and in the early morning hours the police arrive to stop the celebration. Recognizing the four, the police only issue a warning before leaving. Photographer Mick Rock is on hand to capture the moment.

Ron Wood recounts in ZIGZAG later in the year: "Funnily enough we all had a blow with Beck recently. Rod, Jagger and me. I was playing drums, Mick was playing piano, Rod was singing and Beck on guitar. That was the first time that Rod and Jeff had really had a confrontation since [the old days]. There was some animosity between Rod and Jeff. Jeff really isn't that keen on bad vibes. In those days he was kind of thrown in from a number of different ways like accountant, record producer, manager, and so on, and they were all trying to single him out."

JUNE

24TH
Jeff Beck celebrates his 30th birthday.

JULY

Getting back to recording again, Beck returns to Escape Studios, beginning work on his first solo album proper. At this stage, he is recording with members of a group called Zzebra; primarily Loughty Amao (sax and percussion) and Dave Quincy (sax), but the group's rhythm section (keyboard player Tommy Eyre, bassist John McCoy and drummer Liam Genocky) is also reportedly involved. The members of Zzebra are part of a large circle of freelance and studio musicians that makes up another band, Gonzalez, where Max Middleton occasionally

deps as their piano player.

However, no particular direction has been staked out at this juncture except to tape some instrumental jams. These recordings are not returned to, because they require "some decent lyrics and a wailing singer" according to Jeff in a later conversation with NEW MUSICAL EXPRESS. But one track, *Put A Light On Me*, ends up on Zzebra's album *Panic* this year with Jeff on guitar.

FRI 12TH
Jeff is at the Rainbow Theatre in London to hear Average White Band and Billy Cobham. Cobham – whose album *Spectrum* has been a favourite of Jeff's – plays a single London date on his European tour, but his band now features John Abercrombie in place of Tommy Bolin who graced *Spectrum*.

SUN 14TH
Jeff spends a second night out in London this weekend at the Gaumont State Theatre in Kilburn, where Ron Wood debuts as a solo artist backed by a group including Keith Richards, Willie Weeks and Andy Newmark with Rod Stewart as guest.

LATE
Carmine Appice returns to London to set up temporary base for his many projects, one of which is to reunite with Jeff with a view to record an album. Another project is to reconstitute Vanilla Fudge, although without Bogert. Lastly, Appice pursues his tutorial activities (he has already published a drum instruction book called 'Realistic Rock') and plans to open a drum studio in partnership with Deep Purple's Ian Paice.

MON 29TH
American attorney Steve Weiss, who handles Carmine Appice's business affairs, phones Noel Redding in Ashford and offers him the opportunity to play with Beck and Appice.

TUE 30TH
Jeff, Carmine and Noel Redding attempt a rehearsal in London severely hampered by Redding's cold. In fact the rehearsal is a tryout for a new bassist for a re-formed Vanilla Fudge rather than a Beck–Appice group, but it is Rick Grech who eventually gets that job.

AUGUST

Recording sessions at Escape continue with Dave Quincy and Loughty Amao during August.

More important is that Jeff renews his association with Max Middleton this summer, and the two map out the concept for Beck's new album. Jeff and Max will work closely together, either at Escape or at Jeff's Egerton home, before beginning proper recordings in September. One of the first things the two work up is a version of *She's A Woman*, an old Beatles B-side which Max Middleton suggests because the song goes down a storm when he plays it with Linda Lewis's group. She does it straightforward, whereas the arrangement that Jeff and Max set to the tune is given a lilting reggae flavour.

FRI 23RD AND SAT 24TH
Jeff Beck, backed by Upp, videotapes a session for BBC-2's "Music On Two" programme. This instalment's idea is to portray five guitarists with different backgrounds; folk (John Renbourne), jazz (Barney Kessel), classical (John Williams), flamenco (Paco Pena) with Jeff representing the rock category. Subtitled "Five Faces Of The Guitar", the show is hosted by Julian Bream and regular BBC deejay Mike Harding, and produced by Alan Benson. Beck and Upp perform a hitherto unreleased version of the Beatles' *She's A Woman* plus the Andi Clark composition *Get Down In The Dirt*. For the grand finale, all five guitarists briefly contribute to a version of Rodriguez' *Guitar Concerto*.

The programme is telecast on Sunday September 1.

SEPTEMBER

SUN 1ST
BBC-2 televise "Music On Two: The Five Faces Of The Guitar" today from 9 to 10 pm (▶ August 23–24), with Jeff Beck and Upp performing *Get Down In The Dirt* and *She's A Woman* – com-

June 20, 1974: Eric Clapton returns to regular live work with a concert in Copenhagen.

September 1974: George Martin produces Jeff Beck ...

plete with voice bag. Beck's contribution is impressive enough to move NEW MUSICAL EXPRESS (September 7) to write in its 'Teazers' column: "[A] dynamite two-number set from Jeff Beck and new band (including zappy bass display from one Stephen Amazing); ten minutes of better rock than a whole year of 'Old Grey Whistle Tests' has managed to throw up."

•

In the autumn of 1974, Jeff has a revelation when he one day accidentally comes across *Right Over* by Miles Davis on the radio while tinkering in his garage. The track is from Davis' 1971 soundtrack to *Jack Johnson*, features John McLaughlin on guitar, and Jeff claims it will be pivotal in getting the excitement back in his own music again.

MON 9TH
The syndicated US weekly radio show "Rock Around The World" broadcasts Beck, Bogert & Appice's concert at the Rainbow earlier in the year (▶ January 26), with *Laughalong, Lady, Jizz Whizz/Morning Dew, Superstition, Get Ready Your Lovemaker's Coming Home* and *You Shook Me/Rainbow Boogie*.

SUN 15TH
Jeff is initially signed up for Jon Lord and Tony Ashton's one-off concert at the London Palladium tonight. The concert – billed as 'First of the Big Bands' – features almost twenty musicians including Carmine Appice. Beck, however, decides to pull out of the project without explanation at the last minute. Likely he has no regrets judging from the poor reviews the show gets.

MON 16TH–FRI 27TH✱
During the last two weeks of September, Jeff Beck is booked into both CBS Studios and Air Studios. The latter, situated on London's Oxford Street, has been set up by George Martin, who is also hired to produced Beck's new album. Martin is chosen primarily not because of his credentials with the Beatles, but because he has recently done John McLaughlin's ambitious *Apocalypse* LP, where McLaughlin plays with a full-sized orchestra.

George Martin later recalls to the BBC: "He [Beck] hadn't had any success with his solo albums for a long time, and the idea of being produced by me obviously raised an eyebrow with him as much as it did with other people – people actually said to me 'Do you really think you should do this?', and I was advised by someone pretty high in the record business at that time, who said 'Don't touch Jeff Beck, because he's a loser.' I said 'No, I think he's a great guitar player.'"

Recording with Jeff at this time is Carmine Appice, Max Middleton and Phil Chen, a highly rated studio bassist who has also served time with Jimmy James & the Vagabonds, Chapman/Whitney Streetwalkers (a band that also counts Bob Tench among its ranks) and Doors-offspring the Butts Band. Among selections taped at this time are *Scatterbrain* and *Constipated Duck*.

Furthermore, Jeff and Carmine spend their time remixing and touching up the Japan-only *Beck, Bogert & Appice Live* double album with the intention to have it released on both the European and American markets. Appice comments: "... that Japanese engineer's mix wasn't really good." For all their efforts, it is decided not to release the album anyway. (It is not until 20 years later with the advent of the CD-age that this album will be easily obtainable as an import CD.)

The market must be yearning for Jeff Beck material, because MELODY MAKER also reports that Epic plans to release the old Motown tapes he and Cozy Powell did, but this is also stopped.

OCTOBER

EARLY
Around this time, sessions come to a temporary halt when Carmine Appice and Jeff Beck no longer see eye to eye over the essential matter of billing. Whereas Jeff considers this *his* solo album, Carmine and his powerful representatives Steve Weiss and Phil Basile want the two to share billing as a joint Beck–Appice album. In the end, Carmine is pushed out. Although this action sours their relationship – not improved by Appice suing Beck over publishing rights some years later – they eventually patch up their differences. The case is settled out of court.

Carmine explains in DOWNBEAT a few years later: "I'm the guy who started Jeff on his road to jazz-rock. What do you think of that? ... Jeff and I planned to do something along the lines of a Beck–Appice album. It never happened."

Ironically, Appice will join Rod Stewart's group for a long spell in the seventies (co-writing *Da Ya Think I'm Sexy* in the process), sharing the rhythm section with no other than Phil Chen! And – history repeats itself – Appice also replaces Cozy Powell again, this time in Whitesnake in the mid-eighties.

MID TO LATE
With Appice out of the picture, Max Middleton suggests 18-year old drummer Richard Bailey from the group Batti Mamzelle. He and Phil Chen have also held down the bottom in Gonzalez on a number of occasions. Sessions pick up again at a relaxed but efficient pace at Air, and continue throughout October and into the first part of November. Jeff later claims to Jon Tiven that the actual recording was done in a mere dozen days: "We had a week in a rehearsal studio and we'd gotten five numbers done, a couple of them in two days, and it was going so well that it snowballed from there."

Some of the recordings done with Appice are either replaced with new drum tracks or re-recorded. Besides original material by Jeff and Max, four covers are taped, two of which are penned by Stevie Wonder; *Thelonius* (which Wonder gave to Beck way back in May 1972) and the ballad *'Cause We've Ended As Lovers*, which Wonder wrote for his wife Syreeta Wright for her album *Stevie Wonder Presents Syreeta*, released just a month previously. Then there is the reggaefied *She's A Woman* (tentatively called *She's A Reggae Woman*) featuring Jeff's first recorded performance of the voice bag, not counting its presence on the *Beck, Bogert & Appice Live In Japan* album. Finally there is Bernie Holland's poignant ballad *Diamond Dust*. A reported outtake from these sessions is a version of Chuck Berry's *Deep Feeling*, a Hawaiian guitar instrumental that Berry recorded in 1957.

George Martin writes and conducts string parts on two songs, and in the mix-down process decides to segue the tracks on side one *Abbey Road*-style.

Recalling this occasion years later, bassist Phil Chen says in 1989: "... everything was like a feel between Richard Bailey and myself. So I just played what I thought was right – just finding my way through each song somehow. The tracks were all done live".

FRI 25TH
David Bowie's farewell-to-Ziggy concert, "Bowie '73", is shown today on Wide World–In Concert, ABC TV

Ⓒ September 11, 1974: Crosby, Stills, Nash & Young, the Band and Joni Mitchell play London's Wembley Stadium.

Network 11:30 pm–1 am EST (▶ July 3 1973). Filmed by D. A. Pennebaker, the concert briefly features Jeff Beck.

SAT 26TH

Jeff attends a Johnny Winter concert at London's New Victoria Theatre, leaving not only unimpressed but uncomfortable: "I hate to say it, but Johnny Winter didn't do anything for me the other night, and I used to rate him. He came on, and I was so ashamed to be associated with that white rock music when he played. I don't know why, 'cuz it wasn't bad – it just sounded so old."

FACSIMILE FROM NEW MUSICAL EXPRESS, NOVEMBER 9, 1974

Blue-eyed guitar-tormenter JEFF BECK of Egerton, Surrey, lists as his favourite leisure pursuits:

Music and cars and sex ...

– though not necessarily in that order. CHARLES SHAAR MURRAY likes hamburgers, Marvel Comics, and picking his nose – but BECK talked to him

LATE

Charles Shaar Murray and photographer Ian Dickson visit Air's Studio 2 to get a preview of the new album and do an interview for NEW MUSICAL EXPRESS (published November 9).

It is a particularly entertaining Jeff Beck talking, offering a series of colourful and quotable statements. Dismissing Beck, Bogert & Appice once and for all, Jeff fires off: "Kamikaze is exactly the word – it was the biggest fight in rock and roll that you could ever hear. We were grappling with an abysmal lack of material and lack of co-operation all around. I wouldn't want to co-operate and play what they wanted me to play, because I had finished with that style a long time ago. They wanted me to tear my hair out and play the guitar until it melted ... it was a cacophonous nasty horrible noise."

"I want to do stuff that enables me to roast on the guitar, but roast well, and not have to come out with all the old shit that people expect from me."

"Hendrix did it all. He closed the book. When he died, that was it."

"Drums are a bastard thing to play. You can't bluff on drums. You can bluff on a guitar – like I bluff all the time. Bass and drums are unbluffable. The bluffers in the business died off about eight or ten years ago. Bluff guitarists are going to be out of business soon – so I'm probably going to be looking for a job."

For the first time, Jeff acknowledges Jan Hammer as a new inspiration: "[Hammer] is influencing me at the moment. It's only a very crude imitation, but it is Hammer that I'm copying, because his synthesizer sounds like a guitar should sound."

In parting, Beck sums up the interview thus: "Music and cars and sex are my main driving forces, and that's the way I'm gonna keep it."

THU 31ST

Led Zeppelin launch their own record label Swan Song with a big party held at Chislehurst Caves in Kent. Besides the label's signings (Bad Company, the Pretty Things, Maggie Bell), Roy Harper and Jeff Beck are also on the guest list.

NOVEMBER

EARLY TO MID✱

Jeff Beck and George Martin round up sessions at Air in early November, wrapping up Jeff's as-yet-unnamed first solo album. By the middle of the month Martin is working on the final mixes with engineer Phil Brown.

In mid-November Jeff also talks to Rob Mackie of SOUNDS about his new album, for a feature published on November 23. Always his own harshest critic and never quite content with his recordings, already now Jeff is expressing doubt about his first solo album: "There's a lot of varied moods on it ... There's not the magic that I wanted on there. It's very hard to describe, but the album was under my control for the first half, and then there's some stuff on there that I didn't write and I had to be bribed and convinced that, that part was going to be all right. There's some good and some unsuitable."

Preparing a new band to tour the album, Jeff informs: "I think this'll probably be the last band I'll ever have, I want it to be exactly what I want, I don't want four robots or anything like that, but not too big egos either."

SAT 23RD

Jeff is profiled in NEW MUSICAL EXPRESS' ten-week supplement 'The Guitar Book', dated today. "I don't want to show anybody how to bluff. Let 'em learn the proper way. I don't want a trail of people after me learning the wrong way. You want me to give away my secrets? There aren't any. Just don't take any notice of anybody who can play properly and you got it", is Beck's sundry advice to people starting out on guitar.

LATE

By the end of November, Beck is back at Air Studios, but this time to produce more tracks by Upp for their first album for Epic, picking up the threads from the initial Upp sessions at Escape in August 1973. Their album, simply titled *Upp*, is released on Epic about April the following year. For this guitar-less trio, Jeff is also featured on several songs; *Bad Stuff, Friendly Street, It's A Mystery, Give It To You* and finally – of course! – on *Jeff's One*.

DECEMBER

THU 12TH

In a surprise move, Mick Taylor quits the Rolling Stones today to join a group with Jack Bruce and Max Middleton – although the latter's participation is eventually kept brief.

Taylor's departure sparks a series of suggestions and rumours of possible replacements, particularly pointing out Ron Wood and Jeff Beck. Their possible involvement with the Stones is fuelled by a Mick Jagger interview in NEW MUSICAL EXPRESS shortly afterwards: "... there's a lot of people I could dig working with. I've played with Ron a lot. I had one very good night playing with Jeff Beck recently. There's Eric [Clapton] too. They're all great friends of mine."

However, Rod Stewart, also interviewed by NEW MUSICAL EXPRESS right before Christmas this year, hits the nail on the head when asked if Jeff Beck could be a possible Stone: "Oh Christ, never in a million years. The egos! They couldn't be able to get on the same stage together. It'd never work for a second. Now Jeff – well he's a true star – a real presence. To talk about his guitar playing is just unnecessary."

▶ 1975

JANUARY

LATE

With his new album – now given the title *Blow By Blow* – progressing nicely and nearing completion, Jeff flies to New York to have his photo taken for the cover. This is to be designed by Columbia Records art director John Berg, well-known for his artwork for Miles Davis and Chicago among others. In the end, a plain brown-tinted photo from the Beck, Bogert and Appice-days will be used for the back cover, while the front is simply a painted recreation of the back cover photo done by John Collier.

Jeff's new musical direction reportedly causes some concern at Epic, but A & R men Don Ellis and Gregg Geller stand up for Beck and foresee – quite rightly – both an artistic and commercial triumph.

FEBRUARY

EARLY

Keith Richards calls Jeff at home and asks him over to Rotterdam, Holland, where the Rolling Stones are doing loose rehearsals and tentative recordings for a new album in the wake of guitarist Mick Taylor's departure in December the previous year. Not quite sure of what to make of the invitation, Jeff decides to fly over for a weekend.

THU 6TH–SUN 9TH

Jeff Beck, accompanied by Allan Dutton, spends a weekend in Rotterdam with the Rolling Stones. The Stones have set up shop in a large auditorium, and are using their mobile studio to record at their usual lazy pace. They have been here since January 22, and this February weekend is the last before the sessions are curtailed. Besides the basic Stones line-up, trusted right-hand man Ian Stewart is present, and so are Billy Preston, Glyn Johns and engineer Chris Kimsey. Alexis Korner is also said to be around providing fatherly guidance. As it turns out, the purpose of asking Jeff over is to determine if he is a suitable replacement. Two important factors contribute to trying out Jeff; one is Jagger's encounter with him the previous year for the jam with Ron Wood and Rod Stewart, and the other is Ian Stewart's recommendation. Although the combination of Beck and the Stones would appear a bit strange, especially in hindsight, Jeff did in fact fulfill several criteria as Taylor's replacement. First and foremost was his being a contemporary Londoner with a similar background. But when Jeff understands that the Stones may be serious about his joining, he finds the thought too overwhelming, slips a 'sorry'-note under Jagger's hotel room door and catches a plane home.

Jeff tells Steven Rosen a few months later: "I went over there and I found out they wanted me to join. I couldn't believe that. I mean, the money was tempting, I could have made a fortune and never had to work again but I would have been half dead and my reputation would have been shot. I think things have worked out better this way ... I couldn't be happier really." All is not wasted however as Billy Preston immediately arranges for Jeff to appear on a TV show in Los Angeles, while Mick Jagger will indeed call upon Jeff's guitar abilities in the eighties.

Despite being the most sought after vacancy in the music business, surprisingly little is documented of the 2–3 weeks the Stones spend in Rotterdam. The auditions work simply; the Stones call possible candidates and fly them over from England for informal jam sessions.

Guitarists *certain* to have come to the Rotterdam rehearsals – besides Jeff Beck – are Rory Gallagher, Wayne Perkins and Robert A. Johnson (a UK-based American, playing with John Entwistle's Ox). In fact, Johnson is in Rotterdam at the same time as Beck. Guitarists *reported* to appear – some of these contenders brought up by a 'shopping list' published in MELODY MAKER (January 18) – include ex-Beck frontman Bobby Tench, Mountain guitarist Leslie West and Shuggie Otis. Guitarists who did *not* attend the Rotterdam auditions were Ron Wood (who is high in the rumour stakes), Peter Frampton (Bill Wyman's choice) and Chris Spedding. The latter explains to NEW MUSICAL EXPRESS a few months later: "They've [The Stones] been looking for a guitarist for six months – they even had Beck down there, and *he's* not playing with them."

A bootleg from the trial run with Beck exists, including an instrumental version of the Motown song *Heatwave* and – interestingly – an utterly tame and laidback version of Max Middleton's *Freeway Jam*, soon to become a centrepiece of Jeff's live shows. A song the Stones demo in Rotterdam is the Jagger/Richards original *Worried About You*. Unconfirmed sources claims Jeff Beck plays a guitar solo on this tune, a version of which eventually ends up on the song's official release on *Tattoo You* in 1981, but it is definitely Ron Wood who plays the solo on the finished article, although it does have a slight Beck resemblance. Two other oft-bootlegged Stones songs often attributed to Jeff Beck – *Come On Sugar* and *Sexy Night* – definitely do not feature his guitar playing.

After the Rotterdam sessions, the Rolling Stones temporarily go their own ways, and Keith Richards works with American guitarist Wayne Perkins, who is then tipped for the job. When the Rolling Stones travel to Munich to continue recording, Harvey Mandel is brought along and considered the new Stone, but when Ron Wood pops up in Germany at the end of March, he is quickly hired to help the band out for their summer tour of America. Wood, still with the Faces at the time, remains with the Rolling Stones to this day.

SUN 16TH

Tonight is possibly one of the occasions when Jeff steps on stage with Upp at the Marquee. Tonight's advertisement tempts with 'Free admission', likely to promote their new album. Upp are now under Ernest Chapman's wings. Booking agent and later Police manager Ian Copeland – at that time working for John Sherry Enterprises – recounts how Beck's involvement with Upp inadvertently causes problems: "Jeff Beck had befriended them and he produced and played all over their first album, which actually worked against them, since everyone expected him to show up at their club shows. This meant they did good business, at least for a while, but inevitably the band was faced with playing to mainly disappointed Jeff Beck fans."

◉ February 8, 1975: British pub-rock group Dr Feelgood release their debut album "Down By The Jetty".

Newsflash March 1975: Album "Blow By Blow" released ...

MID ✱

Nat Weiss, John McLaughlin's American agent and a business acquaintance of Ernest Chapman, suggests the idea of combining Beck and McLaughlin for a double headlining North American tour in the spring.

With an imminent album release, Beck needs a group for touring purposes and loosely rehearses with Max Middleton and drummer Bruce Gary this winter (Gary is also involved with the new Jack Bruce Band featuring Mick Taylor, and so, in fact, is Middleton). Although the rhythmic combination of Phil Chen and Richard Bailey has worked beautifully in the studio, Jeff wants a more roadworthy rhythm section when he goes on tour. Anyway, Phil Chen is committed elsewhere and Beck feels Bailey, at only nineteen, is too young and his drumming too delicate to provide the needed power in a live situation.

THU 20TH

Chaka Khan and Rufus hold a press reception at Ronnie Scott's in London, and Jeff is attending the record biz occasion, as are Bobby Tench, Roy Wood, Rick Price, Jon Anderson, Patrick Moraz, Charlie Whitney and Roger Chapman.

SAT 22ND

Tonight Linda Lewis – with a band featuring husband Jim Cregan and Max Middleton – plays Ronnie Scott's, and at the end of the evening Jeff Beck saunters onstage together with Bobby Tench, Roger Chapman and singer Claire Hamill for a jam. The audience includes Mick Ronson, Rick Wakeman and film director Ken Russell.

MARCH

LATE

Jeff puts together an ad hoc group for his upcoming American tour. Max Middleton is considered a natural, both because of his earlier stage experience with Jeff but also because of his musicianship and knowledge of the *Blow By Blow* material.

At the end of March, Beck then flies to New York to find a suitable rhythm section. Jon Paris, later Johnny Winter's bassist, is pegged to audition but conflicts in his schedule means he misses the opportunity. Ultimately, Jeff's band is completed by studio bassist Wilbur Bascomb and legendary drummer Bernard "Pretty" Purdie – well-known from countless Aretha Franklin and James Brown recordings among others.

From New York, Jeff Beck presumably flies straight on to Los Angeles with Max Middleton for a TV appearance with Billy Preston.

MON 31ST

Jeff Beck's first proper solo album, *Blow By Blow*, is issued in the States today, while the British release is held back for another few weeks. The album is wholly instrumental with a highly successful blend of melodious funk with jazzy overtones.

Split between original compositions and inspired cover choices, the songs range from a reggaefied Beatles melody to Stevie Wonder's ballad *'Cause We've Ended As Lovers*, which quickly becomes Jeff's signature song. On the cover, the song is given a 'thank you' to Stevie, and it dedicated to Roy Buchanan, who a year or so later repays the compliment by doing the touchingly titled *My Friend Jeff*.

Music critic Dave Marsh comments in ROLLING STONE (June 5): "Jeff Beck seems finally to have figured out that he is not going to replace the great sixties group which bore his name ... After some trying moments with a couple of abortive bands ... this all-instrumental album points to a newer, healthier direction for the man whose playing is more emblematic of the Yardbirds than either Jimmy Page, who followed him, or Eric Clapton, whom he succeeded ... the tunes blend together pleasantly and the second side, particularly, contains some hints that Beck may finally have found a mode in which he is once more comfortable."

Scattered reviews from across the States also praise Beck's new all-instrumental format; some reviewing the LP in tandem with Eric Clapton's *There's One In Every Crowd*, released at the same time. Paul J. Grant in the Michigan paper THE ANN ARBOR SUN (April 11–25): "The failure of Beck, Bogert & Appice was due to the absence of a convincing vocalist. *Blow By Blow* avoids those traps, gives Jeff room to explore and astound by the simple deletion of all vocals. And the amazing thing is how lyrical the end result is." The Dallas, Texas supplement ICONOCLAST (April 18–29) runs the caption 'Beck/Clapton – Same Roots, Different Directions': "Without debating which approach to music is better, it is impossible to ignore that Jeff Beck is playing far more adventurous music on his new album than Eric Clapton is on his. Beck's album not only reaffirms his stature as a musician, but he has taken a big step in recording his first all instrumental LP. ... The guitar playing is incredible. He is everything you could ask for in a guitarist. He's flashy, but he's able to use restraint. He's funky, but melodically sophisticated. He's imaginative and he retains what has always been his number one asset – an incredibly light touch on the guitar itself. His finesse is remarkable". Kennie Margolis in the New Jersey paper THE AQUARIAN (April 23–May 7) is equally impressed: "Jeff Beck's first all-instrumental album fuses rock, funk and

---

Album
JEFF BECK
BLOW BY BLOW

A1 YOU KNOW WHAT I MEAN (AKA IT DOESN'T REALLY MATTER) (BECK/MIDDLETON) **A2** SHE'S A WOMAN (LENNON/MCCARTNEY) **A3** CONSTIPATED DUCK (BECK) **A4** AIR BLOWER (BECK/MIDDLETON/BAILEY/CHEN) **A5** SCATTERBRAIN (BECK/MIDDLETON)

B1 'CAUSE WE'VE ENDED AS LOVERS (STEVIE WONDER) **B2** THELONIUS (STEVIE WONDER) **B3** FREEWAY JAM (MIDDLETON) **B4** DIAMOND DUST (BERNIE HOLLAND)

Released March 31, 1975 (US Epic PE 33409) and April 1975 (UK Epic EPC 69117) A quadrophonic version is released in the United States in April 1975 (US Epic EQ 33409)
Personnel is Jeff Beck (gtrs, talk box), Max Middleton (ac pno, el pno, synths, mini moog), Phil Chen (bs), Richard Bailey (drms). Orchestral arrangements by George Martin (A5, B4)
Recorded at Air Studio 2, 4th floor, 214 Oxford Street, London and possibly CBS Studios, Whitfield Street, London, September–November 1974.
Produced by George Martin
Engineered by Denim Bridges
Highest Chart Position US: #4
Highest Chart Position UK: –

Ⓒ March 1, 1975: Stevie Wonder's "Fulfillingness' First Finale" is awarded Album of the Year in the 17th annual Grammy Awards.

April 1975: Beck's touring group rehearse in London ...

jazz in such a way that he could play with either Miles Davis, James Brown, or any rock band at any given moment, and come off a master. ... The moody 'bad boy' plays the most erotic guitar around."

Against many odds, *Blow By Blow* is a major commercial success and Jeff's coming tour helps propel the LP to the top of the US charts, to the pleasant surprise of both Beck and Epic.

Home in Britain, however, the album is met with a more mixed reception. Both RECORD MIRROR (March 29) and DISC (April 5) greet the album warmly; "This is not, as the title suggests, just a series of indulgent jam sessions but a superb collection of well-planned, well thought-out instrumentals from The Man That Launched A Thousand Licks ... Overall, a great album that will appeal not only to guitarists, but to any lover of excellent music" writes RECORD MIRROR, while David Fudger in DISC exclaims: "What a treat! With this one Jeff shows all the pale Beck imitators what they should be doing (Woody, Ronson, etc, take note). An instrumental album, the first totally 'Beck' album for a noticeably long time it's the most joyful thing I've heard since Weather Report's *Mysterious Traveller*, and pleasingly more accessible at that."

The dissenting opinions come from NEW MUSICAL EXPRESS and MELODY MAKER, and both show what will be Jeff's frustration with the British music press in the following years: on one hand, Steve Lake (MELODY MAKER, March 22) thinks Beck tries to play jazz but fails because he's inadequate: "Frankly, it's not very good. But then, it's not amazingly bad either – it's just lame, about as lame as all other guitar instrumentals he's ever done ... Jeff Beck proves once again that if you want to improvise within a rock framework, then the structures themselves have got to have some aesthetic interest, and that any old pop song simply *won't* do. *Blow By Blow* is remarkable only for its vacuity". And on the other hand, Beck fan #1, Charles Shaar Murray (NEW MUSICAL EXPRESS, March 29), bemoans the lack of what he terms 'braintwisting kamikaze rock and roll': "Basically, *Blow By Blow* is an exercise in that Snappy–Sammy–Smoot synthesiser and clavinet jazz funk perpetrated by the likes of Herbie Hancock, which is not a genre I'm overly fond of ... Tunes are few and far between, and most of the album consists of the musicians fighting over some helpless riff like dogs scrapping over a bone ... If *Blow By Blow* is a Grand One-Off, then let it be; if it's simply a preview of the future grand strategy then it's time for some mass 'Uh-oh's'. Beck's had the balls to try something different, but it's far from an unqualified success."

In his review in SOUNDS (March 29), Pete Makowski pokes his nose at Steve Lake's accusations and defends Jeff's new record fiercely: "After reading a review of this in a certain muzak paper I've come to the conclusion that I've been listening to a totally different album. I've always regarded Beck, along with Blackmore and Hendrix, as an innovator of the unorthodox electric guitar. He commands his own style – a pyrotechnical genius ... All in all this is Beck's finest, but I'm sure there are even better times to come. It's a solid, refreshing, inventive, mindblasting album. Yes folks, it's a Beck album."

APRIL

TUE 1ST ✱
Jeff Beck and Max Middleton fly out to Los Angeles to appear on the TV show "Midnight Special" at the behest of Billy Preston. Preston has taken a liking to Beck during the Rolling Stones auditions in Rotterdam, and their short collaboration prompts false rumours of a Preston/Beck unit to tour the US this spring. What it eventually boils down to is their one-off appearance on this television show, which is pre-recorded at NBC Studios in Burbank and aired on NBC late Friday night, May 2. Jeff and Max perform two selections from Beck's new album, *You Know What I Mean* and *'Cause We've Ended As Lovers*, backed by a small group with bassist Willie Weeks and drummer Ollie Brown. Jeff also joins Billy Preston on the irresistible funky opening slot, *Nothing From Nothing* (a US #1 for Preston the previous year), and then backs Buddy Miles on a classic from the drummer's Hendrix-era, *Them Changes*. The show is presented by Wolfman Jack, and the other main guests besides Beck are Labelle and Chaka Khan.

EARLY
To hone their live skills, Jeff's new touring quartet settles in London for intensive rehearsals. Pete Makowski of SOUNDS is invited to the second day of rehearsals for an interview (published April 19). Makowski is given a short brief *not* to ask Beck anything about his period with Bogert and Appice, something Makowski had not intended to do anyway, because, as he wittily points out, "BB&A and the current Beck line up are about diverse as Twiggy and Godzilla." Asked about his new direction, Beck answers: "Even when I was younger, I used to get really sick of the twelve bar. I really liked people like Barney Kessel. Right now I'm more into songs and rhythms, people like James Brown. Let's face it, there aren't that many good guitarists around. I couldn't even name a handful." Makowski suggests Robin Trower, but Beck dismisses him with "I can't comment on things like that because I really like Jimi so much that my feelings are biased towards him. People say that Trower's carrying on where Hendrix left ... I don't think so." In parting, Beck sums up his recurring frustration with predictability and consistency: "I'm never satisfied with any of my recordings or my playing, I mean what would be the point of going on if I was? Sometimes I get frustrated because I don't develop ideas I start with. But that's me, I change every day."

The worked out set list relies heavily on the new album – in fact, all of its tracks bar *Scatterbrain* will be performed live on the upcoming tour. But Jeff also finds the opportunity to play some songs that he had to give up when he played in a power trio; reviving a pair of songs from the Tench-era Beck Group, primarily the waltz *Definitely Maybe*, which was last performed live during the August 1972 American tour, and *Got The Feeling* is worked up, too. Also from his back catalogue is a revised, voice-bagged version of *Superstition*. There is room too for a pair of surprises in the set list; a version of bassist Stanley Clarke's *Power* (from his eponymous album from the previous year) and a loose jam usually used as an encore, a mutation on the riff from Upp's *Get Down In The Dirt*.

Most importantly is the fact that this repertoire will consist of wholly instrumental music, not counting a little use of the voice bag.

MON 7TH
Jeff is at Ronnie Scott's to hear the Joe Pass Trio.

UNDATED
New Cross, London
To limber up before they depart for the American East Coast, Beck, Middleton, Bascomb and Purdie play a

April 1975: Jeff Beck commences first 'solo' tour of the US ...

secret warm-up gig at a non-descript pub in New Cross.

THU 17TH ✱
Beck with an entourage containing his new band, a small road crew and manager Ernest Chapman fly out to the States.

WED 18TH–MON 21ST ✱
Beck and his band are holed up in Boston, where they are doing pre-tour preparations. Full rehearsals are done with Dawson Sound, the company that will provide the sound for the upcoming tour. There is also room for a bit of press, as journalist Jim Kozlowski witnesses one of the rehearsals and arranges an interview with Beck, later broadcast on the syndicated American radio show "Rock Around The World" on June 1.

While in the Northeast, Jeff hangs out with local Boston group Aerosmith. The connection is Aerosmith guitarist Joe Perry's girlfriend Elyssa Jerret, who is a friend of Beck from the time she lived in England with Joe 'Jammer' Wright. One night, Perry and Jerret take Jeff out to see Muddy Waters play at the popular Boston club Paul's Mall.

TUE 22ND–WED 23RD
Soundchecks and warm-up shows before Jeff Beck's truly first headlining tour of the States are held at MIT's Kresge Auditorium in Cambridge, across the Charles River from Boston.

THU 24TH
JEFF BECK:
FIRST NORTH AMERICAN TOUR;
FIRST LEG
Century Theater, Buffalo, New York
As Beck and McLaughlin share the bill for this tour with no other support acts, it has been decided to alternate every other night as to who will close the show. After a toss of the coin, Beck opens the proceedings tonight with a spirited hour-long set, before McLaughlin closes the concert. His group – the Mahavishnu Orchestra – is a whole different kettle of fish to the ensemble that won such public and critical acclaim and featured stellar players like Billy Cobham and Jan Hammer. This time, McLaughlin fronts an unwieldly combination of strings (a cello and two violinists, one of them the young Steve Kindler), a regular rock rhythm section (bassist Ralphe Armstrong and drummer Michael Walden), plus keyboards and two sax players. Jeff is particular fond of Walden, who during the tour often psyches up Beck before he's about to step on stage, teasingly calling Jeff a softie and promising to write him a tearful ballad.

For this tour Beck will usually stick to a Fender Stratocaster for the first half of his show, before switching to his ox-blood Les Paul for *'Cause We've Ended As Lovers* and the rest of the set.

🎧 Jeff clearly enjoys playing with Bernard Purdie, as he locks with the drummer's strong grooves on an extended jam borne out of Upp's *Get Down In The Dirt* riff, where the explosive Purdie pummels the drums like a steam hammer.

FRI 25TH
Auditorium Theater, Rochester, New York

SAT 26TH
Springfield Civic Center, Springfield, Massachusetts
After tonight's show both Jeff and John McLaughlin, plus members of their groups, indulge in a jam with the lounge band at the Sheraton Hotel where they are staying.

Beck is also interviewed today by Jon Tiven for a feature in INTERNATIONAL MUSICIAN AND RECORDING WORLD (July 1975). Jeff offers his opinions on a series of subjects, ranging from George Martin ("George is a bit of everything, I was very impressed with the way he handled it"); Don Nix ("Most of the time he was fast asleep"); Beck, Bogert & Appice ("You don't form a band that's five years obsolete and take it seriously"); other guitarists ("[they] annoy me. I listen to Stanley Clarke and Jan Hammer. I like real musicians, not the poseurs who buy suits and fancy guitars") and Tommy Bolin ("He's very good. Plays really nicely on the Billy Cobham album. Sometimes sounds a bit like me"). Jeff is also unusually acidic when asked about Ron Wood's engagement in the Rolling Stones, when he is quoted as saying: "I don't want to talk about it. There's no music there. As you get older you just don't want to hear that rubbish anymore. The Rolling Stones are finished, as far as I'm concerned, and they admit it as well."

SUN 27TH
Capitol Theater, Passaic, New Jersey
The tour is doing well at the box office, as confirmed by AMUSEMENT BUSINESS, which reports that tonight's show draws a full house (3,376 spectators to be precise) for a $20,045 gross.

MON 28TH ✱
On a day off during the tour, Jeff travels out to Long Island to visit Stanley Clarke, the renowned bassist in Return To Forever. The two hit it off immediately, and will later share a fruitful musical collaboration.

Soon after this meeting – possibly in the middle of May – Clarke calls up Beck and asks him to contribute his guitar playing to a pair of songs, which are then taped at Electric Lady Studios in New York City. These cuts boost Clarke's breakthrough album *Journey To Love* (released in September 1975), where Jeff is heard soloing on the title cut plus the loving tribute *Hello Jeff*.

Blow By Blow enters the upper reaches of this week's CASH BOX album charts in the US at an impressive #16.

TUE 29TH
The Playhouse, Hofstra University, Hempstead, New York

WED 30TH
Avery Fisher Hall, Lincoln Center, New York, New York
After their first of two nights at Avery Fisher Hall (the new name given to the city's Philarmonic Hall in the Lincoln Center), CBS Records hosts a party for Jeff Beck and John McLaughlin at the New York Cultural Center, beginning at 11.30 pm. After a while, Jeff leaves the party in the company of Rick Derringer and Carmine Appice.

Generally, throughout this tour, Beck gets some stunning reviews, perhaps the best of his career, and is met with approval by the music critics. Chris Charlesworth of MELODY MAKER (May 10) writes: "Personally, I preferred the raunchier Beck to the comparatively tranquil McLaughlin. Beck's drummer ... drove the English guitarist to great heights on occasions and provided a sound runway for all the various liftoffs ... During *She's A Woman* Beck attempted to sing

---

Set List/Jeff Beck

The Coliseum, New Haven, Connecticut May 4 '75

You Know What I Mean • She's A Woman • Freeway Jam • Definitely Maybe • Thelonius • Superstition • 'Cause We've Ended As Lovers • Power • Got The Feeling • Air Blower • Constipated Duck • Diamond Dust • Jeff's Jam (Get Down In The Dirt)

---

158   ⓒ April 7, 1975: Founding member since the group's inception in 1968, Ritchie Blackmore announces his departure from Deep Purple today.

April/May 1975: Jeff Beck/John McLaughlin play two nights in New York ...

through a tube attached to a pouch slung from his shoulder, but the effect he was looking for was lost amid a howl of vocal feedback. It was his only [vocal] contribution to the evening apart from a brief thank-you at the end. He appeared to be in a hurry to leave the stage and seemed genuinely surprised at the welcome he was given."

The concert is also reviewed by Jerry Leichtling in the VILLAGE VOICE (May 12) under the heading 'Rattle of the Bands', who finds McLaughlin disappointing and "Jeff Beck, well he was better than McLaughlin. Quite a bit better and occasionally terrific, though not altogether successful ... The problem is material. Beck can rip off exciting and inventive licks at will, almost offhandedly, but his sense of context slips away at times. He's at his best working with strong melodies that can be embroidered upon, such as the Beatles' *She's A Woman* rather than slick, repetitive chord patterns. Accordingly, his version of [*'Cause We've Ended As Lovers*] was very beautiful. I mean it was executed with such cat-like sexuality, so sparse and expressive and blue that it glowed with intimacy. It was an incredible number. I could go on for quite some time with sexual come-in-your-pants metaphors. But Beck never really got it on as a rocker. He played some nice slide ... and would at times throw in a Hendrix fuzz-tone smash. But there were only flashes of brilliance."

Jerry Leichtling, however, is disturbed by the closing McLaughlin/Beck jam, which has already become a regular occasion on the nights when Beck closes the show (it seems Jeff is never around to do this when McLaughlin closes): "This jam, yeah, this jam, was so absurd, so stilted, so crazy, it was like a Japanese horror movie dubbed into Swedish ... but Beck, realizing it wasn't happening, had the good sense to walk off stage a couple of times only to be pushed back." (True enough, a surviving live tape proves this to be an unusually long and tedious jam.)

Leichtling meets Beck at the CBS Records party afterwards, and when politely complimenting him about the jam, Jeff replies: "Nice of you to say so, but we both know it was nowhere", prompting Leichtling to end his story with: "He was right, but such honesty among rock stars is so refreshing, let's hope he grabs the brass ring again."

While staying in New York City, Jeff also attends a publicity party for

YOU SHOOK ME

Slide Projector

Slide guitar, the technique where a metal or glass tube – hence "bottleneck" – is stuck on a finger of the fretting hand, has always been an integral part of Jeff Beck's sound right from his pre-Yardbirds days. What made his style different was that he preferred to play slide in standard tuning. Most guitarists using a slide retune their instruments to an open tuning to be able to play chords without fingering. Strictly speaking, it is not impossible to play chords with a slide in regular tuning, rather the open tuning does not invite single string technique so readily. But Jeff had an ulterior motive too, as he explained to GUITAR PLAYER in 1973: "It meant changing over, and that looked terrible on stage, watching a guy change over on guitar. You know I just liked to stand there after a number and look cool; I mean I didn't want to do all this toiletry."

Beck's love of the slide can be traced to the EP which included Muddy Waters' recording of *You Shook Me* with Earl Hooker on guitar, and Ian Stewart had to explain how the sound was produced. Jeff was obviously a natural at doing this from day one; apparently he just put a piece of metal on the middle finger of his left hand and away he went. Using his intuitive tonal understanding, the slide became an awesome weapon in Jeff's hands; hitting micro notes, playing with a violinist's effortless legato, impersonating industrial noise or to generally create sonic havoc.

In the beginning Beck was heavily influenced by the ultra-smooth playing of Earl Hooker, and his first Yardbirds session – *Steeled Blues* – was squarely in the Chicago blues mould, modelled on Hooker's playing. No other British guitarist could match Jeff's utterly convincing reading of Elmore James's *The Sun Is Shining* from the BBC in 1966. And on the British hit, *Evil Hearted You*, the slide sounded like a mournful Hawaiian lap steel. But Beck had discovered other uses of the slide; onstage he sometimes put it on his *right* hand (i.e. picking hand), and combined with his left hand he created the impression of two guitars going at once. The effect was caught on camera as early as the Yardbirds' appearance on "Shindig!" in September 1965.

A turning point was *Beck's Bolero*, where the distinction between slide and regular fingering was blurred; some of the flowing lines were metal to string, while others were flesh to string. When he went solo in 1967, Beck used double-tracked slide on *Tallyman*, while *Love Is Blue* was another slide/finger excercise. Jeff was a bit restrictive with the slide on *Truth* (with the notable exception of the backing to *Shapes of Things*), but *Beck-Ola* featured plenty of slide, just listen to the volley of shots on the fade of *Jailhouse Rock* or the panoramic slide guitar in portions of *Rice Pudding*.

With both the re-formed Jeff Beck Group and in Beck, Bogert & Appice, slide guitar was an important stylistic device both in the studio and on the stage, and on record his carefully crafted guitar orchestrations on *I Can't Give Back The Love I Feel For You* and *Definitely Maybe* on the *Jeff Beck Group* album are standouts.

In the jazz-rock years (1975–1980), the slide was always on hand (pun not intended!) in a live situation, where Jeff was able to convey both spine-chilling moments of beauty or – particularly on the stage versions of *Freeway Jam* – some of the rudest sounds ever emitted from a guitar. On record however, the effect was saved for colouring, although the *El Becko* riff was played on slide.

Post-1980, Beck has used slide extensively, often when doing versions of other people's songs, be it an absolutely masterful version of Santo & Johnny's *Sleepwalk* or the grand interpretation of the Beatles' *A Day In The Life*.

new Arista signing the Bisons, and he also attends another record company bash in honour of Manhattan Transfer later on during this spring tour.

•

This April, founding member Ritchie Blackmore quits Deep Purple after almost seven years. Looking for a replacement, the remaining four in the group draw up lists of their personal choices. Even though Jeff Beck tops the polls, the band is suspicious, as David Coverdale later recalls to NEW MUSICAL EXPRESS: "He's very much his own man." The NME reporter shoots back: "An even more determined Blackmore?", to which Coverdale laughs: "Exactly, excellent! He's very individual. It's generally accepted that he'll form a new band every month, go on the road or record an album, and then disband it."

April 19, 1975: British teeny bopper mania peaks when Bay City Rollers tops both UK single and album charts this week.

May 1975: US tour takes in Boston, Detroit, Chicago ...

MAY

THU 1ST
Avery Fisher Hall, Lincoln Center, New York, New York
The two nights at Avery Fisher Hall, promoted by Howard Stein and Ron Delsener, gross a combined $39,500 at the box office from two sellout crowds totalling 5,600 fans.

FRI 2ND
The Spectrum, Philadelphia, Pennsylvania
A quick rescheduling finds Beck and McLaughlin playing Philadelphia's big Spectrum tonight instead of a Boston appearance, which is moved to the following night. The Philly concert attracts 8,000 fans and grosses $40,000. "It knocks me out when I can fill out the Spectrum ... and walk on stage and get received like you're a god or something ... you can't describe it until you've heard it", Beck enthuses to Gordon Fletcher a few days later.

Also today, Jeff is one of the featured attractions on episode #118 of the US TV show "Midnight Special", broadcast on the NBC network this evening (▶ April 1).

SAT 3RD
Music Hall, Boston, Massachusetts
"If there is such a thing as free form soul music, then this is how you would have to describe Beck's new bag of tricks. Reunited with pianist Max Middleton ... Beck wove some jazzy, improvisational guitar images in and around traditional rock structures" is the praise William Howard in the BOSTON GLOBE (May 6) showers on Beck after tonight's show, before he counters "... however, my worst fears were realized. Time after time he drifted aimlessly through these same tunes, carrying on far too long with his solos, thus losing the remarkable tension he developed so well in the studio", before summing up "... an off-night with Beck can still be a rewarding aural experience." John McLaughlin appears on stage with Jeff for the encore.

Today, NEW MUSICAL EXPRESS reports that Jeff Beck is expected to go back on the road in Britain after his US jaunt, and furthermore that he has a new album in the can, with a release date to be tied in with his projected UK concerts. Neither the tour nor the album sees the light of day, the latter probably meant cleaning up and finishing the songs Beck recorded during spring 1974 before Max Middleton and George Martin came on board.

SUN 4TH
New Haven Veterans Memorial Coliseum, New Haven, Connecticut
Promoted by Cornucopia Productions, the New Haven concert fills 6,000 seats, with box office receipts totalling $28,000 out of a potential $37,000.

🎧 A sterling performance by Jeff, Max, Wilbur and Bernard ushers in *Constipated Duck* (with much space for Bascomb's nimble fingers), before Purdie sets the reggae mood after an extensive round-the-kit display on the intro to *She's A Woman*. For *Freeway Jam* Beck clearly sports the Stratocaster, toying with the vibrato arm quite violently. Before *Superstition*, he plays a teasingly little riff out of the BBA book (the intro to *Lady*). Max Middleton is given an opportunity to shine on an superb unaccompanied interlude on a grand piano – just like he did in the second Beck Group – mixing neo-classicism and ragtimes. This gives way to Jeff's grand version of *'Cause We've Ended As Lovers*, a prime example of Beck the interpreter. Stanley Clarke's *Power* follows, featuring a pleasant round of trading fours between Jeff and Max. As the song is brought to a stop, Jeff jokingly whips out the *I Ain't Superstitious* riff, before *Power* segues into *Got The Feeling*, where the guitar switches between a bell-like clarity, a whiff of wah-wah and a nice distorted tone. *Diamond Dust* is maybe the highlight of the night, where the guitar improvises flowingly and effortlessly over the jazzy groove. The short set then ends with a brief jam on the simple *Get Down In The Dirt* riff.

TUE 6TH
Stanley Theater, Pittsburgh, Pennsylvania
Tonight is sold out, with the box office tallying $22,000.

WED 7TH
Music Hall, Cleveland, Ohio
Recalling his more tempermental days in the Yardbirds, in a fit of anger over his malfunctioning guitar, Jeff throws it to the stage so the body is shattered. As a consequence Beck has to rely on rented guitars from local music stores for a few nights.

Tonight, McLaughlin and the Mahavishnu Orhcestra are first out. A good thing, according to Mark Kmetzko in THE SCENE (May 15–21): "From the moment Jeff Beck plugged in, it was obvious that the real show was about to begin. Working in a totally instrumental framework, and largely from his *Blow By Blow* album, Beck turned in an incredible display of technique, taste and feeling. He definitely rearranged my list of best electric guitarists, I can tell you that. Though there were three other musicians on stage with him, Beck was the only one I watched. It was impossible for me to take my eyes from his hands as they gave the guitar a workout the likes of which I haven't seen in years. Yes, Beck was the star of the show, but he was wise enough to let keyboardist Max Middleton work out, too. His lighter, jazz-oriented lines were a nice contrast to the sheer energy of Beck's outings. Also to be congratulated was veteran drummer Bernard Purdie, who pushed Beck along at an incredible pace."

THU 8TH
Arie Crown Theater, Chicago, Illinois
The Beck/McLaughlin double-bill is hot property as witnessed by tonight's two houses – promoted by Howard Stein – which pull 7,700 fans with a $55,100 gross. Before the show there is an accident involving one of Dawson's road crew, when a wastebasket filled with pyrotechnics (from Hawkwind's concert the previous night) explodes.

In Chicago, freelance writer Gordon Fletcher joins the tour for a few days. Fletcher interviews Jeff at large for features published in CREEM (August 1975) and TRANS-OCEANIC TROUSER PRESS (September/October 1975). In CREEM, Beck shows contentment ("I guess this one [*Blow By Blow*] is my favourite of all the records I've cut – there's sure more music on it – and even though I'm still looking for what I really want I'm quite satisfied with it") and financial security (seconded by Ernest Chapman's comment: "Hell, we never spend any money anyway"). The TROUSER PRESS piece is more indepth, and has Jeff philosophizing on fame and the trappings of stardom: "... I think the public has more respect for you if you stick your neck out and do what you want to do and let them follow you. The Faces and Led Zeppelin are catering to the public – giving them just what they want and they're going home happy as can be – but sooner or later they're gonna want to be led somewhere, however much they hate new things, like you turn over a new page ... like in

May 1975: Single "She's A Woman" released in the UK ...

Antonioni's "Blowup" when everyone was scrambling for a piece of broken guitar, and when they get it, the guy who picks it up in the street doesn't know what to do with it. It's the epitome of life – you want a guitar, you bash your mother in the shins until she gets you one, then it goes flying out the window."

Beck also points out black music's importance to him ("You cannot ignore it") and cites guitarist Freddie Stone, Sly's brother, as a personal favourite.

FRI 9TH
Masonic Temple, Detroit, Michigan
After the first house (where McLaughlin again joins Beck for no less than three encores), Jeff is interviewed by Lowell Cauffiel for a story published in GUITAR PLAYER (November 1975). Cauffiel is very concerned about Jeff's progression from "the cliches on the 1968 album *Truth*" to the "run[s] up the neck in rapid-fire notes – jazz style." A view, admittedly, Beck supports: "[My music] crosses the gap between white rock and Mahavishnu or jazz-rock. It bridges a lot of gaps. It's more digestible, the rhythms are easier to understand than Mahavishnu's. It's more on the fringe." Jan Hammer's influence is again put forward by Beck: "He plays the Moog a lot like the guitar, and his sounds went straight into me. So I started to play like him. I mean, I didn't sound like him, but his phrases influenced me immensely."

SAT 10TH
Mecca-Milwaukee Auditorium, Milwaukee, Wisconsin
The review in THE BUGLE-AMERICAN (May 21) by Dan Kelly claims: "Beck has always been one of the most melodic players in rock. He's improved to the point where even his flash fits in harmonically with the lines he plays. His main melody sounds like thinking something through logically and the flash becomes a new idea. Beck might develop this or drop it, but he lets it come through. He is obviously skillful enough to play anything he wants – sometimes I wish he had more to say in his writing, but I suppose these limitations themselves are part of his overall appeal." But Kelly is also critical of Beck's band, and even confuses the names of the rhythm section, believing they are the two playing on *Blow By Blow*. Beck headlines and McLaughlin comes back for the customary double encore: "I've never heard an ovation as loud or spontaneous as the one which Beck and McLaughlin earned together, and was sorely disappointed that they came back [after the first encore] for a bow rather than a blast."

SUN 11TH
Ambassador Theater, St. Louis, Missouri
Last concert of the first leg of Jeff and McLaughlin's co-headliner tour.

MON 12TH✷
After the series of concerts on the East Coast and in the Midwest, the tour takes a twelve day break, so Beck and Middleton fly home to England, while Bascomb and Purdie presumably return to New York.

FRI 23RD
In Great Britain, two *Blow By Blow* tracks, *She's A Woman* coupled with *It Doesn't Really Matter*, are released as a single. The flip-side is, confusingly, the same song as *You Know What I Mean*. The single is scantly promoted, but it is given its fair share or reviews in the British music press. Like NEW MUSICAL EXPRESS (June 7), whose Andrew Tyler drily notes: "George Martin produced this one. His production is very clean. And Jeff, except when he catches handnail in the bridge a couple of times, is very clean too." John Peel, in SOUNDS (June 14), is more serious and he also loves the song: "Jeff Beck plays superbly here ... The band play with remarkable economy, providing an unswerving and rich canvas on which Jeff can expand at will. He tries a little of this, a little of that, bringing a marvellous technique and equal invention to everything he plays. In two minutes and 50 seconds you get some indication just how far the electric guitar can be taken." All the same, Jeff's lilting reggae treatment of this old Lennon/McCartney tune does not make the singles charts.

SUN 25TH
Jeff is one of the many guests invited to a special party after the last of Led Zeppelin's breathtaking run of five soldout nights at London's Earl's Court. The party is held in a restaurant within the Earl's Court complex. Present also are Jon Anderson and Chris Squire from Yes, Marianne Faithfull, Denny Laine and BBC disc jockeys Alan Freeman and Bob Harris, while Dr. Feelgood and Gonzalez supply the music.

Jeff also attends the Earl's Court concert, but is not impressed at all: "I saw the show and I thought they were filth. It sounds like somebody paralysed his [Jimmy Page's] arms or something ...".

TUE 27TH
This is likely the day when Jeff and Max fly back to the States for the first concert of the second leg of the Mahavishnu–Beck tour, this time covering dates on the West Coast and in the South. McLaughlin and Mahavishnu Orchestra have already played a date alone in New Orleans on the 24th.

WED 28TH
JEFF BECK:
FIRST NORTH AMERICAN TOUR;
SECOND LEG
Exhibition Hall, Phoenix Civic Plaza, Phoenix, Arizona
The Phoenix concert is given an in-depth analysis by Bob Henschen in DOWNBEAT (September 11), where Beck closes the second half: "During the half-hour equipment change, Rod Stewart look-alikes and their suburban Phoenix groupie-alikes waited for the rock Jeff Beck. What they actually got was a taste of jazz and funk. Beck's 'new direction', mistakenly hailed as a Mahavishnu derivative by a myriad of critics, is a logical development for a remarkable talent. ... the alleged Mahavishnu influence [on Beck] pro-

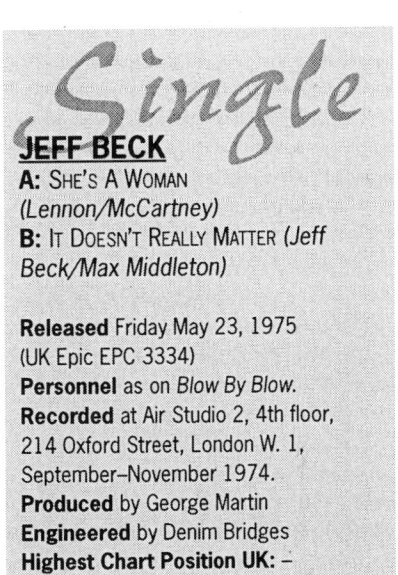

Single
JEFF BECK
A: SHE'S A WOMAN
(Lennon/McCartney)
B: IT DOESN'T REALLY MATTER (Jeff Beck/Max Middleton)

Released Friday May 23, 1975
(UK Epic EPC 3334)
Personnel as on *Blow By Blow*.
Recorded at Air Studio 2, 4th floor, 214 Oxford Street, London W. 1, September–November 1974.
Produced by George Martin
Engineered by Denim Bridges
Highest Chart Position UK: –

May 24, 1975: Earth, Wind & Fire have a double US chart streak with a #1 album ("That's The Way of The World") and a #1 single ("Shining Star").

June 1975: Single "You Know What I Mean" released in the US ...

ved more indirectly compositional than directly stylistic. Beck's guitar technique is completely individual, employing more spaces than McLaughlin's, and with an enduring propensity for the blues. And rhythm. Beck's 75-minute set opened and closed with funky excerpts from his hit album *Blow By Blow* ... In between, Jeff's group played jazz-rock with a vengeance – and adequate acoustics. Hulking Bernard Purdie was a focal point. Rocking back and forth in excellent spirits, Purdie complimented Beck with his usual combination of power and finesse. After the introductory funk numbers, Purdie got the pace motivating for an extended *Freeway Jam*. Soloing at first over the top of a rush-hour pace, Beck then moved the tune into a long slowdown. Using a metal slide to pick above the frets, he dallied brilliantly with a melodic offshoot for almost two minutes before yielding to Middleton's electric piano break, Beck talking back with his guitar between keyboard phrases." Hopes for a Jeff–John jam, however, "were erased by the sudden authority of bright house lights."

THU 29TH
Golden Hall, Convention & Performing Arts Center, San Diego, California

FRI 30TH
Shrine Auditorium, Los Angeles, California

Sold out a week in advance, the Los Angeles concert (promoted by David Forest's Fun Productions) takes in $37,434. Among the 6,290 strong audience is Walter Becker, who is sufficiently impressed by Bernard Purdie to invite him to a future Steely Dan session.

Jeff also talks to Steven Rosen for a cover story in INTERNATIONAL MUSICIAN AND RECORDING WORLD (October 1975). Again there is talk of a hookup with Stevie Wonder: "As a matter of fact, I'm due to go back and play some more with him on his new album. He's got a really good song for me to play on", Beck tells Rosen. However, this intriguing collaboration never gets off the ground (Stevie Wonder will not release a new album until the double album *Songs In The Key of Life* in October next year). Jeff also has a softer view on the Rolling Stones than his harsh comments in the same magazine earlier in the year: "[They have] gone right round the bend, silk trousers and silly hats. It seems like they all have, the Faces, the Stones – not so much the Stones, because I have an affection for them in a funny sort of way".

SAT 31ST
Winterland, San Francisco, California

"Mystery, too, seemed to cloak Beck's musical intentions as he took the stage after intermission. He started his set by riffing off light, quick lines and riding the thunderous rhythm section ... The tentative beginning was a mild surprise to those who remembered Beck's last appearance in San Francisco two years ago ... tonight, as Beck loosened up, he asserted himself through clear, ringing notes, assembled in increasingly complex, far-out combinations. He pulled out a bottleneck for some effects that owed considerably more to Santo & Johnny than to Elmore James. ... The 55-minute performance was capped by the anticipated jam between Beck and Mahavishnu. Beck, obviously excited by McLaughlin's awesome, fiery chops, finally lost his reserve. Waving his hands wildly above his head, he stood there grinning broadly, shouting, while McLaughlin blasted away. Beck offered the jam's theme – a typical Beck dancing, melodic figure – but actually soloed little during the encore, allowing McLaughlin to dominate the five-minute closing segment. The second encore was short and simple. Instead of playing, Beck and McLaughlin took a few extra bows, hugged each other and danced offstage", writes Joel Selvin in ROLLING STONE (July 3).

JUNE

SUN 1ST
Civic Auditorium, San Jose, California

The American radio programme "Rock Around The World" (show #43) features an interview with Jeff Beck today (▶ April 18–21). Photographer Jim Marshall accompanies Jeff for a wild car ride down to San Jose.

MON 2ND

A single of *You Know What I Mean* coupled with *Constipated Duck* is released in the US.

TUE 3RD
Paramount Northwest Theater, Portland, Oregon

John Wendeborn reflects on tonight's concert in the OREGONIAN (June 4): "The Beck sound was a high energy mellowness that featured the guitarist's at times stinging and at other times singing instrumental lines. The sell-out crowd of 3,000 went wild after the initial portion of the show and kept up a roar that resulted in the Beck foursome returning for about 15 minutes of encores ... The total sound was high-powered all the way and showed why Beck is included in the handful of guitar talents who form the bulwark of English music."

WED 4TH
Paramount Northwest Theater, Seattle, Washington

The two reviews in the biggest Seattle papers – published the following day – both praise Beck's return to Seattle.

Patrick McDonald in THE SEATTLE TIMES (June 5) enthuses: "Jeff Beck renewed his credentials as one of the finest electric guitarists ever with a set that has to count among the best of the year ... And his music is now totally instrumental. He no longer has a vocalist to play off of, which is sad in a way because he was good at that, but by expanding his role as sole lead he's also expanded his playing. His style is now much more varied. He's always been technically impressive, but last night even more than ever. The way he shaped and bent notes in *Though We've Ended Now As Lovers* [sic], for instance, was like nothing he's done before ... Beck's playing was completely effortless and he looked like he was enjoying himself immensely. The full house audience was enjoying itself, too – Beck got standing ovations during and after each number and two encores weren't enough. A lot of people left after Beck – indeed, it was a hard act for Mahavishnu to follow."

D. P. Bond of THE SEATTLE POST-INTELLIGENCER (June 5) is also won over: "It was encouraging to see Beck in rare form again, not at all burned

---

Single
JEFF BECK

A: YOU KNOW WHAT I MEAN *(Jeff Beck/Max Middleton)*
B: CONSTIPATED DUCK *(Beck)*

Released Monday June 2, 1975 (US Epic 8-50112)
Personnel as on *Blow By Blow*.
Recorded at Air Studio 2, 4th floor, 214 Oxford Street, London, September–November 1974.
Produced by George Martin
Engineered by Denim Bridges
Highest Chart Position US: –

© June 1, 1975: The Rolling Stones with Ron Wood on guitar begins a coast-to-coast US tour in Baton Rouge, Lousiana.

out as some of his compatriots ... Perhaps the reason for this is that he's never stood still musically, preferring rather to experiment in one style after another. The result has been an ever increasing popularity, which is more than artistically justified ... Some give his recent work a jazz appelation, but I think that's too confining a term. His renditions of Stevie Wonder's *Superstition* and Lennon–McCartney's old tune, *She's A Woman*, were branded with his own distinct style." Bond also comments that Beck elects to perform despite having just received the news of his mother's death, who passed away on June 2nd.

AMERICA'S TOP 30 ALBUMS

#		Title	Artist	Label
1	—	CAPTAIN FANTASTIC	Elton John	MCA
2	1	THAT'S THE WAY OF THE WORLD	Earth, Wind & Fire	Columbia
3	2	TOMMY	Soundtrack	Polydor
4	5	BLOW BY BLOW	Jeff Beck	Epic
5	6	HEARTS	America	Warner Bros
6	7	WELCOME TO MY NIGHTMARE	Alice Cooper	Atlantic
7	4	CHICAGO VIII	Chicago	Columbia
8	3	STRAIGHT SHOOTER	Bad Company	Swan Song
9	9	NUTHIN' FANCY	Lynyrd Skynyrd	MCA
10	10	PLAYING POSSUM	Carly Simon	Elektra
11	14	STAMPEDE	Doobie Brothers	Warner Bros
12	—	FOUR WHEEL DRIVE	Bachman-Turner Overdrive	Mercury
13	17	SPIRIT OF AMERICA	Beach Boys	Capitol
14	20	MISTER MAGIC		
15	19	SURVIVAL		

SAT 7TH
Field House, Regis College, Denver, Colorado

Blow By Blow peaks at #4 in the BILLBOARD chart (dated today) for a solitary week, nestling below Elton John's *Captain Fantastic And The Brown Dirt Cowboy* (which has shot right to the number one slot from outside the Top Thirty this week), Earth Wind & Fire's *That's The Way Of The World* and the soundtrack from *Tommy*. As a nice side effect, the brisk sales of *Blow By Blow* also reactivates Jeff Beck's back catalogue.

SUN 8TH
University of New Mexico, Albuquerque, New Mexico

MON 9TH
Civic Center, El Paso, Texas

Just before tonight's concert, McLaughlin's spare guitar is destroyed in a fall, utterly incredibly as McLaughlin's main, two-necked guitar broke to pieces the night before in Albuquerque. With no more spares, McLaughlin borrows Jeff Beck's extra Les Paul for tonight's show and for the rest of the tour.

WED 11TH
Dallas Memorial Auditorium, Dallas, Texas

Originally slated for Dallas Convention Center, the show is then switched to the city's Memorial Auditorium. The otherwise positive Darlene Richardson (DALLAS MORNING NEWS, June 13) is not sure what to make of Jeff Beck's voice bag contraption, and dubs it an "airbag vocal guitar distorter". The Dallas concert draws a crowd of 7,000 and grosses $36,000.

THU 12TH
Municipal Auditorium, San Antonio, Texas

FRI 13TH
Oklahoma Civic Center Music Hall, Oklahoma City, Oklahoma

SAT 14TH
Tulsa Assembly Centre, Tulsa, Oklahoma

Both Jeff and John have been tentatively booked for the "Arizona '75 Music Festival" in Chandler, Arizona this weekend, with a wide ranging selection of bluegrass, country, gospel and rock and roll groups, but this is eventually cancelled.

David Mandrell's observations in THE TULSA TRIBUNE (June 16) fall in line with what almost every music critic remark on this tour: a rejuvenated and daring yet perfectly accessible Jeff Beck: "[He] was especially enjoyable ... Instead of worrying about being upstaged by the vocalist or limiting himself to blues and rock, Beck has decided to let his guitar do all the work, and by doing so he's solved both problems. Although he was a bit ragged at first, his fingers apparently loosened up, because by the time he played his second encore, he was still surpassing himself with each new number. The key to Beck's effectiveness is that he's a bit eccentric in his playing. Totally unpredictable, Beck is a true original who obviously still has a lot more to say."

SUN 15TH
Music Hall, Houston, Texas

The very last concert of the tour, and John McLaughlin comes out after Beck's closing performance for a final, double-encore. Whereas this tour has become the launching pad for Beck's resurgence, for McLaughlin the tour will be followed by a period of contemplation before he emerges early next year with the all-acoustic format Shakti.

MON 16TH✱
Beck and Middleton fly home.

JULY

FRI 18TH
JEFF BECK:
FIRST NORTH AMERICAN TOUR; THIRD LEG
Edmonton Coliseum, Edmonton, Canada

With *Blow By Blow* still hot, Beck, Bascomb, Middleton, Purdie with Ralph Baker return to the road, this time to cover unchartered territory with dates in Canada, a dip down to the South, then to Hawaii – all as a lead-up to Jeff's first return to Japan since 1973. The set list is kept identical to the earlier USA jaunt.

Tonight's opening attraction is the eclectic country-rock octet Commander Cody And His Lost Planet Airmen.

SAT 19TH
Queen Elizabeth Theater, Vancouver, Canada

"If it weren't for all those nifty licks he tears off one right after another it would be easy to lose Jeff Beck on stage. He's not quite a diminutive figure but he is remarkably free of excessive posturing and wild gestures. Geez, I have friends in North Vancouver who look more like a British Rock Star than he does. The difference is this guitar growing outta his hip and these fingers scrambling intelligently up and down its neck and the combination drives people further back into their seat," compliments Tom Harrison under the headline 'Have Guitar Will Throttle' in GEORGIA STRAIGHT (July 24–31). Harrison concludes: "He no longer needs gimmicks, the gimmicks critics always pointed to when dismissing Beck as curtly as possible, because the effects he goes after are always appropriate."

Commander Cody and his Airmen are again booked to play support but fail to appear, so local Vancouver singer/guitarist Bim opens the show instead. Promoted by John Bauer Concerts, the hall is sold-out (capacity 2,823) with a $22,283 take.

August 1975: Jeff Beck comes down with pneumonia ...

MON 21ST
Winnipeg Arena, Winnipeg, Canada
Vancouver group Chilliwack provide support for Beck's performance at the Arena in Winnipeg, which is another sell-out with an estimated crowd of 8,000 people.

Barbara Cansino of THE WINNIPEG FREE PRESS (July 22) attends the concert: "Jeff Beck, playing with drums, keyboard and bass guitar, gave one of the best rock performances Winnipeg has likely seen ever. Whatever pitfalls Beck might have experienced, they seem irrelevant after Monday night's concert ... The concert was characterized by Beck's incredible mastery of the guitar, and the rapport and synchronization within the group." Encores seem to abound on this tour: "Beck plays so fast, his range is so seemingly limitless, his phrasing so complex, his arrangements so inventive, that the two raging encores seemed more a desire to hang on to an experience because of its musical rarity as much as its excellence."

Writer Jim Millican meets Jeff prior to the show for an interview later published in the Canadian music journal SOUND (March 1976). As many others who meet Beck on this spring and summer tour, Jeff's bad boy image ("I've got my friends to thank for all that") is a recurring theme – especially when Beck reveals himself to be both talkative and an interesting subject. Unusually, Beck is in a retrospective mood, talking about everything from Carmine Appice to the Yardbirds. Jeff cannot praise George Martin's contributions to the new album enough: "Martin was excellent, very good, a very objective person to have around. He controlled any wild ideas we had and pushed them out the window if they weren't conducive to the way the album was going. He's got an incredible presence in a recording studio and I knew, when I played a note or a run or something, that he was aware of the structure. It's nice to work with somebody who knows a G flat from an A minor. He was just an all-round ear with advice and he emulsified the energies that were there and I think that's what a producer should do."

WED 23RD
O'Keefe Center, Toronto, Canada
Small Wonders provide support and there are two shows tonight. Bryan Johnson in TORONTO GLOBE AND MAIL (July 24) gives the concert a strong review under the title 'Jeff Beck a Virtuoso Smith of Heavy Metal'.

A typical Beck night, where his guitar touches all points between fearlessness, pure inspiration and sloppiness. As always, he begins the concert with lightly darting off some unaccompanied riffs, before he signals the opening number *You Know What I Mean*. The slide guitar on *Definitely Maybe* veers from a featherlight touch to a frenetic wobble, and is the night's first highlight. A very fast *Superstition* is so reckless it threatens to go completely off the rails. Max Middleton's excellent introduction to *'Cause We've Ended As Lovers* avoids the boogie woogie routines, and Beck concludes the ballad with a very brief *Jeff's Boogie* with the bluegrass coda thrown in. After a request from the audience for *Lady*, Jeff replies with the two-chorded intro much to the delight of the crowd, but *Power* rambles on good-naturedly with little direction. But on *Got The Feeling* Beck suddenly springs to life again, his guitar playing to the point and full of ideas. The night ends with a loose *Get Down In The Dirt*.

SAT 26TH
Ted Gormley Stadium, City Park, New Orleans, Louisiana
Another unvisited port on the *Blow By Blow* tour is New Orleans, where Jeff Beck plays today in a festival setting in adverse weather conditions. Also on the bill are ZZ Top, Fleetwood Mac, Aerosmith, J. Boy Adams, Trooper and compere Wolfman Jack.

Beck has to perform in pouring rain, and complains to the local underground paper BROKEN BARRIERS (August 20–September 19): "I couldn't fuckin' play, the rain was dripping down on me guitar strings. They were hard to hold." Still, his performance is hitting home: "He did about everything you can expect from a Fender Stratocaster. One moment he's hitting incredibly searing notes in the upper registers, then moves into some bouncy rhythms, changing tempos quickly ... Beck sings *Superstition* through a pickup in his guitar, really stirring up the boogie freaks. ... The set closes out with some good French-inspired march rhythms in a hard rock-mellow jazz context. This is ZZ Top's crowd, but they give the master an enthusiastic standing ovation."

SUN 27TH–TUE 29TH
Flying straight on to Hawaii on the Sunday, Jeff Beck does not feel well because of a swollen throat and a bad cold. He checks into the Kaiser Hospital on Sunday and stays overnight, before he receives treatment from a Dr. Edwin Dierdorff at his hotel room on Tuesday.

(A previously scheduled date at Municipal Auditorium in Atlanta, Georgia on July 28 is cancelled.)

WED 30TH
Honolulu International Center Arena, Honolulu, Hawaii
A 10 minute sound check is held at 3 pm before Beck leaves the stage because of his condition. Despite Jeff's cold, the concert does not only go ahead but is a huge success according to the local review in SUNBUMS (July 1975): "Playing a set that featured almost total lead guitar and no singing, Beck started out with full-tilt energy that made Clapton's slow beat/blues look lethargic. [Jeff] was the man in command, with his guitar coming through loud and clear, as the focal point of a positive new sound that emphasized, for the first time in Beck's career, his extremely proficient and unique guitar playing talents."

Promoted by John Bauer Concerts, the concert pulls 6,700 spectators for a $40,672 gross. The Richie Walker Band play support.

THU 31ST
Because of his bad cold, Beck decides to stay in Hawaii for a few days instead of flying on to Japan as planned.

AUGUST

FRI 1ST
Middleton, Bascomb and Purdie arrive at Haneda airport in Tokyo at 4 pm on flight PA-831 from Hawaii, while Jeff and Ralph Baker stay behind in Honolulu.

September 1975: Recording sessions for new album in London ...

SUN 3RD
JEFF BECK:
FIRST JAPANESE TOUR
"World Rock Festival Eastland"
Okunai-Kyogijo, Makomanai, Sapporo, Japan

A Japanese disc jockey and promoter has organised a travelling festival dubbed the "World Rock Festival Eastland" for a five-city tour of Japan, headlined by a trio of Western artists: the New York Dolls, Felix Pappalardi and Jeff Beck. Today's festival begins at noon and features a host of Japanese groups (Jipang, Sky Rock Blues Band, Close To The Edge, Carmen Maki & OZ, Yonin-Bayashi, Creation and Cosmos Factory) besides the Dolls and Felix Pappalardi (who performs with the local Joe Yamanaka). Jeff Beck is set to close the show, and arrives in Tokyo from Hawaii and flies immediately on a domestic flight to Sapporo, landing just past 7 o'clock. At 8.30 pm Jeff arrives for a quick sound check and play their hour-long set, although Jeff is still hampered by his cold.

MON 4TH
A day off involves just flying from Sapporo to Nagoya, where Beck checks in at the city's Kankou Hotel.

TUE 5TH
"World Rock Festival Eastland"
Ken-Taiikukan, Aichi, Nagoya, Japan

The second concert of the Japanese tour features a different batch of Japanese groups (Far East Family Band, Gedoh, West Road Blues Band) plus Creation; the only local group that will do the whole tour and incidentally will work with Felix Pappalardi later on. Interestingly, this group's latest single is a cover of *Happenings Ten Years Time Ago*.

WED 6TH
After leaving Nagoya in the morning, Jeff arrives in Kyoto at noon, by now feeling so ill that a doctor is called, who diagnoses acute pneumonia and orders him to get complete rest. As today's scheduled concert is another open-air festival and in pouring rain to boot, it is decided to cancel Jeff's appearance. Instead Beck and Baker board the Superexpress to Tokyo.

THU 7TH
"World Rock Festival Eastland"
Korakuen Stadium, Tokyo, Japan

Because of Jeff's illness, a flight home to England is booked, and to allow enough time to make the departure, his appearance today is pushed forward to half past three. After Beck's quick 45 minute show, he goes to hospital first and then to Haneda airport, where he boards flight BA-981 back to London at 9.45 pm.

FRI 9TH
The last concert of the 'World Rock Festival Eastland' goes ahead in Sendai but without Jeff Beck.

•

During the summer Jeff moves from his cottage in Egerton and to a larger place in Wadhurst in East Sussex named River Hall. Described as a 'castle', the stone house was built in 1591 by an arms maker and drawn by an architect who allegedly served under Elizabeth I (1533–1603): "It's three floors and all beamed, and when you walk in the door it's like going back two, three hundred years", Jeff explains in a CIRCUS feature in 1976. Roger Daltrey has a similar country home nearby in Burwash on the Kent–Sussex border, but otherwise it is still a few years before the countryside south of London will be well populated by rock stars.

Beck moves in with girlfriend Celia Hammond and their menagerie of cats and dogs. The old stone house is being slowly refurbished; in fact it is the same place he lives in to this very day. With ample room for all his vehicles, a separate music room and a tranquil country atmosphere, this is Beck's ideal home.

At Wadhurst he recovers from his bout of pneumonia, and gets ready for a follow-up to *Blow By Blow*.

SEPTEMBER

FRI 12TH–TUE 30TH *
On September 12 Jeff Beck returns to the studio to begin work on a new album. Sessions are again held at Air, with the occasional trip to Trident, and for the next three to four weeks he keeps up a fairly intensive recording schedule. Acutely aware of the pressure to make a follow up to match his latest solo success, Jeff spends considerably time putting together this album.

George Martin is enlisted as producer once more, but another Air employee, Chris Bond, is increasingly involved in the control room, to the point where he is later credited as 'Production Assistant'. A series of engineers work on the sessions, including Martin's right-hand man Geoff Emerick, well-known for his work on many Beatles sessions.

NIGHT AFTER NIGHT

Show By Show

To promote *Blow By Blow*, Jeff Beck toured the US with John McLaughlin in the spring of 1975. Jeff had the good sense to give the audiences on this tour a nice contrast to McLaughlin's complex, jazz-based material. In fact, McLaughlin's music in 1975 was less accessible than the original Mahavishnu Orchestra, who combined high-energy, virtuoso musicianship and strong compositions with impeccable improvisations.

For the occasion, Beck assembled a tight little band with Max Middleton, bassist Wilbur Bascomb and ace drummer Bernard 'Pretty' Purdie. This funky group – more the MGs or the Meters than the Mahavishnu – should have done some recordings together if one is to judge by the live tapes in circulation. The colourful Purdie, in particular, seemed to give Jeff much inspiration; his forceful drumming pressed Beck to ascend new heights and also provided a rock steady backcloth of depth and dynamics. Purdie had a long pedigree; he was credited with first coming up with the hi-hat 'bark' and bizarrely also insisted on having overdubbed drums on original Beatles hits. Even if research proves he did indeed add drums to some Tony Sheridan-era Beatles recordings for the American market, Purdie definitely never re-did any of Ringo Starr's drum tracks.

Unfortunately, Jeff Beck never found time or care to take this funky quartet into a studio. A live album from one of the group's sizzling performances would also have made a perfect souvenir, but this was sadly never discussed either. ■

Material seems to come much harder for Beck this time around, who instead relies on his backing men to come up with suitable songs. And instead of using the same ensemble throughout, individual songs are done with different musicians.

A pair of songs are recorded with Max Middleton and Richard Bailey plus new bassist Wilbur Bascomb, both believed to be cut at Trident. One is a song co-credited to Bascomb and Upp's Andi Clark called *Head For Backstage Pass*. (Clark himself does not appear on the track.) The other is the old Charlie Mingus song *Goodbye Pork Pie Hat*. Middleton suggests they

October 1975: Jeff Beck on a bill with the Faces and Aerosmith in the US ...

record the song after hearing Beck fool around with the tune in rehearsals. Jeff in turn is inspired by the acoustic version John McLaughlin did on his *My Goal's Beyond* album.

A key contributor to the rest of the sessions is drummer Michael Walden, who Jeff met during the spring tour with the Mahavishnu Orchestra. Besides being a powerful percussionist and an able keyboardist, Walden also comes up with four songs: *Come Dancing, Sophie, Play With Me* and the acoustic *Love Is Green*. Lastly, the Max Middleton composition *Led Boots* (the title a gentle poke at Jimmy Page) is also recorded at these sessions.

Whereas his recent solo success was relatively easy to concoct – with much of Jeff's solos being first takes and off-the-cuff improvisations – the new album is painstakingly put together with a series of overdubs, edits and spliced tracks. George Martin later describes the process thus: "When [Jeff's new album] came along, it was less [fun], because *Blow By Blow* had been a huge success in the States, and re-established Jeff as being a major force in records ... the sequel to that had all the earmarks of being an even bigger blockbuster, so Jeff was desperately worried about this, and fretted about each solo and took longer to do it. The atmosphere wasn't right, and he wanted to work at home if I gave him the backing tracks, and that sort of thing, so it was a much more worrying album to finish. ... We had nothing to lose when we made *Blow By Blow*, but now we would have."

The sessions likely continue into the very first week of October, too, before Jeff heads back on the road for a few concerts in the States.

OCTOBER

MON 14TH*
Beck and Middleton with Wilbur Bascomb (who has been in England during sessions for the new album) fly to the States for a few dates in the Southeast, thereby completing their criss-crossing of America this year.

WED 15TH AND THU 16TH
JEFF BECK:
FIRST NORTH AMERICAN TOUR;
FOURTH LEG
Civic Centre, Lakeland, Florida
Jeff Beck is sandwiched between Aerosmith and the Faces on their final US trek. The Faces are dinintegrating fast;

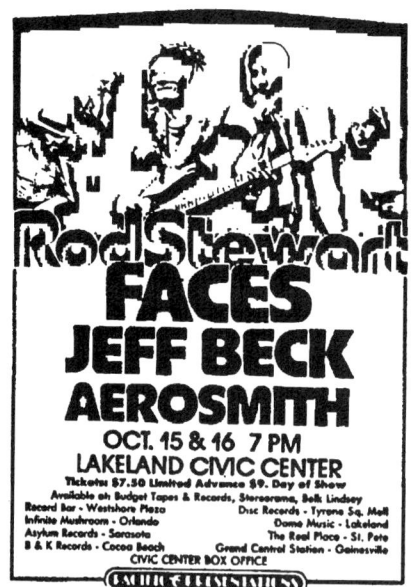

Ronnie Lane has long since left the band to be replaced by Japanese bassist Tetsu Yamauchi and Ron Wood has secured a place in the Rolling Stones. The group is even billed as 'Rod Stewart and the Faces' (common sense dictates this as Stewart is riding the charts with *Atlantic Crossing*). For this tour, The Faces are enlarged with Jesse Ed Davis on guitar and even a string section. An unconfirmed report says Beck jams with the Faces on one of these nights in Lakeland.

Also on the 15th, *Blow By Blow* is certified gold in the US for $1 million in retail sales. (After 1979, gold albums are awarded for more than 500,000 units sold). To date, *Blow By Blow* ranks as Jeff Beck's biggest seller with about two million copies sold worldwide.

SAT 18TH
Gulf Stream Race Track, Hallendale, Florida

SUN 19TH
The Omni, Atlanta, Georgia
After the lightning visit to Florida and Georgia, Jeff breaks up his touring band. Max Middleton returns to England and his band Hummingbird again, taking Bernard Purdie with him for their 1976 album, *We Can't Go On Meeting Like This*.

NOVEMBER

Reputedly further recording sessions are held in London during November to polish and complete Jeff's new album, including overdubbing and mixing. Reportedly, it is Chris Bond who is in charge of these sessions as George Martin is occupied elsewhere.

All in all, Jeff Beck has by now finished an albumful of songs with a tentative release date set for spring next year.

Presumably, it is this month that Jeff also contributes to the second album by his protégés Upp, recorded at Air with Chris Bond at the controls. A trio no more, Upp have expanded to also include guitarist Dave Bunce. Whereas Jeff was all over the group's first album, Jeff only plays a single solo on *I Don't Want Nothing (To Change)* and possibly some rhythm parts on *Dance Your Troubles Away* (the latter contribution is not confirmed, even though the cover states Jeff plays on this tune). The album, titled *This Way Upp*, is released in May 1976, and also features guest appearances by Tom Scott and Gary Coleman.

DECEMBER

THU 18TH
A sign of Jeff Beck's cross-over popularity comes when *Blow By Blow* is voted 'Rock/Blues Album of the Year' in DOWN BEAT's 40th Readers Poll, dated today.

He is also voted second in the category 'Rock/Blues Musician of the Year' (behind Stevie Wonder who garners an overwhelming 1,013 votes to Jeff's 390), while in the jazz guitar (!) category he places tenth. Jeff also picks up many votes in the 'Rock/Blues Group' section.

•

In the annual GUITAR PLAYER Readers' Poll for 1975 (dated January 1976), Beck wins top honours in two categories; for 'Best Guitar LP' (for *Blow By Blow*), and for best guitarist in the general 'Rock' category.

November 1, 1975: The Faces break up after their last-ever performance in Hawaii.

◄ 1976

JANUARY

Reportedly, it is this month that Jeff Beck flies to New York, where he stays at the Navarro Hotel on Central Park South. The purpose of the visit is business, and Jeff is also interviewed by Steve Weitzman for a story published in THE MUSIC GIG (April 1976).

Jeff's new album – still unnamed – is in essence considered finished. The album is even set for a tentative release in March 1976, along with a US tour to begin in April. Beck also reveals that he plans to move to the States for a year.

Weitzman is puzzled by Jeff's disinterested stance, and ponders "... he is indeed an odd creature when compared to the rest of his ilk. He assumes none of your archetypical English rock star poses. Instead, he rests his defenses with a sadness of expression which never really disappears, even when he laughs. Why is Beck sad? Good question. Another good question is, why is Beck bored?" When Jeff states "there's only certain things that can be done on electric guitar and I've covered everything I want to do, really," Weitzman adds "making you think he'd just as soon take up shuffle-board instead".

FEBRUARY

SAT 7TH

NEW MUSICAL EXPRESS reports today: "Don't expect Jeff Beck and singer Frankie Miller to be forming a band together – it wasn't pleasantries the two were exchanging at the Speakeasy last week."

•

This month, Jeff Beck is put in touch with Jan Hammer – presumably at the behest of management and record company – and it is quickly decided to not only include Hammer on Beck's new album, but to make a more permanent Beck–Hammer union for touring purposes.

Since leaving the Mahavishnu Orchestra in 1973, Hammer has also recorded a pair of albums, *Like Children* (with Jerry Goodman) and, solo, *The First Seven Days*. To tour behind the last album, he has put together his own quartet featuring drummer Tony Smith, formerly with Azteca and Malo (Jorge Santana's group), bassist Fernando Saunders, earlier in Detroit's disco group Bohannon, and finally 19-year old violinist Steve Kindler, who briefly played with the very same version of Mahavishnu Orchestra that toured with Jeff the previous spring. Hammer, whose pre-Mahavishnu credentials include stints with regular jazzers like Sarah Vaughan and Elvin Jones, is also a huge fan of funk with a special affection for drummers, a love he shares with Jeff. Hammer is indeed also an able drummer. Managed by Elliot Sears, the Jan Hammer Group go on the road in late 1975 and in early '76 they begin work on their first album.

APRIL

With Jan Hammer on board, a session is booked at Cherokee Studios in Hollywood, California this month. The Hammer composition *Blue Wind* is taped, a rousing, tailor-made duo performance by Jeff and Jan, with Hammer doubling on synthesizers and drums.

Furthermore, Hammer sprinkles four already recorded songs with synthesizers; *Led Boots*, *Come Dancing*, *Play With Me* and *Sophie*. The last is also known to exist as an outtake, with an extended electric piano introduction by Middleton and also a different synthesizer solo than on the final album, which may have been done by Middleton, too, before Hammer got involved. (Interestingly, Hammer is not credited as contributing to *Sophie* in the liner notes of the finished product, although it is unmistakably his synthesizer sound.) Percussionist Ed Greene, who adds extra drums on *Come Dancing*, is also believed to record his bits at Cherokee. The same song also has a very subtle and uncredited horn section overdubbed, interestingly the very first time Beck in his own right has recorded with horns. (The experiment with strings on the previous album is not repeated however.) The sessions are only marred by one of Jeff's white Stratocasters being stolen while in transit from New York's Kennedy Airport to California.

After wrapping up the sessions at Cherokee, the tracks are mixed at three further studios spread around the US: Caribou, Colorado; at Red Gate, Hammer's own recording facility in Brewster, upstate New York, and lastly at Sound Labs in Los Angeles. Hammer is not restricting himself to composing and playing on the new album; he also involves himself in the mixing process, and remixes four of the five songs he is featured on.

The Beck–Hammer union is also finalized, the reasons being obvious: Beck has a successful album to his credit and a crucial follow-up to be released shortly, but he doesn't have a band for his planned American exile, whereas Hammer has his guitar-less Group, but no hit album (but an album to be released shortly in his own name, *Oh Yeah?*), so they decide to join forces. The collaboration is also made easy because Beck's parent company CBS is also handling Nemperor, Hammer's record company.

Although not so obvious, Beck and Hammer's group indeed make up an ersatz Mahavishnu Orchestra with an identical line-up complete with a violin. There's even two alumni from McLaughlin's group, even though Kindler did play with the later, enlarged Mahavishnu Orchestra. Musically, the similiarities are less obvious; the Beck/Hammer constellation employs repetitive, funky motifs as one of their foundations, quite unlike the original Mahavishnu Orchestra which thrived on rhythmic complexity.

MON 5TH

While Jeff is in California this month, he jams with Tommy Bolin at Glen Holly Studios. Reportedly, Beck plays bass guitar in a trio setting, while Bolin plays guitar.

LATE

After completing the new album with mixing sessions in Los Angeles, Beck flies to New York City for a hectic two days before going home to England. Besides picking up a gold album for *Blow By Blow* at an Epic meeting, Jeff also does a series of interviews at the posh St. Regis Hotel. Such extensive advance press preparation is getting to be normal practice as the rock industry turns into a carefully orchestrated big business.

The interviews are printed over the

Ⓒ January 10, 1976: Howlin' Wolf (Chester Burnett) dies in Chicago.

course of a year, and remain some of the most in-depth features published on Beck so far. Jeff talks to Dave Hickey (for a cover story in CIRCUS #136, July 22, 1976), Jean-Charles Costa (cover story in THE MUSIC GIG, August 1976 and a feature in HIT PARADER, November 1976), Billy Altman (CREEM August 1976 plus a reprint in NEW MUSICAL EXPRESS September 11, 1976), Kris Nicholson (BLAST October 1976) and Larry Rother (feature in DOWN BEAT set for February 24, 1977 but not published until June 16, 1977).

The CIRCUS cover story is a long retrospective interview, covering Beck's career from the art school days up till his association with Jan Hammer. Here Jeff vents his feelings about the Beatles: "In the Beatles days I couldn't understand it, but now I see that there was this amazing sort of nucleus of talent there – although I couldn't stand the guitar playing on Beatles records. I used to sit there and just seethe with agony that it wasn't me playing the guitar." Jeff is typically blunt about Mickie Most ("Without a doubt the dumbest thing I ever did"), and has this to say about lyrics in rock: "I never write lyrics. In fact, most lyrics don't mean a bloody thing to me. It's either some contrived piece of rubbish or it's someone's personal love letter that they're singing to themselves. Some of Sly's lyrics hit me now and again, 'cause they've got the grit, you know, and Stevie Wonder can move me, but he's such a great singer he can make anything sound good". Hickey also wants to know if Jeff feels separated from mainstream British rock? "Oh no, not really. I get a great deal of pleasure from the Who still; it amazes me how they continue to turn out valid music without altering their format, and the Kinks as well. I think Ray Davies at present is terribly underrated. No one else is coming close to turning out the kind of intelligent, original pop music that he has of late." But black music is still Beck's greatest inspiration; "There was a lot of really insignificant heavy rock [so instead] I really got hooked on Motown and Philly music ... If I could ever be named along with people with [Stanley] Clarke and Stevie [Wonder] then I don't need anything else, I'm proud enough of that." Jeff also sheds some light on his contemporaries: "Jimmy Page is probably the only other guitar player I've had a sustained relationship with over the years. Eric and I passed like ships in the night, really. And there was Hendrix. I could have had a strong relationship with him but he was too active. I was very much into what Jimi was doing – not technically, or note wise, but the way he was going places with his music made a strong impression on me." In a rare moment, Jeff also talks about his private life, including his newly purchased home in rural Sussex: "[We] keep a bit of English tradition going. It's stupid really. We're fighting a losing battle. It's fantasy, but I love beautiful things, and I love beautiful architecture. And the way people used to live fascinates me. You know, in the fourteenth and fifteenth century. And I have a piece of that: 1500, the castle was built."

In CREEM, Beck sums up the sixties to Billy Altman: "I realize I might burst some bubbles, but it wasn't all that exciting to me. I call the sixties the frustration period of my life. The electronic equipment just wasn't up to the sounds that I had in my head, and it was an endless battle to get my feelings across." Asked about the trio with Bogert and Appice, Jeff replies: "The two of them really drove me around a twist. Always complaining. Such tension in the air – I was doing a bottle of Smirnoff's a day just to survive it all," although he shades his views a bit to Dave Hickey: "I don't repudiate it. It was just kind of a 'dirty weekend group', you know. And when they were kicking they were the hardest fucking white rock group going. Carmine ... jeez, there's no rock drummer except maybe Mooney, who can come close to him in energy. I mean, he explodes!"

But Beck is not fond of going over his life in an interview situation, as he makes clear to Jean-Charles Costa (THE MUSIC GIG): "You know it's really odd when you have to drudge up your whole life for someone in an interview. It's hard for me to remember everything that happened. Sometimes I wonder if anybody remembers what really happened, you know? All the different stories about the Yardbirds ... I don't like to look back really. I try to think about the present, and then just push on into the future." Describing his guitar playing, Jeff eschews technical intricacies and goes for the jugular: "I've always been a very emotional player ... always goin' for that feelin'. I don't like playin' riffs or scales, it's very important to me to get that particular feeling across." In the HIT PARADER feature, Costa asks if Beck is well-treated by his record company and what he feels upon receiving his first gold album? "Yeah, it's kind of nice ... I always used to think they stuck me on the lesser label [Epic versus Columbia], you know?"

DOWN BEAT is preoccupied with portraying an artist who has "embarked on a startlingly new musical direction, leaving behind the rock 'n' roll he had been raised on and experimenting with a more ambitious and challenging jazz-rock sound." The magazine dubs Beck the 'Sonny Rollins of rock 'n' roll', because he takes his time between records and does things at his own pace. Discussing guitarists he is particularly fond of, Jeff picks Roy Buchanan ("a real positive attitude in his music, and a nice raunchy sound"), Les Paul ("the guv'nor of his own field") and John McLaughlin ("I admire him tremendously").

Kris Nicholson conducts the last interview of the day, even following Beck and manager Ernest Chapman into the limousine out to the airport. In parting, Beck tells Nicholson (BLAST MAGAZINE): "I think to bring people's emotions out – as would be done in a great play – is my goal, but I want to do it with music, and the gut feeling it arouses. Music is the best way of expressing emotions ... Everything in the past was playground stuff; now I'm heading for the real thing. I'm not going to grow old wishing I'd done something. That must be the worst killer of all – to know you could've done something that you never did. I know what I want and I've got to do it."

MAY

MID❋
The members of Jan Hammer Group fly to Great Britain to undertake rehearsals with Jeff in time for their American debut in June. A set list is worked out featuring a fair selection of tracks from *Blow By Blow* and *Wired*, plus tunes from Jan Hammer's catalogue. At the outset, few *Wired* tracks will be performed, but throughout the summer more songs from the new album will be added. Jeff does not include any material pre-*Blow By Blow*, and keeps his selections purely instrumental, although Hammer's own songs also features vocals – usually by himself or drummer Tony Smith.

SUN 23RD
The Roundhouse, London
After a weekful of rehearsals, Jeff Beck with the Jan Hammer Group play an unannounced warmup show, sandwiched between Kraan and George Hatchet Band and the headliner, ex-

May 1976: Jeff Beck plays unannounced gig at London's Roundhouse ...

Ten Years After guitarist Alvin Lee, at one the Roundhouse. Rumour of the last-minute addition to the bill begin circling on Friday 21st, and spreads quickly enough to assure the music press is present.

This is Jeff's first British appearance since January 1974. Beck and band play a short set lasting a mere half an hour, beginning with the quartet alone for one number, before Jeff steps onstage for *You Know What I Mean*. They also perform *Diamond Dust* plus a few unspecified tracks from Jeff's forthcoming album.

Steve Clarke, who is reviewing the concert in NEW MUSICAL EXPRESS (May 29), reflects on the difference between Alvin and Jeff: "Beck and Lee were for a time in the late sixties considered part of the same peer group. Closer examination of the two musicians' work would have made it patently obvious that in fact Lee wasn't anywhere near as good a guitarist as Beck. Time, however, was actually working in Beck's favour. Because of his enormous talent, Beck's artistry can actually beat the passing years." Even their physical appearance has changed, according to Clarke: "[Lee's] got progressively more chubby, so that on Sunday night he looked not unlike a second division footballer gone to seed. By the second number he was sweating buckets. Beck on the other hand has worn remarkably well, and still comes on like a skinny kid, cocky, and looking no more wasted than the last time he appeared on a British stage. He seems ageless. And, using his Strat to its fullest phallic potential, is as much the guitar hero in visual terms as he ever was."

Phil Sutcliffe in SOUNDS (May 29) is also suitably impressed: "After Hammer had layed down a frantic keyboard rock number for openers, Beck drifted on looking vague and ill-at-ease but he was soon warmed, reassured that doubt and hesitation wasn't the order of the night, when, after his announcement of a *Blow By Blow* track of which he reckoned to have forgotten the title, drummer Tony Smith practically climbed up his rectum with a funky volley that yelled 'get it ON!'. Beck looked around, smiled, and seemed to accept that all was going to be well after all ... Half a dozen numbers proved he could do the DiMeola just fine. But his most successful piece was a slow instrumental [*Diamond Dust*] in which he began to make that guitar talk, hitting long and clear notes not exactly blue but melancholy and repeatedly taking ob-

PLAY WITH ME

Guitar As Voice

By 1974 Jeff Beck's career had come to a crossroad. His prime importance many felt had been with the Yardbirds, and to a lesser degree on the *Truth* album. The Jeff Beck Group II showed artistic growth, but tried unsuccessfully to implement the old piano–vocal–bass–drums format in a modern setting. And Beck, Bogert & Appice had rather been like walking backwards more than anything else.

Come 1975, Jeff Beck jumped ahead of his contemporaries and a step beyond the competition, as he bounced back with *Blow By Blow*. Throwing out the vocalist, putting the guitar centre stage against a blend of funk grooves and proper melodies, Beck invented a brand new category: The Modern Instrumental Guitar Album. The artistic triumph was capped by commercial success; a #4 album in the American charts which went gold within six months. Not only a contemporary sound, Beck in fact managed to make a timeless album. The songs had a loose feel close to jamming, with Max Middleton's bubbling clavinet and sympathetic Fender Rhodes a perfect foil for the guitar. Backed by the masterful and loose-limbed drumming of Richard Bailey, the album contains such gems as the stately *Diamond Dust* (which finally saw Beck's ambition of making a 'guitar concerto' a reality) and the exquisite *'Cause We've Ended As Lovers*, as well as funkier songs like *You Know What I Mean* and *Thelonius*. The riff Max Middleton's *Freeway Jam* was an air guitar invitation, while *She's A Woman* – done reggae-style in keeping with the times – saw Beck finally putting the voice-bag on record.

Jeff's next album, *Wired*, was a darker and more clinical record. Gone was the carefree feel of *Blow By Blow*, replaced by a meticulous sound picture dominated by some of Jeff's most vicious playing yet. A highlight was the melancholic version of Charlie Mingus' *Goodbye Pork Pie Hat*. The song was transformed into a masterpiece as the guitar ran the spectrum from clean to dirty, from cool to torrid, as Beck sang the solidbody electric. Although *Wired* was likened to "a surgeon's scalpel" by one reviewer, it contained much sparkle to add life. Witness the creaking of vibrato springs during *Blue Wind* (at 3:33 into the song) or Jeff's nervous jabs at the guitar on the intro to *Play With Me* as if he could not wait for the theme to be stated. His playing could be as powerful as ever – the last minute and a half of *Sophie* cook like crazy; Beck trading fours with Jan Hammer on synthesizers. Then there was the brilliant *Blue Wind* where Jan and Jeff shared three choruses each, where Beck truly was a Cliff Gallup of the seventies; his solos like mini-compositions, carefully crafted and yet probably off the top of his head. *Love Is Green* (the title poking fun at *Love Is Blue*) featured Beck gently finger picking a nylon-string guitar, before the electric guitar made its shimmering entrance.

The unimaginative live album with Jan Hammer was an unfocused, dim snapshot of the combustive Beck/Hammer union. Just like the cheap cover, it is a cut and paste job. Instead of pacing the album like their concerts, the sequencing is backwards, so the standard set-opener (*Darkness/Earth In Search Of A Sun*) is song one, side two! Worse still, some of the fiercest live numbers were not included. Maybe it was the production or the song selection or the backwards sequencing, but the album did not sound like it was recorded by a red-hot band that had done dozens of live shows. Where Jeff could could come across as an unchained meteor onstage, here he sounds out of place battling with Hammer's guitar-like synth playing. The exceptions were *Freeway Jam* where Jeff and Jan went toe-to-toe in a sonic tour-de-force, and *She's A Woman*, where Jeff pulled out all his tricks for a stunning break combining Townshend-like chording, dive-bombing slide riffs and upper-register blues jolts.

Although Beck lacked a jazzer's harmonic knowledge, he had a perfect understanding of drama. His combination of rockabilly flash and a blues guitarist's knack of playing a three-note phrase when needed, made him fit right into the fusion maelstrom. Uniquely, Jeff was a rock guitarist crossing over to "jazz", and not vice versa. Still, he kept a distance from the idiom, always knowing he was a natural rocker and not a jazzman.

Both *Blow By Blow* and *Wired* are milestones in electric guitar rock and became hugely influential, paving the way for the whole solo guitarist trend in the late eighties/early nineties epitomized by long hair and infinite chops, but just as often a lack of soul. The twin albums gave Jeff a chance to further develop and explore his sonic language, and by now he had a unique sound all his own – bold and dynamic, emotional and intense, never meaningless and always unpredictable. ∎

June 1976: Jeff Beck and Jan Hammer Group begin extensive US tour ...

tuse melodic routes way beyond the average orthodox of rock guitar. For these few minutes he reminded me what a great instrument the electric guitar is despite the overkill of its mediocre practitioners."

LATE

At the end of May, Jeff Beck becomes an American resident-alien – complete with a Green Card – when he moves to Los Angeles, where he will live for the better part of the next two years.

Jeff is now just another British rock musician who decides to leave the motherland temporarily to avoid paying onerous taxes to the British government.

The change brought about by the Labour Party's taking over from Ted Heath's conservative reign in 1974 includes several new tax laws. One of the laws made effective from April 5, 1974, demands that individuals in the highest bracket are taxed at 83 per cent, and are taxable thus as long as they officially reside in Britain. So-called 'tax exiles' – non-residents like Beck now – are allowed to be in Britain for a limited period, but not to work.

Bringing with him his Alsatian dog Joe, Jeff settles in a house in Bel Air just off Sunset Boulevard. The management stay behind in Britain, but roadie Allan Dutton comes to work with Beck.

Now a hot name with a strong potential, the record company is fully behind him on his American tour, including releasing a special album for radio promotion called *Everything You Always Wanted To Hear By Jeff Beck But Were Afraid To Ask For* (US Epic AS 151), containing a cross-section of his work from *Truth* to *Blow By Blow*. The strategy for the coming months is simple; Jeff will tour and work incessantly. Jeff's itinerary is not a regular tour however, it is rather a 'tour within a tour', a kind of return to his Yardbirds days with a series of one-nighters; sometimes opening and sometimes headlining, playing clubs and playing arenas.

The emphasis will in fact be on several stadium appearances this summer, when America also is in the middle of its Bicentennial celebration. Promoter David Forest explains the logic to ROLLING STONE: "Some of these acts are relinquishing their finesse and being special guests at stadium shows ... And Jeff Beck. Why should he go out and do 30 shows where he's taking a risk when he can do a few stadiums where the draws are guaranteed, there are good promoters and sound and lights, he gets 30 to 40 grand, and he's playing in front of a lot of people?"

SAT 29TH
Winnipeg Convention Center, Winnipeg, Canada
Another one-off warmup date before the tour proper kicks off in Oakland.

JUNE

TUE 1ST
Jeff is reportedly at Hollywood's Roxy Club to hear John McLaughlin's new, all-acoustic group Shakti. Also present are Jaco Pastorius, Billy Cobham, Stanley Clarke and Ray Gomez.

SAT 5TH
JEFF BECK (WITH JAN HAMMER): SECOND NORTH AMERICAN TOUR; FIRST LEG
"Day On The Green #3"
Oakland Stadium, Oakland, California
Jeff Beck drives up from Los Angeles in his own '32 hot rod, and arrives backstage only minutes before his American debut with the Jan Hammer Group. The bill also includes Santana (with Jeff coming onstage for a surprise jam), Nils Lofgren and Journey. Original headliners Jefferson Starship unexpectedly pulled out three weeks ago, and were quickly replaced by two Bay Area bands, Boz Scaggs and Tower Of Power. The highly popular Journey features Jeff's old bandmate Aynsley Dunbar on drums and ex-Santana guitarist Neal Schon. The Bill Graham-staged event at the Oakland Coliseum draws about 43,000 fans – Jeff's biggest audience yet – contributing to a gross of $365,000.

Vivien Goldman is flown over to cover the concert and interview Beck for SOUNDS. The story, published July 17, is headlined 'Jeff Sez Nuthin'! – Exlusive Non-Interview'; a reference to Beck's lack of replies to Goldman's questions. Sample – Goldman: "Jeff, I know you don't like to do interviews, but I've been sent all the way over from England to write this and I'd really appreciate it if you could let me have half an hour of your time, if that's cool with you?" Beck: "Well, it's not cool exactly, but then it's not hot either." All the same, Goldman manages a long and entertaining conversation with Beck on the topic of the values of the music press: "Because I [Beck] don't have a lot to say. If it's going to be in print, it must be worth printing." Goldman counters and suggests that the readers will be interested in reading a chat, but Jeff is adamant: "A chat isn't worth printing." Jeff also reflects on the recent unbilled Roundhouse concert: "... that was a complete reversal! It was a perversion. In other words, if I'd been billed they [the press] would have slated me, but as I made a surprise appearance for half an hour, they said 'Oh! What a surprise!' and they all went crazy." Also on hand is photographer Robert Knight who snaps an oft seen image of Beck; his back to the camera, playing to a sea of faces with his right arm in the air.

For the next seven to eight months, Jeff and Jan basically use a core set of songs for the occasions when they are the opening act, running to about one hour. Many of the summer's performances will be as part of six-hour mini-festivals, which in effect require full sets from the opening acts also. Today's set consists of eight numbers, where Jeff makes his entrance during Jan's cosmic drone *Darkness/ Earth In Search Of A Sun* – as will be customary during his whole time with Hammer. Otherwise there are three songs from *Blow By Blow*, two Jan Hammer-tunes from his '74 album *Like Children (Full Moon Boogie* and *Earth (Still Our Only Home))*, and just two choices from *Wired*; *Sophie* and *Led Boots*. Although more songs will be added as the tour progresses, surprisingly enough *'Cause We've Ended As Lovers* never makes it to Beck and Hammer's set lists.

SUN 6TH
"Day On The Green #4"
Oakland Stadium, Oakland, California
A second day in Oakland finds Jeff Beck on a bill with the J. Geils Band, Blue Öyster Cult, Mahogany Rush, and Sammy Hagar – like yesterday, mainly CBS artists.

FRI 11TH
Celebrity Theatre, Phoenix, Arizona
After the pair of 'Day On The Green' performances, Beck and the Jan Ham-

---

Set List/Beck + Hammer

"Day On The Green #3", June 5 '76

Darkness/Earth In Search of a Sun • You Know What I Mean • Freeway Jam • Sophie • Earth (Still Our Only Home) • Diamond Dust • Full Moon Boogie • Led Boots

June 1976: Album "Wired" released in the US ...

mer Group begin a stretch of headlining dates up and down the West Coast, including a brief Canadian visit. Upp are playing support on this leg of the tour.

Headlining in his own right, Beck's performance usually runs for about 65 minutes, and also includes *Scatterbrain* (complete with the slow blues section from *Air Blower*) and *Blue Wind*. Although a couple of songs are added in the coming months, the set list this year will remain fairly rigid.

Additionally, the Jan Hammer Group function as a built-in opening act, as they always do at least one song before Jeff comes on – even when Beck is the opening act. On the occasions when Jeff and Jan top the bill, Hammer's opening section will usually stretch to half an hour or even more. After a while, this causes some frustration on Jeff's part, who does not get onstage until his cue *(Darkness)* is given.

SAT 12TH
Starlight Amphitheater, Burbank, California

Eric Clapton is a surprise backstage guest today, but he does not appear onstage. Clapton is in California doing some odd sessions for artists as diverse as Ringo Starr and Corky Laing.

SUN 13TH
Golden Hall, Convention & Performing Arts Center, San Diego, California

Robert P. Laurence of THE SAN DIEGO UNION (June 15) writes: "One-time Yardbird Jeff Beck wedded his flashy rock guitar to the classicism of the Jan Hammer Group in a sold-out concert at Golden Hall last night, with interesting if not brilliant results ... A competent, sometimes colorful guitarist, Beck nevertheless suffers from a bland stage personality. He still lacks the arresting presence that makes for a performer of the first rank. Better than a journeyman, he hasn't climbed that extra step to charismatic stardom, the step that would take him from sold-out shows in halls the size of 4,000-seat Golden Hall to auditoriums the size of the 14,000-seat Sports Arena."

MON 14TH

Jeff Beck's second solo album proper, *Wired*, is released in the United States today. The striking cover design by John Berg is a thematic continuation of *Blow By Blow*; a blurred colour shot of Beck clad in white and holding a Stratocaster.

Wired also represents a continuation of Jeff's musical direction on *Blow By Blow*, although this production is far more ambitious and expensive. Besides recording and mixing the album at six different studios, no less than two producers, six musicians plus a horn section and seven engineers are involved. Max Middleton is again an important contributor, but after Jan Hammer overdubs his synthesizers on four already completed songs, Max is reduced from being a soloist to an accompanist. The album is wholly instrumental, and features four songs by Michael Walden, and one apiece from Middleton, Hammer and Andi Clark, plus a version of Charlie Mingus' blues ballad *Goodbye Pork Pie Hat*. One of Walden's compositions is the trio performance *Love Is Green*, where Jeff for the first time on record plays gut string guitar.

Wired is also given a quadrophonic release with a separate catlogue number the following month – the last of Beck's albums to be honoured with such an extra option, as the the quad market proves to be quite limited and the format quickly goes out of fashion. Interestingly, on the quad version some of the songs differ slightly from their regular stereo counterparts: *Head For Backstage Pass* does not fade out so it is about a minute longer, and there is a subtle difference in the mix of *Come Dancing*.

In the US, the album peaks at an impressive #16. Spurred by his Stateside success, *Wired* also manages to enter the British charts with a top placing at #38.

The album receives a mostly positive reaction from the critics. Of the British reviews, Charles Shaar Murray (NEW MUSICAL EXPRESS, June 26) still awaits Jeff's return to straight ahead rock: "Jeff Beck plays Mingus??? Why not? He plays it pretty nice, too: *Goodbye Pork Pie Hat* done with haunting sensitivity and sureness of touch and restrained savagery down the cool end of the heat/light/sound spectrum, an arrow leaving the bow like a leaf falling from a tree. It seems that our Jeffrey has learned to pierce the centre of a tune's target with one shot rather than dropping a cobalt bomb on it and annihilating everything for miles around. It's just stone beautiful is what it is, and it's by far the finest moment on an otherwise somewhat annoying album ... Beck nearly always plays great, and he always sounds like Jeff Beck whatever context he's playing in. Hell, he'd still sound like Jeff Beck even if he was playing a goddam trombone." David Fudger in SOUNDS (July 3) writes: "The album retains a strong blowing element, but Beck is generally more tightly tied to organised tune structures ... The guitar sound is unmistakably Beck and he's taken to the demands of his new setting with the combination of skill and audacity that made him the uniquely daring rock soloist that he is. He's still prepared to interrupt a particularly plaintive and melodious run with a scuffing chord slide, a prancing idiot descending run, or a wavering tremelo arm manoeuvre."

In the US, John Swenson in ROLLING STONE (July 29) writes a flattering review under the headline 'All Wired Up: Beck's Best Yet': "Jazz-rock fusion music has had no greater exponent than Jeff Beck, whose latest album ... demonstrates how vital this genre can be. Even more importantly, *Wired* presents Beck in a context that finally satisfies both his uncompromising standards and commercial neccessity ... Many of Beck's older fans claim he's toned down to play this music, but listening closely, you can hear all the fire and imagination that has characterized every phase of his career. *Wired* is a realization of a style Beck has been working toward for years, and should finally attract the recognition he deserves." Bob Cianci in the New Jersey paper THE AQUARIAN (July 14) is also ecstatic: "Of all the guitarists who could possibly be considered mondo-supremo, the one man who did the most to expand the total electronic possibilities of the electric guitar, the name Jeff Beck reigns head and shoulders above all. Very few of the late sixties–early seventies hotshot lead players ... have been able to move with the trends and progress the way Beck has done, bringing forth a Mahavishnu-like frenzy on this new set ... In short, Jeff has delivered a brilliant LP. Need I say more?"

Elsewhere, there is more scepticism. Neither Lester Bangs in CREEM (September 1976) nor Bob Duncan in

June 5, 1976: The debut album by New York punk pioneers the Ramones enters the US album charts.

June 1976: Jeff Beck plays headlining dates on the West Coast and Canada ...

CIRCUS (August 1976) are fond of Jeff's new direction: "The problem lies mainly in the material. There are too few decent melodies here for Beck to bite and snarl at or soar upon ... What he should do, as he did on *Blow By Blow*, is to get some people equipped as songwriters, arrangers, or players, to talk back to him," laments Bob Duncan. The excellent Lester Bangs is far more to the point and acidic: "Beck is a different man, of course – his rambunctious ego and general el crazola legend speak for themselves – but I do not think there was anything particularly brave, as some people have told me, about a rock guitarist going the Mahaherbiehancoccorea route, as Beck did in *Blow By Blow*, instead of grinding out the let's-fuck blues for the 983rd time or even doing something truly imaginative ... this record remains just like all those other coke-sniffing turquoise-ringed affluent hippies' accoutrements: an item to possess as a matter of fashion, but never, as with even the most stunted of Miles Davis' recent music, to hold to your heart. Because it doesn't hold any."

Jeff's fling with jazz-rock also qualifies for a review in DOWN BEAT (September 9), where Ray Townley awards the album three and a half stars, finding *Wired* "technically clean as a surgeon's scalpel. But it lacks the communicative juices that were dripping like honey from the grooves of *Blow*", while GUITAR PLAYER (September 1976) notes: "If Beck were to have played this material for audiences a few years back, he might have finished his set alone. There's zero boogie appeal."

TUE 15TH
Warner Theater, Fresno, California
A near sellout (1,700 of a 2,000 capacity), tonight's show in Fresno tallies $11,400.

WED 16TH
Meford Armory, Medford, Oregon

Set List/Beck + Hammer

Agradome, Vancouver,
June 19 '76

Darkness/Earth In Search Of A Sun • You Know What I Mean • AIR Blower/Scatterbrain • Freeway Jam • Earth (Still Our Only Home) • Diamond Dust • Full Moon Boogie • Sophie • Led Boots • Blue Wind

---

THU 17TH
Paramount Northwest Theater, Seattle, Washington
Two shows (with Upp) and one sell-out draw a total of 5,065 patrons with a $33,846 receipt at the box office.

FRI 18TH
Paramount Theatre, Portland, Oregon
Promoted by Concerts West like the previous night, the Oregon show with Upp pulls 3,000 for a $17,686 take at the box office.

SAT 19TH
Agradome, Vancouver, British Columbia, Canada
A 6,000 sell-out with a $42,000 gross.

🎧 After being warmed up by the Hammer Group's suitable funky *Oh, Yeah?* (introduced by Hammer's customary 'we're gonna do a different kind of boogie for you'), the audience erupts the moment Beck steps onstage during *Darkness/Earth In Search Of A Sun*, beginning a brilliant concert with Beck playing like a house on fire. The guitar tone is creamy and well-rounded as opposed to the trebly sound his Stratocaster sometimes produces, and Beck is clearly enjoying the occasion, as he takes command from the very start. *You Know What I Mean* follows with a perfectly seamless guitar solo. The three-pronged synth/guitar/violin harmony lines push *Scatterbrain* relentlessly, all the while Tony Smith and Fernando Saunders effortlessly make the song's awkward 5/4 and 9/8 time signatures work. *Sophie* crackles and sparkles with unparalleled energy as Beck plays an especially potent and stunning solo, coming on like an electrified Django. The Hammer-penned song *Earth (Still Our Only Home)* is introduced with a little snatch of a talk-boxed *Superstition* riff, before Jeff plugs into a flanger, out-synthing Hammer's own Moog-runs. But Hammer is a formidable keyboardist, who has no trouble playing complex lines and at the same time understanding the simplicity of real funk. *Diamond Dust* is a majestic elegy, highlighted by Steven Kindler's sensitive violin solo. Before the final number, *Blue Wind*, Hammer teases the listeners by jokily quoting a few bars from Stevie Wonder's *Looking For Another Pure Love*. Throughout the evening, Tony Smith's drumming is a joy; sprightly and funky and powerful.

Like so many other concerts this summer, tonight's inspired and intense performance far surpasses the tepid live results that are released officially next year.

JEFF BECK
WIRED

A1 LED BOOTS (MAX MIDDLETON) **A2** COME DANCING (MICHAEL WALDEN) **A3** GOODBYE PORK PIE HAT (CHARLES MINGUS) **A4** HEAD FOR BACKSTAGE PASS (ANDI CLARK/WILBUR BASCOMB)

B1 BLUE WIND (JAN HAMMER) **B2** SOPHIE (MICHAEL WALDEN) **B3** PLAY WITH ME (MICHAEL WALDEN) **B4** LOVE IS GREEN (MICHAEL WALDEN)

Released July 2, 1976 (UK Epic 86012) and June 14, 1976 (US Epic PE 33849)
Personnel is Jeff Beck (gtrs on all selections, gut string on B4), Max Middleton (clvnt on A1, A4, B2, B3; el pno on A3, B2), Jan Hammer (synths on A1, A2, B1, B2, B3; drms on B1), Wilbur Bascomb (bs on A1, A2, A3, A4, B2, B3, B4), Michael Walden (drms on A1, A2, B2, B3; pno on B4), Richard Bailey (drms on A3, A4), Ed Green (drms on B2), uncredited horns (on B2)
Recorded at Air Studios, 214 Oxford Street, London W1 and Trident Studios, 17 St. Anne's Court, London W1 (September–November 1975), Cherokee Studios, Hollywood, California (April 1976); mixed at Caribou Studios, Nederland, Colorado; Sound Labs, Hollywood, California, and Red Gate Studios, Brewster, New York (spring 1976)
Producer by George Martin
Production assistance by Chris Bond
Remixed by Jan Hammer (A1, A2, B1, B2 plus possibly others) and Michael Walden (B3)
Engineered by Pete Henderson, Dennis MacKay, John Mills, John Arrias, Mark Guerco, Jan Hammer
Mixing engineered by Geoff Emerick, John Mills
Highest Chart Position US: #16
Highest Chart Position UK: #38

June 1976: Jeff Beck opens for Fleetwood Mac in the Midwest ...

THU 24TH
Milwaukee Arena, Milwaukee, Wisconsin

After the West Coast dates, Jeff Beck and the Jan Hammer Group open for Fleetwood Mac in the Midwest, including several stadium concerts. Once fully British, Fleetwood Mac are now LA-based and fronted by Stevie Nicks and Lindsey Buckingham. The group is still touring to promote their eponymous album from the previous August, which eventually will top the US charts in September this year. Also on the bill is singer/guitarist Henry Gross, once of Sha Na Na, and now enjoying some solo success. (Despite Mick Fleetwood's recollection that Beck joins the tour at Pine Knob Music Theater in Clarkston, Michigan on June 21/22, Jeff's name is not found in advertisements for that show.)

It is also Jeff's birthday today – he turns 32.

FRI 25TH
Glen Oak Park Amphitheater, Peoria, Illinois

Jeff Beck with Henry Gross and Fleetwood Mac.

SAT 26TH
Parade Stadium, Minneapolis, Minnesota

Like the previous day, this is also an outdoor concert ('rain or shine!'), but tonight's show – with attendance between 25,000–30,000 people – is nearly cancelled because of heavy downpours. Michael Anthony covers the concert for the MINNEAPOLIS TRIBUNE (June 28), and is witnessing the backstage chaos, including a frantic search for rubber-soled shoes to replace Beck's platforms ("I just wanna play, that's all", Jeff tells the TRIBUNE reporter, while making guitar playing gestures with his fingers.) Henry Gross is dropped because of delays, and the concert finally begins with a Jan Hammer set at around 9.30 (the stadium's curfew at 11.15 pm is extended). Of the actual performance, Anthony writes: "Beck, one of the premiere British guitarists, has formed an association with Hammer. The trust and direction of their work so far – although there were engaging moments in the spacier more lyrical passages of the set – is vague and tentative. Beck, his hair on this occasion resembling Keith Richard's distinctive black artichoke coif, can only be lauded for moving into newer, more complex musical territory. Understandably tired of the Chicago blues, his former metier, Beck is going a step beyond his audience. The result Saturday often seemed a series of exercises on albeit complex chord changes, the kind of thing a student does learning a new form."

SUN 27TH
North Dakota State University, Fargo, North Dakota

Jeff Beck with Henry Gross and Fleetwood Mac.

TUE 29TH
"Superjam '76"
Busch Stadium, St. Louis, Missouri

With a bigger stadium and a larger bill, today finds Beck sharing the spotlight with Jefferson Starship, Ted Nugent, plus Fleetwood Mac. Attendance is 33,500 out of a possible 50,000 with a $350,565 take at the box office.

WED 30TH
"Superjam '76"
Riverfront Coliseum, Cincinnati, Ohio

Jeff Beck plays on an all-British bill with Fleetwood Mac and ex-Traffic guitarist/singer Dave Mason

JULY

FRI 2ND
Indianapolis Convention Center, Indianapolis, Indiana

Snuck between support slots on all-star mega-shows, Jeff and Jan also do several headlining concerts in their own right, like today in Indiana.

Wired is released in Great Britain today, where it eventually makes the charts on July 24, and peaks at #38 during a five-week stay.

SAT 3RD
Masonic Auditorium, Detroit, Michigan

Jeff Beck headline in a WABX presentation. Because of public demand, a second show is added at 10 pm after the first show at 7.30 pm.

SUN 4TH
Groves Stadium, Winston-Salem, North Carolina

Today is America's bicentennial anniversary, and a series of huge rock concerts are staged across the US, starring top draws like Elton John (Massachusetts), Peter Frampton (Georgia), the Eagles and Fleetwood Mac (Florida) and ZZ Top (Tennessee). Although tentatively also booked for a 'Bicentennial Jam' today at Rockford Speedway in Rockford, Illinois with Ted Nugent and Foghat, Jeff Beck and Jan Hammer appear with Blue Öyster Cult, Bob Seger and Aerosmith in North Carolina instead. Despite the strong bill, no more than 14,913 tickets are sold in this arena that has a capacity of 70,000.

Beck will do several shows with Aerosmith in the next months. Aerosmith are about to become one of the biggest concert draws in the States this year, touring to promote the chartbusting *Rocks*. The group's second album, *Get Your Wings* from 1974, features a heavily Yardbirds-inspired version of *The Train Kept A-Rollin'*, with which they usually end their concerts. Jeff therefore decides to insert the powerful *Train* riff as a joke midway through *Blue Wind* – an uncharacteristic throwback to his past, as he otherwise does not do any material pre-1975.

SAT 10TH
"World Series of Rock Game No. 1"
Comiskey Park, Chicago, Illinois

Rick Derringer, Jeff Beck and Jan Hammer, and Aerosmith attract over 60,000 fans – being the biggest crowd Beck has played before so far – making today's concert one of July's absolute top grosses, with gate receipts totalling a staggering $600,915. The huge Comiskey Park is the home of baseball's Chicago White Sox.

Apart from the music, the day has its other moment when a fire breaks out after a mix of firecrackers and cigarettes go awry. Lisa Robinson picks up the story in NEW MUSICAL EXPRESS (July 24): "Jeff Beck had joined the Jan Hammer Group, to rousing cheers, and it was in the midst of his set, when black smoke began to cover [the park]. For a minute, it seemed as though everyone might panic, and many started to leave the stadium. Aerosmith, most of whom had been watching Beck (Joe Perry's idol) from the side of the stage, were rushed outside into their crew bus. It took about twenty minutes for the fire trucks to arrive and put out the blaze, and for

July 1976: Beck/Hammer headline concerts in the Southern States ...

the audience to reassemble. Beck played for most of this time, until the smoke was so thick, and so black, that it was impossible to see."

Aerosmith eventually do their set, and afterwards there is a big party with all the bands at O'Hare Hyatt House.

SUN 11TH
Municipal Stadium, Cleveland, Ohio
Todd Rundgren is added to the Aerosmith/Rick Derringer/Jeff Beck triumvirate.

THU 15TH
City Auditorium, Jackson, Missisippi
After opening for Aerosmith for a few days, Jeff Beck and Jan Hammer strike out on their own again for a swing down South with Upp in support once again.

FRI 16TH
Fox Theater, Atlanta, Georgia
Promoted by Alex Cooley and 96 Rock, one show at 8 pm, with tickets going for $6.50.

SAT 17TH
Dixon-Myers Auditorium North Hall, Memphis, Tennessee

SUN 18TH
Moody Coliseum, Southern Methodist University, Dallas, Texas
Concert presented by radio KFWD in conjunction with the SMU Program Council.

Journey fill in after earlier guests Camel fail to appear, but Upp are also on the bill. The concert is marred by a person throwing firecrackers from the balcony in the hall, but that is not the only menace tonight, according the the reviewer in DALLAS MORNING NEWS (July 20): "Beck's appearance onstage was preceded by a 4-man group (I hate to refer to it as a band because that implies some sort of unity of pur-

pose) that calls itself the Jan Hammer Group. Hammer began the 4-song set by offering what he called 'a different kind of boogie'. That song was bearable, but then the set disintegrated into a wall of noise that was irritating, boring and didn't let up until Beck left the stage. Beck did not seem interested in taking any kind of lead role in the night's proceedings. He became just another member of the group and with Hammer – not Beck – being the principal influence on the music. Beck reduced himself to the role of an imitator. With Hammer, Beck sounded like a bad John McLaughlin and broke this pattern only by trying and failing to duplicate the technique of Peter Frampton. [Beck] is an excellent, crisp rock guitarist. But you wouldn't have known it Sunday night."

Glenn Mitchell in the ICONOCLAST (August 9) is not sure either what to make of the concert: "I enjoyed the Beck set the same way that I enjoyed McLaughlin the times that I saw him: I was intrigued, interested and impressed with the technical proficiency. But I was never caught up in the music, never really moved on anything but a rather detached level. My reaction to Beck – and he is a goddamn breath-taking guitar player, and always has been – was much the same. In fact, the one spontaneous reaction elicited during the whole hour-long set was during the encore when Beck tore into a riff from *The Train Kept A-Rollin'*. Nevertheless, Jeff Beck seems to have a firm grip on the territory he has staked out for himself."

MON 19TH
Hofheinz Pavilion, Houston, Texas
Presented by Concerts West and KILT.

Beck does not get onstage until 11 pm, after warm-up sets by Upp, Journey and the separate portion by Jan Hammer. Bob Claypool of THE HOUSTON POST (July 20) does not get to see the whole concert because of his paper's deadline, but is nevertheless pleased to comment: "The portion of Beck's set that I did see blew away the

cobwebs of all that had gone before ... The set concentrated on Jeff's latest musical plateau – the New Music of electronic jazz-rock, that torrential instrumental genre currently on the rise. Beck fits it perfectly, blending his always-violent guitar lines into the synthesizer playing of Hammer and the frantic fiddling of Kindler. It was heady, soaring stuff."

TUE 20TH
Municipal Auditorium, Austin, Texas
Not amused by Upp and Journey, Paul Beutel of the AMERICAN–STATESMAN (July 22) is then relieved: "But Jeff Beck was worth the wait, amply demonstrating why he is considered one of the top guitarists in rock today ... Beck's guitar work is totally unpredictable and dazzling in his lightning fast precision. He can improvise with or against continually changing rhythmic patterns, sometimes bringing an almost neo-classical sound to his music."

WED 21ST
Civic Center Music Hall, Oklahoma City, Oklahoma
Last night of the independent headlining dates in the South.

FRI 23RD
Arrowhead Stadium, Kansas City, Missouri
More than ten years after sharing the stage with the Beach Boys as a Yardbird at the turn of 1965, Beck is once again sharing the stage with those prime exponents of sunny California pop, now surfing on the wave of another revival with their album *15 Big Ones* (to celebrate their fifteenth anniversary) with even the occasional stage return of Brian Wilson.

This mini-festival also boasts the Doobie Brothers, country-rockers the Ozark Mountain Daredevils and finally Firefall, an offshoot of the Flying Burrito Brothers. Promoted by Cowtown Productions, the stadium is filled to three quarters of its 40,000 potential, but with a strong $240,000 gross.

Robert Bowlin in the KANSAS CITY STAR (July 24) comments on the Beck/Hammer insert halfway during the day: "Large quantities of supercharged progressive jazz were highlighted next with the Jan Hammer Group. The act featured the inimi-

July 1976: Jeff Beck plays support to Aerosmith and the Beach Boys ...

table guitar talents of Jeff Beck, an enigmatic and uncompromising survivor of the 60s. Breezing gracefully through *You Know What I Mean* and *Freeway Jam* ... Beck demonstrated his guitar prowess once and for all. Too bad he didn't get an encore. Presumably the crowd was anxious for the Doobie Brothers."

The meditative fanfare *Darkness/Earth In Search Of A Sun* booms out of the PA system as Beck appears onstage, beginning a surprisingly lacklustre show which never quite gels. The set does feature the newly introduced *Play With Me* as the sole selection from *Wired*, but it is basically a tool for Hammer and Kindler to show-off their instrumental ability. Beck tries desperately to inflate *Freeway Jam* with some helium but it refuses to soar, and for the rest of the 45-minute set right up to *You Know What I Mean*, Jeff, Jan, Steven and Fernando take turns playing their solos without igniting any sparks or stirring the soul.

SAT 24TH
An announced appearance at the Casino Arena in Asbury Park, New Jersey is eventually cancelled.

SUN 25TH
Iowa State Fairgrounds, Des Moines, Iowa
Again with the Beach Boys, the Doobie Brothers and Firefall, plus Gerard. The show attracts 17,994 spectators for a $184,972 gross.

•

After the Iowa concert, Jeff Beck and Jan Hammer evidently take a break with a few weeks rest. Jeff returns to his temporary home in Los Angeles as often as his touring schedule permits. His Bel Air residency is a hangout for many a jam session with Tony Smith and Fernando Saunders. To keep him company, Beck has his Alsatian dog, and of course he also devotes time to his hot rod hobby, buying and restoring several old '32 or '34 Fords during his California exile.

•

During the summer months of 1976, Jeff Beck also has the time to do a pair of session appearances for two musical friends.

One is a recording for Billy Preston, where Beck adds guitar to the funky *Bad Case Of Ego*, released on the singer's eponymous *Billy Preston* (UK A&M/US A&M) album in November. The track also features Tony Maiden (guitar), Kenneth Burke (bass) and Ollie Brown (drums).

The other occurs when Jeff renews his association with Stanley Clarke for the recording of *Life Is Just A Game*. This song will be available only on a special 12" promo single version (coupled with *Hot Fun* on US Nemperor), the track later surfaces on Clarke's popular *School Days* album at the end of the year, but the album version features Icarus Johnson on guitar, although the backing – by Clarke, George Duke (keyboards) and Billy Cobham (drums) – is presumably the same as on the promo single.

UNDATED
A show at the Stanley Theater in Pittsburgh, Pennsylvania is reported to have been included on this tour but remains unconfirmed.

AUGUST

THU 7TH
Wired peaks at #16 in the US album charts today, becoming the highest charting instrumental rock album in the States until the early nineties. Although *Blow By Blow* made #4 the previous year, the use of the voice bag on *She's A Woman* disqualifies it from being purely instrumental.

SAT 21ST AND SUN 22ND
JEFF BECK (WITH JAN HAMMER): SECOND NORTH AMERICAN TOUR: SECOND LEG
Capital Center, Landover, Maryland
Beck and Hammer play support to Jefferson Starship for two nights at the Capital Center, just outside Washington, D. C. Both concerts are reviewed; Charlie McCollum covers the Saturday show for the WASHINGTON STAR (August 23), while Larry Rother reviews the Sunday show in the WASHINGTON POST (August 24).

McCollum: "As good as the Starship was, it was the return of Jeff Beck that offered the most musical interest. Beck has not played in this area for nearly four years and has, in fact, stayed off the tour circuit generally for much of that time. The paucity of live work has not, however, dulled his creative sense. Beck's last two albums ... stand out as the best work he has ever done – even if some of his long-time rock fans are put off by the guitarist's excursions into jazz and other genres. Saturday night, Beck performed with the Jan Hammer Group, a strong jazz act in its own right. Organist Hammer, in particular, gave Beck just the support he needed and the two played off each other's work beautifully. Beck's strong rock lines kept Hammer from wandering into excess, while Hammer's soaring keyboard riffs pushed Beck to the top of his ability."

Rother: "Originally a rock 'n' roller – his lead guitar work with the Yardbirds helped spawn the whole heavy metal genre – Beck is now experimenting with a sound that falls somewhere between jazz and rock ... The combination [of Jeff and Jan] is a most impressive one. Together, Beck and the Hammer group have created a music of breath-taking originality and exceptional intelligence, ranging from the lyrical grace of *Diamond Dust* to the funk of *You Know What I Mean* to the powerful, oriental tinged majesty of *Blue Wind*. Through all of this, Beck shows that he is still the guitar player's guitar player, the master of every lick and trick in the book. His solo on *Darkness*, taking advantage of the Czech-born Hammer's rich, almost classical sense of melody, was a spacey tour de force, the likes of which haven't been heard here since the heyday of Jimi Hendrix. Despite some caustic remarks about playing tunes that 'you kiddies can stamp your little feeties to', Beck made a few concessions to his rock 'n' roll roots. The old Yardbirds standard *Stroll On* [*The Train Kept A-Rollin'*] and a new heavy metal parody called *Led Boots* were performed with fire and flash, serving as additional evidence that the man who is probably the greatest electric guitarist alive was playing close to the top of his form ..."

MON 23RD
Pinecrest Country Club, Shelton, Connecticut
Jeff Beck and Jan Hammer headline.

WED 25TH AND THU 26TH
Nassau Veterans Memorial Coliseum, Uniondale, New York
Jeff Beck supports Jefferson Starship for two sellout shows promoted by Ron Delsener, with a $213,000 gross from 27,000 paying fans. Jeff Beck plays well received sets, and is awarded with two encores the first night; first *Blue Wind* (which breaks into the by now customary *The Train Kept A-Rollin'* riff – to huge cheers from the hall), and then *Led Boots*, preceded by a quick burst of the *I Ain't Superstitious* riff, another teaser from Beck's past. After the second encore, Jeff just puts his guitar on the floor neck down, walks off and leaves the instrument shrieking with feedback.

July 28, 1976: Steve Miller's phenomenally successful "Fly Like An Eagle" earns a gold record in the States.

August 1976: Jeff Beck share the stage with Jefferson Starship ...

The Long Island concerts get a bit of press coverage in England, as Beck is interviewed by Chris Charlesworth of MELODY MAKER (September 11) and Peter Crescenti in SOUNDS (October 9). Concurrently, NEW MUSICAL EXPRESS (September 11) reprints Billy Altman's CREEM interview.

Charlesworth notes: "Jeff Beck doesn't show up in rock polls too much these days, but if a census was taken among his peers the chances are that he would win hands down. Blackmore, for one, names Beck as his favourite player, and even Jimmy Page has acknowledged Beck's talent as being superior to his own. They're right too. On form, Jeff Beck is a stunningly brilliant player who is constantly searching for new ideas." Explaining his partnership with Jan Hammer to Charlesworth, Beck is forthright: "Jan likes to do [his own numbers] to put across the fact that it is his group, and I don't mind it. Sometimes they yell for me and he doesn't like that at all because he feels the set is wasted, and I don't blame him at all. His three numbers set the mood and gets the PA balanced and sorted out before I arrive." Beck also gives insight into why so few numbers are played from *Blow By Blow* on the present tour: "[Hammer] said he was a bit apprehensive at first because he didn't really like *Blow By Blow* because there wasn't anything on that he could have played on." Charlesworth also gets Jeff's views on his Stones audition the previous year: "In three hours I had to play three chords, and I need a little bit more energy behind me than that ... I was thinking, when I was there, that Ron Wood should have been there instead of me ... when I heard that Ronnie was going to join, I thought it was a perfect match." After telling Charlesworth at length how influenced he is by jazz, Beck says in parting: "You know, I've no idea what I do on guitar when I get up there. I don't have a clue musically what it is when I'm working the fretboard, it's all totally by ear. I don't even watch my fingers, which is good because if someone ever poked my eyes out, I'd still be able to get a job."

Peter Crescenti writes, somewhat pompously, that "throughout history, some miracle of the universe has granted certain artists over-sized hearts and souls, invaluable tools that elevate them above most others practising the same art," before naming examples as diverse as da Vinci and Eugene O'Neill – and, "among electric guitarists, Jeff Beck is a maestro." Beck would certainly not subscribe to this comparsion, and assessing his own muisc, he explains to Crescenti: "I don't over-rehearse ('Never', according to roadie Allan Dutton who is also present). If I practise too much, I get incredibly fast, and I find I'm losing the spirit, my soul. I want to see it pouring out, like I would like to see a singer pour it out, like the head and the heart being in the same place." Star trappings are brushed off: "There's so much more to life than just the stage and the music. You've got to take a big slice of real life. People think I live in a limousine, but what they don't know is, I hate it." As for the future, Jeff reveals the plan to make a live album: "It's just a question of convenience, really. Within the next month, I think. It's gonna be good, because I just heard a cassette that we made off the desk, and we got a great sound. If we do a live album, it'll be streets ahead of the studio." A new album is also in the pipeline, but Jeff is now intent on producing it himself: "I can't see any other way. When I'm sitting there with a new guy, training him, I think 'What do I do that for? Why can't I just do it myself?' You can always do things better yourself if you really know what you're after."

FRI 27TH
Cape Cod Coliseum, South Yarmouth, Massachusetts
Massachusetts is a longstanding Beck stronghold, and Jeff Beck and Lynyrd Skynyrd sell-out tonight's Don Law-promoted show (a 7,200 crowd with $46,000 in gate receipts).

SUN 29TH
Palace Theater, Albany, New York
A weird billing finds the Dictators (with Dick Manitoba) opening for Jeff Beck today. A sellout, albeit in a small hall (capacity 2,859), the concert grosses $17,467. A reader's letter in DOWN BEAT (November 3 1977) says: "... I attended a concert in Albany to see and hear Beck with the Jan Hammer Group, and it was one of the most exciting performances I have ever witnessed. ... Beck is the most intelligent and tasteful rock guitarist ever".

TUE 31ST
Astor Theater, Reading, Pennsylvania
A series of concerts are being taped now for a projected live album, and tonight's performance of *Freeway Jam* is later used for the *Jeff Beck with Jan Hammer Live* album.

SEPTEMBER

THU 2ND
Buffalo Memorial Auditorium, Buffalo, New York
Heading into the popular Labor Day weekend, which for many signals the end of summer, Jeff Beck and Jan Hammer again open for the Beach Boys. Promoted by Festivals East, the show is sold out with a 18,000 crowd.

FRI 3RD
Kingdome, Seattle, Washington
Immediately following the East Coast jaunt, Jeff and the Hammer Group fly to Seattle to concentrate on West Coast appearances for a fortnight. Besides opening for Aerosmith, Beck/Hammer also headline several shows on their own. Today at the huge Kingdome is another mini-festival, where Beck appears on a bill with Rick Derringer, Starz (from Long Island) and Aerosmith. The concert reportedly sells out in ninety minutes, although the arena is not filled to its 57,000 capacity (51,091 tickets are sold for a strong $422,698 box office gross). Washington promoter John Bauer explains that 5,000 seats were removed to make room for equipment and better seating.

SAT 4TH
Concord Pavillion, Concord, California
Jeff Beck headline in a Bill Graham presentation with Earthquake and Michael Shrieve's Automatic Man. The show attracts 6,261 fans with a $36,531 take in gate receipts.

Documentation also shows that Beck overdubs a guitar solo today on *Saint And Rascal* for Michael Walden – now also bearing the adopted religious name Narada – presumably done in nearby San Francisco. Other personnel are Will Lee (bass) and David Sancious (keyboards). The song is released on Walden's *Garden of Lovelight* (UK Atlantic/US Atlantic) and credits Beck on the cover, although a source claims it is Ray Gomez who plays the actual solo and Beck's overdub is never used.

WED 8TH
Tempe Stadium, Tempe, Arizona
Aerosmith, Rick Derringer and Jeff Beck play for 17,061 fans and a $92,455 take.

SAT 11TH
Originally booked for an afternoon show at San Diego's Balboa Stadium

September 1976: Jeff Beck joins Aerosmith onstage ...

with Aerosmith, Rick Derringer and Lynyrd Skynyrd, the show is postponed to September 13 at San Diego's Sports Arena. Lynyrd Skynyrd are unable to appear because of injuries sustained in a recent traffic accident involving their guitarist Gary Rossington.

SUN 12TH
Anaheim Stadium, Anaheim, California

Today's sellout concert means a crowd of 55,633 and more than half a million dollars at the box office. The bill is a repeat of the Seattle date the previous week, with Aerosmith being the big draw. Today is also a special occasion as Jeff Beck agrees to indulge in an impromptu jam. Jeff steps onstage during Aerosmith's encore to play on full-throttled versions of *The Train Kept A-Rollin'* and *I Ain't Got You*, the two Yardbirds-related numbers that Aerosmith include in their shows. It is Elyssa Jerret who coaxes Beck to go onstage before *Train Kept* as a birthday surprise for her boyfriend Joe Perry (although Perry in fact turned 26 two days earlier, on the 10th).

This is how Joe Perry later recalls the summer tour with Jeff Beck in GUITAR WORLD: "I remember when we toured with Jeff and the Jan Hammer Group and they were just doing instrumentals. He did stuff on that tour I don't think anybody has touched. He would do these trade-off licks with Jan and bend notes from here to forever. That was inspiring. It was really hard to go on and follow that band, I tell ya. I had been asking him the whole tour to come up and play with us. He'd come up onstage and watch us – actually, he was probably watching the girls in the front row. Finally, in Anaheim, he was onstage and his roadie came up behind him and brought his guitar. He came up and it was great. I had gotten used to him standing there and watching, but it was pretty amazing when he came up and played. I didn't want to play, real-

JOE PERRY, STEVEN TYLER AND JEFF BECK AT ANAHEIM STADIUM, SEPTEMBER 12, 1976. FACSIMILE FROM HIT PARADER, APRIL 1977

ly; I wanted to stand there and watch him play." And in the Aerosmith biography 'Walk This Way', Perry tells Stephen Davis: "It was like me and Brad [Whitford] watching a guitar lesson every night. We'd watch this insanity go on and then have to follow it. To me, it wasn't headlining, it was following. Jeff knew it. A lot of people of his stature wouldn't have opened for us, but he did that summer .. mostly outdoors."

Jeff Beck and Jan Hammer's performance today is also recorded live for a local FM transmission on September 16, which is later bootlegged as *Angel Stadium '76*. (Anaheim Stadium is the home field of baseball's California Angels, and is erroneously referred to as Angels Stadium in this title.)

MON 13TH
San Diego Sports Arena, San Diego, California

Replacing the initial booking at Balboa Stadium, Jeff Beck again opens for Aerosmith with Rick Derringer and Starz. Attendance in San Diego is 11,599, and the earnings total $109,810 in a show promoted by Steve Wolf & Jim Rissmiller in coordination with KCBQ. (This is likely the end of this leg of the tour. A date in Denver has been thought to be the last date of this leg but no evidence of such can be located.)

The set list Jeff Beck has stuck to lately when playing support to bigger acts is strangely low on his own material and consequently high on Jan Hammer songs. Some reviewers make a point of how Beck is reduced to a mere sideman in Hammer's show. Of a set's seven to eight songs, three are the Hammer originals *Darkness/Earth In Search Of A Sun, Earth (Still Our Only Home)* and *Full Moon Boogie* – and in addition Jan does his own opening set *sans* Beck. Of the usual five songs from Beck's catalogue, four are from *Blow By Blow*. The single selection from *Wired* is usually kept as the encore – *Blue Wind* – even that a Hammer composition! In all fairness, Jeff could thank himself for this situation, as this had been the routine for several months. But Beck's frustration is caused not only by the unevenly distributed song selection, but Hammer's increasing stage dominance.

Robert P. Laurence, SAN DIEGO UNION (September 15): "[Beck's] been known to play with some art and finesse, but on Monday he concentrated on churning out decibels, imparting to the evening a certain artistic unity."

CIRCUS magazine publishes an inquiry dated today where guitarists are asked about their choice of axes. Jeff Beck: "I find the Strat technically difficult to play", but prefers it for "really frightening, get down rock," adding "I can't get to love a guitar. They're always playing me up, betraying me".

Also today, a single coupling *Come Dancing* with *Head For Backstage Pass* – both off *Wired* – is released in the States. Although riding on the tails of *Wired*, it flops.

TUE 14TH

Wired is certified gold for sales exceeding one million dollars in the United States today, Beck's second gold album after *Blow By Blow*. [11]

THU 16TH

Part of Jeff Beck and Jan Hammer's performance from Anaheim a few days earlier is broadcast presumably by an LA radio station today (► September 12). Little documentation exists on this radio show, but it is believed that the actual transmission features the Jan Hammer Group on their own in two songs (*Oh, Yeah?* and *Sister

---

Set List/Beck + Hammer

San Diego, California, September 13 '76 (Support to Aerosmith)

Darkness/Earth In Search of a Sun • Earth (Still Our Only Home) • Freeway Jam • Scatterbrain • Diamond Dust • Full Moon Boogie • You Know What I Mean • Blue Wind (including The Train Kept A-Rollin')

Single
JEFF BECK
A: COME DANCING *(Michael Walden)*
B: HEAD FOR BACKSTAGE PASS *(Andi Clark/Wilbur Bascomb)*

Released: September 13, 1976
Personnel as on *Wired*.
Recorded at Air and Trident Studios, London, (September–November 1975) and Cherokee Studios, Hollywood, California, (April 1976)
Produced by George Martin
Highest Chart Position US: –

September 4, 1976: Abba's "Dancing Qeen" hits #1 in the UK single charts, beginning a six-week stay at the top.

September 1976: "Wired" is certified gold in the US ...

GEORGE BENSON AND JEFF BECK AT THE ROCK AWARDS SHOW, SEPT 18 1976. FACIMILIE FROM SOUNDS, OCT 9 1976

Andrea), while Beck is heard on *Darkness/Earth In Search Of A Sun*, *Freeway Jam*, *Scatterbrain* and *Diamond Dust*.

SAT 18TH

Jeff Beck is one of many guests at the second annual Rock Music Awards, simulcast nationwide from the Hollywood Palladium on CBS-TV and hosted by Diana Ross. Staged by Don Kirshner, the show pretends to be an alternative to the Grammy show and also to Dick Clark's American Music Awards. The nominations – five in each category – are made public a few weeks in advance, but met with hilarity by the rock press for the lack of originality and imagination.

Apparently, Jeff Beck is not nominated in any category, but is just attending as a guest at the Palladium and at the post-show party held at the Versailles Rooms in the Beverly Hills Hilton. The party is a veritable 'Who's Who' of music business stars, including Joe Perry, Steven Tyler, Keith Moon, Peter Frampton, Stevie Wonder, George Benson, Mick Jagger, Elton John, Ron Wood, Rod Stewart, Donna Summer and Fleetwood Mac.

THU 30TH

Today is the end of term for choosing nominations for the annual Grammy awards (their term goes from October the previous year through the current September, for that year's awards). Usually, nominations reflect popularity and sales rather than quality. *Wired* is one of five nominations in the category 'Best Pop Instrumental Performance', but eventually the award goes to George Benson's *Breezin'* album.

OCTOBER

FRI 1ST, SAT 2ND, SUN 3RD

It is announced Jeff Beck will appear this weekend as part of a charity event sponsored by the Concern Foundation for Cancer Research characterized as a "rock ' roll tennis festival" at the Los Angeles Tennis Club, also to feature Boz Scaggs, Average White Band, War, and Seals and Crofts but there is no evidence this occurred. A tentative booking on October 1 at the Civic Arena, Pittsburgh, Pennsylvania also does not take place.

THU 7TH
JEFF BECK (WITH JAN HAMMER): SECOND NORTH AMERICAN TOUR; THIRD LEG
Providence Civic Center, Providence, Rhode Island

Following a three-week break, Jeff Beck–Jan Hammer embark on a short 10-city jaunt covering the Northeast.

By now, the set list has been rearranged to include more of Jeff's material. There is apparently a showdown, as Beck later describes to John Tobler: "It started with [Jan] opening for me, doing two numbers to warm up ... And every night, it was a little bit more until he had fifty minutes, and people were saying 'What's going on? Is Jeff playing or what?' ... Then one day we had to have a meeting and tell him that he could do what he liked in his half hour at the start, but after that, he had to back me, but I'm afraid he'd been given this toy which was like a guitar, but with keys on. Later, we had a mother and father of a row, and he realised it was all going to be over, although he wanted the tour to go on for the whole year, so we completely revamped the whole set with a lot more of my stuff, and after that it was great."

The reworked set list re-introduces the crowd pleaser from the 1975 tour, *She's A Woman*, and also two other selections from *Wired*; *Goodbye Pork Pie Hat* and *Come Dancing*, the latter in reality a vehicle for Fernando Saunders on bass. The rarely performed *Play With Me* is shelved, but Jan Hammer succeeds in retaining his numbers in Jeff's set. Presumably, all of the concerts on this leg are recorded for the upcoming live album, and producer/engineer Tom Werman is brought in to oversee the recordings.

FRI 8TH
The Palladium, New York, New York

Under the headline 'Humming Was Impossible', NEW YORK DAILY NEWS' (October 11) music critic Stan Mieses writes: "Jeff Beck didn't wear pink satin pants onstage and he didn't sing. Very few young girls found cause to shriek while he played. While he may not exhibit the spotlite magnetism that makes for a Top Ten Heartthrob, he's on every rock aficionado's Top Five Guitarist list." Mieses is not overtly impressed, though: "Most of the compositions he performed – and they all have the textural density that makes humming the 'tunes' impossible – were from the Hammer Group's two solo albums and Beck's latest record ... While the virtuosity of Hammer on keyboards and Beck on guitar occasionally made these works crescendo and peak with tremendous force and excitement, often it sounded like inspired noodling, and the result was too many notes, and not enough music." Jeff is cajoled into playing a brief snatch of *Rice Pudding* after a request from the crowd, laughing "I didn't know there was somebody here that old!" But that is all that the audience gets of nostalgia: "I'll tell you one thing, if we did all these old tunes, we wouldn't get anywhere, you know what I mean?"

Formerly the Academy of Music, promoter Ron Delsener has taken over and refurbished the venue, and had it re-opened as the Palladium in mid-September. Opening act tonight is the group Heart, fronted by the Wilson sisters Ann and Nancy.

SAT 9TH
The Spectrum, Philadelphia, Pennsylvania

Parts of tonight's show are later used for the *Jeff Beck And Jan Hammer Group Live!* album.

SUN 10TH
Music Hall, Boston, Massachusetts

Heart are billed as 'Special guest stars'.

Presumably, it is during this Boston visit that Jeff Beck is interviewed by Jim Kozlowski for the syndicated radio show "Rock Around The World" for broadcast around the United States the week of October 31.

🎧 The Boston concert displays the new set list, with greater emphasis on Beck's back catalogue. Beck enjoys playing here, and honours Boston ("you people are special, where it all started for me in the US") in an unusually talkative between-song banter. Generally, the group's sound has become more laid back and less cluttered but also less intense. As usual, Jeff works from few set patterns in his soloing, instead relying on spur of the moment inspiration, which tonight produces flashes of brilliance. *You Know What I Mean* is loose and playful, and Jeff's two guitar choruses are a joy to hear. With *Goodbye Pork Pie Hat*, the speed drops to a slow cruise level, and Jeff squeezes some brilliant blues out of his guitar. *She's A Woman* is a display of his unique ability to provide toe-curling suspense; notes hanging in the air, several surprising little left turns, a fluttering of tremolo, a smooth vibrato – all atop an almost futuristic sample-like reggae rhythm.

TUE 12TH
Palace Theater, Waterbury, Connecticut

Also a good concert with a relaxed, spacious groove, where Jeff plays consistently well but without any real highs. *Earth (Still Our Only Home)* zooms in on Jeff's ability to cross blues and jazz. *Scatterbrain* is clean and concise, where the fingerboard is a blur of notes. *Come Dancing* is the night's best with Jeff's Stratocaster ringing clear as a bell, but some of the the other sparring matches in the set between Hammer/Kindler/Beck have a tendency to run on empty. *She's A Woman* swings gently as the guitar is fed through the talk box. The churning rhythm section is excellent throughout, Tony Smith in particular, and the joyful *The Train Kept A-Rollin'* interlude during *Blue Wind* is driven relentlessly by the drummer. Oddly enough, the encore *Led Boots* fails to repeat the impact of the recorded version.

WED 13TH
University of New Hampshire, Durham, New Hampshire

THU 14TH
War Memorial Auditorium, Syracuse, New York

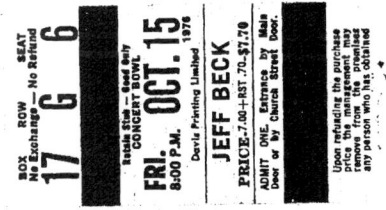

FRI 15TH
Concert Bowl, Maple Leaf Gardens, Toronto, Ontario, Canada

SUN 17TH
US Naval Academy, Annapolis, Maryland

MON 18TH
The Palladium, New York, New York

"Jeff Beck is not – as some have claimed – the best purveyor of fusion music so far. He's only the most tasteful, intelligent rock guitarist yet. And he's merely found in fusion a more complex/complimentary structure, one that suits his erudite chops", writes Michael Rozek in DOWN BEAT (January 13, 1977), reviewing the second Palladium concert in ten days. "After a few increasingly simple Hammer songs, the guitarist sneaked onstage. And a friend of mine who'd come all the way from Nashville to see his rock idol tear it up yelled in my ear, thirty minutes hence, 'He's not tryin'!' His evaluation made perfect sense a moment later, when the aural air snapped – on one tune Beck suddenly cut loose with emotion, channeling years of experience into exactly-right note selection. But then Beck would do something lazy, like leaving out the hard parts of *Goodbye Pork Pie Hat*. Yet soon he was back at beauty again .... It was a rock phenomenon, because you simply heard that Beck was on top of his idiom when he wanted to be. You could hear the freedom that mastery gave him. It was a bit like watching O. J. Simpson or Jim Brown run; in their strides, you can see dominance of an art."

Beck briefly talks with reporter Jean-Gilles Blum of the French ROCK & FOLK magazine after the concert, and informs him that he will mix and release the live tapes and do a tour of Australia early next year before taking a long break.

Guitarist Al DiMeola is backstage and invites Jeff over for a jam at Electric Lady, but Beck politely declines as he is not feeling well and also is going back to England the following day.

TUE 19TH
Jeff flies back to London for a break, presumably staying as long as his tax exile status permits.

SUN 31ST
A Jeff Beck interview is broadcast on "Rock Around The World" (show #177; ► October 10).

Set List/Beck + Hammer

The Palladium, New York, October 8 '76 (headliner)

Darkness/Earth In Search of a Sun • You Know What I Mean • Freeway Jam • Goodbye Pork Pie Hat • Earth (Still Our Only Home) • Scatterbrain • Come Dancing • She's A Woman • Diamond Dust • Full Moon Boogie • Blue Wind (The Train Kept A-Rollin') • Led Boots

THE PUMP

Wang Bar Doodles

Tired of the stereotyped Gibson Les Paul/Marshall combination, Jeff Beck decided to use a Fender Stratocaster when it came to record the *Beck-Ola* album in April 1969. Not only did he feel the Strat provided him with a more personal tone, Jeff was also attracted to the guitar's wang (tremolo) bar which was immediately explored. Originally designed by its inventor Leo Fender to produce a wavering vibrato effect in emulation of the steel guitar, ultimately it was Jimi Hendrix who found sonic possibilities in the Stratocaster that Leo Fender had never dreamed of.

The wang bar would form an integral part of Jeff Beck's sound from *Beck-Ola* onwards, right from the explosive *Jailhouse Rock*, where the tremolo was used to depress a trill on the second guitar solo.

Just like his love of the slide, the wang bar helped him to create a highly flexible phrasing, where the notes would weave seamlessly together. The tremolo was always there, ready to be used in a split-second; a completely natural and integrated part of Beck's way of playing the guitar. Occasionally, he would create whole melodies just by using the bar. Sometimes it would be used prominently (like on *Blue Wind*), sometimes so subtly that it was hard to tell if it was the work of fingers or a bar (like on *New Ways/Train Train*). Sometimes the bar would be used gently (say, when the electric guitar makes its entrance on *Love Is Green*), sometimes abusively (*Going Down*).

Usually, Beck would go one better onstage, where his natural ability with the wang bar would create dazzling and daring moments; the guitar solo on the version of *Freeway Jam* on the *Jeff Beck with the Jan Hammer Group – Live!* album is a prime example. Pushed by Jam Hammer's synthesizers, Beck gave the Stratocaster free reign.

It was post-1980 that Jeff's use of the wang bar would reach new heights, culminating with the haunting *Where Were You* from 1989's *Guitar Shop*. Jeff also proved to be an expert of wang bar use of the old school. On his Gene Vincent tribute *Crazy Legs* he recreated rockabilly gear-shifts effortlessly using a Bigsby vibrato on a Gretsch guitar.

Ultimately it is pointless to dissect Jeff's use of the wang bar, because, like his slide playing, it is such a natural part of his sound. ■

NOVEMBER

It is believed that the live tapes done during the last couple of months are edited and mixed at Scorpio Sound in London this month. Although Jeff is apparently around, he is not allowed to work while in Britain, so Jan Hammer does the mixing. Some doctoring is obviously done to the tapes, as verified by both Tony Smith (who says overdubs were done at Hammer's Red Gate facility) and by Tom Werman, who eventually is credited as 'executive producer' on the finished product, recalls later to GUITAR WORLD: "Regrettably, Jan Hammer insisted on mixing [the live album] or he wouldn't allow the record to come out. He did nothing until the post-tour dinner when he looked at Jeff's manager and said: 'Either I mix the album or there is no album'. Nice fellow, Jan. He didn't even stick his head in the remote truck on any of the dates to see what was going down. Jan is a genius, but that was a bad move."

"I remember being in the studio with Jeff in New Orleans ... pressing the talk-back button and saying, 'Jeff, I think you were a little on top of that' or 'Your tuning is a little suspect there'. And he'd say, 'Okay, let's do it again.' Jeff Beck is a prince. I think he's the nicest major guitar hero I've ever worked with."

DECEMBER

FRI 3RD
JEFF BECK (WITH JAN HAMMER): SECOND NORTH AMERICAN TOUR; FOURTH LEG
Jai Alai Fronton, Miami, Florida
Back in the States again, Jeff Beck commences another leg of the tour, now covering dates in the South and South East. The Miami concert is promoted by Cellar Door Concerts.

Tommy Bolin – with a back-up band including Michael Walden and ex-Vanilla Fudger Mark Stein on keyboards – is tonight's opening act. Bolin, who left Deep Purple a few months previously, is touring in support of his latest album *Private Eyes*. Utterly tragically, after tonight's concert Bolin dies of a drug-related overdose at his hotel room in the morning hours of the 4th.

SAT 4TH
Curtis Hixon Convention Center, Tampa, Florida
Promoted by Beach Club Booking, tonight's one show begins at 8:30 pm, and pulls 5,914 patrons with a fair $33,920 gross.

WED 8TH
The Warehouse, New Orleans, Louisiana

SAT 11TH
Municipal Auditorium, Nashville, Tennessee
Jeff Beck makes his seemingly first ever personal appearance in Nashville. Not a particularly big success either judging by the ticket sales, as Beck and opening act Point Blank (a Dallas, Texas group who have stepped in to take Bolin's place) manage to sell less than half the auditorium's 9,000 capacity for a $27,578 take.

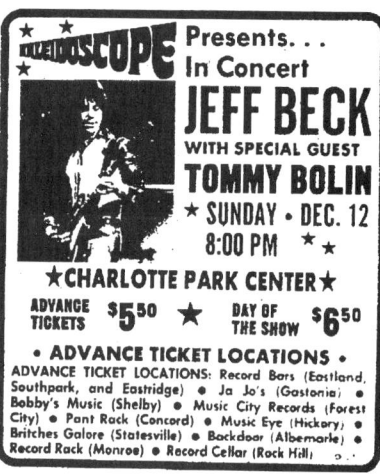

SUN 12TH
Charlotte Park Center, Charlotte, North Carolina
Presented by Kaleidoscope, again with Point Blank. Patrice Carter in the CHARLOTTE OBSERVER (December 13), describes the sensation when Beck steps onstage: "And then! The crowd got what they had been waiting for as Beck came onstage, unannounced. They recognized him immediately. Right off, he launched into a series of lines and riffs that sent those in attendance to new heights. Tony Smith vacated his drums briefly to add color on the cow bells. It was Beck from then on, as he pleased fans until the last strain, after which they begged for more. The group gave them more with an encore, finally ending with *Led Boots*."

Jeff Beck and Jan Hammer's seemingly endless US tour is now nearing completion. After the concert, Patrice Carter asks Jeff backstage what he will do when he and Jan separate after the tour? Beck's monosyllabic reply: "Sleep!"

THU 16TH
In DOWNBEAT's 41st Readers' Poll, dated today, *Wired* is voted 'Rock/Blues Album of the Year' – repeating last year's success with *Blow By Blow* in the same poll – ahead of albums by Earth, Wind & Fire, George Benson *(Breezin')*, New York Mary and Steely Dan *(The Royal Scam)*. Jeff himself also collects 540 votes and easily tops the 'Rock/Blues Musician of the Year' category, with Stevie Wonder second (348 votes) and Frank Zappa third (179 votes). Furthermore, Jeff also places eighth in both the 'Guitar' and 'Rock/Blues Group' polls.

JEFF BECK
Overall Best Guitarist
Best Guitar Album
Best Rock Guitarist

Capping a triumphant year, Jeff Beck also becomes the first triple crown winner in GUITAR PLAYER's annual Readers' Poll 1976 (published this December) – taking top honours in the categories 'Overall Best Guitarist', 'Best Guitar Album' and 'Best Rock Guitarist'. Despite changing trends, this honour comes ten years after Beck was voted best 'Lead Guitarist' in BEAT INSTRUMENTAL – a testimony to his great influence and high standing.

TUE 21ST–FRI 24TH
Back in Britain for the Christmas season, Jeff Beck is present at one of Rod Stewart's four triumphant concerts at Grand Hall, Olympia in London. (The celebrity guest list also includes Linda and Paul McCartney, Marc Bolan and Elton John.) Rod's six man touring band now features Jim Cregan as musical director and weirdly enough Phil Chen on bass and Carmine Appice on drums!

▽ 1977

JANUARY

MID

After a Christmas break, Jeff Beck and the Jan Hammer Group reunite to undertake a tour of New Zealand and Australia, Jeff's first ever trip down under.

By now, Jeff feels his partnership with Jan Hammer is exhausted and he is also tiring of the constant touring. Still, besides the Australasian tour, tentative dates are being lined up in Japan for an April visit.

FRI 21ST
JEFF BECK (WITH JAN HAMMER GROUP):
FIRST AUSTRALASIAN TOUR
Town Hall, Christchurch, South Island, New Zealand

The Paul Dainty Corporation promotes Beck and Hammer's tour of New Zealand and Australia. The support act on the NZ leg Down Under is Ragnarock.

A good tour opening, according to Jude Fahey in THE PRESS (January 22): "Jeff Beck and the Jan Hammer Group gave a spectacular concert in the Town Hall last night ... In spite of recent 'jazz' albums, Beck is still one of us. He was the archetypical rocker, the lad playing guitar for each one of us. No flash, no pretence, all the rock star poses beautifully executed. He was both savage and dynamic, hot licks searing off his guitar blow by blow, but the highlights of his performance were his use of voice box – sparingly, of course – which gave him a direct line with the audience, especially in *She's A Woman*."

SAT 22ND AND SUN 23RD
St. James Theatre, Wellington, North Island, New Zealand

"Jeff Beck looks cosily entrenched in the rut dug out for him by the Jan Hammer Group", begins David Harris in a review in RECORD MIRROR (February 19). "Amid the pristine carvings of Wellington's ornate St. James Theatre, there was a timeless quality that harked back to the Beck of old and regaled the senses acutely ... Beck bent a succession of sounds from his Stratocaster on material from *Wired* – a thankful complement to the gurgles and whirls lashed from Jan's keys. They let go as the set moved on to the midnight hour. They wound up to a rush of gay abandon, Beck slowly commanding with the riffs that have done him proud in the hallowed days of yore. And in the end it was just feedback ..."

TUE 25TH
Town Hall, Auckland, North Island, New Zealand

A visit to Auckland rounds off the brief New Zealand tour.

THU 27TH ✳

Group and guitarist fly on to Australia, where upon their arrival, Tony Smith recalls how they were met at the airport by a motorcade of hot rods, much to the pleasure of Beck!

FRI 28TH
Perth Entertainment Centre, Perth, Australia

The first stop on a five city tour of Australia. Jeff Beck graces the cover of the music paper RAM (issue #50) today. Interestingly, journalist Tina Jorgensen has interviewed an old friend of Beck, Jon Crittle, who used to run the Dandy Fashions boutique on Kings Road in London, but now carves out a living selling antiques in Sydney. Apparently Crittle and Beck shared a love for hot rods and girls, and were close in the years 1967–69.

Although focusing on Jeff's sleazy sides (the story is headlined 'Scandalous Tales & Unsavoury Gossip' and features details of Beck and Crittle's bird pulling competition), Crittle gives great insight into Beck: "He led two lives really; there was his West End existence; the Speakeasy, jamming, pulling chicks; and then he kept this huge flat at Banstead. I was one of the few people to ever go there; he had these two Afghan hounds and the flat was really for them, for his dogs." Crittle maintains that Beck was unlike other rock people: "He was not into dope. He'd trained as some sort of a motor mechanic or something and he was just a car freak; no affectation, no bullshit; not into trendy clothes, he was just a juice freak, oh, and birds; no steady girl though. He was a loner I guess; he came from a working class family in Surrey but he never talked about his parents or family at all. He treated the guitar just like going to work, like going to some factory. I don't think he knew how good a guitarist he was. Jimi Hendrix thought he was the best, but Jeff couldn't give a stuff. ... And when everyone else was out of it on acid and dope he was out of it on booze." "... Jeff was what you'd call in Australia, true blue; no fucking around, no bullshit. I guess he was a simple rocker ..." Jorgensen wants to know if Beck has any spiritual leanings? "No, he never got into anything spiritual. He was all Zen and the Art of Hot Rod Cars. He could never have written anything, a song, or sing. He wasn't at all romantic. Now Clapton, he had a head on his shoulders, but Jeff never had any education, a late developer he was. He could possibly spell his own name, but nothing else; couldn't have understood a contract. Until he started to realise his own talent Jeff just blew with the wind." Crittle has not seen Beck in several years: "I had another breakdown in '69 and didn't see him so much after that. But I remember going up to him ... he'd just bought his first hot rod in America ... and had all these people hanging out of it. But I found him quite aloof. I started to worry then, about how his attitude was changing. I guess he had some sort of moral code. He resisted the dope scene which was hard to do then. He didn't want to know; you'd pass him a joint and he'd pass it on, but he always asked for a bottle."

Australia's other big rock paper, JUKE, also runs Beck on the cover of their January 29 issue, where he shares the mid-page spread with Robin Trower, who is also touring here concurrently.

◎ January 1, 1977: US pop chart toppers – Rod Stewart #1 single ("Tonight's The Night") and Stevie Wonder #1 album ("Songs In The Key of Life")

Newsflash January/February 1977: Jeff Beck tours New Zealand and Australia ...

PAUL DAINTY CORP. PRESENTS ...
THE LEGENDARY JEFF BECK IN CONCERT WITH THE JAN HAMMER GROUP

CONCERT DATES:
PERTH ENTERTAINMENT CENTRE JANUARY 28
ADELAIDE MEMORIAL DRIVE JANUARY 30
MELBOURNE FESTIVAL HALL FEBRUARY 1
SYDNEY HORDERN PAVILION FEBRUARY 4 & 5
BRISBANE FESTIVAL HALL FEBRUARY 7

SUN 30TH
Memorial Drive, Adelaide, Australia

Local guitarist Kevin Borich and his Express are the opening act for tonight's one show at 8.15 pm.

Jeff Beck is also invited to appear live – although presumably only in an interview segment – on Channel 9's "Rock On Sunday" out of Adelaide, which is transmitted today at 5 pm. The show features Beck's choice of music.

Jeff Beck is also briefly interviewed by Greg Kelton for a piece in THE ADVERTISER (February 3), who uses the opportunity to ask Beck about his involvement with the Rolling Stones: "Yeah I had thought of doing a tour with them. If they had offered me the job I would have given it a try, but they went about it in such a roundabout way – really beating around the bush. Instead of coming straight out and asking me to tour with them they called me over to Switzerland [sic] to do some recording work. So I went over there and played with them – about two hours of music – and then thought what the hell. God knows where this tape will end up. So I wrote them a letter saying it was great but I didn't want the job and stuck it under their door. Then I went back to England. The Stones are great people, nice to work with – but I couldn't work at that pace. They are painfully slow."

FEBRUARY

TUE 1ST AND WED 2ND
Festival Hall, Melbourne, Australia

Arriving in Melbourne, Jeff decides to skip the press reception in the afternoon when he is tempted by a local hot rod sale.

The Tuesday concert is covered by both THE HERALD and THE SUN. "Beck strolled casually on stage and got straight into playing without the frills and fancies that accompany many artists these days," writes Debbie Sharpe in the HERALD (February 2), "the combination of Beck, the super rock man, with Jan Hammer and his jazz, was interesting and worked well." Pat Bowring in the SUN (February 2): "[Hammer's] short set moved through pieces which, despite their complexity, never lost their identifiable, dominant theme. Then, almost mid-song, they were joined by the tall, gangling Beck wearing an old shirt and patched jeans. The whole atmosphere changed, with the slick, concise style of Hammer replaced by the raunchiness and bite of Beck." Bowring also interviews Jan Hammer for a story this Wednesday: 'Hammer Gifted, But Beck Is The Star'.

A detailed, full-page review is printed in JUKE (February 12) by P. B. Crabshaw, who is simply ecstatic: "Beck just walked on unannounced, and started working on that guitar. That's what he did throughout his amazing performance. He worked that guitar. He took it through its paces. OK guitar, see if you're up to it! Jeff Beck handled himself and his guitar different to any other guitarist I can remember. The guitar wasn't an extension of himself. He didn't become the guitar as most players do. Neither did he treat his instrument with the tenderness of a lover as most guitarists do. Beck was the master, challenging himself and his instrument to get the maximum performance. He made that guitar do everything you've ever seen or heard a guitar do. He pawed at it, coaxed it, he moved it into all sorts of positions to get that better tone from it, the special sound. Everything that was ever done with a guitar was done during those two hours. He dominated the music virtually throughout that whole time, but without ever losing sight of the other instruments, never overbearing, never showing off. It was simply remarkable. The shirted body, head bent to show only that lanky stringy hair and the familiar pouting line of the mouth, working on that guitar ... Most guitarists play from memory by now, Jeff Beck played intuitively, reaching out, searching for a new way. It was a magic night."

Christie Eliezer of JUKE is backstage to talk to Jeff Beck right before he is about to step on stage: "As [Hammer's] segment kicks off into the cosmics, Beck chattering downstairs shows no visible sign of tension. As the conversation paces along, Beck casually rises, picks up his axe and tossing aside a joke, he disappears through the stage door and under the spotlights as nonchalantly as if he was going to the john. The roar of welcome reaches out and crashes against the wall as he plugs in, and hurls the first flurry of kamikaze notes. The mood within the audience changes. It's no mere sophistication and technique, Beck spices it up with a visceral serving of bite and energy. No doubts about it, the night's gonna start to roast." Despite Beck's coolness before the show, there are too many backstage distractions for Eliezer to conduct a proper interview, but no less than three parallel albums are planned according to Jeff: Firstly a live album ("It was done on the American tour late last year ... You can bet your life they'll be better than the studio album"), secondly an anthology (to be called *Collection,* and lo and behold, the concept will eventually see the light of day in 1991!), and lastly

Set List/Beck + Hammer

Festival Hall, Brisbane, Australia, February 7 '77

Darkness/Earth In Search of a Sun • You Know What I Mean • Goodbye Pork Pie Hat • Come Dancing (bass solo) • She's A Woman • Sophie • Diamond Dust • Freeway Jam

February 1977: Beck/Hammer play last US dates before parting ways ...

the unfinished Beck, Bogert & Appice album ("... I haven't been told, and I don't want to know about it.") Asked about his reputation for forming and folding bands, Jeff replies: "As far as I'm concerned, musicians remain but bands are meant to come and go. It's expected of me now. People say 'what an asshole, he's got no loyalties to his own musicians.' But just look at all the bands who're still hanging in there when they should have split up years ago." What about hit singles? "I'm not interested in that at all. I've done all that once. Now I couldn't bear a hit pushing me into a situation which I know I couldn't handle. I couldn't go out there every night, playing the same thing over and over, having to please the crowds with what they want over here." Jeff also compliments Hammer's group: "It's a gas working with 'em – they're the most challenging band I've ever worked with." (The interview is published in JUKE dated February 19.)

A second night in Melbourne is added because of ticket demand. Support both nights are Jo Jo Zep and the Falcons, for the occasion enlarged by horns.

FRI 4TH AND SAT 5TH
Hordern Pavilion, Sydney, Australia
Beck and Hammer are supported by Chariot for the two-night stand in Sydney.

MON 7TH
Festival Hall, Brisbane, Australia
The last concert in Australia.

TUE 8TH✱
Jeff Beck flies back to his temporary home in Los Angeles.

THU 17TH
The annual Grammy Awards ceremony is presented live on CBS Television tonight, live from Los Angeles. *Wired* is one of five nominees in the 'Best Pop Instrumental Performance' category, but Jeff Beck does not win the accolade, which goes to George Benson and *Breezin'*.

FRI 18TH
JEFF BECK (WITH JAN HAMMER): SECOND NORTH AMERICAN TOUR: FIFTH LEG
Kiel Opera House, St. Louis, Missouri
Jeff Beck and Jan Hammer regroup for a few more dates in the States tagged on following their Australian tour.

"The cliche 'musician's musician' got a shot in the arm and a few shots in the dark last night. Doing all the redefining of what most serious musicians strive for were Jeff Beck and the Jan Hammer Group", begins John S. Cullinane's impressions in the ST. LOUIS POST-DISPATCH (February 19). "The Opera House proved to be an ideal setting for Hammer and Beck to take the stage together. They filled the hall with sound and then some. Worries that the stage wasn't big enough to hold these pre-eminent rock-jazz stars at the same time were dispelled after the first number. Beck, the guitarist, kept eye-to-eye with Hammer, the synthesizer-keyboard player, throughout – as the precise nature of the music dictated. Sometimes they traded solos with the vigour of arch enemies, at other times they blended as brothers, as brothers of music should. The audience spent most of its time either awestruck or clapping thunderously. There was little room for half-hearted reactions to the music ... Hammer's playing, especially the phrasing, was remarkably like Beck's. Before the real thing made a timely appearance, it almost sounded as if Hammer was ghosting Beck's guitar parts ..."

Guitarist Bill Quateman and pianist Ira Kart fill tonight's opening slot.

SAT 19TH
Auditorium Theater, Chicago, Illinois
The Chicago concerts – at 7 and 10.30 pm – are believed to the very last time Jeff Beck and the Jan Hammer Group perform in public, as the two part ways. A tentative Beck–Hammer tour of Japan planned for April is dropped. Even though their relationship is a bit strained after nine months on the road, they will reunite both on stage and in the studio on many occasions in the coming years.

Jan Hammer keeps his group together to record *Melodies* for release at the tail end of 1977. The album features Hammer, Smith, Saunders and Kindler, and among the songs is a vocal version of *Too Much To Lose*, later recorded by Jeff.

Jeff Beck has by now been more or less constantly on the road for over twelve years since he joined the Yardbirds in March 1965 (not counting his enforced lay-off in 1970). With two recent hit albums to his credit and punk rock – whose energy Beck certainly welcomes – exploding, he takes an extended holiday. Interestingly, whereas the new wave movement embraces several sixties acts – primarily the Who, the Kinks and the Small Faces – the Yardbirds apparently are not among the revered.

A new pattern emerges that will repeat itself in the years to come. A short burst of activity will inadvertently be followed by a lengthy period of silence, where Jeff Beck immerses himself in his hot rod building. Beck realizes that he does not have to satisfy the public all the time to secure record sales and command credibilty. Quite the contrary, his time away

---

Album
JEFF BECK WITH THE JAN HAMMER GROUP
JEFF BECK WITH THE JAN HAMMER GROUP – LIVE!

A1 FREEWAY JAM (MIDDLETON) **A2** EARTH (STILL OUR ONLY HOME) (HAMMER) **A3** SHE'S A WOMAN (LENNON/MCCARTNEY) **A4** FULL MOON BOOGIE (HAMMER/JERRY GOODMAN)

B1 DARKNESS (EARTH IN SEARCH OF A SUN) (HAMMER) **B2** SCATTERBRAIN (BECK/MIDDLETON) **B3** BLUE WIND (HAMMER) [INCLUDING AN UNCREDITED 32-BARS OF THE TRAIN KEPT A-ROLLIN' (BRADSHAW/MANN/KAY)]

Released Monday March 21, 1977 (US Epic PE 34433) and Friday March 25✱, 1977 (UK Epic EPC 86025)
Personnel is Jeff Beck (gtrs and 'special effects'), Jan Hammer (el pno, synths, tmbls, vcls on A2), Steve Kindler (vln, string synth on B2, rhygtr on B3), Fernando Saunders (bs, hrmny vcls, rhygtr on A3), Tony Smith (drms, vcls on A4)
Recorded at the Astor Theater, Reading, Pennsylvania, August 31, 1976; the Spectrum, Philadelphia, Pennsylvania, October 9, 1976 plus other locations. Overdub sessions done at unconfirmed studio in New Orleans, Louisiana, late 1976. Remixed at Scorpio Sound Studios, London, presumably November 1976.
Produced by Jan Hammer
Executive production by Tom Werman
Engineered by Dennis Weinreich
Highest Chart Position US: #23
Highest Chart Position UK: –

March 1977: "Jeff Beck With Jan Hammer Group – Live!!" released ...

from the public eye only increases his status. For the time being, Jeff Beck is stuck in his tax exile, and he will spend the rest of 1977 as an American resident, commuting between Los Angeles and New York. And of course he flies home to England whenever his tax free days permit, although he is not allowed to work.

MARCH

MON 21ST

Jeff Beck's very first official live album, the imaginatively titled *Jeff Beck With The Jan Hammer Group – Live!*, is released in the US today, with a British release taking place about the same week.

The cover – like the record's content – seems hastily thrown together, a cut and paste job done with little loving care. Originally conceived as a double, but due to a temporary vinyl shortage, it is kept to a single album. Disturbingly, the record is sequenced backwards from the regular Beck–Hammer routine; the standard set opener *Darkness (Earth In Search Of A Sun)* is put on side two! Hammer also manages to include his two songs featured regularly on tour, *Full Moon Boogie* and *Earth (Still Our Only Home)*. The record further contains three songs from *Blow By Blow* (*Freeway Jam, She's A Woman* and *Scatterbrain*) and only one solitary pick from *Wired* – *Blue Wind* – again a Jan Hammer song. The record peaks on May 14 at a very impressive #23 in the US, but it fails to even chart in the UK. Beck does not bother to promote the album, and leaves the job to Jan Hammer. "Our album came out of 100 dates in Canada, America, Australia and New Zealand ... Our collaboration started as a temporary thing, but it's lasted a year; I think it's time to move on and tour with just my band," Jan explains in CIRCUS.

The British reviews are what is to be expected; Charles Shaar Murray in NEW MUSICAL EXPRESS (March 26) slags the album outright: "Jeff Beck once remarked that he thought Jan Hammer's synthesizer sounded like a guitar ought to sound. His achievement of this goal turns out to be a purely Pyrrhic victory: his guitar now sounds exactly the same as Jan Hammer's synthesizer. Me, I liked it better when it sounded like Jeff Beck's guitar. Fusion music in general and the synthesizer in particular are approaching Terminal Bland-Out for much the same reason. ... Jazz-rock fusion music ends up neither jazz nor rock but a kind of pasteurised Yes-meets-disco which generates much hysteria but little emotion. ... What are intelligent, skilled 30-year-old musicians doing playing this mindless, emotionless crap and kidding themselves that what they're doing is more grown-up than rock and roll? On second thoughts, don't answer that. It hurts too much. Mr. Beck: Wise up!!" Pete Makowski in SOUNDS (March 26) is gentler but not totally convinced, although he awards the album a strong rating of four stars: "Got to admit though, at first I wasn't sure about this album, in fact the first few listens left me quite disappointed. I was expecting some kind of amplified battle of the giants, as it transpires there's no excessive ego trippin' from either party, it's just a happy gatherin'."

In the United States, Steven Rosen in CIRCUS and Karen Rose of TROUSER PRESS are well pleased. Writes Rosen: "Beck forgoes all formality when playing live; his solos may contain certain passages included in the original sounds, but for the most part they are always new and constructed with a mentality only he posesses ... One will not hear any finer or more carefully constructed rock guitar playing than is heard here. *Live!* proves dramatically that Jeff Beck is the hot rod of his field ...", while Rose is happy to report that "when he plays live, Jeff Beck plays rock 'n' roll." Tom Mulhern in GUITAR PLAYER (September 1976) comments drily: "Despite some weak points in the overall sound, the net effect of this recording is rather good." Michael Rozek in ROLLING STONE (June 16) collects a batch of fusion albums, and finds that the *Live!* album "joins all the other fusion busts. It lacks energy ... someone, whether it was Beck or Hammer (who produced), just chose the wrong tapes. Instead of the night of shrieking, wailing and ripping I heard in New York [Rozek attended and reviewed the Palladium show in October 1976], we get singing, sound effects, voice-bag tricks and a general aura of gimmickry."

APRIL

SOUNDS reports how Jeff wanders in at the end of a Motorhead mixing session in London during a return to the motherland late this April.

MAY

SAT 7TH

NEW MUSICAL EXPRESS' Teazers column reports: "Odd couplings of the week: Jeff Beck and Richard Hell together at [New York punk club] CBGBs."

JUNE

SAT 25TH

NEW MUSICAL EXPRESS' Teazers column reports: "Jeff Beck's comment on Cher's visit to Mikell's, a New York jazz club where he was recently at three in the morning: 'Maybe she likes ex-junkie guitar players...'"

SEPTEMBER

Jeff participates briefly in the soundtrack session for the gargantuan filming of *Sgt Pepper's Lonely Hearts Club Band*, starring the Bee Gees and Peter Frampton. George Martin assembles what is essentially Jeff Beck's road band from 1975; Max Middleton, Bernard Purdie and Wilbur Bascomb, plus guitarist Robert Awhai. The sessions commence on September 1st in Los Angeles, and the shooting begins in October.

Beck is only one of many musical guests on the album and his actual contributions have never been confirmed, but it is strongly believed he plays on *Mean Mr Mustard* (sung by Frankie Howerd) and *You Never Give Me Your Money*. The movie and the accompanying soundtrack is premiered in August 1978, and also stars Aerosmith, Alice Cooper, Earth, Wind & Fire, Steve Martin, Paul Nicholas and Billy Preston in smaller roles. Although the film itself is a resounding flop, the album is a big success and makes US #5 in August 1978.

DECEMBER

THU 15TH

In the annual readers poll in DOWNBEAT dated today, Jeff Beck is voted #2 in the category 'Rock/Blues Musician' (after Stevie Wonder), and once again secures enough votes to be regarded as #11 in the 'Guitar' section. Even the lacklustre live collaboration with Jan Hammer is voted #5 in the 'Rock/Blues Album' category.

August 16, 1977: Elvis Presley dies at his Graceland mansion in Memphis at the age of 42.

1978

FEBRUARY

Jeff Beck joins Stanley Clarke on a studio recording in the States. Beck contributes guitar to the songs *Rock and Roll Jelly* and *Jamaican Boy*. The first is actually a power trio workout with Carmine Appice on drums, and is released on Clarke's summer '78 album *Modern Man* (UK Epic/US Nemperor 1978). Released at a time when the fusion period has passed its peak, the reviewer in DOWN BEAT cruelly notes: "Stanley Clarke's *Modern Man* is the kind of synthetic pop ephemera that will be disposed of quicker than used Kleenex ... For jazz, give me Stanley Clarke with Stan Getz or Dexter Gordon. For *Modern Man*, give me a frisbee contest." Still, both Beck and Clarke are voted top in their respective sections ('Guitar' and 'Bass') in – of all things – the PLAYBOY Readers' Jazz Poll this spring. When he is told about the accolade, Beck only shrugs "If that's as far as most Americans' comprehension of jazz goes, then it's rather disturbing, isn't it?"

Jamaican Boy is not issued until Stanley Clarke's half-live/half-studio album *I Wanna Play For You* album (UK Epic/ US Nemperor) at the end of 1979.

APRIL

SAT 29TH

Today's NEW MUSICAL EXPRESS announces Jeff Beck's plans to make a major appearance in Britain, as he is booked to appear on the upcoming Knebworth festival on Sunday June 24, which is also set to star Genesis and others. The following week's paper explains that Beck will put together a new four-piece band for the occasion, and one of the musicians will be Stanley Clarke.

MAY

Jeff Beck returns to England and Wadhurst permanently after his two year tax exile in the United States, but he will still retain his Los Angeles residence for some time.

Looking for material for a new album, Jeff has already called on Jan Hammer. Despite a turbulent working partnership when they toured together in '76 and '77, Jeff is still highly influenced by Hammer, who promptly furnishes him with a demo tape of half a dozen songs at the beginning of the year. Among these titles are believed to be *Star Cycle*, *Too Much To Lose*, *You Never Know*, *Cat Moves* and *Hot Rock*. (*Too Much To Lose* is the lead-off track on Jan Hammer Group's '77 album *Melodies*.)

Jeff Beck then begins recording at the Who's Ramport Studios at Battersea in May with engineer John Porter. Jan Hammer flies in from the States to help Jeff out, and British drummer Simon Phillips – fresh from the Jack Bruce Band – is also brought in. No bassist is hired at this time, so Hammer just overdubs the bass parts on a MiniMoog. Two cuts are quickly finished; *Star Cycle* and *Cat Moves* – both Hammer songs. *Star Cycle* is just a duet between Beck and Hammer, with Hammer supplying keyboards, sequencers and the drums. Attempts to record this with Phillips fails, so in the end Hammer does the drumming himself.

FRI 12TH

Jeff Beck is at the Speakeasy tonight, where Japanese writer Toshi Yajima spots him. Reportedly, Stanley Clarke has come to Britain and the two are presumably planning the upcoming Knebworth appearance, but Clarke is also said to be recording at Air Studios at this time.

JUNE

SAT 24TH

Beck has decided to cancel today's scheduled appearance at the Knebworth festival in Hertfordshire. Besides Stanley Clarke on bass, Beck has been rehearsing with Clarke's regular drummer Darryl Brown, and it is Brown who is blamed for pulling out and forcing Jeff to cancel. Probably, it is the lack of sufficent preparation on his own part which causes Jeff to balk. The festival goes ahead anyhow with Genesis, Tom Petty & The Heartbreakers, Jefferson Starship, Devo, the Atlanta Rhythm Section and also Phil Collins' hobby project Brand X.

JULY

MID

The music press speculates that not only will Jeff Beck and Stanley Clarke form a liasion for recording and touring purposes – including a jaunt around Japan – but the duo will also be augmented by Clarke's old sidekick from Return To Forever, drummer Lenny White. Beck, Clarke and White meet up in Los Angeles this month, but any working relationship never makes it beyond rehearsals.

TUE 25TH

The annual CBS Records convention opens today at the Century Plaza in Beverly Hills, Los Angeles. A meeting place of CBS artists and executives, the week-long event showcases new and old talent. Jeff Beck is at the convention with Celia Hammond.

At the end of Stanley Clarke's performance today, Jeff Beck steps on stage. He joins in on *Rock And Roll Jelly* (which he has recorded with Clarke) and the ballad *Closing*, before surprise guest John McLaughlin appears for an encore of *Goodbye Pork Pie Hat*, with Beck playing back-up to McLaughlin's solo. Other artists milling around at the convention are Billy Cobham, Lenny White, Narada Michael Walden, Tom Scott, Carlos Santana, Chicago, and members of Blue Öyster Cult and REO Speedwagon.

Newsflash October/November 1978: Beck and Hammer record together again ...

AUGUST

Home in Britain again, Jeff records some unspecified backing tracks at his home studio for the new album.

SEPTEMBER

EARLY

Paul McCartney organizes his ambitious Rockestra, and both Jeff Beck and Jimmy Page are briefly involved in this project. Some informal jams are undertaken early this month, before the actual recording takes place the following month. Beck tells the Japanese ROCKIN' magazine (December 1978): "I jammed with Paul McCartney and Jimmy Page in September. It will be included on Paul's new album".

SAT 16TH

Jeff is interviewed at his Wadhurst home by Toshi Yajima for Steve Rosen's 'Beck Book', soon to be published exclusively for the Japanese market. Parts of the interview also run in the Japanese music magazines PLAYER (November 1978) and ROCKIN' (December 1978). Also dropping by Jeff's house today are Max Middleton and Cozy Powell.

A real 'At Home' story, Beck shows Yajima around the estate, his music room and his garage. Talking about his upcoming tour of Japan, Beck outlines how his touring band will include Simon Phillips, Stanley Clarke and Mike Garson on keyboards, who lately has played with Clarke's backing group but of course is best known for his time with David Bowie and the Spiders From Mars.

Asked if he has any message for his Japanese fans, Beck replies: "I was given 4,000 letters, cards and presents. Thank you very much. All letters were in English. Most presents were handmade. I am very happy. Three years ago I went to Japan but I was in a bad condition at that time. My band will go to Japan in late November, and I believe this tour will be great and satisfying."

OCTOBER

TUE 3RD

Unfortunately, Jeff Beck is *not* among the attendees for Paul McCartney's recording of *Rockestra Theme* at Abbey Road today, which nevertheless counts guitarists David Gilmour, Pete Townshend, Hank Marvin, Denny Laine and Laurence Juber. Paul McCartney explains to Paul Gambaccini of ROLLING STONE (July 12, 1979): "A lot of people in music had been thinking about using a rock 'n' roll line-up instead of an orchestra. So I wrote a tune and finally asked people if they'd like to be in the Rockestra. Keith Moon was going to turn up but unfortunately he died a week before. But Beck was gonna come and Clapton and they didn't actually come. Beck was worried about what would happen if he didn't like the track."

•

Recording of Jeff Beck's new album recommences this October, as Jan Hammer returns to Britain again for further sessions at Ramport. Aided by Simon Phillips, an album's worth of songs are recorded. Still no bassist is on board, and again Hammer just plays the bass parts on keyboards.

Two interesting songs put down on tape at this time are *Oceans And Continents*, one of Hammer's songs that he has previously released on *The First Seven Days* LP, and a specially written song by Max Middleton. The latter remains untitled and unfinished, and is notable for a part played by harpist Richard Thomas of the London Philharmonic Orchestra. The score is attempted by freelancer David Snell, but is eventually given up; Middleton later characterizes it as "unplayable".

All the same, by now Jeff Beck has an album recorded (albeit not mixed and readied), including *Star Cycle, Too Much To Lose, You Never Know, Cat Moves, Hot Rock, Oceans And Continents* and Max Middleton's *'Harp Song'*. Jeff Beck has produced the end result himself, and a tentative release date is optimistically set for March 1979 – to coincide with a proposed 15-city US tour.

The sessions are not entirely flawless, as Beck tells John Tobler for BBC Radio in 1982: "... but we really had to force it recording them, because Simon wasn't happening on those at all at the beginning, although eventually it began to get much better."

But the planned album is shelved as Beck is afraid Hammer's presence as instrumentalist and composer will totally dominate the record. Only three of the songs (*Star Cycle, Too Much To Lose, You Never Know*) are retained for Beck's next album a year and half later, and Jeff will also record *Cat Moves* and *Hot Rock* for a Cozy Powell album in 1981.

NOVEMBER

With a tour of Japan coming up, Jeff Beck sets about putting together a new band, and formally joins forces with Stanley Clarke. In fact, the two go out billed as 'Jeff Beck And Stanley Clarke', as the idea is to feature Clarke songs along with Beck material. Jeff also hopes to utilize Clarke for his new album; the plan is that Clarke will overdub bass on the already recorded tracks by Hammer, Phillips and Beck. Jeff brings in Simon Phillips on drums, who is well acquainted with his music. Mike Garson from Clarke's road band is then hired to make the touring band a quartet. For reasons not entirely clear, Garson opts out, but the story has it that Beck dislikes his playing. Max Middleton – presumably busy elsewhere – recommends that Jeff check out pianist Tony Hymas. Actually, Hymas has previously played together with Simon Phillips in the Jack Bruce Band, besides conducting the Ballet Rambert. He has also done low-profile sessions for the likes of Graeme Edge and Chris De Burgh. (Actually, Hymas tends to his job well, as he will become the longest serving sideman to Jeff Beck, touring with him as late as 1995 and contributing to Beck sessions in 1999).

The Japanese tour signals a live comeback for Jeff, as he will tour on and off around the world at a leisurely pace for the next three and half years; visiting Japan twice, the States once, plus doing a European summer tour and finally make a return to the British stage in early 1981.

THU 16TH, FRI 17TH, SAT 18TH ✱

Beck and Clarke plus Tony Hymas and Simon Phillips spend three days in Los Angeles rehearsing.

Jan Hammer's banshee wail *Darkness* is kept as a brief prelude before the real show opener kicks in – the as-yet-unreleased *Star Cycle*. This attention grabber will be kept as set opener for the next two and half years at least. Furthermore, two brand new Hammer songs are premiered, the aforementioned *Cat Moves* and *Hot Rock*. Stanley Clarke is represented with a slew of his original compositions: *School Days, Loupsy Lou* and *Rock 'n' Roll Jelly*, two of which featured Beck in their original recorded arrangements. Beck's back catalogue is heavy on *Blow By Blow* material (*Freeway Jam, Diamond Dust, 'Cause We've*

Ⓢ September 7, 1978: Who drummer and former Beck sessioneer Keith Moon is found dead in his London apartment.

November 1978: Jeff Beck and Stanley Clarke join forces for a tour of Japan ...

Ended As Lovers) and lighter on *Wired* (just *Goodbye Pork Pie Hat* and *Blue Wind*). Only one pre-'75 selection is kept in the set – a surprise second encore on special occasions with *Superstition*.

SUN 19TH
The entourage, which also includes Ralph Baker, flies from Los Angeles on flight PA-003 and arrives at Narita, Tokyo at 9.00 pm. Here they check in at Tokyo Prince Hotel.

JEFF BECK: SECOND JAPANESE TOUR
MON 20TH
Kenmin-Bunka Center, Ibaraki, Japan
For the opening date of the Japanese tour, Beck and Clarke depart at noon on the Hitachi express train from Tokyo and arrive at Ibaraki at exactly 1.18 pm. They are immediately whisked off to the hall for tonight's concert, where a last rehearsal is held from 1.30 until 5.30 pm. Playing without any support group, the eighty minute show starts at 6.40 pm and finishes at eight o'clock. The first night of the tour finds a set list of eleven songs, including the new Jan Hammer songs *Hot Rocks* and *Too Much To Lose*. Tonight, like every other night on the tour, concludes with a double encore of *'Cause We've Ended As Lovers* followed by a ferocious *Blue Wind*.

Afterwards the group checks in at the local Keisei Hotel.

TUE 21ST
A day devoted to travelling, as Beck journeys to Kanazawa where he is booked into the Hakuunnro Hotel.

WED 22ND
Koseinenkin Hall, Ishikawa, Kanazawa, Japan

THU 23RD
Shimin Kaikan, Kurashiki, Japan

Set List/Beck + Clarke

Nippon Budokan Hall, Tokyo, November 30, '78

Darkness/Earth In Search Of A Sun • Star Cycle • Freeway Jam • Cat Moves • Goodbye Pork Pie Hat • bass solo/School Days • Journey To Love • Loupsy Lou • Diamond Dust • Scatterbrain/drum solo • Rock 'n' Roll Jelly • 'Cause We've Ended As Lovers • [Encores:] Blue Wind • Superstition

---

FRI 24TH
Furitu Taiikukan, Osaka, Japan
A slight change in the set list, as *Too Much To Lose* is dropped and replaced by Stanley Clarke's *Journey To Love*, which will be kept for the remainder of the Japanese concerts.

SAT 25TH
Journalist Yuichi Hirayama from ROCKIN' magazine is invited into Beck's hotel room in Osaka, despite Ralph Baker's protests. Hirayama gives Jeff a trophy to honour his #1 spot in PLAYER's readers' poll in the guitar section. Hirayama furthermore presents him with a copy of 'The Beck Book' hot off the press (written by Steven Rosen and only published in Japanese), a red jacket and two Greco guitars, one white (with a vibrato arm) and one black. The white guitar will briefly be put into service by Beck on this Japanese visit. Later in the afternoon, Beck travels to Nagoya.

SUN 26TH
Shi-Kokaido, Nagoya, Japan
For the Nagoya performance, Hammer's *Hot Rock* is exchanged in favour of another, new Hammer composition – *Cat Moves* – which will be kept in for the rest of the tour.

🎵 A fair concert by Jeff and Stanley, although as a whole this quartet neither matches the funk of the Bascomb–Purdie band nor the fire of Jan Hammer's group. Indeed, the spirit of Jan Hammer still haunts Beck's shows, as the elephant trumpeting of *Darkness/Earth In Search Of A Sun* opens tonight's concert before paving way for the brand new but catchy *Star Cycle*. Next up is *Freeway Jam*, where Jeff puts on a slide and quotes all too briefly from *Beck's Bolero*. *Cat Moves* is a strong number, and moves along briskly with excellent support by Clarke and Phillips in the rhythm section. The warmly received *Goodbye Pork Pie Hat* is a highlight and acts as Beck's blues showcase, with his playing remarkably fresh and free of the usual clichés. Here Jeff's guitar is at its boldest, with a self-assured tone and beautiful phrasing. Generally, Beck's selections fare much better than Stanley Clarke's blander numbers. Especially the vocalising on *Journey To Love* is a bit twee and saccharine, and both *Loupsy Lou* and *Rock 'n' Roll Jelly* are stereotyped fusion formulas, the latter built on the same chassis as *Blue Wind*. Clarke's fourth contribution, *School Days*, displays his awesome skills on the electric bass. Simon Phillips kicks off *Scatterbrain* at an impossible speed, causing Jeff to fluff notes left, right and centre, before Phillips plays the obligatory drum solo. After manhandling his guitar with the vibrato arm during the next-to-last number, the strings are dangerously out of tune on the closer *Blue Wind*, which suffers accordingly. Tony Hymas acts as anchor-man throughout, excelling on electric and acoustic pianos (with an extended solo on *Diamond Dust*), but his synth playing is at times victim of aimless knob-twiddling – witness his solo on *Loupsy Lou;* a far cry from Jan Hammer's command of the synthesizer.

TUE 28TH
Shin-nittetu Otani Taiikukan, Kokura, Japan

WED 29TH
Koseinenkin Hall, Osaka, Japan
Because of ticket demand in Osaka for the concert on the 24th, an extra show is added today at the Koseinenkin Hall – where Beck, Bogert & Appice recorded their live album more than five years ago.

THU 30TH
Nippon Budokan Hall, Tokyo, Japan
The audiences at Beck and Clarke's three successful nights in Tokyo are treated to *Superstition* as a second encore, complete with Jeff on the voice bag.

DECEMBER

FRI 1ST
Nippon Budokan Hall, Tokyo, Japan

SAT 2ND
Nippon Budokan Hall, Tokyo, Japan
An extra show – a third night at the popular Budokan arena – is added in Tokyo, because of public demand.

SUN 3RD
While Jeff and his English entourage fly home to London on flight BA-008, Stanley Clarke returns to Los Angeles on flight PA-002. The original idea to keep Stanley Clarke around to do overdubs to the Beck–Hammer–Phillips songs is never realized.

THU 21TH✱
Jeff Beck is backstage at one of Rod Stewart's week-long Christmas shows at Grand Hall, Olympia, London. Jeff chats with Carmine Appice before the show, but leaves before it commences.

December 9, 1978: Rod Stewart scores a US #1 hit with the single "Da Ya Think I'm Sexy".

◀ 1979

MARCH

Although new product is long overdue, Jeff Beck decides to put the new album on hold for the time being, as he fears Jan Hammer's dominant presence will squelch his own contributions.

The release was to tie in with a discussed 15-city headlining tour of the United States, which is also put on hold. This itinerary was to have featured the same Beck–Clarke–Hymas–Phillips line-up as the Japanese tour the previous November.

MAY

SAT 19TH

Eric Clapton and Patti Harrison's wedding party is celebrated at Clapton's Hurtwood Edge estate in Ewhurst, Surrey, and Jeff Beck is one of the many celebrity rock-biz guests.

During the night a big jam evolves in a specially erected marquee in Clapton's garden, and at one point Paul McCartney, George Harrison and Ringo Starr are onstage together. (It has not been verified if Jeff actually participates in this jam.) Also invited and attending the party are Jack Bruce, Ginger Baker, Bill Wyman, Mick Jagger, Keith Richards, Lonnie Donegan, Denny Laine and Jim Capaldi.

JUNE

Jeff Beck re-forms the group that toured Japan the previous autumn for a short European summer tour. Stanley Clarke has in the meantime boosted his rock credibility considerably by being part of the New Barbarians, an ad hoc group fronted by Ron Wood and Keith Richards, who have toured the United States extensively from April 24 to May 21 this spring.

The set list for this summer's round is fairly like the Japan repertoire from November the previous year. Apparently, Beck and Clarke will now stick to the same pattern every night. After setting the mood with *Darkness/ Earth In Search Of A Sun,* the set dives straight into the synthesized intro to *Star Cycle,* before working its way through a cross-selection of Jeff and Stanley's tunes. Both *Cat Moves* and *Hot Rock* are deleted, while *Superstition* is reinstated as a regular encore. Clarke showcases the four compositions he did on the last tour (*Journey To Love, School Days, Loupsy Lou, Rock 'n' Roll Jelly*), three of which actually featured Jeff on the recorded versions (the exception being *School Days*). The only surprise in the course of the concerts comes when Beck and Clarke weave in a few phrases of Jimi Hendrix's *Third Stone From The Sun* theme midway during *Loupsy Lou.*

SAT 30TH
JEFF BECK:
FIRST EUROPEAN TOUR
"Roskildefestivalen"
Roskilde, Denmark

'Roskildefestivalen' is an annual tradition and highly popular festival. This is Jeff's first visit to Denmark since the days of the Jeff Beck Group, who indeed did play the small town of Roskilde on April 21, 1968. Actually, Beck and Clarke are a late addition to the bill, replacing the original main attraction Dire Straits, whose name already appears on the posters. An array of other American, British and Scandinavian groups appear over the weekend (55 in all), including Peter Tosh, Tom Robinson Band, Taj Mahal, Talking Heads and Lindisfarne.

Attendance on the Saturday is a strong crowd of 40,000. Torben Bille from Copenhagen's POLITIKEN is not amused however: "Jeff Beck and Stanley Clarke – the evening's advertised top names – unfortunately proved to be just as enervatingly trivial as one had feared. Here are two musicians undoubtedly talented who judging from this performance had combined forces in order to earn a cheap penny."

Set List/Beck + Clarke

Roskildefestivalen, Roskilde, Denmark, June 30 '79

Darkness/Earth In Search Of A Sun • Star Cycle • Blue Wind • Journey To Love • Freeway Jam • Goodbye Pork Pie Hat • School Days (bass solo) • Diamond Dust • Loupsy Lou • Scatterbrain (drum solo) • Rock 'n' Roll Jelly • 'Cause We've Ended As Lovers • Superstition

---

JULY

SUN 1ST
"Hortensfestivalen '79"
Lystlunden, Horten, Norway

Jeff Beck's one and only visit to Norway takes place in the small coastal town of Horten, south of Oslo. In running order, the festival bill also boasts reggae star Peter Tosh; Lake (a German group); fusion drummer Alphonso Mouzon; UK new-wave group Eddie & The Hot Rods; American singer/guitarist Loudon Wainwright III (who is used to filling the spaces during changeovers); and finally Beck–Clarke. The crowd counts about 12–13,000 festival goers, but the day is plagued by long delays, topped by the one and a half hour it takes before Eddie & The Hot Rods have dismantled their gear and Beck–Clarke's road crew have set up theirs. By the time they get onstage past nine o'clock, many have left the stadium. Battling with a deadline, Leif Gjerstad from DAGBLADET (July 3) has to leave right after Beck and Clarke take the stage: "Of what little I did hear, it seems like what remained of the crowd got a brilliant end to the festival. Judging by *Led Boots* [actually *Star Cycle*] and *Blue Wind,* it sounds like the combi-

Newsflash June 1979: Jeff Beck and Stanley Clarke tour Europe ...

nation of Beck/Clarke delivers what their names promise."

😀 With a well-worn Stratocaster around his neck, Beck opens the concert as night falls with the instantly memorable *Star Cycle*. Tony Hymas sounds more comfortable behind the synthesizer than before, and the guitar and the keyboard lines fit like hand-in-glove. "A brand old tune" Jeff mutters, and then a swirling guitar signals *Blue Wind*, where Hymas shifts between a synthesizer and an electric piano. Jeff is particularily fast-fingered tonight, and he easily straddles the high pitched melody and the growling riff on the bottom strings. The tempo slows a bit for *Journey To Love*. Thankfully, Clarke has stopped singing the la-de-dahs, and the song – with its slight *In Memory of Elizabeth Reed* resemblance – has Beck milking the guitar for every nuance. A little symphony of honking car horns introduces *Freeway Jam*, where a great visual moment occurs when Beck just tosses off the slide halfway through the song, sending it skidding across the stage. Afterwards, Jeff switches to the fat-toned Tele-Gib instead of his trademark Stratocaster. Bereft of a vibrato arm, he adds plenty of slide, behind-the-nut bending and side-of-the-pick harmonics to his sonic spectrum. On *Goodbye Pork Pie Hat*, Jeff lays behind the beat and either fills the spaces with tension or leaves them blank. The Mingus song makes Clarke's showcase *School Days* (which is tacked on the end of *Pork Pie*) all the more banal. Although it starts well – a deep and dark riffing bass – as soon as the main theme enters it falls flat on its face, as Beck and Clarke battle aimlessly in a too-long solo exchange. *Diamond Dust* is a sea of tranquility in this otherwise high-energy hurricane, where Jeff cannot resist slipping in a few bluesy bends. *Loupsy Lou* opens with Phillips alone on a military march snare beat, which bizarrely causes a section of the crowd to sing a brass band theme. Moving from a rock beat to a reggae feel, the song is again victim of too much solo, too little content. All in all, however, this is an excellent concert.

TUE 3RD
"Festival de Jazz-Rock"
Pavillon de Porte de Panton, Paris, France
Jeff Beck and Stanley Clarke are one of the attractions at the 'Festival de Jazz-Rock' in Paris, which also stars a piano duo concert by Chick Corea and Herbie Hancock and Weather Report.

The initials 'F. V.' reviews the concert in ROCK & FOLK (September 1979), and finds Beck and Clarke a shallow experience: "A show which was a demonstration of pure and empty virtuosity. One believes one is at the 'Music Saloon De Jazz-Rock'. Clarke struggles with the bass ... turning jazz-rock into muzak for intellectuals. This night it sounded like they just wanted to leave this lamentable tour. Luckily, Weather Report were ready to console everyone!"

Reportedly, Jeff Beck and Stanley Clarke hang out with the Rolling Stones, who are in Paris recording at EMI's Pathé-Marconi studios. Contributing to these sessions is harp player Sugar Blue, who plays support on Beck's French concerts.

WED 4TH *
Stade Aguillera, Biarritz, France
An unconfirmed date in Biarritz on the west coast of France, just north of the Spanish border.

THU 5TH
Jaap Edenhal, Amsterdam, Holland
According to the advertisement, this is the "enig concert in Nederland" and it is billed as 'the great comeback concert of Jeff Beck' (Jeff hasn't played Holland since the days of Beck, Bogert & Appice in June 1973). The concert draws 3,500 people, and the duo John Schuursma/ Kaz Lux provide support.

Roberto Palombit in MUZIEKKRANT OOR (July 11) is over the moon: "What Beck gets out of the guitar borders on the impossible. Whereas a guitar coryphaeus like Mark Knopfler has a characteristic sound which he employs on every number, Beck pulls endless tonalities from his Stratocaster without any effect equipment ... overall his music was rawer and heavier than what we are used to from

FREEWAY JAM

The Beck & Clarke Expedition

When Jeff Beck went back on the road at the end of 1978 and in the summer of 1979, he teamed up with ex-Return To Forever bassist Stanley Clarke. In many ways, Clarke served the same function as Jan Hammer did with Beck in 1976/1977, lifting some of the responsibilities off Beck's shoulders, as their teaming up meant a jazz-rock supergroup. (A little story from when Beck–Clarke closed the night at an outdoor festival in Norway in 1979 also illustrates the pretentiousness that often went with the jazz-rockers: Peter Tosh played earlier in the day. But wheras Sly Dunbar's mini-kit took a few moments to set up – which he then proceeded to skank to smithereens – assembling Simon Phillips' giant drumset delayed Beck and Clarke's performance with almost an hour.)

As a bassist, Stanley Clarke was a revolutionary, with a slap technique based on the style of Sly Stone's bass player Larry Graham. Clarke also had chops and musical knowledge to spare plus an unabashed love of the spotlight. But his rubbery upper register fusilades sometimes proved too much, when he instead should have been holding down the bottom. Clarke had several successful albums to his credit and he was thus able to front the band on his own. He also had another asset which he shared with Beck, which was a sense of goofiness in his playing. His mind-boggling bass showcase, *School Days*, would elicit just as many smiles as it would jaw-dropping awe from the audience.

Perhaps sensitive from his experiences with the dominant Jan Hammer, Beck never developed his relationship with Stanley Clarke to include his own records. ∎

his latest albums. Beck controlled the whole sound with his fingers ... His guitar work shone like magic." Palombit describes Simon Phillips as a "small forest pygmy ... without doubt the most talented young drummer from England at the moment."

Three songs from tonight are taped and later broadcast on Radio VARA out of Holland. No Jeff Beck compositions are aired, rather these are just the Stanley Clarke numbers *Rock 'n' Roll Jelly*, *School Days* and *Loupsy Lou*.

© June 29, 1979: Ex-Little Feat guitarist Lowell George dies of a drug-related heart attack in Los Angeles.

July 1979: Jeff Beck plays France and Spain with Weather Report ...

SAT 7TH
Konzerthaus, Vienna, Austria
Like his visit to Norway this summer, Austria is another first for Beck.

TUE 10TH
Arènes, Fréjus, France
Fréjus is a small town on the south coast of France, about halfway between Nice and Marseille, but 'les' Arènes is an oft-visited venue for touring rock groups.

Jeff, Stanley and Tony go into sonic overload on *Loupsy Lou* and *Rock 'n' Roll Jelly*, apparently more pre-occupied with producing a series of spacey doodlings with very little musical content, rather than sounding like a proper rock 'n' roll group.

THU 12TH
Arènes, Palavas-les Flots, France
Visiting a small coastal village south of Montpellier by the Mediterranean, Jeff Beck and Stanley Clarke eventually cancel their planned appearance.

This prompts a long, rambling letter from Carles-Didier Rodez in ROCK & FOLK (September 1979). The reader complains of the high ticket prices (50 francs) and the rough security personnel. After Sugar Blue's performance, Jeff Beck gets on stage at 1.15 pm. However, after literally a minute of music, darkness descends on the stage, Beck leaves and someone announces ("Like at Châtelet in 1974, with the same bon homie", snarls Rodcz) that Beck will perform another day and the tickets will be refunded for those who want. (No public excuse is given for the cancellation and Beck–Clarke do not play a 'do good' concert.)

FRI 13TH
Plaza de Toros Las Arenas, Barcelona, Spain
"¿Who is the star of the night? ¡Clearly Jeff Beck!" So is the opinion of Jordi Tarda (writing in POPULAR 1, September 1979): "You think of Eric Clapton and Jimmy Page as the best, but tonight there was no doubt who was the God of the guitar". Equally impressed is Jaume Uriach in Spain's other big music magazine, VIBRACIONES (September 1979), who picks *Scatterbrain* as the night's high-point, where "Tony Hymas accompanies discreetly while Simon Philips bombards the drums". Stanley Clarke, is also given special praise.

The Barcelona concert is at an old bullring and Beck–Clarke with Weather Report, plus Spanish acts Camarón and Dolores, pull a crowd of 15,000 people. The night is exceedingly hot, and after a few numbers Beck takes off his shirt to play barechested.

SAT 14TH
Plaza de Toros de Las Ventas, Madrid, Spain
A second concert with Weather Report is advertised in Madrid today, and is believed to be the end of the European tour. The sun creates havoc with Beck's guitar synthesizer: "I used this one I've got ..., when we were in Spain. The equipment was set up in a bullring which they turned into a concert arena, and the sun was 110 degrees at lunch time. Nobody covered up the synthezier, and it was beating down on the control board. And I'll tell you – that night, when it cooled off, all sorts of things were happening inside it."

SUN 15TH✱
Jeff Beck presumably returns to England.

AUGUST

SAT 18TH
Jeff Beck is backstage at Wembley Stadium today, where the Who (now with Kenny Jones behind the drums) perform supported by Nils Lofgren, AC/DC and the Stranglers.

AUTUMN

To finish a new album, Jeff Beck involves Tony Hymas as composer, much like he depended on Max Middleton to help him with the *Blow By Blow* album five years previous. Hymas spends time at Beck's house, jamming and playing, and one song worked out and recorded at the end of this year is the duet *The Final Piece* (under the working title *'A' Flat*). The ever-doubtful Beck is ready to consign this for the dustbin, but is stopped by an intervention from Cozy Powell. Beck later explains to MELODY MAKER: "I remember after playing it to [Powell] for the first time he just went away glazed and glassy-eyed and I had to have second thoughts!" (Powell plays the song for anyone who cares to listen during Rainbow's February tour next year.)

Ken Scott, who engineered the *Beck-Ola* album back in 1969, is hired as co-producer for the project. Scott's latest credentials include working with US group the Dixie Dregs.

December 3, 1979: Eleven fans are trampled to death prior to a Who concert in Cincinnati, Ohio.

1980

JANUARY/FEBRUARY

At the beginning of the year, Jeff Beck, Tony Hymas and Simon Phillips have booked time at EMI's Abbey Road studio to complete a new Beck album.

A new batch of songs are recorded, all penned by Tony Hymas and Simon Phillips; *The Powers That Be* (later christened *The Pump*), *Golden Days* (a working title for *The Golden Road*), *El Becko* and *Space Boogie*. By the end of February these four songs are completed, but still need bass guitar added.

MARCH

FRI 7TH, SAT 8TH, SUN 9TH

Bass player Mo Foster gets the call to do overdubs for Jeff's upcoming album at Studio 2 at Abbey Road this weekend. Foster is already a seasoned bassist who previously played in Affinity, a band that coincidentally included guitarist Mike Jopp – the very same guy who Beck replaced in the Tridents way back in 1963. Lately, Foster has been an in-demand studio player for a variety of artists ranging from Cliff Richard to Roger Glover's *Butterfly Ball*, and he has already crossed paths with both Tony Hymas (on an album by Joe Breen) and Simon Phillips (sessions for Chris Rainbow and Ray Russell).

His first task is overdubbing bass onto *Space Boogie*. As soon as bass, drums and keyboards are laid down, the guitar solo is laced on top – a challenge as Beck explains to John Tobler: "I had about 50 tries at soloing over that ... When you play that high-speed stuff, you have to be totally involved and the sound has to be around you. You can't just play to a pair of dumb-looking speakers, although I had to in the end because the track was so strong without anything else ... You really need to be in a mood for that kind of stuff. You have to be angry, you have to get that kind of naughtiness going, and then let it out."

FRI 14TH

Mo Foster's second bass overdub session.

TUE 18TH

Mo Foster's third and last bass overdub session.

LATE ✱

Jeff Beck's new album is mixed and readied at EMI's studios at Abbey Road.

MAY

SUN 18TH

Beck sits in with Eric Clapton at the Civic Hall in Guildford, Surrey for a long, loose version of *Ramblin' On My Mind*. Guildford is the regular end-of-tour gig-cum-party for Clapton, and his group now features Albert Lee on guitar and Gary Brooker on keyboards.

Taking up the story, Beck tells John Tobler: "It was very much a spur of the moment thing – that very afternoon, I got a phone call from Eric, and he asked me if I'd like to go to the last gig of his tour. It was a lovely sunny day, so I jumped in my car and drove over to the hall with him and on the way he said: 'Do you want to play tonight?' My heart started pumping, and I thought 'oh God after two years of not playing live to suddenly be on stage with Eric,' so I said I didn't want to play. So he said there was a guitar and an amp there and, if I wanted to, I could play and for the next hour I was thinking: 'What am I going to do? What's he going to be playing?' But he was so reasonable about it. He said, 'Let's just play a blues', and then he beckoned me on and I played."

LATE ✱

The wheels are set in motion for Beck's return to the public, and besides the new album, a tour of the United States is pencilled in for August onwards.

It is decided to use the British quartet Beck–Hymas–Foster–Phillips on the road too, and rehearsals are held at the Roxy Theatre in Willesden, London at the end of May.

JUNE

THU 19TH–TUE 24TH ✱

While attending the NSRA Western Rod Nationals in San Jose, California, Jeff Beck sets aside a day or two for press interviews at his hotel suite in Beverly Hills. Among others, he talks to Mikal Gilmore of ROLLING STONE (October 16), Jas Obrecht of GUITAR PLAYER (October 1980) and Yardena Arar from the Associated Press, which incidentally is conducted on Beck's 36th birthday.

Explaining the long layoff since *Wired*, Beck tells Mikal Gilmore: "Partly it was attributable to the strain of working with Jan. That wasn't my band, you know, it was his; so that made for a touchy situation. Jan wanted us to play as much of his material as mine, I couldn't have that. I had my career to think about. More than anything, though, I just didn't want to go any further in music. After all, I'd been playing guitar for over eighteen years. I wanted to cut the wire completely – to get out and see what it was all about. Then, after a bit, I started to look around, and I realized that most of the music being made now is for children – just a bunch of rubbish with a few nifty riffs that poke through now and then. So that led to a period of wondering. 'Well, what am I going to do when I start back again?'" Asked about contemporary music and guitarists (Gilmore lists Robert Fripp, Tom Verlaine, David Byrne, James 'Blood' Ulmer and Tom Herman as examples of musicians who have expanded the guitar vocabulary), Beck confesses ignorance: "Frankly, I've got better things to do than hang around record shops. And most of the punk stuff I've heard sounds like merely a repeat of what was going on in England years ago, though with less melody and magic ... Still, I've noticed that some of the more experimental new wave groups have started using synthesizers, and that's good. Synthesizers are obviously going to be the catalyst for music and musicians to come. Guitars will probably get phased out." Whereupon Gilmore comments: "Beck chuckles, as if delighted by his own obsolescence. Watching him, I can't help reflecting on how much this one man has single-handedly enlarged the vocabulary and parameter of rock guitar, and what a shame it would be to watch him 'get phased out'."

The GUITAR PLAYER interview warrants a cover story in the magazine's

Newsflash July 1980: First Jeff Beck studio album in four years released ...

October issue, and the in-depth article runs to a colossal seventeen pages. Jas Obrect discusses a wide variety of topics with an articulate and impassioned Beck, be it the limitations of the guitar ("for me it's definitely limited. It seems to be limited for a lot of other players, too, judging by what I've heard on radio"); views on soloing ("I've got no desire to play ten-minute solos. Those were never valid anyway, in my book – never. It was just a cheap way of building up tension in the audience. I remember in the days of Ten Years After and several other groups, really the people were clapping in a sense of relief of tension"); guitar collecting ("I love guitars, but it's funny – I would never take the trouble to make an effort to go out and look for one"); new guitarists ("I've heard Steve Morse of Dixie Dregs ... I was very impressed"); picking techniques ("I don't use picks anymore unless my fingers hurt or I've broken a nail. Usually I use my bare fingers, all of them if I can"); the Yardbirds ("I liked some of the stuff we did with Sam Phillips"); Jimmy Page ("I don't call him, and he doesn't ring me") and Hendrix ("I liked Jimi best when we didn't talk guitars"). Pressed for his favourite recording, Jeff cites *Beck's Bolero*.

MON 30TH

More than two years in the making, Jeff Beck's new album *There And Back* is released concurrently in the United States and Great Britain this week. The monochrome cover portrays Jeff with guitar case in hand. The album is roughly split in two; three tracks from 1978 featuring Jan Hammer and five selections from this spring with Tony Hymas and Simon Phillips as composers. The music is still best classified as fusion, but lacks the looseness of *Blow By Blow* and the variety of *Wired*. *Star Cycle* will later find fame as the theme song to the British pop show "The Tube" (Channel 4) in 1982, while *The Pump* will form part of the soundtrack to "Risky Business", a 1984 movie starring Tom Cruise.

Even though the climate in rock has changed – with punk and new wave being the new rages – since Jeff's last proper studio album four year now, the album makes a strong US #21 and a surprising UK #38.

Reviews of *There And Back* furthermore confirm the changes taking place, as typified by Gregg Turner's hip jive in Creem (October 1980): "The hive of six-string stingers Beck so notoriously mined in the fantabulous 60s has been debunked non-toxic. No poison, just bunk, & in fact, speakin' of bees, this is the most anti-insect album of sounds. Nothing for chrissakes is pollinated. Just this real hapless jazzbo-type funk, no angry, not stinging, no nothin', man. Rage to die. Eight trax – 'scuse me, compositions – of instrumental exploration go nowhere fast. Beck's gee-tar drones and frolics thru these particularly non-abrasive sopoforic passages punctating Jan Hammer's self-indulgence and dullsville sonic 'experimentation'. This mishmash of electronics and guitar's just real wimpy, lightweight stuff." After letting off this barrage, Turner lightens up: "Production overall's pretty good for what alla this baloney amounts to; somehow very sympathetic with motif and execution. ... El Becko's actually OK too. Beck's playing sorta listenable and it's quite possible that somewhere in the middle it starts to cook. Yeah, so maybe ..." David Fricke in Rolling Stone (September 4) essentially shares the same view, and is particularly disappointed by the contributions by Beck's former synthesist: "... the star opens *There And Back* with three strikes against him, all of them work of fuzak keyboardist Jan Hammer ... formulaic Hammer compositions, i.e. terminally predictable excercises in cosmic Mahavishnu-style virtuosity, lazy MOR fodder or neo-Funkadelic jive ... *There And Back* is a disappointingly static record from a consummate riffer whose speciality was always leading the pack. These days, Jeff Beck seems content to be a spectator, watching the parade go by."

The British reviews are generally more positive. Hugh Fielder in Sounds (July 12) begins ironically: "Quite what Jeff Beck's been up to in the three years since his last album which was live you have to go back four to find a studio album, I'm not too sure. But he ain't been writing much, that's for sure. He comes up with precisely one half-credit out of the eight tracks on this album. Needless to say it's the one track that contains the cool sustained magic that only Beck is capable of. With just keyboards for accompaniment it closes the album and leaves you gnashing your teeth over what could have been." Steve Gett in Melody Maker (July 12) also finds this composition the highlight of the album: "*The Final Peace* is magic. Accompanied only by Tony Hymas on keyboards, he coaxes out more feeling within three and a half minutes than most guitarists achieve on a whole album. *There And Back* is strictly for Beck devotees, while *The Final Peace* is a must for everyone who ever wanted to hear electric guitar played with feeling."

JULY

FRI 4TH

UK release date for *There And Back*.

EARLY

To promote *There And Back* in England, Epic has booked a solid afternoon in the coffee lounge at London's

---

Album

JEFF BECK
THERE AND BACK

A1 Star Cycle *(Jan Hammer)* **A2** Too Much To Lose *(Jan Hammer)* **A3** You Never Know *(Jan Hammer)* **A4** The Pump *(Hymas/Phillips)*

B1 El Becko *(Hymas/Phillips)* **B2** The Golden Road *(Hymas/Phillips)* **B3** Space Boogie *(Hymas/Phillips)* **B4** The Final Piece *(Beck/Hymas)*

Released Monday June 30, 1980 (US Epic 35654) and Friday July 4, 1980 (UK Epic 83288)
Personnel is Jeff Beck (gtrs), Jan Hammer (synths, sequencers A1, A2, A3, drms on A1), Tony Hymas (kybds A4, B1, B2, B3, B4), Simon Phillips (drms on all except A1, B4) and Mo Foster (bs on A4, B1, B2, B3).
Recorded at Ramport Studios, Thessally Road, Battersea and EMI Studios, Abbey Road, London, May, October and November 1978, late 1979 and spring 1980.
Produced by Ken Scott and Jeff Beck
Engineered by John Porter (at Ramport)
Highest Chart Position UK: #38
Highest Chart Position US: #21

© May 30, 1980: Ex-Derek & The Dominos bassist Carl Radle, who was with Gary Lewis on the Yardbirds 'Dick Clark' tour in 1966, dies in Tulsa, Oklahoma.

July 1980: "There And Back" met with mixed critical response ...

Waldorf Astoria. Here Beck talks to Nick Kent of NEW MUSICAL EXPRESS, Steve Gett of MELODY MAKER and Chris Welch of MUSICIANS ONLY (all dated July 19). John Tobler conducts a separate interview with Jeff at the time, for stories published in the British NEW MUSIC NEWS (August 3) and the American magazine TROUSER PRESS (November 1980).

Nick Kent, once a big Beck fan, is crestfallen at meeting his old hero. Kent paints a fascinating portrait of Jeff in the new post-punk world, and he is not kind: "Beck is constantly at pains to articulate himself properly throughout the interview. Although his complexion has a leathery, badly sunburnt quality to it and his face has a disctintly lived-in quality, his features – topped off by the yokel thatch of old – remain unchanged, characterised most of all by a pair of moon-shaped glaring eyes, stung with a mixture of suspicion and disinterest. From a distance, his demeanour seems terminally sullen. Face to face, he appears merely confused, the moody pout that frames his lower jaw going slack whilst his eyes lower their guard, making him seem one of those unfortunate souls plagued by a kind of depressive melancholia." It is particularly Beck's lack of interest in what is happening elsewhere in the musical world which bothers Kent: "Robert Fripp's guitar experiments merit far more attention; Tom Verlaine has achieved the maverick shaping of both a form and a guitar style that, although arguably more academic, nonetheless completely trashes Beck's blinkered conceits; Neil Young's playing on *Live Rust* steals the fire that Beck could once kindle. Beck confesses ignorance regarding all those players. The new wave music that moved him to view rock as a revived force he can't pinpoint in terms of individual bands and players. In fact, I've never encountered a musician more adrift in his own trough of musical incompetence. And possibly he realises this. He reminisces with fervour about the Yardbirds and the *Truth*-era band that granted him his reputation, whilst the fusion squad – Walden, Hammer, Stanley Clarke – he refers to in guarded terms that could well mask the realisation that his dalliances with the latter crew have driven him up a cul-de-sac." At one point in the interview Beck wakes up: "Rock was totally destroyed for me by all that [heavy metal], for a good long while ... The new wave stuff I've heard – a lot of it – has really brought the spirit back into the form. Like, there has been a renaissance of getting back to basics. It makes me remember when I was kid just getting into the guitar and being totally into Cliff Gallup ... I idolised him, learnt his solos note-for-note. I even remember drawing pictures of him", prompting Kent to write: "Beck's dialogue suddenly takes on a fervent, wide-eyed tone. That sense of awe – forever lurking in the heart of the true fan – is the most crucial moment during the whole three quarters of an hour, because it stands at direct odds with his otherwise depressing sense of confusion." Kent finishes by describing Beck's career as "one long contradiction", and sums up what he considers to be his grim future prospects: "Too wayward to settle into some anonymous group role, too instinctively 'flash' to be the humble craftsman, Jeff Beck will always remain out on a tangent, very much alone. Is it really any wonder that he is unable to find the necessary perspective to deliver the goods at least one last time?"

The other interviews have a far more positive attitude. Chris Welch, who has not talked to Beck since September 1973, now writes for the new rock paper MUSICIANS ONLY. A bit more technically angled, here Beck talks about guitars and equipment besides the new album and touring: "I don't miss the road. I want my cake and eat it, I want to suddenly be there – onstage playing without the aggravation of getting there." Despite being vague about his musical direction to Welch, Jeff is firm on one point: "I don't see my future lying in jazz. If I put one brick in the altar of rock and helped rock guitar move on a bit, then I'm happy with that achievement. But no way do I want to be classified as a jazz-rock musician. As soon as you play a few speedy runs you wind up in the jazz guitar poll."

Steve Gett of MELODY MAKER gets the story about his favourite song, *The Final Piece*: "I had asked Tony if he could write me a featured guitar piece, and then having asked him that stupid question I was very embarrassed because that is something I should be able to do. So then I told him that I wanted some really spaced out chords so that I could work in-between them, and that's exactly what we did. I just made up the guitar on that, it wasn't really planned at all. He wrote a melody to which I didn't rigidly stick – I just cried a few times on the guitar."

John Tobler has his interview with Beck published both in England and America, and in TROUSER PRESS Beck disclaims his ability as a proper jazz musician: "If I were going to pursue jazz I'd have to have a lot more understanding of it under my belt. It's too late for me to start delving back to old, great jazz records – Ornette

LED BOOTS

Here And Gone

When Jeff Beck returned to the studio in 1978 to record a follow-up to *Wired*, he again recruited Jan Hammer to help him out. Although Hammer supplied enough songs to fill a whole album, Jeff was reluctant to let him dominate the proceedings and shelved the project until another songwriting source was found; ultimately that being Tony Hymas and Simon Phillips.

Ironically, Jan Hammer's three contributions to *There And Back* are the album's highlights. *Star Cycle* was a new concept, a sequenced loop over which Hammer and Beck soloed with abandon, meshing together in an undistinguishable frenzy, while the mighty *You Never Know* featured Hammer's astonishing guitar-like synth solo – perhaps the best guitar solo Beck *never* played.

The Hymas/Phillips contributions on the other hand, lacked Hammer's strong melodic element. Both *El Becko*, a kind of metal flamenco, and the wobbly *Space Boogie* packed some punch, but the popular *The Pump* came over as quite ordinary. Especially disappointing were *The Final Piece* – a random slice of doodlings – and *The Golden Road*, an unfocused fusion attempt which refused to stick in the mind. Much of the music on *There And Back* is like the cover – dark, humourless and in stark black and white. Nevertheless, Jeff Beck was still a strong, viable commercial property despite the threat from punk and new wave, and *There And Back* triumphantly scored a US near-top twenty. Indeed, the yearly overview of the 'Best Selling Albums of 1980' in ROLLING STONE shows *There And Back* comfortably nesting at #56.

Uniquely, Jeff had now dropped playing with a plectrum altogether and used his bare fingers instead. Subscribing to Ry Cooder's view that "playing with a pick is like showering with a swimsuit", the meat-to-the-metal approach not only looked darn cool, but gave Jeff's playing an extra physical, emotional edge. ■

August 1980: US tour begins in Oregon ...

Coleman and stuff like that. It's just beyond my grasp now, so it's natural to go back to the way I've always played, which is from the gut or spur-of-the-moment type stuff." He then analyzes the downfall of the Yardbirds: "We had a really good crack at [it] in the States, and we could have been enormous. If we'd just hung together for another year we'd have spanned into the '67 period, when you got Sly and the Family Stone, and if the Yardbirds had had enough solid financial backing behind them, we'd have been all right. We were limited by bad management, and the gigs were wrongly chosen. All we had was Bill Graham's Fillmore East and West, and there were very few other gigs for us." When Tobler questions Jeff's ability as composer, Beck replies: "I used to steal songwriting credits, but I do try to write. I got a pocket tape recorder and I thought that would be it, I'd carry it around and whenever I got the inspiration, just put down the idea – but I would play the stuff back the next day and hate it. Very few things have come from my own creativity, right from square one, so to speak. I play better when something's already written; I might change it beyond all recognition, but I'm at least using the nucleus of someone's idea as a springboard. I haven't given up trying, though. I've got some stuff that maybe you'd like if you heard it. It never reaches anyone's ears but mine." Lastly, Jeff also confesses trouble with his frontman role in a live situation: "I'm not that much of a show-off that I can handle a load of people for an hour and a half. It's a tough game: you've done all your tricks in the first two or three numbers, or you burn it up in a nice atmosphere, and then you've got to do something else. An album's bad enough, but at least you can program it and put it together over a long time."

FRI 11TH✱
Jeff Beck is guest on Paul Gambaccini's "Roundtable", a weekly BBC Radio One chat show with news about music and new releases.

FRI 18TH
A rather unnecessary single coupling *The Final Piece* with *Space Boogie* is released in Great Britain. [409]

MON 28TH
Meanwhile in the US, the record company chooses to issue the single *Too Much To Lose* backed with *The Final Piece*. Not surprisingly, neither the British nor the American singles cause any chart action.

UNDATED
Sometime during 1980 Beck adds his guitar to three cuts (*Affair Across A Crowded Room*, *Children Only Play (Do You Remember?)*, and *Last Days Of An Empire*) on singer/actor Murray Head's album *Jokes/Voices* (UK Polydor). The album is produced by Paul Samwell-Smith, and it reappears two years later as *How Many Ways*. The album is recorded at Ridge Farm, a 17th century mansion in Dorking, Surrey with a hi-tech studio installed in the barn.

AUGUST

To prepare for Beck's first American concerts since February 1977, rehearsals with Tony Hymas, Mo Foster and Simon Phillips are held at the Nomis Complex in Shepherd's Bush, followed by a full-stage rehearsal at the Lyceum on the Strand.

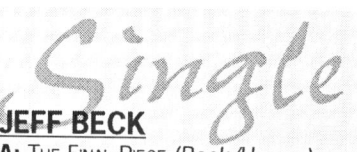

JEFF BECK
A: THE FINAL PIECE *(Beck/Hymas)*
B: SPACE BOOGIE *(Hymas/Phillips)*

Released Friday July 18, 1980 (UK Epic EPC 8806)
Personnel is Jeff Beck (gtrs), Tony Hymas (kybds), Mo Foster (bs on B) and Simon Phillips (drms on B)
Recorded at EMI Studios, Abbey Road, late 1979 and spring 1980
Produced by Ken Scott and Jeff Beck
Highest Chart Position UK: –

Single

JEFF BECK
A: TOO MUCH TO LOSE *(Hammer)*
B: THE FINAL PIECE *(Beck/Hymas)*

Released Monday July 28, 1980 (US Epic 8-50914)
Personnel is Jeff Beck (gtrs), Jan Hammer (kybds on A), Tony Hymas (kybds on B) and Simon Phillips (drms on A)
Recorded at Ramport Studios October–November 1978 (A) and EMI Studios, Abbey Road, late 1979 (B)
Produced by Ken Scott and Jeff Beck
Highest Chart Position US: –

Obviously worried about the strain of fronting his own group, a streamlined set list is put together. The situation is similar to Jeff's American tour in 1975, where the spotlight is on him alone, with no Jan Hammer or Stanley Clarke to fall back on. The whole of *There And Back* will be performed live, although *The Golden Road* does not always make the short-list every night. From Beck's past come *Led Boots*, *Blue Wind*, *Diamond Dust* (where Tony Hymas plays an extended keyboard intro) and *Scatterbrain* (Simon Phillips' drum extravaganza). A double encore will be employed throughout the tour; first *Goodbye Pork Pie Hat/You Never Know*, followed by a pleasant revival of *Going Down*, which Jeff sings.

No regular opening act is planned for this jaunt, instead local groups or national artists on tour are added in the support slots.

TUE 26TH✱
Jeff Beck's entourage leaves for the States.

WED 27TH AND THU 28TH
Pre-tour rehearsals are held at the Paramount Northwest Theater in Oregon on the East Coast.

FRI 29TH
JEFF BECK:
FOURTH NORTH AMERICAN TOUR;
FIRST LEG
Paramount Northwest Theater, Portland, Oregon
Opening night finds Jeff Beck back at the same theatre he played for the first time almost exactly eight years ago, in August 1972. (He also performed here in 1973, 1975 and 1976.)

SAT 30TH
Lane County Fairground Exhibition Building, Eugene, Oregon

SUN 31ST
Opera House, Spokane, Washington

SEPTEMBER

MON 1ST
Orpheum Theater, Vancouver, British Columbia, Canada

TUE 2ND
Seattle Center Arena, Seattle, Washington
'Beck Plays Uneven Concert in Return to Seattle' goes a headline in THE SEATTLE TIMES (September 3). Patrick McDonald observes: "It's been four

September 1980: Jeff Beck plays concerts in California ...

years since Jeff Beck, the great rock guitarist, played Seattle, so it was good to see him again last night at the Arena – although the concert was less impressive than it might have been. Beck still displayed amazing speed and agility, but his new material ... lacked the dynamics and lyricism of his earlier work. The drumming, by Simon Phillips, was like rolling thunder especially when he pounded both bass drums at the same time. And Mo Foster's electric bass was constantly thumping, creating wave upon wave of low, visceral sounds that washed over everything, including the guitar. ... The new tunes, such as *Star Cycle* and *The Pump* tended to be short, crisp and jazzy with few intriguing licks. *The Golden Road*, was slower and more cerebral, and was the best of the new. The quiet, moving *The Final Piece* also was nice. The older, lyrical tunes such as *'Cause We've Ended As Lovers* and *Diamond Dust* displayed Beck's gifts more fully. Even the faster tunes from the past, such as *Blue Wind*, were more interesting. Beck reworked all the tunes, old and new, by bending and shaping the notes differently and changing the tempos. Beck is the one artist who never stands still. Perhaps Beck stayed away a little too long ... There was a good-sized audience there last night but not a capacity crowd. For Beck, a rock star with almost mythic reputation, that was a surprise."

FRI 5TH
Greek Theater, University of California, Berkeley, California

Conrad Silvert in the THE SAN FRANCISCO CHRONICLE (September 8) is full of praise of tonight's concert: "It is a testament to Beck's discipline and imagination that his music was so fresh and new sounding the whole set through. Except for the throwaway encore of *I'm Going Down* (his final encore) all his music was purely instrumental – no words, no flamboyant posturing about the stage, only the pure, elemental sound of Beck's guitars. Many instrumental bands, even great ones, suffer from the same problem, they play music that would make the greatest backing tracks in the world, if only there were a lead singer to flesh out the sound and bring it to life. Beck needn't worry about that, because his approach is like that of a lead vocalist who constantly gives the music a dynamic contour. Early in the set, he established several of his trademarks on a song called *Star Cycle* – the descending doublestops that tailed off before suddenly bursting into an upbeat acceleration; the modern yet blues-drenched phrasing; the chucka-chucka rhythm riffs that propelled the band and at the same time kept them perfectly in line. Beck is precision personified."

Although Silvert does find a pair of ballads inserted halfway punctuates the momentum, he sums up: "Through it all, no matter how sophisticated he became or how he eventually got down to basics, Beck cut a classic figure visually. He was an ageless, almost Peter Pan-like character. Standing there in his black leather pants, bending his legs slightly at the knees, taking sharp little hop-steps in his white shoes, flashing quicksilvery smiles in every direction, he was clearly enjoying himself. It proved to be infectious. Jeff Beck was unpretensious, thoroughly professional, and he knocked everybody dead."

SAT 6TH
Open Air Amphitheater, San Diego State University, San Diego, California

Barry Alfonso, writing for the SAN DIEGO UNION (September 8), is another critic who welcomes Beck back: "The years have not been kind to many veteran rock artists. The list of top-flight musicians who made their reputations in the early '60s only to decline in creativity is a long one – Stephen Stills and Eric Clapton are two obvious examples of this. It's been difficult for rock talents to endure both aesthetically and commercially. Jeff Beck, who appeared with his band Saturday night ... has fared better than most. ... Against a backdrop of tiny twinkling lights, Beck and his three sidemen served up an equally glittering set, drawing from both his current album and his earlier years. ... Even better was the band's vigorous treatment of another Beck favourite, *Blue Wind*. Unleashing choppy chords as he wove about the stage, Beck proved that the rocker in him hasn't died yet."

Set List/Jeff Beck

Greek Theater, Los Angeles, September 9 '80

Star Cycle • El Becko • Too Much To Lose • The Pump • 'Cause We've Ended As Lovers • Space Boogie • The Golden Road • Diamond Dust • Scatterbrain • The Final Piece • Blue Wind • Goodbye Pork Pie Hat/You Never Know

With no Hammer or Clarke to share a spotlight or a song with, Jeff Beck is pushed out front by his *There And Back* band. The good thing is that this group works as a true team. Jeff is in a cheerful mood tonight, chatting with the crowd between songs: "We're gonna get a little schmoozy here, so if you've got a girl friend, grab hold of her" is Beck's advice to the crowd before he soars into an ethereal, jazzy *'Cause We've Ended As Lovers*. The bubbly *Space Boogie* is great, much better than the recorded version, with Mo Foster's hydraulic bass lines well to the fore and with Phillips pounding the bass drums incessantly. In *Too Much To Lose* Beck lets fusion be fusion and rips off a wild solo firmly rooted in the blues. And herein lies the very attraction of Jeff Beck playing jazzier songs; he is able to inject a natural giddiness into the music. Simon Phillips' drum-o-rama halfway through *Scatterbrain* is exciting but does tend to go on a bit. *Led Boots* is forceful, but where most of Jeff's songs improve on stage, this song does not come close the sheer fury of the recorded version. For an encore, the quartet comes back to do a striking *Goodbye Pork Pie Hat/ You Never Know* medley, followed by a rocking *Going Down*, sung by Jeff.

SUN 7TH
Santa Barbara County Bowl, Santa Barbara, California

MON 8TH AND TUE 9TH
Greek Theatre, Los Angeles, California

For the two night stand at LA's Greek Theater, local folkie Jimmy Spheeris is an unannounced opening act, causing Don Snowden in THE LOS ANGELES TIMES (September 10) to wryly comment: "Throwing [Spheeris] before a pack of rabid Beck fans would appeal to the people who booked Daniel into the lions' den." Snowden also questions Beck's music, which "suffered

October 1980: Jeff Beck is on the cover of Guitar Player magazine ...

from an overemphasis of technical mastery – rather than inspiration", although he is quick to point out Beck's strengths: "Beck is still fundamentally a guitarist who slams out chords like a dyed-in-the-wool rocker and never resorts to the supersonic scale runs that are de rigeur among fusion guitarists. His playing during his first local performance in three years was full of unpredictable twists, turns and textures that have made him perhaps the most influential rock guitar stylist this side of Hendrix." The problem, according to the review, is "that Beck has merely traded in the 4/4 confines of rock for a set of more technically complex limitations. The other members of his quartet were largely content to back Beck with standard fusion grooves rather than challenge him with the improvisatory interplay that might have generated some real sparks. Beck approached his frontman duties with a distant, perfunctory manner that unfortunately permeated the second encore, a throughly half-hearted rendition of *Going Down.*"

David Weiss in THE LOS ANGELES HERALD EXAMINER (September 10) is disturbed with the young and reckless audience Beck attracts: "You had to be there. In fact you had to be there with psycho-active drugs coursing their way through your veins. The event was Jeff Beck ... where teenagers and arrested developers howled like coyotes at every mind-bending electric guitar riff that ol' Beck-Ola served up. Not to say J. B. can't play most rock guitarists to at least a standoff. His electrically sustained phraseology is nothing to sneeze at nor is his dexterity. But when push comes to shove the guitar man had better hope that paraquet never eats up all the supply of available herb, because his effect on people depends to some extent at least on the effects of that ego distorting drug." The rest of the review is more occupied with Weiss's worries about the crowd's drug habits, rather than Beck's music: "The phenomenon works something like this: 1) Young music fan takes drug 2) loss of personality ensues followed by paranoia 3) rock star enters, playing mock heroic eardrum splitting loud music 4) patrons are ego emboldened vicariously at concert to big success."

WED 10TH
Today's concert at the Red Rocks Amphitheater in Morrison (Denver), Colorado is cancelled due to heavy rains and is not re-scheduled either.

FRI 12TH
Austin Municipal Auditorium, Austin, Texas

The Canadian group the Kings provide support. The reviewer in THE AMERICAN-STATESMAN (September 14) fails to see the attraction of Jeff Beck: "Playing off the idea that fast is good, loud is good, and a decent set of lights will help distract attention from the fact that you aren't doing anything in particular, Beck ran through instrumental number after number, striking the familiar poses with the guitar, shaking his rooster haircut, and, occasionally, playing guitar over the din of his keyboard, bass and drums accompaniment. This is not Beck the rocker: it's Beck the jazz-fusion hack, and although he doesn't do it as well as Larry Coryell, John McLaughlin, Terje Rypdal ... he does have the advantage of a following that's been with him since the '60s, a group of fanatics for whom Beck is the ultimate guitar hero, a man who can do no wrong. But as long as he limits himself to the tuneless exploration of four-note themes, material that rarely contains any melody or changes on which to take off, and improvisations that are little but scalar excercises, substituting awesome technology for music, he's not going to get my vote. I only had to look at the crowd to realize how much I'm outvoted, but the turgid mess on stage left me cold."

SAT 13TH
Dallas Convention Center Arena, Dallas, Texas

SUN 14TH
Sam Houston Coliseum, Houston, Texas

MON 16TH✵
With a scheduled fortnight's break, Beck returns to Great Britain.

WED 18TH
Jeff Beck appears as a guest on the syndicated American radio show "Modern Music" based on an interview taped earlier. Around this time, too, Beck also appears on another another syndicated radio talk show, "Innerview", hosted by Jim Ladd to promote the tour and the release of *There and Back.*

OCTOBER

THU 2ND✵
Jeff Beck flies to America to resume the tour.

FRI 3RD
JEFF BECK:
FOURTH NORTH AMERICAN TOUR;
SECOND LEG
Sunrise Musical Theater,
Fort Lauderdale, Florida

Back on the road again, the *There And Back* band seemingly stick to the same live routine, although *Freeway Jam* is also added to the set list.

SAT 4TH
Lakeland Civic Center, Lakeland, Flordia

SUN 5TH
Fox Theatre, Atlanta, Georgia

TUE 7TH
Capitol Theater, Passaic, New Jersey

WED 8TH
The Spectrum, Philadelphia, Pennsylvania

THU 9TH
The Cage, University of Massachusetts, Amherst, Massachusetts

FRI 10TH
The Fieldhouse, State University of New York, Plattsburgh, New York

SAT 11TH
Cape Cod Coliseum, South Yarmouth, Massachusetts

Ex-Aerosmith guitarist Joe Perry and his group, the Joe Perry Project, open for Beck in New England.

"A young crowd ... decked out in Ted Nugent, Rush and ZZ Top T-shirts came to worship the electric guitarist who, as a member of the Yardbirds, pioneered the ear-splitting 'heavy metal' style those bands have tried to incorporate. What the kids heard left them in the dust. Always one of the most innovative stylists to

December 1980: Jeff Beck tours Japan for the fourth time in his career ...

emerge from the rock era, Beck has returned to the concert trail as a sophisticated jazz-rock stylist who, while still throwing enough pyrotechnics around to keep his old audience satisfied, now plays with a new intelligence, subtlety and grace that his imitators cannot approach. Unlike the guitarists he has inspired, Beck was not just flashy but fiery; he was overpowering but never overbearing, not merely dazzling but brilliant," writes Tony Lioce in THE PROVIDENCE JOURNAL (October 13), and concludes: "Despite his reputation as a moody, sullen frontman, Beck introduced numbers, clowned with his sidemen and chatted with the crowd – which may have been perplexed by the complexities of the music he played, but which seemed to have a grand time regardless, and which might even have learned a thing or two about how articulate and marvelous an instrument the electric guitar can be."

SUN 12TH
The Palladium, New York, New York
There are two concerts tonight.

TUE 14TH
D.A.R. Constitution Hall, Washington, D.C.
D.C. locals Bill Holland & Rents Due are the opening act at tonight's sell out show. The enthusiastic review in the WASHINGTON STAR (October 15) declares: "Beck put on a dazzling display of the art of making the Fender Stratocaster sounding like anything and everything – from a screaming banshee to a crowded freeway to a chorus of angels or a single voice. His current band basically is a fusion one with the thumping bass of Mo Foster, super modern keyboard accompaniment by Tony Hymas and break neck rolls and fills played by drummer Simon Phillips. If the newer, headier *There And Back* music ... left some of Beck's young crowd behind, Beck regrouped his flock with the easily recognizable and likeable *Freeway Jam*. During the introduction Beck and Hymas jostled with each other through traffic producing sounds which sounded amazingly like the Southeast Southwest Freeway at 5.30 pm. Horns honked, tires and brakes screeched, engines roared – all from one guitar ..."

WED 15TH
Stanley Theater, Pittsburgh, Pennsylvania

THU 16TH
Cobo Arena, Detroit, Michigan

FRI 17TH
Assembly Hall, University of Illinois at Urbana-Champaign, Champaign, Illinois

SAT 18TH
SIU Arena, Southern Illinois University, Carbondale, Illinois

SUN 19TH
Granada Theater, Chicago, Illinois

MON 20TH✱
With a successful North American tour behind him, Jeff Beck flies home to Great Britain.

DECEMBER

TUE 1ST✱
Presumably fly off to Japan.

WED 2ND
Installed in Tokyo, Jeff Beck holds a press conference at the hotel where he stays. During the day, Jeff and his group also rehearse. The set list is similar to the recent US tour except for the sequencing.

THU 3RD
The Japanese instrument maker Greco gives two miniature guitars to Jeff, which he uses on this tour for the encore number *Going Down*.

THU 4TH
JEFF BECK:
THIRD JAPANESE TOUR
Nippon Budokan Hall, Tokyo, Japan
Jeff Beck, Tony Hymas, Mo Foster and Simon Phillips begin a tour of Japan, his fourth since Beck, Bogert & Appice were here in 1973. There will be no opening acts.

Set List/Jeff Beck

Bunka-Taiikukan, Yokohama, December 16 '80

Star Cycle • El Becko • Too Much To Lose • The Pump • 'Cause We've Ended As Lovers • Space Boogie • The Final Piece • Led Boots • Freeway Jam • Diamond Dust • Scatterbrain • Blue Wind • Goodbye Pork Pie Hat/You Never Know • Going Down

---

FRI 5TH
Furitu Taiikukan, Osaka, Japan

MON 8TH
Kyuden Kinen Taiikukan, Fukuoka, Japan

TUE 9TH
Shimin Kaikan, Kurasiki, Japan

WED 10TH
Festival Hall, Osaka, Japan

THU 11TH
Shi-Kokaido, Nagoya, Japan

FRI 12TH
Kenmin-Kaikan, Miyagi, Japan

SUN 14TH
Doritu-Sangyo-Kyoshin-Kaijo, Sapporo, Japan

TUE 16TH
Bunka-Taiikukan, Yokohama, Japan

WED 17TH
Nippon Budokan Hall, Tokyo, Japan
After the show, Jeff and his group throw a party.

🎧 To paraphrase Jimmy Page, "when [Beck] is on, he's probably the best there is", and tonight's closing segment with a short *Goodbye Pork Pie Hat* leading into a pulsating *You Never Know* lives up to that praise. The guitar is elastic and flexible, as Jeff twists and turns the melody lines upside down and inside out, doing cartwheels on the fretboard with a breathtaking freshness. Finally, Beck tears into *Going Down*, giving space for bass and piano solos besides his own two choruses of inspired over-the-topisms.

THU 18TH
Nippon Budokan Hall, Tokyo, Japan
An extra show has been added to the Japanese itinerary due to public demand, and tonight is Jeff Beck's very last concert of an eventful fifteen-year recording and touring career, which has seen him move from psychedelia and blues-rock via funk-pop and jazz-rock to heavy metal.

LATE
Beck, Hymas, Foster and Phillips return home to England for a Christmas break.

Ⓒ December 8, 1980: John Lennon is assassinated by Mark David Chapman in New York City.

▶▶ Fast forward

In March 1981 Jeff Beck took the road band with Tony Hymas, Simon Philips and Mo Foster for a last outing, when he toured England for the first time since 1974 – culminating with a London concert with Jimmy Page joining him onstage for the encore. In September that year Beck made a guest spot with Eric Clapton at the *Secret Policeman's Other Ball*, a benefit show for Amnesty International.

1982, however, was a very quiet year as Jeff Beck slipped from the public eye, as he would invariably do time and again in the following years. Instead, he would devote time to his cars. As Jeff later explained to MUSICIAN (September 1989): "We had three good summers in a row – and then I'm in the garage!"

In September 1983, the triumvirate of Yardbirds guitarists; Eric Clapton, Jeff Beck, Jimmy Page, united for a unique presentation inspired by Ronnie Lane's battle with his illness. Under the banner ARMS (Action Research into Multiple Sclerosis), the three played at London's Royal Albert Hall with a stellar backing band. The idea was so successful that the ARMS-show also took to the road in the US for a handful of dates in December of the same year.

Then, in an attempt to rekindle the flame of the original Jeff Beck Group, he teamed up with Rod Stewart for a long US tour in the summer of 1984. However, after only four or five concerts, Beck took his hat and walked off. The year also found Jeff doing high-profile appearances on records by Tina Turner (on her comeback smash *Private Dancer)*, the Honeydrippers (a US #4 with their mini-album of old rhythm and blues covers), Mick Jagger *(She's The Boss,* which featured Jeff extensively) and, of course, Rod Stewart (the UK #27/US #6 hit *Infatuation).*

It was not until the summer of 1985 that Jeff himself put out *Flash.* Produced by Nile Rodgers, it was not a wholly successful experiment, coupling drum machines and vocals (by Jimmy Hall and also Beck) with the guitar in a more subdued role. But Jeff and Rod made the single charts together with *People Get Ready* (US #48), and Beck was rewarded with his first Grammy for *Escape* (1986), which also saw him tour Japan in June with Jan Hammer.

Both 1987 and 1988 found Beck at a low ebb. He played on Mick Jagger's second solo album, *Primitive Cool,* and also rehearsed with Jagger's touring group in the autumn of '87 but ultimately backed out in a typical Beck manouvre. In November the same year, he injured his right hand thumb seriously while working in his garage.

1989, on the other hand, turned out to be an active year. For the first time since his *There And Back* band, Jeff formed a small group for both recording and touring purposes. The trusted Tony Hymas was back on keyboards, while the flamboyant Terry Bozzio filled Jeff's need for a strong backbeat. (Actually, the trio recorded briefly together the previous year for a soundtrack to the feature film *Twins.)* Recording at a laid back pace during the first half of 1989, the trio toured Japan in August, followed by a US tour co-headlining with fellow Epic stablemate Steve Ray Vaughan in October–December. This was accompanied by the release of *Jeff Beck's Guitar Shop With Terry Bozzio and Tony Hymas* (US #49), a highly acclaimed all-instrumental album which garnered Beck a second Grammy award in 1990. The trio visited Europe in the spring, ending with a return to the British stage as Beck's second decade as a touring and recording artist drew to a close.

In November 1991 the career overview *Beckology* was released, a 3 CD set elegantly packaged in a Fender guitar case cardboard replica. The box set trawled Beck's entire career from the Tridents onwards, but overall it was unevenly distributed; a perhaps overly large helping of Yardbirds material at the expense of rare or unreleased Beck tracks coupled with some conspicious omissions.

In 1992 Jeff came back with no less than two separate releases; one a soundtrack from the television film *Frankie's House* (a collaboration with Jed Leiber), the other a tribute to his idols Cliff Gallup and Gene Vincent with *Crazy Legs,* recorded in a genuine fifties style. The same year he also contributed to Roger Waters' *Amused to Death.*

Another two-year period of semi-retirement followed 1992, but Jeff re-formed the band with Hymas and Bozzio and added bassist Pino Palladino for a US trek with Carlos Santana in August–October 1995, although no new material was forthcoming. Concurrently, Jeff also tried to record an album, but one by one attempts with Stewart Copeland (in 1994) Richard Bailey (also in 1994) Hymas/Bozzio (in 1995) and Steve Lukather (in 1996/97) were shelved.

In 1998 Jeff decided to steer his attention to touring with a brand new set list rather than recording, and put together a brand new group with Jennifer Batten (guitar/midi guitar), Randy Hope Taylor (bass) and Steve Alexander (drums). In July of that year they hit the road in Europe, playing a series of dates and visiting many out-of-the-way towns in countries like Germany, Austria, Italy and France. In October 1998 this was followed by a tour of South America, adding Mexico, Uruguay, Brazil and Argentina to Beck's tour logbook.

In 1999 a new album, *Who Else!* (US #99) was finally released – his first in ten years! – which had Jeff dabbling with techno, Irish music but also adding blues, jazz rock and an eastern flavour to the eclectic mix. A full-scale two-legged US tour was undertaken to promote the album, and in October of that year he also played London.

Throughout the last two decades Jeff Beck's stature as an innovative guitarist and important stylist was acknowledged again and again. Not only did his name rank high in the plethora of polls conducted in those years, but there were other signs too; in January 1992 the Yardbirds were inducted in the Rock n' Roll Hall of Fame, and in 1995 Jeff Beck was inducted into GUITAR PLAYER's 'Gallery of The Greats'. In their appreciation, the magazine wrote: "Beck incessantly strives to create new sounds and techniques, and he consistently shatters conventional notions of guitar playing. A true musician." ■

QUOTE RIGHTLY SO

"I'm all for anything that creates new ideas for guitars. I watched Jeff Beck ... He gets a fabulous sound. I imagine he tunes the strings right down, then waggles his fingers across the strings. Either that or he's got iron-strong fingers! But he gets a marvellously full sound. I think Jeff's work, especially on records, is outstanding."
Hank Marvin, BEAT INSTRUMENTAL, May 1965

"Jeff Beck of the Yardbirds uses one [fuzz bender] with a bottleneck and gets a sound like a violin – really tasteful. He's about the best exponent."
Stevie Winwood, MELODY MAKER, February 1966

"Jeff Beck is the greatest bottleneck guitarist in the country."
Steve Marriott, RECORD MIRROR, February 1966

"Guys like ... Jeff Beck would completely knock them out in the States. They wouldn't know what hit them if those cats went over to America and started sitting in around Chicago."
Mike Bloomfield, MELODY MAKER, October 1966

"Beautiful guitar."
Jimi Hendrix on Beck's Bolero, NME, April 1967

"I like Eric Clapton and some of the things Jeff Beck does and that cat Vic Briggs."
Jimi Hendrix, MELODY MAKER, April 1967

"I think [Beck's] great. When he's having a shining night he's really fantastic. He plays things of pure genius."
Jimmy Page, NEW MUSICAL EXPRESS, April 1970

"My all-time favourite guitarist – which is strange because I can never play like him and don't want to. But I really admire what he does and he's played so many good solos it's difficult to pick one above the others. But with this particular number [Jeff's Boogie] he carved his own little world in a way. As always, every note was in context, right on target. I know so many guitarists who've tried to copy it."
Mick Box (Uriah Heep), 'Whatever Turned Me On', NEW MUSICAL EXPRESS, August 1972

"Jeff was a considerable influence on me as a kid. I even had a Jeff Beck T-shirt at one time, and I used to follow him about and plague him backstage. We've become mates since, but I still don't think he knows I was the kid who used to tag around after him."
Dave "Clem" Clempson (Humble Pie, Colloseum), NEW MUSICAL EXPRESS, May 1973

"The Yardbirds have been a very heavy influence on me. If they could get back together with Jeff Beck, they would be the biggest group in the world."
Alice Cooper, NEW MUSICAL EXPRESS, June 1973

"But Jeff Beck is great to listen to, because he takes a chance, and when it comes off it's so emotional. When he gets feedback going right it's like an orchestra playing instead of just a guitar with a lot of brilliant runs."
Ritchie Blackmore, GUITAR PLAYER, July/August 1973

"Jeff Beck always comes up with something interesting."
Rory Gallagher, February 1974

"When you see Beck and he's good – and I know he's an erratic player – then he's the best. But there's no guarantee you're gonna see him at his best, that's the trouble. I just know that you can see Beck and there wouldn't be anyone else to touch him."
Jimmy Page, MELODY MAKER, September 1974

"I like Jeff Beck's guitar playing. I think he's really good – he did a song of mine, Tallyman. That was ages ago. I thought it was very out of charachter for him, but he's an incredible guitarist, probably my favourite guitarist. I don't know, he's just got it."
Graham Gouldman, MELODY MAKER, March 1975

"If I could play like that I'd rule the world. I'm producing him [Beck], sitting there and watching him and seeing things I don't believe. I'm watching his hands do things, converting it in my mind, and I'd say 'You can't get that note out of that right there'. I couldn't believe it. Jeff came off with some of the most ungodly, off-the-wall sounds that I've ever heard. And I'm sure there's no other guitar player that can do the same thing."
Steve Cropper, NEW MUSICAL EXPRESS, January 1976

"Jeff is a fine player – I've heard him do some beautiful things."
George Benson, DOWN BEAT 'Blindfold Test', October 1976

"I like Jeff, yeah. I have listened to Wired, and there are a couple of solos on there that I like. And I like some of his stuff on Rough And Ready."
Frank Zappa, GUITAR PLAYER, January 1977

"Jeff Beck (is) an inconsistent player in that when he's on, he's probably the best there is."
Jimmy Page, GUITAR PLAYER, July 1977

"Most of those [early influences] relating directly to my guitar playing were English guitarists – most notably Eric Clapton and Jeff Beck."
Todd Rundgren, GUITAR PLAYER, October 1977

"I also like flashy players – Jeff Beck, Peter Frampton."
José Feliciano, GUITAR PLAYER, July 1978

"The first guitar player I ever remember really flipping over was Jeff Beck when he was in the Yardbirds. He was the first guy who really caught my ear and that I wanted to be like."
Kerry Livgren (Kansas), GUITAR PLAYER, August 1978

"Well, there's no question that Beck's Bolero had an impact on me. A lot of my instrumentals were probably motivated by my original hearing of that, though I had written some instrumentals with a bolero-type feel prior to my ever hearing Beck."
Ted Nugent, GUITAR PLAYER, August 1979

"Jeff is amazing. Being able to work with him for the year-and-a-half that I did, I learned a lot of lines from him; it was like an one hour course in technique every night. I was entertaining the audience, but I was in school, too."
Tim Bogert, GUITAR PLAYER, September 1979

"Jeff Beck plays slow and absolutely tasty, which is his talent. Even if he never rehearses, he will probably always be a tasteful guitarist, unless he goes a bit too mad with the weird style he has got at the moment."
Michael Schencker, GUITAR PLAYER, January 1981

Appendix 1 — "Quote Rightly So"

"Her [Chrissie Hynde] favourite guitar player is Jeff Beck."
James Honeyman-Scott, GUITAR PLAYER, April 1981

"Jeff Beck has wonderful technique, because he also uses the talkbox ... I've sort of gone ape for Jeff Beck at the moment. I've got about every album he's made. And he's just terrific."
Peter Frampton, GUITAR PLAYER, November 1981

"He was excellent in the studio, although he did take a little time to get himself together on his solos, be he's a gut player – he doesn't come in with any plan or preconceived notions, and he'll sit down with a battered guitar, and make the most incredible sounds come out of it. Sometimes, he'd be playing badly, and you knew nothing would come, and he'd get angry with himself, but other times, he'd just pick the thing up and create things which other people just couldn't do. And very inventive stuff too."
George Martin, 'THE RECORD PRODUCERS', 1982

"Listen to Jeff Beck on Truth. That's what I'd like to do. I'm really into tone on guitar, and Jeff Beck was my epitome of tone."
Gary Richrath (REO Speedwagon), GUITAR PLAYER, February 1982

"I'd be remiss is I did not include Jeff Beck's Blow By Blow and Wired. As electric guitar solo albums, these two are my ultimates for a tasty stylist who makes a complete musical statement without wasting a note. Beck's records always struck me as those of a man who knew his limitations, and made popular guitar records that were chancy, career-wise, but never missed the mark of quality and craftsmanship, and never failed to pull off the intended. He rolled with the changes and came up smelling like a rose every time."
Rik Emmett (Triumph), GUITAR PLAYER, May 1982

"So he's [Jeff Beck] an exception, and he's an exceptional guitarist. Truth especially is a landmark to me because for the time that it came out, it was the heaviest guitar that you could get on earth. That album had great production, and Beck used very economical playing to accentuate the sound effects on the guitar. He plays licks on there that strike me as being perfect."
Steve Morse, GUITAR PLAYER, June 1982

"Jeff Beck was an influence too – extremely. I couldn't believe what he could do. I remember seeing him put the guitar down, make it feedback, and play a whole tune without even touching the fingerboard."
Brian May, GUITAR PLAYER, January 1983

"Jeff Beck is still one of my main influences. I like Jeff Beck's style for his emotional content and the sound he gets. I don't like predictable guitar playing. You never know what he's going to come out with next, which is what is great about him."
Gary Moore, Guitar World, May 1983

"I like Jeff's playing, and because he's taken something from me. We all take from somebody. We all have to learn somewhere."
Les Paul, Guitar World, May 1983

"If you can bring out your uniqueness through your music, that gives you an edge – you don't have to figure out something tricky – and that's what Beck does ... Another thing: Beck's able to remove himself from the competition. We have the Eddie Van Halens, the Randy Rhoadses, and all the guys who put eight fingers on the fretboard ... Jeff Beck can play music that's not competitive; he doesn't have to worry about who's the fastest gun."
Rick Derringer, INTERNATIONAL MUSICIAN & RECORDING WORLD, August 1984

"I've never seen anybody play guitar like Beck, with the exception of Hendrix. Beck knocks me out. The guitar is like a part of his body. He holds it and it's making music, and then he puts it down on the ground and it's still making music. Stevie Ray has that, too. It's amazing,"
Nile Rodgers, GUITAR PLAYER, November 1984

"I was really influenced by Jeff Beck. He was like the first person to play in that Indian style. He made his guitar sound like different instruments and no-one else was doing that. He definitely changed my approach."
Gary Moore, GUITAR WORLD, November 1984

"I'm more interested in what Joe Blokes down the road in this garage band is doing than, say, what the new Jeff Beck album is like. Not that I don't respect Jeff Beck, who's an incredible musician. But I think we've seen what he can do, and there's a lot of guitar players out there that we haven't heard."
The Edge, GUITAR PLAYER, June 1985

"I ... think of Jeff as probably being the finest guitar player I've ever seen. And I've been around. I still think that, if I really sit down and mull it over. There's something cool and mean about Becky that beats everyone else. I have to hand it to him, in that respect."
Eric Clapton, GUITAR PLAYER, July 1985

"Jeff Beck was much more from the body, much more from lower down. Lovely. I slightly prefer Jeff's playing, actually."
Paul Samwell-Smith, GUITAR PLAYER, October 1985

"Jeff's my favourite guitar player today."
Nils Lofgren, GUITAR PLAYER, December 1985

"There are guys out there who can play real good without boring people. Jeff Beck is one of them. He's more of a technical guy, but when he wants to rock and roll he sure knows how to do it with his guts."
Angus Young, GUITAR WORLD, March 1986

"The Yardbirds were the other strong influence. They came in right behind the Stones and the Beatles. They were really in another league; they could really play. Beck could play his head off back then."
Earl Slick, GUITAR PLAYER, May 1986

"Jeff Beck with the Yardbirds, and in the Truth era, as well as now. His tones are so amazing."
Eric Johnson, GUITAR PLAYER, May 1986

"Jeff Beck: An innovator – a master toucher and emoter of guitar fluidity."
Ted Nugent, GUITAR WORLD, March 1987

"Jeff Beck is just fabulous. I went to see him in concert one night in Dallas, and he played the Blow By Blow, Wired and There & Back albums back to back. I sat right on the edge of my seat for three hours. He played monstrous guitar. I'd love to pick his brain. I love the technique he plays with and the feel and everything."
Clint Strong (Merle Haggard's Strangers), GUITAR PLAYER, August 1987

"Jeff Beck was the other guy [besides Hendrix] for me at that time. He had a lot of restraint, taste and control."
David Torn, GUITAR PLAYER, November 1987

"Quote Rightly So" — Appendix 1

"The baddest guitar player on the face of the earth. Period. As far as feel goes, he can play anything he wants to play with superb distinction. One note or a thousand notes, it's at his command, with flawless grace. ... He's a guitaristic treasure."
Doug Wimbish, GUITAR WORLD, **January 1988**

"The Yardbirds' Jeff's Boogie is pretty tough stuff. That song has probably the finest collection of unique licks and tricks. At that point, Jeff's licks and tricks were so far ahead of any American player. He epitomized the image of the lead guitar hero. And Jeff's Boogie, that shook me so much. I can play it note-for-note, but it took me a long time to figure all that out."
Joe Walsh, GUITAR PLAYER, **April 1988**

"Jeff Beck is the prime example. Here's a guy who, in my opinion, is the world's greatest guitar player."
Miles Copeland, GUITAR PLAYER, **May 1988**

"I haven't been in too many situations where it was a head-cutting contest. It might be interesting to experience that. I'd like to play alongside Jeff Beck sometime. I think if I ever wanted to put myself in the position of going against somebody, that's the one situation where I'd imagine being challenged. It would be interesting to see for myself how I'd rise to that. I think that would be wild."
Robben Ford, GUITAR PLAYER, **September 1988**

"Jeff Beck influenced me so much. When I was a kid, I sat down with Truth and really learned what he was playing."
Jeff Golub, GUITAR PLAYER, **December 1988**

"If Jeff Beck wanted a rhythm player, I'd jump on that in a second."
Jennifer Batten, GUITAR PLAYER, **July 1989**

"When B.B. King plays one note without any reference point, it speaks to me. And Jeff Beck has got that, too. I'd like to be able to put all that fire or venom or love in one note and have it be recognizable as that."
Reeves Gabrels, GUITAR PLAYER, **November 1989**

"Pete Green and Jeff Beck were the only other players [in the sixties] who could touch on material and then go away from it. Jeff particularly. There's a standing joke with him and me about the song Wee Wee Baby off the Folk Festival of Blues album. Buddy Guy kicks it off, and it's like a random start, no one seems to know how it's going to go – and Jeff's got that down."
Eric Clapton, GUITAR WORLD, **December 1989**

"I listened to Jeff Beck a lot from the Blow By Blow period. I wore out two copies of that record. Just the combination of guitar and amp and his fingers. He just made the guitar do what he heard."
David Grissom, GUITAR PLAYER, **December 1991**

"Jeff is truly on of the greats ... Jeff was playing all this amazing shit while simultaneously talking to me. I wanted to pack it up that day, send the amps home and find a nice, little job."
Slash, GUITAR WORLD, **November 1992**

"I'm not a fan of many rock guitar players. Jeff Beck's my favorite; a damned fine player."
David Gilmour, GUITAR WORLD, **February 1993**

"Jeff Beck is my hero anyway. And also a good friend, I'm proud to say. If you know him, it's even wilder to see what he does. ... You get offstage from jamming with Jeff Beck and you think 'Okay, I know I'm gonna wake up now.' It's every guitarist's ultimate dream."
Steve Lukather, GUITAR WORLD, **July 1993**

"Another player I have to mention is Jeff Beck. Seymour Duncan sent me copies of Jeff Beck's new records. The rockabilly record knocked my socks off. The Gene Vincent thing, I swear to God, is the most authentic re-make of anything I've ever heard in my life. Hats off to him. He's got the sound, and he got 98 percent of the licks absolutely perfect."
Danny Gatton, GUITAR PLAYER, **July 1993**

"Jeff Beck has always been one of my favourites,"
John Paul Jones, GUITAR PLAYER, **February 1995**

"Cause We've Ended As Lovers is a milestone in melodic electric guitar playing. I don't know how many millions of hours I've jammed with Jeff Beck records. He's undoubtedly one of the absolute greatest when it comes to that – maybe he is the greatest on that kind of thing."
Joe Satriani, GUITAR PLAYER, **January 1996**

"If you gotta play ... it's gotta be for real. That's why I like Jeff Beck. He's always on the cutting edge of sound, even to this day, but when he plays something, it's still him playing. Every time I hear him, I think he's done it all, and he still comes up with something new."
Harvey Mandel, GUITAR PLAYER, **April 1996**

"He's [Beck] number one in that style. A killer. He plays that guitar, man, like nobody I know."
John McLaughlin, GUITAR PLAYER, **April 1996**

"Jeff Beck is probably one of my favourite players. This man just hits notes and you think, 'How come that note's not on my guitar?' And he gets this incredible sustain for no reason. He's so fresh, so un-show business. That's what I love about Jeff."
Ritchie Blackmore, GUITAR PLAYER, **December 1996**

"Jimi certainly knew about English musicians before he came over. He knew about Eric Clapton; he admired John Mayall's Bluesbreakers and Cream. And Jeff Beck's name would come up often. In my mind I'm sure he preferred Jeff's playing to Eric's."
Kathy Etchingham (Jimi Hendrix's ex-girlfriend), MOJO, **January 1998**

"Jeff Beck always comes to mind. He's an incredible proficient guitarist, but he isn't Mr. Pendant ... Jeff Beck's Wired was electric and neonlike. It sounded incredibly contemporary but also sort of futuristic."
Kim Thayil, ROLLING STONE, **April 1999**

"It's a lot easier to appreciate Jeff Beck if you're a guitar player. He just has such natural control over the instrument. It's the ability to make it do something that you've never heard anybody else do."
Slash, ROLLING STONE, **April 1999**

In 1990 THE OBSERVER ran an informal weekly poll dubbed "The Experts' Expert", and when the choice came to lead guitarists, Jeff Beck was chosen by seven out of the eight guitar players: **David Gilmour** ("the most consistently brilliant guitarist over the past 25 years has been Jeff Beck"), **Brian May** ("Jeff Beck is the greatest living guitarist"), **Midge Ure** of Ultravox ("Jeff Beck is such an unassuming character ... He just lets his playing say it all for him"), **Hank Marvin** ("Jeff Beck has done a lot of interesting things and much that's important for rock guitar"), **Gary Moore** ("Jeff Beck is the only guitarist of the generation I grew up with who has continued to move forwards"), **Tony Iommi** ("I've always rated Jeff Beck") and **Phil Collen** of Def Leppard ("Jeff Beck has been truly great during his entire career").

Appendix 2

THE NUTS 'N' BOLTS OF JEFF BECK

THE FORMATIVE YEARS

Guitars: After building guitars himself and trying his hand at acoustic instruments, Jeff Beck's first electric guitar was a Japanese Guyatone. This company produced a wide range of guitars in the late fifties, but no exact details of the model Beck played have been documented. Beck then advanced to a Fender Stratocaster-imitation called a Futurama, a guitar made in Czechoslovakia and imported to the UK by Selmer.

The first important guitar Jeff bought was a Burns, which practically got him into the Del-Tones, his first steady group. The model was possibly the Burns Vibra-Artiste, which was produced in the years 1960–62.

In 1961 Jeff bought a sunburst Fender Stratocaster on hire-purchase. The guitar had a rosewood neck, which indicates that it was made post-1959 (prior to this year, all Fender guitars had maple necks). After seeing a publicity picture of Gene Vincent & the Blue Caps (including guitarist Johnny Meeks) sporting no less than four blonde Fenders, Beck felt inspired to try to repaint his guitar. The result was not particularly successful, and as he wanted to spend money on a car, the Stratocaster was sold.

Jeff's close mate, John Owen, had a **Fender Telecaster** which Beck borrowed over time and which eventually became his. Jeff certainly used this guitar in the Nightshift, then brought it with him to the Tridents and then into the Yardbirds. Apparently Owen got Jeff's Burns instead, and when Owen sold the Burns, Jeff felt the instrument belonged to him. This plain blonde Telecaster, presumably bought brand new in 1961 ("£107 it cost [Owen]", Beck recalled) sported a rosewood neck and the standard white pickguard. The Telecaster perfectly reflected Beck's personality; a sturdy, no-nonsense guitar with a cool, timeless design.

THE TRIDENTS (ca. 1963–1965)

Guitars: For the time Jeff was in the Tridents, he was known to have played the Fender Telecaster that he got through the exchange deal with John Owen.

Amp: For amps, Jeff employed John Lucas' Vox AC 30, although other amps were certainly put in service too. The AC 30 was a very popular combo amplifier; i.e. a speaker cabinet with a built-in amplifier unit.

Effects: Jeff toyed with his first outboard effects when he played with the Tridents. He had two echo units; first a German model called the Klempf Echolette and later the Italian made Binson Echorec.

THE YARDBIRDS (Feb 1965–Nov 1966)

Guitars: When Jeff joined the Yardbirds, he brought with him the blonde Fender Telecaster he used with the Tridents. However, by now the guitar was outfitted with a black pickguard. As this was not standard, Jeff may indeed have cut the scratch plate himself. It was easily recognizable because of wear after heavy pick use, which suggests it was not an original Fender guard, as they usually withstood pick abuse well. Jeff was seen playing this guitar on many occasions in his first months with the Yardbirds, for example at high-profile appearances like in Paris on

The 'John Owen' Fender Telecaster with rosewood neck (June 1965)

The 'John Walker' Fender Esquire with black pickguard (September 1965)

June 20, 1965 and at the 5th National Jazz & Blues Festival on August 6, 1965. The Telecaster was certainly used on *Heart Full of Soul* and the first batch of Yardbirds recordings done in the spring of 1965. Jeff retired the guitar a while later, and this was reportedly – albeit then with a white scratchplate again – given to Jimmy Page in the autumn of 1966. Page later outfitted the guitar with glue-on reflecting circles (around Christmas 1966) and then painted it in psychedelic patterns (spring 1967). It was used throughout the Page-era Yardbirds, and also to record the first Led Zeppelin album, receiving its crowning moment when Page dusted it off to play the guitar solo on *Stairway To Heaven*.

Jeff also briefly used a striking **red Fender Telecaster** upon joining the Yardbirds, apparently a guitar belonging to the management, as both Dreja and Clapton used this guitar on several occasions. Another guitar that seemed to be property of the Yardbirds management was a **Fender Jazzmaster**, which Jeff reportedly used at times, but this instrument usually was reserved for Dreja. (There exists a press photo of the Yardbirds dressed in dark suits and ties, taken during their first American tour in September 1965, with Jeff clutching a **Fender Jaguar**; likely a studio prop and never actually used by any of the group.) Jeff also strummed a **Guild acoustic 12-string**, which was used onstage to re-create the harpsichord part in *For Your Love*. The guitar was damaged beyond repair during the group's first US tour. In fact, Jeff has never played acoustic guitar in public again besides a special encore strum on the ARMS tour in 1983.

A guitar that forever is tied to Jeff Beck was the **Fender Esquire** (serial #1056), he bought from John Maus of the Walker Brothers. The Esquire differed from the Tele in that it had only one single pickup, but it still had a three-way selector, which functioned as a pre-set tone control. This specimen was also unique because Maus had hand-carved the front of the body like a Stratocaster. The Yardbirds and the Walker Brothers shared a date together on May 20, 1965, and it was around that time Beck bought the guitar (supposedly for £70), although he probably ran into Maus at other times too, as Jeff was chummy with Gary Leeds of the Walkers. The guitar came with its original white pickguard, which Jeff shortly afterwards changed to a more stylish black one, likely during the Yardbirds' first American tour. Jeff used this guitar probably on all Yardbirds recordings from September 1965 until February 1966, including ground breaking tracks like *I'm A Man*, *The Train Kept A-Rollin'* and *Shapes of Things*.

About late February 1966 Jeff acquired a sunburst Gibson Les Paul Sunburst, dated 1958, which he bought from Selmer's music shop in Charing Cross Road, London for about £175. For convenience, the instrument is herein referred to as Beck's **Gibson Les Paul #1***. The change to a Les Paul was inspired by seeing Eric Clapton use a similar model around London clubs, but interestingly Beck acquired his model before Clapton

---

* The numbering system here is used to easily identify Jeff Beck's succession of Les Pauls and Stratocasters; the numbers do not indicate nor include every guitar Beck has owned.

The Nuts 'n' Bolts in Jeff Beck's Guitar Shop — Appendix 2

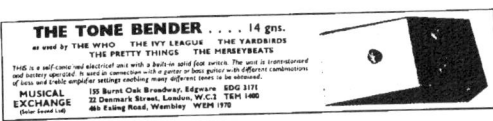

Advertisement for the Sola Sound Tone Bender, Beat Instrumental July 1965

recorded the seminal John Mayall's Bluesbreakers 'Beano' album in April 1966, which defined the classic Les Paul blues-rock sound.

Although commonly referred to as a Les Paul 'Standard', this was not the name the Gibson company originally designated for the Sunburst model. The Les Paul line was introduced as early as 1952 but underwent a few changes in the following years, one of which was replacing the original single-coil pickups with the more powerful humbuckers; pickups with double-coils. Jeff's particular model was a rather plain-looking dark reddish sunburst with a black pickguard. The first sonic evidence of Jeff with this Les Paul was a BBC session on February 28, 1966, and the first documented eyewitness sighting of Beck and the Gibson was in concert in Bristol, England on March 9, 1966 and on British TV on March 10, 1966. The Les Paul became Jeff's preferred choice thereafter and was employed during the remainder of his tenure with the Yardbirds, including the third and fourth US tours (August–September and October–November 1966 respectively). The Esquire was retained as back-up guitar and occasionally brought out. From March 1966 until his departure from the band later that year, the Les Paul was also used almost exclusively for recording, including the Yardbirds album and the singles *Over Under Sideways Down*, *Happenings Ten Years Time Ago* plus future B-side *Beck's Bolero*. The guitar was subject to some rough treatment however, and received an almost fatal blow when Beck smashed it in Texas on October 30, 1966. Leaving the splintered remnants plus the Fender Esquire behind in the care of road manager Henry Smith, Jeff jumped on a plane out of Texas and out of the Yardbirds and headed for California.

The *Blowup* movie saw Jeff playing a hollow-body two-pickup electric; described as either a Hofner or a Framus. Beck's dislike of hollow-body guitars is well-known, and as it happened the guitar in the movie was just a prop – actually made to Steve Howe's specs – that he willingly smashed to smithereens.

As for strings, Jeff kept to super light gauges as soon as he could get hold of these (with the top E being a skinny 00.7!), but with the action set fairly high to accommodate slide playing.

Amps: While in the Yardbirds, Jeff was prone to use Vox valve amplifiers, primarily their robust Vox AC 30 Treble Boost model with 2 x 12" speakers. Also used was the bigger brother, the AC 50, which had a separate amp and speaker cabinet.

Throughout the Yardbirds' first US tour (September 1965), the group relied entirely on borrowed amplification equipment from other acts. For their second US tour (December 1965–January 1966), the group were supplied with use of Vox equipment in Chicago which meant that trustworthy amps were available and sometimes flown out, but where it was prohibitively expensive or impractical to ship these amps, it was still common for them to have to resort to borrowed equipment. Top of the line was the Vox Super Beatle, which Jeff performed with on the third US tour (August – September 1966). In the US, the Super Beatle consisted of a trapezoid-shaped amplifier atop a chrome-plated stand with wheels and a speaker cabinet that could be tilted. The amp was particularly powerful with a rating of 240 watts, and came with a preamp including a built-in fuzzbox and mid-range boost plus tremelo and reverb, all controlled by a footswitch. The Yardbirds were still burdened with other hired equipment on their third and fourth US tours, where they were seen with both Standel and Jordan amplifiers. These were transistorized, and the latter company's Boss amp bragged of its "undistorted sound", hardly an amp after Beck's heart!

Honouring Jeff Beck's victory in BEAT INSTRUMENTAL'S polls in December 1966, Marshall ran an advertisement to congratulate the Who, Stevie Winwood and Jeff Beck – who "all use Marshall". Although Beck later utilised Marshalls extensively, no conclusive proof documents that he used a Marshall with the Yardbirds.

Effects: Jeff Beck popularized the fuzzbox like no other guitarist, and his groundbreaking use of this effect on *Heart Full of Soul* (just recorded prior to the Rolling Stones' fuzz declaration *Satisfaction*) featured a box borrowed from Jimmy Page and made by Roger Mayer. Afterwards, Beck acquired and also endorsed the Sola Sound Tone Bender (an 'Electronic Fuzz Unit'), designed by Gary Hurst. The Tone Bender was produced commercially from early 1965, sold for 14 guineas and sported a one-off switch plus two selectors to adjust 'level' and 'attack' controls. Other prominent Yardbirds recordings featuring fuzz guitar were *Mister You're A Better Man Than I* and *Over Under Sideways Down*. Jeff also experimented with a Leslie speaker for *Still I'm Sad*. Named after its inventor Don Leslie, it was a rotating speaker usually used with organs to produce a swivelling sound.

THE JEFF BECK GROUP (Jan 1967–Aug 1969)

Guitars: The Gibson Les Paul #1 that was damaged in October the previous year was repaired in time for Jeff Beck's return to the studio and the stage at the beginning of 1967. At the same time the guitar underwent reparations, the pickup covers were removed to reveal two cream-coloured double-coiled humbuckers. This

Gibson Les Paul #1, post-smash, pre-strip (February '67)

Gibson Les Paul #1, post-smash, post-strip (July '68)

was probably again due to Eric Clapton who did a similar operation on his Les Paul, and claimed it improved the sound immensely. (Baring the pickups has later proved to be of no tonal consequence at all.) Beck used the Les Paul on the *Hi Ho Silver Lining* and *Tally Man* singles, but he was still attached to the Esquire which he kept about his apartment but also carried around on the road as a spare.

Jeff sometimes borrowed Ron Wood's **'Danecaster'** on several occasions during 1967 (like at the Saville Theatre on July 2), a Frankensteinian combination of a Telecaster body fitted with a Danelectro 12-string neck. Producing a particularly huge sound, the guitar was built by Marshall's of Ealing.

In early 1968 Beck stripped the Les Paul down to the wood. First photographic evidence of the sanded-down guitar is from the European tour in April 1968. The instrument was used to record the *Truth* album in April and May 1968.

For this album it sounded like Beck also used a guitar with a vibrato arm (like on the coda to *Morning Dew*) – possibly a Fender Stratocaster – and Jeff played Mickie Most's Gibson Jumbo acoustic guitar on *Greensleeves*. More interesting was the use of a Sho-Bud pedal steel, which Jeff put to brilliant use on the reworked *Shapes Of Things*, although he did not employ the actual pedals but just used the instrument as a lap steel. During the first US tour with his group, Beck used the stripped-down Les Paul while occasionally plugging in a Fender guitar, probably his old Esquire or an unspecified Telecaster.

For the second American tour in October–December 1968, Jeff arrived in Chicago on October 11 with the stripped Les Paul, only to see it being damaged after the concert by a careless road manager. The Fender Esquire was still kept as a backup. Although the Les Paul was sufficiently repaired to be quickly usable, dealer and guitarist Rick Nielsen was backstage in Chicago and witnessed the accident. Nielsen flew to Philadelphia on October 26, and sold several guitars to Beck. Primarily Jeff bought his **Gibson Les Paul Sunburst #2** for $350. Believed to be from 1958, this specimen was distinguished by a beautiful flamed top, commonly called tiger-striping. Here, too, the pickup covers were taken off to reveal a cream-coloured back pickup and a 'zebra' front pickup; i.e. cream-and-black coloured. This guitar was likely debuted the very same night (according to Beck, "It was [bought] right before a gig, and I played the guitar that night, right out of the box"), and remained Beck's favourite stage guitar until the break-up of his band in August 1969, lasting through the Jeff Beck Group's second, third, fourth and fifth North American tours. Perhaps it was

Fender Stratocaster #1 (September '71)

Nielsen, too, who furnished Beck with a natural Fender Stratocaster, which also was reportedly seen for the first time in Jeff's hands during this American tour. (Although of course Beck had a Stratocaster years earlier when he played with the Del-Tones, the guitar is here numbered **Fender Stratocaster #1** for the sake of reference.) It is strongly believed that this maple-necked Stratocaster dated from 1954. The guitar was stripped of its sunburst paint to reveal the natural wood finish, and it was always easily recognizable because of the broken pickguard on the lower horn. During the second US tour, Beck also posed with a recent-model **Gibson SG Standard** – with enlarged pickguard and a Gibson Vibrola tremolo arm; this guitar was not seen again.

Unfortunately, the Les Paul #2 was never preserved properly on record. When it came time to make a second album –

Gibson Les Paul #2 (March 1969)

Beck-Ola – in the spring of 1969, Jeff Beck favoured Fender Stratocaster #1. By now he had tired of the common Les Paul sound and felt that a Stratocaster better suited his personality and playing style. Sadly, Les Paul #2 was stolen in New York – possibly at just the time the group abruptly ended their last tour and were returning home to Britain in August 1969. The guitar was never recovered.

Jeff fell in love with Ernie Ball's rock 'n' roll strings, which were only obtainable in America in 1967. After meeting Jimi Hendrix, he also went up a notch or two in string gauges to a 00.9 top E-string.

Amps: When Jeff went back on the road in March 1967 he very briefly used Vox 'Beatle' amps in rehearsals and also for the first club dates, but by May he had switched to Marshall amplifiers, which he would invariably stick to for the following two years. Jeff initially had a pair of 200-watt Marshall amplifiers, one on each side of the stage, a simple way of distributing the sound in the pre-PA-miking days. He also used 50-watt and 100-watt Marshall tops in those years.

For the first US tour in June–August 1968 Beck had to rely on hired amplifiers, usually high-wattage Fender equipment but also Marshalls. For the second US tour in October–December 1968 he used Marshall equipment exclusively; two 200-watt tops with four speaker cabinets, each with four 12 inchers – the classic Marshall stack. During the third US tour (March 1969) Beck again travelled with Marshall amps, but was also using Rickenbacker Transonic Series 200 amps, which put out 350 watts and consisted of an amplifier mounted atop a speaker cabinet on a rolling stand. (Led Zeppelin also employed the cumbersome Transonics on their first US tour in 1968/'69.) During the quick fourth US visit in May 1969, Jeff was saddled with Kustom amps, known for their 'tuck and roll' covering.

Effects: Various fuzzboxes were used in the first Jeff Beck Group. Those included the Sola Sound which he had served him so well in the Yardbirds, a Colorsound Tone Bender and probably a Supa-fuzz, which was produced by Marshall. In time for the recording of Truth in April–May 1968, Beck got a Vox Cry Baby wah-wah pedal, an effect already used by Eric Clapton (Tales of Brave Ulysses) and Jimi Hendrix (Burning of the Midnight Lamp). Beck used it to great effect on I Ain't Superstitious and You Shook Me.

JEFF BECK GROUP II (April 1971–July 1972)

Guitars: When Jeff and Cozy Powell put together a second Beck Group in the early months of 1971, Jeff used the natural Fender Stratocaster #1 with the broken pickguard and also his old stripped Les Paul #1. Both guitars were used for the recording of Rough And Ready in 1971.

Les Paul #1 was later sent to a repairman in Memphis, where the guitar was completely overhauled. The initials J. B. were engraved at the 22nd fret and the neck was inlaid with some frilly flower motifs. The original Gibson logo was replaced by an old style Gibson script logo, and additional damage was done when the original pickups were taken out and new ones were put in. Jeff still has this guitar in his collection, but it is very rarely played.

For the Jeff Beck Group sessions (January 1972) he reportedly used Stratocaster #1 throughout, and Beck's use of the vibrato arm was clearly audible on songs like Going Down. He also experimented with an electric sitar (a Coral model), as heard on I Can't Give Back The Love I Feel For You.

When the new Jeff Beck Group began touring in the summer (Europe) and autumn (USA) of 1971 and then spring 1972 (UK, Germany and the USA again), Jeff also used Stratocaster #1 exclusively. But at the end of the Cozy Powell-era Beck was seen with a **Fender Stratocaster #2**, a blonde model with rosewood neck. The guitar must have been very recent, perhaps brand-new, because this particular Stratocaster bears all the features of a 1970–1971 model; a 'third period' Stratocaster with large headstock, black logo but with the capitalised subtitle 'With Synchronized Tremolo' missing – which was dropped by the Fender factory in 1970. This guitar was used by Jeff during the group's short English tour in July 1972.

During the very brief transitional period with Max Middleton, Kim Milford/Bobby Tench, Tim Bogert and Carmine Appice in

Fender Stratocaster #2 (October 1972)

The Nuts 'n' Bolts in Jeff Beck's Guitar Shop — Appendix 2

Gibson Les Paul #3 (May 1973)

his group (September 1972), Jeff also employed Stratocaster #2.

Amps: For the time with his second Beck Group, Jeff used mainly Marshall amps and speaker cabinets for recording and stage work, but an old Vox AC 30 and scattered Fender amps were also used in the studio. As the road work increased, Jeff invested in a new rig; a Sunn Coliseum Lead amplifier combined with a Univox cabinet with 6 x 12" speakers (model UX 1516) – although he also used Sunn speaker cabinets. The Univox likely made its debut during the US tour in May 1972, and proved trustworthy enough on the road for Beck to keep it more or less identical for the next five years or so.

Effects: Both in the studio and onstage Beck pedalled the occasional fuzzbox or booster (Coloursound Tone Bender and Coloursound Overdriver, both of them descendents of the London-based Sola Sound company), a Cry Baby wah-wah (e.g. on *Definitely Maybe*), a Maestro Echoplex and a Leslie rotating speaker (heard on *Raynes Park Blues*).

BECK, BOGERT & APPICE (Sept 1972–Feb 1974)

Guitars: After the brief tenure with Max Middleton and Kim Milford, Jeff, Tim and Carmine regrouped as a power trio. From their public inception on September 16, 1972 (at Kennington Oval) until December of that year, Beck carried almost exclusively Stratocaster #2. The guitar was of course equipped with a vibrato arm, and Beck kept four out of the regular five springs (the actual protecting backplate was removed). The Stratocaster was used to record their only official album; *Jeff Beck, Tim Borgert, Carmine Appice*, in December 1972 and January 1973. (In a recording situation other guitars were also used, like electric sitar on *Oh To Love You*.) Interestingly, photographic evidence shows Beck onstage with a pre-1959 Gibson Les Paul Special in Detroit on November 7, 1972; a guitar characterized by its two 'soap bar' pickups and yellow-ish finish.

But it was in January 1973 that Jeff Beck acquired his **Gibson Les Paul #3,** bought from Strings & Things in Memphis for five-hundred dollars. This was in fact a 1954 Gibson Les Paul Gold-top, serial #27048, which a previous owner had already modified with two humbuckers instead of the original P90 single-coil pickups. Furthermore, the guitar had been repainted in a dark brown-to-black finish ("oxblood" is how Beck himself described the colour), had Schaller tuning pegs installed, but the distinct bridge/tailpiece was original. The instrument was unveiled for the first time on February 1, 1973, at the start of a college tour of the UK. From now on until the demise of Beck, Bogert & Appice in February 1974, Jeff would use this guitar on every live performance. Although originally equipped with pickup covers, these were taken off sometime between June and September 1973; beneath the covers were two double black-coloured bobbins. With the entrance of Les Paul #3, Stratocaster #2 was lost from view.

Jeff was asked by Melody Maker why he switched from a Stratocaster to a Les Paul ('Any Questions?', May 5, 1973): "I started playing the Fender Stratocaster in late 1971, after my Gibson [#2] was stolen, but abandoned it when I found a Gibson I really liked, although I might start playing the Stratocaster again, as I have now had it fitted with a Gibson pick-up [likely Fender Stratocaster #2]. ... My attraction for the Les Paul is that it is better built and I prefer it."

When the trio began working on a new album in London in September 1973, Seymour Duncan – an American guitarist turned repairman – was present at one of the sessions. Duncan worked at the newly-opened Fender Sound House in London, and built Beck a hybrid **'Tele-Gib'** consisting of a 1959 Telecaster body and a 1963/1964 Telecaster neck plus a pair of humbuckers from an old Gibson Flying V; the bridge pickup cream-coloured and the neck pickup a 'zebra' with one cream and one black bobbin. The instrument was a present to Jeff, who quickly repaid the service when he donated his classic Yardbird-era Fender Esquire to Duncan. (The Esquire now was stripped of its original blonde finish to reveal the wood graining, and had also received a replacement neck from 1955.)

Amps: During the whole Beck, Bogert & Appice era, Jeff stuck to a Sunn Coliseum Lead amplifier onstage, usually atop Univox speaker cabinets. Curiously, Jeff also endorsed Univox amplifiers, but no evidence shows that he actually used those onstage. For studio work, different amps were certainly tried out.

Effects: Jeff ran a very basic set-up at the beginning of Beck, Bogert & Appice, but both a booster and a wah-wah pedal were put in use. Jeff used a Uni-Vibe flanger – similar to the effect Roger Mayer had built for Jimi Hendrix – on the studio version of *Livin' Alone*.

Jeff Beck endorses Univox amps, Guitar Player, March/April 1973

The most visible and discussed outboard effect Beck ever used was the talk box, which he first introduced on Beck, Bogert & Appice's mammoth US tour beginning in March 1973. (It was to be another year and a half however, before Beck would record with the voice bag.) The model Jeff used was called 'The Bag' and was manufactured by Kustom, in fact, the first commercially available talk box, of which about only 100 were made. The Bag itself resembled a Mexican wineskin strapped over Beck's shoulder, easily identified in live pictures of him during this era. Inside the Bag was a horn driver powered by the amp's speaker output. A plastic tube fastened to the driver emitted the sound to the mouth to modify the signal, and it was then amplified by a regular microphone connected to the PA system. It was guitarist Mike Pinera who tipped off Beck to the Bag. Pinera had used it successfully on the album *Metamorphosis* by Iron Butterfly, and Jeff probably met Pinera as Bogert and Appice were friends of his. The exposure he gave the effect likely inspired both Joe Walsh (who used a similar device on *Rocky Mountain Way*, his US #23 hit from October 1973) and Peter Frampton (on his multi-platinum album *Frampton Comes Alive* in 1976). Indeed, Frampton had already dabbled with a forerunner – the Talkin' Accentuator – made by Nashville pedal-player Pete Drake.

When Beck, Bogert & Appice went on their last tour together in January 1974, Beck used the newly introduced phase shifter (probably the Small Stone model by Electro-Harmonix or the popular MXR P90); an effect which sought to recreate the Leslie speaker.

Appendix 2: The Nuts 'n' Bolts in Jeff Beck's Guitar Shop

"BLOW BY BLOW" ERA
(Aug 1974–Oct 1975)

Guitars: In the autumn of 1974 Jeff Beck set about recording *Blow By Blow*. His arsenal of guitars included Les Paul #3, the 'Tele-Gib' (heard on *'Cause We've Ended As Lovers*), a spare Fender Esquire and finally a beautiful old instrument, Beck's **Fender Stratocaster #3**. A 3-tone sunburst with maple neck, it is believed to be a 1956 model, and was perhaps the main guitar on *Blow By Blow*. For some reason, this guitar is apparently not taken on the road when Jeff and John McLaughlin embark on a long US trek in April–June 1975. Indeed, the guitar does not resurface later either.

For the US tour Jeff played the faithful Stratocaster #1 and Les Paul #3, commonly opening his shows with the Fender before switching to the Gibson for *'Cause We've Ended As Lovers*. He also brought with him the the 'Tele-Gib'. After an on-stage intermezzo in Cleveland in May, Jeff's Stratocaster was smashed and he consequently has to rely on borrowed guitars from local music stores thereafter. John McLaughlin also presented him with a gift – Jeff's **Fender Stratocaster #4**. Purchased from Norman's Rare Guitars in Reseda, California, this blonde rosewood-necked guitar was reportedly an early sixties model, and was later stolen in transit between London and New York. Used briefly on the John McLaughlin tour, this instrument was also depicted on the cover of *Wired*. When Beck took his *Blow By Blow*-band to Japan in August 1975, he alternated between Les Paul #3 and Stratocaster #4.

Amps: For the McLaughlin US tour, Beck had one small post-CBS Fender Champ amp miked to the max into two Marshall 100-watt tops with Marshall or Fender cabinets. Later on in the tour he found the Champ to be too clean, and used Marshalls in the whole amp/speaker chain. He also used an elaborate monitor system, to enable him to hear the guitar properly.

Effects: The *Blow By Blow* album displayed a wide range of tones, with Beck using every effect at his command, be it fuzzboxes, wah-wah pedals or the Bag. On tour he brought with him a Coloursound Tone Bender, a Mu-Tron Octave Divider (it gives a note below the one that is played), a DeArmond wah-wah/volume and a specially-made volume booster.

"WIRED" ERA
(Sept 1975–Feb 1977)

Guitars: Throughout the *Wired* era Beck preferred to use Fender Stratocasters almost exclusively. Stratocaster #1 was still around, albeit now with a new feature installed; a rosewood neck with Fender's new bullet truss rod system. When John

The 'Steve Marriott' Fender Stratocaster #7 (July 1979)

McLaughlin heard the news of how Stratocaster #4 was stolen, he bought Jeff another similar blonde/rosewood model; **Fender Stratocaster #5**. While most of *Wired* was done on various Fenders, a nylon string acoustic guitar was used to record *Love Is Green*.

Touring with Jan Hammer in 1976, Jeff depended on Fender Stratocasters; indeed he gave up playing Les Pauls on-stage altogether after changing between Fenders and Gibsons for the last ten years. At the very first concerts (including London on May 23 and the Oakland, California festival on June 5/6), Beck used the revised Stratocaster #1. But once the heavy touring schedule got under way, Jeff got himself a workhorse; **Fender Stratocaster #6** – yet another blonde – certainly a pre-1971 body, but with a post-1971 neck as it had a bullet truss rod system and hence correctly a 3-bolt neck mounting. But photos show the neck was oddly enough joined to the body with an old style 4-bolt plate.

Following his concert in Memphis on July 17, 1976, a fan gave Jeff an old Fender Esquire from about 1952/'53 as a present. The guitar was in immaculate condition.

Amps: The extensive touring with Jan Hammer in 1976–1977 found Beck returning to Univox cabinets, but with a Marshall amplifier on top.

Effects: The Bag was used throughout the time with Hammer, initially only during *Full Moon Boogie*, and then later in the year when *She's A Woman* was introduced to the set. The MXR Phaser, a Mu-tron III envelope filter, a Coloursound Octivider, a wah-wah, an echo unit and the Coloursound Tone Bender also made up Beck's effect display. The Coloursound Ring Modulator (manufactured since March 1973) was used in the studio on songs like *Sophie*, and was also featured on tour and heard on the joint Beck/Hammer *Live!* album.

JEFF BECK + STANLEY CLARKE
(Nov 1978–July 1979)

Guitars: In either 1977 or '78, Jeff Beck acquired his **Fender Stratocaster #7**. The guitar belonged to Steve Marriott, has a maple neck dated 1954, and bears the serial #0062. Beck himself describes that guitar as his personal favourite. Although he would be careful with it, he took it on a European tour with Stanley Clarke in the summer of 1979, along with the 'Tele-Gib'. Jeff also had his **Fender Stratocaster #8**. Initially bought at Norman's Rare Guitars, this butchered guitar consisted of a rosewood neck circa 1959/1960, an early 1960 body, serial #56599, and with all-black Schechter hardware; one volume and one tone pot plus three separate pickup switches rather than the Strat's customary three-way selector. Jeff played this guitar both at the CBS Records convention in July 1978 and on the Japanese tour in November 1978, but the guitar was never used again on-stage. Jeff also brought with him both Stratocaster #7 and the Fender Esquire to Japan (the latter is believed to be the guitar which is now enshrined in the Hard Rock Cafe collection). Finally, Jeff tried out the Roland GS/GR 500 Guitar Synth in Japan and also briefly in Europe the following summer, but found it to be unreliable.

Beck's personal collection at this time furthermore included a white Ibanez Original Model (also kept as a backup guitar in Japan in November '78), an Ibanez Flying V model and a Fender Precision Bass.

His string gauges now went .009, .011, .017, .024, .036 and .046.

Amps: For the 1978 Japan tour, Jeff used two Marshall Super Leads with Marshall speaker cabinets.

Effects: Roland OD-1 Overdrive, Coloursound Overdriver, Tychobrahe Paraflanger, Roland Space Echo RE-201 and the Bag.

"THERE AND BACK" ERA
(May 1978–March 1981)

Guitars: The Fender Stratocaster #7 was the main guitar for both recording *There And Back* and touring in support of the album in 1980, but the 'Tele-Gib' was also seen on the road. During the Japanese tour in November 1980, Jeff was also given a pair of Greco guitars (one of them a miniature used on the encore *Going Down*). Grecos were in fact made by Fuji Gen Gakki, the very same company which produces Ibanez guitars. Beck also owned a Stick – a recent invention which demanded a two-handed playing technique – which was a gift from his manager.

Amps: On tour, Beck took with him his old 100-watt Marshall valve amps from the Rod Stewart days.

Effects: Touring with the *There And Back* band in the States and Japan in the autumn of 1980, Beck had minimal accessories; basically an Ibanez Overdrive and a Tychobrahe Paraflanger, plus the Roland Space Echo. ∎

Appendix 3

LIVE PERFORMANCES 1965–1980

This appendix lists all venues for all live performances – arranged by country, state and city – Jeff Beck has undertaken or has been booked to play in the years 1965–1980, beginning with the Yardbirds. Hence, live performances with the Tridents January–March 1965 are not included. Please refer to the general text for futher information.

- An asterisk (*) indicates dates and/or venues not confirmed.
- (YB w/o Beck) indicates Yardbirds dates that went ahead between March 1965–December 1966 despite Beck's absence while still officially a member of the Yardbirds
- (Canc) indicates shows that were initially booked and/or announced but were ultimately cancelled.

AUSTRALIA

City/Venue	Date
Adelaide (South Australia)	
Memorial Drive	30 January 1977
Brisbane (Queensland)	
Festival Hall	7 February 1977
Melbourne (Victoria)	
Festival Hall, West Melbourne	1, 2 February 1977
Perth (Western Australia)	
Perth Entertainment Centre	28 January 1977
Sydney (New South Wales)	
Hordern Pavilion, Sportsground, Paddington	4, 5 February 1977

AUSTRIA

City/Venue	Date
Vienna	
Konzerthaus	7 July 1979

BELGIUM

City/Venue	Date
Antwerp	
Arenahall, Deurne	1 October 1972
Bilzen	
"Bilzen Festival" (Canc)	23, 24 August 1969
Brussels (▶ Woluwe-St-Lambert)	
Vorst Nationaal (Forest National)	25 November 1973
Gent	
[unconfirmed venue]	13 October 1967
Woluwe-St-Lambert (metropolitan Brussels)	
"Wolu-City 2", Kentucky Palace	29 May 1966

CANADA

City/Venue	Date
Edmonton (Alberta)	
Edmonton Coliseum	18 July 1975
Montreal (Quebec)	
"Montreal Pop Festival" (Canc)	22 August 1969
Toronto (Ontario)	
Rock Pile	27 October 1968
Electric Circus	9 March 1969
Rock Pile (Canc)	9 August 1969
Massey Hall	8 May 1972
Concert Bowl, Maple Leaf Gardens	13 April 1973
O'Keefe Center	23 July 1975
Concert Bowl, Maple Leaf Gardens	15 October 1976
Vancouver (British Columbia)	
Agradome (Canc)	4 April 1969
Queen Elizabeth Theater	19 July 1975
Agradome	19 June 1976
Orpheum Theater	1 September 1980
Winnipeg (Manitoba)	
Winnipeg Arena	21 July 1975
Winnipeg Convention Center	29 May 1976

DENMARK

City/Venue	Date
Copenhagen	
KB Hallen (YB w/o Beck)	7 April 1966
Brondby Pop Club	20 April 1968
Pop-puk	21 April 1968
Le Carousel	28 April 1968
Brondby Pop Club	5 October 1968
Star Club (Canc)	6 October 1968
Odense	
Fyens Forum (YB w/o Beck)	7 April 1966
Roskilde	
Fjordvilla	21 April 1968
Fjordvilla (Canc)	6 October 1968
"Roskildefestivalen"	30 June 1979
Trelleborg	
Parken	20 April 1968

ENGLAND (▶ UNITED KINGDOM)

FRANCE

City/Venue	Date
Besançon	
Palais Des Sports	23 November 1973
Biarritz	
Stade Aguillera	4 July 1979*
Fréjus	
Arènes	10 July 1979
Lille	
Salle Des Fêtes, Fâches-Thumesnil	21 November 1973
Marseilles	
L'Omnibus	3 April 1966
Mulhouse	
[unconfirmed venue] (Canc)	11 October 1972
Palaiseau	
Point Gamma, L'Ecole Polytechnique	4 May 1968
Palavas-les Flots	
Arènes (Canc)	12 July 1979
Paris	
Palais Des Sports	20 June 1965
Theatre Olympia (Canc)	14 December 1965
Golf Drouet	4 February 1966
Palace de la Mutualité	5 February 1966

207

Appendix 3 — Live performances 1965–1980

La Locomotive Club	1 April 1966
Le Weekend Club	26 June 1966
[unconfirmed venue] (Canc)	13 July 1966
[unconfirmed venue]	5 May 1968
Le Bataclan	20 February 1973
Théâtre Olympia	14 June 1973
Théâtre Du Châtelet (Canc)	22 November 1973
"Festival de Jazz-Rock" Pavillon de Porte de Panton	3 July 1979

Provins
"Provins Rock Festival"	27 June 1966

Lyon*
Palais D'Hiver	27 November 1973

unconfirmed location South of France
[unconfirmed venue]	2 April 1966

GERMANY (FEDERAL REPUBLIC OF GERMANY)
(West Germany prior to Oct 1990)

City/Venue	Date
Berlin (West Berlin)	
Waldbühne	9 June 1973
Essen	
Grugahalle (Canc)	17 February 1974
Frankfurt	
K-52	9 November 1965
Zoom Club	16 October 1971
Kongresshalle	8 April 1972
Jahrhunderthalle	8 October 1972
"Summer Rock Festival", Radrennbahn	10 June 1973
Germersheim	
"Whitsuntide Festival" (Canc)	22 May 1972
Hamburg	
Musikhalle	7 April 1972
Musikhalle	6 October 1972
Musikhalle	8 June 1973
Hanover	
Niedersachsenhalle	7 October 1972
Ludwigshafen	
"3rd British Rock Meeting" Sandreenbahn Altrip (Canc)	22, 23 September 1973
Friedrich-Ebert-Halle (Canc)	16 February 1974
Munich	
Big Apple	12 November 1965
Circus Krone-Bau	13 April 1972
Circus Krone-Bau	3 October 1972
Deutsches Museum (Canc)	14 February 1974
Nuremberg	
Messehalle	4 October 1972
Offenbach	
Stadthalle (Canc)	13 February 1974
Offenburg	
[unconfirmed venue]	14 April 1972*
Ravensburg	
Oberschwabenhalle (Canc)	15 February 1974
Stuttgart	
Killesberg	12 April 1972
Killesberg*	5 October 1972
Wurzburg	
"Wurzburg Giant Pop Festival"	9 July 1972

FINLAND

City/Venue	Date
Turku	
"Ruis-Rockfestival", Runsala-parken	22 August 1971

HOLLAND (► THE NETHERLANDS)

ITALY

City/Venue	Date
San Remo	
"16th Festival of Italian Songs" Casino Municipale	28, 29 January 1966
Milan	
[unconfirmed venue]	mid-August 1965*

JAPAN

City/Venue	Date
Fukuoka	
Kyuden Kinen Taiikukan	8 December 1980
Ibaraki	
Kenmin-Bunka Center	20 November 1978
Kanazawa	
Koseinenkin Hall, Ishikawa	22 November 1978
Kokura	
Shin-nittetu Otani Taiikukan	28 November 1978
Kurashiki	
Shimin Kaikan	23 November 1978
Shimin Kaikan	9 December 1980
Kyoto	
"World Rock Festival Eastland", Yagai-Ongakudo, Maruyama (Canc)	6 August 1975
Miyagi	
Kenmin-Kaikan	12 December 1980
Nagoya	
Shi-Kokaido	16 May 1973
"World Rock Festival Eastland", Ken-Taiikukan, Aichi	5 August 1975
Shi-Kokaido	26 November 1978
Shi-Kokaido	11 December 1980
Osaka	
Koseinenkin Hall	18, 19 May 1973
Furitu Taiikukan	24 November 1978
Koseinenkin Hall	29 November 1978
Furitu Taiikukan	5 December 1980
Festival Hall	10 December 1980
Sapporo	
"World Rock Festival Eastland" Okunai-Kyogijo, Makomanai	3 August 1975
Doritu-Sangyo-Kyoshin-Kaijo	14 December 1980
Sendai	
"World Rock Festival Eastland", Trail Land, Sugo (Canc)	9 August 1975
Tokyo	
Nippon Budokan Hall	14 May 1973
"World Rock Festival Eastland" Korakuen Stadium	7 August 1975
Nippon Budokan Hall	30 Nov, 1–2 Dec 1978
Nippon Budokan Hall	4, 17, 18 Dec 1980
Yokohama	
Bunka–Taiikukan	16 December 1980

THE NETHERLANDS

City/Venue	Date
Amsterdam	
Concertgebouw	30 September 1972
Jaap Edenhal	5 July 1979
Geleen	
"Pink Pop Festival", Voetballstadion	11 June 1973
Haarlem	
Concertgebouw (YB w/o Beck)	11 April 1966
Rotterdam	
[unconfirmed venue]	3 March 1968
Ahoy Hal	11 September 1971
Grote Zaal, DeDoelen	2 October 1972*

Live performances 1965-1980 — Appendix 3

NEW ZEALAND

City/Venue	Date
Auckland	
Town Hall	25 January 1977
Christchurch	
Town Hall	21 January 1977
Wellington	
St. James Theatre	22, 23 January 1977

NORWAY

City/Venue	Date
Horten	
"Hortensfestivalen 79", Lystlunden	1 July 1979

SCOTLAND (▶ UK)

SPAIN

City/Venue	Date
Barcelona	
Plaza de Toros Las Arenas	13 July 1979
Madrid	
Plaza de Toros de la Ventas	14 July 1979

SWEDEN

City/Venue	Date
Gothenburg	
Cue Club	24 April 1968
Jönköping	
Rigoletto	26 April 1968
Rigoletto	4 October 1968
Kristinehamn	
[unconfirmed venue]	27 April 1968
Stockholm	
Gyllene Cirkeln	25 April 1968
[unconfirmed venue]	1–3 October 1968
Uddevalla	
[unconfirmed venue]	25 April 1968

SWITZERLAND

City/Venue	Date
Arosa	
Arosa Ski Resort	September 1971*
Basel	
[unconfirmed venue] (Canc)	10 October 1972
Bern	
[unconfirmed venue] (Canc)	13 October 1972
Chur	
Hotel Drei Könige	15 April 1968
Luzern	
Kursaal	16 April 1968
St. Gallen	
Africana Music-Club	17 April 1968
Zurich	
[unconfirmed venue] (Canc)	11 October 1972

UNITED KINGDOM OF GREAT BRITAIN

ENGLAND

When two county designations follow the first refers to the location prior to April 1 1974 reorganization act and the second listing to the current designation after that date.

City/Venue	Date
Altrincham (Cheshire/Greater Manchester)	
Stamford Hall	15 June 1965
Ashton-under-Lyne (Lancashire/Greater Manchester)	
Mecca Palais	23 June 1966
Aylesbury (Buckinghamshire)	
Grosvenor Ballroom/Borough Assembly Hall	9 March 1965
Grosvenor Ballroom/Borough Assembly Hall (Canc)	20 April 1965
Axminster (Devon)	
Guildhall	15 October 1965
Barnstaple (Devon)	
Queen's Hall	14 October 1965
Bath (Somerset/Avon)	
Pavilion	5 July 1965
Pavilion	1 November 1965
Pavilion	14 March 1966
Pavilion	25 July 1966
Pavilion	8 April 1968
Pavilion (Canc)	16 December 1968
Bedford (Bedfordshire)	
Granada Cinema	13 May 1965
Granada Cinema	2 December 1965
Bexley (Kent/Greater London)	
Black Prince Hotel	7 April 1968
Bicester (Oxfordshire)	
Garrison Theatre	5 April 1968
Billingham (Durham/Cleveland)	
Kave Dwellers Club (Canc)	24 June 1965
Birmingham (Warwickshire/West Midlands)	
Marquee Dance Club, City Centre	19 April 1965
University of Birmingham	18 June 1965
Silver Blades Ice Rink	25 April 1966
Birmingham Theatre	15 May 1966
Gay Tower Ballroom	13 June 1966
Odeon Cinema	6 October 1966
Caravelle Club, Viewing Lounge Birmingham Airport	7 June 1967
Midnight City	25 June 1967
[unconfirmed venue]	8 December 1967
Mothers, Erdington (Canc)	19 December 1968
Mothers, Erdington (Canc)	13 April 1970
Top Rank Suite	14 July 1972
Town Hall	23 January 1974
Bishop's Stortford (Hertfordshire)	
Rhodes Center	9 April 1966
Blackpool (Lancashire)	
Empress Ballroom, Winter Gardens	11 June 1965
North Pier Pavillion	8 August 1965
North Pier Pavillion	3 July 1966
Bletchley (Buckinghamshire)	
Wilton Hall	23 March 1968
Bognor Regis (Sussex/West Sussex)	
Shoreline Club	27 May 1967
Borehamwood (Hertfordshire)	
Links Club	26 March 1965
Borley (Essex)	
Country Club	7 June 1965
Boston (Lincolnshire)	
Starlight Room, Gliderdome	19 June 1965
Starlight Room, Gliderdome	22 July 1967
Bournemouth (Hampshire/Dorset)	
[unconfirmed venue] (Canc)	7 June 1965
Odeon Cinema (Canc)	1 August 1965
Hard Rock (Canc)	15 February 1973
Bracknell (Berkshire)	
Sports Centre	16 September 1967
Bradford (Yorkshire/West Yorkshire)	
Gaumont Cinema	22 November 1965
University of Bradford* (Canc)	26 May 1966
Westbrook Hall, Bradford Technical College	22 April 1967

Appendix 3 Live performances 1965–1980

[unconfirmed venue] 11 May 1968
Brighton (Sussex/East Sussex)
Top Rank 18 March 1966
University of Sussex 14 December 1967
University of Sussex *(Canc)* 9 February 1972
University of Sussex 8 March 1972
The Dome 16 January 1974
Bristol (Gloucestershire/Avon)
Corn Exchange 30 June 1965
Colston Hall *(Canc)* 15 November 1965
Colston Hall 3 December 1965
Corn Exchange 9 March 1966
University of Bristol *(Canc)* 23 April 1966
Locarno Ballroom 26 May 1966
Colston Hall 7 October 1966
Chinese R&B Club, Corn Exchange 16 May 1967
Bristol Polytechnic *(Canc)* 31 January 1972
Bristol Polytechnic 4 March 1972
Colston Hall 24 January 1974
Brixton (▶ London)
Bromley (Kent)
Bromley Court Hotel 21 April 1965
Bromley Court Hotel 29 June 1966
Bury (Lancashire/Greater Manchester)
Palais de Danse 25 June 1966
Buxton (Derbyshire)
Pavilion Gardens Ballroom 14 May 1966
Pavilion Gardens Ballroom 23 July 1966
Camberley (Surrey)
Agincourt Ballroom *(Canc)* 14 March 1965
Agincourt Ballroom *(Canc)* 10 April 1966
Cambridge (Cambridgeshire)
Corn Exchange 10 April 1965
Corn Exchange 10 July 1965
ABC Cinema 25 November 1965
Corn Exchange 5 March 1966
Canterbury (Kent)
University of Kent *(Canc)* 1 February 1972
University of Kent 16 March 1972
Carlisle (Cumberland/Cumbria)
Cosmopolitan Club 17 April 1966
Market Assembly Hall 20 May 1967
Chalk Farm (▶ London)
Chatham (Kent)
Ritz Theatre 24 November 1965
Town Hall 7 March 1966
Chelmsford (Essex)
Corn Exchange 24 April 1965
Cheltenham (Gloucestershire)
Whaddon Football Ground 16 July 1965
Chertsey (Surrey)
[unconfirmed venue] 17 September 1967
Chesham (Buckinghamshire)
Co-op Hall 16 March 1968
Chesterfield (Derbyshire)
ABC Cinema 19 November 1965
Victoria Ballroom 24 March 1966
Cheshunt (Hertfordshire)
Wolsey Hall 10 March 1965
Chiselhurst (Kent)
Chiselhurst Caves 1 July 1966
Cleethorpes (Lincolnshire/Humberside)
Memorial Hall *(Canc)* 26 June 1965
"1965 East Coast Festival of Jazz & Modern Music",
  Boating Lake Ground 31 July 1965
Winter Gardens 21 October 1965
ABC Cinema 5 November 1965

Winter Gardens 1 April 1968
Colchester (Essex)
University of Essex 16 June 1967
Coventry (Warwickshire/West Midlands)
Coventry Theatre 9 May 1965
Coventry Theatre 28 November 1965
[unconfirmed venue] 30 October 1967
Lanchester Technical College* 18 November 1967
[unconfirmed venue] 2 June 1968
"Arts Festival", Lanchester College* *(Canc)* 1 February 1969
Lanchester Polytechnic *(Canc)* 12 February 1972
Cromer (Norfolk)
Royal Links Pavilion 29 April 1967
Cray (Kent)
Iron Curtain Club, St. Mary 25 February 1966
Crayford (Kent)
Town Hall 26 April 1966
Croydon (Surrey/Greater London)
Fairfield Hall 5 March 1965
Dartford (Kent)
[unconfirmed venue] 29 September 1967
[unconfirmed venue] 8 March 1968
Victoria and Bull Pub 10 May 1968
Derby (Derbyshire)
Gaumont Cinema 20 November 1965
Bass Recreational Grounds 9 July 1966
Doncaster (Yorkshire/South Yorkshire)
Top Rank Suite 25 May 1966
Droitwich (Worcester)
Winter Gardens 25 April 1965
Dunstable (Bedfordshire)
California Ballroom 9 October 1965
California Ballroom 30 April 1966
California Ballroom 19 August 1967
Queensway Civic Hall 1 February 1973
Durham (County Durham)
University of Durham 24 June 1966
Ealing (▶ London)
East Dereham (Norfolk)
Wellington Club, Dereham Exchange 16 December 1967
East Grinstead (Sussex)
Whitehall 3 July 1965
East Ham (▶ London)
Eltham (▶ London)
Egham (Surrey)
[unconfirmed venue] 3 February 1968
Exeter (Devon)
ABC Cinema 5 December 1965
ABC Cinema *(Canc)* 4 March 1967
University of Exeter 4 November 1967
Farnborough (Hampshire)
Assembly Hall, Farnborough Technical College
 20 March 1965
Assembly Hall, Farnborough Technical College
 9 July 1965
Town Hall *(Canc)* 10 April 1966
Folkestone (Kent)
Toft's* 26 August 1967
Gorleston (Norfolk)
Floral Hall 2 November 1966
Floral Hall 14 June 1967
Gosport (Hampshire)
Thorngate Halls 11 March 1965
Grantham (Lincolnshire)
Drill Hall 2 October 1965
Cat Ballou 17 March 1968

Live performances 1965–1980 — Appendix 3

Gravesend (Kent)
Co-op Hall — 22 July 1966
Great Malvern (▶ Malvern)
Great Yarmouth (Norfolk)
Winter Gardens — 15 July 1965
Greenford (Middlesex/Greater London)
Starlite Ballroom *(Canc)* — 18 April 1965
Starlite Ballroom — 4 July 1965
Starlite Ballroom — 12 June 1966
Starlite Ballroom — 7 May 1967
Starlite Ballroom — 9 July 1967
Starlite Ballroom — 20 August 1967
Grimsby (Lincolnshire/Humberside)
Mecca Gaiety Ballroom *(Canc)* — 27 May 1966
Guildford (Surrey)
Ricky Ticky Club, Plaza Ballroom — 29 April 1965
Wooden Bridge Hotel — 15 October 1967
Hammersmith (▶ London)
Hanley (▶ Stoke-on-Trent)
Harrow (▶ London)
Hartlepool (Yorkshire/Cleveland)
Queens Rink Ballroom — 22 September 1967
Hassocks (Sussex/East Sussex)
Ultra Club, Downs Hotel — 4 April 1965
Ultra Club, Downs Hotel *(Canc)* — 19 June 1966
Hastings (Sussex/East Sussex)
The Witchdoctor — 6 October 1965
Pier Pavilion — 10 July 1966
Heacham near Hunstanton (Norfolk)
Public Hall — 6 May 1967
Hendon (▶ London)
Hereford (Herefordshire/Hereford & Worcester)
Hillside Ballroom — 12 March 1965
High Wycombe (Buckinghamshire)
Town Hall — 13 April 1965
Town Hall — 22 June 1965
Town Hall — 19 October 1965
Town Hall — 28 March 1966
Town Hall *(Canc)* — 12 April 1966
Town Hall *(Canc)* — 10 May 1966
Town Hall — 12 May 1967
Town Hall *(Canc)* —
Hinckley (Leicestershire)
St. George's Ballroom — 3 April 1965
St. George's Ballroom *(Canc)* — 11 December 1965
St. George's Ballroom *(Canc)* — 12 March 1966
St. George's Ballroom — 15 April 1967
St. George's Ballroom — 30 September 1967
Hounslow (Middlesex)
Zambesi Club *(Canc)* — 30 October 1965
Zambesi Club — 11 June 1966
Hull [aka Kingston Upon Hull] (Yorkshire/Humberside)
Skyline Ballroom — 7 July 1967
Ipswich (Suffolk)
Manor House — 12 April 1965
Gaumont Cinema — 16 May 1965
[unconfirmed venue] *(Canc)* — 11 April 1966
Gaumont Cinema — 2 October 1966
Isleworth (Middlesex)
Middlesex Borough College — 4 June 1966
Kidderminster (Worcester/Hereford & Worcester)
Town Hall — 14 July 1966
Kingston-upon-Thames (Surrey/Greater London)
Granada Cinema — 6 May 1965
Drill Hall — 13 May 1967
Kingston Technical College* — 9 December 1967
Kirklevington (Yorkshire)
Kirklevington Country Club — 29 October 1967
Kirklevington Country Club — 12 May 1968
Knebworth (Hertfordshire)
"Knebworth Festival" *(Canc)* — 24 June 1978
Lancaster (Lancashire)
University of Lancaster *(Canc)* — 18 February 1972
University of Lancaster — 10 March 1972
University of Lancaster — 19 January 1974
Leeds (Yorkshire/West Yorkshire)
University of Leeds *(Canc?)* — 25 June 1965
Refectory, University of Leeds — 23 October 1965
Majestic Ballroom — 23 March 1966
Odeon Cinema — 24 September 1966
Refectory, University of Leeds — 7 October 1967
Refectory, University of Leeds — 11 March 1972
Union, University of Leeds — 10 February 1973
Refectory, University of Leeds — 12 January 1974
Leicester (Leicestershire)
DeMontfort Hall — 13 February 1973
Lewisham (▶ London)
Leyton (▶ London, now Waltham Forest)
Liverpool (Lancashire/Merseyside)
Empire Theatre — 25 September 1966
Union, University of Liverpool — 25 May 1967
Union, University of Liverpool — 7 February 1973
Empire Theatre — 20 January 1974
London & Greater London
Marquee — 8 March 1965
Palais, Wimbledon — 19 March 1965
Marquee — 29 March 1965
London Architectural Association — 9 April 1965
Cook's Ferry Inn, Edmonton — 15 April 1965
Lakeside Ballroom, Hendon — 22 April 1965
King's Court Hotel (Bayswater) — 23 April 1965
Marquee — 26 April 1965
Granada Cinema, Walthamstow — 1 May 1965
Odeon Cinema, Lewisham — 2 May 1965
Marquee — 3 May 1965
Granada Cinema, East Ham — 7 May 1965
Granada Cinema, Tooting — 14 May 1965
Marquee — 17 May 1965
Marquee — 8 June 1965*
Palais, Wimbledon — 2 July 1965
Fender Club, Harrow — 4 June 1965
Marquee — 6 July 1965
Marquee — 12 October 1965
Baths, Leyton — 30 October 1965
Baths, Eltham — 8 November 1965
Granada Cinema, East Ham — 27 November 1965
Marquee — 15 March 1966
Streatham Ice Rink *(Canc)* — 24 March 1966
Palais, Wimbledon — 22 April 1966
Marquee — 3 May 1966
Bluesville Club, Manor House — 27 May 1966
Ram Jam Club, Brixton *(Canc)* — 9 June 1966
Marquee — 21 June 1966
Ram Jam Club, Brixton — 2 July 1966
Royal Albert Hall, Kensington — 23 September 1966
Astoria Theatre, Finsbury Park — 3 March 1967
Saville Theatre — 5 March 1967
Marquee — 11 April 1967
Upper Cut Club, Forest Gate — 28 April 1967
Roundhouse, Chalk Farm — 12 May 1967
Blue Opera Club, Feathers Hotel, Ealing — 15 May 1967
Marquee — 6 June 1967
Cook's Ferry Inn, Edmonton — 19 June 1967
Saville Theatre — 2 July 1967
Cook's Ferry Inn, Edmonton — 25 September 1967

Appendix 3   Live performances 1965-1980

Marquee	26 September 1967
UFO, Roundhouse, Chalk Farm	29 September 1967
The Speakeasy	26 October 1967
North East London Polytechnic, Walthamstow	
	15 December 1967
Marquee	12 December 1967
[unconfirmed venue], Hammersmith	17 February 1968
Marquee	20 February 1968
Middle Earth, Covent Garden	9 March 1968
North East London Polytechnic, Walthamstow	
	22 March 1968
Marquee	9 April 1968
"Bluesville '68", Manor House	7 June 1968
"Bluesville '68", Manor House	6 September 1968
Middle Earth, The Roundhouse, Chalk Farm	21 December 1968
Wood Tavern, Hornsey *(Canc)*	25 December 1968
Marquee	14 January 1969
Lyceum (The Strand)	25 April 1969
Marquee *(Canc)*	6 June 1969
College of Printing *(Canc)*	11 February 1972
Roundhouse, Chalk Farm *(Canc)*	20 February 1972
College of Printing	3 March 1972
Waltham Forest Technical College, Waltham Forest	
	18 March 1972
Roundhouse, Chalk Farm	19 March 1972
Roundhouse, Chalk Farm	23 July 1972
"Rock at The Oval" Oval Cricket Ground, Kennington	
	16 September 1972
Great Hall, Imperial College (University of London)	
	3 February 1973
Sundown, Edmonton	16 February 1973
Crystal Palace Bowl	15 September 1973
Rainbow Theatre (formerly Astoria Theatre), Finsbury Park	
	26 January 1974
[unconfirmed venue], New Cross	April 1975*
Roundhouse, Chalk Farm	23 May 1976
Lowestoft (Suffolk)	
Royal Hotel	27 March 1965
Nautilus Club	9 September 1967
Loughborough (Leicestershire)	
Loughborough College	13 March 1965
Loughborough University Of Technology	8 February 1973
Luton (Bedfordshire)	
Ritz Theatre	23 November 1965
Maidstone (Kent)	
Royal Star Ballroom	11 April 1965
Malvern (Worcestershire/Hereford & Worcester)	
Winter Gardens	22 March 1966
Winter Gardens	5 July 1966
Winter Gardens	25 April 1967
Winter Gardens	5 September 1967
Manchester (Lancashire/Greater Manchester)	
University of Manchester	6 March 1965
Twisted Wheel	13 March 1965
Oasis Club *(Canc)*	25 June 1965
Oasis Club	7 August 1965
Oasis Club	24 October 1965
Palace Theatre *(Canc)*	5 December 1965
Jigsaw Club	19 March 1966
Manchester Technical College	29 April 1966
ABC Cinema, Ardwick	28 September 1966
New Century Hall	2 September 1967
University of Manchester*	2 March 1968
University Of Manchester *(Canc)*	27 November 1971
University of Manchester	1 March 1972
Hardrock	11 February 1973
Free Trade Hall	11 January 1974
March (Cambridgeshire)	
Marcam Hall	6 November 1965
Margate (Kent)	
Dreamland Ballroom	1 July 1965
Dreamland Ballroom	28 May 1966
Matlock (Derbyshire)	
Matlock Bath Pavilion	11 November 1967
Middleton (Lancashire/Greater Manchester)	
Co-op Hall* *(Canc)*	4 March 1966
Morecambe (Lancashire)	
Marine Ballroom, Central Pier	18 June 1965
Floral Hall Ballroom	28 July 1965
Marine Ballroom, Central Pier	22 October 1965
Mudeford (Dorset)	
Country Club	2 June 1965
Nelson (Lancashire)	
Imperial Ballroom	26 March 1966
New Brighton (Cheshire)	
Tower Ballroom	8 December 1965
Newbury (Berkshire)	
Corn Exchange	17 June 1966
Newcastle-upon-Tyne (Northumberland/Tyne & Wear)	
Top Rank Ballroom	19 July 1965
City Hall	1 October 1966
Club-Au-Go-Go	16 November 1967
Student Union, Newcastle Polytechnic	9 February 1973
City Hall	10 January 1973
Northampton (Northamptonshire)	
ABC Cinema	29 November 1965
Norwich (Norfolk)	
Oford Cellar	31 May 1967
[unconfirmed venue]	27 January 1968
University of East Anglia *(Canc)*	27 March 1968
[unconfirmed venue]	14 September 1968
Nottingham (Nottinghamshire)	
The Dungeon	2 April 1965
Sherwood Rooms	26 October 1965
Beachcomber Club	23 April 1967
Beachcomber Club	9 May 1967
Brittania Rowing Club	15 September 1967
Beachcomber Club*	10 November 1967
Brittania Rowing Club*	9 February 1968
Brittania Rowing Club*	24 March 1968
Oldham (Lancashire/Greater Manchester)	
Astoria Ballroom	25 March 1965
Oswestry (Shropshire)	
Plaza Ballroom	17 April 1965
Plaza Ballroom*	15 March 1968
Oxford (Oxfordshire)	
[unconfirmed venue] *(Canc)*	17 March 1965
University of Oxford, Queen's College	18 June 1966
Town Hall	23 December 1967
Oxford Polytechnic	14 February 1973
Peterborough (Huntingdon & Peterborough/Cambridgeshire)	
Palais	5 June 1965
Plymouth (Devon)	
ABC Cinema	4 December 1965
Poole (Dorset)	
Poole College	3 November 1967
Portsmouth (Hampshire)	
Guildhall	4 May 1965
The Birdcage, Kimbell's Ballroom, Southsea *(Canc)*	
	17 July 1965
Guildhall *(Canc)*	25 July 1965
Savoy Ballroom, Southsea	2 August 1965
Guildhall	30 November 1965
South Parade Pier, Southsea	17 March 1972

Live performances 1965–1980 — Appendix 3

South Parade Pier, Southsea *(Canc)*	17 February 1973
Guildhall	25 January 1974
Preston (Lancashire)	
[unconfirmed venue] *(Canc)*	29 March 1966
Purley (Oxfordshire/South Oxfordshire)	
Orchid Ballroom	3 November 1965
Ramsgate (Kent)	
Supreme Ballroom	8 July 1967
Reading (Berkshire)	
University of Reading*	14 October 1967
University of Reading*	2 February 1973
Richmond-Upon-Thames (Surrey)	
Crawdaddy Club, RAA Club House	28 March 1965
Crawdaddy Club, RAA Club House	27 June 1965
"5th National Jazz & Blues Festival", RAA Grounds	6 August 1965
Romford (Essex)	
Elm Park	6 June 1965
Romsey (Hampshire)	
Gaiety Ballroom	2 December 1967
Rugby (Warwickshire)	
Town Hall	8 September 1967
St. Albans (Hertfordshire)	
Market Hall	21 April 1967
Salisbury (Wiltshire)	
City Hall	23 June 1965
City Hall *(Canc)*	21 April 1966
City Hall	16 June 1966
City Hall	30 November 1967
Scunthorpe (Lincolnshire/Humberside)	
Drill Hall	26 June 1965
Baths Hall	19 February 1966
Sheffield (Yorkshire/South Yorkshire)	
Student Union, University of Sheffield	2 March 1972
City Hall	22 January 1974
Sincilbank (Lincolnshire)	
"Top Pop Festival" Lincoln City Football Grounds	30 May 1966
Slough (Buckinghamshire/Berkshire)	
Adelphi Cinema	30 April 1965
Adelphi Cinema	6 December 1965
Slough College	11 December 1967
Solihul (Warwickshire/West Midlands)	
Civic Hall	3 June 1967
Southall (Middlesex)	
Southall Community Centre	18 April 1965
Southampton (Hampshire)	
Guildhall	5 April 1965
ABC Cinema	26 November 1965
Top Rank Suite	4 May 1966
Gaumont Cinema	9 October 1966
University of Southampton	21 October 1967
Guildhall *(Canc)*	3 February 1972
University of Southampton	14 March 1972
Top Rank Suite	14 July 1972
Southend-On-Sea (Essex)	
Odeon Cinema	12 May 1965
Southport (Lancashire/Merseyside)	
Floral Hall	16 April 1966
Stafford (Staffordshire)	
Rugby Club	12 June 1965
Staines (Surrey)	
Town Hall	8 October 1965
Ricky Tick Club	11 March 1966
Stevenage (Hertfordshire)	
Locarno Ballroom	17 November 1965
Stockport (Cheshire/Greater Manchester)	
Manor Lounge *(Canc)*	10 June 1965
The Tabernacle, Hillgate	28 May 1967
The Tabernacle*, Hillgate	3 September 1967
Stockton-On-Tees (Durham/Cleveland)	
ABC Cinema	18 November 1965
ABC Cinema	29 September 1966
Stoke-On-Trent (Staffordshire)	
Gaumont Cinema, Hanley	8 May 1965
Heavy Steam Machine, Hanley	6 February 1973
Stourbridge (Worcestershire)	
Town Hall	20 October 1965
Town Hall	20 July 1966
Sunbury (Surrey)	
"8th National Jazz & Blues Festival", Kempton Park Racecourse	10 August 1968
Swindon (Wiltshire)	
McIlroys Ballroom	8 April 1965
Odeon Cinema	11 May 1965
Locarno Ballroom	30 September 1965
Tamworth (Staffordshire)	
Assembly Rooms	27 October 1967
Taunton (Somerset)	
Gaumont Cinmea	18 May 1965
Tolworth (Surrey)	
Toby Jug	5 February 1969
Tooting (▶ London)	
Torquay (Devon)	
Town Hall	15 July 1967
Truro (Cornwall)	
Town Hall	30 July 1967
Tunbridge Wells (Kent) aka Royal Tunbridge Wells	
Assembly Hall	27 April 1965
Uxbridge (Middlesex, now Greater London)	
Burton's Ballroom	23 March 1965
Burton's Ballroom	8 June 1965
Burton's Ballroom	3 June 1967
Walthamstow (now Waltham Forest, ▶ London)	
Warrington (Lancashire/Cheshire)	
Paar Hall	14 June 1965
Watford (Hertfordshire)	
Trade Union Hall	18 October 1965
Wembley (Middlesex/Brent, Greater London)	
"NME Poll-Winners Concert", Empire Pool	1 May 1966
"NME Poll-Winners Concert", Empire Pool *(Canc?)*	7 May 1967
Weston-super-Mare (Avon)	
Winter Gardens	17 October 1965
Winter Gardens	18 May 1968
Wimbledon (▶ London, now Merton)	
Windsor (Berkshire)	
Ricky Tick Club, Thames Hotel	16 April 1965
Ricky Tick Club, Thames Hotel	30 July 1965
Ricky Tick Club, Thames Hotel	7 October 1965
Ricky Tick Club, Thames Hotel	10 June 1966
"6th National Jazz & Blues Festival", Royal Windsor Racecourse *(Canc)*	30 July 1966
"7th National Jazz & Blues Festival", Royal Windsor Racecourse	13 August 1967
Woburn Abbey (Bedfordshire)	
"Festival of the Flower Children", Woburn Abbey Park	28 August 1967
Woking (Surrey)	
Atlanta Ballroom *(Canc)*	15 March 1965
Wolverhampton (Staffordshire/West Midlands)	
Gaumont Cinema	20 May 1965
Queen's Ballroom	25 October 1965

Appendix 3 Live performances 1965-1980

Queen's Ballroom	21 March 1966
College of Technology	30 March 1968
Civic Hall	14 January 1974
Woodstock (Oxfordshire)	
Blenheim Park	23 July 1967
Worcester (Worcestershire)	
University of Worcester *(Canc)*	5 February 1972
Worthing (Sussex/West Sussex)	
Pier Pavilion	17 June 1965
Assembly Hall	5 August 1965
Pier Pavilion	21 April 1966
Assembly Hall	21 July 1966
Pier Pavilion	23 March 1967
Assembly Hall	13 April 1967
Assembly Hall	24 August 1967
Assembly Hall	11 April 1968

Isle Of Man
Douglas

Palace Theatre *(Canc)*	28 July 1966
Palace Theatre	17 June 1967

Scotland
Given first are original county names as known prior to April 1 1974 followed by their current region names, if different.

Aberdeen (Aberdeenshire/Grampian)

Capitol Theatre	30 March 1965
Ayr (Ayrshire/Strathclyde)	
Ayr Ice Rink	16 July 1966
Cowdenbeath (Fife)	
Palais de Danse	15 July 1966
Dumfries (Dumfries/Galloway)	
Drill Hall	28 May 1965
Dunfermline (Fife)	
Kinema Ballroom	21 July 1965
Dundee (Angus/Tayside)	
Top 10 Club, Palais	23 May 1965
Dunbar (East Lothian)	
Victoria Ballroom	17 July 1966
Edinburgh (Mid-Lothian)	
Caley Cinema *(Canc)*	9 January 1974
Caley Cinema	29 January 1974
Elgin (Morayshire/Grampian)	
Town Hall	7 July 1966
Falkirk (Stirlingshire/Central)	
"Great Caledonian Express" Grangemouth	
	23 September 1972
Glasgow (Lanarkshire/Strathclyde)	
Paisley Ice Rink	27 May 1965
Barrowland Ballroom *(Canc)*	31 May 1965
Odeon Cinema	30 September 1966
Electric Garden *(Canc)*	4 October 1971
Apollo Theatre *(Canc)*	8 January 1974
Apollo Theatre	28 January 1974
Kirkcaldy (Fife)	
Raith Ballroom	21 May 1965
Raith Ballroom	8 July 1966
Montrose (Angus/Tayside)	
Locarno Ballroom	25 May 1965
Newtongrange (Mid-Lothian)	
New Hall	30 May 1965
Perth (Perthshire/Tayside)	
City Hall	22 May 1965*
City Hall	15 July 1966
Selkirk (Selkirkshire/Borders)	
Victoria Hall	19 May 1967

Stirling (Stirlingshire/Central)	
Plaza Ballroom *(Canc)*	23 May 1965
Wick (Caithness/Highland)	
Assembly Rooms	24 May 1965

Wales
Ammanford (Glamorgan/West Glamorgan)

Regal Ballroom	13 May 1966
Cardiff (Glamorgan/South Glamorgan)	
Capitol Theatre	19 May 1965
Capitol Theatre	8 October 1966
University of Cardiff	1 December 1967
Top Rank Suite	18 February 1973
Top Rank Suite	17 January 1974
Colwyn Bay (Flintshire/Clwyd)	
Pier	1 July 1967
Haverfordwest (Carmerthen/Dyfed)	
[unconfirmed venue]	25 November 1967
Llanelli (Carmerthen/Dyfed)	
Glen Ballroom	4 April 1968
Llandudno (Flintshire/Clwyd)	
The Pier *(Canc)*	15 August 1965
Neath (Glamorgan/West Glamorgan)	
Ritz Entertainments Club, Skewen	12 May 1966
Rhyl (Flintshire/Clwyd)	
Majestic Ballroom	11 October 1965
Swansea (Glamorgan/West Glamorgan)	
Top Rank Suite	6 October 1967
Top Rank Suite	12 February 1973

UNITED STATES

State/City/Venue	Date
Alabama	
Decatur	
Decatur High School Auditorium *(YB w/o Beck)*	
	3 November 1966
Arizona	
Phoenix	
VIP Club, Jaycees Hall	4 September 1965
TraveLodge	28 October 1971
Exhibition Hall, Arizona Civic Plaza	28 May 1975
Celebrity Theater	11 June 1976
Tempe (metropolitan Phoenix)	
Tempe Stadium	8 September 1976
Tucson	
Thrift City	21 August 1966
Community Center	9 August 1972
Arkansas	
Little Rock	
Robinson Auditorium	11 September 1965
Barton Coliseum *(YB w/o Beck)*	4 November 1966
Barton Coliseum	10 November 1972
Magnolia	
Southern State College Field House *(YB w/o Beck)*	
	2 November 1966
California	
Anaheim	
Anaheim Convention Center *(Canc)*	19 April 1969
Anaheim Stadium	12 September 1976
Avalon (Santa Catalina Island)	
Casino Terrace Ballroom	23 August 1966
Berkeley	
Berkeley Community Theater	14 August 1972
Greek Theater, University of California	

Live performances 1965-1980 — Appendix 3

Burbank	5 September 1980
Starlight Amphitheater	12 June 1976
Chico	
Chico Teen Center, Silver Dollar Fairgrounds	30 December 1965
Concord	
Concord Pavilion	4 September 1976
Fresno	
Warnor Theater	15 June 1976
Long Beach	
Long Beach Auditorium	29 October 1971
Long Beach Arena	6 May 1973
Los Angeles (▶ also Santa Monica)	
The Hulabaloo	5–7, 9 January 1966
Shrine Auditorium	26, 27 July 1968
Shrine Auditorium	2, 3 August 1968
Shrine Auditorium	29, 30 November 1968
Hollywood Palladium	13 August 1972
Hollywood Palladium	3 May 1973
Shrine Civic Auditorium	30 May 1975
Greek Theater	8, 9 September 1980
Marysville	
Skateland	30 December 1965
Oakland	
"Day On The Green #3", Oakland Stadium	5 June 1976
"Day On The Green #4", Oakland Stadium	6 June 1976
Pismo Beach	
Rose Garden Ballroom (YB w/o Beck)	31 August 1966*
Riverside	
The Haze (Canc)	18 April 1969
Sacramento	
Memorial Auditorium	8 January 1966
San Bernadino	
Swing Auditorium, National Orange Showgrounds	31 October 1971
Swing Auditorium, National Orange Showgrounds	11 August 1972
San Diego	
Conventional Hall (Canc)	29 August 1966
Palm Springs Pop Festival (Canc)	2 April 1969
Community Concourse	10 August 1972
San Diego Sports Arena	5 May 1973
Golden Hall, Convention & Performing Arts Center	29 May 1975
Golden Hall, Convention & Performing Arts Center	13 June 1976
Balboa Stadium (Canc)	11 September 1976
San Diego Sports Arena	13 September 1976
Open Air Amphitheater, San Diego State University	6 September 1980
San Francisco	
Carousel Ballroom (YB w/o Beck)	25 August 1966
Fillmore Auditorium	23 October 1966
Fillmore West	19–25 July 1968
Fillmore West	5–8 December 1968
Fillmore West (Canc)	10–13 April 1969
Winterland	30 October 1971
Winterland	28, 29 April 1973
Winterland	31 May 1975
San Jose	
San Jose Civic Auditorium (Canc)	30 August 1966
Santa Clara Fairgrounds (Canc)	20 April 1969
San Jose Civic Auditorium	12 August 1972
San Jose Civic Auditorium	1 May 1973
San Jose Civic Auditorium	1 June 1975
San Leandro	
Rollarena (YB w/o Beck)	26 August 1966
Santa Barbara	
Earl Warren Showgrounds (YB w/o Beck)	27 August 1966
Robertson Gymnasium, University of California	2 May 1973
Santa Barbara County Bowl	7 September 1980
Santa Monica (metropolitan Los Angeles)	
Santa Monica Civic Auditorium (YB w/o Beck)	7 September 1966
Stockton	
Stockton Civic Auditorium (YB w/o Beck)	1 September 1966
Ventura	
Ventura High School Auditorium (YB w/o Beck)	27 August 1966

Colorado

Colorado Springs	
City Auditorium	16 August 1972
Denver (also ▶ Morrison)	
Field House, Regis College	7 June 1975
Convention Center Complex (Canc)	24 July 1973
[unconfirmed venue]	September 1976*
Morrison	
Red Rocks Amphitheater (Canc)	10 September 1980

Connecticut

Bridgeport	
Kennedy Stadium (Canc)	19 July 1969
New Haven	
Woolsey Hall, Yale University	9 May 1969
New Haven Veterans Memorial Coliseum	4 May 1975
Shelton	
Pine Crest Country Club	23 August 1976
Waterbury	
Palace Theater	17 May 1972
Palace Theater	16 April 1973*
Palace Theater	12 October 1976
Westport	
Staples High School Auditorium	22 October 1966

District of Columbia

Washington (also ▶ Alexandria, Virginia; Landover & Laurel, Maryland)	
Washington Coliseum (YB w/o Beck)	26 November 1966
DAR Constitution Hall	21 October 1972
Georgetown University	31 March 1973
DAR Constitution Hall	14 November 1980

Florida

Dania	
Pirate's Cove, Pirate's World	18, 19 July 1969
Pirate's Cove, Pirate's World	3 November 1972
Jacksonville	
Jacksonville Raceway	21 October 1972
Fort Lauderdale	
Sunrise Musical Theater	3 October 1980
Hallendale (greater Miami)	
Gulf Stream Race Track	18 October 1975
Hollywood (greater Miami)	
Hollywood Speedway Sportatorium	20 October 1972
Hollywood Speedway Sportatorium	14 July 1973
Lakeland (greater Tampa)	
Lakeland Civic Center	15, 16 October 1975
Lakeland Civic Center	4 October 1980
Miami	
Thee Image	15, 16 November 1968
Thee Image (Canc)	28-30 March 1969

Appendix 3   Live performances 1965–1980

Miami Jai-Alai Fronton   3 December 1976
Orlando
Orlando Sports Stadium   5 August 1972
Tampa
Curtis Hixon Hall   4 August 1972
Curtis Hixon Hall   13 July 1973
Curtis Hixon Convention Center   4 December 1976

Georgia
Atlanta
Municipal Auditorium* (Canc)   11 September 1965
Municipal Auditorium* (Canc)   12 November 1972
Municipal Auditorium   16 July 1973
Municipal Auditorium (Canc)   28 July 1975
Fox Theater   16 July 1976
Fox Theater   5 October 1980

Hawaii
Honolulu
Honolulu International Center Exhibit Hall (YB w/o Beck)
                                                  4 September 1966
Honolulu International Center Arena   8 May 1973
Honolulu International Center Arena   30 July 1975

Illinois
Carbondale
SIU Arena, Southern Illinois University   18 November 1980
Champaign
Assembly Hall, University of Illinois-Champaign
                                                  17 November 1980
Chicago
Arie Crown Theater, McCormick Place   18 September 1965
Arie Crown Theater, McCormick Place   11 December 1965
Aragon Ballroom   22 January 1966
Civic Opera House   6 August 1966
'Lectric Theater   11 October 1968
Kinetic Playground (Canc)   21 February 1969
Kinetic Playground   14, 15 March 1969
Kinetic Playground (Canc*)   1, 2 August 1969
Arie Crown Theater, McCormick Place   13 May 1972
Arie Crown Theater, McCormick Place   8 August 1972
International Amphitheater   4 April 1973
Arie Crown Theater, McCormick Place   8 May 1975
Cominskey Park   10 July 1976
Granada Theater   19 November 1980
DeKalb
Field House, Northern Illinois University
                                                  8 November 1972
Peoria
Glen Oak Park Amphitheater   25 June 1980
Rockford
Rock River Roller Palace   11 December 1965

Indiana
Hamilton
Cold Springs Resort   12 August 1966
Indianapolis
Indiana Fairgrounds Coliseum (YB w/o Beck)
                                                  11 November 1966
Indiana Fairgrounds Coliseum   6 April 1973
Indianapolis Convention Center   2 July 1976
Monticello
Indiana Beach Ballroom   12 August 1966
Richmond
Richmond Civic Hall (YB w/o Beck)   21 November 1966
Terre Haute
Memorial Field House, Indiana State University (YB w/o Beck)
                                                  9 November 1966
Valpariso
Valpariso Armory   21 January 1966

Iowa
Arnolds Park
Roof Garden Ballroom   9 August 1966
Cedar Rapids
Danceland Ballroom   18 December 1965
Clear Lake
Surf Ballroom   19 December 1965
Davenport
Col Ballroom   5 August 1966
RKO Orpheum Theater (YB w/o Beck)   8 November 1966
Des Moines
Iowa State Fairgrounds   25 July 1976

Kansas
Chanute
Chanute Auditorium (YB w/o Beck)   7 November 1966
Emporia
Renfro's   15 December 1965
Kansas City
Memorial Building Auditorium (YB w/o Beck)
                                                  5 November 1966
Wichita
Cotillion Ballroom   15 August 1966

Kentucky
Bowling Green
Diddle Arena, University of Western Kentucky (YB w/o Beck)
                                                  15 November 1966
Frankfort
Capitol Plaza (Canc)   12 May 1972
Paintsville
Paintsville High School Gymnasium (YB w/o Beck)
                                                  14 November 1966

Louisiana
Alexandria
Parrish Coliseum, Louisiana State University (YB w/o Beck)
                                                  1 November 1966
Baton Rouge
Independence Auditorium (Canc)   10 November 1968
New Orleans
The Warehouse   11 November 1972
Ted Gormley Stadium City Park   26 July 1975
The Warehouse   8 December 1976

Maryland
Annapolis
Annapolis National Guard Armory   15 January 1966
US Naval Academy   17 October 1976
Baltimore
Eudowood Gardens   15 January 1966
Baltimore Civic Center (YB w/o Beck)   10 September 1966
Baltimore Civic Center Arena (YB w/o Beck)
                                                  13 November 1966
Baltimore Civic Center   16 March 1969
Columbia
Merriweather Post Pavilion   15 July 1973
Landover (greater Washington DC)
Capital Centre   21, 21 August 1976
Laurel (greater Washington DC)
"Laurel Jazz & Pop Festival", Laurel Race Course
                                                  12 July 1969

Live performances 1965–1980 — Appendix 3

Massachusetts
Amherst
The Cage, University of Massachusetts 9 October 1980
Boston
Boston Tea Party 26–29 June 1968
Boston Tea Party 22–24 October 1968
Symphony Hall *(Canc)* 2 March 1969
Boston Tea Party 6–8 May 1969
Music Hall 8 December 1971
Aquarius/Orpheum Theater 18 May 1972
Aquarius/Orpheum Theater 24 October 1972
Music Hall 28 March 1973
Music Hall 3 May 1975
Music Hall 10 October 1976
Lowell
Commodore Ballroom 22 July 1969
South Yarmouth (Cape Cod)
Cape Cod Coliseum 27 August 1976
Cape Cod Coliseum 11 October 1980
Springfield
Springfield Civic Center 26 April 1975
Worcester
The Comic Strip 21 October 1966
Worcester Memorial Auditorium *(Canc)* 28 February 1969

Michigan
Alma
Alma College 12 October 1968
Ann Arbor
Fifth Dimension 7 July 1968
Detroit
Michigan State Fair Coliseum *(YB w/o Beck)* 18–20 November 1966
Grande Ballroom 5, 6 July 1968
Grande Ballroom 1-3 November 1968
Grande Ballroom 21, 22 March 1969
Grande Ballroom 26 July 1969
Grande Ballroom *(Canc)* 25, 27 July 1969
Cobo Arena 7 May 1972
Ford Auditorium 7 November 1972
Cobo Hall Arena* 8 April 1973
Masonic Auditorium 9 May 1975
Masonic Auditorium 3 July 1976
Cobo Arena 16 November 1980
Flint
IMA Auditorium 12 December 1965
Manitou Beach
Green's Pavilion, Lakeview Park 10 August 1966
Saginaw
Daniel's Den 26 December 1965

Minnesota
Detroit Lakes
Detroit Lakes Pavilion 8 August 1966
Minneapolis
Dayton's Minneapolis Auditorium 5 August 1966
Minneapolis Labor Temple 23 March 1969
Minneapolis Armory *(Canc)* 14 May 1972
Minneapolis Armory 5 April 1973
Parade Stadium 26 June 1976
Mentor
Maple Lake Pavilion 7 August 1966

Mississippi
Jackson
City Auditorium 15 July 1976

Missouri
Kansas City
Music Hall *(Canc)* 5 November 1969
Arrowhead Stadium 23 July 1976
St. Louis
Kiel Auditorium *(YB w/o Beck)* 10 November 1966
Kiel Auditorium *(Canc)* 22 February 1969
Kiel Auditorium *(Canc)* 20 May 1972
Kiel Auditorium 3 April 1973
Ambassador Theater 11 May 1975
"Superjam '76", Busch Stadium 29 June 1976

Montana
Great Falls
4-H Building, Montana State Fairgrounds 14 August 1966

New Hampshire
Durham
Fieldhouse, University Of New Hampshire 15 April 1973
University Of New Hampshire 13 October 1976

New Jersey
Asbury Park
Casino Arena *(Canc)* 24 July 1976
Cherry Hill
Cherry Hill Arena *(Canc)* 30 March 1973
Passaic
Capitol Theater 27 October 1972
Capitol Theater 30 March 1973
Capitol Theater 27 April 1975
Capitol Theater 7 October 1980

New Mexico
Albuquerque
Civic Auditorium 15 August 1972
University Of New Mexico 8 June 1975
Santa Fe
J.P.'s Palace 17 August 1966*

New York
Albany
Palace Theater 1 April 1973
Palace Theater 29 August 1976
Bethel
"Woodstock Music & Art Fair" *(Canc)* 17 August 1969
Buffalo (▶ also Wheatfield)
Century Theater 30 October 1972
Century Theater 24 April 1975
Buffalo Memorial Auditorium 2 September 1976
Commack (Long Island)
Long Island Arena 4 May 1972
Ellenville (The Catskills)
Tamarack Lodge 21 July 1969
Flushing (Queens)
Singer Bowl, Flushing Meadow Park 13 July 1969
Hempstead (Long Island)
Physical Fitness Center, Hofstra University 28 October 1972
Playhouse, Hofstra University 29 April 1975
New York
The Rolling Stone 17 September 1965
Fillmore East 14, 15 June 1968
"Daytop Under The Stars", Daytop Village, Staten Island 16 June 1968
The Scene 18–23 June 1968
Fillmore East 18, 19 October 1968

217

Appendix 3 Live performances 1965–1980

Fillmore East	31 October 1968
Fillmore East	2, 3 May 1969
Fillmore East	3 July 1969
Wolman Memorial Rink, Central Park	14 July 1969
Academy of Music	5, 6 November 1971
Carnegie Hall	5 May 1972
Gaelic Park (The Bronx)	2 August 1972
Felt Forum, Madison Square Garden	9, 10 April 1973
Avery Fisher Hall, Lincoln Center for the Performing Arts	
	30 April–1 May 1975
The Palladium	8 & 18 October 1976
The Palladium	12 November 1980

Plattsburgh
Fieldhouse, State University of New York	
	10 October 1980

Randalls Island
"New York Pop Festival", Downing Stadium	
	5 July 1969

Rochester
Rochester Institute of Technology	29 October 1972
Community War Memorial	7 April 1973
Auditorium Theater	25 April 1975

Schnectady
Aerodome	2 July 1969

Stony Brook (Long Island)
Gymnasium, State University of New York at Stony Brook	
	16 February 1969
Gymnasium, State University of New York at Stony Brook	
	7 March 1969

Syracuse
War Memorial Auditorium	14 October 1976
Lowe's State Theater	29 March 1973

Uniondale (Long Island)
Nassau Veterans Memorial Coliseum	25, 26 August 1976

West Hempstead (Long Island)
Island Garden	7 March 1969

Wheatfield
The Peppermint Stick	25 December 1965

North Carolina
Charlotte
Charlotte Park Centre	12 July 1973
Charlotte Park Centre	12 December 1976

Greensboro
Coliseum	22 October 1972

Winston-Salem
Memorial Coliseum (YB w/o Beck)	25 November 1966

North Dakota
Fargo
North Dakota State University	27 June 1976

Ohio
Akron
Akron Civic Theater (YB w/o Beck)	12 November 1966

Athens
Grover Center, Ohio University (YB w/o Beck)	
	12 November 1966

Berea
Union Ballroom, Baldwin-Wallace College (YB w/o Beck)	
	2 December 1966

Cincinnati
Music Hall (Canc)	4 November 1971
Riverfront Coliseum	30 June 1976

Cleveland (▶ also University Heights)
La Cave	9, 10 July 1968
The Grande	22, 23 November 1968
The Grande	8 March 1969
Allen Theater	6 May 1972
Music Hall	7 May 1975
Municipal Stadium	11 July 1976

Columbus
Veterans Memorial Auditorium	2 April 1973

Dayton
O'Hara Arena	11 May 1972

Lima
Springbrook Gardens Teen Center (YB w/o Beck)	
	4 December 1966

Mentor
Mentor Hullabaloo	13 October 1968

University Heights (metropolitan Cleveland)
Gymnasium, John Carroll Univ	12 April 1973

Oklahoma
Bartlesville
Civic Center (YB w/o Beck)	6 November 1966

Oklahoma City
Oklahoma State Fairgrounds grandstand	3 September 1965
Wedgewood Amusement Park	19, 20 August 1966
[unconfirmed venue]	10 November 1968
Oklahoma Civic Center Music Hall	13 June 1975
Oklahoma Civic Center Music Hall	21 July 1976

Tulsa
Tulsa Assembly Center Exhibit Hall	18 August 1966
Tulsa Assembly Center Arena (YB w/o Beck)	
	6 November 1966
Tulsa Assembly Center	14 June 1975

Oregon
Eugene
Lane County Fairground Ex. Building	30 August 1980

Medford
Medford Armory	16 June 1976

Portland
Paramount Northwest Theater	18 August 1972
Paramount Northwest Theater	27 April 1973
Paramount Northwest Theater	3 June 1975
Paramount Northwest Theater	18 June 1976
Paramount Northwest Theater	29 August 1980

Salem
Salem Armory-Auditorium (YB w/o Beck)	3 September 1966

Pennsylvania
Philadelphia (also ▶ Upper Darby)
Electric Factory	25, 26 October 1968
"1st Spectrum Summer Music Festival", The Spectrum	
	11 July 1969
The Spectrum	19 May 1972
The Spectrum	11 July 1973
The Spectrum	2 May 1975
The Spectrum	9 October 1976
The Spectrum	8 October 1980

Pittsburgh
Pittsburgh Civic Arena	28 December 1965
Pittsburgh Civic Arena (YB w/o Beck)	22 November 1966
Stanley Theater	1 August 1972
Syria Mosque	11 April 1973
Stanley Theater	6 May 1975
Stanley Theater	July 1976*
Civic Arena (Canc)	1 October 1976
Stanley Theater	15 November 1980

Reading
Astor Theater	31 August 1976

Live performances 1965–1980 — Appendix 3

Scranton
CYO Hall* (Canc) — 16 September 1965
Upper Darby (metropolitan Philadelphia)
Tower Theater — 26 October 1972

Rhode Island
Newport
"Newport Jazz Festival", Festival Field — 4 July 1969
Providence
Palace Theater — 25 October 1972
Providence Civic Center — 4 April 1973
Providence Civic Center — 7 October 1976

Tennessee
Cookeville
Memorial Gymnasium, Tennessee Technological University, Cookeville (YB w/o Beck) — 16 November 1966
Martin
Field House, University of Tennessee (YB w/o Beck) — 17 November 1966
Nashville
Municipal Auditorium — 11 December 1976
Knoxville
Knoxville Civic Coliseum — 4 November 1972
Memphis
Skateland Frayser — 10 September 1965
The Clearpool — 10 September 1965
Mid-South Coliseum — 11 May 1972
Ellis Auditorium — 17 July 1976

Texas
Amarillo
Checkmate Young Adult Club — 13 August 1966
Tri-State Fairground Coliseum (Canc?) — 28 October 1966
Austin
Austin Municipal Auditorium — 20 July 1976
Austin Municipal Auditorium — 12 September 1980
Beaumont
Municipal Auditorium (YB w/o Beck) — 31 October 1966
Dallas
Dallas Memorial Auditorium — 29 October 1966
Lou Ann's — 17 July 1968
McFarlin Memorial Auditorium Southern Methodist University — 9 November 1968
McFarlin Memorial Auditorium Southern Methodist University (Canc) — 26 April 1969
Majestic Theater — 7 August 1972
State Fair Coliseum (Canc) — 21 July 1973
Dallas Memorial Auditorium — 11 June 1975
Moody Coliseum, Southern Methodist University — 18 July 1976
Dallas Convention Center Arena — 13 September 1980
El Paso
El Paso Civic Center — 9 June 1975
Fort Worth
Will Rogers Memorial Coliseum — 27 December 1965
Harlingen
Municipal Auditorium — 30 October 1966
Houston
The Catacombs — 12, 13 July 1968
Music Hall — 8 November 1968
Continental Ballroom (Canc) — 27 April 1969
Music Hall — 6 August 1972
Civic Center (Canc) — 19 July 1972
Music Hall — 15 June 1975
Hofheinz Pavilion — 19 July 1976
Sam Houston Coliseum — 14 September 1980

San Antonio
Municipal Auditorium (Canc) — 20 July 1973
Municipal Auditorium — 12 June 1975

Vermont
Burlington
Memorial Auditorium (Canc) — 22 November 1968

Virginia
Alexandria
Alexandria Roller Rink — 23 December 1965
Alexandria Roller Rink (YB w/o Beck) — 9 September 1966
Alexandria Roller Rink — 20 October 1968
Alexandria Roller Rink — 1 March 1969

Washington
Seattle
Seattle Center Coliseum — 1 January 1966
Eagles Auditorium — 27 November 1968
Seattle Center Arena (Canc) — 3 April 1969
Paramount Northwest Theater — 18 August 1972
Seattle Center Arena — 26 April 1973
Paramount Northwest Theater — 4 June 1975
Paramount Northwest Theater — 17 June 1976
Kingdome — 3 September 1976
Seattle Center Arena — 2 September 1980
Olympia
Evergreen Ballroom — 31 December 1965*
Spokane
Spokane Coliseum (Canc) — 5 April 1969
Opera House — 31 August 1980
Tacoma
Univ of Puget Sound Field House — 31 December 1965

Washington, D.C. (▶ District Of Columbia)

West Virginia
Beckley
Raleigh County Armory (YB w/o Beck) — 24 November 1966
Charleston
Charleston Civic Center (YB w/o Beck) — 24 November 1966
Huntington
Cabell County Memorial Field House (YB w/o Beck) — 27 November 1966

Wisconsin
Milwaukee
Riverside Theater — 10 May 1972
Auditorium Theater — 10 May 1973
Milwaukee Arena — 24 June 1976

Appendix 4

RADIO & TV APPEARANCES 1965–1980

This appendix lists all known radio and TV appearances by Jeff Beck in the years 1965 to 1980. Please note that the entries are listed chronologically based on the actual (first) *transmission* dates. This index omits radio and TV appearances that have been cancelled or not aired, also radio and TV performances where Jeff Beck was unable to appear. Also not included are the many syndicated radio broadcasts in the USA of previously aired BBC recordings. It should also be specifically noted that many *non-performing* TV- and radio appearances Jeff Beck has done over the years, particularly in the United States, have proven impossible to fully document and are not included in this list. An asterisk (*) indicates performed songs not confirmed. Please refer to the general text for futher information.

Radio appearances:

1965

Tmx date	Rec date	Location	Programme	Songs	Country	Channel
12 March	8 March*	EMI, London	"The Friday Spectacular"	For Your Love*	UK	Radio Lux
20 March	16 March	Playhouse, London	"Saturday Club"	I'm Not Talking 2'30	UK	BBC Light
				Guitar Boogie 2'27		
				My Girl Sloopy 3'30		
				For Your Love 2'18		
				Just Like I Treat You 2'36		
23 March	23 March	Studiolympia	"Pop Inn"	Interview	UK	BBC Light
29 March	29 March	London*	"Teen Scene"	[unknown]	UK	Radio London
10 April	22 March	Maida Vale 4, London	"Top Gear"	Someone To Love Me 1'35	UK	BBC Light
				I Ain't Got You 2'00		
				For Your Love 2'15		
				I'm Not Talkin' 2'30		
				Steeled Blues 2'00		

• [BBC Transcription Service: "Top Of The Pops" # 23 (7 May 1965) with *I Ain't Got You, For Your Love* and *I'm Not Talking*]

Tmx date	Rec date	Location	Programme	Songs	Country	Channel
11 April	6 April*	London*	"Ready–Steady–Radio"	[unknown]	UK	Radio Lux
17 April	9 April	Piccadilly 1, London	"Saturday Swings"	Too Much Monkey Business 2'28	UK	BBC Light
				Hush a Bye 1'58		
				I'm A Man 4'00		
				Runaround [Bottle Up And Go] 2'37		
				For Your Love 2'18		
				Spoonful 3'23		
30 April	30 April	Playhouse, London	"Joe Loss Pop Show"	For Your Love 2'12	UK	BBC Light
				I Ain't Done Wrong 3'05		
				I'm Not Talking 2'21		
1 June	1 June	Paris Cinema, London	"Pop Inn"	Interview only	UK	BBC Light
5 June	1 June	Maida Vale 5, London	"Saturday Club"	I Wish You Would 2'38	UK	BBC Light
				Steeled Blues 2'33		
				Heart Full of Soul 2'23		
				Respectable 3'02		

• [BBC Transcription Service: "Top Of The Pops" # 32 (7 July 1965) with *I Wish You Would* and *Heart Full of Soul*]

Tmx date	Rec date	Location	Programme	Songs	Country	Channel
8 June	5 June	Paris Cinema, London	"The Top Ten Game"	Interview	UK	BBC Light
12 June	4 June	Maida Vale 4, London	"Saturday Swings"	Pretty Girl 2'02	UK	BBC Light
				Steeled Blues 2'38		
				Heart Full of Soul 2'23		
				I'm Not Talking 2'27		
				I Ain't Done Wrong 2'55		
				Louise 3'00		
20 June	9 June	Paris Cinema, London	"The Ken Dodd Show"	Heart Full of Soul 2'23	UK	BBC Light
25 June	21 June*	EMI, London	"The Friday Spectacular"	Heart Full of Soul*	UK	Radio Lux
26 June	9 June	Aeolian 2, London	"Top Gear"	I Ain't Done Wrong 3'05	UK	BBC Light
				I've Been Trying 2'35		
				Heart Full of Soul 2'25		
				Guitar Boogie 2'30		

• [BBC Transcription Service; "Top Of The Pops" # 35 (30 July 1965) with *I Ain't Done Wrong* and *Heart Full of Soul*]

Tmx date	Rec date	Location	Programme	Songs	Country	Channel
2 July	2 June	Playhouse, London	"Joe Loss Pop Show"	Heart Full of Soul 2'19	UK	BBC Light
				For Your Love 2'11		
				I Ain't Got You 1'54		

• [BBC Transcription Service: "Top Of The Pops" # 32 (9 July 1965) and # 35 (30 July 1965) with *For Your Love* (sources unconfirmed)]

Tmx date	Rec date	Location	Programme	Songs	Country	Channel
4 July	3 July	Playhouse, London	"Easy Beat"	I Ain't Done Wrong 2'55	UK	BBC Light
				Heart Full of Soul 2'20		
11 July	6 July	London	"Ready–Steady–Radio"	[unknown]	UK	Radio Lux

Radio & TV appearances — **Appendix 4**

Tmx date	Rec date	Location	Programme	Songs	Country	Channel
8 Aug*	6 Aug	5th Nat.J&B, Richmond	"Ready–Steady–Radio"	[unknown]	UK	Radio Lux
13 Aug	9 Aug	Playhouse, Manchester	"The Beat Show"	Heart Full of Soul 2'22 Love Me Like I Love You 2'55 I Ain't Done Wrong 2'45	UK	BBC Light
14 Aug	5 Aug	Maida Vale 4, London	"Saturday Swings"	I Ain't Done Wrong 2'56 Hush A Bye 1'45 San-Ho-Zay 2'48 Heart Full of Soul 2'20 I've Been Trying 3'13 Love Me Like I Love You 3'42	UK	BBC Light
30 Aug	6 Aug	Playhouse, London	"You Really Got ..."	I Wish You Would 2'34 For Your Love 2'21 Love Me Like I Love You 2'56 I'm A Man 4'31 Too Much Monkey Business 2'29 Heart Full of Soul 2'29	UK	BBC Light

• [BBC Transcription Service: "Top Of The Pops" # 45 (8 October 1965) with *Love Me Like I Love You*, *I'm A Man* and *Too Much Monkey Business*]

Tmx date	Rec date	Location	Programme	Songs	Country	Channel
2 Oct	27 Sept	Aeolian 1, London	"Saturday Club"	My Girl Sloopy 2'15 Evil Hearted You 2'20 The Stumble 1'55 Still I'm Sad 2'55 The Train Kept A-Rollin' 2'45	UK	BBC Light

• [BBC Transcription Service: "Top Of The Pops" # 49 (11 November 1965) with *Evil Hearted You*, *Still I'm Sad* and *My Girl Sloopy*]

Tmx date	Rec date	Location	Programme	Songs	Country	Channel
7 Oct	4 Oct	Playhouse, Manchester	"The Beat Show"	Still I'm Sad 2'53 Heart Full of Soul 2'22 Evil Hearted You 2'20	UK	BBC Light
10 Oct	9 Oct	Playhouse, London	"Easy Beat"	Evil Hearted You 2'15 Still I'm Sad 2'55	UK	BBC Light
18 Oct	8 Oct	S2, Broadcast House	"This Must Be The Place"	For Your Love 2'20 Heart Full of Soul 2'25 Still I'm Sad 3'00 Evil Hearted You 2'25	UK	BBC Light
27 Dec	16 Nov	Brdcst. House, London	"Sound of Boxing Day"	The Train Kept A-Rollin' 2'41 Mister You're A Better Man ... 3'12 Smokestack Lightning 5'04 Still I'm Sad 3'09	UK	BBC Light

• [BBC Transcription Service: "Top Of The Pops" # 62 (4 February 1966) with *Smokestack Lightning*, *Mister You're A Better Man* and *The Train Kept A-Rollin'*]

Tmx date	Rec date	Location	Programme	Songs	Country	Channel
[unknown]	[unknown]	London*	[unconfirmed]	The Train Kept A-Rollin' Mister You're A Better Man ...	UK	[unknown]

1966

Tmx date	Rec date	Location	Programme	Songs	Country	Channel
22 Feb	22 Feb	Paris Cinema, London	"Pop Inn"	Interview	UK	BBC Light
5 March	28 Feb	Playhouse, London	"Saturday Club"	Mister You're A Better Man ... 3'05 Shapes Of Things 2'20 I've Been Trying 3'10 Dust My Blues 2'55	UK	BBC Light

• [BBC Transcription Service: "Top Of The Pops" # 71 (8 April 1966) with *Mister You're A Better Man Than I*, *Shapes Of Things* and *Dust My Blues*]

Tmx date	Rec date	Location	Programme	Songs	Country	Channel
13 March	12 March	Paris Cinema, London	"Easy Beat"	Mister You're A Better Man 3'05 Shapes Of Things 2'20	UK UK	BBC Light BBC Light
4 May	4 May	Playhouse, London	"Parade Of The Pops"	Shapes Of Things 2'15 Mister You're A Better Man 3'05	UK	BBC Light
21 May	6 May	Piccadilly 1, London	"Saturday Swings"	Jeff's Boogie 2'22 Mister You're A Better Man ... 3'11 The Sun Is Shining 3'33 Over Under Sideways Down 2'11 Baby, Scratch My Back 3'15 Shapes Of Things 2'24	UK	BBC Light

• [BBC Transcription Service: "Top Of The Pops" # 81 (17 June 1966) with *Scratch My Back*, *Over Under Sideways Down*, *The Is Shining* (3 vocal verse edit) and *Shapes of Things*]

Tmx date	Rec date	Location	Programme	Songs	Country	Channel
31 May	31 May	Paris Cinema, London	"Pop Inn"	Interview	UK	BBC Light
12 June	11 June	Paris Cinema, London	"Easy Beat"	Rack My Mind 3'05 Over Under Sideways Down 2'10	UK	BBC Light

Appendix 4   Radio & TV appearances

Tmx date	Rec date	Location	Programme	Songs	Country	Channel
1 July	9 June	Paris Cinema, London	"Joe Loss Pop Show"	Over Under Sideways Down 2'15 Shapes Of Things 2'25 Jeff's Boogie 2'10	UK	BBC Light
10 Sept	8–9 Sept*	USA	"Don Moss On The ..."	Interview	UK	Radio Lux

1967

Tmx date	Rec date	Location	Programme	Songs	Country	Channel
18 March	7 March	Playhouse, London	"Saturday Club"	Let Me Love You Baby 3'10 Stone Crazy 3'25 I Ain't Superstitious 1'42 Hi Ho Silver Lining 2'55 (I Know) I'm Losing You 2'15	UK	BBC Light

• [BBC Transcription Service: "Top Of The Pops" # ? (ca. April 1967) with Stone Crazy, Hi Ho Silver Lining and (I Know) I'm Losing You]

Tmx date	Rec date	Location	Programme	Songs	Country	Channel
2 May	2 May	Paris Cinema, London	"Pop Inn"	interview	UK	BBC Light
15 May	15 May	Playhouse, London	"Monday, Monday"	Let Me Love You 3'25 Rock My Plimsoul 3'10 Hi Ho Silver Lining 2'55	UK	BBC Light
8 July	4 July	Playhouse, London	"Saturday Club"	Rock My Plimsoul 4'18 This Morning 5'10 Tallyman 2'52	UK	BBC Light

• [BBC Transcription Service: "Top Of The Pops" # 141 (11 August 1967) with Rock My Plimsoul, This Morning and Tallyman]

Tmx date	Rec date	Location	Programme	Songs	Country	Channel
[Syndic'ted]	14 July	Bush House, London	"The Young Scene" # 13	Interview	UK	BBC Trans
11 Aug	14 July	Knsngtn House, London	"Top Of The Pops" # 141	Interview	UK	BBC Trans
16 Oct	9 Oct	Paris Cinema, London	"David Symonds Show"	Rock My Plimsoul 3'30	UK	BBC Radio 1
19 Oct	9 Oct	Paris Cinema, London	"David Symonds Show"	Let Me Love You 3'06	UK	BBC Radio 1
20 Oct	9 Oct	Paris Cinema, London	"David Symonds Show"	Walking By The Railings 2'21	UK	BBC Radio 1
5 Nov	1 Nov	Maida Vale 4, London	"Top Gear"	I Ain't Superstitious Beck's Bolero Loving You Is Sweeter Than Ever You Shook Me You'll Never Get To Heaven	UK	BBC Radio 1

• [BBC Transcription Service: "Top Of The Pops" # ? (ca. Dec 1967) with I Ain't Superstitious, Loving You Is ... and You'll Never Get To Heaven]

1968

Tmx date	Rec date	Location	Programme	Songs	Country	Channel
15 Feb	15 Feb	Brdcst. House, London	"Late Night Extra"	Interview 2'45	UK	BBC Radio 1/2
17 Feb	15 Feb	Brdcst. House, London	"Scene And Heard"	Interview	UK	BBC Radio 1
26 June*	26 June*	Boston, USA	[unconfirmed]	Interview	USA	WBCN-FM
20 July	19 July	San Francisco, USA	"Scene And Heard"	Interview	UK	BBC Radio 1
17 Aug	15 Aug	London	"Scene And Heard"	Interview	UK	BBC Radio 1
29 Sept	17 Sept	Piccadilly 1, London	"Top Gear"	You Shook Me Shapes Of Things Sweet Little Angel Mother's Old Rice Pudding	UK	BBC Radio 1

• [BBC Transcription Service: "Top Of The Pops" # ? (October 1968) with Shapes of Things, Sweet Little Angel and Mother's Old Rice Pudding]

Tmx date	Rec date	Location	Programme	Songs	Country	Channel
Oct	Oct	Stockholm, Sweden	[unconfirmed]	Interview	Sweden	SR P3
3 Nov	17 Sept	Piccadilly 1, London	"Top Gear"	Rock My Plimsoul	UK	BBC Radio 1
(syndic'ted)	17 Sept	Piccadilly 1, London	"Progressive Pop"	Sweet Little Angel	UK	BBC Trans

1969

Tmx date	Rec date	Location	Programme	Songs	Country	Channel
22 March*	22 March*	Detroit, USA	[unconfirmed]	Interview	USA	WKNR-FM
26 July*	26 July	Detroit, USA	[unconfirmed]	Interview	USA	WKNR-FM

1972

Tmx date	Rec date	Location	Programme	Songs	Country	Channel
14 Jan	14 Dec '71	BBC Studio T1, London	"Sound Of The Seventies"	Going Down Got The Feeling	UK	BBC Radio 1
11 Feb	14 Dec '71	BBC Studio T1, London	"Sound Of The Seventies"	Ice Cream Cakes	UK	BBC Radio 1

Radio & TV appearances — **Appendix 4**

Tmx date	Rec date	Location	Programme	Songs	Country	Channel
8 July	29 June	Paris Cinema, London	"In Concert"	New Ways/Train Train Ice Cream Cakes Going Down Definitely Maybe Let Me Love You Morning Dew Ain't No Sunshine Tonight I'll Be Staying Here With You	UK	BBC Radio 1
14 Oct*	14 Oct	London	"Scene And Heard"	Interview	UK	BBC Radio 1
29 Oct	29 June	Paris Cinema, London	"The BBC Presents"	Same as BBC "In Concert" with Tonight I'll Be Staying Here With You omitted.	USA	[syndicated]

1973

Tmx date	Rec date	Location	Programme	Songs	Country	Channel
12 Jan	14 Dec '71	BBC Studio T1, London	"Sequence"	Going Down	UK	BBC Radio 1
June*	14 June	Paris, France	"Musicorama"	[unknown]	France	Radio Europe 1

1974

Tmx date	Rec date	Location	Programme	Songs	Country	Channel
10 March	5 Feb	London	"My Top 12"	Interview	UK	BBC Radio 1
[syndic'ted]	5 Feb	London	"Pop Profile"	Interview	UK	BBC Trans
9 Sept	26 Jan	Rainbow, London	"Rock Around The World"	Laughalong Lady Jizz Whizz/Morning Dew Superstition Your Lovemaker's Coming Home You Shook Me/Rainbow Boogie	USA	[syndicated]

1975

Tmx date	Rec date	Location	Programme	Songs	Country	Channel
1 June	18–21 Apr.	Boston, USA	"Rock Around The World"	Interview	USA	[syndicated]

1976

Tmx date	Rec date	Location	Programme	Songs	Country	Channel
16 Sept	12 Sept	Anaheim, USA	[unconfirmed]	Darkness/Earth In Search of A Sun Freeway Jam Scatterbrain Diamond Dust	USA	[local FM]
31 Oct	10 Oct*	Boston, USA	"Rock Around The World"	Interview	USA	[syndicated]

1979

Tmx date	Rec date	Location	Programme	Songs	Country	Channel
July*	5 July	Amsterdam, Holland	[unconfirmed]	Rock 'n' Roll Jelly School Days Loupsy Lou	Holland	FM-Radio VARA

1980

Tmx date	Rec date	Location	Programme	Songs	Country	Channel
11 July	July*	London	"Roundtable"	Interview	UK	BBC Radio 1
18 Sept	June*	Los Angeles	"Modern Music"	Interview	USA	[syndicated]
Oct*	Sept*	Los Angeles	"Innerview"	Interview	USA	[syndicated]

Appendix 4 — Radio & TV appearances

TV appearances:

1965

Tmx date	Shoot date	Location	Programme	Songs	Country	Channel
18 March	18 March	BBC, Manchester	"Top Of The Pops"	For Your Love	UK	BBC 1
18 March	18 March	TV Centre, Manchester	"Scene At 6:30"	For Your Love	UK	Granada TV
19 March	19 March	Kingsway, London	"Ready, Steady, Go!"	For Your Love	UK	Rediffusion
25 March	25 March	BBC, Manchester	"Top Of The Pops"	For Your Love	UK	BBC 1
25 March	24 March	TWW Centre, Bristol	"Discs-A-Go-Go"	For Your Love*	UK	TWW
1 April	1 April	BBC, Manchester	"Top Of The Pops"	For Your Love	UK	BBC 1
2 April	2 April	Wembley	"Ready, Steady, Goes Live!"	For Your Love*	UK	Rediffusion
9 April	9 April	Wembley	"Ready, Steady, Goes Live!"	For Your Love*	UK	Rediffusion
16 April	16 April	Wembley	"Ready, Steady, Goes Live!"	For Your Love*	UK	Rediffusion
4 June	4 June	Wembley	"Ready, Steady, Go!"	Heart Full of Soul*	UK	Rediffusion
11 June	11 June*	Wembley	"Ready, Steady, Go!"	Heart Full of Soul*	UK	Rediffusion
14 June	14 June*	TV Centre, Manchester	"Scene At 6:30"	Heart Full of Soul*	UK	Granada TV
19 June	13 June	Alpha, Birmingham	"Thank Your Lucky Stars"	Heart Full of Soul	UK	ABC TV
30 June	30 June	TWW Centre, Bristol	"Discs-A-Go-Go"	Heart Full of Soul*	UK	TWW
8 July	8 July	BBC TV Centre, London	"Top Of The Pops"	Heart Full of Soul	UK	BBC 1
9 July	6 July	Wembley	"Ready, Steady, Go!"	Heart Full of Soul*	UK	Rediffusion
30 July	30 July	Wembley	"Ready, Steady, Go!"	My Girl Sloopy*	UK	Rediffusion
27 Aug	27 Aug	Wembley	"Ready, Steady, Go!"	[unconfirmed]	UK	Rediffusion
23 Sept	10–11 Aug	Twickenham, London	"Shindig!"	Heart Full of Soul / For Your Love	USA	ABC TV
28 Sept	28 Sept	TV Centre, Manchester	"Scene At 6:30"	Evil Hearted You*	UK	Granada TV
29 Sept	29 Sept	TWW Centre, Bristol	"Discs-A-Go-Go"	Evil Hearted You*	UK	TWW
1 Oct	1 Oct	Wembley	"Ready, Steady, Go!"	Evil Hearted You*	UK	Rediffusion
2 Oct	26 Sept	Alpha, Birmingham	"Thank Your Lucky Stars"	Evil Hearted You*	UK	ABC TV
21 Oct	21 Oct	BBC, Manchester	"Top Of The Pops"	Evil Hearted You or Still I'm Sad*	UK	BBC 1
29 Oct	29 Oct	Wembley	"Ready, Steady, Go!"	Evil Hearted You* / Still I'm Sad*	UK	Rediffusion
21 Nov	13 Nov	Brussels, Belgium	"Adamo Show"	Still I'm Sad / For Your Love	Belgium	RTB TV
3 Dec	23 Sept	NCRV Bussom, Holland	"Tiener Magazine"	For Your Love	Holland	NOS-1/NCRV
6 Dec	22–23 Sep	NBC, New York	"Hullabaloo"	I'm A Man	USA	NBC TV
9 Dec	6 Aug	5th Nat.J&B, Richmond	"Shindig Goes To London"	For Your Love/My Girl Sloopy	USA	ABC TV
16 Dec	10–11 Aug	Twickenham, London	"Shindig!"	I'm A Man	USA	ABC TV
23 Dec	10–11 Aug	Twickenham, London	"Shindig!"	I Wish You Would	USA	ABC TV

1966

Tmx date	Shoot date	Location	Programme	Songs	Country	Channel
4 Jan*	4 Jan*	KHJ-TV, Los Angeles	"9th Street West"	I'm A Man*	USA	Channel 9 TV
8 Jan	3 Jan	KABC, Hollywood	"Shivaree"	I'm A Man / Heart Full of Soul	USA	ABC TV
28 Jan	28 Jan	San Remo, Italy	"The 16th Festival of ..."	Questa Volta	Italy	RAI-1 TV
29 Jan	29 Jan	San Remo, Italy	"The 16th Festival of ..."	Pafff...Bum	Italy	RAI-1 TV
15 Feb	10 Jan*	KCOP-TV, Hollywood	"The Lloyd Thaxton Show"	Shapes of Things / For Your Love	USA	KCOP-TV
12 Feb	3 Feb	Paris, France	"Music Hall de France"	Shapes of Things*	France	TV ORTF-2
18 Feb	18 Feb	Wembley	"Ready, Steady, Go!"	Shapes of Things / Mister You're A Better Man Than I	UK	Rediffusion
26 Feb	20 Feb	Alpha, Birmingham	"Thank Your Lucky Stars"	Shapes of Things*	UK	ABC TV
1 March	1 March	London*	"Five O'Clock Club"	Shapes of Things*	UK	Rediffusion
2 March	2 March*	TWW Centre, Bristol	"Now!"	Shapes of Things*	UK	TWW
4 March	4 March*	Wembley	"Ready, Steady, Go!"	Shapes of Things*	UK	Rediffusion
10 March	10 March	BBC TV Centre, London	"Top Of The Pops"	Shapes of Things	UK	BBC 1
16 March	16 March	TV Centre, Manchester	"Scene At 6:30"	Shapes of Things*	UK	Granada TV
17 March*	17 March	Southend	"Pop The Question"	Interview	UK	Southern TV
31 March	31 March	BBC TV Centre, London	"Top Of The Pops"	Shapes of Things	UK	BBC 1
1 April	1 April	Paris, France	"Ready, Steady, Allez"	Shapes of Things*	UK	Rediffusion
15 April	17 March	Kensington, London	"Where The Action Is"	Shapes of Things / The Train Kept A-Rollin'	USA	ABC TV
29 April	29 April	Wembley	"Ready, Steady, Go!"	Jeff's Boogie	UK	Rediffusion
11 May	17 March	Kensington, London	"Where The Action Is"	I Wish You Would / Mister You're A Better Man Than I	USA	ABC TV

Radio & TV appearances — Appendix 4

Tmx date	Shoot date	Location	Programme	Songs	Country	Channel
15 May	1 May	Empire Pool, Wembley	"Poll Winners Concert Pt 2"	The Train Kept A-Rollin' / Shapes of Things	UK	ABC TV
27 May	27 May	Wembley	"Ready, Steady, Go!"	Over Under Sideways Down*	UK	Rediffusion
8 June	8 June	BBC TV Centre, London	"A Whole Scene Going"	Over Under Sideways Down	UK	BBC 1
9 June	9 June	BBC TV Centre, London	"Top Of The Pops"	Over Under Sideways Down	UK	BBC 1
16 June	9 June	BBC TV Centre, London	"Top Of The Pops"	Over Under Sideways Down	UK	BBC 1
2 July	27 June	Paris, France	"Music Hall de France"	[unconfirmed]	France	ORTF-1 TV
22 July	22 July	Wembley	"Ready, Steady, Go!"	Farewell / Lost Woman	UK	Rediffusion
29 July	27 July	TV Theatre, London	"Hey Presto–It's Rolf!"	Rack My Mind 3'00	UK	BBC 1
13 Aug	15 June*	London	"It's A Mod Mod World"	Over Under Sideways Down / Turn Into Earth	US	WABC TV
11 Oct*	11 Oct*	London*	[unconfirmed]	Jeff's Boogie	UK	[TV]
11 Nov	24–26 Oct	ABC, Los Angeles	"The Milton Berle Show"	Happenings Ten Years Time Ago	USA	ABC TV

• [Possibly a second instalment on 9 Dec, but it is unclear if this is a repeat of tonight's appearance or a separate taping.]

Tmx date	Shoot date	Location	Programme	Songs	Country	Channel
17 Nov	19 Oct	Lime Grove, London	"Top Of The Pops"	Happenings Ten Years Time Ago	UK	BBC 1

Note: Song titles performed on early episodes of "Ready Steady Go!" are largely unavailable. It was often the routine, that in addition to their current hit, featured bands would perform an additional song. Rumoured but undocumented possibilities for these 'missing songs' by the Yardbirds include: Bo Diddley's *I'm A Man* and *Who Do You Love* and Howlin' Wolf's *Smokestack Lightning* among others.

1967

Tmx date	Shoot date	Location	Programme	Songs	Country	Channel
27 April	27 April	Lime Grove, London	"Top Of The Pops"	Hi Ho Silver Lining	UK	BBC 1
18 May	18 May	Lime Grove, London	"Top Of The Pops"	Hi Ho Silver Lining	UK	BBC 1
20 May	17 May	Hilversum, Holland	"Moef-Ga-Ga"	Hi Ho Silver Lining	Holland	NOS-1/AVRO
28 June	23 May	Rak Group, London	"Man Alive"	Interview	UK	BBC 2
29 Sept	14 Sept	Hilversum, Holland	"Moef-Ga-Ga"	Tallyman	Holland	NOS-1/AVRO

1968

Tmx date	Shoot date	Location	Programme	Songs	Country	Channel
March	March	London*	[unconfirmed]	Love Is Blue	UK	[TV]
14 April*	14 April*	Zürich, Switzerland	"Hits A Go Go"	Love Is Blue*	Swtzrlnd	SRG-TV

1969

Tmx date	Shoot date	Location	Programme	Songs	Country	Channel
24 July*	26 June	Lime Grove, London	"Top Of The Pops"	Goo Goo Barabajagal	UK	BBC 1
Late '69	14–18 Ap*	London	[unconfirmed]	Plynth/Rice Pudding (edit)	Sweden	STV-2

1972

Tmx date	Shoot date	Location	Programme	Songs	Country	Channel
25 March	25 March	Bremen, W-Germany	"Beat Club"	Definitely Maybe	Germany	Radio Bremen

1973

Tmx date	Shoot date	Location	Programme	Songs	Country	Channel
27 Feb*	20 Feb	Paris, France	"Pop Deux"	Superstition / I'm So Proud / Morning Dew / Black Cat Moan	France	ORTF TV
8 June	Late April*	Los Angeles*	"In Concert"	Superstition/Morning Dew (edit)	USA	ABC TV
?	?		"The Trouble With Rock"	[unknown]	USA	[TV]

1974

Tmx date	Shoot date	Location	Programme	Songs	Country	Channel
1 Sept	23–24 Aug	London	"BBC Music On Two"	Get Down In The Dirt 4'04 / She's A Woman 5'10	UK	BBC 2
25 Oct	3 July '73	London	"Bowie '73"	The Jean Genie/Around And Around	USA	ABC TV

Appendix 4 — Radio & TV appearances

1975

Tmx date	Shoot date	Location	Programme	Songs	Country	Channel
2 May	April 1*	Los Angeles	"Midnight Special" #118	You Know What I Mean 'Cause We've Ended As Lovers Nothing From Nothing Them Changes	USA	NBC TV

1977

Tmx date	Shoot date	Location	Programme	Songs	Country	Channel
30 Jan	30 Jan*	Adelaide, Australia	"Rock On Sunday"	Interview	Australia	Channel 9 TV

Playhouse, London = Playhouse Theatre, Northumberland Avenue, London
Playhouse, Manchester = Playhouse Theatre, Hulme, Manchester
Manchester studio = BBC's studio location on Dickenson Road, Rusholme, Manchester

BBC Trans/BBC Transcription = BBC Transcription Service, i.e. the BBC recordings which were prepared for overseas broadcasts. Confusingly, Transcription Service also used the programme name "Top Of The Pops" for their radio-shows.
BBC 1/2 = BBC Radio 1/Radio 2
TWW = Television Wales and West

COVER SONGS ON THE BBC

This index attempts to catalogue the various *cover songs* performed on different BBC programmes by Jeff Beck in his career with the Yardbirds, the two Jeff Beck Groups and as a solo artist, and is restricted to songs which were not released officially. Hence this index excludes for example *I'm A Man* – a cover song released as a US single in November 1965, but includes *For Your Love* – a cover song released officially, but without Jeff Beck. Although the scope of this book is limited to the years 1965–1980, Jeff Beck, in fact, has not recorded any specially made recordings for the BBC since 1974.

The index lists song title; composer; group with whom Jeff recorded the BBC version; original performer (year); date of BBC transmission(s) plus a commentary.

Ain't No Sunshine (Bill Withers)
Jeff Beck Group II
Bill Withers (1971)
BBC Radio One, 8 July 1972
• Performed live by the Jeff Beck Group II during 1972, this was a US #3 hit for Bill Withers in 1971 and also won him a Grammy.

Baby Scratch My Baby (James Moore)
The Yardbirds
Slim Harpo (aka James Moore) (1966)
BBC Light, 21 May 1966
• Introduced to the Yardbirds' set list while it was fresh from its run in the US R&B charts for Slim Harpo at the start of 1966. It was later re-arranged to become *Rack My Mind* on The Yardbirds LP.

Dust My Blues (J. Bihari, E. James)
The Yardbirds
Elmore James (1951)
BBC Light, 5 March 1966
• A variation of Robert Johnson's 1936 recording *I Believe I'll Dust My Broom*, this well-worn blues standard was introduced to the Yardbirds' set list in 1965 as Jeff Beck's featured showcase.

Get Down In The Dirt (Andi Clark)
Jeff Beck
Upp (1974)
BBC TV 2, 1 September 1975
• Also featured as the regular encore jam on the Beck/McLaughlin 1975 US tour.

For Your Love (Graham Gouldman)
The Yardbirds
The Yardbirds (1965)
BBC Light, 20 March 1965; 10 April 1965: 17 April 1965: 30 April 1965; 2 July 1965; 30 August 1965; 18 August 1965, BBC TV 1, 18 March 1965; 15 March 1965; 1 April 1965
• The Yardbirds' most-performed song on the BBC.

Guitar Boogie (Chuck Berry)
The Yardbirds, Jeff Beck
Chuck Berry (1958) (adapted from Arthur Smith's *Guitar Boogie Shuffle*)
BBC Light, 20 March 1965; 26 June 1965
• Introduced to the Yardbirds' set list along with Jeff Beck's entry into the band in March 1965 and was one of five songs recorded for Beck's first BBC radio session. This instrumental of course eventually became *Jeff's Boogie*, which closely copied Berry's arrangement.

Hush A Bye (All The Pretty Little Horses) (traditional)
The Yardbirds
Traditional slave song (circa 1860s)
BBC Light, 17 April 1965, 14 August 1965
• A folk song performed solo by Keith Relf on acoustic guitar with only a bongo accompaniment, but never performed live.

I Ain't Got You (Calvin Carter)
The Yardbirds
Jimmy Reed (1956)
BBC Light, 10 April 1965, 22 July 1965
• *I Ain't Got You* was the B-side of the Yardbirds second single *Good Morning Little Schoolgirl*. Although Reed scored many US R&B hits between 1955 and 1961 – two of which crossed over to make the top ten in the pop charts – *I Ain't Got You* was not a hit.

(I Know) I'm Losing You (Norman Whitfield, Eddie Holland, Cornelius Grant)
Jeff Beck Group
The Temptations (1966)
BBC Light, 18 March 1967
• This song was part of the Jeff Beck Group's set list in 1967, and was originally done by the Temptations with David Ruffin on vocals, one of Rod Stewart's faves. Stewart later recorded the song for his breakthrough album *Every Picture Tells A Story* in 1971.

Radio & TV appearances — **Appendix 4**

I Wish You Would (William 'Billy Boy' Arnold)
The Yardbirds
Billy Boy Arnold (1955)
BBC Light, 5 June 1965; 30 August 1965
• *I Wish You Would* was the Yardbirds first single in 1964, originally recorded by Chicago harp-player/singer Billy Boy Arnold.

I've Been Trying (Curtis Mayfield)
The Yardbirds
The Impressions (1965)
BBC Light, 26 June 1965; 14 August 1965; 5 March 1966
• Introduced to the Yardbirds' repertoire in June 1965, this was – unusually for the Yardbirds – a ballad with weight on harmony vocals.

Just Like I Treat You (Willie Dixon)
The Yardbirds
Howlin' Wolf (1962)
BBC Light, 20 March 1965
• One of Howlin' Wolf's more obscure numbers, which presumably was also performed while Eric Clapton was a Yardbird.

Let Me Love You Baby (Willie Dixon)
Jeff Beck Group
Buddy Guy (1961)
BBC Light, 18 March 1967; 15 May 1967
• A Buddy Guy number that Jeff Beck and Rod Stewart re-wrote to become *Let Me Love You*.

Louise (John Lee Hooker)
The Yardbirds
John Lee Hooker (1960)
BBC Light, 12 June 1965
• A number also recorded by the group for their *Five Live Yardbirds* album, this John Lee Hooker song was another left-over from the Clapton-era.

Loving You Is Sweeter Than Ever (Calvy Hunter, Stevie Wonder)
Jeff Beck Group
The Four Tops (1966)
BBC Light, 5 November 1967
• Like the Temptations, the Four Tops were also a Tamla-Motown act, and this US #45/UK #21 hit also bore an early Stevie Wonder co-writing credit.

Pretty Girl (Ellas McDaniel)
The Yardbirds
Bo Diddley (aka Ellas McDaniel) (1963)
BBC Light, 12 June 1965
• A Bo Diddley song recorded previously by the group for their *Five Live Yardbirds* album.

Respectable (O'Kelly, Ronald & Rudolph Isley)
The Yardbirds
The Isley Brothers (1960)
BBC Light, 5 June 1965
• Originally the gospel-infested follow-up to the Isley Brothers' successful hit *Shout* from 1959, this was also recorded by the Yardbirds for their *Five Live Yardbirds* album with Eric Clapton.

Runaround (unconfirmed)/***Bottle Up And Go*** (Tommy McClennan)
The Yardbirds
Tommy McClennan (1940)
BBC Light, 17 April 1965
• While BBC files list the unidentified *Runaround* for this session, it seems they essentially do an impromptu, largely instrumental adaptation of Tommy McClennan's *Bottle Up And Go*, also done by the likes of Josh White and Leadbelly.

San-Ho-Zay (Freddy King, Sonny Thompson)
The Yardbirds
Freddy King (1961)
BBC Light, 14 August 1965
• Although listed as *San Jose* and as composed by the Yardbirds in the BBC files, this was certainly Beck's version of Freddy King's classic guitar instrumental and minor US R&B hit in 1961.

Smokestack Lightning (Chester Burnett)
The Yardbirds
Howlin' Wolf (1956)
BBC Light, 27 December 1965
• This song was a centrepiece of the Yardbirds' repertoire during their entire life span. The version recorded by the Yardbirds and Beck for the BBC clocks in at over 5 minutes.

Someone To Love Me (James Pryor)
The Yardbirds
Snooky Pryor (1956)
BBC Light, 10 April 1965
• Dressed in an arrangement by Eric Clapton, this song was possibly considered as a B-side to *For Your Love* early in 1965 prior to Clapton's exit from the band. It remained in the Yardbirds' set, however, as evidenced by this BBC recording shortly after Jeff's arrival. With lyrics re-written as *Lost Woman* the song then appeared on their 1966 LP *The Yardbirds*.

Spoonful (Willie Dixon)
The Yardbirds
Howlin' Wolf (1960)
BBC Light, 17 April 1965
• This Howlin' Wolf song was also covered by the Paul Butterfield Blues Band on Elektra's *What's Shakin'* anthology (1966) and by Cream on their debut album *Fresh Cream* (1966).

Stone Crazy (Buddy Guy)
Jeff Beck Group
Buddy Guy (1962)
BBC Light, 18 March 1967
• The second Buddy Guy number recorded for the BBC by Jeff Beck on his first radio session with Rod Stewart.

Sweet Little Angel (Jules Taub, Riley B. King)
Jeff Beck Group
B.B. King (1956)
BBC Light, 29 September 1967
• A song that was part of the Jeff Beck Group's group set list during 1967 and 1968, it was also popularized by Earl Hooker.

The Stumble (Freddy King, Sonny Thompson)
The Yardbirds, Jeff Beck
Freddy King (1962)
BBC Light, 2 October 1965
• An instrumental which was also covered by Peter Green and John Mayall on *A Hard Road* in 1967. Beck himself recorded the song for the soundtrack to *Twins* in 1988.

The Sun Is Shining (Elmore James)
The Yardbirds
Elmore James (1960)
BBC Light, 21 May 1966
• An Elmore James song which Beck brought with him from the Yardbirds and into his first Jeff Beck Group.

Too Much Monkey Business (Chuck Berry)
The Yardbirds
Chuck Berry (1956)
BBC Light, 9 April 1965; 30 August 1965
• A US R&B top ten in 1956, this Chuck Berry number was also recorded by the Yardbirds for their *Five Live Yardbirds* album.

Walking By The Railings (Jeffrey Rod*)
Jeff Beck Group
BBC Light, 20 October 1967
• This song is said to be a variation of Elmore James' *Talk To Me, Baby*, which the Jeff Beck Group featured in their live set during 1967 and 1968 and is possibly another of their rewritten blues.

You'll Never Go To Heaven (If You Break My Heart)
   (Burt Bacharach, Hal David)
Jeff Beck Group
Dionne Warwick (1964)
BBC Light 5, November 1967
• This was a UK #20 and US #34 in 1964 for Dionne Warwick.

Appendix 5

RECORDING SESSIONS 1965-1980

This appendix catalogizes all Jeff Beck's recording sessions in the years 1963 to 1980. Please note that the entries are listed chronologically based on the actual known recording dates. This list covers only sessions that feature Jeff Beck as the main artist or where he is featured as an integral part of a band, and hence various guest appearances are not included. This index also omits radio and TV recordings. An asterisk (*) indicates assumed dates. Please refer to the general text for futher information.

Artist	Date	Studio	Songs recorded	First release
The Tridents	late 1963	Regent Sound, London	Keep Your Hands Off My Baby	(unreleased)
The Tridents	late 1963	Regent Sound, London	Trouble In Mind	Beckology, 1991
The Tridents	1964	Oriole, London	Wandering Man Blues	Beckology, 1991
The Tridents	1964	Oriole, London	That Noise	(unreleased)
The Yardbirds	15* March 1965	Advision, London	Steeled Blues	UK/US single B-side, 1965
The Yardbirds	15* March 1965	Advision, London	I Ain't Done Wrong	Five Yardbirds EP, 1965
The Yardbirds	13* April 1965	Advision, London	I'm Not Talking	Five Yardbirds EP, 1965
The Yardbirds	13* April 1965	Advision, London	My Girl Sloopy	Five Yardbirds EP, 1965
The Yardbirds	April 1965	Advision, London	Heart Full of Soul (sitar version)	Shapes of Things Box, 1984
The Yardbirds	20* April 1965	Advision, London	Heart Full of Soul (issued vers.)	UK/US single A-side, 1965
The Yardbirds	26* July 1965	Olympic, London	Still I'm Sad (backing track)	UK single A-side, 1965
Jeff Beck	Aug 1965	Olympic*, London	Steelin'	Blues Anytime, 1968
Jeff Beck	Aug 1965	Olympic*, London	Chuckles	Blues Anytime, 1968
The Yardbirds	23 Aug 1965	Advision, London	Evil Hearted You	UK/US single A-side, 1965
The Yardbirds	23 Aug 1965	Advision, London	Still I'm Sad (overdub)	UK single A-side, 1965
The Yardbirds	23 Aug 1965	Advision, London	Heart Full of Soul (Italian)	(unreleased)
The Yardbirds	7-8* Sept 1965	RCA, Hollywood	I'm A Man	(unreleased)
The Yardbirds	12 Sept 1965	S. Phillips Studio, Memphis	The Train Kept A-Rollin'	Having A Rave Up, 1965
The Yardbirds	12 Sept 1965	S. Phillips Studio, Memphis	Mister You're A Better Man	Having A Rave Up, 1965
The Yardbirds	19 Sept 1965	Chess, Chicago	I'm A Man	US single A-side, 1965
The Yardbirds	21 Sept 1965	CBS, New York	The Train Kept ... (overdub)	Having A Rave Up, 1965
The Yardbirds	21 Sept 1965	CBS, New York	Mister You're A ... (overdub)	Having A Rave Up, 1965
The Yardbirds	21 Sept 1965	CBS, New York	I'm A Man ... (overdub)	Having A Rave Up, 1965
The Yardbirds	21 Sept 1965	CBS, New York	New York City Blues	US single B-side, 1966
The Yardbirds	1 Dec 1965	Advision*, London	Still I'm Sad (Italian)	(unreleased)
The Yardbirds	21-22 Dec 1965	Chess, Chicago	Shapes of Things	UK/US single A-side, 1966
The Yardbirds	7 Jan 1966	CBS, Hollywood	Shapes of Things (overdub)	UK/US single A-side, 1966
The Yardbirds	10 Jan 1966	RCA, Hollywood	Shapes of Things (mastering)	UK/US single A-side, 1966
The Yardbirds	17-19* Jan 1966	CBS, New York	Pafff ... Bum	Italian single B-side, 1966
The Yardbirds	17-19* Jan 1966	CBS, New York	Questa Volta	Italian single A-side, 1966
The Yardbirds	28-30* March 1966	Advision, London	Jeff's Blues	Shapes of Things Box, 1984
The Yardbirds	28-30* March 1966	Advision, London	What Do You Want	Shapes of Things Box, 1984
The Yardbirds	28-30* March 1966	Advision, London	Pounds And Stomps	Shapes of Things Box, 1984
The Yardbirds	28-30* March 1966	Advision, London	Someone To Love Me Pt. 2	Shapes of Things Box, 1984
The Yardbirds	28-30* March 1966	Advision, London	Chris' Number	Shapes of Things Box, 1984
The Yardbirds	28-30* March 1966	Advision, London	Crimson Curtain	Shapes of Things Box, 1984
The Yardbirds	28-30* March 1966	Advision, London	Like Jimmy Reed Again	Shapes of Things Box, 1984
The Yardbirds	28-30* March 1966	Advision, London	Here 'Tis	Shapes of Things Box, 1984
The Yardbirds	19-20 April 1966	Advision, London	Over Under Sideways Down	UK/US single A-side, 1966
The Yardbirds	19-20 April 1966	Advision, London	Jeff's Boogie	UK/US single B-side, 1966
Jeff Beck/Jimmy Page	16-17* May 1966	IBC, London	Beck's Bolero	single B-side, 1967
Jeff Beck/Jimmy Page	16-17* May 1966	IBC, London	[untitled]	(unreleased)
The Yardbirds	31 May-3 June 1966	Advision, London	Lost Woman	The Yardbirds, 1966
The Yardbirds	31 May-3 June 1966	Advision, London	The Nazz Are Blue	The Yardbirds, 1966
The Yardbirds	31 May-3 June 1966	Advision, London	I Can't Make Your Way	The Yardbirds, 1966
The Yardbirds	31 May-3 June 1966	Advision, London	Rack My Mind	The Yardbirds, 1966
The Yardbirds	31 May-3 June 1966	Advision, London	Farewell	The Yardbirds, 1966
The Yardbirds	31 May-3 June 1966	Advision, London	Hot House Of Omagarashid	The Yardbirds, 1966
The Yardbirds	31 May-3 June 1966	Advision, London	He's Always There	The Yardbirds, 1966
The Yardbirds	31 May-3 June 1966	Advision, London	Turn Into Earth	The Yardbirds, 1966
The Yardbirds	31 May-3 June 1966	Advision, London	What Do You Want	The Yardbirds, 1966
The Yardbirds	31 May-3 June 1966	Advision, London	Ever Since The World Began	The Yardbirds, 1966
The Yardbirds	26* July 1966	IBC, London	Happenings Ten Years Time	UK/US single A-side, 1966
The Yardbirds	20* Sept 1966	Advision. London	Psycho Daisies	UK single B-side, 1966
The Yardbirds	Early Oct 1966	Sound Techniques, London	Stroll On	Soundtrack, 1967
Jeff Beck	19 Jan 1967	De Lane Lea, London	Hi Ho Silver Lining	UK/US single A-side, 1967
Jeff Beck Group	June 1967	De Lane Lea, London	Tallyman	UK/US single A-side, 1967
Jeff Beck Group	June 1967	De Lane Lea, London	Rock My Plimsoul (#1)	UK/US single B-side, 1967

Recording sessions   Appendix 5

Artist	Date	Location	Title	Release
Jeff Beck Group	5 + 7 Dec 1967	Abbey Rd, London	I've Been Drinking	UK single B-side, 1968
Jeff Beck	5 Feb 1968	De Lane Lea, London	Love Is Blue	UK single A-side, 1968
Jeff Beck Group	20 March 1968	EMI/Abbey Rd*, London	Shapes of Things	Truth, 1968
Jeff Beck Group	14–16 May 1968	EMI/Abbey Rd, London	Let Me Love You	Truth, 1968
Jeff Beck Group	14–16 May 1968	EMI/Abbey Rd, London	Morning Dew	Truth, 1968
Jeff Beck Group	14–16 May 1968	EMI/Abbey Rd, London	You Shook Me	Truth, 1968
Jeff Beck Group	14–16 May 1968	EMI/Abbey Rd, London	Greensleeves	Truth, 1968
Jeff Beck Group	14–16 May 1968	EMI/Abbey Rd, London	Rock My Plimsoul (#2)	Truth, 1968
Jeff Beck Group	14–16 May 1968	EMI/Abbey Rd, London	Blues de Luxe	Truth, 1968
Jeff Beck Group	14–16 May 1968	EMI/Abbey Rd, London	I Ain't Superstitious	Truth, 1968
Jeff Beck Group	25 May 1968	EMI/Abbey Rd, London	Ol' Man River*	Truth, 1968
Jeff Beck Group	May 1968	EMI/Abbey Rd*, London	Long Blues	(unreleased)
Jeff Beck Group	February* 1969	?, London	All Shook Up (#1)	(unreleased)
Jeff Beck Group	February* 1969	?, London	Throw Down A Line	(unreleased)
Jeff Beck Group	March 1969	?, London	Blues Title	(unreleased)
Jeff Beck Group	14–18* April 1969	De Lane Lea, London	All Shook Up (#2)	Beck-Ola, 1969
Jeff Beck Group	14–18* April 1969	De Lane Lea, London	Spanish Boots	Beck-Ola, 1969
Jeff Beck Group	14–18* April 1969	De Lane Lea, London	Girl From Mill Valley	Beck-Ola, 1969
Jeff Beck Group	14–18* April 1969	De Lane Lea, London	Jailhouse Rock	Beck-Ola, 1969
Jeff Beck Group	14–18* April 1969	De Lane Lea, London	Plynth	Beck-Ola, 1969
Jeff Beck Group	14–18* April 1969	De Lane Lea, London	The Hangman's Knee	Beck-Ola, 1969
Jeff Beck Group	14–18* April 1969	De Lane Lea, London	Rice Pudding	Beck-Ola, 1969
Jeff Beck & Donovan	16–17* May 1969	Advision, London	Goo Goo Barabajagal	UK/US single A-side, 1969
Jeff Beck & Donovan	16–17* May 1969	Advision, London	Trudy (Bed With Me)	UK/US single A-side, 1969
Jeff Beck & Donovan	16–17* May 1969	Advision, London	Stromberg Twins	(unreleased)
Jeff Beck & Donovan	16–17* May 1969	Advision, London	Suffer Little Children	(unreleased)
Jeff Beck & Donovan	16–17* May 1969	Advision, London	Homesickness	H.M.S. Donovan, 1970
Jeff Beck & Donovan	16–17* May 1969	Advision, London	From Here On, Your Guess ...	(unreleased)
Jeff Beck (Group)	4* August 1969	?, London	Gospel Title	(unreleased)
Jeff Beck (Group)	4* October 1969	?, London	Instrumental	(unreleased)
Jeff Beck (A.N. Other)	3–5 Feb 1970	Record Plant, New York	Working In The Coal Mine	Music From Free Creek, 1973
Jeff Beck (A.N. Other)	3–5 Feb 1970	Record Plant, New York	Cherry Picker	Music From Free Creek, 1973
Jeff Beck (A.N. Other)	3–5 Feb 1970	Record Plant, New York	Big City Woman	Music From Free Creek, 1973
Jeff Beck (A.N. Other)	3–5 Feb 1970	Record Plant, New York	Cissy Strut	Music From Free Creek, 1973
Jeff Beck	April 1970	?, London	[untitled]	(unreleased)
Jeff Beck/Cozy Powell	1–10* June 1970	Tamla, Detroit	Reach Out, I'll Be There	(unreleased)
Jeff Beck/Cozy Powell	1–10* June 1970	Tamla, Detroit	(I Know) I'm Losing You	(unreleased)
Jeff Beck/Cozy Powell	1–10* June 1970	Tamla, Detroit	Can't Give Back The Love	(unreleased)
Jeff Beck/Cozy Powell	1–10* June 1970	Tamla, Detroit	Just Like You Never Loved Me	(unreleased)
Jeff Beck/Cozy Powell	1–10* June 1970	Tamla, Detroit	Don't Give A Hoot	(unreleased)
Jeff Beck Group II	April/July 1971	Island, London	Got The Feeling	Rough And Ready, 1971
Jeff Beck Group II	April/July 1971	Island, London	Situation	Rough And Ready, 1971
Jeff Beck Group II	April/July 1971	Island, London	Short Business	Rough And Ready, 1971
Jeff Beck Group II	April/July 1971	Island, London	Max's Tune (Raynes Park ...)	Rough And Ready, 1971
Jeff Beck Group II	April/July 1971	Island, London	I've Been Used	Rough And Ready, 1971
Jeff Beck Group II	April/July 1971	Island, London	New Ways/Train Train	Rough And Ready, 1971
Jeff Beck Group II	April/July 1971	Island, London	Jody	Rough And Ready, 1971
Jeff Beck Group II	3–14* Jan 1972	TMI, Memphis	Ice Cream Cakes	Jeff Beck Group, 1972
Jeff Beck Group II	3–14* Jan 1972	TMI, Memphis	Glad All Over	Jeff Beck Group, 1972
Jeff Beck Group II	3–14* Jan 1972	TMI, Memphis	Tonight I'll Be Staying Here ...	Jeff Beck Group, 1972
Jeff Beck Group II	3–14* Jan 1972	TMI, Memphis	Sugar Cane	Jeff Beck Group, 1972
Jeff Beck Group II	3–14* Jan 1972	TMI, Memphis	I Can't Give Back The Love ...	Jeff Beck Group, 1972
Jeff Beck Group II	3–14* Jan 1972	TMI, Memphis	Going Down	Jeff Beck Group, 1972
Jeff Beck Group II	3–14* Jan 1972	TMI, Memphis	I Got To Have A Song	Jeff Beck Group, 1972
Jeff Beck Group II	3–14* Jan 1972	TMI, Memphis	Highways	Jeff Beck Group, 1972
Jeff Beck Group II	3–14* Jan 1972	TMI, Memphis	Definitely Maybe	Jeff Beck Group, 1972
Jeff Beck Group II	23–25* May 1972	Electric Lady, New York	Superstition (#1)	(unreleased)
Jeff Beck Group II	23–25* May 1972	Electric Lady, New York	Maybe Your Baby	(unreleased)
Jeff Beck Group II mk2	1–2* July 1972	Electric Lady, New York	Superstition (#2)	(unreleased)
Jeff Beck Group II mk2	1–2* July 1972	Electric Lady, New York	Lose Myself With You	(unreleased)
Beck, Bogert & Appice	9–13* Oct 1972	CBS, London	poss. Superstition*	(unreleased)
Beck, Bogert & Appice	9–13* Oct 1972	CBS, London	poss. Why Should I Care*	(unreleased)
Beck, Bogert & Appice	11–22* Dec 1972	Chess, Chicago	Superstition	Beck, Bogert, Appice, 1973
Beck, Bogert & Appice	11–22* Dec 1972	Chess, Chicago	Why Should I Care	Beck, Bogert, Appice, 1973
Beck, Bogert & Appice	11–22* Dec 1972	Chess, Chicago	Lose Myself With You	Beck, Bogert, Appice, 1973
Beck, Bogert & Appice	11–22* Dec 1972	Chess, Chicago	Livin' Alone	Beck, Bogert, Appice, 1973
Beck, Bogert & Appice	11–22* Dec 1972	Chess, Chicago	I'm So Proud	Beck, Bogert, Appice, 1973

Appendix 5   Recording sessions

Artist	Date	Studio	Songs recorded	First release
Beck, Bogert & Appice	8–19* Jan 1973	Village Recorders, LA	Black Cat Moan	Beck, Bogert, Appice, 1973
Beck, Bogert & Appice	8–19* Jan 1973	Village Recorders, LA	Lady	Beck, Bogert, Appice, 1973
Beck, Bogert & Appice	8–19* Jan 1973	Village Recorders, LA	Sweet Sweet Surrender	Beck, Bogert, Appice, 1973
Beck, Bogert & Appice	Jan* 1973	?, US	Oh To Love You	Beck, Bogert, Appice, 1973
Beck, Bogert & Appice	Jan* 1973	?, UK	Oh To Love You (overdub)	Beck, Bogert, Appice, 1973
Jeff Beck (solo session)	April/May 1973	Escape, Kent	[unconfirmed]	(unreleased)
Beck, Bogert & Appice	3–14* Sept 1973	Apple, London	Got To Find My Woman (#1)	(unreleased)
Beck, Bogert & Appice	3–14* Sept 1973	Apple, London	Missing Word (Prayin')	(unreleased)
Beck, Bogert & Appice	3–14* Sept 1973	Apple, London	Jizz Whizz (#1)	(unreleased)
Beck, Bogert & Appice	17–21* Sept 1973	De Lane Lea, London	Got To Find My Woman (#2)	(unreleased)
Beck, Bogert & Appice	17–21* Sept 1973	De Lane Lea, London	Jizz Whizz (#4)	(unreleased)
Beck, Bogert & Appice	24–28* Sept 1973	Escape, Kent	Jizz Whizz (#3)	(unreleased)
Beck, Bogert & Appice	2–12* Oct 1973	De Lane + Escape	Solid Lifter	(unreleased)
Beck, Bogert & Appice	2–12* Oct 1973	De Lane + Escape	Satisfied	(unreleased)
Beck, Bogert & Appice	2–12* Oct 1973	De Lane + Escape	All In Your Mind	(unreleased)
Beck, Bogert & Appice	2–12* Oct 1973	De Lane + Escape	Laughalong	(unreleased)
Beck, Bogert & Appice	2–12* Oct 1973	De Lane + Escape	Get Ready Your Lovemaker's ...	(unreleased)
Beck, Bogert & Appice	2–12* Oct 1973	De Lane + Escape	Livin' Life Backwards	(unreleased)
Beck, Bogert & Appice	2–12* Oct 1973	De Lane + Escape	Getting Somewhere, Getting ...	(unreleased)
Beck, Bogert & Appice	10–21* Dec 1973	CBS, London	[unconfirmed]	(unreleased)
Beck, Bogert & Appice	Jan 1974	Island, London	[unconfirmed]	(unreleased)
Beck, Bogert & Appice	1–15* Feb 1974	Island, London	[unconfirmed]	(unreleased)
Jeff Beck (w/Zzebra)	July/Aug 1974	Escape, Kent	[unconfirmed]	(unreleased)
Jeff Beck (w/C. Appice)	16–27* Sept 1974	Air + CBS, London	Scatterbrain (#1)	(unreleased)
Jeff Beck (w/C. Appice)	16–27* Sept 1974	Air + CBS, London	Constipated Duck (#1)	(unreleased)
Jeff Beck	Oct/Nov 1974	Air, London	You Know What I Mean	Blow By Blow, 1975
Jeff Beck	Oct/Nov 1974	Air, London	She's A Woman	Blow By Blow, 1975
Jeff Beck	Oct/Nov 1974	Air, London	Constipated Duck (#2)	Blow By Blow, 1975
Jeff Beck	Oct/Nov 1974	Air, London	Air Blower	Blow By Blow, 1975
Jeff Beck	Oct/Nov 1974	Air, London	Scatterbrain (#2)	Blow By Blow, 1975
Jeff Beck	Oct/Nov 1974	Air, London	'Cause We've Ended As Lovers	Blow By Blow, 1975
Jeff Beck	Oct/Nov 1974	Air, London	Thelonius	Blow By Blow, 1975
Jeff Beck	Oct/Nov 1974	Air, London	Freeway Jam	Blow By Blow, 1975
Jeff Beck	Oct/Nov 1974	Air, London	Diamond Dust	Blow By Blow, 1975
Jeff Beck	Oct/Nov 1974	Air, London	Deep Feeling*	(unreleased)
Jeff Beck	12–30* Oct 1975	Trident, London	Head For Backstage Pass	Wired, 1976
Jeff Beck	12–30* Oct 1975	Trident, London	Goodbye Pork Pie Hat	Wired, 1976
Jeff Beck	12–30* Oct 1975	Air, London	Come Dancing	Wired, 1976
Jeff Beck	12–30* Oct 1975	Air, London	Sophie	Wired, 1976
Jeff Beck	12–30* Oct 1975	Air, London	Play With Me	Wired, 1976
Jeff Beck	12–30* Oct 1975	Air, London	Love Is Green	Wired, 1976
Jeff Beck	12–30* Oct 1975	Air, London	Led Boots	Wired, 1976
Jeff Beck	Nov 1975	Air, London	[unconfirmed](overdubs)	Wired, 1976
Jeff Beck	April 1976	Cherokee, Hollywood	Led Boots (overdub)	Wired, 1976
Jeff Beck	April 1976	Cherokee, Hollywood	Come Dancing (overdub)	Wired, 1976
Jeff Beck	April 1976	Cherokee, Hollywood	Play With Me (overdub)	Wired, 1976
Jeff Beck	April 1976	Cherokee, Hollywood	Sophie (overdub)	Wired, 1976
Jeff Beck	April 1976	Cherokee, Hollywood	Blue Wind	Wired, 1976
Jeff Beck	April* 1976	Red Gate, New York	[unconfirmed](mixing)	Wired, 1976
Jeff Beck	Nov* 1977	?, New Orleans	[unconfirmed](overdubs)	Beck/Hammer – Live!!, 1977
Jeff Beck	May 1978	Ramport, Battersea	Star Cycle	There And Back, 1980
Jeff Beck	Oct/Nov 1978	Ramport, Battersea	Too Much To Lose	There And Back, 1980
Jeff Beck	Oct/Nov 1978	Ramport, Battersea	You Never Know	There And Back, 1980
Jeff Beck	Oct/Nov 1978	Ramport, Battersea	Cat Moves	(unreleased)
Jeff Beck	Oct/Nov 1978	Ramport, Battersea	Hot Rock	(unreleased)
Jeff Beck	Oct/Nov 1978	Ramport, Battersea	Oceans And Continents	(unreleased)
Jeff Beck	Oct/Nov 1978	Ramport, Battersea	'Harp Song'	(unreleased)
Jeff Beck	Autumn 1979	Abbey Rd*, London	The Final Piece	There And Back, 1980
Jeff Beck	Jan/Feb 1980	Abbey Rd, London	The Pump	There And Back, 1980
Jeff Beck	Jan/Feb 1980	Abbey Rd, London	The Golden Road	There And Back, 1980
Jeff Beck	Jan/Feb 1980	Abbey Rd, London	El Becko	There And Back, 1980
Jeff Beck	Jan/Feb 1980	Abbey Rd, London	Space Boogie	There And Back, 1980
Jeff Beck	7–9, 14, 18 Mar 80	Abbey Rd, London	[unconfirmed](bass overdubs)	There And Back, 1980

BOOKS CONSULTED

Aeppli, Felix: *Heart of Stone – The Definitive Rolling Stones Discography* (Pierian Press 1985)
Aerosmith with Stephen Davis: *Walk This Way* (Avon Books 1997)
Anon.: Booklet in *The Yardbirds Box 7 LP Set* (Charly Records 1984)
Anon.: *Rolling Stone Rock Almanac* (Papermac 1984)
Bacon, Tony: London Live (Miller Freeman Books 1999)
Badman, Keith/Rawlings, Terry: *Quite Naturally The Small Faces* (Complete Music Publications 1997)
Barnes, Richard: *The Who Maximum Rhythm & Blues* (Eel Pie 1982)
Burdon, Eric: *I Used To Be An Animal, But I'm All Right Now* (Faber & Faber 1986)
Carson, Annette: *Jeff Beck – Crazy Fingers* (Privately published 1999)
Celmins, Martin: *Peter Green – Founder of Fleetwood Mac* (Castle Communications 1995)
Charlesworth, Chris: *Deep Purple* (Omnibus 1983)
Clayson, Adam: *Call up the Groups!* (Blandford 1985)
Cole, Richard/Trubo, Richard: *Stairway To Heaven – Led Zeppelin Uncensored*
Coleman, Ray: *Brian Epstein – The Man Who Made The Beatles* (Penguin 1990)
Coleman, Ray: *Survivor – the Eric Clapton Biography* (Sidgewick & Jackson 1985)
Copeland, Ian: *Wild Thing* (Simon & Schuster 1995)
Cross, Charles R./Flannigan, Erik (with Neil Preston): *Led Zeppelin – Heaven And Hell* (Harmony 1991)
Cross/Kendall/Farren: *Encyclopedia of British Beat Groups of the Sixties* (Omnibus 1980)
Davies, Dave: *Kink* (Boxtree 1996)
Dawson, Dinky/Alan, Carter: *Life On The Road* (Billboard Books 1998)
des Barres, Pamela: *I'm With The Band* (Jove Books 1983)
Finneran, Bill (compiler): *The Yardbirds* [collection of press clippings] (Privately published, 1999)
Fleetwood, Mick/Davis, Stephen: *My Life And Adventures with Fleetwood Mac* (Sidgewick & Jackson 1990)
Fletcher, Tony: *Dear Boy – The Keith Moon Biography* (Omnibus Press 1998)
Foster, Mo: *17 Watts?* (Sanctuary Music Library 1997)
Frame, Pete: *Rock Family Trees* (Omnibus 1980)
Frame, Pete: *Rockin' Around Britain* (Omnibus 1999)
Garner, Ken: *In Session Tonight – The Complete Radio 1 Recordings* (BBC 1993)
George, Nelson: *Where Did Our Love Go? – The Rise And Fall of the Motown Sound* (Omnibus Press 1985)
Gomelsky, Giorgio/Cohen, Phil: *The Yardbirds: Train Kept A-Rollin' CD booklet* (Charly 1993)
Gray, John: *Rod Stewart – The Visual Documentary* (Omnibus 1991)
Groom, Chris: *Rockin' And Around Croydon* (Wombeat 1999)
Grushkin, Paul: *The Art of Rock* (Artabras 1987)
Guiness Book of British Hit Albums 2nd Edition
Guiness Book of Rock Stars 2nd Edition
Halbrook, Ed (compiler): *The Yardbirds* [fanzine/collection of press clippings] issues #1-11 (Privately published, 1980s)
Hinman, Doug with Jason Brabazon: *You Really Got Me: An Illustrated World Discography of The Kinks 1964–1993* (Privately published, 1994)
Hinman, Doug: *All Day And All Of The Night: The Kinks In Concert, on TV, radio and More* (Unpublished manuscript)
Hinton, Brian: *Nights In Wight Satin* (Isle of Wight Cultural Services Department 1990)
Hunter, Ian: *The Diary of a Rock N' Roll Star* (Panther 1974)
Joynson, Vernon: *Fuzz, Acid And Flowers* (Borderline Production 1996)
Joynson, Vernon: *The Tapestry of Delights* (Borderline Productions 1995)
Lewis, Dave: *Led Zeppelin – A Celebration* (Omnibus 1991)
Lewis, Dave/Pallett, Simon: *Led Zeppelin – The Concert File* (Omnibus Press 1997)
Lewisohn, Mark: *The Beatles – Complete Recordings* (EMI/Paul Hamlyn 1989)
Lewisohn, Mark: *The Complete Beatles Chronicle* (Pyramid Books 1992)
Martin, George: *All You Need Is Ears* (St. Martin's Press 1979)
MacKay, Richard/Ober, Mike: *Yardbirds World* (Yardbirds World Publications, 1989)
MacKay, Richard: *Over, Under, Sideways Down: Yardbirds World 2* (Yardbirds World Publications, [1992?])
Ober, Mike: *Then Play On* (Privately published, 1992)
McLagan, Ian 'Mac': *All The Rage* (Sidgewick & Jackson 1998)
McMichael, Joe/Lyons, Irish Jack: *The Who Concert File* (Omnibus Press 1997)
Mitchell, Mitch/Platt, John: *The Hendrix Experience* (Pyramid 1990)
Mylett, Howard: *Jimmy Page – Tangents Within A Framework* (Omnibus 1983)
Napier-Bell, Simon: *You Don't Have To Say You Love Me* (Ebury Press 1998)
Nix, Don: *Road Stories and Recipes* (Schirmer Books 1997)
Platt, John/McCarty, Jim/Dreja, Chris: *The Yardbirds* (Sidgewick & Jackson 1983)
Povery, Glenn/Russell, Ian: *Pink Floyd – In The Flesh* (Bloomsbury 1997)
Rawlings, Terry/Badman, Keith/Neill, Andrew: *Good Times, Bad Times* (Complete Music 1997)
Rawlings, Terry: *Rock On Wood. Ronnie Wood – The Origin Of A Rock & Roll Face* (Boxtree 1999)
Redding, Noel/Appleby, Carol: *Are You Experienced?* (Fourth Estate 1990)
Roberty, Marc: *Clapton – The Complete Chronicle* (Pyramid Books 1991)
Roberty, Marc: *Eric Clapton – A Visual Documentary* (Omnibus 1986)
Roberty, Marc: *Eric Clapton – The Complete Recording Sessions 1963–1992* (Blandford 1993)
Rogan, Johnny: *The Kinks* (Proteus 1984)
Rosen, Steve: *The Beck Book* (English summary by Toshiaki Igarashi)
Rou Jensen, Anders: *Mellem Drømme & Drøn* (Chr Erichsens Forlag 1995)
Russo, Greg: *Yardbirds – The Ultimate Rave-Up* (Crossfire Publications 1997)
Santoro, Gene: *Beckology* CD booklet (1991)
Schreuders, Pier; Lewisohn, Mark; Smith, Adam: *The Beatles London* (Hamlyn 1994)
Shapiro, Harry; Glebbeck, Ceasar: *Jimi Hendrix – Electric Gypsy* (Heinemann 1990)
Shaw, Greg: *The Doors On The Road* (Omnibus Press 1997)
The Billboard Book of Number one Hits
Tobler, John; Grundy, Stuart: *The Guitar Greats* (BBC 1983)
Tobler, John; Grundy, Stuart: *The Record Producers* (BBC 1982)
Tremlett, George: *The Rod Stewart Story* (Futura 1976)
Various: *Rock Guitarist Vol. Two* (Guitar Player Books 1978)
Various: *Rock Guitarists Vol. One* (Guitar Player Books 1977)
Various: *Yardbirds Official Fanclub newsletter* February/March 1966 as reprinted in *Yardbirds World* [fanzine] issues #5 November 1983 (Privately published)
Wyman, Bill: *Stone Alone* (Viking 1990)

BIBLIOGRAPHY

Notable Jeff Beck magazine features and interviews 1965–2000.

• *Disc Weekly* March 27, 1965 "Hit it off? Of course we do!" Jeff with an one-off column in *Disc* Weekly

• *Disc Weekly* May 15, 1965 "It's All in Fun says Jeff" Jeff commenting the on-going Kinks/Yardbirds UK tour. Interview by Penny Valentine

• *Beat Instrumental* June 1965. "Jeff Beck Supplies 'Oriental' Touch". The Yardbirds interviewed by John Emery

• *Disc Weekly* July 10, 1965 "The Honest Truth". Short profile. Interview by Mike Ledgerwood

• *Beat Instrumental* October 1965. "Yardbirds Session". The Yardbirds interviewed by Brian Clark

• *KRLA Beat* October 9, 1965. "Yardbirds Wail!" The Yardbirds profiled and interviewed by Louise Crisione

• *Beat Instrumental* January 1966 "Yardbirds Move On" Jeff Beck interviewed by John Emery

• *Melody Maker* March 5, 1966: "Beck and Superpop" Jeff answers the question "just what is expected of the top-liners?"

• *Beat Instrumental* April 1966. "Chart Climbing Yardbirds Still Love The Blues". Jeff Beck and Jim McCarty interviewed by Brian Clark

• *Record Mirror* June 11, 1966: "Guess What! I Can't Play a Sitar Properly, Says Jeff Beck" Story by Richard Green

• *Disc and Music Echo* June 25, 1966 "We're Cheesed Off With Fans!" Interview by Richard Lennox

• *Beat Instrumental* July 1966. "Big Band For Jeff Beck?" Interview by Mike Crofts

• *Teen Set* March 1967 "The Yardbirds Talk To Carol Gold (And Carol Gold Talk To The Yardbirds!)" Interview by Carol Gold

• 'The Jeff Beck Column' ran monthly in *Beat Instrumental* from September 1966 until March 1967

• *Melody Maker* March 25, 1967 "For Jeff, This 'Fiasco' Has a Silver Lining!" Interview by Chris Welch. Also interview with Mrs Winnifred Cook, Ray Cook's mother

• *New Musical Express* April 15, 1967 "Guitarist Beck Has Hit As a Singer!" Interview by Keith Altham

• *Record Mirror* April 29, 1967 "Jeff Won't Be Making Another Disc Like 'Hi Ho Silver Lining'..." Interview by Peter Jones

• *Melody Maker* May 6, 1967 "'Hi Ho Silver Lining' Is Just Not Jeff" Interview

• *Disc and Music Echo* May 20, 1967 "Jeff Beck: Chap With A Chip and A Hi-Ho Hit" Interview

• *New Musical Express* May 27, 1967 "Jeff Beck Not Nearly So Wicked As He Thinks He Is!" Interview by Keith Altham

• *Beat Instrumental* June 1967 "Jeff Beck Session"

• *Record Mirror* August 26, 1967 "I Don't Suppose I'll Get Married – All I Want Is My Music" Interview by Derek Boltwood

• *Hit Parader* August 1967 "Jeff's Future Beckons" Interview by Valerie Wilmer

• *Teen Set* (undated) 1967 "Carol's Chronic Crises" Interview by Carol Gold

• *Beat Instrumental* September 1967 "Nothing But Trouble For Jeff" Interview

• *Muziek Express* (Holland) October 1967 "Beck In Een Trans Atlantische Romance" Story by Vicki Hibbert

• *Disc and Music Echo* March 2, 1968 "Hendrix And Cream Are Out, Says Jeff" Interview

• *Record Mirror* March 2, 1968 "Has Jeff Recorded a Yuccchhh Ballad?" Interview by Derek Boltwood

• *Disc* March 23, 1968 "Me – Jeff Beck" Interview by Steve Webbe

• *Beat Instrumental* April 1968 "My Change of Style Is Not A Permanent Thing" Interview by Pete Goodman

• *Ekstrabladet* (Denmark) April 20, 1968 "Jeff Beck love er ikke blue" From Press Conference, Copenhagen, Denmark, April 1968

• *Go* July 12, 1968 "Jeff Beck Slams British Music Scene" Interview by Loraine Alterman

• *Record Mirror* July 20, 1968 "The Legendary Jeff Beck in America" Transatlantic phone interview by Derek Boltwood

• *Disc and Music Echo* July 20, 1968 "Now Jeff is the Darling of America" Transatlantic phone interview

• *Guitar Player* October 1968 "Beck Is Back" Interview with John Sharkey

• *The Heights* [undated] October 1968 "The Heaviest Thing I Lift Is A Cup Of Tea" Interview by Richard T Schmidt

• *Toronto Globe And Mail* October 28, 1968: "Beck Could Become Blues Guitar God of The Sixties" Interview by Ritchie Yorke

• *Hullabaloo* December 1968 "Jeff Beck" Profile

• *Hit Parader* February 1969 "Beck Group" Profile

• *Melody Maker* February 1, 1969 "When Jeff Was Scared To Go On Stage". Interview by Chris Welch

• *Beat Instrumental* March 1969: "Profile: Jeff Beck" Interview by M.H

• *Eye* April 1969 "With The Jeff Beck Group – A Week-end Gig In San Francisco" Interview. Photos by Baron Vollman

• *Montclarion* May 21, 1969 "The Shape of Jeff Beck" Interview by William Higbie

• *Jazz & Pop* June 1969 (Cover story) "Jeff Beck" Interview by David Walley and Patricia Kennedy

• *Disc and Music Echo* July 5, 1969 "Donovan, Jeff, And Instant Hit" Jeff interviewed about the Donovan session

• *New Musical Express* August 16, 1969 "Beck's Group Split May Stop More Work With Don[ovan]" Interview by Alan Smith

• *Record Mirror* September 6, 1969 "Transfer Fees For Musicians?" Jeff Beck and Tony Newman talk about their future plans. Interview by Ian Middleton

Bibliography — Appendix 6

- *Zigzag* September 1969 "So You Want To Be A Rock And Roll Star" (Cover story) Interview by Pete Frame and Dick Lawson

- *Beat Instrumental* December 1969 "Changing Scene For Jeff Beck" Interview

- *Melody Maker* May 23, 1970 "Detroit Is My Scene Now, Says Jeff Beck" Interview by Royston Eldridge

- *Melody Maker* July 18, 1970 "Coming Soon: Jeff Beck's New Tamla Motown Sound" (Interview with Mickie Most)

- *Zigzag* May 1971 "My Beck Pages" Rod Stewart on Jeff Beck by Mac Garry

- *Sounds* May 1, 1971 "Talk-in With Jeff Beck" (Cover story) Interview by Royston Eldridge

- *Rock* May 7, 1971 "Jeff Beck Is Back" Interview by Royston Eldridge (Reprint of Sounds article May 1, 1972)

- *Rolling Stone* #85 June 24, 1971 "Jeff Beck Is Back In Action" Interview by Chris Hodenfield

- *Circus* November 1971 "Bad Boy Beck Returns" Story by Danny Goldberg; based on Sounds May 1 interview

- *Sounds* December 18, 1971 "Beck Breaks Silence" Interview by Dick Meadows

- *Circus* February 1972 "What Next, Jeff Beck?" Interview by Beverly Magid

- *Melody Maker* January 1, 1972 "Beck's Boogie In The Basement" Interview by Chris Welch

- *New Musical Express* April 8 and 15, 1972 "Beck On Trial" Two-part interview by Tony Stewart

- *Extra* (France) June 1972 Interview by Bruno Eucat

- *New Musical Express* August 5, 1972 "Beck With A Vanilla Flavour" Story and interview by Danny Holloway

- *New Haven Rock Press* #7 1972 "Jeff Beck Speaks! He Also Plays Guitar" Interview by Jon Tiven

- *Sounds* September 30, 1972 "It's Full Circle For Beck" Interview with Jeff Beck and Tim Bogert by Martin Hayman

- *Muziekkrant Oor* (Holland) August 30, 1972 "Yardbirds waren 100 procent professioneel" Interview with Jeff Beck by Willem Hoos

- *Melody Maker* September 30, 1972 "Get Beck!" Interview by Chris Welch

- *Pop Music* (France) October 19, 1972 "B.B.A. le noveau Jeff Beck" Interview by Jean-Noël Coghe

- *Rolling Stone* October 26, 1972 "Jeff Beck: Back In The Fudge Again" Interview by Paul Bernstein

- *New Musical Express* October 28 and November 4, 1972 "Beck Looks Back" Two-part interview by Nick Kent

- *Disc* November 4, 1972 "Hi Ho Golden Lineup" Interview by Robert Brinton

- *Zoo World* November 11, 1972 "The New Jeff Beck Group Again!" Interview by Cameron Crowe

- *Sounds* November 18, 1972 "The Thorn In Jeff's Side" Interview by Ray Telford

- *Record Mirror* December 23, 1972 "Beck: Everything And The Kitchen Sink!" Interview by Robin Mackie

- *New Musical Express* December 23, 1972 "Beck Burts Into Flames" Interview by Bill Phillips

- *Best* 55 (France), February 1973 "Le Reveil de Jeff Beck" Jeff Beck interviewed by Herve Muller

- *New Musical Express* February 10, 1973 "Rock 'n' Roll Vandals" Jeff Beck and Carmine Appice interviewed by Charles Shaar Murray

- *Melody Maker* February 10, 1973 "Under Two Flags" Chris Welch reports on BBA pre-tour rehearsals

- *Sounds* February 10, 1973 "Beck Bogert Appice; Two Flags, One Purpose" Report by Martin Hayman (part one)

- *Sounds* February 17, 1973 "A Heavy Metal Boogie Show" Report by Martin Hayman (part two)

- *Record Mirror* February 17, 1973 "Beck: Off The Starting Block At Last" Jeff Beck and Carmine Appice interviewed by Robin Mackie

- *Time Out* February 16–22, 1973 "Jeff Beck: Unbalanced" Interview by Andrew Furnival

- *Disc* February 24, 1973 "The Men At Beck's Call" Carmine Appice interviewed by Andrew Tyler

- *Maxipop* (France) #26 February 27, 1973 "B.B.A. Le Viex Rêve" Interview by Jacques LeBlanc

- *Circus* March 1973 "Stevie Wonder's Summer With Jeff Beck and The Stones" Story by Janis Schacht and Howard Bloom

- *Muziekkrant Oor* (Holland) March 28, 1973 "Jeff Beck: Soms is een fles wodka de enige manier in vorm te komen" Interview (uncredited)

- *Sounds* March 31, 1973 "Out For Some Action" Interview by Ray Telford

- *New Musical Express* March 31, 1973 "Beck's New Boogie" Track-by-track preview of BBA's album by Jeff Beck. Story by Charles Shaar Murray

- *Crawdaddy* August 1973 "Rock and Roll Vandals" Interview by Lenny Kaye

- *Disc* May 5, 1973 "Talk Beck" Interview by Robert Brinton

- *Melody Maker* May 5, 1973 "Hello, Hello, It's Great To Be Beck" Interview by Chris Welch

- *Sounds* July 7, 1973 "The Jeff Beck Story" Interview by Steve Rosen from Los Angeles

- *Rock* July 23, 1973 "Mrs. Beck's Little Boy Jeff Does It Again" Interview by Cameron Crowe

- *Rock & Folk* (France) August 1973 "Jeff Beck: Des Chats Et Trois Voitures" Jeff Beck and Carmine Appice interviewed by Claude-Alvarez Pereyre

- *Creem* August 1973 "Word Of Wisdom From Jeff Beck"

- *Melody Maker* September 22, 1973 "Beck's Block Buster" (Cover story)

- *Melody Maker* September 29, 1973 "Heavyweight Champions Of The World" In the studio with BBA. Story by Chris Welch

Appendix 6   Bibliography

- *New Musical Express* September 29, 1973 "The Axman Cometh" In the studio report by Charles Shaar Murray

- *Sounds* September 29, 1973 "Beck Bogert & Appice: A Perfect Medium" Interview by Pete Erskine

- *Record Mirror* October 13, 1973 "When We've Got The Sound Right" Interview by John Beattie

- *Sounds* December 29, 1973 "Tim Bogert Talk In" Interview by Pete Erskine

- *Guitar Player* December 1973 "Jeff Beck" (Cover story) Interview by Steve Rosen

- *Melody Maker* January 5, 1974 "We're An Emotional Band" Interview by Jeff Ward

- *Sounds* January 12, 1974 "Straight To The Veins" Interview by Rob Mackie

- *Circus* April 1974 "BBA II – Behind The Jet-Set Rock LP" Interview with Carmine Appice and Tim Bogert by Ellen Mandell

- *Trans-Oceanic Trouser Press* #4 July/August 1974 "Beck Basic" Story by Karen Rose and Nick Taquinto

- *New Musical Express* November 9, 1974 "Music And Cars And Sex ..." Interview by Charles Shaar Murray

- *New Musical Express* November 23, 1974 "Just Don't Take Any Notice Of People Who Can Play Properly ..." [NME Guitar Book insert] Interview by Charles Shaar Murray

- *Sounds* November 23, 1975 "Daleks Need Not Reply" Interview by Rob Mackie

- *Sounds* April 19, 1975 "A Blow By Blow Meet With Beck" (Cover story) Interview by Pete Erskine

- *International Musician And Recording World* July 1975 "Jeff Beck" Interview by Jon Tiven

- *Creem* August 1975 "Jeff Beck: Convalescence (Or Growing Up?)" Story by Gordon Fletcher

- *Trans-Oceanic Trouser Press* September/October 1975 "One To One With Beck" Interview by Gordon Fletcher

- *International Musician And Recording World* October 1975 "Jeff Beck" (Cover story) Interview by Steve Rosen

- *Guitar Player* "Jeff Beck" November 1975 Interview by Lowell Cauffiel

- *Circus* Raves #123 December 1975 "Jeff Beck Goes Back To Black" Story by Mick Houghton

- *Sound* (Canada) March 1976 "Jeff Beck: Is He Really Rock's Bad Boy?" Interview by Jim Millican

- *The Music Gig* April 1976 "Jeff Beck" Interview by Steve Weitzman

- *Sounds* July 17, 1976 "Jeff Sez Nothin'!" Report by Vivien 'Scoop' Goldman

- *Circus* #136 July 22, 1976 "Live 'Wired'" (Cover story) Interview by Dave Hickey

- *Creem* August 1976 "Jeff Beck Gets Mellow (Well... Sort Of)" Interview by Billy Altman

- *Beat Instrumental* August 1976 "Wired-up With Jeff Beck" Interview by Charles Stevenson [Steve Rosen]

- *Melody Maker* September 11, 1976 "Live Wired Beck" Interview by Chris Charlesworth

- *New Musical Express* September 11, 1976 "Beck Biting" (Interview reprint from *Creem* August 1976)

- *Sounds* October 9, 1976 "The Jeff Beck Sheet" Interview by Peter Crescenti

- *Blast* October 1976 "Jeff Beck Wired Into The Driver's Seat" Interview by Kris Nicholson

- *Hit Parader* November 1976 "Beck Don't Look Back (or Progress is Obsession)" Interview by Jean Charles Costa

- *Ram* (Australia) #50 January 28, 1977 "Scanadlous Tales & Unsavoury Gossip Dept: Jeff Beck, Hot Rods ... Hot Licks ..." John Crittle on Jeff Beck. Interview by Tina Jorgensen

- *The Advertiser* (Australia) February 3, 1977 "Nobody Laughs At Jeff Now" Interview by Greg Kelton

- *Juke* (Australia) #93 February 19, 1977 "Beck's Is Better" Interview by Christie Eliezer

- *Circus* #157 June 9, 1977 "More Lively Than Wired" Jan Hammer on Jeff Beck. Interview by Fred Schruers

- *Down Beat* June 16, 1977 "The Progression Of A True Progressive" Interview by Larry Rother

- *Player* (Japan) November 1978. Interview by Toshi Yajima

- *Trouser Press Collectors' Magazine* May/June 1980 "Jeff Beck"

- *Musicians Only* July 19, 1980 "The Case of Jeff Beck – The Vanishing Trick" (Cover story) Interview by Chris Welch

- *New Musical Express* July 19, 1980 "Beck's Ball Of Confusion" Interview by Nick Kent

- *Melody Maker* July 19, 1980 "There With Beck" Interview by Steve Gett

- *New Music News* August 3, 1980 "Beck's Blah-Blah" Interview by John Tobler

- *Rolling Stone* #328 October 16, 1980 "The New, Subdued Jeff Beck" Interview by Mikal Gilmore

- *Guitar Player* October 1980 "Jeff Beck (Rock Legend Fusion Pioneer)" (Cover story) Interview by Jas Obrecht

- *Trouser Press* November 1980 "Here And Beck" Interview by John Tobler

- *The Guitar Greats* (BBC Publications 1983) "Jeff Beck" Interview by John Tobler and Stuart Grundy

- *Guitar World* September 1981 "Everything You Always Wanted To Know About ... A Guarded Tour Through Music History" (Cover story) Interview by John Swenson

- *Fender Stratocaster 30th Anniversary* January 1984. Interview by Tony Bacon

- *Music* April 5–18, 1984 "Jeff Beck Back With Fresh Energy" Story by John Tobler

- *International Musician And Recording World* May 1984 ('Guitar Heroes Special') "Jeff Beck" Interview by John Tobler

- *AutoWeek* August 5, 1984 "Fast Cars and Rock 'n' Roll" Interview by Michael Nickele

Bibliography — Appendix 6

- *International Musician And Recording World* August 1984 "The Original Grandmaster Flash" Profile by Philip Bashe and John Tobler

- *Guitar World* September 1984 "Guitar Safari – Beck Records A Smokin' New Album" Report by Bob Davis

- *Guitar World* January 1985 "Beck – Twenty Years Of Rock And Roll Power" (Cover story) Interview by Gene Santoro (Part one)

- *Guitar World* March 1985 "The Jeff Beck Scrapbook" Interview by Gene Santoro (Part two)

- *Musician* #79 May 1985 "Number One With A Slow Bullet: Confessions Of A Reluctant Guitarist" (Cover story) Interview by David Fricke

- *Guitar Player* November 1985 "Beck on Beck" (Cover story) Interview by Jas Obrecht

- *The Times* March 22, 1986 "Ambitious In His Artistry" Interview by David Sinclair

- *Goldmine* #191 November 20, 1987 "Jeff Beck, There And Beck" Story by David Terralavoro

- *Guitar World* June 1989 "Beck Is Back!!!" Intrview by Steve Weitzman

- *Guitarist* July 1989 "Beck In The Studio" Report by Mo Foster

- *Musician* #131 September 1989 "Jeff Beck's Chop Shop" (Cover story) Interview by Scott Isler

- *Guitar* #11 September 1989 "Jeff Beck Breatkthrough" Interview by John Stix

- *Guitarist* October 1989 "Jeff Beck – Reluctant Hero" (Cover story) Interview by Neville Martin

- *Q* Magazine October 1989 "Just Say No!" Interview by David Sinclair

- *ME/Sounds* (Germany) "Im Oldtimer-Museum Von Jeff Beck: Der Auto Erotiker" Interview by Gunter Matejka

- *Rolling Stone* #566 November 30, 1989 "Guitar Slingers Shoot It Out" Report by Ted Drozdowski

- *Rolling Stone* #570 January 25, 1990 "Alone Together" Jeff Beck and Stevie Ray Vaughan. Interview by Steve Pond

- *Guitar World* January 1990 "Jeff Beck: Strat Cat" Interview by Brad Tolinski

- *Guitar Player* February 1990 "Jeff Beck Talks Shop" (Cover story with Stevie Ray Vaughan) Interviews by Matt Resnicoff and Joe Gore

- *Fachblatt Musik Magain* (Germany) ? 1990 "Jeff Beck Again" Story by Steven Rosen

- *Guitar Club* (Italy) October 1990 "Jeff Beck: Magia Del Suono" Interview by Paolo Battigelli

- *Guitar For The Practicing Musician* October 1990 "Jeff Beck In The Listening Room" by John Stix. Also Jon Bon Jovi interview

- *Fachblatt Musik Magazin* (Germany) "Technik Ist Nicht Alles" Beck, Hymas and Bozzio interviewed by John Christiansen

- *Guitar World* July 1991 "Jeff Beck & Buddy Guy: Strat Cats" (Cover story) Interview by Charles Shaar Murray

- *The Guitar Magazine* "Strat's The Way I Like It" Jeff on the Fender Stratocaster

- *Musician* #170 December 1992 "Jeff Beck Goes Backward & Forward" Interview by Matt Resnicoff

- *Guitar Player* April 1993 "Jeff Beck – The Dark Knight Returns" (Cover story) Interview by Chris Gill

- *Guitar Player* May 1993 "Muddy Waters Tribute" Jeff Beck on Paul Rodgers' project. Report by Chris Gill

- *Guitar World* May 1993 "Jeff Beck-A-Lula" Interview by Dan Forte

- *Guitar Magazine* June 1993 "Beck To The Future?" Interview by Douglas J. Noble with Andy Roberts

- *Guitarist* (UK) July 1993 "Wayward Wind" Interview by Eddie Allen

- *Vox* July 1993 "Regrets, We've Had A Few" (Cover story with Gary Moore). Interview by Paul Colbert

- *Jukebox Magazine* (France) October 1993 Story and interview by Jean-William Thoury

- *Musician* October 1993 "Jeff Beck Unlocks His Secret" Interview by Matt Resnicoff

- *Guitar Player* November 1993 "Taking The Dangerous Curves" Interview by Chris Gill

- *FAZ* (Germany) "Jeff Beck" December 3, 1993 Story by Peter Kemper

- *Guitar World* January 1994 "Tribute To Hendrix" Jeff Beck on the 'Stone Free' project

- *20th Century Guitar* November 1995 "Jeff Beck" (Cover story) Profile by Roger Diller

- *Best* (France) March 1999 "Jeff Beck" Interview by Laurent Lavige

- *Rock & Folk* (France) March 1999 "Jeff Beck" Interview by Jerome Soligny

- *Total Guitar* April 1999 "Jeff Beck – Who Else?" Interview by Jon Jannaway

- *Guitarist* April 1999 "Who Else – But Jeff Beck?" (Cover story) Interview by Neville Marten

- *Guitar* April 1999 "Baby, It's The Guitar Man" (Cover story) Interview by Bob Gulla

- *Mojo* April 1999 "Heartful of Soul … And Two Sugars Please" Interview by Charles Shaar Murray

- *Fuzz* (Sweden) April + May 1999 "Jeff Beck – Vem Annars?" (Cover story in April) Two part interview by Paul Guy

- *Guitar World* April + May 1999 "Beck To The Future"/ "Blow By Blow" Two part interview by Alan Di Perna

- *Guitar Player* May 1999 "Beck 2000" Interview by Lisa Sharken

- *Guitar One* May 1999 "The Original Beck" Interview by Dave Rubin

- *Goldmine* August 13, 1999 "Still Freeway Jamming 35 Years After The Yardbirds" Interview by Dave Thompson

- *Guitar World* October 1999 "Heavy Friends" Jeff Beck and Jimmy Page interviewed by Brad Tolinski

INDEX

A New Day Ahead 119
Abercrombie, John 152
AC/DC 190
Ace Kefford Stand 106
Action 45, 52
Adam Faith and the Roulettes 20
Adams, Brian 127
Adams, J. Boy 164
Aerosmith 62, 151, 158, 164, 166, 173, 174, 176, 177, 184
Affinity 191
Akkerman, Jan 145, 146
Aktual Facts 22
Alan Elsden and His Jazz Band 23
Aldrich, Ronnie 52
Alex Harvey & His Soul Band 17
Alexander, Steve 198
Alexys & the Third Generation 40
Alfandry, Michael 142
Alfonso, Barry 195
Alice Cooper 29, 127, 184
Alix, Jack 39
All Stars 29, 94
Alldis, Barry 82
Allison, Jerry 29
Allison, Mose 17, 19
Allman, Duane 70
Alphabeats 12
Alquin 142
Altham, Keith 25, 53, 70, 71, 73, 91
Altman, Billy 168, 176
Amandia 65
Amao, Loughty 152
Amazing, Stephen 144, 153
Amazing Blondel 109
Amboy Dukes 105
Ambrose 70, 72
Ambrose, Dave 70, 71, 72, 106
American Dream 94
Anderson, Andy 29
Anderson, Eric 131
Anderson, Jon 156, 161
Andrews, Bernie 91
Andrews, Chris 29, 35, 50
Animals 27, 32, 35, 45, 50, 54, 78, 79
Anthony, Michael 173
Antoine 44, 46
Antonioni, Michelangelo 59, 60, 61, 161
Appice, Carmine 77, 80, 101, 103–7, 119–153, 157, 158, 164, 168, 180, 185, 187
Aquarian Age 84
Arar, Yardena 191
Argent 111, 123, 124, 146
Armisegger, Rolf 84
Armstrong, Ralphe 158
Arnold, P. P. 77, 80, 111
Arthur Brown's Kingdom Come 115
Arthur Greenslade & the Gee Men 19
Asher, Peter 82
Ashford, 100, 106, 107, 108, 152
Ashton, Tony 153
Atkins, Chet 10, 26, 113
Atlanta Rhythm Section 185
Attack 70, 75
Aufrey, Hughes 46
Auger, Brian 26, 34, 35, 69, 72, 106, 111
Automatic Man 176
Avalon, Frankie 32, 33, 37
Average White Band 126, 152, 178

Avory, Mick 22, 23
Awhai, Robert 184
Azteca, 167

Bacharach, Burt 81
Bachelors 45
Bachman Turner Overdrive 151
Back Door 144, 145, 146
Bad Company 154
Badfinger 49
Badger 150
Bageris, Bob 118
Bailey, Richard 153, 156, 165, 169, 198
Baker, Ginger 37, 54, 91, 188
Baker, Ralph 143, 147, 163–165, 187
Baldry, Long John 27, 34, 59, 60
Ball, Dave 106, 109, 139
Ball, Dennis 106, 107, 109
Ballet Rambert 186
Ballets 37
Band Of Gypsies 106
Bandits 11
Bangs, Lester 171
Banks, Pete 67, 134
Barber, Chris 81
Barclay James Harvest 115
Baronets 84, 92
Barron Knights 51, 75
Barrett, Syd 77, 81, 127
Barsamian, Jacques 46
Barsalona, Frank 55, 86, 87
Barton, Cliff 29
Bascomb, Wilbur 157, 160, 161, 163–165
Basile, Phil 102, 124, 143, 153
Batten, Jennifer 59, 198
Batti Mamzelle 153
Bauer, John 163, 164, 176
Beach Boys 40, 41, 51, 55, 73, 174, 175, 176
Beatles 16, 20, 24, 26, 39, 48, 52, 61, 62, 72, 75, 83, 92, 96, 138, 143, 152, 153, 156, 159, 165, 168
Beatstalkers 22
Beattie, John 146
Beau Brummels 23, 28, 38, 40, 42
Bebb, Bill 69, 76
Beck, Annetta 10
Beck, Arnold Herbert 29
Beck, Bogert & Appice 124, 126–128, 130–134, 136, 138–151, 153, 154, 156, 169, 183, 187, 189, 197
Becker, Walter 162
Beckett 144
Bee Gees 75, 78, 80, 82, 184
Bee, Johnny 40
Beefheart, Captain 110
Beggars Opera, 112, 126, 127
Beiderbecke, Bix 110
Bell, Madeleine 79, 81, 99
Bell, Maggie 110, 146, 154
Benjamin, Benny 109
Benson, Alan 152
Benson, George 111, 178, 180, 183
Bentley, Jack 69
Berg, John 155, 171
Bernstein, Paul 124, 129
Berry, Chuck 29, 16, 19, 38, 39, 40, 50, 96, 143, 153
Beson, Irving 65
Better Days 139
Beutel, Paul 174

Big Bertha, 107, 109, 119
Biggles 125
Bim 163
Bird, Ronnie 44
Birds 18, 23, 66, 67
Bisons 159
Black Oak Arkansas 129, 138, 140, 145
Black Sabbath 122, 140
Black, Cilla 50, 83
Blackmore, Ritchie 12, 122, 159
Blake, Doug 84, 96, 123
Blakely, Alan 75
Blind Faith 101, 102, 104
Blond On Blond 95
Bloomfield, Mike 96, 116
Blossom Toes 77
Blue, Sugar 189, 190
Blue Cheer 90, 96
Blue Flames 69
Blue Things 38
Blue Öyster Cult 101, 123, 129, 170, 173, 185
Blues Image 104
Blues Organization 49
Blum, Jean-Gilles 179
Blunstone, Colin 142
Bogert, Tim 80, 101–103, 105, 107, 119, 120, 122, 123, 125, 126, 128, 129, 131, 133, 134, 136, 139, 142, 143, 144, 146–149, 151
Bohannon 167
Bolan, Marc 67, 180
Bolin, Tommy 149, 152, 158, 167, 180
Boltwood, Derek 77, 78, 83, 88
Bond, Chris 165, 166
Bond, D. P. 162
Bond, Graham 37, 52
Bones, Ray 76
Bonham, John 100, 102, 121, 125, 151
Boone, Pat 43
Borealis 103
Bosworth, Penny 116
Bowie, David 45, 73, 142, 143, 144, 153, 186
Bowlin, Robert 174
Box, Mick 127
Boxer 152
Boyd, Eddie 33, 34
Bozzio, Terry 198
Bramlett, David 106
Brand X 185
Bream, Julian 152
Breen, Joe 191
Brennan, Rose 28
Brian Auger's Oblivion Express 111
Brian Auger's Trinity 26, 34, 69, 72, 106
Brian Poole & the Tremeloes 22, 37, 53
Brin Smythe 30
Brinton, Robert 121, 127, 128, 139
Britton, Bobbie 23
Brooker, Gary 191
Brooks, Elkie 40
Brown, Arthur 77, 91, 115
Brown, Darryl 185
Brown, James 91, 150, 156, 157
Brown, Maxine 40
Brown, Ollie 157, 175
Brown, Patricia Rose 11, 13
Brown, Pete 128, 131, 146, 151
Brown, Phil 154
Brown, Ricky 100
Browne, Duncan 109
Brownsville Station 56
Bruce & the Spiders 23

Bruce, Jack 37, 54, 67, 75, 106, 128, 132, 151, 154, 156, 185, 186, 188
Buchanan, Roy 114, 127, 138, 156, 168
Buckingham, Lindsey 173
Buckinghams 38
Buckley, Lord 64
Buckley, Sean 73
Buckley, Tim 92
Buddy Miles Express 107
Buffalo Springfield 41, 84
Bumblies 23
Bunce, Dave 166
Bunn, Roger 146
Burden, Billy 27
Burdon, Eric 26, 35, 75, 78, 79, 140
Burke, Kenneth 175
Burke, Solomon 77
Burnette, Johnny 12
Burton, James 29, 127
Butterfield, Paul 139
Butts Band 153
Buxton, Glen 127
Buzzy Linhart's Seventh Sons 86
Byrds 23, 30, 41, 42, 51
Byrne, David 191

Cactus 107, 109, 113, 119, 120, 122, 132, 137, 139, 145
Calder, Tony 29
Cale, J. J. 121
Camarón and Dolores 190
Camel 174
Campbell, Glenn R 67
Canned Heat 41, 97, 112, 145
Cansino, Barbara 164
Capaldi, Jim 150, 188
Caravan 23, 61, 62, 63, 64, 65, 98
Carmen, Eric 66, 92
Carter, Patrice 180
Carr, Roy 35, 115
Carroll, Steve 12
Cash, Dave 74
Cast 97
Cattini, Clem 67, 82
Cauffiel, Lowell 161
CCS 109
Cecil, Malcolm 120
Chain Reaction 61
Chaman, Clive 110, 112, 117, 118, 120, 122, 146
Chaman, Stanley 110
Chandler, Chas 26, 35, 66, 109
Chapman, Ernest 110, 111, 113, 117, 119, 120, 124, 127, 131, 132, 143, 151, 155, 156, 158, 160, 168
Chapman, Roger 156
Chapman/Whitney Streetwalkers 153
Charging Rhino of Soul 88
Chariot 78, 183
Charles, Ray 51, 78
Charlesworth, Chris 158, 176
Cheap Trick 92
Checkmates [UK] (see also Diane Ferraz & the Checkmates) 52
Checkmates [US] 56
Chen, Phil 37, 153, 156, 180
Cher 184
Chicago 115, 155, 185
Chicken Shack 77, 142
Chilliwack 164
Choir 66, 92
Christgau, Robert 95
Christian, Neil 12

Christie, Lou 40
Cianci, Bob 171
Cinquetti, Gigliola 43
Clanton, Jimmy 62
Clapton, Eric 10, 12, 14–18, 22, 25, 28, 30, 34, 35, 38, 40, 44, 45, 52–54, 66, 67, 71, 75–81, 83, 84, 87, 88, 90, 91, 94, 96, 97, 99, 101, 102, 106, 109, 111, 116, 121, 124, 127–130, 141, 144, 154, 156, 164, 171, 181, 186, 188, 190, 191, 195, 198
Clark, Andi 144, 152, 165, 171
Clarke, Gerry 32
Clarke, Stanley 157, 158, 160, 170, 175, 185–190, 193, 194
Clarke, Steve 151, 169
Clark-Hutchinson 144
Claude, Francis 37
Claypool, Bob 174
Clayton Squares 45, 48, 52
Cliff Bennett & the Rebel Rousers 44
Clifford, Mike 57
Close To The Edge 165
Cobham, Billy 149, 150, 152, 158, 170, 175, 185
Cochise 107
Cochran, Eddie 29, 10
Cocker, Joe 91, 98, 104, 121
Cockney Rebel 122
Coghe, Jean-Nöel 92
Cole, B. J. 107
Cole, Richard 92, 95
Coleman, Bill 85
Coleman, Gary 166
Collier, John 155
Collins, Phil 185
Colosseum 112
Colyer, Ken 13, 52
Commotions 31
Conliffe, Brian 55, 61
Conn, Mervyn 26, 27, 28
Connolly, Billy 126
Cook, Ray 13, 68, 69
Cook, Winifred 69
Cool, King 106
Cooley, Alex 174
Coombes, Rod 70, 71, 72, 142
Copeland, Ian 155
Copeland, Stewart 198
Copley, Jim 144
Corea, Chick 189
Cornick, Glenn 27, 102
Coryell, Larry 87, 106, 196
Cosgrove, Tommy 106
Cosmos Factory 165
Costa, Jean-Charles 168
Costello, Pat 93
Cotton, James 39
Coulson, Clive 126, 143
Country Joe & the Fish 62
Couriers 62
Coutore, Joe 139
Coverdale, David 159
Cox, Mick 87
Crabby Appleton 146
Crabshaw, P. B. 182
Cradle 108
Crawdaddies 20
Crazy World of Arthur Brown 80
Cream 54, 71, 73, 75, 77, 82, 83, 87, 106, 112–116, 118–121, 123, 126, 128, 133, 134, 136, 138
Creation [Japan] 165
Creation [UK] 50, 80, 82, 84, 85, 86

236

Cregan, Jim 156, 180
Crescenti, Peter 176
Crescents 12
Crickets 29
Criscione, Louise 30
Crittle, Jon 181
Cromelin, Richard 124, 140
Cropper, Steve 114, 115, 117, 132
Crosby, Stills & Nash 104
Crossland, Al 35
Crusaders 12
Cullinane, John S. 183
Cumulus 111
Curved Air 112

Dallas, Karl 116
Daltrey, Roger 165
Danes 57
Danger, Cal 11
Dankworth, Johnny 27
Dark Knights 55
Darrell, Guy 74
Dave Berry & the Cruisers 27, 45
Dave Clark Five 17, 26, 35
Dave Dee, Dozy, Beaky, Mick & Tich 53, 54
Davies, Dave 22, 23, 35, 40, 66
Davies, Mandy Rice 52
Davis, Clive 111, 113
Davis, Jesse Ed 166
Davis, Spencer 35, 76, 107
Davis, Miles 153, 155, 157, 172
Davison, Harold 54, 59
Day, Rusty 105, 107
De Burgh, Chris 186
De Nave, Connie 29
De Shannon, Jackie 30, 46
Dee, Simon 15, 75, 84
Deep Purple 71, 91, 122, 140, 151, 152, 159, 180
Delsener, Ron 160
Deltones 10, 11, 12
Dene Hunter & the Newtones 23
Denning, Chris 75
Denson, Ed 62
Derek & the Dominos 62
Derringer, Rick 113, 145, 158, 173, 174, 176, 177
Detroits 35
Devo 185
Dewhurst, R. J. 143
Dias, Denny 132
Dick Rabbit 97
Dickens, Charles 45
Dictators 176
Diddley, Bo 13, 16, 19, 22, 33, 34, 46, 143
Dierdorff, Edwin 164
DiMeola, Al 179
Diane Ferraz & the Checkmates 75
Dion & the Wanderers 42
Dire Straits 188
Distant Cousins 62
Divine 95
Dixie Dregs 190, 192
Dixie, Ethel Florence 29
Dixon, Willie 12, 19, 39, 74
Dodd, Ken 23, 24, 34
Doerr, Lana 55
Dogfox 94
Dolenz, Mickey 76
Don & Dee Dee Ford 20
Donegan, Lonnie 188
Donovan 69, 85, 93, 99–101, 103, 104, 109, 128, 144
Doobie Brothers 174, 175
Doone, Lorna 130
Dorian Passante Zero 144
Dorsey, Lee 69, 106

Doud, Earle 106
Douglass, Greg 62
Dr. Feelgood 161
Dr. John 106, 143, 145, 151
Dreja, Chris 16, 20, 28, 32, 33, 35, 39, 42, 43, 46, 47, 50, 52, 53, 55, 57, 58, 59, 64
Driscoll, Julie 34, 72
Drummond, Norrie 59
Duke, George 175
Dunbar, Aynsley 72, 75–78, 90, 98, 170
Dunbar, Sly 189
Duncan, Bob 171
Duncan, Ian 10
Duncan, Lesley 99
Duncan, Seymour 66
Dunne, Mickey 81
Dupree, Simon 16, 76, 80
Dutton, Allan 137, 155, 170, 176
Dyke, Roy 150
Dylan, Bob 36, 105, 113, 117, 142

Eagles 173
Earth & Fire 144
Earth Opera 87, 93
Earth Quake 176
Eastman, Linda 62
Eclipse 120
Eddie & the Hot Rods 188
Edgar Broughton Band 98
Edge, Graeme 186
Edmed, John 10
Edwin Hawkins Singers 102
Eire Apparent 87
Eldridge, Royston 107, 110
Electric Light Orchestra 120, 126, 146
Eliezer, Christie 182
Elliot, Mama Cass 51
Ellis, Dave 122
Ellis, Don 151, 155
Elvidge, Dave 12
Elving, Ulf 91
Emerick, Geoff 165
Emerson, Keith 106, 139
English, Scott 67
Entwistle, John 53
Epstein, Brian 24, 27, 72, 75
Equals 76
Ernie, Long Tall 142
Erskine, Pete 120, 137, 145, 146
Ertegun, Ahmet 146
Ertegun, Neshui 107
Escapades 55
Essex 24
Essex, David 128
Etchison, Michael 95
Eucat, Bruno 117
Evans, Bill 121
Evans, Mal 24
Everly Brothers 34, 112, 126, 134
Evy 24
Exception 75
Executives 22, 35
Eyes of Blue 48
Eyre, Tommy 152

Fabulous Rhinestones 119
Faces 105, 106, 111, 144, 155, 160, 162, 166
Fahey, Jude 181
Fairport Convention 20, 78, 91, 111, 112, 140, 142
Faith 88
Faithfull, Marianne 23, 161
Fame, Georgie 27, 28, 36, 38, 50, 69, 73
Family 142
Fanatics 24, 45

Fantastic Epics 38
Far East Family Band 165
Farlowe, Chris 51, 79, 91
Farr, Gary 36, 125
Farr, Rikki 21, 26, 112, 115, 116, 125
Feel For Soul 73
Feiten, Buzzy 106, 130
Fendermen 80
Fennelly, Michael 146
Fernandez, Tony 151
Fever Tree 92
Fielder, Hugh 192
Fielding, Howard 121
Findlay, Krissie 66, 68
Finn, Mickey 21
Firefall, 174, 175
Fisher, Eddie 12, 65
Fisher, Matthew 107
Five of Us 57
Flare 110, 111, 112
Flash 113, 123, 134, 144
Flatt & Scruggs 88
Fleetwood Mac 77, 104, 164, 173, 178
Fletcher, Gordon 160
Fletcher, Tony 49, 144
Flock 38
Flying Burrito Brothers 174
Fläsket Brinner 111
Focus 126, 143
Foghat 123, 124, 129, 130, 173
Fontana, D. J. 95
Fontana, Wayne 36, 75
Fordyce, Keith 17, 18
Forest, David 162, 170
Foster, Mo 191, 194, 195, 197, 198
Four & Seven Eighths 52
Four Pennies 37
Four Seasons 38, 40
Four Tops 74, 108
Fourmost 28
Fowley, Kim 30, 41
Foxx, Inez and Charlie 36
Frame, Pete 104
Frampton, Peter 80, 105, 137, 144, 155, 173, 174, 178, 184
Frankenstein & His Monsters 52
Franklin, Aretha 156
Frantics 56
Free 118
Freeman, Alan 17, 45, 161
Freiberg, David 100
French, Pete 119, 122, 132, 146
Fricke, David 192
Fripp, Robert 191, 193
Frog, Wynder K. 150
Frost 88
Frugal Sounds 50
Fry, John 132
Fudger, David 157, 171
Fuller, Jesse 14
Furnier, Vincent 29
Furnival, Andrew 134
Fury, Billy 35, 36
Fusion 83, 184
Future 40, 79

Gallagher, Rory 112, 140, 155
Gallup, Cliff 9, 10, 11, 88, 130, 169, 193, 198
Galvanters 74
Gambaccini, Paul 186, 194
Ganley, Dave 139
Gants 31
Garber, Stephen 123
Gardner, Kim 67, 68, 80, 94, 100, 150
Garner, Erroll 117
Garrett, Amos 139
Garry, Mac 104
Garson, Mike 186

Gary Farr & the T-Bones 36
Gary Lewis & the Playboys 40, 62, 65
Gary Summers & the Highlanders 22
Gary, Bruce 156
Gass 111
Gaye, Marvin 150
Gebber, Eric 123
Gedoh 165
Geesin, Ron 98
Gell, David 23
Geller, Gregg 155
Gellerman, Alan 123
Gene Vincent & the Blue Caps 10, 122
Genesis 146, 185
Genocky, Liam 152
George Hatchet Band 169
George, Gloria 74
Gerard 175
Germain, Jean-Claude 24
Gershwin, George 46
Gerson, Ben 101
Gerstein, Richard 119
Gett, Steve 192, 193
Getz, Stan 185
Gibb, Russ 88, 97, 103
Gibsons 74
Gilford, Barry 12
Gilmore, Mikal 191
Gilmour, David 81, 186
Ging, Keith 148
Giuliano, Charles 114
Gjerstad, Leif 188
Glover, Roger 191
Godfrey, Mick 10
Goffin, Gerry 74, 92
Gold 88
Gold, Carol 61, 73
Golden Earring 126, 142, 145
Goldie & the Gingerbreads 21, 25, 26, 36
Goldman, Vivien 170
Gomelsky, Giorgio 14, 16, 17, 19, 20, 24, 26, 28–34, 37, 38, 39, 43, 46, 47, 48, 111
Gomez, Ray 170, 176
Gonzalez 152, 153, 161
Good, Jack 111
Goodman, Jerry 167
Gordon, Dexter 185
Gouldman, Graham 19, 28, 34, 75
Graham Bond Organization 37
Graham, Bill 40, 57, 62, 86, 89, 92, 113, 170, 176, 194
Graham, Harold 35
Graham, Larry 189
Grand Funk Railroad 38, 101
Grant, Eddy 76
Grant, Keith 26
Grant, Paul J. 156
Grant, Peter 66–69, 71, 84, 86, 87, 89, 91, 93–97, 100, 101, 104, 105, 106, 108, 110, 111
Grant, Steve 93
Grass Roots 142
Grateful Dead 86, 87, 107
Grease Band 98
Grech, Rick 144, 152
Green, Ed 167
Green, Herbie 129
Green, Peter 54, 72, 77, 79, 81, 109, 111
Green, Richard 30, 54, 60, 68, 83
Gregg, Brian 12
Grignard, Ferre 50
Grimes, Hamish 14, 16
Grolin, Carsten 92
Gross, Bob 99

Gross, Henry 173
Groundhogs 142
Groupe 31
GTOs 95
Guess Who 102
Gunnel, Rik 13
Guy, Buddy 12, 14, 34, 35, 39, 69, 74, 77, 89, 120, 140
Gypsy 112

Hagar, Sammy 170
Hales, Ron 127
Haley, Bill 50
Hall, Jimmy 137, 198
Hammer, Jan 142, 149, 154, 158, 161, 167, 168, 170, 171, 173–188, 192, 193, 194, 198
Hammond, Celia 90, 96, 165, 185
Hancock, Herbie 68, 121, 157, 189
Handa, Kenicki 141
Hangmen 39
Hanson, Gösta 85
Harding, Mike 120, 152
Haricotes Rouges 24
Harley, Steve 122
Harper, Roy 151, 154
Harpo, Slim 48
Harris, Bob 161
Harris, David 181
Harris, Eddie 144
Harris, June 55, 65, 84, 87
Harris, Rolf 54
Harris, Terence "Jet" 67
Harrison, George 20, 24, 40, 66, 76, 81, 144, 188
Harrison, Patti 76, 188
Harrison, Tom 163
Hart, Tim 126
Hartley, Keef 75, 116
Harvey, Les 147
Haskell, Jeffrey 145
Hawkwind, 109, 125, 160
Hayman, Martin 117, 125, 128, 134
Hayward, Al 129
Head, Murray 120, 194
Heard 40
Heart 178
Heath, Ted 82, 170
Heaven 116, 117
Hebb, Bobby 62
Hell, Richard 184
Help Yourself 112
Hemmings, David 59
Hendrix, Jimi 66, 67, 70–73, 78–83, 87, 96, 97, 100, 102, 104, 106, 107, 109, 113, 116, 127, 129, 133–136, 140, 143, 150, 154, 157, 159, 168, 175, 181, 188, 192, 196
Henschen, Bob 161
Herd 12
Herman, Tom 191
Herman's Hermits 20, 24, 36, 52
Hickey, Dave 168
Hicks, Tony 66
Higbie, William 99
Hill, Jack W. 31
Hinton, Joe 108
Hipster Image 23
Hirayama, Yuichi 187
Hirondelles 84
Hitchings, Duane 122, 132
Hobos 27
Hodenfield, Chris 110
Hoffman, Dezo 16
Hoggard, Stuart 150
Holland, Bernie 146, 153

Appendix 7   Index

Holliday, Doc 75
Hollies 22, 23, 28, 32, 33, 36, 44, 51, 75, 76, 79
Holloway, Danny 122
Holly, Buddy 29, 38
Holy Smoke 110
Home 121, 122
Honeycombs 37
Hooker, Earl 12, 74, 81, 150, 159
Hooker, John Lee 22, 138, 140
Hoos, Willem 112
Hope, Alan (aka Kerry Rapid) 11, 26
Hopkin, Mary 108
Hopkins, Nicky 29, 49, 71, 81, 82, 83, 85, 89, 91–101, 103, 121
Hornsby, Paul 70
Hot Chocolate 109
Hounds 85
Howard, Johnny 12
Howard, William 160
Howe, Steve 59, 61, 78
Howerd, Frankie 184
Howes, Arthur 21
Hugg, Brian 32
Hughes, David 115
Hughes, Jimmy 74
Hughes, Mary 30, 41, 57, 58, 59, 61–65, 70, 77, 84
Huhn, Tom 139
Hull, Dave 41
Humble Pie 112, 122, 140, 141
Hummingbird 146, 166
Humperdinck, Engelbert 70, 83
Hunt, Dennis 140
Hunt, Marsha 106
Hutton, Danny 30, 132
Hyland Brian 62
Hymas, Tony 186, 187, 189, 190, 191, 192, 194, 197, 198

Ian Cambell Folk Group 49
Ike & Tina Turner 59, 60, 78
Ikettes 59
Impressions 26, 114
Incredible String Band 80, 112
In-Mates Trio 86
Insexts 76
Iron Butterfly 70, 104
Isadore, Conrad 146
Isley Brothers 22
Isaacs, James 137
Iveys 49
Ivy League 26, 35, 36

J. Geils Band 119, 145, 170
Jack Bruce Band 156, 185, 186
Jackson, Milt 78
Jacobs, David 17
Jagger, Mick 14, 107, 143, 152, 154, 155, 178, 188, 198
Jake, Shakey 39
Jamerson, James 108, 109
James Gang 129
James, Dick 108
James, Elmore 16, 44, 48, 74, 77, 80, 88, 159, 162
James, Mike 73
Jammer, Joe [Wright] 150, 158
Jan Hammer Group 167, 168, 170, 171, 173–178, 181, 183, 184, 185

Jarvie, Roger 10, 11, 12
Jay Hawkers 39
Jeff & Jon 21
Jeff Beck Group [I] 62, 69, 71–76, 78–105, 107, 118, 123, 124, 125, 138, 188
Jeff Beck Group [II] 110–117, 119–122, 134, 136
Jeff Beck Sound 72, 78, 84
Jeff Beck's Million Dollar Bash 83
Jefferson Airplane 58, 100
Jefferson Starship 170, 173, 175, 185
Jensen, Kid 125
Jerebine, Doug 84, 96
Jerret, Elyssa 158, 177
Jerry Allen and his Trio 20
Jethro Tull 27, 84, 91, 92, 96, 97, 101, 102, 104
Jets 24
Jimi Hendrix Experience 78, 80, 96
Jimmy James & the Vagabonds 15, 37
Jipang 165
Joe Perry Project 196
John Mayall's Bluesbreakers 15, 28, 37, 39, 45, 72, 74, 75, 77
John Rosasco Quartet 42
John, Bobby 59
John, Elton 108, 109, 163, 173, 178, 180
Johnny Kidd & the Pirates 12
Johnny Wollaston Band 23
Johns, Andy 146, 147
Johns, Bibi 91
Johns, Glyn 155
Johnson, Bryan 164
Johnson, Derek 115
Johnson, Duncan 84
Johnson, Icarus 175
Johnson, Judi 17
Johnson, Robert A. 155
Johnson, Valerie 70
Jokers [Dutch] 47
Jokers [US] 62
Jones Boys 38
Jones, Brian 26, 46, 78, 97
Jones, Douglas 140
Jones, Elvin 167
Jones, Gloria 146
Jones, John Paul 49, 54, 67, 85, 91
Jones, Kenny 98, 190
Jones, Leslie 13
Jones, Paul 73, 82, 91
Jones, Peter 72
Tom Jones, 44, 72, 83
Joplin, Janis 89, 93, 99, 106
Jopp, Mike 13, 191
Jorgensen, Tina 181
Journey 170, 174
Joyful Wisdom 94
Juber, Laurence 186
Juicy Lucy 121
Just IV 58

Kane, Eden 10
Karstein, Jimmy 62, 64
Kart, Ira 183
Karthago 126
Kartune 80
Kay, Barbara 28
Kay, John 142
Kaye, Lenny 139
Kaye, Tony 150
Kefford, Chris "Ace" 106, 107
Kehm Karahn 67
Keith Conway & the Aristocrats 27
Kelly, Dan 161

Keltner, Jim 40
Kelton, Greg 182
Kemp, Rick 126
Ken Birch Band 86
Ken Turner Band 23
Kennedy, Ray 125, 127, 131, 140
Kennely, Patricia 93
Kenny Ball's Jazzmen 76
Kensington Market 93
Kent, Nick 114, 125, 128, 134, 145, 193
Kessel, Barney 65, 157
Khan, Chaka 156, 157
Kimsey, Chris 155
Kindler, Steve 158, 167, 172, 174, 175, 179, 183
King Crimson 121, 151
King Solomon's Minds 97
King, Albert 74, 90, 92, 131
King, B. B. 12, 74
King, Ben E. 110, 115
King, Ed 113
King, Freddie (Freddy) 27, 33, 55, 115, 117
King, Jonathan 51
Kingbees 49
Kings 196
Kings of Rhythm Orchestra 59
Kinks 18, 20–24, 29, 36, 45, 50, 51, 52, 78, 92, 112, 168, 183
Kirk, Roland 101
Kirshner, Don 178
Kleek 79
Klimaks 27
Klingman, Moogy 106
Kmetzko, Mark 160
Knickerbockers 52
Knight, Robert 141, 170
Knocker 13
Knopfler, Mark 189
Koda, Cub 56
Konquerer Worm Blues Band 55
Koo Koo Bird Bicycle Band 80
Kooper, Al 90
Korner, Alexis 37, 109, 121, 155
Kossoff, Paul 118
Kozlowski, Jim 158, 178
Kruzade 50
Kraan 126, 169
Kyle, Hugh 149

Labelle 157
Ladd, Jim 196
Lafontaine, Renée 37
Laine, Denny 77, 81, 161, 186, 188
Laing, Corky 132, 171
Lake 188
Lane, Ronnie 98, 151, 166, 198
Laurence, Robert P. 171, 177
Law, Don 88, 129, 176
Lawton, April 130
Le Blanc, Jacques 136
Le Gault, Lance 111
Leander, Mike 75
Leandros, Vicky 82
Lebrun, Christian 142
Led Zeppelin 62, 94, 95, 97, 99, 101–104, 106, 114, 125, 126, 128, 140, 154, 160, 161
Ledgerwood, Mike 10, 26, 68
Lee, Albert 12, 144, 191
Lee, Alvin 81, 87, 102, 116, 128, 169
Lee, Brenda 32
Lee, Ric 102

Lee, Will 176
Leeds, Gary 26
Leiber, Jed 198
Leichtling, Jerry 159
Lennon, John 10, 20, 67, 76, 197
Lennox, Richard 51
Leon and Malia, 141
Lewallen Brothers 57
Lewis, Jerry 32
Lewis, Jerry Lee 33, 91, 97, 110
Lewis, Linda 125, 152, 156
Ligertwood, Alex 110, 111, 115
Lind, Bob 46
Lindisfarne 126, 188
Linhart, Buzzy 86
Lioce, Tony 197
Little Anthony & the Imperials 40, 65
Little Boy Blues 38
Little, Carlo 29, 100, 107
Liversidge, April 44
Lloyd, Charles 90, 93
Lofgren, Nils 170, 190
Logan, Nick 100
Lomax, Jackie 150
London Philharmonic Orchestra 79, 186
Loog Oldham, Andrew 28, 60
Looking Glass 118
Lord Sutch & Heavy Friends 100, 107
Lord, Jon 71, 94, 153
Loss, Joe 21, 22, 24, 51, 52
Lucas, John 13
Lucas, Paul 13, 14
Lukather, Steve 198
Lulu 25, 26, 28, 72, 73, 75, 76, 83, 143
Lux, Kaz 189
Lynch, Kenny 29
Lynyrd Skynyrd 176, 177

Mabbs, Valerie 115
Mackie, Rob 120, 154
Mad Angel 139
Magritte, René 101
Mahal, Taj 188
Mahavishnu Orchestra 128, 139, 142, 144, 158, 161, 166, 167
Mahogany Rush 170
Maiden, Tony 175
Makowski, Pete 157, 184
Malo, Ron 33
Malo 119, 167
Mamas & the Papas 51
Man 125
Mandel, Harvey 155
Mandel, Mike 106
Mandell, Ellen 151
Mandrell, David 163
Manfred Mann 27, 36, 37, 45, 52, 76
Manhatten Transfer 159
Maniax 34
Manitoba, Dick 176
Mansfield, Jayne 29
Marchetti, Gianni 42
Marcus, Steve 101
Margolis, Kennie 156
Margouleff, Bob 120
Mark Leeman Five 15, 16, 18, 20, 21, 23, 34, 36, 37
Mar-Keys 115
Markham, Pigmeat 131
Markley, Bob 30
Markowitz, Roy 106
Marmalade 73, 78
Marriott, Steve 66, 67, 100, 104
Marsh, Dave 156
Marshall, Jim 162

Martell, Vinnie 101
Martha & the Vandellas 17
Martin, Dewey 41
Martin, Steve 184
Martin, George 153, 154, 158, 160, 161, 164, 165, 166, 184
Marvellettes 17
Marvin, Hank 10, 40, 66, 81, 186
Mason, Dave 80, 86, 173
Mason, Jeff 11
Mathieu, Mireille 46
Matthew, Brian 17, 18, 23, 33, 50, 69, 150, 151
Matthews, Barry 10
Maureen & the Thunderbirds 53
Mauriat, Paul 82
Maus, John 80
May, Brian 45
Mayall, John 12, 54, 85, 90
Mayfield, Curtis 23, 24, 44, 114, 115, 124, 131, 142, 151
Mayer, Roger 10
MC5 95, 104
McCallum, David 32
McCartney, Linda 180
McCartney, Paul 26, 36, 67, 76, 82, 143, 180, 186, 188
McCarty, Jim [US guitarist] 40, 107
McCarty, Jim 18, 26, 32, 35, 39, 43, 51, 53, 56, 58, 64, 109, 110
McCollum, Charlie 175
McCoy, John 152
McCoys 19, 51, 94
McCullough, Henry 120
McDermott, Galt 97
McDonald, Patrick 162, 194
McGear, Mike 36
McGowan, Cathy 18
McKay, Scotty 39, 62
McKendree Spring 142
McKenna, Val 21
McKennon Mendelssohn Mainline 94
McLagan, Ian 98
McLaughlin, John 127, 128, 142, 143, 153, 156, 158, 160, 163, 166, 168, 170, 174, 185, 196
McMonigle, Hank 141
Meadows, Dick 114
Means, Andrew 122
Meat 97
Medicine Head 115
Meijers, Constant 126, 142
Melly, George 146
Mendelsohn, John 117
Mercado, Mike 74
Mersey Lads 32
Messengers 46
Meters 106
Michaels, Mark 89
Michel, Patrice 115
Michna, Andrea 39
Mick O'Neil and the Soultones 15
Mickey They And Them 38
Middleton, Ian 105
Middleton, Max 110, 112, 113, 114, 117–121, 123, 124, 130, 145, 146, 151–157, 160–167, 169, 171, 186, 190
Midnight Shift 97
Mieses, Stan 178
Mike Cotton Sound 27
Miles, Buddy 87, 94, 107, 157
Milford, Kim 120, 122, 123, 130, 131

238

Millenium 146
Miller, Frankie 167
Miller, Jimmy 110, 111, 147
Miller, Steve 39, 62, 100
Miller-Goldberg Blues Band 39
Millican, Jim 164
Mills, John 145
Mindbenders 69
Mingus, Charlie 165, 169, 171
Mint Tattoo 89
Miracles 26
Misunderstood 67
Mitch Ryder & the Detroit Wheels 40
Mitchell, Eddy 46, 50
Mitchell, Glenn 174
Mitchell, Mitch 106, 115, 130
Moby Grape 89, 96
Mockingbirds 28
Modugno, Domenico 43
Mojo Men 40
Mojos 72
Money, Zoot 35, 51, 69, 78
Monkees 62, 68, 73, 76
Monopoly 75
Montrose, Ronnie 124
Moody Blues 15, 23, 27, 44, 95
Moon, Chris 107
Moon, Keith 49, 53, 76, 107, 120, 128, 143, 144, 151, 178, 186
Moore, Barbara 74
Moore, Scotty 29, 88, 95
Moran, Johnny 82, 89
Moraz, Patrick 156
Morgan's 37
Morrison, Van 97, 122
Morse, Steve 192
Morton, Shadow 151
Most Brothers 67
Most, Mickie 49, 66, 67, 71, 73–77, 81, 82, 83, 85, 93, 94, 98, 99, 104, 105, 107–111, 122, 129, 138, 144, 168
Mother Earth 96
Mothers of Invention 79, 102, 146
Motorhead 184
Motown Trinity 76
Mott The Hoople 16, 131, 151
Mountain 96, 97, 111
Moustique 24
Mouzon, Alphonso 188
Move 73, 80, 107
Muir, John 114
Mullen, Jim 146
Muller, Herve 128, 147
Muni, Scott 32
Munx 92
Murphy, Willy 97
Murray, Charles Shaar 120, 125, 126, 132, 134, 135, 136, 145, 149, 154, 157, 171, 184
Murray, David 108
Murray, Jan 65
Murray, Pete 17
Mutineers 46

Napier-Bell, Simon 47, 48, 50, 52, 53, 55, 58, 65, 66, 111
Nash, Graham 32, 76
Nash, Johnny 142
Nashville Teens 75
Nazareth, 142
Nazgul 113
Nelson, Ricky 29
Nesmith, Mike 76
Neuman, Alfred E. 11

New Barbarians 188
New Breed 61
New Colony Six 38
New Nadir 84
New York Dolls 144, 165
New York Mary 180
Newman, Tony 27, 75, 96, 100, 101, 103, 104, 105, 152
Newmark, Andy 152
Nicholas, Paul 184
Nicholson, Kris 168
Nicks, Steven 173
Nico 65
Nielsen, Rick 92, 94
Nightshift 12, 13
Nighy, Martin 11
9.30 Fly 114
Nite People 75, 82, 91
Nix, Don 62, 113, 115, 120, 132, 158
Noone, Peter 52
NRBQ 98
Nugent, Ted 105, 173, 196

O'List, David 70, 77, 107
Obrecht, Jas 191
Oldfield, Michael 125, 128
Olsson, Nigel 108
Omruds 34
Open Roads 39
Orbison, Roy 68, 69
Orpheus 102
Osibisa 112, 130
Other, A. N. (aka Jeff Beck) 106
Otis, Shuggie 155
Out Group 38
Outer Limits 52
Outlaw Blues Band 95
Owen, John 10, 11, 13
Ox 155
Ozark Mountain Daredevils 174

Page Boys 56
Page, Jimmy 10–14, 16, 18, 19, 28, 29, 38, 40, 49, 51–55, 57, 59, 60, 61, 64–67, 74, 79, 81, 86, 87, 88, 91, 94, 99, 100, 102, 106, 107, 109, 110, 114, 116, 124, 126, 128, 140, 141, 151, 156, 161, 166, 168, 176, 186, 190, 192, 197, 198
Paice, Ian 144, 152
Palace Guard 41
Palladino, Pino 198
Ben 12
Palmer, Carl 144
Palmer, Janice 70
Palombit, Roberto 189
Pappalardi, Felix 132, 165
Paramount Jazz Band 23, 28
Parchment People 81
Paris, Jon 55, 156
Pass, Joe 157
Pastorius, Jaco 170
Paul Butterfield Blues Band 39, 42
Paul Revere & the Raiders 30
Paul, Les 23, 59, 64, 88, 95, 139, 150, 168
Paul, Steve 87, 113
Pawnbrokers 55
Peacock, Steve 125
Peck, Jedd 106
Peel, John 24, 81, 91, 94, 114, 115, 116, 126, 135, 161
Peeps 27
Pegg, Dave 20

Peking Omnibus Company 80
Pena, Paco 152
Pennebaker, D. A. 143
Penny Wise 85
Pentangle 77
Pereyre, Claude-Alvarez 142
Perkins, Carl 116, 118, 129, 150
Perkins, Wayne 155
Perry, Joe 88, 158, 173, 177, 178, 196
Peter & Gordon 23, 30, 32, 39
Peter Jay & the New Jaywalkers 59
Peter Wheat & the Breadmen 58
Peter, Paul & Mary 34
Philbin, John 56
Phillips, Bev 81
Phillips, Bill 131
Phillips, Eddie 80
Phillips, Sam 31, 32, 192
Phillips, Simon 185, 186, 187, 189, 191, 192, 194, 195, 197, 198
Piblokto!, 146
Pieces 152
Piercy, Denny 27, 48
Pilnick, Phil 150
Pinera, Mike 120, 137
Pink Fairies 109
Pink Floyd 69, 77, 80, 81, 90, 111, 146
Pitney, Gene 23, 43, 44
Pitt, Kenneth 73
Plague 39
Plant, Robert 91, 102, 110, 121, 146
Platt, John 53, 64
Poco 123
Poets 22
Point Blank 180
Pollux 24
Ponti, Carlo 73
Poole, Malcolm 106
Poor Souls 22
Porter, John 185
Potter, Bob 11
Potter, Nic 107
Potter, Ted 11
Powell, Cozy 106–109, 112–115, 117, 119–122, 132, 139, 153, 186, 190
Powell, Jimmy 75, 76
Power Stop 80
Powerhouse Six 45
Prentice, Ron 19
Presley, Elvis 29, 30, 95, 100
Preston, Billy 113, 155, 156, 157, 175, 184
Pretty Things 21, 28, 33, 38, 67, 84, 109, 154
Price, Alan 78, 80
Price, Rick 156
Primitives 110
Prince, Viv 67
Proby, P. J. 111
Procol Harum 76, 96, 103
Profile 50
Pryor, Snooky 18, 46, 54
Pudding 67, 74, 77, 80, 83
Pudding Chair Sometime 80
Pulin, Chuck 114, 120, 138
Punter, Graham 134
Purify, James & Bobby 81

Quarry, Bill 57, 58
Quateman, Bill 183
Quatro, Suzi 108
Queen 35, 45, 51, 66, 163
Quicksilver Messenger Service 100
Quiet Melon 100
Quincy, Dave 152

Quintones 110
Quiver 125
Quotations 70

Radle, Carl 62
Raelettes 78
Ragnarock 181
Rainbow [Ritchie Blackmore's] 122, 190
Rainbow, Chris 191
Ramatam 123, 130
Rankin, Kenny 87
Rapid, Kerry (aka Alan Hope) 11, 26
Rapin, Guillaume 115
Raspberries 66
Rasputin, O. 15
Rats 83
Ravan, Genya 120
Reality 112
Red Dogs 38
Red, White & Blues Band 55
Redbone 113, 114
Redding, Noel 73, 78, 96, 100, 106, 109, 152
Redgrave, Vanessa 59
Redway, Mike 20
Reed, Jimmy 16, 46
Reed, Lou 126, 143, 145, 146
Reeves, Greg 107
Reid, Terry 59, 93, 103, 104
Reizner, Lou 90
Relf, Jane 34
Relf, Keith 16, 27, 28, 29, 33, 35, 37, 39, 42, 44, 46–49, 51, 53–60, 64, 65, 66, 109
Reneri, Ray 38
Renbourne, John 152
REO Speedwagon 138, 185
Retaliation 76, 77, 98
Return To Forever 158, 185
Rhinoceros 99
Rhodes, Emitt 41
Richard, Cliff 83, 96, 191
Richard[s], Keith 10, 40, 66, 107, 152, 155, 173, 188
Richard, Little 70, 129
Richardson, Darlene 163
Richie Walker Band 164
Riddle, Sam 41
Riot Squad 21
Roadrunners 16, 25
Rob & the Clansmen 22
Robb Storme Group 68
Roberts, Art 38
Robinson, Lisa 123, 173
Robinson, Peter 16, 28
Robinson, Smokey 108
Rock And Roll Trio 32
Rockestra 186
Rod, Jeffrey 75
Rodez, Carles-Didier 190
Rodgers, Nile 77, 198
Rodgers, Paul 131
Rodney Walsh & the Hot Rods 12
Roffery, Richard 139
Roffery, Ted 139
Rolling Stones 12, 13, 15, 23, 30, 46, 47, 48, 50, 59, 60, 92, 95, 98, 100, 110, 114, 119, 120, 122, 147, 154, 155, 157, 158, 162, 166, 182, 189
Rolly et Harry 37
Ronnie Jones & the Nightimers 15
Ronson, Mick 83, 143, 145, 156
Ronstadt, Linda 106
Rookes, Linda 83
Roosters 12
Rose, Karen 184

Rose, Tim 80, 84, 138
Rosen, Steven 102, 140, 147, 155, 162, 184, 186, 187
Ross, Diana 150, 178
Rossington, Gary 177
Rotary Connection 92
Rother, Larry 168, 175
Roulettes 52
Rowlands, John 71
Roxy Music 150
Rozek, Michael 179, 184
R-Tistics 38
Rudis, Al 118
Ruff, Ray 56
Rufus 156
Rundgren, Todd 106, 119, 174
Rush 196
Rush, Otis 12
Russell, Ken 156
Russell, Leon 151
Russell, Ray 191
Ryan Twins 36, 68
Ryan, Barry 37, 53
Ryder, Mitch 40, 75, 107
Rypdal, Terje 196

Sabres 76
Sam Apple Pie 125
Sam Gopal Indian Blend 74
Sam The Sham & the Pharaohs 62
Sampson, Les 109
Samwell-Smith, Paul 19, 26, 28, 36, 37, 39, 46, 47, 49, 50–53, 59, 66, 82, 194
Sancious, David 176
Sanders, Pete 92, 95, 97, 101, 106
Santa Barbara Machine Head 94
Santana 111, 170
Santana, Carlos 119, 185, 198
Santana, Jorge 167
Santo & Johnny 159, 162
Sarstedt, Peter 10
Sarstedt, Rick 10
Saunders, Fernando 167, 172, 175, 178
Savages 12
Savile, Jimmy 17
Savill, Les 80
Savoy Brown 96, 97, 102
Sawyer, Pam 108
Scaffold 36
Schmidt, Richard T. 93
Schon, Neal 170
Schuursma, John 189
Schwall, Jim 104
Scott, Ken 190
Scott, Kerby 42
Scott, Tom 166, 185
Scourtis, Ted 61, 88
Scruggs, Earl 95
Searchers 34
Sears, Elliot 167
Seatrain 112
Sebastian, John 101, 143
Section 145
Seekers 40, 48
Seger, Bob 173
Selvin, Joel 162
Senate 110
Sensational Alex Harvey Band 146
Settlers 50, 68
Sha Na Na 115, 120, 173
Shades 18
Shadows 10, 40, 67, 83
Shakers 85
Shakti 163, 170
Shangri-Las 39
Shankar, Ravi 51
Sharke, John 90
Sharkey, Geoff 127

Appendix 7   Index

Sharpe, David 182
Shaw, Sandie 72
She Trinity 50
Sheffields 52
Shelton, Robert 86
Sherry, John 155
Short Back & Sides 85
Short, Brian 110, 112
Shotgun Express 67, 70
Showmen 57
Shrieve, Michael 176
Siegal-Schwall Band 89, 118
Silkie 23, 34
Sill, Judee 124
Silver Metre 97, 106
Silverhead 144
Silvert, Conrad 113, 195
Simba 52
Simon & Garfunkel 40
Simper, Nick 107
Simpson, Valerie 108
Sir Raleigh & the Coupons 41
Skid Row 112
Skidmore, Catherine 129
Sky Rock Blues Band 165
Slade 112, 140
Sly & the Family Stone 89, 150, 194
Small Faces 45, 48, 50, 52, 68, 69, 73, 78, 96, 98, 100, 104, 183
Small Wonders 164
Smith, Alan 104
Smith, Gary 29, 32
Smith, Henry 61
Smith, Pennie 128
Smith, Tony 167, 168, 169, 172, 175, 179, 180, 181
Smoke 86
Snake Eye 127
Sneakers 78
Snowden, Don 195
Soft Machine 112
Soft White Underbelly 101
Solo, Bobby 29, 43
Solomon, Linda 138
Somerville, Phil 12
Sonny & Cher 65
Sorcerers 106
Soul Agents 14
Soul Bucket 79
Soul Concern 79
Soul Society 80
Soulents 16
Sounds Incorporated 27, 75, 96
Spector, Phil 30, 78
Spedding, Chris 144, 155
Spencer Davis Group, 27, 45, 73
Spheeris, Jimmy 195
Spiders 29
Spiders From Mars 143, 186
Spirit 95
Springfield, Dusty 46, 73, 76, 83
Squire, Chris 144, 161
Squires, Rosemary 20
St. John, Barry 15
St. Willie Cool School 75
Staggerlees 18
Stamp, Chris 83
Stanhall, Viv 107
Stanley & the Fendermen 57
Staple Singers 145, 148
Starr, Ringo 128, 143, 171, 188
Starz 176, 177
Statesmen 18
Status Quo 121, 126, 140
Steam Packet 34, 67, 69
Steamhammer 97, 100
Stearns, Rob 12
Steeleye Span 126, 140

Steely Dan 132, 140, 162, 180
Stein, Howard 113, 118, 119, 160
Stein, Mark 101, 180
Stephens, Leigh 96, 97
Steppenwolf 101
Stevens, Cat 61, 72, 73, 110
Stevenson, Charles 140
Stewart, Al 98
Stewart, Billy 33
Stewart, Ian 12, 13, 67, 98, 155
Stewart, Rod 14, 34, 67–73, 75, 76, 77, 79, 86, 87, 88, 90, 95, 96, 98, 100, 102–106, 108, 120, 124, 129, 135, 138, 144, 152–155, 161, 166, 178, 180, 187, 198
Stewart, Tony 116, 120, 121
Stills, Stephen 195
Stone The Crows 110, 147
Stone, Freddie 161
Stone, Sly 40, 151
Strangeloves 38
Stranglers 190
Stratton-Smith, Tony 106
Stredder, Margaret 74
Street, Danny 49, 110
Stud 116
Summer, Donna 178
Summers, Andy 35
Supertramp 112
Supremes 19, 80, 108, 110, 150
Surfs 23
Sutch, Screaming Lord 13, 50, 100, 107
Sutcliffe, Phil 169
Suzuki, Tomoo 141
Sweet Dirt 144
Sweetwater 95, 97
Swenson, John 171
Swingle Singers 85
Switch 80
Symonds, David 25, 34, 80
Syn 67

T Rex 142
Tages 84, 85
Talking Heads 188
Tallarico, Steven (aka Steven Tyler) 62, 107
Tarda, Jordi 190
Tasavallan Presidentii 111
Taylor, James 145
Taylor, Mick 74, 76, 154, 155, 156
Taylor, Randy Hope 198
T-Bones 16
Telford, Ray 130, 136
Tempest, Roy 35
Temptations 19, 69, 74, 108
Ten Wheel Drive 120
Ten Years After 81, 84, 85, 91, 94, 95, 101, 102, 104, 143, 192
Tench, Bob 103, 111, 112, 113, 117–124, 129, 146, 151, 152, 153, 155, 156
Tender Trap 83
Terry & the Pack 38
Terry Lightfoot & His Jazzmen 17
Them 17, 45, 157
Thin Lizzy 127, 142
Third Ear Band 116, 120
Thirsty Too 122
Thomas, Jimmy 59
Thomas, Richard 186
Thompson, Paul 150
Thornton, Big Mama 34, 90

Three Dog Night 132
Thunderballs 40
Tigrett, Isaac 115
Tillery, Sweet Linda 95
Time Box 79
Tiven, Jon 119, 123, 153, 158
Toad 94
Tobler, John 29, 109, 132, 151, 178, 186, 191, 193
Tom Cats 17
Tom Petty & the Heartbreakers 185
Tom Robinson Band 188
Tommy James & the Shondells, 146
Tomorrow 59, 78, 79, 80, 84
Tony King Sound 79
Toot, Barend 126
Tosh, Peter 188
Toussaint, Allen 150
Tower Of Power, 140, 170
Townsend, Rob 142
Townshend, Pete 36, 40, 66, 75, 76, 79, 81, 128, 186
Toys 76
Trad Lads 28
Traffic 73, 80, 86, 95, 110, 147
Tranquility 119
Transatlantics, 29
Travis, Merle 10
Trees 46, 116
Tremeloes 21, 75
Triangle [France] 147
Triangle [UK] 54
Trice, Jack 38, 56
Tridents 13, 14, 26, 66, 68, 81, 128, 191, 198
Trindl, Gene 41
Tripplehorn, Tommy 62, 64
Troggs 24, 52, 73, 146
Troiano, Domenic 129
Trooper 164
Trower, Robin 151, 157, 181
Troy, Doris 20, 24
Truncles 75
Tucky Buzzard 113, 126, 127
Turner, Tina 198
Turner, Gregg 192
Turnstile 95
Turtles 38, 75
Twink 78, 84, 94
Tyler, Andrew 115, 134, 161
Tyler, Steven (aka Steven Tallarico) 62, 107, 178
Tyrannosaurus Rex 83, 91

Unbelievable Uglies 55
Undermined 53
Unit Four Plus Two 2, 38, 45
Unwanted Pregnancies 35
Upp 144, 146, 148, 152, 154, 155, 157, 158, 165, 166, 171, 174
Uriach, Jaume 190
Uriah Heep 109, 126, 127, 142
Ursa Major 129, 130

Valentine, Hilton 35
Valentine, Penny 21, 23, 75, 76
Van Der Graaf Generator 107
Van Matre, Lynn 118
Vanilla Fudge 80, 95, 97, 101, 102, 105, 107, 122, 124, 125, 132, 138, 151, 152

Vann, Billy 79
Vashti 38
Vaughan, Sarah 167
Vaughan, Steve Ray 198
Vee, Bobby 17
Vejetables 40
Velvet Underground 65
Venet, Jack 52
Verlaine, Tom 191, 193
Vestine, Henry 41
Vibrations 17, 19
Vickers, Mike 82
Vigon 44
Vilaubi, Larry 140
Vincent, Gene 29, 10, 11, 40, 122, 150, 198

Wainwright III, Loudon 188
Wais, Alain 142
Wakeman, Rick 146
Walden, Michael 158, 166, 171, 176, 180, 185, 193
Walker Brothers, 22, 26, 45, 48, 70
Walker, Billy 72, 115, 120
Walker, John 22, 76, 80
Walker, Johnnie 107
Waller, Gordon 39
Waller, Mickey 14, 26, 68, 69, 70, 72, 78, 79, 81, 86, 87, 95, 96, 97, 100, 106, 107
Walley, David 93
Walsh, Joe 129, 137
Walton, Kent 18
War 151, 178
Ward, Jeff 147
Warhorse 106
Warm Sounds 72
Warren Davis Monday Band 72
Warwick, Dionne 103
Washington D.C.'s, 78
Waters, Muddy 12, 38, 81, 85, 150, 158, 159
Waters, Roger 198
Wayne, Bruce 101
Weather Report 157, 189, 190
Webbe, Steve 83
Webster, Charles 122
Weeks, Willie 152, 157
Weiss, David 196
Weiss, Larry 67
Weiss, Nat 156
Weiss, Steve 101, 104, 124, 132, 152, 153
Weitzman, Steve 167
Welch, Chris 68, 69, 76, 77, 82, 96, 114, 115, 120, 125, 133, 135, 137, 145, 193
Welch, Raquel 33
Welz, Joey 39
Wendeborn, John 162
Werman, Tom 178, 180
West Coast Pop Art Experimental Band 30
West Road Blues Band 165
West, Bruce & Laing 132
West, Keith 78, 79
West, Leslie 111, 132, 151, 155
Wet Willie 137, 140, 141
White, Alan 144
White, Chris 146
White, Lenny 185
White, Tony Joe 109, 145
Whitesnake 122, 153
Whitney, Charlie 156
Whyton, Wally 45
Wickham, Vicki 46
Wild Yama Rama Chuck Band 95
Wilde, Marty 52, 69
Wiles, Brian 12
Williams, John 111, 152

Wind & Fire 180
Wings 186
Winston Fumbs 74
Wint 13
Winter, Edgar 124, 145
Winter, Johnny 96, 104, 154, 156
Winwood, Steve 35, 66, 73, 79, 144
Wishbone Ash 140, 142, 146
Withers, Bill 116, 120
Wold, Barbera 39
Wolf, Peter 88, 94
Wolfman Jack 157, 164
Wolman, Baron 95
Wonder, Stevie 51, 74, 99, 110, 118–122, 125, 130, 131, 134, 139, 140, 141, 143, 144, 150, 153, 156, 162, 163, 166, 168, 172, 178, 180, 184
Wood, Ron 10, 23, 66–73, 75, 79–82, 84–89, 92–106, 110, 152, 154, 155, 158, 166, 176, 178, 188
Wood, Roy 120, 156
Woods, Stu 106
Worsøe, Arne 85, 92
Wright, Geoff 71
Wright, Nicholas 73
Wright, Syreeta 108, 153
Wyman, Bill 13, 46, 155, 188

XLs, 55

Yajima, Toshi 185, 186
Yamanaka, Joe 165
Yamauchi, Tetsu 166
Yardbirds, 14–62, 64–75, 79, 80, 81, 83–91, 93, 99, 104, 107, 109, 111, 112, 114, 115, 118, 128, 131, 135, 138, 143, 150, 156, 159, 160, 164, 168, 170, 175, 183, 192, 193, 194, 196, 198
Yes 59, 144, 150, 161
Yes n' No 24
Yonin-Bayashi 165
Yorke, Ritchie 94
Young Rascals 52, 80
Young, Muriel 45
Young, Neil 110, 193
Young, Roy 110

ZZ Top 164, 173, 196
Zappa, Frank 79, 95, 125, 146, 150, 180
Zarathustra 97
Zehringer, Rick 94
Zelkowitz, Goldie 36
Zephyr 104
Zero 46, 48, 49, 144
Zito, Tom 138
Zombies 34
Zoot Money's Big Roll Band 35, 69, 78
Zzebra 152